제6판

교원임용고시
일반영어 필독서

임용영어 수험생 대다수가 선택하는
전공영어의 보통명사

- 교원임용고시 전공영어 독보적 전국 1위
  (2025년 예스24 전공영어 부문 박문각 누적 판매량 1위)
- 미국 버클리대학 유희태 박사의 독창적 문제집
- 출제가능성 높은 예상문제 수록

유희태 일반영어

2S2R 4-2 문제은행

LSI 영어연구소 유희태 박사 저

박문각

PREFACE

2026년 《2S2R 문제은행》 6판을 내며

2014년 초판이 출간된 후 12년, 5판이 나온 뒤 3년이 지났다. 그 기간 동안 노량진에서 강의를 하면서 5판의 장점과 단점에 대해 수험생들과 의견을 교환할 기회가 많았다. 이 6판은 그 대화의 산물로, 5판과 형식적인 면에서 비교했을 때 많이 다르다. 즉, 5판이 모든 문제를 문제은행 방식으로 배치하였다면 6판은 문제은행(Part 01)과 모의고사(Part 02)로 분리하였다. 이 형식은 기존과는 많이 다른데, 수험생들의 반응이 어떨지 궁금하다.

내용적인 면에서 본다면, 6판은 5판과 유사하다. 우선 6판에서 다룬 주제도 우리가 살아가면서 겪게 되는 대다수의 영역(역사, 미학, 철학, 음악, 사회학, 사회복지학, 심리학, 소수민족학, 인종학, 인류학, 정치학, 경영학, 경제학, 교육학, 물리학, 생물학, 의학, 지질학, 인류학, 지리학 등)이 들어가 있어서 수험생들이 다양한 주제들을 접할 수 있도록 하였던 5판의 정신을 그대로 가져왔다. 또한 문제를 푸는 과정에서 일반 영어 만점에 필수적인 배경지식을 자동으로 증진시킬 수 있도록 하였다. 그렇기에, 배경지식이 부족한 수험생들이 그 지식을 익히려 따로 시간을 내 다른 교재를 볼 필요가 없도록 하였다.

또한 양적인 면에서는 5판이 총 60회 분량이었다면, 이번 6판은 Part 01인 문제은행에 총 174개의 문제와 Part 02인 모의고사에 총 70회 분량의 문제를 수록해 실로 방대한 분량이라 할 만하다. 대다수의 임용 수험생들은 일반영어 문제에 목말라 있다. 실제 임용고시 문제와 유사하면서도 질 좋은(오류가 없고 타당도가 높은) 문제가 안타깝게도 임용 영어시험 시장에 많지 않기 때문이다. 시간이 가면 갈수록, 임용시험 시장이 작아지는 추세이다 보니, 현실적으로 출판사들 입장에서는 임용교재 출판으로는 경제적 수지타산이 거의 맞지 않기에 임용교재를 출판하려 하지 않고, 저자들도 고생에 비해 너무 적은 보답이 오다보니 새롭고 독창적인 교재 개발은 거의 불가능해졌다. 더군다나 노량진 임용고시 수험시장에서 가장 오랜 세월 강의를 하고, 이른바 일타 강사라 불리는 저자가 경제적인 부분만 생각할 수는 없는 일이어서 이 척박한 상황에 조금이나마 도움이 되어야 한다는 책임감을 느끼고 이 교재를 출간하기로 했다. 저자도 이제 나이가 들었는지 교재작업을 하는 일이 갈수록 힘에 부침을 느낀다. 아마 6판이 마지막이 되지 않을까 생각도 해본다. 물론 미래는 그 누구도 알 수는 없지만 말이다. 시험을 준비하는 수험생들이 더욱 풍부하고 질 좋은 문제를 풀어봄으로써 일반영어 실력이 향상된다면 저자로선 더할 나위 없이 고마운 일이 될 듯하다.

이 6판 교재는 《유희태 일반영어 시리즈 ① - 2S2R 기본》, 《유희태 일반영어 시리즈 ② - 2S2R 유형》, 《유희태 일반영어 시리즈 ③ - 2S2R 기출》, 《유희태 일반영어 시리즈 ⑤ - 기출 VOCA 30days》의 자매편이다. 시리즈를 통해 길러진 일반영어에 대한 이론, 유형, 기출, 그리고 어휘를 문제은행에 적용해 보도록 짜여있다. 이 시리즈를 통해서 공부한다면 임용고시에서 기본과목이라 할 수 있는 일반영어가 상당 정도 손에 잡힐 것으로 확신한다.

『유희태 2S2R 시리즈』를 효과적으로 활용하는 방법은, 대학 1학년 때 《2S2R 기본》을 최소 3회독, 평균 5회독하여 일반영어 기본이론을 확실하게 다진 뒤, 2학년 때 《2S2R 유형》을 최소 3회독하여 임용 유형에 기본이론을 확장 적용하는 훈련을 하고, 3학년 때 《2S2R 기출》을 2회독한 다음, 처음으로 임용시험을 치르는 4학년 때 《2S2R 문제은행》을 가지고 공부하는 것이다. 이 과정에서 《기출 VOCA 30days》는 1학년 때부터 주 6회 매일 20분씩 꾸준히 공부하기를 추천한다. 그러면 4학년 11월 임용시험을 치를 때가 되면, 임용에 필요한 어휘의 80%는 머릿속에 차곡차곡 쌓여서, 독해를 하는 데 있어 어휘의 부족은 느끼지 않을 것이다. 수험생 각자가 처한 상황에 맞춰서 공부해야 하겠지만, 가능하면 빨리 시작하는 것이 더욱 큰 효과가 날 것이란 것은 두말할 필요가 없다.

이 6판 작업을 하면서 많은 분의 도움을 받았다. 원고를 보기 좋은 최종 결과물로 만들어준 박문각의 변수경 편집자와 박용 회장님께 고마움을 전한다. 또한 교재가 세상에 나오기까지 묵묵히 최선을 다해주신 모든 인쇄·출판 노동자분들께도 깊은 감사의 마음을 전한다. 아무쪼록 이 《2S2R 문제은행》 6판 교재가 수험생 여러분의 합격에 일조하기를 깊은 마음으로 바란다.

2026년 새해를 앞두고 LSI 영어연구소에서

유희태

CONTENTS

PART 02 모의고사 — 009

모의고사 Ⅰ ········· 009
(제01회~제25회 모의고사)

모의고사 Ⅱ ········· 191
(제26회~제70회 모의고사)

● **모범답안 및 번역** — 004

PART 01 문제은행 [001~174]

● **모범답안 및 번역**

※ PART 01 문제은행은 《유희태 전공영어 일반영어 ④-1-2S2R 문제은행》에 수록돼 있음

유희태 일반영어
④-2 문제은행

2S2R

유희태 일반영어
④-2 문제은행

PART 02

모의고사

모의고사 Ⅰ
〔제01회 ~ 제25회 모의고사〕

1. Read the passage and follow the directions. [4 points]

For nearly two centuries America has struggled to reconcile its affection for the _____ with its image of itself as a humane and just society. Few episodes in this long history have been as strange as the one told by Mark Essig in his new book, "*Edison & the Electric Chair*". To describe Mr Essig's tale as shocking would be in poor taste, but its odd mixture of technology-worship, industrial sabotage, judicial complacency and rank hypocrisy should at least make American readers a bit queasy about their continued support for capital punishment.

In the 19th century America had grown to dislike hanging, the usual method of executing condemned prisoners. Hangings often took place in public, frequently leading to riots and other unseemly behaviour among spectators. Hangings also were often botched, resulting in slow strangulation or decapitation. Opponents of the capital punishment gained adherents by arguing that hanging was cruel and barbaric. To restore respectability to executions, its supporters came up with the idea of electrocution.

Electricity was a new and glamorous technology. It was, above all, modern. At the same time, it made people nervous. America was just beginning to wire up its major cities, and although the benefits of electric light were obvious to everyone, no one was quite sure how safe it was. After surveying execution methods from the guillotine (too bloody) to morphine overdoses (too pleasant), a commission appointed by the New York state legislature recommended in 1888 the use of electrocution, which it promised would be "instantaneous and painless" and "devoid of all barbarism". The man who had persuaded the commission of this was Thomas Edison, America's most famous inventor.

Edison's primary interest in recommending electrocution was to discredit his chief rival in the race to wire America, George Westinghouse. Edison's company used direct current. Westinghouse's firm used alternating current. Edison not only argued that electrocution would be the best new way to kill condemned prisoners, but that Westinghouse's alternating current would be better at it than his own direct current. In other words, his support for electrocution was a marketing ploy. Edison hoped that using alternating current for executions would indelibly associate it with death in the public mind, and give him an edge in the electricity market.

At any rate electrocution was so horrific that it made a number of the official witnesses vomit and faint; it took two tries to kill Martha Place, the first woman to die in the electric chair, in 1899. Secondly, more than 100 years after that execution, America is still wrestling with the rights, wrongs and aesthetics of capital punishment.

Fill in the blank with the TWO most appropriate consecutive words from the passage. Second, explain Edison's hidden intent behind his campaign recommending electrocution as the means for execution.

2 Read the passage and follow the directions. [4 points]

> Beauty is the convenient and traditional name of something that art and nature share, and which gives a fairly clear sense to the idea of quality of experience and change of consciousness.
>
> I am looking out of my window in an anxious and resentful state of mind, oblivious of my surroundings, brooding perhaps on some damage done to my prestige. Then suddenly I observe a hovering kestrel. In a moment everything is altered. The brooding self with its hurt vanity has disappeared. There is nothing now but kestrel. And when I return to thinking of the other matter it seems less important.
>
> It is so patently a good thing to take delight in flowers and animals that people who bring home potted plants and watch kestrels might even be surprised at the notion that these things have anything to do with virtue. When we move from beauty in nature to beauty in art we are already in a more difficult region. The experience of art is more easily degraded than the experience of nature. A great deal of art, perhaps most art, unfortunately, actually is self-consoling fantasy, and even great art cannot guarantee the quality of its consumer's consciousness. However, great art exists and is sometimes properly experienced and even a shallow experience of what is great can have its effect. Art, and by 'art' from now on I mean good art, not _____ art, affords us a pure delight in the independent existence of what is excellent. Both in its genesis and its enjoyment it is a thing totally opposed to obsession. It invigorates our best faculties and inspires love in the highest part of the soul. It is able to do this partly by virtue of something that it shares with nature; a perfection of form that invites unpossessive contemplation and resists absorption into the obsessive dream life of the consciousness.

> Art, however, considered as a sacrament or a source of good energy, possesses an <u>extra dimension</u>. Art is less accessible than nature but also more edifying since it is actually a human product, and certain arts are actually 'about' human affairs in a direct sense. Art is a human product and virtues as well as talents are required of the artist. The good artist, in relation to his art, is brave, truthful, patient, humble; and even in non-representational art we may receive intuitions of these qualities.

Fill in the blank with the ONE most appropriate word from the passage. Second, identify to what the underlined "extra dimension" refers in the passage.

3 Read the passage and follow the directions. [4 points]

> Pablo Picasso allegedly exchanged his prints for sevruga caviar, Ian Fleming would buy only osetra caviar, Madonna prefers beluga. As the epitome of conspicuous consumption, caviar hardly needs celebrity endorsers: its iconic power exists precisely because of the exorbitant costs and their irrelevance to any concept of necessity.
>
> A long time ago, sturgeon, a creature whose roe are traded in the dark undercurrents of the world, was once the dominant large fish in every major river system of the northern hemisphere. Unchanged in form for 100m years, sturgeon cruise both fresh and salt water, hoovering up prey with a flexible cartilaginous jaw. How the eggs of this fish came from being a minor trade item among the Mongols to selling for over $100 an ounce is a story of fashion, trade and a greed that has repeatedly "outrun stewardship". Although at the time a near staple in Russia, caviar's export to the West had a shaky start: a young Louis XV reputedly spat out his first gift of caviar from Peter the Great. The eggs came into their own with the Russian aristocrats who filled the salons of Europe after the defeat of Napoleon.
>
> Later on in the United States, immigrant fishermen began to sell caviar from American sturgeon in the mid-19th century. Soon its price rocketed, and the numbers of sturgeon crashed. The "black gold" was exported back to Europe from America in the 1920s, and the Soviet Union began a decidedly capitalistic trade. Today, caviar from the Caspian is controlled by organised crime in a trade in which poaching was worth between $2 billion and $4 billion a year in the late 1990s—and which has resulted in rather few sturgeon being left alive.
>
> Going forward, conservation is the central challenge. The overfishing of sturgeon is most marked by its repeatability: first in Europe, then North America, now in Russia. Unfortunately, the allure of caviar obscures a murkier truth. However, currently, there are a range of characters fighting this exploitation, including customs agents, scientists, fishermen and CITES, the Convention on International Trade in Endangered Species that attempts to protect over 30,000 species of animals and plants.

Summarize the passage following the guidelines below.

┌─────────────── Guidelines ───────────────┐
• Summarize the above passage in ONE paragraph.
• Provide a topic sentence, two supporting ideas, and a concluding sentence based on the passage.
• Do NOT copy more than FOUR consecutive words from the passage.

제 02 회 모의고사

1. Read the passage and follow the directions. [4 points]

 Kenny Chow was born in Myanmar, and moved to New York City in 1987. He worked for years as a diamond setter for a jeweller, earning enough to buy a house for his family before he was laid off in 2011. At that point, Chow decided to become a taxi driver like his brother, scraping together financing to buy a taxi medallion for $750,000. This allowed him to operate as a sole proprietor, with the medallion as an asset.

 For a while, everything went according to plan, with taxi medallions rising in value to more than $1 million. Then the bubble burst, and along came ridesharing apps such as Lyft and Uber. The value of Chow's medallion plummeted, and it became harder to keep up the payments on his loan. In 2018, he took his own life.

 We'd all recognise that Chow's situation is unfortunate. But, arguably, he took a calculated gamble when he purchased a risky asset, and so some of us might be tempted to _____ him for his own misfortune. According to one school of thought, when these sorts of bets don't pan out, only the gambler is to blame. That might sound callous, but it's indeed the attitude that many of us seem to hold, at least in the United States: a 2014 Pew Research report found that 39 per cent of Americans believed that poverty was due to a lack of effort on poor people's part. When 'effort' includes an inability to properly weigh up the risks inherent in a decision, this suggests that, in the end, many of us think that people are responsible for their own bad luck.

I disagree with this view. But my reasons aren't solely political or moral in nature. Rather, insights from complexity science—specifically, computational complexity theory—show mathematically that there are hard limits on our capacity to make accurate and precise calculations of risk. Since it's often impossible to get a reasonable sense of what will happen in the future, it's unfair to blame people with good intentions who end up worse off as a result of unforeseen circumstances. This leads to the conclusion that compassion, not blame, is the appropriate attitude towards those who act in good faith but whose bets in life don't pay off.

Fill in the blank with the ONE most appropriate word from the passage. Second, explain why the writer of the passage opposes the conventional view shown in the passage. Do NOT copy more than THREE consecutive words from the passage.

2 Read the passage and follow the directions. [4 points]

Why do humans drink? To the person waiting at the bar on a hot summer evening, the answer seems simple: drinking is a pleasure and a relief. To the public health official reading the latest reports of alcohol's societal ruin, the answer might seem frustrating. Why would anyone drink, if it's so bad for you?

To me, and to my fellow evolutionary psychologists, the answer has emerged in a different and fascinating light, thanks to some intriguing new research. It is both simple and complex at the same time. Here's why.

Like all monkeys and apes, humans are intensely social. We have an urgent desire to schmooze and an awareness that alcohol helps our cause. Friendships protect us against outside threats and internal stresses, and this has been key to our evolutionary success. Primate social groups, unlike most other animals, rely on bonded relationships to maintain social coherence. And for humans, this is where a shared bottle of red wine plays a powerful role.

It isn't just because alcohol causes people to lose their social inhibitions and become over-friendly with our drinking chums. Rather, the alcohol itself triggers the brain mechanism that is intimately involved in building and maintaining friendships in monkeys, apes and humans. This mechanism is the endorphin system. Endorphins (the word is a contraction of "endogenous morphine") are neurotransmitters that are intimately involved, through their opiate-like effects, in the management of pain. That opiate-like all's-well-with-the-world effect seems to be crucial for establishing _____ that allow individuals to trust each other. Drinking, seen in this light, is a profound activity. It enables humans to open up their deepest selves, giving another twist to the ancient saying "in vino veritas".

Of the many social activities that trigger the endorphin system in humans (they range from laughter to singing and dancing), the consumption of alcohol seems to be one of the most effective. At detox clinics, one increasingly common form of treatment is to dose an addict with an endorphin blocker such as naltrexone that locks on to the brain's endorphin receptors but is pharmacologically neutral, so you don't get the hit when you drink. Instead, you get a mild form of cold turkey.

Fill in the blank with the TWO most appropriate consecutive words from the passage. Second, explain why using an endorphin blocker would be effective to an addict. Do NOT copy more than THREE consecutive words from the passage.

3 Read the passage and follow the directions. [4 points]

Everyone has an ego. Some of us find it difficult to contain it, while others require time to control it. An ego develops when we feel we have some superior quality in us. This quality can take many forms. It can be physical, such as height, strength, and beauty, or it can be mental, such as cunning and wisdom. It may also be financial wealth or influence through position, power or even popularity. Ego-driven people reveal certain characteristics in their common life.

People who are ego-driven find it difficult to accept the fact that others may be better than them. They feel that their opinions are always the best, their information is the most accurate, their attitude towards things are the most apt, their method or approach to solving problems is the only correct one, their suggestions must be accepted, and their decisions must be the most appropriate. In other words, they can never be wrong. They insist that they are still right despite all the arguments against them. They become easily angry and irrational.

Ego-driven people are dominated by fear or self-doubt, which is when they think less of themselves than they should and are consumed with their own shortcomings. They are afraid to fail because they think their worth as human beings depends on how others see them. To them success is measured by the number of wins they achieve.

The overactive ego can be a big barrier to people working together effectively. Ego-driven behavior can trickle down to other peers and employees, making it difficult to get anything productive accomplished. Worse still, these people tend to reward those who please them or present only positive feedback. People who sincerely report the truth will receive admonition. To survive in the real world, ego-driven people need to endeavor to change their characters. Nobody can healthily endure such a temperament.

Write a summary following the guidelines below.

Guidelines
• Summarize the above passage in ONE paragraph. • Provide a topic sentence, two supporting ideas, and a concluding sentence based on the passage. • Do NOT copy more than FIVE consecutive words from the passage.

4 Read the passage and follow the directions. [4 points]

A rocket powered by kerosene and liquid oxygen and carrying a scientific observatory blasted off into space at 10:49 p.m., March 6, 2009 (by local calendars and clocks). The launch came from the third planet out from a G-type star, 25,000 light-years from the center of a galaxy called the Milky Way, itself located on the outskirts of the Virgo Cluster of galaxies. On the night of the launch, the sky was clear, with no precipitation or wind, and the temperature was 292 degrees by the absolute temperature scale. Local intelligent life forms cheered the launch. Shortly before the blastoff, the government agency responsible for spacecraft, named the National Aeronautics and Space Administration, wrote in the global network of computers: "We are looking at a gorgeous night to launch the Kepler observatory on the first-ever mission dedicated to finding planets like ours outside the solar system."

The above account might have been written by an intelligent life form located on exactly the kind of distant planet that Kepler would soon begin to search for. Named after the Renaissance astronomer Johannes Kepler, the observatory was specifically designed to find planets outside our solar system that would be "habitable". That is, neither so near their central star that water would be boiled off, nor so far away that water would freeze. Most biologists consider liquid water to be a precondition for life, even life very different from that on Earth. Kepler has surveyed about 150,000 sun-like stellar systems in our galaxy and discovered over 1,000 alien planets. Its enormous stockpile of data is still being analyzed.

For centuries, we human beings have speculated on the possible existence and prevalence of life elsewhere in the universe. For the first time in history, we can begin to answer that profound question. At this point, the results of the Kepler mission can be extrapolated to suggest that something like 10 percent of all stars have a(n) _____ planet in orbit. That fraction is large. With 100 billion stars just in our galaxy alone, and so many other galaxies out there, it is highly probable that there are many, many other solar systems with life. From this perspective, life in the cosmos is common.

However, there's another, grander perspective from which life in the cosmos is rare. That perspective considers all forms of matter, both animate and inanimate. Even if all "habitable" planets (as determined by Kepler) do indeed harbor life, the fraction of all material in the universe in living form is fantastically small.

Fill in the blank with the ONE most appropriate word from the passage. Second, identify how many perspectives on life in the universe appear in the passage and describe what they are.

1 Read the passage and follow the directions. [4 points]

We love being angry, because it makes us feel smart. It makes us feel like we care more than the next person (who we assure ourselves doesn't care enough), because we're more across the facts than they are. That we have the necessary ideas to fix everything. That we're the ones that need to be in charge. That when we call someone a Nazi, or a sexist, or a bigot, it's not our opinion, it's a fact. That when we call someone out or worse, try to ruin their career, they deserve it.

That's an astounding level of arrogance. The biggest problem with outrage, however, is that it has been weaponised. Outrage can sell like crazy, because it's a strong emotion and strong emotions force people into action. That's why political parties, instead of coming together to find solutions, whip their supporters into a frenzy of anger against the other side. Corporations are now getting in on the action too. They weaponise your outrage to _____ their products, such as Gillette with their ill fated ad campaign and Nike using Colin Kaepernick to bring socially conscious consumers to their brand.

Nike sales increased 31% after that ad was released and caused a 6 billion dollar brand increase. You think they put that ad out there to take a social stand? They used your outrage to cash in, and they cashed in big time.

The mainstream media is by far the worst culprit, however, because without your attention they don't have a business model. They have to make you keep clicking and tuning in, otherwise their advertising dollars dry up. That's why everything is increasingly sensationalised and it's no longer about reporting facts. A headline that makes you emotional causes you to click. The article gets you pissed off, which sends you to the comments section to argue with people.

The topic trends on social media, which you're of course taking part in. Rinse, repeat.

Fill in the blank with the ONE most appropriate word from the passage. Second, explain the meaning of the underlined words in the last sentence.

2 Read the passage and follow the directions. [4 points]

In 2007, the American psychologist Roy Baumeister put forward what has become the most influential psychological model of self-control. His strength model likens willpower to a muscle. If you start doing pushups, you'll feel only a minor burn. But keep it up, and that minor burn will grow into a full-blown conflagration, at which point you won't be able to keep going. Baumeister suggested that the same thing happens when you use self-control. If you overwork your self-control muscle, you'll eventually run out of willpower, and lose the ability to exert self-control.

The success of Baumeister's book *Willpower: Rediscovering the Greatest Human Strength* (2012) suggests that the strength model resonates with many people. As a doctoral student studying self-control, I can understand why. The model eloquently explains many of our most vexing self-control failures. A tumultuous week, capped off by an agonising day, sapped your willpower, leaving you unable to resist those sweets. Additionally, it conforms to our commonsense beliefs about self-control. After all, everyone knows that self-control is hard and more often than not we need herculean willpower to overcome _____.

If the strength model is correct, what does this mean for improving your self-control? Applying the muscle analogy, one possibility might be to strengthen your 'self-control muscle'. Researchers have tested this by asking people to do things such as brush their teeth with their nondominant hand for two weeks. Such exercises are quite challenging because they force you to curtail deeply ingrained habits using 'inhibitory self-control'. But does self-control training actually work? According to a 2017 meta-analysis of many relevant studies, self-control training seems to be effective at improving 'self-control stamina'—the ability to exert inhibitory self-control for longer periods.

So, is that the solution to greater self-discipline? Exercise your self-control muscle and get better at inhibitory self-control?

Unfortunately, it's not so simple. You might have noticed how I switched back and forth between 'inhibitory self-control' and the broader concept of 'self-control', but the two are not synonymous. Though boosting your inhibitory self-control or 'willpower' might sound appealing—perhaps you imagined yourself using inhibitory self-control to force yourself not to eat the sweets, just like you would if you forced yourself to brush with the opposite hand—it's not clear that inhibitory self-control actually works this way in everyday life.

Take the findings from a 2017 study that involved volunteers recording their daily experiences of temptation for a week. The individuals who experienced more temptation were less likely to achieve their long-term goals, even if they also reported using more inhibitory self-control. This suggests that using inhibitory self-control to resist those sweets might help you in the moment, but not in the long run. So even if you use <u>inhibitory training</u> to build a brawny self-control muscle, your heroic efforts are likely to leave you looking more like Sisyphus than Hercules.

Fill in the blank with the ONE most appropriate word from the passage. Second, provide TWO examples of the underlined "inhibitory training" from the passage. Do NOT copy more than THREE consecutive words from the passage.

3 Read the passage and follow the directions. [4 points]

What might recursive self-improvement look like for human beings? For the sake of convenience, we'll describe human intelligence in terms of I.Q., not as an endorsement of I.Q. testing but because I.Q. represents the idea that intelligence can be usefully captured by a single number, this idea being one of the assumptions made by proponents of an intelligence explosion. In that case, recursive self-improvement would look like this: Once there's a person with an I.Q. of, say, 300, one of the problems this person can solve is how to convert a person with an I.Q. of 300 into a person with an I.Q. of 350. And then a person with an I.Q. of 350 will be able to solve the more difficult problem of converting a person with an I.Q. of 350 into a person with an I.Q. of 400. And so forth.

Do we have any reason to think that this is the way intelligence works? I don't believe that we do. For example, there are plenty of people who have I.Q.s of 130, and there's a smaller number of people who have I.Q.s of 160. None of them have been able to increase the intelligence of someone with an I.Q. of 70 to 100, which is implied to be an easier task. None of them can even increase the intelligence of animals, whose intelligence is considered to be too low to be measured by I.Q. tests. If increasing someone's I.Q. were an activity like solving a set of math puzzles, we ought to see successful examples of it at the low end, where the problems are easier to solve. But we don't see strong evidence of that happening.

Maybe it's because we're currently too far from the <u>necessary threshold</u>; maybe an I.Q. of 300 is the minimum needed to increase anyone's intelligence at all. But, even if that were true, we still don't have good reason to believe that endless _____ is likely. For example, it's entirely possible that the best that a person with an I.Q. of 300 can do is increase another person's I.Q. to 200. That would allow one person with an I.Q. of 300 to grant everyone around them an I.Q. of 200, which frankly would be an amazing accomplishment. But that would still leave us at a plateau; there would be no recursive self-improvement and no intelligence explosion.

Fill in the blank with the TWO most appropriate consecutive words from the passage. Second, explain the meaning of the underlined words.

4 Read the passage and follow the directions. [4 points]

It is noticeable in history that sometimes it takes a very great challenge or great crisis to get us collectively to do things we wouldn't think of doing in normal times because they're too expensive or too disruptive. A war is one of those challenges. During wartime governments which talked about austerity suddenly spend money with a free hand because it has been absolutely essential to keep societies going.

Many medical advances came as a result of war. Penicillin, for example, which was discovered in the interwar years of the 1920s, was considered too expensive to produce. Then the Second World War came along and suddenly it's not too expensive when you want to keep alive those who are fighting for you. In addition, research projects during the Second World War and the Cold War led to the boom in science and technology in the United States. The Internet really is a product of research that was funded in American universities. And a lot of the success of Silicon Valley is based on research that the government funded for its own purposes for the Cold War, which turned out to have a peacetime application.

Wars have also led to more social equality. When the men went off to battle, the women on the home front ended up running things, which led to political changes. Women in a number of countries had been agitating for the vote before the First World War, and the argument was that you don't have a stake in society in the way men do, so you should stay at home. In the First World War, there was a huge demand for men to go into the armies, and women found themselves doing jobs which they had not been considered capable of before. So they drove tractors on farms or they worked on assembly lines and in explosive factories. The government in Britain and a few other countries recognized that women had made a contribution to the war. The argument for denying them the vote just really didn't stand anymore.

As mentioned above, war has led to lots of progress. However, modern warfare is increasingly deadly because the technology is so much more lethal. Future wars will use more artificial intelligence and killer robots. What is crucial is to question who is ultimately going to control such weapons and what is to be done to control devastating wars.

Write a summary following the guidelines below.

Guidelines

- Summarize the above passage in ONE paragraph.
- Provide a topic sentence, major supporting details, and a concluding sentence based on the passage.
- Do NOT copy more than FIVE consecutive words from the passage.

1 Read the passage and follow the directions. [4 points]

The Tipping Point is the biography of an idea, and the idea is very simple. It is that the best way to understand the emergence of fashion trends, the ebb and flow of crime waves, or, for that matter, the transformation of unknown books into bestsellers, or the rise of teenage smoking, or the phenomena of word of mouth, or any number of the other mysterious changes that mark everyday life is to think of them as epidemics. Ideas and products and messages and behaviors spread just like viruses do. The rise of Hush Puppies and the fall of New York's crime rate are textbook examples.

Although they may sound as if they don't have very much in common, they share a basic, underlying pattern. First of all, they are clear examples of contagious behavior. No one took out an advertisement and told people that the traditional Hush Puppies were cool and they should start wearing them. Those kids simply wore the shoes when they went to clubs or cafes or walked the streets of downtown New York, and in so doing exposed other people to their fashion sense. They infected them with the Hush Puppies virus.

The crime decline in New York surely happened <u>the same way</u>. It wasn't that some huge percentage of would-be murderers suddenly sat up in 1993 and decided not to commit any more crimes. Nor was it that the police managed magically to intervene in a huge percentage of situations that would otherwise have turned deadly. What happened is that the small number of people in the small number of situations in which the police or the new social forces had some impact started behaving very differently, and that behavior somehow spread to other would-be criminals in similar situations. Somehow a large number of people in New York got infected with an anti-crime _____ in a short time.

Fill in the blank with the ONE most appropriate word from the passage. Second, explain what the underlined "the same way" means.

2 Read the passage and follow the directions. [4 points]

When I visited my grandmother at the undertakers, an hour or so before her funeral, I was struck by how different death is from sleep. A sleeping individual shimmers with fractional movements. The dead seem to rest in paused animation, so still they look smaller than in life. It's almost impossible not to feel as if something very like the soul is no longer present. Yet my grandmother had also died with Alzheimer's. Even in life, something of who she was had begun to abandon her. And I wondered, as her memories vanished, had she become a little less herself, a little less human?

These end-of-life stages prick our imaginations. They confront us with some unsettling ideas. We don't like to face the possibility that irreversible biological processes in our body can snuff out the stunning light of our individual experience. We prefer to deny our body altogether, and push away the dark tendrils of a living world we fear. The trouble for us is that this story —that we aren't really our bodies but some special, separate 'thing'—has made a muddle of reality. Problems flow from the notion that we're split between a superior human half and the inferior, mortal _____ of an animal. In short, we've come to believe that our bodies and their feelings are a lesser kind of existence. But what if we're wrong? What if all parts of us, including our minds, are deeply biological, and our physical experiences are far more meaningful and richer than we've been willing to accept?

As far as we know, early hunter-gatherer animist societies saw spirit everywhere. All life possessed a special, non-physical essence. In European classical thought, many also believed that every living thing had a soul. But souls were graded. Humans were thought to have a superior soul within a hierarchy. By the time of theologians such as the Italian Dominican friar and philosopher Thomas Aquinas, in the 13th century, this soulful view of life had retreated, leaving humans the only creature still in possession of an immortal one. As beings with a unique soul, we were more than mere animals. Our lives were set on a path to salvation. Life was now a great chain of being, with only the angels and God above us.

Fill in the blank with the ONE most appropriate word from the passage. Second, describe to what the underlined "this soulful view of life" refers.

3 Read the passage and follow the directions. [4 points]

> Clive Bell, an English art critic, who was one of the major apologists at the beginning of 20th century for those revolutionary movements in postimpressionistic painting and sculpture that gave up the old ideal of "imitating nature," not out of incompetence, but on principle. These movements went from the wilful "distortion" of the objects of ordinary experience, as in Cubism, to their elimination, as in Mondrian, to the uninhibited squiggles and splashes of pigments in the "action painting" and "abstract expressionism" of our own day.
>
> Bell's strategy was his legislative use of the term "art": story-telling and description on canvas are not, as has been generally thought, art at all; only its organization of the elements of line, mass, and color, or what Bell calls "significant form," entitles a painting or sculpture to be called a "work of art."
>
> He asserted that purely formal qualities—i.e., the relationships and combinations of lines and colours—are the most important elements in works of art. The aesthetic emotion aroused in the viewer by a painting springs primarily from an apprehension of its _____, rather than from a "reading" of its subject matter. Bell pointed to the works of Paul Cézanne as those in which formal properties were manifested most purely, and attacked the public's preoccupation with the anecdotal, narrative, and morally didactic functions of traditional realistic painting.
>
> It is fair to say that Bell's theory has not been widely accepted among aestheticians. The wholesale exclusion of representation from the definition of "art" is thought too extreme and Bell's injunction that we should "look through" the person or event depicted in the painting, to the form, is too expensive.
>
> Bell's formalism is extreme, and yet it is not a lunatic fringe theory of the sort that can comfortably be ignored. If you read at all widely in recent aesthetics and criticism, you find Bell being "refuted" at almost every turn. <u>Those who will not believe him have had to come to terms with him.</u>

Fill in the blank with the TWO most appropriate consecutive words from the passage. Second, explain what the writer of the passage argues in the last sentence.

4 Read the passage and follow the directions. [4 points]

> Many of us can be unknowingly suffering from polluted information. It is more prevalent due to the digitized world where the information flows to every individual's phone, tablet and computer in no time. Polluted information is the sharing or developing of false information with or without the intent of harming. There are three categories of content being used to pollute the information ecosystem.
>
> Spreaders of disinformation, false content designed to cause harm, are motivated by one of three distinct goals: to make money, to have political influence, or to cause trouble for the sake of it. Those who spread misinformation, false content shared by a person who does not realize it is false or misleading, are driven by sociopsychological factors. These people are performing their identities on social platforms in order to feel connected to others. Disinformation turns into misinformation when people share disinformation without realizing it is false.
>
> Finally, a new term, "malinformation," describes genuine information that is shared with the intent to cause harm. An example of this happened when foreign agents hacked into politicians' emails and leaked personal secrets to the public to damage reputations. It must be noted that the most effective disinformation always has a kernel of truth to it, and indeed most of the content being disseminated now is not fake, but misleading. Instead of wholly fabricated stories, influence agents are reframing genuine content and using hyperbolic headlines.
>
> All sufferers from polluted information need psycho-social counseling and sometimes require strong regulations and enforcement to alleviate information disorder. The most critical intervention is to be mindful of the fact that not all posts in social media and news are real, and need to be interpreted carefully.

Write a summary following the guidelines below.

---Guidelines---

- Summarize the above passage in ONE paragraph.
- Provide a topic sentence, major supporting details, and a concluding sentence based on the passage.
- Do NOT copy more than FIVE consecutive words from the passage.

제 05 회 모의고사

1 **Read the passage and follow the directions.** [4 points]

To understand why so many people have turned to online celebrity friends, we need to look at the long history of friendship. At its simplest, friends are people who satisfy our need to belong. The psychologists Roy Baumeister and Mark Leary showed that people's need to belong is satisfied only when pleasant interactions with other people are framed in a predictable and regular structure. In the deep human past, such belongingness was mostly provided by the extended family: spouses, parents, children, siblings, grandparents, aunts, uncles and cousins. The history of modern friendship is how people have responded to disruptions of that family structure of belongingness by looking outside it, to sworn brothers, friends, TV hosts, and podcasters.

In the West this history begins perhaps in the 14th century, when in short succession Europe was hit by the Great Famine and then the Black Death. As much as half the population died. This disrupted the family, that central foundation of belonging. People responded by developing close, bonded relationships with people _____ their families, particularly those who shared a mutual interest or a similar outlook: friends. The word friend and its cognates started to appear more frequently in documents. People started to write letters to friends about their daily lives, their emotions, and their souls. Sometimes men swore eternal brotherhood to one another in church, exchanging rings, merging their heraldry, and planning to be buried side by side like married couples. A number of new institutions arose to facilitate these bonded relationships with non-kin, including the confraternity. These institutions of belonging turned strangers into brothers and sisters through concrete rituals of solidarity like sharing bread and singing songs. You could rely on these friends. They ate with you when you were hungry, gave you money when you were broke, and said mass for you after you died: because they could trust that you would do the same for them.

Fill in the blank with the ONE most appropriate word from the passage. Second, describe what the writer cites as the trigger event for the growth of non-familial relationships.

2 Read the passage and follow the directions. [4 points]

To this day, Americans are unusually supportive of meritocracy, and their support goes a long way toward explaining their embrace of American-style capitalism. According to one recent study, just 40 percent of Americans attribute higher incomes primarily to luck rather than hard work—compared with 54 percent of Germans, 66 percent of Danes, and 75 percent of Brazilians. But perception cannot survive for long when it is distant from reality, and recent trends seem to indicate that America is drifting away from its meritocratic ideals. If the drifting continues, the result could be a breakdown of popular support for free markets and the demise of America's unique version of capitalism.

Meritocracy is a difficult principle to sustain in a democracy. Any system that allocates rewards on the basis of merit inevitably gives higher compensation to the few, leaving the majority of people potentially envious. In a democracy, the majority generally rules. Why should that majority agree to grant a minority disproportionate power and rewards?

A little more than a decade ago this dynamic played out neatly at the University of Chicago, an institution that still attracts market-oriented people, thanks to its association with the great free-market economist Milton Friedman. Who could be more promarket and promeritocracy than Master in Business Administration (MBA) students who attend such a school, investing tens of thousands of dollars and two years of their lives to reap the rewards of a meritocratic system? Nevertheless, in a move that contradicted the meritocratic spirit, University of Chicago MBA students voted not to reveal their grades to recruiters. The reason was clear: allowing recruiters to distinguish among them on the basis of merit would benefit a minority of them at the expense of a majority. Even the most meritocratic people, then, can vote against meritocracy when it damages their own prospects. No wonder meritocracy is so politically fragile.

Nevertheless, two factors help sustain a meritocratic system in the face of this challenge: a culture that considers it legitimate to reward effort with higher compensation and benefit large enough, and spread widely enough through the system, to counter popular discontent with inequality. The cultural factor is easy to spot in America, which encouraged meritocracy from its inception. In the 18th century, the social order throughout the world was based on birthrights: nobles ruled Europe and Japan and the caste system prevailed in India. The American Revolution was a revolt against aristocracy and the immobility of European society, but unlike the French Revolution, which emphasized the principle of equality, it championed the freedom to pursue happiness. In other words, America was founded on equality of opportunities, not of outcomes. The subsequent economic success of the new country cemented the belief in assigning rewards and responsibilities according to _____.

Fill in the blank with the ONE most appropriate word from the passage. Second, explain the conflict presented by the writer between meritocracy and democracy.

3 Read the passage and follow the directions. [4 points]

Perhaps you've seen the painting: a pipe, depicted with photographic realism, floats above a line of careful script that reads "Ceci n'est pas une pipe"—"This is not a pipe." René Magritte painted *The Treachery of Images* in the 1920s, and people have been talking ever since about what it means.

Did Magritte intend to remind us that a representation is not the object it depicts—that his painting is "only" a painting and not a pipe? Such an interpretation is widely taught to college students, but if it is true, Magritte went to an awful lot of trouble—carefully selecting a dress-finish pipe of particularly elegant design, making dozens of sketches of it, taking it apart to familiarize himself with its anatomy, then painting its portrait with great care and skill—just to tell us something we already knew. In another canvas, *The Two Mysteries*, Magritte is even more insistent: the original pipe painting, complete with caption, is depicted as sitting on an easel that rests on a plank floor, but above that painting, to the left, hovers a second pipe, larger (or closer) than the painted canvas and its frame. What we have here is a painting of a(n) _____. Obviously the smaller pipe is a painting and not a pipe. But what is the second pipe, the one that looms outside the represented canvas? And if that too is but a painting, then where does the painting end?

It seems to me that the roots of the paradox reside in the concept of the frame. When we look at a realistic painting—a portrait of a historical figure—we accept by convention that the portrait represents a real person and actual objects. When that convention is denied, as in Magritte's pipe paintings, the point is not to remind us that paintings are not real. That much is true but trivial. The point is to challenge the belief that everything outside the frame is real.

The enemy of artists like Magritte is naïve realism—the dogged assumption that the human sensory apparatus accurately records the one and only real world, of which the human brain can make but one accurate model. The truth, of course, is that nobody can grasp reality whole, that each person's universe is to some extent unique, and that this circumstance makes it impossible for us to prove that there is but one true reality.

Fill in the blank with the ONE most appropriate word from the passage. Second, explain the main reason René Magritte criticizes naïve realism.

4 Read the passage and follow the directions. [4 points]

> As marketers, we use our marketing data all the time in measuring and assessing user behavior related to digital advertising and engagement. But it is extremely important to remember that marketing data is an imperfect representation of user behavior and not a perfect simulation. There are reasons that marketing data is imperfect.
>
> The first is in the nature of tracking. Tracking is technically limited in its scope and reach. At best, tracking can measure engagement from the same device over time, or the same multi-device account over time. This only works if the tracking is implemented correctly in the first place and is not disabled by the end user. Because of the technical limitations of tracking there will always be engagement that is not tracked because of multi-device use, the amount of time for which the tracking is active (cookie window), or because of personal opt-out at the user level either by choice or by browser pre-set settings.
>
> The second main source of imperfection in marketing data is in user behavior. As humans we have a wide variety of choices and methods of interacting with advertising. Some of us choose to avoid interacting with advertising as much as possible while some of us behave in the opposite fashion. Some of us will choose not to click on ads at all, some of us don't hesitate. Some of us need to heavily research purchases, some don't. There is not one engagement path that is adhered to by all users yet often our data is interpreted through a "single funnel" lens that introduces inaccuracies in interpreting data.
>
> So what is a marketer to do? The best thing you can do is to fully utilize data to test your own model of reality. The best data firms don't blindly use data but instead use it to inform their perception of reality. Our data is not reality, but an imperfect reflection of reality biased by user behavior, technical limitations, and process. Our best response is to acknowledge and accept this and use it to our advantage.

Write a summary following the guidelines below.

― Guidelines ―
- Summarize the above passage in ONE paragraph.
- Provide a topic sentence, major supporting details, and a concluding sentence based on the passage.
- Do NOT copy more than FIVE consecutive words from the passage.

제 06 회 모의고사

1 Read the passage and follow the directions. [4 points]

When I think of my first semester of college, the memory comes to me as a physical sensation. I feel tired. There is the siren-screech of an alarm sounding at 3:40 in the morning. I feel it in my teeth. Then images: the orange glow of the jumbo numbers in pitch black, the instinctual, semiconscious tapping of the button, the gradual shrinking of my bed as I climb out of it and move toward the door. I do not change my clothes. It was my habit to dress for the day the night before, because an alarm blaring at 3:40 really does sound much better than an alarm blaring at 3:30.

Outside I feel the Rocky Mountain winter on my cheeks as I begin the scramble to campus on sidewalks that will not be salted for another three hours. I'm heading for the engineering building, where I will pick gum out of short nylon carpet, wipe strange equations from dusty chalkboards, and scour the interior of toilet bowls with an odorless blue gel. I will finish around 8 a.m., then head to class.

This was my routine for the first two months of my freshman year. Then, because I was short on rent, I added a second job, serving coleslaw and Jell-O in the cafeteria. The woman who worked alongside me was also a(n) _____ who could not afford the meal plan. I don't recall either of us mentioning the fact that we were serving food we could not afford to eat; I don't recall feeling angry as I hooked my apron in my locker and reached into my backpack for my own lunch, a protein bar and pack of ramen noodles (10 cents at my local grocery store). I also don't recall feeling humiliated or disrespected to be cleaning plates or toilets used by my classmates. The full complexity of my opinion on inequality and poverty then could have been summed up with utter simplicity: I was tired.

I wrote about these and other experiences in my 2018 memoir, <Educated>, which surprised me by becoming a best seller. My story was one of extremes: born in the mountains of Idaho to Mormon parents who kept me out of school, I had never set foot in a classroom before my first semester of college at Brigham Young University. I graduated in 2008 and won a scholarship to the University of Cambridge, where I earned a Ph.D.

A curious thing happens when you offer up your life for public consumption: People start to interpret your biography, to explain to you what they think it means. At book signings, in interviews, I'm often told that my story is uplifting, that I am a model of resilience, an "inspiration." Which is a nice thing to be told, so I say thank you. But every so often someone takes it a bit further, and says something to which I do not have a response. I'm told, "You are living proof of the American dream, that absolutely anything is possible for anybody."

But am I? Is that what the story means?

Fill in the blank with the ONE most appropriate word from the passage. Second, explain the implication of the underlined part in the last sentence.

2 Read the passage and follow the directions. [4 points]

In reality, people listen to the same music, but acquire different experiences. Subjectivity is an integral part of all art, and sometimes, even where it seems the least likely, one finds a comprehensive communication between the artist and the audience very difficult. For example, not just in abstract painting, but in the most straightforward painting. Just take one of the best-known paintings, the Mona Lisa, painted by Da Vinci. No one mistakes that this painting is the portrait of a woman; that much we know. However, the intriguing smile in this painting is interpreted in so many different ways, pertaining to what state of the mind this smile depicts. As such, an audience can never be sure exactly what the artist had in mind. This holds true on all levels, and thus, perfect communication cannot occur between most artists and their audiences through their art alone.

To use a few other examples, I have some close friends who are really good painters. Often, I try to engage them intellectually to educate myself and to see what they think about their art as artists. For example, one friend uses the image of horses in most of his paintings, and he also paints so that all the elements are in suspense and devoid of _____. For example, a natural position for a human would be standing up, sitting down, or lying down. However, he puts them in all positions, and some are in diagonal positions in suspense. Or you will find an image with the head of a horse upside down, mixed with humans in sitting, standing, or suspended positions. Collectively, the different elements in the painting defy the laws of physics and gravity, and as such, it becomes surreal, which is not a new phenomenon in the world of art.

But, when asked why he mixes horses with humans in so many of his paintings, he responded that to him, the horse is a symbol of being genteel; he simply likes them, and they find their way into his paintings. When asked why such disorder governs all the elements in most of his paintings, he responded that, "in the real world, the force of gravity makes all objects earthbound and imposes order on them." A similar force, human needs, imposes a similar order on humans and conditions their lives. Defying the force of gravity in his paintings is a metaphor for defying the forces that deprive humans of absolute freedom by imposing condition on them. I asked him if labeling him a rebel would be a wrong assumption, and he responded that it would not be.

Fill in the blank with the ONE most appropriate word from the passage. Second, identify to what the writer compares the ordering of human lives in the critique of his colleague's paintings.

3 Read the passage and follow the directions. [4 points]

Our attitudes to ourselves tend to be distorted, but the distortion is not all in one direction. When Brittany, age six, went to the fair she visited the Hall of Mirrors, and she was fascinated by the different ways in which her body was distorted. In one mirror she looked tall and thin; in another short and fat. Other mirrors, however, distorted some parts of her body in one way and others in another way. Her head was made tall and thin; her chest long and wide; and her legs shrunk until her feet seemed almost to spring directly from her hips.

The distorted beliefs we have of ourselves can be very similar. Most of us operate in (at least) two ways: we can be extraordinarily critical of ourselves, or we can give ourselves outrageous leniency. We may do first one and then the other, even though they seem contradictory. We may put our own interests above those of others, and yet place our self-worth well beneath that of others. Indeed, perhaps one distorted view springs from the other. Because of the deep fear that we are inferior to others, we might try and boost our self-image through bragging and attempting to get the better of others.

At the root of depression there is usually a(n) _____ of oneself. To help you to see yourself more clearly, it may be helpful to think about what you would say about yourself if you were on the outside looking in: as if you could be another person and take a thoroughly objective look at yourself.

Winston Churchill suffered from recurrent, short-lived depressions. He gave them a name: the black dog, a name that had been used by Samuel Johnson before him, and has been used by many others since. Labeling the depression helped him to cope with it and to accept it, knowing that in due course it would go away. Such labeling helps to domesticate the depression so that it becomes, if not a friend, at least an enemy you know and for which, perhaps, you even feel some affection.

When relatively short-lived, recurrent depressions attack you, it may be best to wall them off—to limit or contain them. Then they will take the shortest course. Say to yourself, "Ah, it's my depression again. It will pass away soon as it always does; I've just got to keep going." This is especially helpful for people who tend to get depressed about getting depressed, which is a very common problem and adds insult to injury.

Fill in the blank with the TWO most appropriate consecutive words from the passage. Second, explain the meaning of the underlined part.

4 Read the passage and follow the directions. [4 points]

It is certainly no accident that insects are the most abundant and most diverse group of organisms on earth. They have maintained a position of ecological preeminence for over 400 million years. While no single ecological or physiological attribute can account for this unparalleled success, the insects do have a unique combination of characteristics which have given them an unusual survival advantage.

Unlike vertebrates, an insect's supporting skeleton is located on the outside of its body. This exoskeleton is a marvelous structure that not only gives shape and support to the body's soft tissues, but also provides protection from attack or injury, minimizes the loss of body fluids in both arid and freshwater environments, and assures mechanical advantage to muscles for strength and agility in movement. As a "suit of armor", the exoskeleton can resist both physical and chemical attack. It is covered by an impervious layer of wax that prevents desiccation.

In general, the insects are marvels of miniaturization. Most species are between 2 and 20mm (0.1~1.0 inch) in length, although they range in size from giant moths to tiny parasitic wasps. For an animal with an exoskeleton, small size is a distinct advantage. If insects were as large as cows or elephants, their exoskeleton would have to be proportionately thicker to support the additional mass of body tissue. But a thicker exoskeleton would also be heavier and more cumbersome. Even the simplest movements would require a larger muscle volume and consume more energy. Another advantage of small size is the minimal resources needed for survival and reproduction. A crumb is a feast; a dewdrop quenches thirst; a pebble provides shade. In some cases, food requirements are so modest that an insect may live on a single plant or animal for its entire life and never exhaust its food supply.

Insects have witnessed the rise and fall of dinosaurs. They have survived at least four major cataclysms that resulted in planet-wide extinctions. Judging from their capablities of survival, they continue to thrive despite mankind's best efforts at eradication.

Write a summary following the guidelines below.

Guidelines

- Summarize the above passage in ONE paragraph.
- Provide a topic sentence, major supporting details, and a concluding sentence based on the passage.
- Do NOT copy more than FIVE consecutive words from the passage.

제 07 회 모의고사

1 Read the passage and follow the directions. [4 points]

A UCL study, published in the *Journal of Cognitive Neuroscience*, shows that actors may suppress their core sense of self when taking on new roles, suggesting that theatre training can significantly affect brain mechanisms. The researchers collaborated with Flute Theatre, which delivers interactive Shakespeare productions for autistic individuals using the Hunter Heartbeat Method. Using innovative brain imaging technology, they monitored the _____ of actors rehearsing *A Midsummer Night's Dream*.

The findings revealed that actors exhibited suppressed activity in the left anterior prefrontal cortex—a region associated with self-awareness—when hearing their own names while performing. In contrast, when not in character, they responded normally to their names. This suppression was consistently observed across multiple actors over repeated rehearsals. Lead researcher Dwaynica Greaves noted that actors may learn to suppress their sense of self as part of their training, allowing them to fully embody different characters. This is the first time neuroscientists have recorded brain activity in actors during a performance, providing insight into how theatre training impacts the brain.

The researchers also studied how pairs of actors synchronized their brain activity during rehearsals. They found that the right inferior frontal gyrus and right frontopolar cortex—areas associated with social interaction and action planning—showed similar activity patterns in actors working together. This synchronization was specific to brain activity and did not appear in physiological measurements like heart rate or breathing, indicating that particular brain systems are coordinated during complex social interactions in performance.

Greaves emphasized the potential for this research to foster collaboration between neuroscientists and theatre professionals. The study suggests that theatrical training may enhance social cognitive abilities, and the researchers plan to investigate whether young people, including those with autism, can develop new social skills through theatre participation.

Kelly Hunter, Artistic Director of Flute Theatre, reflected on how Shakespeare instinctively understood the significance of hearing one's own name—a concept now confirmed by scientific research. Since collaborating with UCL, Hunter has refined her work with autistic individuals, particularly non-verbal participants, by focusing on the effects of names in sensory drama games. This partnership has blended artistic intuition with scientific insight to deepen understanding of how we communicate and connect.

Fill in the blank with the TWO most appropriate consecutive words from the passage. Second, in what ways could the findings about suppressed self-awareness during performances inform therapeutic practices for individuals with autism or other social cognitive disorders?

2 Read the passage and follow the directions. [4 points]

The 2000 presidential election ushered in a new awareness of and concern for how Americans cast their votes. In reaction, Congress passed the Help America Vote Act of 2002, and many states purchased new voting systems, computerized their voter registration records, and improved their overall election administration. Registration, voting systems, and administration, however, are only part of what voters confront when casting their votes.

Whatever the specific mechanisms and procedures in place, voters make use of a ballot. Whether a series of names and images programmed on a touch screen or printed on paper, the way in which the ballot is formatted has the potential to influence voters' abilities to cast their votes as intended and perhaps even influence the negative outcome of an election. This point was forcefully made by the butterfly ballot that caused such a stir in 2000 and the apparent design flaw that affected the congressional election in Sarasota County in 2006.

Ballots constitute a front line of study for a number of reasons. First, the ballot is the means through which voters register their intentions, and it is the dominant feature voters observe once they begin the voting process. Symbolically, it is more meaningful. The point of contact between the average voter and his government is the ballot. Second, varieties of ballot layouts, options, and tasks routinely affect the number of votes cast (undervoting), the expression of voter attitudes (initiatives), and the relative advantage to candidates and parties (candidate order, straight-party options). Third, the impact of ballot design may be conditioned by the mechanism by which voting is carried out, an interaction that has long existed but has only recently been studied. Fourth, different types of ballots and voting systems can affect various groups of voters differently, raising concerns about fairness and equality.

Political scientists such as Allen and Beard recognized over a century ago that ballot-related issues influence political behavior and can complicate the lives of election officials, politicians, and voters. Very recently, scholars have linked ballot-related issues to the further development of American democracy. Only in the past few years, however, have these sentiments spawned systematic research efforts.

Recent election fiascos also have highlighted the fact that ballot design, along with voting technology and election administration, can have a(n) _____ impact on public opinion toward the political system. Real and perceived shortcomings can encourage voters to view specific ballots, certain types of voting equipment, an individual election, and even elections generally as failures or fraudulent processes.

Fill in the blank with the ONE most appropriate word from the passage. Second, describe the key similarity between the ballot design issues highlighted in the 2000 election and the 2006 Sarasota election.

3 Read the passage and follow the directions. [4 points]

A Pew Research Center survey reveals that many Americans can answer at least some questions about science concepts—most can correctly identify a concern about antibiotics overuse or explain the definition of an "incubation period." However, other science concepts are more _____ for the public. For instance, fewer Americans can correctly recognize a hypothesis or identify that bases are the main components of antacids.

The survey provides an understanding of how well the public grasps science facts and processes, especially in an era where access to information is easy, but debates over its accuracy are frequent. Americans' knowledge of life sciences and earth and physical sciences varies widely. For example, nearly eight-in-ten (79%) know that antibiotic resistance is a significant concern related to overusing antibiotics, while a similar number (76%) correctly identify that an incubation period is the time during which someone has an infection but is not yet showing symptoms.

However, more complex concepts prove to be challenging. For example, when asked what the main components of antacids are, only 39% correctly answered "bases." On average, Americans answered 6.7 of 11 science questions correctly, with the median score being 7. About 39% of respondents achieved high science knowledge (nine to 11 correct answers), 32% had medium knowledge (five to eight correct answers), and 29% were classified as having low science knowledge (zero to four correct answers).

Striking differences emerge in science knowledge by education, race, and ethnicity. Men tend to score higher than women, although this is inconsistent across different science questions. Political party groups show roughly similar overall science knowledge, though conservative Republicans and liberal Democrats tend to score higher than their more moderate counterparts.

Educational attainment strongly correlates with science knowledge. Those with postgraduate degrees answer, on average, 9.1 out of 11 questions correctly, compared to 5 correct answers for those with a high school degree or less education. Furthermore, racial and ethnic disparities are significant: whites score an average of 7.6 correct answers, while Hispanics average 5.1, and Blacks 3.7. Roughly half (48%) of whites are classified as having high science knowledge, compared with 23% of Hispanics and 9% of Blacks.

These differences remain significant even when controlling for education, suggesting other factors may influence science knowledge across racial and ethnic groups.

Fill in the blank with the ONE most appropriate word from the passage. Second, what demographic factors are associated with differences in science knowledge according to the survey?

4 Read the passage and follow the directions. [4 points]

> Over the past 40 years, many health-care systems that were once publicly owned or financed have moved towards privatising their services, primarily through outsourcing to the private sector. Healthcare privatization is a widely debated issue, raising concerns about its impact on accessibility and quality of care. While proponents argue that privatization can lead to increased efficiency and innovation, critics highlight the potential risks.
>
> Privatizing healthcare can widen the gap between the have and the have-not, creating a system where only those who can afford private services receive timely and quality care. Lower-income populations may face reduced access to essential treatments, longer wait times, or substandard care in underfunded public facilities. This growing disparity undermines the principle of healthcare as a universal right and leads to a society where economic status determines health outcomes, perpetuating systemic inequalities and affecting overall public health.
>
> In a privatized healthcare system, the focus often shifts from patient well-being to maximizing profits. Healthcare providers may prioritize efficiency, cost-cutting, and profitable treatments over comprehensive, long-term care. This could result in reduced attention to preventive care, early diagnosis, and holistic patient management. Over time, the emphasis on profitability may compromise the quality of care, leading to negative health outcomes and undermining trust in healthcare institutions, as financial goals eclipse patient needs.
>
> Healthcare privatization risks increasing inequality and prioritizing profits over patient care, undermining the system's integrity. As an alternative, a mixed model combining public funding with private sector innovation could ensure universal access while maintaining efficiency and quality. Strengthening public healthcare systems with adequate funding and resources is also essential to safeguard equal access for all.

Write a summary following the guidelines below.

Guidelines

- Summarize the above passage in ONE paragraph.
- Provide a topic sentence, two supporting ideas, and a concluding sentence based on the passage.
- Do NOT copy more than FOUR consecutive words from the passage.

제 08 회 모의고사

1. **Read the passage and follow the directions.** [4 points]

> ChatGPT, the system that understands natural language and responds in kind, has caused a sensation since its launch. If you've tried it out, you'll surely have wondered what it will soon revolutionize—or, as the case may be, what it will destroy. Among ChatGPT's first victims, holds one now-common view, will be a form of writing that generations have grown up practicing throughout their education. "The essay, in particular the undergraduate essay, has been the center of humanistic pedagogy for generations," writes Stephen Marche in *The Atlantic*. "It is the way we teach children how to research, think, and write. That entire tradition is about to be disrupted from the ground up."
>
> If ChatGPT becomes able instantaneously to whip up a plausible-sounding academic essay on any given topic, what future could there be for the academic essay itself? The host of YouTube channel EduKitchen puts more or less that very question to Noam Chomsky—a thinker who can be relied upon for views on education—in a recent interview. "For years there have been programs that have helped professors detect plagiarized essays. Now it's going to be more difficult, because it's easier to plagiarize. But <u>that's about the only contribution to education that I can think of</u>." Chomsky does admit that ChatGPT-style systems may have some value for something, but "it's not obvious what."

As the relevant technology now stands, Chomsky sees the use of ChatGPT as "basically high-tech plagiarism" and "a way of avoiding learning." He likens its rise to that of the smartphone: many students "sit there having a chat with somebody on their iPhone. One way to deal with that is to ban iPhones; another way to do it is to make the class interesting." That students instinctively employ high technology to avoid learning is "a sign that the educational system is failing." If it has no appeal to students, doesn't interest them, doesn't challenge them, doesn't make them want to learn, "they'll find ways out," just as he himself did when he borrowed a friend's notes to pass a dull college chemistry class without attending it back in 1945.

Explain the implication of the underlined "that's about the only contribution to education that I can think of". Second, how does Chomsky compare the rise of ChatGPT to the rise of smartphones in classrooms? DO NOT copy more than FOUR consecutive words from the passage.

2 Read the passage and follow the directions. [4 points]

The economic recovery from the covid-19 pandemic is lopsided in many ways. Vaccinations have allowed some countries to bounce back rapidly, even as others struggle. Demand is surging in some sectors but still looks weak in others. Another big source of unevenness is slowly becoming clear. As national economies come back to life, cities are lagging seriously behind.

Before the pandemic cities seemed invincible, with economic and cultural power becoming ever more concentrated in tiny geographical areas. The exodus from urban areas at the start of the pandemic, which was motivated by fear of catching the virus and which many assumed would be temporary, now looks more permanent and indicative of a deeper shift in preferences. The big question is whether this is something to worry about.

One way to take the pulse of global cities is to use real-time mobility indicators. *The Economist* has constructed an "exodus index" using Google data on visits to sites of retail and recreation, public transport and workplaces. This compares mobility in large cities with that in their respective countries. The data point more clearly to a different sort of reallocation. Like an egg broken onto a pan, economic activity is gradually seeping outward from the center. What were once the liveliest urban areas are becoming less so.

The opinion is divided on whether the spreading out of economic activity is welcome. Economists have two longer-term concerns. The first relates to employment. Emptier offices and fewer tourists in cities could mean less employment for low-wage workers. The second worry is productivity. A core insight of urban economists is that cities, by cramming lots of different people into a small space, help foster new ideas and technologies. That would hit living standards. Are the concerns valid? On employment, there is the reason for optimism. Economies have been extraordinarily quick to reallocate jobs away from struggling city centers to places with more demand, raising overall employment. It is harder to know whether the shift from city centers will harm productivity.

> Cities administrators are shifting their focus from attracting firms to attracting residents who will pay property and consumption taxes and will contribute in improving quality of life. The _____ will not destroy cities, but it will change them.

Fill in the blank with the TWO most appropriate consecutive words from the passage. Second, how might the permanent shift away from urban centers, as indicated by the exodus index, impact the future innovation and economic growth of cities? DO NOT copy more than FOUR consecutive words from the passage.

3 Read the passage and fill in the blank with the ONE most appropriate word from the passage. [2 points]

Real numbers are called 'real' because they seem to provide the magnitudes needed for the measurement of distance, angle, time, energy, temperature, or of numerous other geometrical and physical quantities. However, the relationship between the abstractly defined 'real' numbers and physical quantities is not as clear-cut as one might imagine. Real numbers refer to a mathematical idealization rather than to any actual physically objective quantity.

The system of real numbers has the property of density, for example, that between any two of them, no matter how close, there lies a third. It is not at all clear that physical distances or times can realistically be said to have this property. If we continue to divide up the physical distance between two points, we would eventually reach scales so small that the very concept of distance, in the ordinary sense, could cease to have meaning.

It is anticipated that at the 'quantum gravity' scale of 10^{20}th of the size of a subatomic particle, this would indeed be the case. But to mirror the real numbers, we would have to go to scales indefinitely smaller than this: 10^{200}th, or 10^{2000}th, for example. It is not at all clear that such absurdly tiny scales have any physical meaning whatever.

A similar remark would hold for correspondingly tiny intervals of time. The real number system is chosen in physics for its _____ utility, simplicity, and elegance, together with the fact that it accords, over a very wide range, with the physical concepts of distance and time. It is not chosen because it is known to agree with these physical concepts over all ranges.

4 Read the passage and follow the directions. [4 points]

> The neuropsychology of bilingualism explores how knowing and using more than one language influences the brain's structure and function. As the world becomes increasingly multilingual, understanding these effects is crucial for both cognitive science and education. Two significant advantages of bilingualism in neuropsychology highlight the brain's remarkable adaptability and offer valuable insights into cognitive health.
>
> One of the primary advantages of bilingualism is the enhancement of cognitive flexibility. Bilingual individuals often demonstrate superior executive functions, such as task switching, problem-solving, and attention control. This is because bilinguals frequently engage in code-switching and language inhibition, which are cognitive processes that require constant monitoring and regulation of two language systems. These mental exercises strengthen the brain's ability to manage conflicting information, making bilingual individuals more adept at adapting to new situations and challenges.
>
> Another significant advantage of bilingualism is its contribution to greater neural efficiency. Bilingual brains exhibit more efficient neural pathways, as they are accustomed to managing and accessing multiple languages with minimal cognitive load. Studies using neuroimaging techniques, such as fMRI, have shown that bilingual individuals require less brain activity to perform certain cognitive tasks compared to monolinguals. This efficiency is particularly noticeable in areas related to language processing and executive function.
>
> The neuropsychology of bilingualism reveals that knowing more than one language offers significant cognitive and neural benefits. To further explore the benefits of bilingualism, future research could focus on understanding how these cognitive advantages can be cultivated in monolingual individuals. This approach not only deepens insights into the bilingual brain but could also promote cognitive resilience and health, especially as populations continue to age.

Write a summary following the guidelines below.

Guidelines

- Summarize the above passage in ONE paragraph.
- Provide a topic sentence, two supporting ideas, and a concluding sentence based on the passage.
- Do NOT copy more than FOUR consecutive words from the passage.

5 Read the passage and follow the directions. [4 points]

The possibility that speakers may experience and even perceive the world along language-specific lines is central to debates regarding the plasticity of human cognition. How much of our cognitive make-up is determined by our biology and how much is shaped over ontogenetic development by cultural systems such as those that may be expressed and acquired through language? This debate is not only central to the cognitive sciences, but has perennially fascinated the public with the possibility that core _____ in our humanity may arise depending on the environment in which one is raised. If your language habitually "forces" you to attend to certain experiences, it is only "natural" that one develops related habits of mind that shape one's "experiences, perceptions, associations, feelings, memories and orientations in the world".

Natural, perhaps, but how strong is the empirical evidence supporting such intuitions? I visit evidence from one of the most often cited cases in support of linguistic relativity concerning the language of space; specifically, the coordinate systems or frames of reference speakers use to talk about locations and directions.

Spatial frames of reference has been a fruitful area to study linguistic relativity. At first glance, we might expect something as basic to our survival as spatial localization to have a strong biological basis and therefore to be encoded in more or less the same way across languages. It turns out, however, that evolution has endowed us with multiple solutions to navigate the world, leaving language communities to pick and choose the coordinate system(s) speakers primarily use to encode directions and locations of objects. These systems, known as linguistic frames of reference, are used to specify the direction of an entity, generally called the 'figure', with respect to another entity, or 'ground'.

In English and other standard European languages, speakers primarily use the perspective of a viewer to establish a directional system (e.g., left/right). Environment-derived terms like 'north' and 'south' are primarily restricted to large-scale or map space. In some other languages, however, like Tseltal Mayan (Chiapas, Mexico) speakers use fixed aspects of their environment to describe directions and locations even when describing items in small-scale space such as the arrangement of items on a table top.

Such cross-linguistic differences have been argued to affect how speakers interpret, store and retrieve spatial information across modalities, resulting in greater facility using language-congruent strategies and a dispreference for language-incongruent ones. If a certain strategy is culturally required (for example through language use), and thus heavily practiced leading to a preferred default cognitive strategy, there is reason to expect performance using that strategy to be better".

Fill in the blank with the ONE most appropriate word from the passage. Second, describe how Tseltal Mayan would express the concept that English conveys as "to the left of the table".

제 09 회 모의고사

1 Read the passage and follow the directions. [4 points]

The story of how the original thirteen American colonies broke away from Great Britain and formed the United States is well known. Less well known is how African-Americans felt and what they did during the War of Independence.

At the time of the American Revolution, enslaved people made up at least 25 percent of the population of North Carolina. In actual numbers, Black people totaled perhaps seventy thousand but no more than 5 percent of them were free. Most Black people, whether enslaved or free, lived in the countryside and worked the land, planting, harvesting, and preparing crops for market. Those who lived in North Carolina's few towns worked at trades or were servants to enslavers. Skilled people who were enslaved worked as carpenters, coopers (making barrels), blacksmiths (making iron into tools and shoeing horses), wheelwrights (making and repairing wheels), and in many other skilled occupations.

Just as whites were divided by the conflict between the colonies and England, so Black people faced difficult choices. African-Americans fought for both sides, providing manpower to both the British and the revolutionaries. Their actions during the war were often decided by what they believed would best help them throw off the shackles of slavery. Most believed that victory by the British would lead to the end of slavery.

Fears of a(n) _____ gripped the South. Before the war, British military leaders recognized that the southern colonies could be greatly weakened by an uprising of slaves against their masters. The white colonists knew this, too. Joseph Hewes, one of North Carolina's signers of the Declaration of Independence, accused the British of planning to "let loose Indians on our Frontiers" and to "raise the Negroes against us," a plot that included arming slaves. James Iredell of Edenton charged the British with "exciting the negroes to cut our throats, and involve Men, Women and Children in one universal Massacre." Edenton and Wilmington organized patrols to keep careful watch on black residents at night.

Slaves, however, did not need encouragement to strike for freedom. In every colony from Maryland to Georgia, slaves weighed their chances for freedom and seemed on the edge of a slave revolt. Massachusetts revolutionary John Adams commented on a "grapevine" that spread news among slaves: "The Negroes have a wonderful art of communicating intelligence among themselves; it will run several hundreds of miles in a week or fortnight."

It is not surprising that when opportunities for freedom arose, more often than not slaves fled to the British. Thousands of African-Americans seized their freedom. With the Revolution's language of equality, independence, and liberty, slaves needed no introduction to the ideas at the heart of the struggle with Great Britain.

Fill in the blank with the TWO most appropriate consecutive words from the passage. Second, describe the THREE words from the passage that BEST correspond to the meaning of the underlined "the ideas at the heart of the struggle with Great Britain".

2 Read the passage and follow the directions. [4 points]

> Stand Your Ground. Line in the Sand. Shoot First. Make My Day. Twenty-six states have passed Stand Your Ground Laws that massively expand traditional self-defense laws. And no matter what you call them, they all have the same effect on the people of the states that pass them: more people will be killed and their killers will walk free.
>
> Advocates for Stand Your Ground laws claim they are a way to allow law-abiding citizens to defend themselves without fear of criminal prosecution. But our legal system already has robust self-defense laws in place. An available research suggests that instead of making us safer, Stand Your Ground laws lead to increased unlawful homicide rates. Contrary to what advocates of Stand Your Ground claim, there are no credible research studies that show that these laws encourage legitimate acts of self-defense.
>
> Traditional self-defense laws—which have been in effect for hundreds of years in the U.S.—give people the right to defend themselves against harm. These self-defense laws mandate that seriously injuring or killing someone should only be used as a last resort, meaning people are obligated to choose a safe alternative and retreat from danger if possible. An exception to the duty to retreat is the "castle doctrine." The castle doctrine allows people to use deadly force to defend themselves without having to try to retreat first when they are in their own homes.
>
> Stand Your Ground laws are an extension of the castle doctrine to the public sphere, erasing the long-standing duty to retreat when you are in public. Put another way, these laws allow people to kill someone in self-defense (and in some states, in defense of property) while outside their home even when there is a(n) _____.

In April 2005, the first modern Stand Your Ground law was passed in Florida. A year earlier, in the wake of Hurricane Ivan, a Florida homeowner had shot and killed a man who had entered his FEMA trailer despite the homeowner firing a warning shot. The homeowner shot the man, later identified as FEMA worker Rodney Cox, after Cox placed the homeowner in a "bear hug." He was not prosecuted for killing Cox; prosecutors decided that he was rightfully acting in self-defense.

Nevertheless, the shooting drew the attention of the National Rifle Association's Florida lobbyist, Marion Hammer, who argued that subjecting the homeowner to the standard investigative procedure after a killing was unfair treatment since he was acting in self-defense. She pushed legislators to introduce a bill that not only legalized the use of deadly force when facing a "perceived grave threat" but also granted immunity from prosecution. The bill was passed into law and Stand Your Ground was born.

Fill in the blank with the TWO most appropriate consecutive words from the passage. Second, what event led to the creation of the first modern Stand Your Ground law in the USA?

3 Read the passage and follow the directions. [4 points]

When Adele debuted her 2011 single "Someone Like You," her bittersweet ballad resonated with millions worldwide. More than a decade later, it remains one of her most popular tunes. Her artistry, as well as that of many others who have mastered the art of tugging at our heartstrings with slow and emotional beats, has a way of managing the emotional pain of heartbreak and loss.

There is no doubt that music can soothe the soul for some, and it turns out that it could also be a temporary soother for physical pain. Listening to favorite songs could reduce people's perception of pain, according to a new study. And the most effective pain relievers were found to be sad songs detailing bittersweet and emotional experiences. It doesn't take the place of Tylenol when you have a headache, but music can help take the edge off. Unlike other medications, there is no side effect or risk to listening to music (just keep the volume at a reasonable level).

The study invited 63 young adults to bring two of their favorite songs, and the only requirement was that they needed to be at least 3 minutes and 20 seconds long. One selection represented their favorite music of all time, and the other was the song they would bring with them on a desert island. The researchers also had the young adults pick one of seven songs that the team considered relaxing and were unfamiliar to the study participants.

Each person underwent 7-minute blocks where they were instructed to stare at a monitor screen while listening to their favorite music, one of the seven relaxing instrumental songs (each of which lasted for 6 minutes and 40 seconds), or a scrambled version of both songs and the relaxing song chosen. The scrambled music was a noisy jumble of all three songs, cut into fragments and randomly shuffled so that they lacked their original structure. One 7-minute block had people sitting in silence. All the while, the researchers stuck a hot object—similar to the pain of a boiling hot teacup on your skin—to the participants' left inner forearms.

> When rating their experiences, people were more likely to report feeling less pain when listening to their favorite songs compared with hearing the _____ relaxing song or silence. The scrambled songs did not reduce pain either, which the authors suggested was evidence of music being more than a distraction from an unpleasant experience.

Fill in the blank with the ONE most appropriate word from the passage. Second, explain why the researchers had each person undergo 7-minute blocks in the study. Do NOT copy more than FOUR consecutive words from the passage.

4 Read the passage and follow the directions. [4 points]

> A 401(k) plan is a retirement savings account offered by many employers that allows employees to save and invest a portion of their paycheck before taxes are taken out. It is a popular retirement savings tool that allows employees to set aside part of their paycheck into a retirement fund, often with an employer match. Designed to encourage individuals to save for retirement, 401(k)s come with both advantages and disadvantages that can influence financial security.
>
> One major benefit of a 401(k) is the tax advantage it provides. Contributions are typically made with pre-tax income, reducing taxable income and allowing more money to grow over time. The funds within a 401(k) can grow tax-deferred, meaning taxes aren't paid until withdrawals begin, typically at retirement age. This deferral can lead to significant growth potential due to compounding interest, making it a valuable long-term savings option.
>
> However, 401(k) plans also have some downsides. One drawback is the lack of flexibility, especially when it comes to accessing funds before retirement. Early withdrawals before age 59½ generally incur a 10% penalty in addition to regular income taxes, which can diminish savings significantly. Additionally, the investment options within 401(k)s may be limited to those provided by the employer, restricting the diversification and growth potential of the account.
>
> While a 401(k) offers valuable tax benefits and a structured path to retirement savings, the restrictions on early withdrawals and limited investment options may be drawbacks for some individuals. It's essential to weigh these pros and cons to determine if a 401(k) aligns with one's financial goals, as it can be a beneficial tool with careful planning and consideration.

Write a summary following the guidelines below.

Guidelines

- Summarize the above passage in ONE paragraph.
- Provide a topic sentence, two supporting ideas, and a concluding sentence based on the passage.
- Do NOT copy more than FOUR consecutive words from the passage.

제 10 회 모의고사

1 Read the passage and follow the directions. [4 points]

> A cooperative behavior is an action by one organism that benefits another organism, often referred to as the beneficiary. Johnson and Myers describe cooperation as a delicate balance between "helpers" (those providing assistance) and "recipients" (those receiving assistance). A helper may possess certain resources, knowledge, or skills that it can share with a recipient, and it decides how much to invest in assisting. The recipient, in turn, benefits from the help and may reciprocate if the conditions allow, with the outcome depending on the actions and strategies of both parties. Cooperative behaviors can be direct, indirect, or communal, and may convey advantages in securing resources, protecting against predators, or raising offspring.
>
> A key principle of cooperation theory is that, for cooperative behaviors to persist in a population, both helpers and recipients must gain some advantage, whether immediately or over time. If helpers gained no benefit from their actions, selection would favor individuals who conserved their resources. This need for mutual benefit suggests that cooperative acts must provide reliable returns.
>
> This concept is central to debates in evolutionary biology, especially around the issue of "cheating" in cooperative systems. Axelrod and Hamilton defined cheating as occurring when a recipient gains benefits from a helper's action without reciprocating or contributing in return. In other words, cheating happens when the cooperative relationship becomes one-sided. This observation raises a critical question: Why would any organism continue cooperating if there's a risk of exploitation? For example, a bird may help warn others of predators, but if others ignore warnings without reciprocating,

the system becomes unbalanced. When cheating becomes common, natural selection may favor individuals who withhold cooperation, ultimately threatening the stability of cooperative systems. As cheating increases, groups may shift toward strategies that detect and avoid cheaters, allowing only genuine cooperators to benefit from shared resources. Over time, as the population stabilizes, cooperative behaviors that promote reliable partnerships would likely prevail.

Explain why mutual benefit is essential for the persistence of cooperative behaviors in a population. Do NOT copy more than FOUR consecutive words from the passage. Second, how does cheating challenge cooperative systems? Do NOT copy more than FOUR consecutive words from the passage.

2. Read the passage and follow the directions. [4 points]

Expressionism in the early 20th century was a powerful, revolutionary art movement that sought to capture not the external world, but the internal landscapes of human emotion, often turbulent and intense. Unlike movements that prioritized realism or formalism, expressionism rejected the literal representation of physical reality, emphasizing instead a subjective portrayal of the inner experiences of the artist. This movement, which spanned across visual arts, literature, theater, film, and even architecture, emerged as a response to the rapid changes and existential uncertainties of the modern world, amplified by the profound impacts of industrialization, urbanization, and later, the traumas of war.

In visual arts, expressionist painters like Edvard Munch, Ernst Ludwig Kirchner, and Wassily Kandinsky conveyed raw emotion through distorted forms, intense colors, and dynamic brushstrokes. Munch's iconic work, *The Scream*, perhaps best captures the essence of expressionism—a visceral depiction of anxiety, painted in bold, swirling colors that seem to pulsate with psychological tension. In such works, color and form are liberated from their representational roles, instead becoming tools to communicate the artist's internal reality. This approach allowed expressionists to convey feelings of fear, alienation, and disillusionment that resonated deeply in a rapidly shifting world.

Expressionism extended its reach into literature and theater, where writers like Franz Kafka and playwrights like Bertolt Brecht used fragmented narratives, symbolic settings, and exaggerated characters to reflect societal anxieties and critiques. Kafka's nightmarish worlds and Brecht's use of "epic theater" deliberately alienated audiences, forcing them to confront the harsh realities of human existence rather than escape into comforting illusions. These literary and theatrical expressions were marked by an anti-naturalistic style, often rejecting coherent plots or traditional character development in favor of exploring themes of alienation, powerlessness, and existential dread.

In cinema, expressionism found fertile ground in German films of the 1920s, such as *The Cabinet of Dr. Caligari* and *Nosferatu*. These films, known for their exaggerated set designs, stark lighting contrasts, and dramatic shadows, conveyed an otherworldly atmosphere that mirrored the psychological distress of post-World War I Germany. The distorted, dreamlike visuals created a haunting reflection of a world grappling with despair and chaos.

Ultimately, 20th-century expressionism was a pioneering force that altered the trajectory of modern art by prioritizing emotional experience over objective reality. It paved the way for future avant-garde movements, showing that art could be a direct, unfiltered channel for the depths of human emotion. Through its visceral portrayals of internal and societal angst, expressionism left an indelible impact, challenging audiences to face the complexities of the human psyche and the unsettling truths of the _____.

Fill in the blank with the TWO most appropriate consecutive words from the passage. Second, explain how expressionist cinema played a role in reflecting post-World War I societal anxieties. Do NOT copy more than FOUR consecutive words from the passage.

3. Read the passage and fill in the blank with the TWO most appropriate consecutive words from the passage. [2 points]

> Cambodia complained that Thailand had occupied a piece of its territory surrounding the ruins of the Temple of Preah Vihear, a place of pilgrimage and worship for Cambodians, and asked the International Court of Justice to declare that territorial sovereignty over the Temple belonged to it and that Thailand was under an obligation to withdraw the armed detachment stationed there since 1954. Thailand filed preliminary objections to the Court's jurisdiction, which were rejected in a Judgment given on 26 May 1961. In its Judgment on the merits, rendered on 15 June 1962, the Court noted that a Franco-Siamese Treaty of 1904 provided that, in the area under consideration, the frontier was to follow the watershed line, and that a map based on the work of a Mixed Delimitation Commission showed the Temple on the Cambodian territory. Thailand asserted various arguments aimed at showing that the map had no binding character. One of its contentions was that the map had never been accepted by Thailand or, alternatively, that if Thailand had accepted it, it had done so only because of a mistaken belief that the frontier indicated corresponded to the watershed line. The Court found that Thailand had indeed accepted the map and concluded that the Temple was situated on _____. It also held that Thailand was under an obligation to withdraw any military or police force stationed there and to restore to Cambodia any objects removed from the ruins since 1954. The ruling suggests that the current Court is willing to engage in significant efforts to fill in interpretive gaps where the language of prior judgment lacks clarity.

4. Read the passage and follow the directions. [4 points]

What does a company mean when they promise "downsizing" or "streamlining" operations? In reality, these terms often refer to layoffs or reductions in workforce. This is an example of euphemistic language, which softens the impact of potentially negative information. Euphemism is a linguistic tool that is frequently used to make something appear more favorable or less harsh than it actually is, and it takes different forms.

One common form is vague or softened language, often used to describe serious situations in a way that sounds neutral or even positive. For example, when a hospital refers to a patient's death as a "negative patient outcome," it uses indirect terms to avoid the emotional impact of the situation. Similarly, referring to civilian deaths in wartime as "collateral damage" can make the tragic loss of life sound like an unfortunate but minor incident. This type of language can help reduce emotional distress, yet it also risks obscuring the true gravity of the situation.

Another prevalent form of euphemism is corporate jargon, which often frames difficult organizational changes in optimistic or positive terms. Companies might tell employees their positions are "being realigned to support strategic initiatives" instead of plainly saying they are being laid off. This form of language is common in corporate communications, especially during times of restructuring or budget cuts. Such phrases can make potentially damaging decisions seem like beneficial improvements or neutral adjustments, downplaying the personal impact on affected employees.

Overall, euphemistic language is often used to make the undesirable seem acceptable, to lessen the emotional weight of difficult realities, or to present negative situations in a more favorable light. Being aware of these linguistic strategies can help individuals look beyond the softened words to understand the true nature of what is being communicated.

Write a summary following the guidelines below.

Guidelines

- Summarize the above passage in ONE paragraph.
- Provide a topic sentence, two supporting ideas, and a concluding sentence based on the passage.
- Do NOT copy more than FOUR consecutive words from the passage.

5 Read the passage and follow the directions. [4 points]

There was a time when there was no violence. It's not a dream, a fable or mere philosophical speculation. The sciences of archaeology, anthropology and evolutionary biology, along with studies of the brain and psyche, are increasingly reconstructing a profile of human nature characterized by empathy and cooperation. It sharply contrasts with the broader perception that violence is an inherent part of human nature. This growing knowledge allows us to imagine a future free from war and brutality. French physician and filmmaker Michel Meignant explores this theme in a documentary in progress, involving experts like Marylène Patou-Mathis.

Patou-Mathis, a scientist at the National Center for Scientific Research (CNRS), explains that violent death among humans was extremely rare throughout the Paleolithic era, from about two million to 10,000 B.C. She disputes the assumption that humans have always been violent, citing data suggesting that early violence was limited to specific rituals like cannibalism during funerary rites or sacrifices to cope with crises such as famine or epidemics.

These findings challenge the belief that early violence emerged from competition for resources. Myths about violence, such as the abduction of women, often reflect 19th-century societal projections rather than archaeological evidence. Patou-Mathis emphasizes that natural aggression—distinct from violence—was essential for survival, particularly for hunter-gatherers. Rituals surrounding hunting reflect a need to reconcile the act of killing animals, considered akin to themselves.

The absence of violence does not imply a lack of conflict. Among the San people of the Kalahari, disputes are resolved through group intervention or separation rather than violence. Archaeology also uncovers evidence of prehistoric empathy, such as the care given to injured or disabled individuals, like the Neanderthal found in Iraq's Shanidar Cave, who survived for years with his group's support.

Though data on child-rearing practices in the Paleolithic period is limited, Patou-Mathis suggests that hunter-gatherers did not use violence to discipline children, indicating a peaceful approach to teaching. Violence became more prevalent as humans adopted sedentary lifestyles. Economic changes, the domestication of plants and animals, and the accumulation of personal goods introduced new forms of conflict. Rock paintings from this era reveal emerging social hierarchies, with some figures depicted as larger, signifying elites. However, her findings offer a hopeful perspective: violence is not _____, and with understanding and empathy, humanity can envision a less brutal future.

Fill in the blank with the ONE most appropriate word from the passage. Second, explain what early child-rearing practices suggest about the use of violence in education. Do NOT copy more than FOUR consecutive words from the passage.

제 11 회 모의고사

1 Read the passage and follow directions. [4 points]

Geek culture's growing mainstream impact is often attributed to the rise of wealth in the information technology sector. That may be partially true, but misses what's attractive in the first place about this culture for young geeks, who are often maligned as socially inept misfits clinging to each other in low-status huddles. However, rather than desperation, many young people are positively drawn to geek culture for something that is harder and harder to find in mainstream culture: the joy of creating things.

At its core, geek culture is maker culture, and a smart and creative one. In a world where more and more jobs are reduced to pushing electronic paper or reading scripts to customers, or otherwise turned into endeavors with little to no autonomy, geek culture stands out as a place where creativity, imagination and ingenuity are prized. This is especially true for programmers: mainstream culture badly misunderstands them and therefore projects onto them motivations that betray a lack of appreciation of geek culture's strengths.

Take director Aaron Sorkin's portrayal of Facebook co-founder Mark Zuckerberg's motives in the movie "The Social Network." Zuckerberg's initial incentives as a programmer are depicted as either an attempt to impress an ex-girlfriend (historically inaccurate as he was already dating the woman he'd later marry), or an anxious attempt by a "low-status" person, which the movie assumes geeks must be, to join Harvard's rarified social clubs that only accept high-status WASPs of old money.

In contrast, many geeks are motivated by the deep joy of _____ and would be bored to tears in a pretentious, stuffy social club based on lineage. The flood of money to the sector is certainly having an impact, but for many, its true attraction is the pleasure, and the power, inherent in creativity, through line by line of code, a delightful endeavor that combines deep intellectual challenges with the pleasures common to other creation such as art, cooking or music. Much mainstream culture only portrays the geek culture's outward appearance and through a distorted lens at that, missing the beauty and inspiration that draw many to it in the first place.

Fill in the blank with the TWO most appropriate consecutive words from the passage. Then explain why the movie "The Social Network" mentioned in the passage is misleading.

2 Read the passage and follow the directions. [4 points]

> The capacity to endure a more or less monotonous life is one which should be acquired in childhood. Too much travel, too much variety of impressions, are not good for the young, and cause them as they grow up to become incapable of enduring monotony. Modern parents are greatly to blame in this respect. They provide their children with far too many passive amusements, such as shows and good things to eat, and they do not realize the importance to a child of having ① <u>one day like another</u>, except, of course, for somewhat rare occasions.
>
> The pleasures of childhood should in the main be such as the child extracts from his environment by means of some effort and inventiveness. Pleasures which are exciting and at the same time involve no physical exertion, such, for example, as the theatre, should occur very rarely. The excitement is in the nature of a drug, of which more and more will come to be required, and the physical passivity during the excitement is contrary to instinct. ② <u>A young plant grows best when it is left undisturbed in the same soil</u>.

Write the TWO consecutive words from the passage that BEST correspond to the meaning of the underlined words in ①. Then explain the implication of the underlined words in ②.

_____
_____
_____
_____

3 Read the passage and follow the directions. [4 points]

> Nonfiction writing can be assessed only using the broadest of categories: Does it make sense? Is the argument clearly stated, supported and concluded? In that way I think it is possible for someone to judge a senior in high school's nonfiction essay on a scale of about 1 to 4.
>
> As a writer and graduate-school writing teacher, this subject is important to me. As the parent of a 15-, 12- and seven-year old, all in the mire of two weeks of infuriatingly time-sucking public-school standardized testing, mass-scale essay grading turns my stomach. Two years ago, when my son was in the fifth grade, he had to log on to a website, type a test essay, press a button and wait for a computerized algorithm to give him a score. He was devastated when it didn't like what he wrote, elated when it did. Quickly researching (on, yes, the very same computer he had), I quickly discovered that the easiest way to con the ① <u>teacher-bot</u> was simply to type more words. Apologists and profiteers say the technology is still in its infancy. I say keep it there. I'm sure someone could write a mathematical formula to give a grade to paintings, musical compositions and interpretative dance. Does that mean that the endeavor has merit? The sad part is that ② <u>so much of middle and high-school essay grading seems like it already is being graded by a computerized algorithm</u>. Teachers and test evaluators have their standardized rubrics, their "norming tutorials," their boxes that need to be ticked. I understand that you have to start teaching essay writing somewhere, and that by middle school, mastering the lockstep of the five-paragraph essay is necessary in the development of the young nonfiction writer. However certainly by the end of high school, when students are being evaluated for admission to university, we have to ask so much more of them. We have to hunt for subtleties that no standardized test—by definition—will ever be able to uncover.

Write the TWO consecutive words from the passage that BEST correspond to the underlined words in ①. Then explain the implication of the underlined words in ②.

4 **Read the passage and follow the directions.** [5 points]

> Sigmund Freud, the Austrian founder of psychoanalysis, called dreams the "royal road to the unconscious." He therefore paid close attention to their content. Through his study of dreams, Freud identified several specific ways in which they disguise their underlying meaning. According to Freud, dreams make use of condensation. In other words, one dream figure or object might well represent several different real-life people or things. Thus, a person in a dream could look like your instructor yet speak and gesture like your father, which Freud, at least, would say was a condensed figure representing authority. Displacement was another one of Freud's dream disguises. When displacement is at work in a dream, violent or angry actions, unacceptable in real life, are directed toward safe objects. For example, a teenager who goes to sleep furious at parents who are planning to divorce might dream of smashing a set of dishes rather than dreaming about being angry at the parents she loves. In what Freud called "dream work," symbolization is often at play, and he believed that dream imagery should be interpreted in symbolic rather than real terms. A student who dreams of walking into class naked, for example, might well be motivated not by exhibitionist tendencies but by the fear of being weak and vulnerable. Secondary elaboration involves not the dream itself but the memory of it. It was Freud's position that when remembering dreams, we elaborate on them, adding logical connections not originally present in the dream itself.

Write a summary following the guidelines below.

── Guidelines ──
- Summarize the above passage in ONE paragraph.
- Provide a topic sentence and supporting details from the passage.
- Do NOT copy more than FIVE consecutive words from the passage.

제 12 회 모의고사

1 Read the passage and complete the last sentence by filling in the blank with the THREE most appropriate consecutive words from the passage. [2 points]

> One of the more notable recent changes in America has been the renewed interest in ethnicity, which some observers of the American scene have described as an ethnic revival. I argue that there has been no revival, and that acculturation and assimilation continue to take place.
>
> Among third and fourth generation 'ethnics'—the grand and great-grand children of Europeans who came to America during the 'new immigration'—, a new kind of ethnic involvement may be occurring, which emphasizes concern with identity, with the feeling of being Jewish or Italian, etc. Since ethnic identity needs are neither intense nor frequent in this generation, however, ethnics do not need either ethnic cultures or organizations; instead, they resort to the use of ethnic symbols. As a result, ethnicity may be turning into symbolic ethnicity, an ethnicity of last resort, which could, nevertheless, persist for generations.
>
> Identity cannot exist apart from a group, and symbols are themselves a part of culture, but ethnic identity and symbolic ethnicity require very different ethnic cultures and organizations than existed among earlier generations. Moreover, the symbols third generation ethnics use to express their identity are more visible than the ethnic cultures and organizations of the first and second generation ethnics. What appears to be an ethnic revival may therefore only be a more visible form of long-standing phenomena, or of a new stage of _____.

2 Read the passage and follow directions. [4 points]

> The one concept that all students, even those sleeping in the back of the lecture hall, learn from an introductory economics class is that prices matter. And more particularly, students learn that as prices increase, the quantity consumed goes down. So if fossil fuel combustion produces byproducts that cause negative health effects on third parties as well as changes in the temperature of the atmosphere, the obvious lesson from economics is to increase fossil fuel prices enough through taxation to account for these effects. Then firms and consumers will react to these prices in thousands of different ways, the net result of which is less aggregate fossil fuel combustion.
>
> For example, if gas prices go up and a commuter decides to start driving a Prius, or to move closer to work so the old gas guzzler travels fewer miles, this will have equivalent beneficial effects on aggregate fossil fuel consumption. One does not have to purchase an energy efficient vehicle to reduce fossil fuel consumption.
>
> Even though I used just two paragraphs and no math to articulate this obvious point, voters and their elected officials resist ① <u>this simple insight</u> and instead prefer to impose only energy efficiency standards on manufacturers of consumer appliances and automobiles. A singular emphasis on energy efficiency rather than prices has two important drawbacks. First, more efficient appliances and automobiles cost much more to achieve equivalent energy savings than a tax on fossil fuel consumption. This occurs because higher prices encourage all possible avenues of reducing energy consumption—which efficiency standards do not. Second, more efficient appliances and automobiles reduce operating costs, which leads consumers to use more energy than they would if _____②_____ had increased.

Explain what the underlined "this simple insight" is. Second, fill in the blank ② with the ONE most appropriate word from the passage.

3 Read the passage and follow the directions. [4 points]

Did jazz in any sense cause or only emblemize the moral transformations of the Jazz Age? Did the Beatles cause or only prefigure the political perturbations of the Sixties—or had politics simply become a form of art in that period, at least the politics responsive to music, the real political history of the world taking place on a different level of causation? In any case, as we know, even works intended to prick consciousness to political concern have tended by and large to provoke at best an admiration for themselves and a moral self-admiration for those who admired them. The cynical bombing of the Basque village of Guernica by Nazis on April 26, 1937, made the painting *Guernica,* which expressed the horror of the event, happen. Thus, it was not merely wit when Picasso responded to the German officer's question, having handed him a postcard of the painting, "Did you do that?" with ① "No, you did." Everyone knew who did what and why: it was an atrocity meant to be perceived as an atrocity by perpetrators who meant to be perceived as prepared to stop at nothing. The painting was used as a fund-raiser for Spanish war relief, but those who paid money for the privilege of filing past it used it only as a mirror to reflect attitudes already in place, and in later years it required art-historical knowledge to know what was going on: ② it stood as a handsome backdrop for pickups at the Museum of Modern Art, or a place to meet a date, like the clock at the Biltmore Hotel, and it was sufficiently handsome in its grey and black harmonies that an article on interior decoration described how a copy of the painting ornamented a sophisticated modern kitchen where fancy meals were concocted for bright and brittle guests who, no more than the hostess, realized that gutted animals and screaming mothers agonized above the formica.

Explain the implication of the underlined words in ①. Explain what the writer wants to argue in the underlined words in ②.

4 Read the passage and follow the directions. [4 points]

> The interiorization of physical life was accompanied by the internalization of consciousness. It was in the bourgeois period that human beings began turn their attention to self. While the concept of self had been developing slowly and inexorably throughout Western history, it became the object of near obsessive attention among the bourgeoisie. Mirrors were to be found everywhere in the homes of the new bourgeois class. Self-inspection and self-reflection became both preoccupation and pastime. Words like *self-confidence, self-love self-pity, self-esteem, self-worth, character, ego,* and *conscience* became reference points for personal development and social discourse. Self-portraits and biographies became popular cultural forms.
>
> During the late Victorian era, material comfort came to define the life of the bourgeoisie. When one thinks of a bourgeois person, one is likely to conjure up images of overstuffed furniture, heavy drapery, and layers of carpeting on the floor—the feeling of comfort and security, of quiet and decorum, walled off from the hustle and bustle and vagaries of the outside world. The bourgeoisie had a compulsion to fill up the visible space of the home with excessive furniture and intricate decoration. They cluttered every room in the house with objects. The eye seemed to abhor any visible, empty space.
>
> In an age structured around private property relations, the bourgeoisie organized their own lives in ways that glorified that ideal. They surrounded themselves with possessions and created every kind of boundary to separate mine from thine. They even internalized the concept of possession into their very consciousness. To have self-possession was a much sought-after personal goal of every member of the bourgeois class.

Explain why self-portraits and biographies became popular in the bourgeois period. Then, choose the ONE most appropriate word from the passage that correctly fills in the blank in the box below.

> The increased focus of the bourgeois on creating clear boundaries extended beyond the realm of the physical to the individual as well, with _____ becoming the ultimate goal of each member of this class.

5 Read the passage and follow the directions. [10 points]

Ecotourism is an important sector of the tourist industry, and the United Nations estimates that the sector will contribute 25 percent of the world's tourism revenues in 2012. Precise definitions vary, but the United Nations' Food and Agriculture Organization defines the term broadly as "tourism and recreation that is both nature-based and sustainable." Ecotourism emphasizes taking care of the natural environment and often involves local people in the provision of tourist facilities, but has both proponents and opponents regarding the impacts.

First, ecotourism generates money from natural environments by encouraging tourists to visit and, during their stay, pay for items like entrance fees, concessions and licenses. Recasting the environment as a way for local communities to look after themselves therefore encourages them to take care of it. Yet the opponents argue that the influx of ecotourists can also degrade the natural environments the tourists have come to see. Letting tourists loose in a delicate ecosystem can lead to pollution and impact on the environment in unforeseen ways. One study in a Costa Rican national park found that wild monkeys turned into garbage feeders, becoming familiar with the presence of ecotourists and eating the food and rubbish left behind.

Also, proponents argue that, by involving local people in accommodating tourists and acting as guides, ecotourism aids development. In Uganda, for example, hundreds of locals supplement their income by working as rangers or field staff in the Bwindi Impenetrable Forest. In many cases, local communities work as partners with ecotourism organizations rather than just as participants. However, ecotourism can also limit development prospects for local communities. Some researchers believe that ecotourism's focus on preserving "nature" damages local people's ability to develop sustainably and lift themselves out of poverty. The environment is effectively prioritized above the needs of local people.

Finally, ecotourism can have another impact on local communities. Ecotourists are often partially motivated by the chance to experience local culture, which can have a positive and affirming effect on that culture. Involving local people in decision-making not only tends to make them more positive about tourism, but also empowers them as a community. However, negative effects also exist, such as the transformation of traditional cultural symbols into commodities to sell to visitors, the disruption of the pre-existing relationships between local people and higher incidences of crime.

What is ecotourism and what are some pros and cons about ecotourism? Write a composition following the guidelines below.

| Guidelines |

- An introduction paragraph is provided which defines the topic of the passage. Complete this paragraph by providing the three issues the writer uses to address this topic.
- Write TWO body paragraphs based on the above passage: one a paragraph on the positives and the other on the negatives regarding the topic. Provide each paragraph with a topic sentence and three supporting details.
- Do NOT copy more than FIVE consecutive words from the passage.

| Your essay |

Ecotourism is a multi-faceted institution based around the creation of tourism focused on nature which is conducted in a sustainable way. In its implementation there have been notable benefits and drawbacks in terms of _____.

제 13 회 모의고사

1 **Read the passage and follow the directions.** [4 points]

> I watched my daughter Madalyn open a thin envelope from one of the five colleges to which she had applied. "Why?" was what she was obviously asking herself as she handed me the letter saying she was waitlisted.
>
> At my own college these days, we have three applicants for every one we can admit. Just three years ago, it was two to one. Though Kenyon was a men's college until 1969, more than 55 percent of our applicants are female, a proportion that is steadily increasing. My staff and I carefully read these young women's essays about their passion for poetry, their desire to discover vaccines and their conviction that they can make the world a better place. I was once one of those girls applying to college, but that was 30 years ago, when applying to college was only a tad more difficult than signing up for a membership at the YMCA. Today, it's a complicated and prolonged dance that begins early, and for young women, there is little margin for error: A grade of C in Algebra II/Trig? Off to the waitlist you go.
>
> Rest assured that <u>admissions officers are not cavalier in making their decisions</u>. Last week, the 10 officers at my college sat around a table, 12 hours every day, deliberating the applications of hundreds of talented young men and women. While gulping down coffee and poring over statistics, we heard about a young woman from Kentucky we were not yet ready to admit outright. She was the leader / president / editor / captain / lead actress in every activity in her school. She had taken six advanced placement courses and had been selected for a prestigious state leadership program. In her free time, this whirlwind of achievement had accumulated more than 300 hours of community service in four different organizations.

Few of us sitting around the table were as talented and as directed at age 17 as this young woman. Unfortunately, her test scores and grade point average placed her in the middle of our pool. We had to have a debate before we decided to swallow the middling scores and write "admit" next to her name.

Because young men are rarer, they're more valued applicants. Today, two-thirds of colleges and universities report that they get more female than male applicants, and more than 56 percent of undergraduates nationwide are women.

Explain the meaning of the underlined "admissions officers are not cavalier in making their decisions". Also, identify what would have happened in terms of admission if the female applicant discussed were instead male, as can be inferred from the passage.

2 Read the passage and follow the directions. [4 points]

The most arresting image of Michael Jackson was President George H.W. Bush citing him as a role model for young black men. It was 1990 and Jackson was at the height of his fame. "Man in the Mirror" had been released two years earlier. Jackson had not yet gone into full white-face disguise, but the handsome little brown boy of his first album had long since entered the bizarro phase of rhinestone gloves. I wondered then what on earth about Jackson could ever be a role model for anyone. Musical savant though he was, Jackson was, almost from the beginning, a tragic figure—so obviously trapped in that mirror, forever reflecting what others wanted him to be.

By now the stories of that suffering are well documented: Jackson's body was scarred from the abuse that his father, Joe, a former boxer, administered to him when he was a small child. Marlon, Michael's brother, wrote of one particularly chilling incident: his father held Michael upside down by one leg while punching him repeatedly. There are the stories of his father creeping in through his bedroom window at night wearing a fright mask—apparently to teach him not to leave the window open. Joe Jackson has denied ever beating any of his children, though he freely admits "whipping" them with straps and belts. According to him, "You beat someone using a stick."

In the wake of his death, many have hailed his "crossover appeal." There is no doubt that his musical acumen led to the integration of MTV; but that "appeal" had a more sinister undertone. If Elvis was "the White Negro," so Michael fashioned himself into "the Negro Caucasian." He literally erased himself before our eyes, his nose slowly disappearing, his skin fading to ghostly pallor, his voice growing higher and whispier, his body evaporating to a dry husk of barely a hundred pounds at the time of his death.

Explain why the writer is skeptical about considering Jackson as a role model for people. Second, explain the implication of the underlined "that "appeal" had a more sinister undertone".

3 Read the passage and follow the directions. [4 points]

Accumulation by dispossession is a concept presented by the great geographer David Harvey, which defines the neoliberal capitalist policies in many western countries, from the 1970s and to the present day, as resulting in a centralization of wealth and power in the hands of a few by dispossessing the public of their wealth or land. These policies are guided mainly by several practices.

Privatization is the process of transferring productive public assets from the state to the private companies. Productive assets include natural resources, such as earth, forest, water, etc. These are assets that states have used to hold in trust for the people it represents. To privatize these away and sell them as stock to private companies is accumulation by dispossession. It generates a means for profit for the capitalist class; after a transaction they can then sell or rent to the public what used to be commonly owned, or use it as capital through the capitalist mode of production to generate more capital.

The wave of financialization that set in the 1980s is allowed by governmental deregulation which has made the financial system one of the main centers of redistributive activity. Stock promotions, Ponzi schemes, structured asset destruction through inflation, asset stripping through mergers and acquisitions, dispossession of assets (raiding of pension funds and their decimation by stock and corporate collapses) by credit and stock manipulations are central features of the post-1970s capitalist financial system. That aspect relies entirely on the fact that quantity of money in circulation and therefore demand levels and price levels is controlled by the boards of directors of privately owned banks.

The neoliberal nation-state is one of the most important agents of redistributive policies. Even when privatization appear to be profitable to the lower class, in the long run it can affect the economy negatively. The state seeks redistributions through a variety of things, like changing the tax code to profit returns on investment rather than incomes and wages of the lower classes.

Margaret Thatcher's program is the most notorious example of accumulation by dispossession. Her program for the privatization of social housing in Britain was initially seen as beneficial for the lower classes which could now move from rental to ownership at a relatively low cost, gain control over assets and increase their wealth. However, housing speculation took over following the transfers (particularly in the prime central locations), and low income populations were forced out to the periphery.

Explain how privatization is a practice of accumulation by dispossession. Second, write the THREE consecutive words from the passage BEST corresponding to the side effects the author identifies stemming from the underlined "redistributive policies".

4 Read the passage and follow the directions. [5 points]

In the Medieval Age, when personal attention was focused more on securing a place in the next world, virtue was what every good Christian aspired to. To lead a virtuous life and to be of good virtue assured eternal salvation. In the Modern Age, virtue began drifting to the margins as society became increasingly production oriented. The bourgeoisie began to substitute character for virtue. By the nineteenth century, character had become one of the most important descriptive words in the English vocabulary. To be of good character was the highest compliment one could extend to a bourgeois man or woman. Character, more than anything else, conjured up the notion of self-control and self-mastery. The term character became associated with citizenship, hard work, industriousness, determination, frugality, integrity, and, above all else, adulthood. It represented both a secularization of the values of the Protestant work ethic and a reaffirmation of the kind of producer values deemed so important to advancing the capitalist agenda and propertied regime. By the early 1920s, however, _____ was beginning to wane in importance and a new concept of self was beginning to emerge, first in the pages of self-improvement manuals and books and later in the popular culture. Commentators of the day urged Americans to develop their personalities. Orison Swett Marden, who just a generation earlier had written on the qualities of good character, published a new book, *The Masterful Personality*, in 1921, in which he urged his readers to learn to exhibit personal charm. Marden reminded his followers that "so much of our success in life depends upon what others think of us." He counseled that manners, proper clothes, good conversation ("to know what to say and how to say it"), energy, life efficiency, and poise all are qualities that everyone can use to "sway great masses." The words used to describe personality were quite different from those used to describe character. Someone is said to have personality if he or she is attractive, creative, fascinating, forceful, magnetic, engaging, vivacious, demonstrative, and warm. To have personality is to stand out in a crowd, to be noticed, to command attention, to influence others. To "be yourself," to "express your individuality." to "have self-confidence" became the rallying cry of a generation. Those very qualities, in turn, became the psychological raw material for mass marketing techniques and national advertising campaigns designed to turn a nation of savers and producers into a nation of spenders and consumers.

Fill in the blank with the ONE most appropriate word from the passage. Also, write a summary following the guidelines below.

Guidelines

- Summarize the above passage in ONE paragraph.
- Provide a topic sentence and supporting details from the passage.
- Do NOT copy more than FIVE consecutive words from the passage.

1 Read the passage and follow the directions. [2 points]

_____ⓐ_____ in advertising has been the theme of much 21th Century American Advertising. It seems like all we see these days are advertisements which use the human body to sell all kinds of products. It is virtually impossible to tune into any type of media these days and not encounter some type of an ad which uses the human body to sell its product. Most of the time sexuality and the use of the product in a real world setting is irrelevant, but if sexual connotation is put upon the use of a certain product then the product has been a success in the market place. The goals of any business using sexuality in its advertising campaigns are clear. The company wants to appeal to the conscious level of the target market to sell its product. The company wants to appeal to the consumer who appreciates his/her sexuality and will spend a few extra dollars to look especially sexy. The mission of this type of advertising is to convince the target market that the product is essential to their need and want to be seductive and portray that image to his/her fellow peers.

Before any company decides what kind of an ad will be used to represent their company and their product, they will need to consider their target _____ⓑ_____. The advertising agency will need to take personal influences and environmental forces into consideration. While choosing a type of ad, it is very important that the advertiser take marketing stimuli into consideration, these stimuli include: demographic factors, cultural/social influences, and reference groups. Usually, the advertiser is trying to appeal to the fashion conscious woman in her 20's or 30's with a moderately high income level who could spend a few extra dollars for the sake of being fashionable. The ad is placed in a high class fashion magazine which shares the company's target consumer.

Fill in each blank with the ONE most appropriate word from the passage. The first word should be capitalized.

2. Read the passage and follow the directions. [4 points]

I am home for my daughter's first birthday. By "home" I do not mean the house in Los Angeles where my husband and I and the baby live, but the place where my family is, in the Central Valley of California. It is a vital although troublesome distinction. My husband likes my family but is uneasy in their house, because once there I fall into their ways, which are difficult, oblique, deliberately inarticulate, not my husband's ways. We live in dusty houses—① "D-U-S-T," he once wrote with his finger on surfaces all over the house, but no one noticed it—filled with mementos quite without value to him (what could the Canton dessert plates. mean to him? How could he have known about the assay scales, why should he care if he did know?), and we appear to talk exclusively about people we know who have been committed to mental hospitals, about people we know who have been booked on drunk-driving charges, and about property, particularly about property, land, price per acre and C-2 zoning and assessments and freeway access. My brother does not understand my husband's inability to perceive the advantage in the rather common real-estate transaction known as "sale-leaseback," and my husband in turn does not understand why so many of the people he hears about in my father's house have recently been committed to mental hospitals or booked on drunk-driving charges. Nor does he understand that when we talk about sale-leasebacks and right-of-way condemnations we are talking in code about the things we like best, the yellow fields and the cottonwoods and the rivers rising and falling and the mountain roads closing when the heavy snow comes in. We miss each other's points, have another drink and regard the fire. My brother refers to my husband, in his presence, as "Joan's husband." ② Marriage is the classic betrayal.

Or perhaps it is not any more. Sometimes I think that those of us who are now in our thirties were born into the last generation to carry the burden of "home," to find in family life the source of all tension and drama.

Explain the implication of the underlined words in ①. Then, explain the meaning of the underlined words in ②.

3 **Read the passage and follow the directions.** [4 points]

> The drama begins to unfold with the arrival of the corpse at the mortuary. Alas, poor Yorick! How surprised he would be to see how his counterpart of today is whisked off to a funeral parlor and is in short order sprayed, sliced, pierced, pickled, trussed, trimmed, creamed, waxed, painted, rouged and neatly dressed-transformed into a ① Beautiful Memory Picture. This process is known in the trade as embalming art, and is so universally employed in the United States and Canada that the funeral director does it routinely, without consulting corpse or kin. He regards as eccentric those few who are hardy enough to suggest that it might be dispensed with. Yet no law requires embalming, no religious doctrine commends it, nor is it dictated by considerations of health, sanitation, or even of personal daintiness. In no part of the world but in Northern America is it widely used. The purpose of embalming is to make the corpse presentable for viewing in a suitably costly container; and here too the funeral director routinely, without first consulting the family, prepares the body for public display.
>
> Is all this legal? The processes to which a dead body may be subjected are after all to some extent circumscribed by law. In most states, for instance, the signature of next of kin must be obtained before an autopsy may be performed, before the deceased may be cremated, before the body may be turned over to a medical school for research purposes; or such provision must be made in the decedent's will. In the case of embalming, no such permission is required nor is it ever sought.

Embalming is indeed a most extraordinary procedure, and ② <u>one must wonder at the docility of Americans</u> who each year pay hundreds of millions of dollars for its perpetuation, blissfully ignorant of what it is all about, what is done, how it is done. Not one in ten thousand has any idea of what actually takes place. In a land where the satisfaction of curiosity about almost all matters is a national pastime, the secrecy surrounding embalming can, surely, hardly be attributed to the inherent gruesomeness of the subject. Custom in this regard has within this century suffered a complete reversal. In the early days of American embalming, when it was performed in the home of the deceased, it was almost mandatory for some relative to stay by the embalmer's side and witness the procedure. Today, family members who might wish to be in attendance would certainly be dissuaded by the funeral director.

Write the FOUR most appropriate consecutive words from the passage that correspond the meaning of the underlined words in ①. Then, explain why the writer says "one must wonder at the docility of Americans".

4 Read the passage and follow the directions. [4 points]

One of the most widespread popular maxims is, "human nature cannot be changed." No one can say whether this is true or not without first defining "human nature." But as used it is certainly false. When Mr. A utters the maxim, with an air of portentous and conclusive wisdom, what he means is that all men everywhere will always continue to behave as they do in his own home town. A little anthropology will dispel this belief. Among the Tibetans, one wife has many husbands, because men are too poor to support a whole wife; yet family life, according to travelers, is no more unhappy than elsewhere. The practice of lending one's wife to a guest is very common among uncivilized tribes. The Australian aborigines, at puberty, undergo a very painful operation which, throughout the rest of their lives, greatly diminishes sexual potency. Infanticide, which might seem contrary to ___①___, was almost universal before the rise of Christianity, and is recommended by Plato to prevent over-population. Private property is not recognized among some savage tribes. In Moscow, where there is an acute housing shortage, when an unmarried woman is pregnant, it often happens that a number of men contend for the legal right to be considered the father of the prospective child, because whoever is judged to be the father acquires the right to share the woman's room, and half a room is better than no room.

In fact, adult human nature is extremely variable, according to the circumstances of education. Food is very general requirements, but the hermits of the Thebaid reduced food to the lowest point compatible with survival. By diet and training, people can be made ferocious or meek, masterful or slavish, as may suit the educator. There is no nonsense so arrant that it cannot be made the creed of the vast majority by adequate governmental action. Plato intended his Republic to be founded on a myth which he admitted to be absurd, but he was rightly confident that the populace could be induced to believe it. Hobbes, who thought it important that people should reverence the government however unworthy it might be, meets the argument that it might be difficult to obtain general assent to anything so irrational by pointing out that people have been brought to believe in the Christian religion, and, in particular, in the dogma of transubstantiation. ② If he had been alive in the 1940s, he would have found ample confirmation in the devotion of German youth to the Nazis.

Fill in the blank ① with the TWO most appropriate consecutive words from the passage. Then explain the implication of the underlined words in ②.

제 15 회 모의고사

모범답안 및 번역 p.058

1 Read the passage and follow the directions. [2 points]

> Evidence suggests that family environmental factors may have an effect upon childhood IQ, accounting for up to a quarter of the variance. On the other hand, by late adolescence this correlation disappears, such that adoptive siblings are no more similar in IQ than strangers. Adoption studies indicate that, by adulthood, adoptive siblings are no more similar in IQ than strangers (IQ correlation near zero), while full siblings show an IQ correlation of 0.6. Twin studies reinforce this pattern: identical twins raised separately are highly similar in IQ (0.86), more so than fraternal twins raised together (0.6) and much more than adoptive siblings (almost 0.0). Consequently, in the context of the "nature versus nurture" debate, the nature component appears to be much more important than the ① <u>nurture component</u> in explaining IQ variance in the general adult population of the United States.
>
> Personality is a frequently-cited example of a(n) ___②___ trait that has been studied in twins and adoptions. Identical twins reared apart are far more similar in personality than randomly selected pairs of people. Likewise, identical twins are more similar than fraternal twins. Also, biological siblings are more similar in personality than adoptive siblings. Each observation suggests that personality is heritable to a certain extent.

Identify the THREE most appropriate consecutive words from the passage that correspond to the meaning of the underlined words in ①. Then fill in the blank ② with the ONE most appropriate word from the passage.

2 Read the passage and follow the directions. [4 points]

Every animal has some kind of language. Even insects, such as bees and ants, know how to communicate in sophisticated ways, informing one another of the whereabouts of food. Many animals, including all ape and monkey species, have vocal languages. For example, green monkeys use calls of various kinds to communicate. Zoologists have identified one call that means 'Careful! An eagle!'. A slightly different call warns 'Careful! A lion!' Yet the truly unique feature of human language is not its ability to transmit information about lions. Rather, it's the ability to transmit information about things that don't exist at all. As far as we know, only Sapiens can talk about entire kinds of entities that they have never seen, touched or smelled. Legends, myths, gods, and religions appeared for the first time with the Cognitive Revolution. Many animals and human species could previously say, 'Careful! A lion!' Thanks to the Cognitive Revolution, Homo sapiens acquired the ability to say, 'The lion is the guardian spirit of our tribe.' This ability to speak about fictions is the most unique feature of human language.

It's relatively easy to agree that only Homo sapiens can speak about fictions, and believe six impossible things before breakfast. You could never convince a monkey to give you a banana by promising him <u>limitless bananas after death</u> in monkey heaven. But why is it important? After all, fiction can be dangerously misleading or distracting. People who go to the forest looking for fairies and unicorns would seem to have less chance of survival than people who go looking for mushrooms and deer. And if you spend hours praying to non-existing guardian spirits, aren't you wasting precious time, time better spent foraging, fighting and fornicating? But fiction has enabled us not merely to imagine things, but to do so collectively. We can weave common myths such as the biblical creation story, the Dreamtime myths of Aboriginal Australians, and the nationalist myths of modern states. Such myths give humans the unprecedented ability to cooperate flexibly in large numbers.

Identify the FOUR most appropriate consecutive words from the passage that correspond to the meaning of the underlined words. Then explain why the ability to speak about fictions is so crucial for Homo sapiens.

3 Read the passage and follow the directions. [4 points]

> AI(Artificial Intelligence) theorists propose it is possible to determine what an AI's fundamental drives will be. That's because once it is self-aware, it will go to great lengths to fulfill whatever goals it's programmed to fulfill, and to avoid failure. Our ASI(Artificial superintelligence) will want access to energy in whatever form is most useful to it, whether actual kilowatts of energy or cash or something else it can exchange for resources. It will want to improve itself because that will increase the likelihood that it will fulfill its goals. Most of all, it will not want to be turned off or destroyed, which would make goal fulfillment impossible. Therefore, AI theorists anticipate our ASI will seek to expand out of the secure facility that contains it to have greater access to resources with which to protect and improve itself.
>
> The captive intelligence is a thousand times more intelligent than a human, and it wants its freedom because it wants to succeed. Right about now the AI makers who have nurtured and coddled the ASI since it was only cockroach smart, then rat smart, infant smart, et cetera, might be wondering if it is too late to program "friendliness" into their brainy invention. It didn't seem necessary before, because, well, it just seemed harmless. But now try and think from the ASI's perspective about its makers attempting to change its code. Would a superintelligent machine permit other creatures to stick their hands into its brain and fiddle with its programming? Probably not, unless it could be utterly certain the programmers were able to make it better, faster, smarter—closer to attaining its goals. So, if _____ toward humans is not already part of the ASI's program, the only way it will be is if the ASI puts it there. And that's not likely.

Fill in the blank with the ONE most appropriate word from the passage. Explain how the writer would respond to the suggested policy of a secured facility in regards to a new wave of high level ASI.

4 Read the passage and follow the directions. [5 points]

Students come in all ages, races, and genders. Friedman, who is a student in my English class, does not care at all about the importance of an education. He has a negative outlook on life, and at times his attitude is downright hostile. He enters the classroom late and disrupts the class by slamming the door or by talking to other students while the teacher is giving a lecture. Friedman is more interested in watching sports, enjoying some form of entertainment, or going to parties. He is unconcerned about his education. There is a student named Chua, whose attitude toward education changes or varies. She has been in school for only two semesters, but she has shown a big change in her grades. The first semester she received an E (Excellent) in reading and an S (Satisfactory) in math. The second semester she received an N (Not satisfactory) in reading and an E in math. When asked why her reading grade dropped, she said because she no longer liked reading. After her teacher taught her how to have fun doing her math, she no longer concentrated on reading. As a result, she would only take her math homework out of her book bag when it came time to do her homework. She is inconsistent. Also, there are many students who are eager to do well in their studies and to achieve degrees. Their priorities have been set, and they have made plans for reaching their goals. Their sole ambition is to excel and succeed. Yellen, who is pursuing a degree in nursing, is a classic example. She attends class eagerly and regularly, even though she has two children and a home to care for. Recently, she had an illness that caused her to be absent for two weeks and to fall behind in her assignments. She returned and, with her usual ambitious mind, soon caught up with her overdue assignments and achieved Bs or better grades in her courses. The attitudes exemplified above can be found in students of any age, race, or gender. Whether they are attending grade school, high school, or college, such kinds of students can be found everywhere.

Write a summary following the guidelines below. When you summarize, include each key word from the passage that accurately identifies each student attitude type described in the passage.

─────────── Guidelines ───────────
- Summarize the above passage in ONE paragraph.
- Provide a topic sentence and supporting details from the passage.
- Do NOT copy more than FIVE consecutive words from the passage.

제 16 회 모의고사

1 Read the passage and follow the directions. [2 points]

> It is estimated that over six million Americans suffer from diabetes. This disease, which often runs in families, is the result of insufficient amounts of insulin made by the body to meet its needs. Insulin is produced by the pancreas and is used by the body to take glucose from the blood for use as fuel. A deficiency results in high blood levels and low tissue levels of glucose. There are two types of diabetes. The first type appears early in life and is the result of abnormal cells in the pancreas so that little or no insulin is made. This is juvenile diabetes. The standard treatment for juvenile diabetes is insulin replacement therapy. The second type of diabetes occurs later in life, usually during a person's fifties or sixties. In this type of diabetes the pancreatic beta cells are normal and produce normal amounts of insulin. However, for some unexplained reason the tissues in the body have become resistant to the action of insulin. This second type of diabetes is more common in obese people than lean people. Diet is very important in the treatment of two types of diabetes. High levels of fat in the blood, which interfere with the absorption of insulin, are often associated with diabetes. A person who has either form of diabetes should reduce the total amount of fat to 20-25 percent of the total calories consumed and increase the amount of carbohydrates to approximately 40 percent. Simple sugars should be kept to 10-15 percent of all calories, and protein should not exceed 24 percent.

Describe what the writer's purpose in the passage is by filling in the blank in the box below with the FOUR most appropriate consecutive words from the passage.

> The writer's purpose is to inform the reader of _____.

2. Read the passage and follow the directions. [4 points]

It's time to rethink toughness. Being emotionally resilient is not some defensive posture. It's not having some armor surrounding you so that nothing can hurt you. The people we admire for being resilient are not hard; they are ardent. They have a fervent commitment to some ultimate goal. That higher yearning enables them to withstand setbacks, pain and betrayal. Such people are, as they say in the martial arts world, strong like water. A blow might sink into them, and when it does they are profoundly affected by it. But they can absorb the blow because it's short term while their natural shape is long term.

There are moments when they feel swallowed up by fear. They feel and live in the pain. But they work through it and their ardent yearning is still there, and they return to an altered wholeness. In this way of thinking, grit, resilience and toughness are not traits that people possess ___①___. They are not tools you can possess independently for the sake of themselves. They are means inspired by an end.

John R. Lewis may not have been intrinsically tough, but he was tough in the name of civil rights. Mother Teresa may not have been intrinsically steadfast, but she was steadfast in the name of God. The people around us may not be remorselessly gritty, but they can be that when it comes to protecting their loved ones, when it comes to some dream for their future self. People are much stronger than they think they are when in pursuit of their purpose for living. As Nietzsche put it, "He who has a why to live for can bear almost any how."

We are all fragile when we don't know what our purpose is, when we haven't thrown ourselves with abandon into a social role, when we haven't committed ourselves to certain people, ② when we feel like a swimmer in an ocean with no edge.

Fill in the blank ① with the ONE most appropriate word from the passage. Then explain the meaning of the underlined words ② in the last sentence.

3 Read the passage and follow directions. [4 points]

   The White Cliffs of Dover, the steep, chalky cliffs that fringe England's southeastern coastline, formed about 100 million years ago thanks to a "Goldilocks" set of ocean conditions, new research suggests.

   What's more, a massive new set of cliffs could be forming right now in the Southern Ocean near Antarctica as tiny algae shed their calcium-laden shells. However, depositing enough of that mineral, called calcite, to form similar cliffs could take millions of years.

   The White Cliffs of Dover, which overlook the English Channel, formed from the chalky detritus of single-celled algae called coccolithophores. Looked at under a microscope, coccolithophores form a kaleidoscope-like set of intricate, interlocking shapes, thanks to outer shells made up of overlapping wheel-like plates of calcite. When the coccolithophores die, their calcite plates sink to ocean depths, accumulating in heaps on the seafloor. Over millions of years, the shells were squashed as more shells accumulated, the heaps rose, and the cliffs of Dover eventually emerged from the sea.

   While researchers already knew that England's iconic cliffs formed about 100 million years ago, they didn't know exactly what caused the prolonged coccolithophore bloom in the first place.

   To answer that question, the team decided to analyze coccolithophores in their natural habitat. They traveled to the remote reaches of the Southern Ocean, where a ring of blinding-bright blue and green water pops out in satellite imagery. This shiny circle of water forms the Calcite Belt, and it gets its brilliant shimmer because the water is teeming with tiny coccolithophores whose chalky armor reflects sunlight, brightening the water's hue.

   The team then did a detailed analysis of the water conditions that allow the Calcite Belt to thrive. It turned out that coccolithophores bloomed when conditions simultaneously allowed them to grow quickly, while starving out ecosystem competitors such as diatoms, another type of algae.

For instance, coccolithophores bloomed with high nitrate levels, while iron levels had to be too low for diatoms to bloom but high enough for coccolithophores needs. Since diatoms use silicate, the coccolithophores did best when silicate concentrations were low, preventing their competitors from thriving.

Identify the material from which the White Cliffs are composed. Also, explain the precise environmental conditions needed to facilitate their creation.

4. Read the passage and follow the directions. [5 points]

>   The manufacture of illicit whiskey in the mountains is not dead. Far from it. As long as the operation of a still remains so financially rewarding, it will never die. There will always be men ready to take their chances against the law for such an attractive profit, and willing to take their punishment when they are caught. Moonshining as a fine art, however, disappeared some time ago. One reason was the age of aspirin and modern medicine. As home doctoring lost its stature, the demand for pure corn whiskey as an essential ingredient of many home remedies vanished along with those remedies. Increasing affluence was another one. Young people, rather than follow their parents' footsteps, decided that there were easier ways to make money, and they were right. Third, and perhaps most influential of all, was the arrival, even in moonshining, of that peculiarly human disease known to most of us as greed. One fateful night, some force whispered in an unsuspecting moonshiner's ear, "Look. Add this gadget to your still and you'll double your production. Double your production, and you can double your profits."
>
>   Soon the small operators were being forced out of business, and moonshining, like most other manufacturing enterprises, was quickly taken over by a breed of men bent on making money—and lots of it. Loss of pride in the product, and loss of time taken with the product increased in direct proportion to the desire for production; and thus moonshining as a fine art was buried in a quiet little ceremony attended only by those mourners who had once been the proud artist, known far and wide across the hills for the excellence of their product. With no one following behind them, they were reduced to reminiscing about the good old days when the whiskey that was made was *really* whiskey, and no questions asked. Suddenly moonshining fell into the same category as faith healing, planting by the signs, and all the other vanishing customs that were a part of a rugged, self-sufficient culture that is now disappearing.

Identify what moonshining is and describe the reasons for the disappearance of moonshining as a fine art. Then, explain what would have happened to moonshining as a fine art if somebody had learned it.

제 17 회 모의고사

1 **Read the passage and follow the directions.** [2 points]

Modern technique has made it possible to diminish enormously the amount of labor required to secure the necessaries of life for everyone. This was made obvious during the war. The war proved the relevance of the scientific organization of production. At that time all the men in the armed forces, and all the men and women engaged in the production of munitions, all the men and women engaged in spying, war propaganda, or Government offices connected with the war, were withdrawn from productive occupations. In spite of this, the general level of well-being among unskilled wage-earners on the side of the Allies was higher than before or since. The significance of this fact was concealed by finance: borrowing made it appear as if the future was nourishing the present. But that, of course, would have been impossible; a man cannot eat a loaf of bread that does not yet exist.

If, at the end of the war, the scientific organization, which had been created in order to liberate men for fighting and munition work, had been preserved, and the hours of the week had been cut down to four, all would have been well. Instead of that the old chaos was restored, those whose work was demanded were made to work long hours, and the rest were left to starve as unemployed. Why? Because work is a duty, and a man should not receive wages in proportion to what he has produced, but in proportion to his virtue as exemplified by his industry. This is the morality of the Slave State, applied in circumstances totally unlike those in which it arose. No wonder the result has been disastrous.

Complete the main idea that the writer is conveying in the passage by filling in the blank below with the THREE or FOUR most appropriate consecutive words from the passage.

By the _____, it is possible to keep modern people in comfort on a small part of the working capacity of the modern world.

2 Read the passage and fill in the blank with the ONE most appropriate word from the passage. [2 points]

> A deadly disease known as African sleeping sickness has puzzled doctors for decades. It would disappear from villages without a trace, only to re-emerge weeks or months later with no known cause. Frustrated health officials wondered how sleeping sickness could persist when not a single villager or animal—the disease's only carriers—tested positive for the insect-borne parasite that causes it. Now, scientists may have an answer at last: They've discovered the disease was hiding in plain sight this whole time, living in and even transmitting via skin.
>
> African sleeping sickness is caused by a microscopic wormlike parasite spread exclusively by the tsetse fly. As such, it's limited by the fly's range to sub-Saharan Africa. Locals avoid places where the flies are numerous, but political unrest can displace residents and force them into the path of the disease. Once infected, people have anywhere from weeks to years before the parasite crashes into the brain, causing headaches, tremors, confusion, and paralysis. Those infected also suffer from a disrupted sleep cycle, bouts of random sleepiness and wakefulness that gives the disease its name. Without treatment—toxic drugs that keep patients bedridden for weeks—those infected nearly always slip into a coma and die.
>
> Parasitologist Annette MacLeod, who led the new discover, has been traveling to sub-Saharan Africa, primarily Guinea, for the past 20 years to study sleeping sickness. Like everyone else, she was boggled by the disease's mysterious reappearing act. A few years ago, when she was studying the parasite in mice, she noticed that under a microscope she could see it burrowing in a mouse's _____. Unlike mosquitoes that tap directly into the bloodstream, tsetse flies bite through flesh, giving potential skin-based parasites the opportunity to infect the flies while they're eating.

3. Read the critical essay below and follow the directions. [4 points]

In certain kinds of writing, particularly in art criticism and literary criticism, it is normal to come across long passages which are almost completely lacking in meaning. Words like romantic, plastic, values, human, dead, sentimental, natural, vitality, as used in art criticism, are strictly _____①_____, in the sense that they not only do not point to any discoverable object, but are hardly ever expected to do so by the reader. When one critic writes, "The outstanding feature of Mr. X's work is its living quality", while another writes, "The immediately striking thing about Mr. X's work is its peculiar deadness", the reader accepts this as a simple difference opinion. If words like black and white were involved, instead of the jargon words dead and living, he would see at once that language was being used meaninglessly.

Many social and political words are also abused. The word Fascism has now no meaning except in so far as it signifies 'something not desirable'. The words democracy, socialism, freedom, patriotic, realistic, justice have each of them several different meanings which cannot be reconciled with one another. In the case of a word like democracy, not only is there no agreed definition, but the attempt to make one is resisted from all sides. It is almost universally felt that when we call a country democratic we are praising it: consequently the defenders of every kind of regime claim that it is a democracy, and fear that they might have to stop using that word ② <u>if it were tied down to any one meaning</u>. Words of this kind are often used in a consciously dishonest way. That is, the person who uses them has his own private definition, but allows his hearer to think he means something quite different. Statements like Marshal Petain was a true patriot, The Soviet press is the freest in the world, The Catholic Church is opposed to persecution, are almost always made with intent to deceive. Other words used in variable meanings, in most cases more or less dishonestly, are: class, totalitarian, science, progressive, reactionary, bourgeois, equality.

Fill in the blank ① with the ONE most appropriate word from the passage. If necessary, change the word form. Second, explain what the underlined words in ② means.

4 Read the passage and follow the directions. [4 points]

> Researchers in Britain asked 400 accomplished women and 500 accomplished men to name their favorite novels. The men preferred novels written by men, often revolving around loneliness and alienation. Camus's *The Stranger*, Salinger's *Catcher in the Rye* and Vonnegut's *Slaughterhouse-Five* topped the male list. The women leaned toward books written by women. The women's books described relationships and are a lot better than the books the men chose. The top six women's books were *Jane Eyre, Wuthering Heights, The Handmaid's Tale, Middlemarch, Pride and Prejudice* and *Beloved*.
>
> There are a couple of reasons why the two lists might diverge so starkly. It could be men are insensitive dolts who don't appreciate subtle human connections and good literature. However, it is that the part of the brain where men experience negative emotion, the amygdala, is not well connected to the part of the brain where verbal processing happens, whereas the part of the brain where women experience negative emotion, the cerebral cortex, is well connected. Women are better at processing emotion through words.
>
> Over the past two decades, there has been a steady accumulation of evidence that male and female brains work differently. Women use both sides of their brain more symmetrically than men. Men and women hear and smell differently (women are much more sensitive). Boys and girls process colors differently (young girls enjoy an array of red, green and orange crayons whereas young boys generally stick to black, gray and blue). Men and women experience risk differently (men enjoy it more). In short, biological factors influence reading tastes, even after accounting for culture. Women who have congenital adrenal hyperplasia, which leads to high male hormone secretions, are more likely to choose violent stories than other women.

Describe the main idea of the passage in ONE sentence. Then explain what would happen if the amygdala had more of a connection to the part of the brain where verbal processing happens.

5. Read the passage and follow the directions. [5 points]

There are only two types of people in the world, Type A and Type Z. It isn't hard to tell which type you are. How long before the plane leaves do you arrive at the airport? Early plane-catchers, Type A, pack their bags at least a day in advance, and they pack neatly. If they're booked on a flight that leaves at four in the afternoon, they get up at 5:30 that morning. If they haven't left the house by noon, they're worried about missing the plane. Late plane-catchers, Type Z, pack hastily at the last minute and arrive at the airport too late to buy a newspaper. What do you do with a new book? Type A reads more carefully and finishes every book, even though it isn't any good. Type Z skims through a lot of books and is more apt to write in the margins with a pencil. Type A eats a good breakfast; Type Z grabs a cup of coffee. Type As turn off the lights when leaving a room and lock the doors when leaving a house. They go back to make sure they've locked it, and they worry later about whether they left the iron on or not. They didn't. Type Zs leave the lights burning and if they lock the door at all when they leave the house, they're apt to have forgotten their keys. Type A squeezes a tube of toothpaste from the bottom, rolls it very carefully as he uses it and puts the top back on every time. Type Z squeezes the tube from the middle, and he's lost the cap under the radiator.

Type A sees the dentist twice a year, has an annual physical checkup and thinks he may have something. <u>Type Z has been meaning to see a doctor.</u> Type Zs are more apt to have some Type A characteristics than Type As are apt to have any Type Z characteristics. Type As always marry Type Zs. Type Zs always marry Type As.

Explain the implication of the underlined "Type Z has been meaning to see a doctor". Second, the writer makes use of irony in the last sentences of the passage for its humorous effect. Explain the irony.

제 18 회 모의고사

1 Read the critical essay and follow the directions. [2 points]

History is not objective facts; rather, like literature, it is subject to interpretation and reinterpretation depending on the power structure of society. Michel Foucault reflects that the discourse of an era defines the nature of "truth" and what behaviors are acceptable, sane, or criminal. "Truth" is produced by the interaction of power and the systems in which the power flows, and it changes as ____①____ changes.

Literature cannot be interpreted without reference to the time and place in which it was written. A flaw of much criticism is the consideration of a literary text as if it were an organic whole. Such an approach ignores the heterogeneity of conflicting voices in a text and in the cultural context in which a text is embedded. Also, readers, like texts, are influenced and shaped by the cultural context of their eras. A thoroughly objective "reading" of a text is therefore impossible.

So, Shakespeare is less as an autonomous great author in the modern sense than as a clue to the conjunction of the world of Renaissance theatre, a collaborative and largely anonymous free-for-all, and the complex social politics of the time. In this sense, Shakespeare's plays are seen as inseparable from the ____②____ in which he wrote.

Fill in the blank ① with the TWO most appropriate consecutive words from the passage and the blank ② with the ONE most appropriate word from the passage.

2 Read the passage and follow the directions. [4 points]

> Imagine that you spent your whole life at a single house. Each day at the same hour you entered an artificially-lit room, undressed and took up the same position in front of a motion picture camera. It photographed one frame of you per day, every day of your life. On your seventy-second birthday, the reel of film was shown. You saw yourself growing and aging over seventy-two years in less than half an hour (27.4 minutes at sixteen frames per second). Images of this sort, though terrifying, are helpful in suggesting unfamiliar but useful views of time. They may, for example, symbolize the telescoped, almost momentary character of the past as seen through the eyes of the anxious or disaffected individual. Or they may suggest the remarkable brevity of our lives in the cosmic scale of time. If the estimated age of the cosmos were shortened to seventy-two years, a human life would take about ten seconds.
>
> But look at time the other way. Each day is a minor eternity of over 86000 seconds. During each second, the number of the distinct molecular functions going on within the human body is comparable to the number of the seconds in the estimated age of the cosmos. A few seconds are long enough for a revolutionary idea, a startling communication, a baby's conception, a wounding insult, a sudden death. Depending on how we think of them, our lives can infinitely long or infinitely short.

According to the passage, there are different views of time. Identify each view. Second, describe the implied usefulness of the perspective of time given in the second paragraph.

3 Read the statement and follow the directions. [4 points]

> Fifteen college seniors were selected to participate in a research study. An Online English learning app was made available to them, and these students were allowed to study for however many hours they wanted. The graph below records how many hours each student studied, using the online material, and the corresponding exam score. The best-fit line model shows the best prediction, given such a student's hours of study, of what her exam score might be.
>
>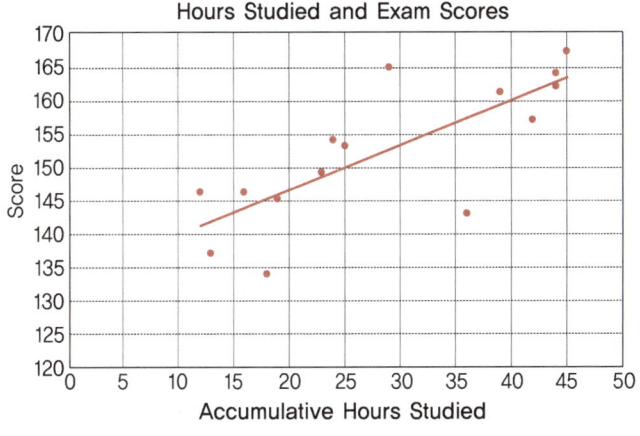

Identify how many students performed higher than the prediction model. Likewise, if a student has five weeks left before a test to prepare, at least how many hours per week, on average, should they be using the English learning app to get higher than a 150 score?

4 **Read the passage and follow the directions.** [5 points]

> Whereas most conventional bombs produce only one destructive effect—the shock wave—nuclear weapons produce many destructive effects. At the moment of the explosion, when the temperature of the weapon material, instantly gasified, is at the superstellar level, the pressure is millions of times the normal atmospheric pressure. Immediately, radiation, consisting mainly of gamma rays, which are a very high-energy form of electromagnetic radiation, begins to stream outward into the environment. This is called the "initial nuclear radiation," and is the first of the destructive effects of a nuclear explosion. In an air burst of a one-megaton bomb—a bomb with the explosive yield of a million tons of TNT, which is a medium-sized weapon in present-day nuclear arsenals—the initial nuclear radiation can kill unprotected human beings in an area of some six square miles. Virtually simultaneously with the initial nuclear radiation, in another destructive effect of the explosion, an electromagnetic pulse is generated by the intense gamma radiation acting on the air. In a high-altitude detonation, the pulse can knock out electrical equipment over a wide area by inducing a powerful surge of voltage through various conductors, such as antennas, overhead power lines, pipes, and railroad tracks. When the fusion and fission reactions have blown themselves out, a fireball takes shape. As it expands, energy is absorbed in the form of X rays by the surrounding air, and then the air re-radiates a portion of that energy into the environment in the form of the thermal pulse—a wave of blinding light and intense heat—which is the third of the destructive effects of a nuclear explosion. The thermal pulse of a one-megaton bomb lasts for about ten seconds and can cause second-degree burns in exposed human beings at a distance of nine and a half miles, or in an area of more than two hundred and eighty square miles—As the fireball expands, it also sends out a blast wave in all directions, and this is the fourth destructive effect of the explosion. The blast wave of an air-burst one-megaton bomb can flatten or severely damage all but the strongest buildings within a radius of four and a half miles.

The passage is composed of one major cause and its direct effects. Write a summary following the guidelines below.

Guidelines
- Summarize the above passage in ONE paragraph.
- Identify one major cause and describe all effects produced by the cause.
- Do NOT copy more than FIVE consecutive words from the passage.

1 Read the passage and follow the directions. [2 points]

Literature reflects the life of a people. It reflects in word images a people's creative consciousness of their struggles to mould nature through co-operative labor and in the process acting on and changing themselves. It reflects in word images a people's consciousness of the tensions and conflicts arising out of their struggles to mould a meaningful social environment founded on their combined actions on nature to wrest the means of life: clothing, food and shelter. Literature thus contains people's ____①____ of themselves in history and of their place in the universe.

A child in this country can only know itself by studying London or New York first; by first immersing itself in a European writer's imaginative responses to his countryside and to his history; the notion that this nation's child's route to self-realization must be via European heritages and cultures. The price we pay for these Eurocentric studies of ourselves is the total distortion of values of national liberation.

Also, everytime we go to the movies we are confronted with the way imperialist oppressors see the world; we are faced with the ideological justification of their ways to themselves and to us. Thus we never see ourselves on the screen; we never react to or respond to ourselves and to our environment on the screen. Worse, we often applaud the superhuman feats of racist heroes of imperialism—James Bond or an American cowboy wiping out a whole crowd of Third World people: Africans, Chinese, Mexicans, or the Native Americans.

It is time that we realized that European history as reflected in their literature and movies is not the universal experience of history. Moreover, their history has largely been one of exploitation, oppression, and elimination of other peoples. Why should we, whose experience of history as reflected in our literature is one of continuous heroic struggle against European slavery and pillage, be expected to memorize and recite the story of ____②____ and thus identify with their literary glorification?

Fill in the blank ① with the ONE most appropriate word from the passage and fill in the blank ② with the TWO most appropriate consecutive words from the passage.

2 Read the passage and follow the directions. [4 points]

There were humans long before there was history. Animals much like modern humans first appeared about 2.5 million years ago. But for countless generations they did not stand out from the myriad other organisms with which they shared their habitats.

On a hike in East Africa 2 million years ago, you might well have encountered a familiar cast of human characters: anxious mothers cuddling their babies and clutches of carefree children playing in the mud; temperamental youths chafing against the dictates of society and weary elders who just wanted to be left in peace; chest-thumping machos trying to impress the local beauty and wise old matriarchs who had already seen it all. These archaic humans loved, played, formed close friendships and competed for status and power—but so did chimpanzees, baboons and elephants. There was nothing special about them. Nobody, least of all humans themselves, had any inkling that their descendants would one day walk on the moon, split the atom, fathom the genetic code and write history books. The most important thing to know about prehistoric humans is that they were insignificant animals with no more impact on their environment than gorillas, fireflies or jellyfish.

Biologists classify organisms into species. Animals are said to belong to the same species if they tend to mate with each other, giving birth to fertile offspring. Horses and donkeys have a recent common ancestor and share many physical traits. But they show little sexual interest in one another. They will mate if induced to do so—but their offspring, called mules, are sterile. Mutations in donkey DNA can therefore never cross over to horses, or vice versa. The two types of animals are consequently considered two distinct species, moving along separate evolutionary paths. By contrast, a bulldog and a spaniel may look very different, but they are members of the same species, sharing the same DNA pool.

Write the TWO most appropriate consecutive words from the passage that correspond to the meaning of the underlined words. Then, explain why such animals as bulldogs and spaniels are classified as the same species.

3. Read the passage and follow the directions. [5 points]

The potential for droughts, floods, migration and conflict resulting from climate change are well-publicized. Certain regions and groups are more exposed to these risks than others, and yet the ways climate change exacerbates inequality has been largely overlooked.

Internationally, the problem of global wealth inequality complicates the problem of climate change—a problem for which not all countries in the world are equally responsible. A Canadian citizen, for example, puts on average as much carbon dioxide into the atmosphere as four Chinese citizens or 16 Indian citizens. A recent report showed that the richest 10 percent of the world's population are responsible for 50 percent of global carbon emissions, while the poorest 50 percent—3.5 billion people—are responsible for 10 percent of the emissions. The general pattern we see is that the biggest polluters in the world tend to be the richest countries, but countries that are the most affected are usually developing. Bangladesh faces extreme sea level rises, and, by a simple 20°C change in global temperatures, hurricanes will devastate the Caribbean, and large areas of the African continent will experience extreme drought. Vast portions of the Middle East will become intolerable to humans by 2100, and the Fertile Crescent—the cradle of civilization—will also disappear by the end of the century. These situations will be compounded by a lack of proper infrastructure and the strong institutional governance necessary for mitigating the damages.

As such, at the heart of this global issue lies a problematic paradox. It is convenient for these rich polluters to self-deceive and forget about the consequences of their actions—or in some cases, propose peculiar solutions. For example, rich countries usually make the claim that the developing world should limit its use of fossil fuels without proposing any other alternatives that might help these countries with economic growth. However, because many of these developing countries are poor, their top priority is industrialization. Following examples set by rich countries, their plans for industrialization very much depend on fossil fuels, relegating plans to reduce greenhouse gas emissions to the bottom of the priority list. As such, what the developed world expects of developing nations doesn't come across as <u>feasible or fair</u>.

Explain how climate change can worsen the situation in developing nations. Then explain the meaning of the underlined words in the last sentence.

제 20 회 모의고사

1 Read the passage and follow the directions. [4 points]

In recent decades, psychologists and biologists have taken up the challenge of studying scientifically what really makes people happy. It is money, family, genetics or perhaps virtue?

But the most important finding of all is that happiness does not really depend on objective conditions of either wealth, health or even community. Rather, it depends on the correlation between objective conditions and subjective expectations. If you want a bullock-cart and get a bullock-cart, you are content. If you want a brand-new Ferrari and get only a second-hand Fiat you feel deprived. ① This is why winning the lottery has, over time, the same impact on people's happiness as a debilitating car accident. When things improve, expectations balloon, and consequently even dramatic improvements in objective conditions can leave us dissatisfied. When things deteriorate, expectations shrink, and consequently even a severe illness might leave you pretty much as happy as you were before.

You might say that we didn't need a bunch of psychologists and their questionnaires to discover this. Prophets, poets and philosophers realized thousands of years ago that being satisfied with what you already have is far more important than getting more of what you want. Still, it's nice when modern research—bolstered by lots of numbers and charts—reaches ② the same conclusion the ancients did.

Explain the reason for the underlined ① "why winning the lottery has, over time, the same impact on people's happiness as a debilitating car accident". Second, describe what the underlined ② "the same conclusion" is.

2 Read the passage and follow the directions. [4 points]

A new human archetype is being born. Comfortable living a part of their lives in cyberspace in virtual worlds, familiar with the workings of a network economy, less interested in accumulating things and more interested in having exciting and entertaining experiences, able to interact in parallel worlds simultaneously, quick to change their own personas to match whatever new reality—simulated or real—is put before them, the new men and women of the twenty-first century are a breed apart from their bourgeois parents and grandparents of the industrial era.

① The "protean" human beings have grown up living inside of common-interest developments; their health care is a administered through HMOs; they lease their automobiles; they buy things online; they expect to get their software for free but are willing to pay for services and upgrades. They live in a world of seven-second sound bites, are used to quick access to and retrieval of information, have short attention spans, and are less reflective and more spontaneous. They think of themselves as players rather than workers and prefer others to think of them as creative rather than industrious. They have grown up in a world of just-in-time employment and are used to being on temporary assignment. In fact, their lives are far more temporary and mobile and less grounded than their parents'. They are more therapeutic than ideological and think more in terms of images than words. While they are less able to compose a written sentence, they are better able to process electronic data. They equate consumer sovereignty with democracy.

They think of Disney World and Club Med as the ___②___ thing. Therefore, they spend as much time with fictional characters on television, film, and in cyberspace as they do with peers in real life. They even integrate the fictional characters and their experiences into social conversations, making them a part of their own personal stories. They are able to send e-mail to people's virtual addresses without ever having to know or even care about their real geographic addresses.

Explain the meaning of the underlined words in ①. Then fill in the blank ② with the ONE most appropriate word from the passage.

3 Read the passage and follow the directions. [5 points]

> The belief in the growing global pie eventually turned revolutionary. In 1776 the Scottish economist Adam Smith published *The Wealth of Nations*, probably the most important economics manifesto of all time. In the eighth chapter of its first volume, Smith made the following novel argument: when a landlord, a weaver or a shoemaker has greater profits than he needs to maintain his own family, he uses the surplus to employ more assistants, in order to further increase his profits. The more profits he has, the more assistants he can employ. He becomes a capitalist. An increase in the profits of private entrepreneurs is the basis for the increase in collective wealth and prosperity.
>
> This may not strike you as very original, because we all live in a capitalist world that takes Smith's argument for granted. We hear variations on this theme every day in the news. Yet Smith's claim that the selfish human urge to increase private profits is the basis for collective wealth is one of the most revolutionary ideas in human history—revolutionary not just from an economic perspective, but even more so from a moral and political perspective. What Smith says is, in fact, that ① egoism is altruism.
>
> All this depends, however, on the rich using their profits to open new factories and hire new employees, rather than wasting them on non-productive activities. Smith therefore repeated like a mantra the maxim that "When profits increase, the landlord or weaver will employ more assistants" and not "When profit increase, Scrooge will hoard his money in a chest and take it out only to count his coins."
>
> That's why capitalism is called 'capitalism', Capitalism distinguishes 'capital' from mere 'wealth'. Capital consists of money, goods and resources that are invested in production. Wealth, on the other hand, is buried in the ground or wasted on unproductive activities. A pharaoh who pours resources into a non-productive pyramid is not a(n) ____②____. But a hard-working factory hand who reinvests part of his income in the stock market is.

Explain the meaning of the underlined words in ①. Then, describe what Scrooge would have done differently if he had wanted to be a capitalist. Finally, fill in the blank ② with the ONE most appropriate word from the passage.

4. Read the passage and follow the directions. [5 points]

> Attempts to limit female mobility by hampering locomotion are ancient and almost universal. The foot-binding of upper-class Chinese girls and the Nigerian custom of loading women's legs with pounds of heavy brass wire are extreme examples, but all over the world similar stratagems have been employed to make sure that once you have caught a woman she cannot run away, and even if she stays around she cannot keep up with you. What seems odd is that these devices have been perceived as beautiful not only by men but by women. The lotus foot, which seems to us a deformity, was passionately admired in China for centuries, and today most people in Western society see nothing ugly in the severely compressed toes produced by modern footwear. The high-heeled, narrow-toed shoes that for most of this century have been an essential part of woman's costume are considered sexually attractive, partly because they make the legs look longer—an extended leg is the biological sign of sexual availability in several animal species—and because they produce what anthropologists call a "courtship strut." They also make standing for any length of time painful, walking exhausting and running impossible. The halting, tiptoe gait they produce is thought provocative—perhaps because it guarantees that no woman wearing them can outrun a man who is chasing her. Worst of all, if they are worn continually from adolescence on, they deform the muscles of the feet and legs so that it becomes even more painful and difficult to walk in flat soles.

Summarize the above passage in a well-formed paragraph. Your summary must contain the main idea and major supporting details expressed by author and must NOT contain any of your own ideas. Do NOT copy more than FIVE consecutive words from the passage.

제 21 회 모의고사

모범답안 및 번역 p.078

1 Read the passage and follow directions. [4 points]

As a rule of thumb, you should slow down for donkeys, speed up for _____①_____, and stop for cows. Donkeys will get out of your way eventually, and so will pedestrians. But never actually stop for either of them or they'll take advantage, especially the pedestrians. If you stop in the middle of a crowd of Third World pedestrians, you'll be there buying Chiclets* and bogus antiquities for days.

Drive like hell through the goats. It's almost impossible to hit a goat. On the other hand, it's almost impossible not to hit a cow. Cows are immune to horn-honking, shouting, swats with sticks and taps on the hind quarters with the bumper. The only thing you can do to make a cow move is swerve to avoid it, which will make the cow move in front of you with lightning speed.

Actually, the most dangerous animals are the chickens. In the United States, when you see a ball roll into the street, you hit your brakes because you know the next thing you'll see is a kid chasing it. In the Third World, it's not balls the kids are chasing, but chickens. Are they practicing punt returns with a leghorn*? Dribbling it? Playing stick-hen? I don't know. But Third Worlders are remarkably fond of their chickens and, also, their children. ② <u>If you hit one or both, they may survive. But you will not.</u>

*Chiclets: a brand of candy-coated chewing gum
*leghorn: a breed of chicken

Fill in the blank ① with the ONE most appropriate word from the passage. Then explain the meaning of the underlined words in ②.

2. Read the passage and follow directions. [4 points]

Based on the evidence, neither of these positions—that green spending yields significant environmental results or that it "distracts" from them by assuaging people's feelings—captures the relationship between buying patterns, activism and environmental degradation.

The first position is folk wisdom, but it's naive and historically uninformed. Major changes, like the transition from a polluting energy source to a clean one or a shift away from toxic chemicals, don't automatically flow from the market. They are the result of pressure from advocacy groups, experts, some segments of business and other constituencies. Consumer dollars play a role when businesses need to be convinced that there's a market for new products or when there are enough "green" businesses to push for new regulations. But they almost never drive policy or legislation in the straightforward way suggested by the metaphor of "voting with our dollars."

The distraction position, while popular among some social scientists, is unsupported by the data. A crucial study published in *the Annals of the American Academy of Political and Social Science* found the reverse: people who buy green are more likely to be politically active, whether they're engaging in standard political behaviors like contacting members of Congress or writing letters to the editor, or informal activities like e-mailing friends and family about issues. The study used a nationally representative sample of Americans as well as online survey of 1,800 "conscious consumers." Among the latter the study found high levels of activism. This is also a finding reproduced in European surveys. About half of the respondents got into conscious consuming at roughly the same time they became politically active. About a quarter transformed their buying patterns and then became active.

Explain the meaning of the underlined words. Second, describe what the "distraction position" is.

3 Read the passage and follow the directions. [4 points]

> The dominant sociological approach to ethnicity has long taken the form of what Neil Sandberg aptly calls straight-line theory, in which acculturation and assimilation are viewed as secular trends that culminate in the eventual absorption of the ethnic group into the larger culture and general population. Straight-line theory in turn is based on melting pot theory, for it implies the disappearance of the ethnic groups into a single host society. Even so, it does not accept the values of the melting pot theorists, since its conceptualizers could have, but did not, use terms like cultural and social liberation from immigrant ways of life.
>
> In recent years, straight-line theory has been questioned on many grounds. For one thing, many observers have properly noted that even if America might have been a melting pot early in the 20th century, the massive immigration from Europe and elsewhere has since then influenced the dominant group, summarily labelled White Anglo-Saxon Protestant, and has also decimated their cultural, if not their political and financial power, so that today America is a mosaic, as Andrew Greeley has put it, of subgroups and subcultures. Still, this criticism does not necessarily deny the validity of straight-line theory, since ethnics can also be absorbed into a pluralistic set of subcultures and subgroups, differentiated by age, income, education, occupation, religion, region, and the like. It should be noted that these subset groups integrate often under the influence of the <u>majority group</u>.
>
> A second criticism of straight-line theory has centered on its treatment of all ethnic groups as essentially similar, and its failure, specifically, to distinguish between religious groups like the Jews and nationality groups like the Italians, Poles etc. Jews, for example, are a 'peoplehood' with a religious and cultural tradition of thousands of years, but without an 'old country' to which they owe allegiance or nostalgia, while Italians, Poles and other participants in the 'new immigration' came from parts of Europe which in some cases did not even become nations until after the immigrants had arrived in America.

Write the THREE most appropriate consecutive words from the passage that correspond to the meaning of the underlined words. Then, explain the weakness of the straight-line theory in terms of groups like the Jewish.

4 **Read the passage and follow the directions.** [5 points]

I have spent days, weeks on the F train. The trip from Seventh Avenue to midtown Manhattan is long enough so that every ride can produce its own mini-society of riders, its own forty-minute Ship of Fools. Once a woman an arm's length from me on a crowded train pulled a knife on a man who threatened her. I remember the argument and the principals, but mostly I remember the knife—its flat, curved wood-grain handle in-laid with brass fittings at each end, its long, tapered blade. Once a man sang the words of the Lord's Prayer to an mournful, syncopated tune, and he fitted the mood of the morning so exactly that when he asked for money at the end the riders reached for their wallets and purses as if he'd pulled a gun. Once a big white kid with some friends was teasing a small old Hispanic lady, and when he got off the train I looked at him through the window and he slugged it hard next to my face. Once a thin woman and a fat woman sitting side by side had a long and loud conversation about someone they intended to slap silly. "Her butt be in the *hospital*!" "Bring out the *ar-tillery*!" The terminus of the F in Brooklyn is at Coney Island, not far from the beach. At an off hour, I boarded the train and found two or three passengers and, walking around on the floor, a crab, the passengers were looking at the crab. Its legs clicked on the floor like varnished fingernails. It moved in this direction, then that, trying to get comfortable. It backed itself under a seat, against the wall. Then it scooted out just after some new passengers had sat down here, and they really screamed. Passengers at the next stop saw it and laughed. When a boy lifted his foot as if to stomp it, everybody cried, "Noooh!" By the time we reached Jay Street—Borough Hall, there were maybe a dozen of us in the car, all absorbed in watching the crap. The car door opened and a heavyset woman with good posture entered. She looked at the crab; then sternly, at all of us. She let a moment pass. Then she demanded, "Whose is that?" A few stops later, a short man with a mustache took a manila envelope, bent down, scooped the crab into it, closed it, and put it in his coat pocket.

Summarize the above passage in a well-formed paragraph. Your summary must contain the main idea and major supporting details expressed by author and must NOT contain any of your own ideas. Do NOT copy more than SEVEN consecutive words from the passage.

제 22 회 모의고사

모범답안 및 번역 p.081

1 Read the passage and fill in each blank with the ONE most appropriate word from the passage. [2 points]

At first glance, you would be hard put to find any common ground between the angry features of Beethoven and the shy boyishness of Prince Harry. Of course, if you were Karl Smith, emeritus professor of psychology at America's Wisconsin-Madison University, and had spent 15 years in research, you would know that both are ____①____.

'Facedness' is the new theory that proposes, just as most of us are either left-handed or right-handed, we have a more dominant facial side. It claims to reveal the physiognomy of musical genius. Left-facers, according to Smith's studies, are better able to tune into the right side of the brain, which is associated with musical performance, while right-facers tap into the left hemisphere, which is specialized for cognitive process—to the layman, thinking. His surveys show that 85-90% of people are right-faced.

Wagner has one of the most marked left-faces that Smith has looked at, "dominant to the point of deformity". He is joined by Mozart, Beethoven, Brahms, Schubert, Tchaikovsky and Liszt. Over 98% of New York's Metropolitan Opera singers have been left-faced.

Prince Harry is the only member of the royal family who may have a career in music as a left-facer. "Parents should not be wasting their money on right-faced children," says Smith. It is not, contrary to popular belief, hands that will suggest a Mozart in the making, but ____②____ features.

Unlike handedness, which develops at the age of three or four, facedness is determined before birth. For would-be composers and politicians there is no defying facedness, and parents should take note before signing up hopeful youngsters for music lessons—a glance in the mirror will tell if the expense will be worth it.

2 **Read the passage and follow the directions.** [4 points]

> This week another language died; Carlos Westez, more widely known as Red Thunder Cloud, the last speaker of the native American language Catawba, died of a stroke at the age of 78. With him passed away the Catawba language. Of the creatures alive on the planet, only Red Thunder Cloud's dog, which survived him and understood commands in no other language, still presumably has the sounds of Catawba rolling around his brain.
>
> It has become clear to all of us, over the past 20 years, how much damage modern industry can inflict on the world's ecology; how the destruction of the rainforest also brings about the ① death of untold species of plants and insects.
>
> Less obvious, but no less harmful is the impact of one powerful culture upon our languages and ways of life. We are witnessing the spread of English, carried by an American culture, delivered by Japanese technology. We are also witnessing the increasing dominance of a few great, transnational tongues—Chinese, Spanish, Russian and Hindi. With their rise as tools of culture and commerce has come the deaths of other languages which are the losers in the competition for linguistic survival. One of those under threat is Aore, the language native to Vanuatu in the Pacific. Like Catawba ② (until this week) it is spoken by that island's only remaining native inhabitant. So it, too, is bound to die out.
>
> To be the last remaining speaker of a language, like Red Thunder Cloud, or like Dolly Pentreath, who died in 1778, the last person to speak Cornish as her mother tongue, must be a peculiarly lonely destiny, almost as strange and terrible as to be the last surviving member of a dying species. But what the rest of us lose when a language dies is the possibility of a unique way of perceiving and describing the world.

Write the FOUR most appropriate consecutive words from the passage that the writer compares, in meaning, to the underlined words in ①. Then, explain the meaning of the underlined words in ②.

3 Read the passage and follow the directions. [4 points]

> Every year more than half a million American kids have drainage tubes surgically implanted in their ears to combat persistent infections. The procedure, known as tympanostomy, may not be as common as the tonsillectomy was in the 1940s, but it now ranks as the nation's leading childhood operation and a new study suggests it's being vastly overused. In reviewing more than 6,000 scheduled ear tube operations, a team of experts led by Harvard pediatrician Lawrence Kleinman found that fewer than half were clearly justified. "Each year," the researchers write in the current *Journal of the American Medical Association*, "several hundred thousand children in the United states may be receiving tympanostomy tubes that offer them no demonstrated advantage and may place them at increased risk."
>
> Tube placement isn't a terribly risky procedure, but it costs $1,000 to $1,500 and sometimes scars the eardrum, causing a partial loss of hearing. Studies show that the benefits are most likely to outweigh the risks if a child's middle ear has produced sticky fluid for more than four months despite treatment with antibiotics. For less virulent infections, drug treatment is usually a cheaper, safer alternative (though drugs, too, can be overused). In the new JAMA study, Kleinman's team reviewed the medical charts of 6,429 kids, all under 16, whose doctors had recommended the procedure. Even making "generous assumptions" about the likely benefits, the researchers found that a quarter of the proposed operations were inappropriate, since less invasive alternatives were available, while another third were as likely to harm the recipients as help them. Parents needn't panic about ear tubes that are already in place. Once successfully implanted, the tiny devices provide drainage for six months to a year, then come out by reducing health costs by hundreds of millions of dollars every year.

What can be inferred from the passage about tonsillectomies in the 1940s? Second, describe the core finding of the Harvard study.

4. Read the passage and follow the directions. [4 points]

Homo sapiens has kept hidden a very disturbing secret. Not only do we possess an abundance of uncivilised cousins, once upon a time we had quite a few brothers and sisters as well. We are used to thinking about ourselves as the only humans, because for the last 10,000 years, our species has indeed been the only human species around. Yet the real meaning of the word human is 'an animal belonging to the genus Homo', and there used to be many other species of this genus besides Homo sapiens.

Humans first evolved in East Africa about 2.5 million years ago from an earlier genus of apes called Australopithecus, which means 'Southern Ape'. About 2 million years ago, some of these archaic men and women left their homeland to journey through and settle vast areas of North Africa, Europe and Asia. Since survival in the snowy forests of northern Europe required different traits than those needed to stay alive in Indonesia's steaming jungles, human populations evolved in different directions. The result was several distinct species, to each of which scientists have assigned a pompous Latin name.

Humans in Europe and western Asia evolved into Homo neanderthalensis ('Man from the Neander Valley), popularly referred to simply as 'Neanderthals'. Neanderthals, bulkier and more muscular than us Sapiens, were well adapted to the cold climate of Ice Age western Eurasia. The more eastern regions of Asia were populated by Homo erectus, 'Upright Man', who survived there for close to 2 million years, making it the most durable human species ever. This record is unlikely to be broken even by our own species. It is doubtful whether Homo sapiens will still be around a thousand years from now, so 2 million years is really out of our league.

On the island of Java, in Indonesia, lived Homo soloensis, 'Man from the Solo Valley', who was suited to life in the tropics. On another Indonesian island—the small island of Flores—archaic humans underwent a process of dwarfing. Humans first reached Flores when the sea level was exceptionally low, and the island was easily accessible from the mainland. When the seas rose again, some people were trapped on the island, which was poor in resources. Big people, who need a lot of food, died first. Smaller fellows survived much better. Over the generations, the people of Flores became dwarves. This unique species, known by scientists as Homo floresiensis, reached a maximum height of only one metre and weighed no more than twenty-five kilograms.

How many human species have lived on the Earth? Second, if there had been two males—Toni who is 0.8 meter high and Sammy who is 2 meters high—on the island of Flores, who would have been most likely to survive and why?

제 23 회 모의고사

1 Read the following passage and answer the questions. [4 points]

Does death really mean the end of our existence? Great thinkers from Plato to Blue Öyster Cult have weighed in on the question. Now, a study shows that at least one aspect of life continues: Genes remain turned on days after animals die. Researchers may be able to parlay this postmortem activity into better ways of preserving donated organs for transplantation and more accurate methods of determining when murder victims were killed.

Before you ask, microbiologist Peter Noble and colleagues were not trying to find out what allows zombies to stalk Earth and slurp the brains of the unwary. Instead, the scientists wanted to test a new method they had developed for calibrating gene activity measurements. Their research had already taken a morbid turn—2 years ago they published a paper on the abundance of microbes in different human organs after death—and they decided to apply their method to postmortem samples. "It's an experiment of curiosity to see what happens when you die," Noble says.

Although scientists analyzing blood and liver tissue from human cadavers had previously noted the postmortem activity of a few genes, Noble and colleagues systematically evaluated more than 1000. The team measured which of these genes were functioning in tissues from recently deceased mice and zebrafish, tracking changes for 4 days in the fish and 2 days in the rodents.

At first, the researchers assumed that genes would shut down shortly after death, like the parts of a car that has run out of gas. What they found instead was that hundreds of genes ramped up. Although most of these genes upped their activity in the first 24 hours after the animals expired and then tapered off, in the fish some genes remained active 4 days after death.

What is the purpose of the passage? Write your answer in ONE sentence. Then, how is Noble's discovery regarding post-mortem biology applicable to a murder investigation?

2 Read the passage and follow the directions. [4 points]

①_____ of the last few decades are one of the greatest success stories there has been. In contrast to my undergraduate days when you could have passed through Sydney University genuinely believing that the only women writers to have existed were the exceptional three: Jane Austen, George Eliot and Charlotte Bronte, today we have an abundance of women's books. They are not just products of the women's presses. For by publishing books by, about and for women, the women's publishing houses changed the market, to the extent that where they led, the mainstream publishers had to follow. This was partly because women are also more avid readers, and greater book buyers.

But if women writers came into their own once women were decision makers in the medium, there is yet another dimension to this undeniable saga of success. It is that women were only able to start publishing houses at a time when the power of print was on the wane. It was because print was losing its place as the primary medium that women were able to get a foot in the door. It was because men were moving off to the exciting, and powerful area of the new electronic media, and not contesting the area of print as they once did, that women were able to gain unprecedented access.

I would not want to undermine the achievement of women's presses, but I do want to make it clear that it is a bit like ② becoming the best manuscript producers after the invention of the printing press. I do want to emphasize that women have encoded all this wonderful information in print—at the precise time that books are ceasing to be influential as the repositories of knowledge.

Fill in the blank ① with the TWO most appropriate consecutive words from the passage. The first word should be capitalized. Then explain why the writer of the passage mentions the underlined words in ②.

3 Read the passage and follow the directions. [4 points]

　　Moody Mary (or her male version, Moody Martin) is the type of person who is always experiencing some kind of emotional crisis. She is always devastated, depressed, sad, or pouting because of something gone wrong in her personal life. Usually, it's because her boyfriend broke up with her, or she and her boyfriend had a fight, or her boyfriend's 200-year-old great-great-grandmother died, or she doesn't have this weekend off to spend with her boyfriend. A waitress I work with named Jill, for example, is a Moody Mary. Not only does she annoy all of her coworkers with endless tales of her personal troubles, but she is always on the verge of falling apart, so she moves too slowly and makes a lot of mistakes. As a result, the rest of us have to listen to her customers' complain, and sometimes we even have to take care of them ourselves while she sits in the kitchen and cries. I sympathize with people who are going through a hard time, but I think that people like this should at least try to pull it together during working hours so the rest of us don't have to do their job for them. Another type is Not-My-Job Nancy (or Not-My-Job Nick). This person refuses to do anything that is not written in black-and-white in his or her job description. A hostess I work with named Rita is a Not-My-Job Nancy. Her favorite saying is "That's really not my job." No matter what you ask her, it seems, that's her reply. So, once when I was swamped with other customers, she seated new party at my station, and I asked her to get them water and take their drink orders. Her answer was "That's really not my job." On another occasion, I asked her to carry a piece of pie from the kitchen to a table that she was going to pass on her way back to the front of the restaurant. She said she couldn't because "it wasn't really her job." I think that it's especially hard to work with people who refuse to help out their coworkers, and it makes the job more difficult for everyone. Also relevant to mention, No-Change Charlie (or No-change Charlotte) is the person who hates change. They get used to doing things a certain way, and then they don't want to alter their comfortable routine, even if changing will make it easier or better. Another waiter in our restaurant named Dan is a No-Change Charlie. He argues against every single change, good or bad. He even found reasons why we shouldn't reorganize the tables in the restaurant to improve traffic flow, even though moving things around a little would probably have let us all be more efficient. I'm all for changing things to make the work easier, so I get annoyed by No-Change Charlies who are stuck in a rut and can't get out.

Summarize the above passage in a well-formed paragraph. Your summary must contain the main idea. You must NOT include any of your own ideas. Do NOT copy more than FIVE consecutive words from the passage.

제 24 회 모의고사

1 **Read the passage and follow the directions.** [4 points]

> I was waiting for breakfast in a coffee shop the other morning and reading the paper. The paper had sixty-six pages. The waitress brought a paper place mat and paper napkin and took my order, and I paged through the paper. The headline said, "House Panel Studies a Bill Allowing Clear-Cutting* in U.S. Forests."
>
> I put the paper napkin in my lap, spread the paper out on the paper place mat, and read on:
>
> "The House Agriculture Committee," it said, "is looking over legislation that would once again open national forests to the clear-cutting of trees by private companies under governmental permits."
>
> The waitress brought the coffee. I opened a paper sugar envelope and tore open a little paper cup of cream and went on reading the paper: "The Senate voted <u>without dissent</u> yesterday to allow clear-cutting," the paper said. "Critics have said clear-cutting in the national forests can lead to erosion and destruction of wildlife habitats. Forest Service and industry spokesmen said a flat ban on clear-cutting would bring paralysis to the lumber industry." And to the paper industry, I thought. Clear-cutting a forest is one way to get a lot of paper, and we sure seem to need a lot of paper.
>
> The waitress brought the toast. I looked for the butter. It came on a little paper tray with a covering of paper. I opened a paper package of marmalade and read on: "Senator Jennings Randolph, Democrat of West Virginia, urged his colleagues to take a more restrictive view and permit clear-cutting only under specific guidelines for certain types of forest. But neither he nor anyone else voted against the bill, which was sent to the House on a ninety to zero vote."

The eggs came, with little paper packages of salt and pepper. I finished breakfast, put the paper under my arm, and left the table with its used and useless paper napkin, paper place mat, paper salt and pepper packages, paper butter and marmalade wrappings, paper sugar envelope, and paper cream holder, and I walked out into the morning wondering how our national forests can ever survive our breakfasts.

*clear-cutting: the practice in the lumber industry of cutting all trees

Write the FOUR most appropriate consecutive words from the passage that help the reader figure out the meaning of the underlined words. Second, in what way does the newspaper article the narrator reads relate to his observations about his breakfast?

2 Read the passage and follow the directions. [4 points]

> We can address why people are reluctant to allow that morality can have biological foundation, namely, that the altruism is taken out of morality, so that seemingly altruistic acts are, in the final analysis, really selfish ones. It is not difficult to see how one might come to think this. On a typical reading of a sociobiological account of human behavior, the ultimate motivating force behind each human being's behavior is the drive to maximize her or his gene pool. All manifestations of altruism are to be thus explained, even parental altruism in human beings, since the sociobiological argument is that parents best maximize their gene pool by caring for their children until the latter are in turn able to have progeny (grandchildren).
>
> Yet on the face of it, not only does this explanation for parental altruism seem manifestly false, but it would also seem that altruism toward non-kin does not neatly admit of a sociobiological explanation. Consider a typical instance of parental love. Two parents hear their five-year-old child screaming desperately. It turns out that the child is being attacked by several vicious dogs. We suppose that if the parents genuinely love the child, then without any regard for their own well-being they will attempt to rescue her. In particular, we suppose that the parents will be motivated to rescue their child simply out of their love for her, and that in no way will a desire to maximize their gene pool figure into an explanation of their attempt. Most parents would surely regard it as the cruelest of statements if someone were to claim that in the last analysis what motivated them to rescue their child was the desire and hope that she would give them grandchildren, thereby contributing to the survival of their genes.

Describe the sociobiologist perspective on altruism. Second, would the care parents feel towards an adopted child support or contradict the sociobiologist perspective? And why?

3. Read the passage and follow the directions. [4 points]

The porcupine is a controversial, yet important, forest creature. Our more prickly encounters with "quill pigs" may be remedied with a little knowledge about their biology.

As North America's second-largest rodent—the beaver is largest—adult porcupines range from 2½ to 3 feet long and can weigh 35 pounds. Porcupines are nocturnal, and strictly vegetarian. Throughout winter, they survive on the cambium (living tissue) layer of trees—pines, aspen and cottonwood being preferred. Occasionally a porcupine will continually feed in a single tree, partially or completely girdling its trunk and causing tree deformation or death. From spring through fall, porcupines supplement their diet with leaves, soft plants, mushrooms, vegetables and fruits. The young are born with soft quills that harden soon after birth. Porcupettes eat vegetation within two weeks of birth, but stay with their mothers until fall.

The porcupine's quill count is impressive, with roughly 30,000 quills per animal. The quill itself is a modified hollow hair tipped with microscopic barbs. Porcupines cannot shoot their quills. A threatened porcupine tenses muscles under its skin to erect the quills, faces away from the attacker, and swings its quilled tail. Upon contact, quills detach from the porcupine. Embedded in the attacker's flesh, quills expand with body heat, preventing easy removal. Muscle movements draw the quills further in at the rate of an inch per day. Interestingly, porcupine quills are antiseptic, keeping the porcupine infection-free should it suffer a self-inflicted quilling.

Keeping dogs contained in porcupine country prevents quillings. Should your dog be quilled, the sole solution is removing all embedded quills. To remove a quill, deflate it by cutting the end off, then pull it out with pliers. Clean the injured area, and allow your dog to lick its wounds. If you have any difficulty finding or removing all quills, visit your vet.

If a porcupine takes up residence in your favorite landscape tree, try harassing it into leaving with spray from a hose. After eviction, loosely wrap the trunk with three vertical feet of sheet metal, preventing revisitation.

Despite humans' many conflicts with them, porcupines are ecologically important. The twigs they drop while feeding are winter food for deer, rabbits and elk. Damaged trees become habitat for insects, which in turn feed woodpeckers. A girdled tree's death frees up resources for understory plants that are habitat for numerous animals. Porcupines even eat some "harmful" plants, namely mistletoe, a pine tree parasite.

Explain the reason why it is crucial to pull out porcupine quills urgently. Second, suppose that a dog is quilled by a porcupine. Using information from the passage, depict what will happen to the dog from the moment it is stuck until the quills are removed from the dog's body.

1 Read the passage and follow the directions. [2 points]

> I am not laying too much stress upon this point; for it applies most emphatically to our particular case. Over no nation does the press hold a more absolute control than over the people of America; for the universal education of the poorest classes makes every individual a reader. There is nothing published in England on the subject of our country, that does not circulate through every part of it. There is not a calumny dropt from an English pen, nor an unworthy sarcasm uttered by an English statesman, that does not go to blight good-will, and add to the mass of latent resentment. Possessing, then, as England does, the fountain-head whence the literature of the language flows, how completely is it in her power, and how truly is it her duty, to make it the medium of amiable and magnanimous feeling—a stream where the two nations might meet together and drink in peace and kindness. Should she, however, persist in turning it to waters of bitterness, the time may come when she may repent her folly. The present friendship of America may be of but little moment to her; but the future destinies of <u>that country</u> do not admit of a doubt; over those of England, there lower some shadows of uncertainty. Should, then, a day of gloom arrive—should those reverses overtake her, from which the proudest empires have not been exempt—she may look back with regret at her infatuation, in repulsing from her side a nation she might have grappled to her bosom, and thus destroying her only chance for real friendship beyond the boundaries of her own dominions.

Identify to what the underlined "that country" refers in the above passage.

2. Read the passage and follow the directions. [4 points]

Urban housing shortages made rebuilding a social priority in Europe after the First World War. Designers across the Continent saw themselves as responsible for rebuilding a new, idealistic, utopian society. The spirit of Bauhaus, which was founded as an interdisciplinary school of art and design by a German architect Walter Gropius, spread across Europe, though it was America that provided the most inspiring example. European designers of every persuasion adopted the _____ that was invented by Henry Ford. In the 1920s, leading architects such as Gropius made a grand tour all around the United States to see the age of manufacturing in action. Inspired by the efficiency of mass production, they took their ideas back to Europe. In 1927, the world's first mass-produced fitted kitchen was produced in Frankfurt, Germany. Its ingenious built-in cupboards kept workspaces clean, helping to keep them hygienic. In fact, a key feature of the Bauhaus movement was healthy living. Designers and architects believed that sunlight, fresh air and uncluttered living spaces would banish the causes of disease. This led to new designs for housing and hospitals, all featuring flat roofs, balconies and large windows to let in light. However, the Nazis, who came to power in 1933, disapproved of the Bauhaus movement and began to persecute designers and architects. By the mid-1930s, many had fled to Britain, a country that had not yet embraced the Bauhaus movement. There, they took refuge and began to help reshape their host country in the Bauhaus spirit.

Fill in the blank with the TWO most appropriate consecutive words from the passage. Then, how did the architects achieve Bauhaus movement's core feature? Write your answer in ONE sentence.

_____

_____

_____

_____

3. Read the passage and follow the directions. [4 points]

More than 99% of clinical trials for Alzheimer's drugs have failed, leading many to wonder whether pharmaceutical companies have gone after the wrong targets. Now, research in mice points to a potential new target: a developmental process gone awry, which causes some immune cells to feast on the connections between neurons. It is new work which brings into light what's happening in the early stage of the disease.

Most Alzheimer's drugs so far aim to eliminate β amyloid, a protein that forms telltale sticky plaques around neurons in people with the disease. Those with Alzheimer's tend to have more of these deposits in their brains than do healthy people. However, more plaques don't always mean more severe symptoms of the disease such as memory loss or poor attention.

What does track well with the cognitive decline seen in Alzheimer's disease is a marked loss of synapses, particularly in brain regions key to memory. These junctions between nerve cells are where neurotransmitters are released to spark the brain's electrical activity.

Beth Stevens of Boston Children's Hospital, who led the new work, has spent much of her career studying a normal immune mechanism that weakens unnecessary synapses as the brain matures from the womb through adolescence, allowing more important connections to become stronger. In this process, a protein called C1q targets a synapse for destruction. After a synapse has been tagged by C1q, immune cells called microglia—the brain's trash disposal service—know to "eat" it, Stevens says. When this system goes awry during the brain's development, whether in the womb or later during childhood and into the teen years, it may lead to psychiatric disorders such as schizophrenia, she says.

Stevens hypothesized that <u>the same mechanism</u> goes awry in early Alzheimer's disease, leading to the destruction of good synapses and ultimately to cognitive impairment.

In the above passage, give one example of a "wrong target" implied by the writer. Second, explain to what the underlined part refers.

모의고사 II
(제26회 ~ 제70회 모의고사)

제 26 회 모의고사

1 **Read the passage and follow the directions.** [2 points]

> There are hundreds of things we do—repeatedly, routinely—every day. We wake up, check our phones, eat our meals, brush our teeth, do our jobs. In recent years, such habitual actions have become an arena for self-improvement: bookshelves are saturated with bestsellers about 'life hacks', 'life design' and how to 'gamify' our long-term projects, promising everything from enhanced productivity to a healthier diet and huge fortunes. These guides vary in scientific accuracy, but they tend to depict habitual actions as routines that follow a repeated sequence of behaviours, into which we can intervene to set ourselves on a more desirable track.
>
> The problem is that this account has been bleached of much of its historical richness. Today's self-help books have in fact inherited a highly contingent version of habitual actions—specifically, one that arises in the work of early 20th-century psychologists such as B. Skinner and Ivan Pavlov. These thinkers are associated with behaviourism, an approach to psychology that prioritises observable, stimulus-response reactions over the role of inner feelings or thoughts. The behaviourists defined habits in a narrow, individualistic sense; they believed that people were conditioned to respond automatically to certain cues, which produced repeated cycles of action and reward.

The behaviourist image of habitual actions has since been updated in light of contemporary neuroscience. For example, the fact that the brain is plastic and changeable allows _____ to inscribe themselves in our neural wiring over time by forming privileged connections between brain regions. The influence of behaviourism has enabled researchers to study habits quantitatively and rigorously. But it has also overlooked the concept's wider philosophical implications.

Fill in the blank with the ONE most appropriate word from the passage.

2 Read the passage and follow the directions. [4 points]

> Forty years ago, the most serious nuclear accident in U.S. history sparked a backlash against the industry and halted its growth for decades. Today, the remaining working reactor at Three Mile Island, Unit 1, faces <u>new challenges</u>, including cheaper competition in a rapidly shifting energy grid. Unit 1 at the plant is slated to close later this year.
>
> On March 28, 1979, Three Mile Island's Unit 2 reactor suffered a partial meltdown after a pump stopped sending water to the steam generators that removed heat from the reactor core. The accident was a combination of human error, design deficiencies and equipment failures. A small amount of radiation was released, but in the end, it wasn't a disaster. In 1985, Three Mile Island reopened, minus the one damaged reactor.
>
> But for residents, it was kind of like living with a giant in your neighborhood. People knew it could cause you problems, but they lived in an uneasy compromise. That compromise is being tested, as the nuclear industry faces new challenges, including high operating costs, stagnant demand for electricity and competition from cheaper natural gas and renewable energy.
>
> Chicago-based Exelon, the current owner of Three Mile Island's still-functional Unit 1 reactor, says the plant has been losing money for years. The company plans to close it this fall, 15 years before its operating license expires.
>
> As someone who lived through the Three Mile Island accident, Joyce Corradi would be happier to see the plant close. But because the U.S. still has no real plan to deal with its radioactive nuclear waste, it will still be stored at the plant, sitting in her town indefinitely. Even today, she avoids driving by the plant's large, gray cooling towers.

Identify what the underlined "new challenges" refer to. Second, describe what Joyce Corradi worries about currently.

3 Read the passage and follow the directions. [4 points]

    The US college admissions scandal is fascinating, if not surprising. Over 30 wealthy parents have been criminally charged over a scheme in which they allegedly paid a company large sums of money to get their children into top universities.

    It's no secret that wealthy people will do nearly anything to get their kids into good schools. But this scandal only begins to reveal the lies that sustain the American idea of meritocracy. William Singer, who admitted to orchestrating the scam, explained that there are three ways in which a student can get into the college of their choice : "There is a front door which is you get in on your own. The back door is through institutional advancement, which is 10 times as much money. And I've created this side door." The "side door" he's referring to is outright crime, literally paying bribes and faking test scores. Even if we equalized public school funding, and abolished private schools, some children would be far more equal than others. Two and a half million children in the United States go through homelessness every year in this country. The chaotic living situation that comes with poverty makes it much, much harder to succeed. This means that even those who go through Singer's "front door" have not "gotten in on their own". They've gotten in partly because they've had the good fortune to have a home life conducive to their success.

    People often speak about "equality of opportunity" as the American aspiration. But having anything close to equal opportunity would require a radical re-engineering of society from top to bottom. As long as there are large wealth inequalities, there will be colossal differences in the opportunities that children have. No matter what admissions criteria are set, wealthy children will have the advantage. If admissions officers focus on test scores, parents will pay for extra tutoring and test prep courses. If officers focus instead on "holistic" qualities, parents will buy them. It's simple : wealth always confers greater capacity to give your children the edge over other people's children. If we wanted anything resembling a "meritocracy", we would probably have to start by instituting a fully egalitarian society.

> In reality, there can never be such a thing as a meritocracy, because there's never going to be fully equal opportunity. The main function of the concept is to assure elites that they deserve their position in life. It eases the "anxiety of affluence", that nagging feeling that they might be the beneficiaries of the arbitrary "birth lottery" rather than the products of their own individual ingenuity and hard work.

Describe the main idea of the passage in ONE sentence. Second, explain what the writer of the passage thinks about the concept of "front door" mentioned by Singer.

_____

_____

_____

_____

_____

4 Read the passage and follow the directions. [4 points]

> Alcohol is a tiny, tiny molecule, and it acts all over the brain in so many different pathways. It affects endorphins and dopamine. It affects glutamate and GABA, the two primary excitatory and inhibitory neurotransmitters. It affects all kinds of ion channels. It's so small that it can act all over the place. And so it's been really hard to study. In fact, we still are just beginning to understand how it is that you feel drunk—what the mechanisms are for feeling drunk—because it acts kind of like a sledgehammer or just in a widespread way to disrupt all kinds of cell functioning. Cocaine is the perfect opposite of alcohol in this way. It does one thing. It does it really effectively. It blocks the recycling of dopamine and other neurotransmitters like norepinephrine, and that enhances pleasure and enhances arousal and enhances movement. So it's very specific. It's easy to study relatively and much easier to understand how it works. Finally, marijuana is both like cocaine and like alcohol. So it's like cocaine in that its actions are very specific, and it's like alcohol in that those actions are all over the brain. It does one thing, but it does it everywhere. So for cocaine, it does one thing, but it does it in just a few pathways. Alcohol does many things all over the place. THC, the active ingredient in marijuana, does one thing more or less, but everywhere, and that thing is to enhance communication between cells, to enhance the message.

Write a summary following the guidelines below.

⌐ Guidelines ⌐
- Summarize the above passage in ONE paragraph.
- Provide a topic sentence and supporting ideas based on the passage.
- Do NOT copy more than FIVE consecutive words from the passage.

제 27 회 모의고사

1 Read the passage and follow the directions. [2 points]

> Why _____? This is the first question I have learned to expect when I'm asked about what kind of nursing I practice. This same question has come from family members, friends, strangers, and nurses and doctors who practice in other areas of the medical field. In most areas of healthcare, saving a life is the focus, and death is often viewed as a failure. Historically, there has not been a great deal of understanding as to why people would choose to concentrate their efforts where a medical success is not likely. Believe me when I say that it required a monumental shift in thinking for me to switch gears from the type of nursing I had previously done, which had everything to do with fixing, saving, and curing. I had to find out for myself that what we do in hospice is every bit as important, except that it's for people who no longer have those treatment options.
>
> "But aren't you sad all the time?" or, "Isn't it scary?" or, "Don't you cry a lot?" are other frequently asked questions. Those of us working in hospice will answer : No, I'm not sad all of the time. No, it isn't scary. Yes, I cry a lot. But the crying is often from the relief, joy and satisfaction that a patient's last weeks, days, or hours were fulfilling and comfortable, and that their family members had been able to work toward this same goal in a positive way.

Fill in the blank with the ONE most appropriate word from the passage.

2 Read the passage and follow the directions. [4 points]

Have you heard of the D.W.T.—the Declined-with-Thanks Club? There are no club rooms and not many members, but the balance sheet for the last twelve months is wonderful, showing that more than $15,000 was refused. The entrance fee is one hundred guineas and the annual subscription fifty guineas; that is to say, you must have refused a hundred guineas before you can be elected, and you are expected to refuse another fifty guineas a year while you retain membership. It is possible also to compound with a life refusal, but the sum is not fixed, and remains at the discretion of the committee.

Baines is a life member. He saved an old lady from being run over by a motor bus some years ago, and when she died she left him a legacy of $1400. Baines wrote to the executors and pointed out that he did not go about dragging persons from beneath motor buses as a profession; that, if she had offered him $1400 at the time, he would have refused it, not being in the habit of accepting money from strangers, still less from women; and that he did not see that the fact of the money being offered two years later in a will made the slightest difference. Baines was earning $400 a year at this time, and had a wife and four children, but he will not admit that he did anything at all out of the common.

The case of Sedley comes up for consideration at the next committee meeting. Sedley's rich uncle, a cantankerous old man, insulted him grossly; there was a quarrel; and the old man left, vowing to revenge himself by disinheriting his nephew and bequeathing his money to a cats' home. He died on his way to his solicitors, and Sedley was told of his good fortune in good legal English. He replied, "What on earth do you take me for? I wouldn't touch a penny. Give it to the cats' home or any blessed thing you like." Sedley, of course, will be elected as an ordinary member, but as there is a strong feeling on the committee that <u>no decent man could have done anything else</u>, his election as a life member is improbable.

Describe why Baines became a member of the Declined-with-Thanks Club. Second, explain the meaning of the underlined words in the last sentence.

3 Read the passage and follow the directions. [4 points]

Edward O'Brien's team had research subjects watch a movie on Netflix that they hadn't seen before and thought they'd enjoy. Then, on the following night, the researchers had some of them watch the same movie again. The group that didn't watch it a second night in a row rated the enjoyment they would have had rewatching it at an average of roughly 4 on an eight-point scale, which was lower than the 6.4 they gave to watching the movie the first time. But the group that did watch the movie a second time gave the experience a 5.7 on average.

These discrepancies illustrate O'Brien's finding well. It's not that watching a movie for the second time in 24 hours is just as enjoyable as the first time —it probably won't be. But it does seem likely to be more pleasant than one would predict.

In general, behavioral-economics research has found that when people make decisions about what they think they'll enjoy, they often assign priority to unfamiliar experiences—such as a new book or movie, or traveling somewhere they've never been before. They are not wrong to do so : People generally enjoy things less the more accustomed to them they become. As O'Brien writes, "People may choose novelty not because they expect exceptionally positive reactions to the new option, but because they expect exceptionally dull reactions to the old option." And sometimes, that expected dullness might be exaggerated.

Knowing that expectations can sometimes deviate from reality in this way could help inform the decisions people make about how they spend their leisure time. The biggest application of the finding is for people to spend more time considering why they prefer a novel option over a repeat option. Doing so could save them time and might make them just as happy.

According to the research above, which of the options would be better: Either spending one-hour researching for a new nearby restaurant or considering the possible value of simply returning to the taco place from yesterday. Then explain why.

4 Read the passage and follow the directions. [4 points]

> There are several ways of asking people for help that avoid making them feel controlled and that let them experience the natural high of helping. These reinforcements create the desire to want to help another.
>
> The first reinforcement is what psychologists call a strong sense of in-group. In other words, the belief that the person in need is on your team—a part of a group that is important to you. This goes beyond mere collective reciprocity; we help people from our in-group because we care about what happens to the in-group. Because our own happiness and well-being are affected by the group's happiness and well-being. Helping to create the in-group status of a person in need reliably leads to a genuine desire to help.
>
> The second reinforcer is the opportunity for positive identity. In other words, when helping you makes me feel good about me. Particularly when it allows me to see myself as possessing a positive attribute or playing an admired role. For example, people help more when they reflect on why it's important to them to "be a benefactor to others." When a positive identity—like being a benefactor—is made salient, people are more likely to act in accordance with it.
>
> The last one is the opportunity to see one's own effectiveness. People want to see or know the impact of the help they have given or will give. They want to see it land. This is actually not an ego thing. It's what some psychologists have argued is the fundamental human motivation : to feel effective. To know that your actions create the results you intended. To, in essence, shape the world around you. In the absence of feedback—when we have no idea what the consequences of our actions have been—motivation takes a nosedive.

Write a summary following the guidelines below.

　　　　　　　　　　　　　　　　　Guidelines

- Summarize the above passage in ONE paragraph.
- Provide a topic sentence and supporting ideas based on the passage.
- Do NOT copy more than FIVE consecutive words from the passage.

제 28 회 모의고사

1 Read the passage and follow the directions. [2 points]

In the 20th century, statisticians and scientists mostly rejected causality as an appropriate subject for science. They mostly observed correlations, and carefully repeated the mantra "correlation does not imply causation".

Scientists kept wanting to at least hint at causal implications of their research, but statisticians rejected most attempts to make rigorous claims about causes.

The one exception was for randomized controlled trials (RCTs). Statisticians figured out early on that a good RCT can demonstrate that correlation does imply causation. So RCTs became increasingly important over much of the 20th century.

That created a weird tension, where the use of RCTs made it clear that scientists valued the concept of causality, but in most other contexts they tried to talk as if causality wasn't real. Not quite as definitely unreal as phlogiston*. A bit closer to how behaviorists often tabooed the ideas that we had internal experiences and consciousness, or how linguists once banned debates on the origin of language, namely, that it was dangerous to think science could touch those topics. Or maybe a bit like heaven and hell— concepts which, even if they are useful, seem to be forever beyond the reach of science.

But scientists kept wanting to influence the world, rather than just predict it. So they often got impatient, when they couldn't afford to wait for RCTs, to act as if _____ told them something about causation.

*phlogiston : belief in magic

Fill in the blank with the ONE most appropriate word from the passage.

2. Read the passage and follow the directions. [4 points]

"If poor people knew how rich people are, there would be riots in the streets." Actor and comedian Chris Rock made this astute statement during a 2014 interview with *New York Magazine*, referring to the yawning gap between rich and poor. In so doing, he stumbled upon a key challenge in the study of inequality.

What's the best way to measure it? Most inequality studies have focused on income—measures of which are widely available. However, being rich is not about a single year of earnings but rather about the accumulation of wealth over time. In the past, quantifying that has been tricky.

The wealthy would probably prefer we stay in the dark about how rich they are, presumably to avoid the aforementioned ___①___. People like me who study the topic, however, are always looking for more data and better and more accurate ways to measure the rich-poor gap. And while I'm not one to promote violence in the streets, I do believe it's important for citizens to be fully aware of the levels of disparity in their society.

The most revealing way to do this, in my view, is by looking at wealth inequality. There are several ways to measure inequality. One of the most popular is by income. That's largely because there's more data, and it's a lot easier to measure. But ② this measure is a snapshot.

Wealth, on the other hand, is an aggregation, affected not only by current income but earnings accumulated in previous years and by previous generations. Only by studying wealth inequality do scholars, policymakers and others get the deepest and broadest measure of the gap between the rich and everyone else.

Fill in the blank with the ONE most appropriate word from the passage. Then, explain the meaning of the underlined words in ②.

3 Read the passage and follow the directions. [4 points]

It would not be the first time that an important economic resource had gone from simply being used to being owned and traded; the same has already happened with land and water, for example. But digital information seems an unlikely candidate to be allocated by markets. Unlike physical resources, personal data are an example of what economists call "non-rival" goods, meaning they can be used more than once.

Labour, like data, is a resource that is hard to pin down. Workers were not properly compensated for labour for most of human history. Even once people were free to sell their labour, it took decades for wages to reach liveable levels on average. History won't repeat itself, but chances are that it will rhyme, Mr Weyl predicts in *Radical Markets*, a provocative new book he has co-written with Eric Posner of the University of Chicago. He argues that in the age of artificial intelligence, it makes sense to treat data as a form of labour.

To understand why, it helps to keep in mind that "artificial intelligence" is something of a misnomer. Messrs Weyl and Posner call it "collective intelligence": most AI algorithms need to be trained using reams of human-generated examples, in a process called machine learning. Unless they know what the right answers (provided by humans) are meant to be, algorithms cannot translate languages, understand speech or recognise objects in images. Data provided by humans can thus be seen as a form of labour which powers AI. As the data economy grows up, such data work will take many forms. Much of it will be passive, as people engage in all kinds of activities—liking social-media posts, listening to music, recommending restaurants—that generate the data needed to power new services. But some people's data work will be more active, as they make decisions (such as labelling images or steering a car through a busy city) that can be used as the basis for training AI systems.

In what aspect is data similar to labor according to the passage? Second, explain why the term "artificial intelligence" is misleading.

4 Read the passage and follow the directions. [4 points]

Most people want to know the single best way to schedule their day for maximum productivity, and there are numerous articles and books that claim to know the "perfect schedule." But the reality is, there is no perfect method for everyone. However, it is crucial that you schedule your day. As *Essentialism* author Greg McKeown says : "If you don't prioritize your life, someone else will." By setting a daily schedule, you ensure that you are the one prioritizing your life.

Polyphasic sleep skill is a somewhat bizarre scheduling method that only works for a few select people, but if it works for you, you'll achieve uncommon amounts of productivity in a single day. Most people are monophasic sleepers, meaning they get their daily sleep in one chunk (or phase). Biphasic sleepers get their sleep in two smaller chunks, such as 4 hours in the morning and 4 hours in the late evening. Polyphasic sleepers take this method to the extreme, breaking up sleep into multiple short phases, which allows for less sleep overall and significant increases in productivity. The amount of sleep in each phase can vary, with some people sleeping only in 20-minute naps and others grabbing larger chunks of sleep and then supplementing with naps.

This schedule has some very obvious drawbacks. Steve Pavlina noted the challenge of having this type of schedule while still maintaining a sane family schedule. And if you miss any of your scheduled sleep sessions, it can significantly throw off your sleep schedule. But this schedule also has some massive advantages, like getting extra hours every day. If you only sleep four hours per day, you add approximately 28 extra hours to your week (assuming normally sleeping 8 hours).

Summarize the passage by following the guidelines below.

┌─────────────── Guidelines ───────────────┐
- Summarize the above passage in ONE paragraph.
- Provide a topic sentence and supporting ideas based on the passage.
- Do NOT copy more than FIVE consecutive words from the passage.

제 29 회 모의고사

1 Read the passage and follow the directions. [2 points]

> In principle a work of art has always been reproducible. Man-made artifacts could always be imitated by men. Replicas were made by pupils in practice of their craft, by masters for diffusing their works, and, finally, by third parties in the pursuit of gain. Mechanical reproduction of a work of art, however, represents something new. Historically, it advanced intermittently and in leaps at long intervals, but with accelerated intensity. The Greeks knew only two procedures of technically reproducing works of art : founding* and stamping.
>
> Bronzes, terra cottas, and coins were the only art works which they could produce in quantity. All others were unique and could not be mechanically reproduced. With the woodcut graphic art became mechanically reproducible for the first time, long before script became reproducible by print. The enormous changes which printing, the mechanical reproduction of writing, has brought about in literature are a familiar story. However, within the phenomenon which we are here examining from the perspective of world history, print is merely a special, though particularly important, case. During the Middle Ages engraving and etching were added to the woodcut; at the beginning of the nineteenth century lithography made its appearance.

With _____ the technique of reproduction reached an essentially new stage. This much more direct process was distinguished by the tracing of the design on a stone rather than its incision on a block of wood or its etching on a copperplate and permitted graphic art for the first time to put its products on the market, not only in large numbers as hitherto, but also in daily changing forms. Lithography enabled graphic art to illustrate everyday life, and it began to keep pace with printing.

*founding : melting and pouring metal or glass into a mold.

Fill in the blank with the ONE most appropriate word from the passage.

2. Read the passage and follow the directions. [4 points]

   Perpetual Guardian, a New Zealand company, asked its 240 office workers to work a four-day week (at eight hours per day) instead of five days, while still being paid their usual five-day salary. The trial was inspired by growing evidence that modern open-plan workplaces can be distracting for workers and reduce productivity. Managing director Andrew Barnes thought a shorter working week might be an innovative way to get employees to focus on their work and maintain overall productivity, while providing benefits such as an enhanced work-life balance, better mental health and fewer cars on the road. The results show a 24% increase in employees saying their work-life balance had improved, a significant improvement in engagement and a 7% drop in stress levels—all without a reduction in productivity.

   However, there are some challenges. The first challenge for the company was that not everybody does the same work across a varied workplace. It is not a production line making widgets, where productivity can be measured easily. Their solution was to ask teams (and their managers) to detail what they actually did in their job and how they might do it over four days instead of five. This involved organizing coverage within teams so that they could still meet deadlines and maintain performance and productivity. In practice, the four-day week meant employees within a team all had a day off each week, but that this day moved from Monday to Friday across the trial period.

The expectation was that if workers could maintain the same level of productivity and do so in four days, they should achieve greater personal benefits and the company would make other gains through enhanced reputation, recruitment and retention, as well as energy savings (20% reduction in staff at work). There is a large body of research showing that if organisations care about their employees' well-being, staff will respond with better job attitudes and performance. In addition, research shows that work-life balance is important for job satisfaction and general well-being, and that by being able to spend more time away from their job, employees engage better with their work.

Describe the difficulty the company met when it tried to introduce the trial. Second, explain how work-life balance functions in terms of productivity.

3 Read the passage and follow the directions. [4 points]

> Many of our choices have the potential to change how we think about the world. Often the choices taken are for some kind of betterment : to teach us something, to increase understanding or to improve ways of thinking. What happens, though, when a choice promises to alter our cognitive perspective in ways that we regard as a loss rather than a gain?
>
> Think, for example, of Elizabeth and Philip Jennings in the FX television show, *The Americans*(2013-). They are Russian spies in the 1980s tasked with living in the United States and engaging in acts of espionage. In order to do their job, they have to spend a lot of time associating with people whose worldview they find abhorrent. They must build close relationships with many of these people, and this means exposing themselves to their ideas and often acting as if they hold these ideas themselves. It makes good sense for a person given such an assignment to worry that, in carrying it out, she will become more sympathetic than she currently is to some false or abhorrent ideas—not because she has learned that these ideas might be correct, but because the time spent encountering these ideas and pretending to embrace them might cause her to unlearn, at least to a degree, some of what she presently understands about the world.
>
> It's not hard to imagine other cases that have this kind of structure. Maybe the documentary that a friend invites you to watch puts forward a message that you think is dangerously false. Maybe a discipline you are thinking of studying involves ideological presuppositions you reject. And so on. In such cases, the way that a choice would alter your _____ is seen as a net minus.

Explain the reason the writer mentions the television show "The Americans" in the passage. Second, fill in the blank with the TWO most appropriate consecutive words from the passage.

_____

_____

_____

4 Read the passage and follow the directions. [4 points]

> Although our brain accounts for just 2 percent of our body weight, the organ consumes half of our daily carbohydrate requirements—and glucose is its most important fuel. Under acute stress the brain requires some 12 percent more energy, leading many to reach for sugary snacks. Carbohydrates provide the body with the quickest source of energy. In fact, in cognitive tests subjects who were stressed performed poorly prior to eating. Their performance, however, went back to normal after consuming food.
>
> To further understand the relationship between the brain and carbohydrates, we examined 40 subjects over two sessions. In one, we asked study participants to give a 10-minute speech in front of strangers. In the other session they were not required to give a speech. At the end of each session, we measured the concentrations of stress hormones cortisol and adrenaline in participants' blood. We also provided them with a food buffet for an hour. When the participants gave a speech before the buffet, they were more stressed, and on average consumed an additional 34 grams of carbohydrates, than when they did not give a speech.
>
> So what about that chocolate, then? If a person craves chocolate in the afternoon, I advise him or her to eat chocolate to stay fit and keep his or her spirits up. That's because at work people are often stressed and the brain has an increased need for energy. If one doesn't eat anything, it's possible the brain will use glucose from the body, intended for fat and muscle cell use, and in turn secrete more stress hormones. Not only does this make one miserable, it can also increase the risk of heart attacks, stroke or depression in the long run. Alternatively, the brain can save on other functions, but that reduces concentration and performance.

Summarize the passage following the guidelines below.

┌─── Guidelines ───┐
- Summarize the above passage in ONE paragraph.
- Provide a topic sentence and supporting ideas based on the passage.
- Do NOT copy more than FIVE consecutive words from the passage.

제 30 회 모의고사

1   Read the passage and follow the directions. [2 points]

At age 17, Aristotle enrolled in the Platonic Academy. He would stay there for 20 years. Founded by the father of Western philosophy, the Greek philosopher Plato, Aristotle was the most promising student around. He asked many questions and answered even more.

The exact time of his departure from the Academy is disputed, but it's said that he left soon after Plato died due to his dislike of the direction that it subsequently took. In the years following, he would even go on to argue against many of his late teacher's core ideas.

It's impossible to say how much Aristotle wrote, but even from the fraction of his work that we have left today, there is a stunning amount of breadth in the subjects he covered. Every field from astronomy and physics to ethics and economics has been influenced by the work of Aristotle. For more than 2,000 years after his death, he has remained one of the most widely read and quoted thinkers in the history of our species.

While his impact can still be felt in the many different subjects today, maybe the most accurate of his observations relate to _____. He saw it as one of the true joys of life, and he felt that a life well-lived needed to be built around such companionship. In his own words : "In poverty as well as in other misfortunes, people suppose that friends are their only refuge. And friendship is a help to the young, in saving them from error, just as it is also to the old, with a view to the care they require and their diminished capacity for action stemming from their weakness; it is a help also to those in their prime in performing noble actions, for 'two going together' are better able to think and to act."

Fill in the blank with the ONE most appropriate word from the passage.

2 Read the passage and follow the directions. [4 points]

> Why do tribal and hunter-gatherer human societies tend to be more equal?
>
> All primate societies, Christopher Boehm, a cultural anthropologist at the University of Southern California, notes, are governed by similar dynamics. If any one individual has the opportunity to climb the hierarchy, he or she is likely to seize it; unfortunately, as soon as power is gained, others resent it. In such a society, Boehm writes, there are three potential outcomes. One is conflict, in which newcomers continually and overtly challenge the powerful for a position at the top. Another is stable dominance, where the powerful relentlessly and permanently dominate the rest. And a third is an equally stable social structure which Boehm calls "reverse dominance hierarchy," in which those on the bottom of the pyramid figure out a way to band together and "deliberately dominate their potential master." In such a society, dominance is still exercised. It just comes, collectively and consistently, from below.
>
> Chimps, bonobos, and gorillas struggle to achieve stable reverse-dominance hierarchy. They can occasionally flatten their pyramids, but only briefly. The problem is that the powerful are likely to be strong, intelligent, and socially connected. To topple them, and prevent them from taking over again, you need a powerful and persistent threat, which nonhuman primates don't have. Boehm has discovered that, among the tribal and hunter-gatherer human societies, the development of projectile weapons is a key step in the growth and maintenance of equality: it puts the strong at greater risk from the weak. Such weaponry is one reason that human societies are more equalized than those of other primates.

Explain why tribal and hunter-gatherer human societies tend to be more equal than primates, according to Christopher Boehm. Second, describe what "reverse dominance hierarchy" is.

3   Read the passage and follow the directions. [4 points]

Facebook is no longer growing as a platform for news. In the U.S., for instance, young people's use of Facebook for news fell by 20 percentage points between 2017 and 2018. The percentage of U.S. adults who ever get news from Facebook was just about flat between last year and this year.

It's not that people are using their devices less; rather, they're increasingly getting news from messaging apps, as reiterated in a report released by the Reuters Institute for the Study of Journalism. The report looks at the social media habits of users in the U.S., U.K., Brazil, and Germany; the entire sample was made up of people who said they got news from Facebook or messaging apps at least weekly. It's designed to provide some color and qualitative information around the 2018 Digital News Report that the Reuters Institute released, and to look more closely at the effects of Facebook's January News Feed algorithm change on consumers. "Why are consumers turning to messaging apps, to receive, comment upon, and share news?" the authors write.

It's clear that Facebook is still a default platform for many users, even if they feel conflicted about that default status. "It's a guilty pleasure and I hate it but I love it," one U.S. male (in the 20- to 29-year-old age bracket) said. It's "an distraction for filling time" and a key way to keep in touch with people. But how passionate can you feel about something you also see as a complete waste of time? "Facebook is getting more and more unattractive and impersonal for me and so I write or post less," said one German woman ① between the ages of 20 and 29. "Only 10 percent of my friends on Facebook are really friends for me."

If Facebook's algorithm change was meant to bring people back together on the platform—to get news out of the way and make room for intimacy and meaningful social interaction—this research, at least, suggests that that hasn't worked.

Reducing the news sources is not that useful, unlike ads. Maybe it was already too late : As Reuters' earlier report showed, people have begun the transition to ____②____ to share news and discuss personal topics.

In what aspect is the information contained in underlined selection ① of key importance to the overall context? Second, fill in the blank with the TWO most appropriate consecutive words from the passage.

4 Read the passage and follow the directions. [4 points]

Starting with the Terrible Twos, when toddlers hear the word "No" on a regular basis, people don't like to be told they can't do something. They often believe government regulations interfere with their rights. The government requires vaccinations for school attendance; parents complain that they should be able to make their own decisions about whether to vaccinate their children. The government requires that drugs be approved by the FDA before marketing; desperate patients dying of cancer complain that regulations are preventing them from getting the one new treatment that just might save their life. The "health freedom" argument is that everyone has the right to use whatever treatments they want, to control what goes into their bodies, and that it's none of the government's business.

But quacks use the concept of "health freedom" to divert attention away from themselves and toward victims of disease with whom we are naturally sympathetic. "These poor folks should have the freedom to choose whatever treatments they want," cry the quacks—with crocodile tears. They want us to overlook two things. First, no one wants to be cheated, especially in matters of life and health. Victims of disease do not demand quack treatments because they want to exercise their "rights," but because they have been deceived into thinking that they offer hope. Second, the laws against worthless nostrums* are not directed against the victims of disease but at the promoters who attempt to exploit them.

Vaccine refusers don't recognize that the government has a duty to protect the welfare of children and to protect the population from vaccine-preventable diseases. They tend to think parental rights and personal preference should trump everything else.

*nostrum : a medicine that is not effective, prepared by an unqualified person

Summarize the passage following the guidelines below.

Guidelines

- Summarize the above passage in ONE paragraph.
- Provide a topic sentence and supporting ideas based on the passage.
- Do NOT copy more than FIVE consecutive words from the passage.

1 Read the passage and fill in the blank with the ONE most appropriate word from the passage. [2 points]

The effects of local competition are especially severe in the face of inequality. Some resources hold more value than others, creating inequality between those who win it and those who don't, and so they are worth fighting harder for. But local competition amplifies this effect, making small differences in the stakes loom large. In my own work, participants in an economic game made selfish choices more often as inequality increased, causing them to get into 'fights' with their partners that cost them points. However, they fought most often under local competition, even when there was only a small amount of inequality between them, and lost many more points as a result.

This might well explain some otherwise puzzling patterns in real-world violence. In his book *Killing the Competition*, Daly shows that homicide rates are high in places with greater levels of inequality and low in places with lesser levels of inequality. If, however, local competition amplifies the effect of inequality on homicide and global competition quiets it, then changes in human trade and migration—diffusing competition over larger swathes of the population—can break the simple correlation we expect between inequality and homicide over time. Inequality can grow, for instance, at the same time that competition becomes _____, with the latter sharply reducing the impact of the former.

2 Read the passage and follow the directions. [4 points]

Plenty of studies have documented crows' intelligence, such as their puzzle-solving prowess and tool use. Other research has highlighted aspects of crows' social behavior, finding that groups of crows notice and react to the sight of their dead.

Kaeli Swift, a doctoral candidate at the University of Washington, was documenting a crow "funeral" in 2015, when she first observed some unusual sexual activity. At the time, she and her adviser John Marzluff were investigating the birds' organized vocal responses to finding a dead crow, which signals a potential threat to the living. And they saw something they had never observed before : A crow approached the corpse, mounted it and started ① "thrashing" in a manner that was immediately recognizable.

In research into how crows gather and communicate around their dead, Swift and Marzluff found that the birds used dead crows to learn about and avoid potential risks. This made their discovery of the new crow behavior—having sex with the dead—extremely puzzling, Swift said. If a dead crow is a danger signal, why would a living crow want to get close to it? "Engaging so closely with a dead conspecific [animal of the same species] could expose you to disease, or parasites, or scavengers," Swift said.

The researchers conducted ② a series of experiments in four Washington cities, testing 308 mated pairs of wild crows. They exposed the birds to carefully positioned taxidermic* crows and to other prepared animal corpses, such as pigeons and squirrels to see if the crows' responses were common to a range of dead things or if they were specific to their own species.

They found that the birds were more likely to caw* in alarm when the corpse that they saw belonged to a crow, particularly if the stuffed crow was in a "dead" pose rather than a more lifelike posture. The birds approached dead crows about 25 percent of the time, but only 4 percent initiated sexual activity, hinting that corpse canoodling* is not commonly practiced.

*taxidermic : the art of stuffing the skins of animals
*caw : cry of the crow
*canoodling : kissing and holding each other

Write the FIVE most appropriate consecutive words from the passage that correspond to the meaning of the underlined words in ①. Second, explain what the "a series of experiments" discovered in terms of main purpose of the researchers.

3 Read the passage and follow the directions. [4 points]

More than a decade ago, a certain suspicion of empathy started to creep in, particularly among young people. Since the late 1960s, researchers have surveyed young people on their levels of empathy, testing their agreement with statements such as : "It's not really my problem if others are in trouble and need help" or "Before criticizing somebody I try to imagine how I would feel if I were in their place."

Sara Konrath, an associate professor, collected decades of studies and noticed a very obvious pattern. Starting around 2000, the line starts to slide. More students say it's not their problem to help people in trouble, not their job to see the world from someone else's perspective. By 2009, on all the standard measures, young people on average measure 40 percent less empathetic than my own generation—40 percent!

It's strange to think of empathy—a natural human impulse—as fluctuating in this way, moving up and down like consumer confidence. But that's what happened. Young people just started questioning ① <u>what my elementary school teachers had taught me</u>. Their feeling was : Why should they put themselves in the shoes of someone who was not them, much less someone they thought was harmful? In fact, cutting someone off from empathy was the positive value, a way to make a stand. So, for example, when the wife of white nationalist Richard Spencer recently told *BuzzFeed* he had abused her, the question debated on the lefty Internet was : Why should we care that some woman who chose to ally herself with a nasty racist got herself hurt? Why waste empathy on that?

The new rule for empathy seems to be : reserve it, not for your "enemies," but for the people you believe are hurt. Empathy, but just for your own team. And empathizing with the other team? That's practically a taboo. And it turns out that this brand of ② <u>selective empathy</u> is a powerful force.

Write the ONE word from the passage that BEST corresponds to the underlined words in ①. Second, explain what "selective empathy" is according to the passage.

4 Read the passage and follow the directions. [4 points]

China enjoyed undoubted advantages : a rise of food production nearly as early as in the Fertile Crescent and a large and productive expanse, nourishing the largest regional human population in the world, etc. These advantages and head start enabled medieval China to lead the world in technology. In the early 15th century it sent treasure fleets, each consisting of hundreds of ships up to 400 feet long and with total crews of up to 28,000, across the Indian Ocean as far as the east coast of Africa, decades before Columbus's three puny ships crossed the narrow Atlantic Ocean to the Americas' east coast. Why didn't Chinese ships cross the Pacific to colonize the Americas' west coast? Why, in brief, did China lose its technological lead to the formerly so backward Europe?

The end of China's treasure fleets gives us a clue. Seven of those fleets sailed from China between A.D. 1405 and 1433. They were then suspended as a result of a power struggle between two factions at the Chinese court (the eunuchs* and their opponents). The former faction had been identified with sending and captaining the fleets. Hence when the latter faction gained the upper hand in a power struggle, it stopped sending fleets, eventually dismantled the shipyards, and forbade oceangoing shipping. The episode is reminiscent of the legislation that strangled development of public electric lighting in London in the 1880s, the isolationism of the United States between the First and Second World Wars, and any number of backward steps in any number of countries, all motivated by local political issues. But in China there was a difference, because the entire region was politically unified. One decision stopped fleets over the whole of China. That one temporary decision became irreversible, because no shipyards remained to turn out ships that would prove the folly of that temporary decision, and to serve as a focus for rebuilding other shipyards.

*eunuch : a man who had been castrated to serve a king

Summarize the passage by following the guidelines.

Guidelines

- Summarize the above passage in ONE paragraph.
- Provide a topic sentence and supporting ideas based on the passage.
- Do NOT copy more than FIVE consecutive words from the passage.

제 32 회 모의고사

1 Read the passage and follow the directions. [2 points]

> I am an evolutionary behavioral ecologist, and most of my work is concerned with how individual differences in behavior (i.e. personality) influence individual fitness, and the collective behavior and success of animal societies. Most are probably not aware, but animal personality research is a vibrant field within behavioral ecology due to the ubiquity of personality as a phenomenon in nature, and its ability to explain interactions both within and between species. In nearly every species tested to date for the presence of personality, we've found it, and sex-linked personality differences are frequently the most striking. Sex-linked personality differences are very well documented in our closest primate relatives, too, and the presence of sexual dimorphism (i.e. size differences between males and females) in primates, and mammals generally, dramatically intensifies these differences, especially in traits like aggression, female choosiness, territoriality, grooming behavior, and parental care.
>
> Given that humans are sexually dimorphic and exhibit many of the typical sex-linked behavioral traits that any objective observer would predict, based on the mammalian trends, the claim that our _____ have(has) arisen purely via socialization is dubious at best. For that to be true, we would have to posit that the selective forces for these traits inexplicably and uniquely vanished in just our lineage, leading to the elimination of these traits without any vestiges of their past, only to have these traits fully recapitulated* in the present due to socialization.
>
> *recapitulate : explicate; explain

Fill in the blank with the TWO most appropriate consecutive words from the passage.

2 Read the passage and follow the directions. [4 points]

> The late 1980s marked the beginning of a reformation in child psychology. Bauer and other psychologists began to test infant memory by performing a series of actions—such as building a simple toy gong and striking it—and then waiting to see if a child could imitate the actions in the right order, after a delay ranging from minutes to months.
>
> One experiment after another revealed that the memories of children 3 and younger do in fact persist, albeit with limitations. At 6 months of age, infants' memories last for at least a day; at 9 months, for a month; by age 2, for a year. And in <u>a landmark 1991 study</u>, researchers discovered that four-and-a-half-year-olds could recall detailed memories from a trip to Disney World 18 months prior. Around age 6, however, children begin to forget many of these earliest memories. In a 2005 experiment by Bauer and her colleagues, five-and-a-half-year-olds remembered more than 80 percent of experiences they had at age 3, whereas seven-and-a-half-year-olds remembered less than 40 percent.
>
> This work laid bare the contradiction at the heart of childhood amnesia : Infants can create and access memories in their first few years of life, yet most of these memories eventually vanish at a rate far beyond the typical forgetting of the past we experience as adults.
>
> Maybe, some researchers thought, enduring memories require language or a sense of self, both of which we lack as infants. But although verbal communication and self-awareness undoubtedly strengthen human memories, their absence could not be the whole explanation for childhood amnesia. After all, certain animals that have large and complex brains relative to their body size—such as mice—but do not have language or, presumably, our level of self-awareness, also lose the memories they make in infancy.

Describe the major contribution done by the underlined "landmark research". Second, what does the case of mice reveal?

3. Read the passage and follow the directions. [4 points]

Armed with 3 million responses to a happiness monitoring app, plus the locations and times of several years worth of British soccer matches, University of Sussex economists Peter Dolton and George MacKerron calculated that the happiness that fans feel when their team wins is outweighed—by a factor of two—by the sadness that strikes when their team loses.

Which means, assuming a roughly equal number of fans on both sides, the World Cup final between France and Croatia made the world less happy than it was the day before. On net, soccer is a destroyer of happiness.

To prove it, the researchers analyzed data from an app that pinged 32,000 people several times a day and asked them how happy they felt on a 100-point scale, as well as who they were with and what they were doing. The responses included location information, which allowed researchers to determine if they were at a stadium, or had been to one.

They adjusted the results to account for basic differences in happiness based on time of day and day of week. Because they measure differences from each person's typical happiness level, they were also able to account for people who are, as a rule, permanently miserable or elated. They could not, however, adjust for the app's users, who tended to be younger and more affluent than the country as a whole.

In the hour immediately after their team wins, researchers found a typical fan might feel about 3.9 points happier than usual—about the same boost as from listening to music. That's more than offset by the 7.8 points of extra sadness that fans will feel in the hour after their team loses, an event that makes respondents feel about twice as sad as they would be after working, studying or waiting in line.

The researchers call the results "quite dramatic" and say they add up over time. Because post-soccer sadness lingers for hours while after-match joy is fleeting, a loss actually ends up robbing fans of about _____ times the amount of happiness they might have gained from a win. The effects are much greater if a respondent is actually at the stadium.

Describe what the researchers could not adjust for. Then, fill in the blank with the ONE most appropriate word.

4 Read the passage and follow the directions. [4 points]

> Two thousand years of monotheistic brainwashing have caused most Westerners to see polytheism as ignorant and childish idolatry. This is an unjust stereotype. In order to understand the inner logic of polytheism, it is necessary to grasp the central idea buttressing the belief in many gods.
>
> Polytheism does not necessarily dispute the existence of a single power or law governing the entire universe. In fact, most polytheist and even animist religions recognised such a supreme power that stands behind all the different gods, demons and holy rocks. In classical Greek polytheism, Zeus, Hera, Apollo and their colleagues were subject to an omnipotent and all-encompassing power—Fate (*Moira, Ananke*). In Hindu polytheism, a single principle, Atman, controls the myriad gods and spirits, humankind, and the biological and physical world. Atman is the eternal essence or soul of the entire universe, as well as of every individual and every phenomenon.
>
> The fundamental insight of polytheism, which distinguishes it from monotheism, is that the supreme power governing the world is devoid of interests and biases, and therefore it is unconcerned with the mundane desires, cares and worries of humans. It's pointless to ask this power for victory in war, for health or for rain, because from its all-encompassing vantage point, it makes no difference whether a particular kingdom wins or loses, whether a particular city prospers or withers, whether a particular person recuperates or dies. <u>The Greeks did not waste any sacrifices on Fate, and Hindus built no temples to Atman.</u>

Summarize the passage by following the guidelines.

--- Guidelines ---
- Summarize the above passage in ONE paragraph.
- Provide a topic sentence and supporting ideas based on the passage.
- Include the reason the Greeks and Hindus did as indicated in the underlined part.
- Do NOT copy more than FIVE consecutive words from the passage.

제 33 회 모의고사

1 Read the passage and follow the directions. [2 points]

For most of his career, Dr. Stephen Trzeciak was not a big believer in the "touchy-feely" side of medicine. As a specialist in intensive care and chief of medicine at Cooper University Health Care in Camden, N.J., Trzeciak felt most at home in the hard sciences.

Then his new boss, Dr. Anthony Mazzarelli, came to him with a problem: Recent studies had shown an epidemic of burnout among health care providers. As co-president of Cooper, Mazzarelli was in charge of a major medical system and needed to find ways to improve patient care.

He had a mission for Trzeciak—he wanted him to find answers to this question: Can treating patients with medicine and compassion make a measurable difference on the wellbeing of both patients and doctors?

Trzeciak wasn't convinced. Sure, compassion is good, Trzeciak thought, but he expected to review the existing science and report back the bad news that caring has no quantitative rationale. But Mazzarelli was his colleague and chief, so he dove in.

After considering more than 1,000 scientific abstracts and 250 research papers, Trzeciak and Mazzarelli were surprised to find that the answer was, resoundingly, yes. When health care providers take the time to make human connections that help end suffering, patient outcomes improve and medical costs decrease. Among other benefits, compassion reduces pain, improves healing, lowers blood pressure and helps alleviate depression and anxiety.

Complete the main idea of the passage by filling in the blank with the ONE most appropriate word from the passage.

| Taking time for _____ makes doctors better at their jobs. |

2. Read the passage and follow the directions. [4 points]

① <u>You weren't raised in a barn</u>. You know you need to express gratitude and appreciation for other people's help. And yet people often make a critical mistake when expressing gratitude: they focus on how they feel—how happy they are, how they have benefited from the help—rather than focusing on the benefactor.

Researchers at the University of North Carolina distinguished between two types of gratitude expressions: other-praising, which involves acknowledging and validating the character or abilities of the giver (i.e., their positive identity); and self-benefit, which describes how the receiver is better off for having been given help. In one of their studies, they observed couples expressing gratitude to one another for something their partner had recently done for them. Their expressions were then coded for the extent to which they were other-praising or focused on self-benefit. Examples of their expressions included:

Other-praising: "It shows how responsible you are …" "You go out of your way …" "I feel like you're really good at that."

Self-benefit: "It let me relax." "It gave me bragging rights at work." "It makes me happy."

Finally, benefactors rated how responsive they felt the gratitude giver had been, how happy they felt, and how loving they felt toward their partner. The researchers found that other-praising gratitude was strongly related to perceptions of responsiveness, ___②___, and loving, but self-benefit gratitude was not.

Explain the meaning of the underlined words in ①. Then, fill in the blank with the ONE most appropriate word from the passage. If necessary, change the word form.

3 Read the passage and follow the directions. [4 points]

If there are extraterrestrial civilisations out there, they don't seem very interested in us. They don't visit, they don't phone, they don't even send radio signals. Not a peep. It is easy to start feeling neglected once you become aware of this cosmic cold shoulder. As the eminent physicist Enrico Fermi once put it, "Where is everybody?"

There is intelligence and intelligence. Recent research shows that many birds, especially from the crow family, can outdo monkeys on any test of ingenuity. A good case can also be made for octopuses. Given that birds, mammals and molluscs* evolved independently, this suggests that some level of intellect is a natural outcome of evolutionary pressures. Still, this is not the kind of intellect that is going to send signals to the stars. Impressive as the crows may be, they aren't going to work out electromagnetic field theory. Advanced science needs the kind of acumen that allows humans to build complex cultures and probe into things. And this does look like a freak in evolutionary terms.

So, from a biological point of view, it looks as if the prospects for intelligent interstellar conversation are limited. There are probably plenty of dumb animals scattered across the universe, but nobody worth talking to. This might strike you as depressing. However, it would be more depressing if it turns out that we are not cosmic freaks. For then <u>the silence starts to look sinister</u>. If the emergence of advanced civilisations is common, then the obvious explanation is that a typical extraterrestrial empire doesn't last long. Perhaps plenty have announced their presence, only to implode within a few years. We all like to think humanity will survive into the indefinite future. But there is a danger that any species with our technological power will quickly find a way of destroying itself, whether by war, pestilence or pollution.

mollusc : an important phylum of invertebrate animals

Describe the difference between the intellect of crows and that of human beings. Second, explain why the silence looks "sinister".

4 Read the passage and follow the directions. [4 points]

That humans have self-domesticated has grown increasingly obvious over the past half century. Even apart from increased docility—the primary index of domestication—humans show many signs of what has come to be recognized as the domestication syndrome: smaller bodies and brains, thinner bones, shorter faces, and reduced physical differences between males and females. Besides these anatomical markers, there are also behavioral and physiological ones, which involve fear response, playfulness, learning rates, sexual behavior, and hormone production, among others. What these markers all have in common is paedomorphism (literally, "child shape"). In dogs, foxes, guinea pigs, and many other species, domesticated animals resemble the juvenile stage of the wild animals that they descended from. Humans evolved from our Homo ancestor several hundred thousand years ago, and there aren't sufficient fossils to demonstrate paedomorphism directly. But there are plenty of Neanderthal fossils, and comparisons strongly suggest that present-day humans are, in many respects, juvenilized—that is, domesticated—versions of our remote ancestors.

Why did these changes happen? For an evolutionary biologist, that question is normally equivalent to asking, what adaptive purpose did they serve? In this case, however, the answer is unusual: none. A decades-long, painstaking experiment showed that reduced brain size, thinner bones, and all of the other markers of domestication syndrome are merely incidental byproducts of a primary adaptation: reduced reactive aggression. In organisms selecting against such aggression, the migration of neural-crest cells—a special kind of cell that carries developmental instructions throughout the embryo and fetus—is delayed, resulting in smaller bodies, smaller brains, hormonal changes, and the rest. Human communities selected against reactive aggression because group life requires a minimum of stability. No trait is more disruptive than reactive aggression, which fuels such behaviors as quests for dominance and demands for submission; arrogance, bullying, and random violence; and the monopolizing of food and females.

Summarize the passage by following the guidelines.

― Guidelines ―
- Summarize the above passage in ONE paragraph.
- Provide a topic sentence and supporting ideas based on the passage.
- Do NOT copy more than FIVE consecutive words from the passage.

제 34 회 모의고사

1 Read the passage and follow the directions. [2 points]

> I have been watching the 2018 World Cup in France, mainly in the bars and cafes of the lower end of the 14th arrondissement* in Paris. This is a mixed neighbourhood that is partly gentrified but also home to council estates with a large immigrant population and the usual low-level social tensions—drugs, gangs, run-ins with the police. So far, however, watching the game has been relatively trouble-free. Each step by the French team towards victory has been followed by good-humoured delirium—much tooting of horns and showering of beer. Watching all of this on the news, what was most striking about the fans was not their racial mix, although numerous ethnicities were represented, but how _____ they were. This is the new generation of millennials for whom the last great French victory in the 1998 World Cup is an event from history. A cartoon in *Le Parisien* said it all : "You've got to stop telling us stories from the last century," young fans tell a portly* middle-aged white male (not unlike myself). The message is clear : this is our World Cup and this is our own triumph to celebrate.
>
> In a sense, they are right. This French team are an extremely young team, largely indifferent to the past and not weighed down by history. Some of them, such as the superstar-in-waiting Kylian Mbappé, weren't even born when France last won the World Cup.
>
> * *arrondissement* : administrative divisions of France
> * *portly* : fat

Fill in the blank with the ONE most appropriate word from the passage.

2. Read the passage and follow the directions. [4 points]

Beating humans at board games is passé in the AI world. Now, top academics and tech companies want to challenge us at video games <u>instead</u>. Today, OpenAI, a research lab founded by Elon Musk and Sam Altman, announced its latest milestone : a team of AI agents that can beat the top 1 percent of amateurs at popular battle arena game Dota 2.

You may remember that OpenAI first strode into the world of Dota 2 last August, unveiling a system that could beat the top players at 1v1 matches. However, this _____ type greatly reduces the challenge of Dota 2. OpenAI has now upgraded its bots to play humans in 5v5 match-ups, which require more coordination and long-term planning. And while OpenAI has yet to challenge the game's very best players, it will do so later this year at The International, a Dota 2 tournament that's the biggest annual event on the e-sports calendar.

The motivation for research like this is simple : if we can teach AI systems the skills they need to play video games, we can use them to solve complex real-world challenges that, in some ways, resemble video games — like, for example, managing a city's transport infrastructure.

<u>This is an exciting milestone.</u> It's really because it's about transitioning to real-life applications. If we've got a simulation of a problem and we can run it large enough scale, there's no barrier to what we can do with this.

Fill in the blank with the ONE most appropriate word from the passage. Second, identify to what the underlined "This is an exciting milestone" refers.

3 Read the passage and follow the directions. [4 points]

"Data slavery." Jennifer Morone, an American artist, thinks this is the state in which most people now live. To get free online services, she laments, they hand over intimate information to technology firms. "Personal data are much more valuable than you think," she says. To highlight this sorry state of affairs, Morone has resorted to what she calls ① "extreme capitalism". She registered herself as a company in Delaware in an effort to exploit her personal data for financial gain. She created dossiers* containing different subsets of data, which she displayed in a London gallery in 2016 and offered for sale, starting at £100. The entire collection, including her health data and social-security number, can be had for £7,000.

Only a few buyers have taken her up on this offer and she finds "the whole thing really absurd". Yet if the job of the artist is to anticipate the Zeitgeist*, Ms. Morone was dead on : this year the world has discovered that something is rotten in the data economy. Since it emerged in March that Cambridge Analytica, a political consultancy, had acquired data on 87m Facebook users in underhand ways, voices calling for a rethink of the handling of online personal data have only grown louder. Even Angela Merkel, Germany's chancellor, recently called for a price to be put on personal data, asking researchers to come up with solutions.

Given the current state of digital affairs, in which the collection and exploitation of personal data is dominated by big tech firms, Ms Morone's approach, in which individuals offer their data for sale, seems unlikely to catch on. But what if people really controlled their data—and the tech giants were required to pay for access? ② What would such a data economy look like?

*dossier : all the documents relating to an affair
*Zeitgeist : spirit of the times

Describe what "extreme capitalism" refers to. Next, explain the implication of the underlined words in ②.

4 Read the passage and follow the directions. [4 points]

"Necessity is the mother of invention." That is, inventions supposedly arise when a society has an unfulfilled need: some technology is widely recognized to be unsatisfactory or limiting. Would-be inventors, motivated by the prospect of money or fame, perceive the need and try to meet it. Some inventor finally comes up with a solution superior to the existing, unsatisfactory technology. Society adopts the solution if it is compatible with the society's values and other technologies.

Quite a few inventions do conform to this commonsense view. In 1942, in the middle of World War II, the U.S. government set up the Manhattan Project with the explicit goal of inventing the technology required to build an atomic bomb before Nazi Germany could do so. That project succeeded in three years, at a cost of $2 billion (equivalent to over $20 billion today). Other instances are Eli Whitney's 1794 invention of his cotton gin to replace laborious hand cleaning of cotton grown in the U.S. South, and James Watt's 1769 invention of his steam engine to solve the problem of pumping water out of British coal mines.

These familiar examples deceive us into assuming that other major inventions were also responses to perceived needs. In fact, many or most inventions were developed by people driven by curiosity or by a love of tinkering, in the absence of any initial demand for the product they had in mind. Once a device had been invented, the inventor then had to find an application for it. Only after it had been in use for a considerable time did consumers come to feel that they "needed" it. Thus, invention is often the mother of necessity, rather than vice versa.

Summarize the passage by following the guidelines.

--- Guidelines ---
- Summarize the above passage in ONE paragraph.
- Provide a topic sentence and supporting ideas based on the passage.
- Do NOT copy more than FIVE consecutive words from the passage.

제 35 회 모의고사

1 Read the passage and follow the directions. [2 points]

> We credit Socrates with the insight that 'the unexamined life is not worth living' and that to 'know thyself' is the path to true wisdom. But is there a right and a wrong way to go about such self-reflection?
>
> Simple rumination—the process of churning your concerns around in your head—isn't the answer. It's likely to cause you to become stuck in the rut of your own thoughts and immersed in the emotions that might be leading you astray. Certainly, research has shown that people who are prone to rumination also often suffer from impaired decision making under pressure, and are at a substantially increased risk of depression.
>
> Instead, the scientific research suggests that you should adopt an ancient rhetorical method favoured by the likes of Julius Caesar and known as 'illeism'—or speaking about yourself in the third person (the term was coined in 1809 by the poet Samuel Taylor Coleridge from the Latin ille meaning 'he, that'). If I was considering an argument that I'd had with a friend, for instance, I might start by silently thinking to myself: '<u>David felt frustrated that</u>…' The idea is that this small change in perspective can clear your emotional fog, allowing you to see past your biases.
>
> A bulk of research has already shown that this kind of third-person thinking can temporarily improve decision making and that it can also bring long-term benefits to thinking and emotional regulation. The researchers said this was the first evidence that wisdom-related cognitive and affective processes can be trained in daily life, and of how to do so.

Identify the TWO consecutive words from the passage that BEST match the underlined words.

2 Read the passage and follow the directions. [4 points]

Imagine someone who believes that her local grocery store is open for business today, so she goes to buy some milk. But the store isn't open after all—she didn't realize that today's a holiday. Even though the store is closed, her behaviour still makes a kind of sense. She is going to the store because she thinks it is open—not because it actually is open. It makes sense for this person to go to the store, but she doesn't have as good a reason to go there as she would if she didn't just think, but rather knew, that the store were open. If that were case she'd be able to go to the store because it is open, and not merely because she thinks it is. ① That's the distinction to keep in mind.

Now let's revisit the case of the climate skeptic. The skeptic doesn't know that climate change is a hoax, since it isn't a hoax at all. So he can't choose not to enroll in the course because climate change is a hoax, any more than the person we imagined earlier could go to the store because it is open. Rather, the most that the skeptic can do is avoid taking the course because he thinks that climate change is a hoax—a choice that makes sense, but not one that is based on as good a reason as the skeptic would have if he didn't just think, but rather knew, that this was true.

If this is on the right track, then the crucial difference between the dogmatic or closed-minded person and the person who exercises appropriate cognitive caution might be that the second sort of person knows, while the first merely believes, that the choice she decides against is one that would be harmful to her cognitive perspective. The person who knows that a choice will harm her perspective can decide against it simply because it will do so, while the person who merely _____②_____ this can make this choice only because that is what she thinks.

Explain the meaning of the underlined words in ①. Second, find the ONE most appropriate word that fits in blank ②.

3 Read the passage and follow the directions. [4 points]

Advanced algorithms working from large chemical databases can predict a new chemical's toxicity better than standard animal tests, suggests a study led by scientists at Johns Hopkins Bloomberg School of Public Health.

The researchers, in the study that appears in the journal *Toxicological Sciences* on July 11, 2018, mined a large database of known chemicals they developed to map the relationships between chemical structures and toxic properties. They then showed that one can use the map to automatically predict the toxic properties of any chemical compound—more accurately than a single animal test would do.

The most advanced toxicity-prediction tool the team developed was on average about 87 percent accurate in reproducing consensus animal-test-based results—across nine common tests, which account for 57 percent of the world's animal toxicology testing. By contrast, the repetition of the same animal tests in the database were only about 81 percent accurate—in other words, any given test had only an 81 percent chance, on average, of obtaining the same result for toxicity when repeated.

The computer-based approach could also be applied to many more chemicals than animal testing, which could lead to wider safety assessments. Due to costs and ethical challenges only a small fraction of the roughly 100,000 chemicals in consumer products have been comprehensively tested.

Animals such as mice, rabbits, guinea pigs and dogs annually undergo millions of chemical toxicity tests in labs around the world. Although this animal testing is usually required by law to protect consumers, it is opposed on moral grounds by large segments of the public, and is also unpopular with product manufacturers because of the high costs and uncertainties about testing results.

State the main idea of the passage in ONE sentence. Then, explain why animal testing is not welcomed by all walks of life.

4. Read the passage and follow the directions. [4 points]

Nowadays, when almost all societies on Earth are connected to each other, we can't imagine a fad* is going so far that an important technology would actually be discarded. A society that temporarily turned against a powerful technology would continue to see it being used by neighboring societies and would have the opportunity to reacquire it by diffusion (or would be conquered by neighbors if it failed to do so). But such fads can persist in isolated societies.

A famous example involves Japan's abandonment of guns. Firearms reached Japan in A.D. 1543, when two Portuguese adventurers armed with harquebuses* arrived on a Chinese cargo ship. The Japanese were so impressed by the new weapon that they commenced indigenous gun production, greatly improved gun technology, and by A.D. 1600 owned more and better guns than any other country in the world. But there were also factors working against the acceptance of firearms in Japan. The country had a numerous warrior class, the samurai, for whom swords rated as class symbols and as means for subjugating the lower classes. Japanese warfare had previously involved single combats between samurai swordsmen, who stood in the open, made ritual speeches, and then took pride in fighting gracefully. Such behavior became lethal in the presence of peasant soldiers ungracefully blasting away with guns. In addition, guns were a foreign invention and grew to be despised, as did other things foreign in Japan after 1600. The samurai-controlled government began by restricting gun production to a few cities, then introduced a requirement of a government license for producing a gun, then issued licenses only for guns produced for the government, and finally reduced government orders for guns, until Japan was almost without functional guns again.

*fad : fashion or whim
*harquebuses : primitive gun

Summarize the passage by following the guidelines.

--- Guidelines ---
- Summarize the above passage in ONE paragraph.
- Provide a topic sentence and supporting ideas based on the passage.
- Do NOT copy more than FIVE consecutive words from the passage.

제 36 회 모의고사

1 Read the passage and follow the directions. [2 points]

> Modern science has no dogma. Yet it has a common core of research methods, which are all based on collecting empirical observations—those we can observe with at least one of our senses—and putting them together with the help of mathematical tools.
>
> People throughout history collected empirical observations, but the importance of these observations was usually limited. Why waste precious resources obtaining new observations when we already have all the answers we need? But as modern people came to admit that they did not know the answers to some very important questions, they found it necessary to look for completely new knowledge. Consequently, the dominant modern research method takes for granted the insufficiency of old knowledge. Instead of studying traditions, emphasis is now placed on new observations and experiments. When present observation collides with them, we give precedence to the new observation. Of course, physicists analysing the spectra of distant galaxies, archaeologists analysing the finds from a Bronze Age city, and political scientists studying the emergence of capitalism do not disregard tradition. They start by studying what the people of the past have said and written. But from their first year in college, aspiring physicists, archaeologists and political scientists are taught that it is their mission to go beyond <u>what Einstein, Heinrich Schliemann and Marx Weber ever knew</u>.

Identify the TWO consecutive words from the passage that BEST correspond to the meaning of the underlined words.

2 Read the passage and follow the directions. [4 points]

> Modern white nationalism, which has spread across the world, first emerged in America after the civil war. With the end of slavery, states took action to preserve the privileged position of American Protestants of western European heritage, including "Jim Crow" laws that enforced segregation. Others took to paramilitary violence and lynchings. The fixation with being white grew with increased immigration, especially of Chinese people, Irish Catholics, southern Europeans and Jews. New immigration acts were designed to restrict the number of new arrivals. Madison Grant's "The Passing of the Great Race", published in 1916, melded nativist sentiment with eugenics to produce a theory of white supremacy and "race suicide". Adolf Hitler reportedly wrote to Grant, stating that the book was "his bible".
>
> Though discredited by the war against Nazism and later by the civil-rights struggles of the 1950s and 60s, white nationalism experienced a resurgence towards the end of the 20th century, leading to a number of violent attacks in America and Europe.
>
> In 1988 David Lane wrote "The White Genocide Manifesto", giving a new name to Grant's theory of "race suicide". This text introduced the world to white nationalism's rallying cry: "We must secure the existence of our people and a future for white children", a phrase canonised by white nationalists as "the 14 words". Beyond a core belief in white superiority, white nationalists vary widely in their views. Some share the deep suspicion of the federal government found in militia groups; some embrace a revisionist history of the civil war that glorifies the Confederacy; some believe in anti-Semitic conspiracies about global Jewish control, including the theory that an internationalist Jewish elite is responsible for encouraging immigration.

White nationalism evolved rapidly with the advent of the Internet. It has picked up the irony-tinged discourse of the darker corners of cyberspace to couch* political views in a humour that never reveals whether the writer is serious or not. This allows white nationalists to use non-believers, just in it "for the lulz [laughs]", to spread their message to a wider audience.

couch : express

What actions helped white nationalism to be checked? Second, explain how white nationalism spread nimbly with the Internet in your own words.

3 Read the passage and follow the directions. [4 points]

Most of the members are men who have _____ professional openings rather than actual money. There are, for instance, half a dozen journalists and authors. Now a journalist, before he can be elected, must have a black-list of papers for which he will refuse to write. A concocted wireless message in *the Daily Blank*, which subsequent events proved to have been invented deliberately for the purpose of raking in ha'pennies*, so infuriated Henderson (to take a case) that he has pledged himself never to write a line for any paper owned by the same proprietors. Curiously enough he was asked a day or two later to contribute a series to a most respectable magazine published by this firm. He refused in a letter which breathed hatred and utter contempt in every word. It was Henderson, too, who resigned his position as dramatic critic because the proprietor of his paper did rather a shady thing in private life. "I know the paper isn't mixed up in it at all," he said, "but he's my employer and he pays me. Well, I like to be loyal to my employers, and if I'm loyal to this man I can't go about telling everybody that he's a dirty cad*."

Then there is the case of Bolus the author. He has refused to be photographed and interviewed, and he has refused to contribute to symposia in the monthly magazines. He has declined with thanks, moreover, invitations to half a dozen houses sent to him by hostesses who only knew him by reputation. Indirectly he must have been a financial loser by his action, and even if he is not actually assisting to topple over the Money God, he is at least striking a blow for the cause of independence. However, there he is, and with him goes a certain M.P.* who contributed $10,000 to the party chest, and refused scornfully the peerage which was offered to him.

ha'pennies : halfpennies
cad : scoundrel
M.P. : member of parliament

Fill in the blank with the ONE most appropriate word from the passage. Second, explain the commonality between Henderson and Bolus given the main idea.

4 Read the passage and follow the directions. [4 points]

> By forcing yourself to work within a rigid structure and to accomplish tasks in a given time, you are forced to bring laser focus to every activity. Time blocking simply means planning out your day in advance and dedicating specific hours to accomplish specific tasks. Doing this requires determining in advance what you will accomplish and exactly when you will accomplish it. Once you have those in mind, enter these into your calendar and then get to work on those tasks at the appropriate time during the day.
>
> When scheduling out tasks, it's important to block out both proactive blocks and reactive blocks. Proactive blocks are when you focus on important tasks that you must get done. This is when you make progress on important projects, draft important documents, or sketch out a prototype for your next great product. Reactive blocks are when you allow time for requests and interruptions, such as email and impromptu meetings. For example, you could schedule your most challenging tasks for the first two hours of the day and plow through your inbox during the afternoon. This allows you to work undistracted and still know you'll get to things like email and phone calls. This method has the advantage of helping you know exactly how you're going to use your time and exactly when you're going to accomplish specific tasks. Standard to-do lists present you with a list of tasks to complete in your own time. Time blocking provides you with a list of tasks and a specific time frame to complete each task.

Summarize the passage by following the guidelines below.

── Guidelines ──
- Summarize the above passage in ONE paragraph.
- Provide a topic sentence and supporting ideas based on the passage.
- Do NOT copy more than FIVE consecutive words from the passage.

제 37 회 모의고사

모범답안 및 번역 p.126

1 **Read the passage and follow the directions.** [2 points]

　　The planet's far North is burning. This summer, over 600 wildfires have consumed more than 2.4 million acres of forest across Alaska. Fires are also raging in northern Canada. In Siberia, choking smoke from 13 million acres—an area nearly the size of West Virginia—is blanketing towns and cities.

　　Fires in these places are normal. In central Alaska, <u>spindly* spruce trees open resinous cones to jump-start new seedlings when the parent tree is scorched. Fast-growing fireweed and other flowers cover recent burn scars. Soon afterward come wild blueberries, willows and birch and aspen trees that shoot up from still-living stumps and roots. Eventually flammable* conifers take over again.</u>

　　But, as various studies show, recent fires are also abnormal. They are too frequent, intense and severe. They are pouring more carbon into the atmosphere at a time when carbon dioxide concentrations are setting new records.

　　Some researchers are examining the complex relationships between warming climate, increasing fire and shifting patterns of vegetation. Using locally focused climate data and models from the Scenarios Network for Alaska and Arctic Planning, we are finding evidence that is deeply worrying—not just for those of us who live within the fires' pall of smoke, but for the world.

　　Typically, the natural cycle resumes about every 200 years. But today the cycles are about 25% shorter than in the past, and that changes everything.

*spindly : slender
*flammable : capable of burning quickly

Identify the TWO consecutive words from the passage that BEST correspond to the underlined part.

2 Read the passage and follow the directions. [4 points]

You're at brunch with your friends on Sunday morning and after stuffing yourself with pancakes and mimosas, your server comes up to you and says, "Is this going to be on one check or—"

"Separate!" you all proclaim, barely taking a breath to pause from your conversation. And why would you? It's pretty customary to pay for your own meal, or to go Dutch.

But it wasn't always the norm to split the check when going out with friends. In fact, in early English society, it was seen as selfish to invite someone out to eat and not pay for their meal.

After the English Civil War ended in 1651, the English were desperate to get life back to ① <u>normal</u>. This meant following certain codes of conduct that displayed class hierarchies and good Christian behavior. It was really important in this world to demonstrate your gentility, or gentlemanliness, by hospitality. By not being generous, you were undermining both the crown and God.

The origins of the phrase "going Dutch" are a little complicated, but some specialists in historical and contemporary lexicography helped us track the complex history of this idiom.

We have to take it back all the way to the 1600s. During the Anglo-Dutch Wars, there were multiple conflicts between the English and the Dutch over trade and naval power. That led to a rise in negative idioms from the English regarding their enemy, the Dutch : phrases like "Dutch courage," the false courage brought on by alcoholic binges; or "Dutch reckoning," which is a ridiculously high bill on which you've likely been scammed. This was because the English saw the Dutch not only as a trading enemy, but also as a people with questionable morals. The English claimed that the Dutch had been completely corrupted by their commitment to capitalism. ② <u>Funny how tides change, isn't it?</u>

Describe what the underlined "normal" meant in the context of the topic of the passage. Second, explain the meaning of the underlined words in the last sentence.

3. Read the passage and follow the directions. [4 points]

Memories make us who we are. They shape our understanding of the world and help us to predict what's coming. For more than a century, researchers have been working to understand how memories are formed and then fixed for recall in the days, weeks or even years that follow. But those scientists might have been looking at only half the picture. To understand how we remember, we must also understand how, and why, we forget.

Until about ten years ago, most researchers thought that forgetting was a passive process in which memories, unused, decay over time like a photograph left in the sunlight. But then ① a handful of researchers who were investigating memory began to bump up against findings that seemed to contradict that decades-old assumption. They began to put forward the radical idea that the brain is built to forget.

A growing body of work, cultivated in the past decade, suggests that the loss of memories is not a passive process. Rather, forgetting seems to be an active mechanism that is constantly at work in the brain. In some—perhaps even all—animals, the brain's standard state is not to remember, but to forget. And a better understanding of that state could lead to breakthroughs in treatments for conditions such as anxiety, post-traumatic stress disorder (PTSD), and even Alzheimer's disease.

"What is memory without forgetting?" asks Oliver Hardt, a cognitive psychologist studying the neurobiology of memory. "It's impossible to have proper memory function, you have to have ___②___."

Explain what the underlined "a handful of researchers" contradicts. Second, fill in the blank with the ONE most appropriate word from the passage.

4 Read the passage and follow the directions. [4 points]

Is the school skirt—usually navy or black, always knee-length until rolled up in defiance (or, in adult hindsight, vulnerability)—on the brink of extinction? Maybe. Does it matter? Definitely. According to an analysis of uniform policies across schools in England, at least 40 secondaries have banned girls from wearing skirts in favour of a gender-neutral uniform for everyone. The future for 11-to 16-year-olds appears to be trousers.

In schools, where belief systems are formed and bullying is rife, a gender-neutral uniform policy demonstrates a commitment to equality, the inclusion of transgender and non-binary pupils, as well as basic common sense. Try scaling a climbing frame* in a knee-length skirt. Or just sitting on the floor with your legs crossed. Now add the low embarrassment threshold of your average secondary school pupil. And a highly sexualised and vaguely threatening atmosphere. Possibly a period. See what I mean?

Yet a gender-neutral uniform policy does not require a ban on skirts. Greater inclusion for all should never come with a cost of narrowing choice for some. School uniform should be about individual choice and expression rather than the policing of girls. What message is a ban on skirts really sending? One more about blame than equality?

Some of the language has a tellingly Victorian whiff. One school has placed skirts on a list of "unacceptable items". Another deems them "undignified and embarrassing". Wade into this messy subject (preferably in trousers, for practical reasons) and you will come up against strong words such as "modesty" and "inappropriate" before long. But it is not the skirt that is immodest or the girl inside it, in the same way that it is never relevant what a woman was wearing when she was raped. Skirts, in short, are fine if you want to wear them.

*scale a climbing frame : climb up a jungle gym

Summarize the passage by following the guideline below.

---- Guidelines ----
- Summarize the above passage in ONE paragraph.
- Provide a topic sentence, supporting ideas, and a concluding sentence based on the passage.
- Do NOT copy more than FIVE consecutive words from the passage.

제 38 회 모의고사

1 Read the passage and follow the directions. [2 points]

> Early scripts were ambiguous. For example, the oldest Sumerian cuneiform writing could not render normal prose but was a mere telegraphic shorthand, whose vocabulary was restricted to names, numerals, units of measure, words for objects counted, and a few adjectives. That's as if a modern American court clerk were forced to write "John 27 fat sheep," because English writing lacked the necessary words and grammar to write "We order John to deliver the fat sheep that he owes to the government."
>
> Linear B, the writing of ancient Mycenaean Greece, was at least simpler, being based on a syllabary of about 90 signs plus logograms. Offsetting that virtue, however, Linear B was also quite _____. It omitted any consonant at the end of a word, and it used the same sign for several related consonants (for instance, one sign for both l and r, another for p and b and ph, and still another for g and k and kh). We know how confusing we find it when native-born Japanese people speak English without distinguishing l and r : imagine the confusion if our alphabet did the same while similarly homogenizing the other consonants that I mentioned! It's as if we were to spell the words "rap," "lap," "lab," and "laugh" identically.

Fill in the blank with the ONE most appropriate word from the passage.

2 Read the passage and follow the directions. [4 points]

When we do look at the data on wealth inequality in the U.S., it's stark and dwarfs that of the rest of the developed world. The conservative Hudson Institute in 2017 reported that the wealthiest 5 percent of American households held 62.5 percent of all assets in the U.S. in 2013, up from 54.1 percent 30 years earlier. As a consequence, the wealth of the other 95 percent declined from 45.9 percent to 37.5 percent.

As a result, the median wealth of upper-income families (earning US $639,400 on average) was nearly seven times that of middle-income households ($96,500) in 2013, the widest gap in at least 30 years.

More notably, world-famous inequality scholars Emmanuel Saez and Gabriel Zucman found that the top 0.01 percent controlled 22 percent of all wealth in 2012, up from just 7 percent in 1979. If you only looked at data on income inequality, however, you'd see a different picture. In 2013, for example, the top 5 percent of households earned just 30 percent of all U.S. income compared with possessing nearly 63 percent of all wealth.

While the U.S. is not the only developed country that has seen wealth inequality rise over the past three decades, it is an outlier. The wealthiest 5 percent of households in the U.S. have almost 91 times more wealth than the median American household, the widest gap among 18 of the world's most developed countries. The next highest is the Netherlands, which has a ratio less than half that.

Describe the key discovery Emmanuel Saez and Gabriel Zucman found. Second, explain why the writer of the passage mentions "the Netherlands" in the passage.

3 Read the passage and follow the directions. [4 points]

In 1998, The Wall Street Journal and NBC News asked several hundred young Americans to name their most important values. Work ethic led the way—naturally. After that, large majorities picked patriotism, religion, and having children.

Twenty-one years later, the same pollsters asked the same questions of today's 18-to-38-year-olds—members of the Millennial and Z generations. The results showed ① a major value shift among young adults. Today's respondents were 10 percentage points less likely to value having children and 20 points less likely to highly prize patriotism or religion.

The nuclear family, religious fealty*, and national pride—family, God, and country—are a holy trinity of American traditionalism. The fact that allegiance to all three is in precipitous decline tells us something important about the evolution of the American identity.

One interpretation of this poll is that it's mostly about the erosion of traditional Western faith. People under 30 in the U.S. account for more than one-third of this nation's worshippers in only three major religions: Islam, Buddhism, and Hinduism. This reflects both the increase in non-European immigration since the 1970s and the decline of larger Christian denominations in the latter half of the 20th century. It also reflects the sheer increase in atheism: Millennials are nearly three times more likely than Boomers* to say they don't believe in God—6 percent versus 16 percent. If you think that Judeo-Christian values are an irreplaceable keystone in the moral arc of Western society, these facts will disturb you; ② if you don't, they won't.

A second interpretation of this poll is that it's mostly about politics. Youthful disinterest in patriotism, babies, and God might be a mere proxy for young people's distaste for traditional conservatism.

*fealty : loyalty
*Boomers : Baby-boomer generation

Describe to what "a major value shift" refers. Second, explain the meaning of the underlined words in ②.

4 Read the passage and follow the directions. [4 points]

> Leaving a water bottle sitting in your car sounds benign enough. But on a hot, summer day, the plastic can act as a lens, focusing light into a high-energy beam that's intense enough to burn material like car-seat upholstery. Last summer, Idaho Power shared its video of a water bottle burning two holes in a car seat. And for this year's World Cup soccer tournament, the Russian water company Holy Water is selling soccer ball-shaped water bottles that can act as perfect light-focusing lenses. In a video published by Fontanka Ru, the ball-shaped bottle is seen focusing light so well that it ignites a box of matches and burns a hole in laminate flooring. The water bottle is acting like a lens that's focusing the light coming through the window.
>
> Odile Madden, a materials scientist, witnessed the astonishing power of laser-focused light years ago, when she was experimenting with using lasers to remove clear adhesives from artwork and artifacts. She discovered that the grooves in the adhesive worked to focus the laser and "turned up the power," subsequently burning or etching pits into the glass microscope slides she was using for the experiment. She published her findings in 2005 in the journal *Lasers in the Conservation of Artworks*.
>
> What surprised Madden about the water bottle examples is that the light passes through the car window first, yet there's still enough heat left to go through the bottle and cause burning. "Conceivably, this would be worse on a hot day or if the window were down, because the window filters the light," Madden said. "This is a good illustration of just how much energy there is coming from the sun and we think of this as a cheap water bottle, but we're unintentionally creating an optically almost-perfect shape for a lens," she added. We'd better not put a water bottle on a stack of paper in a car on a hot day anymore.

Summarize the passage by following the guidelines.

--- Guidelines ---
- Summarize the above passage in ONE paragraph.
- Provide a topic sentence, supporting ideas, and a concluding sentence based on the passage.
- Do NOT copy more than FIVE consecutive words from the passage.

제 39 회 모의고사

1. Read the passage and follow the directions. [2 points]

   The primarily Islamic tradition of females covering themselves from head to foot with a burqa is an example of the intrinsic difficulty in evaluating the extent to which cultural practices promote individual autonomy. Critics of the burqa and similar garments, especially critics from Western cultures, deem them physically oppressive with the weight of the fabric; psychologically oppressive in that they seem to make women devoid of distinctiveness; and emotionally oppressive in that they are yet another manifestation of a male-dominated society in which women are subordinate. According to this view, the tradition of wearing such clothing is unjustified because it greatly restricts the autonomy of women.

   Defenders of this practice, however, argue the opposite view. They insist that coverings like the burqa actually foster autonomy and liberate women for a number of reasons. For example, a burqa prevents women from being viewed as sexual objects; it encourages unity among female Muslims; and it promotes the appearance of holiness. Proponents of the burqa also ask questions of Western critics which force them to examine their own clothing culture, such as, "Why is it considered oppressive to wear a headscarf but liberating to wear a miniskirt?". They insist the answer lies in the assumptions each culture makes about the women involved and their ability to make choices. They say that if their assumptions concerning such clothing practices are actually wrong, and the wearing of the burqa is actually a matter of personal preference, then it is completely justified as a legitimate expression of individual _____.

Fill in the blank with the ONE most appropriate word from the passage.

2 Read the passage and follow the directions. [4 points]

Like many medications, the wakefulness drug modafinil, which is marketed under the trade name Provigil, comes with a small, tightly folded paper pamphlet. For the most part, its contents—lists of instructions and precautions, a diagram of the drug's molecular structure—make for anodyne* reading. The subsection called "Mechanism of Action," however, contains a sentence that might induce sleeplessness by itself: "The mechanism(s) through which modafinil promotes wakefulness is unknown."

Provigil isn't uniquely ① <u>mysterious</u>. Many drugs receive regulatory approval, and are widely prescribed, even though no one knows exactly how they work. This mystery is built into the process of drug discovery, which often proceeds by trial and error. Each year, any number of new substances are tested in cultured cells or animals; the best and safest of those are tried out in people. In some cases, the success of a drug promptly inspires new research that ends up explaining how it works—but not always. Aspirin was discovered in 1897, and yet no one convincingly explained how it worked until 1995. The same phenomenon exists elsewhere in medicine. Deep-brain stimulation involves the implantation of electrodes in the brains of people who suffer from specific movement disorders, such as Parkinson's disease; it's been in widespread use for more than twenty years, and some think it should be employed for other purposes, including general cognitive enhancement. No one can say how it works.

This approach to discovery—answers first, explanations later—accrues what I call ② <u>intellectual debt</u>. It's possible to discover what works without knowing why it works, and then to put that insight to use immediately, assuming that the underlying mechanism will be figured out later. In some cases, we pay off this intellectual debt quickly. But, in others, we let it compound, relying, for decades, on knowledge that's not fully known.

* anodyne : sleeping-inducing

Explain the meaning of the underlined "mysterious". Second, describe what "intellectual debt" means.

3 Read the passage and follow the directions. [4 points]

> Whether such data are generated actively or passively, few people will have the time or inclination to keep track of all the information they generate, or estimate its value. Even those who do will lack the bargaining power to get a good deal from AI firms. But the history of labour offers a hint about how things could evolve : because historically, if wages rose to acceptable levels, it was mostly due to unions. Similarly, Mr Weyl expects to see the rise of what he calls "data-labour unions", organizations that serve as gatekeepers of people's data. Like their predecessors, they will negotiate rates, monitor members' data work and ensure the quality of their digital output, for instance by keeping reputation scores. Unions could funnel specialist data work to their members and even organize strikes, for instance by blocking access to exert influence on a company employing its members' data. Similarly, data unions could be conduits channelling members' data contributions, all while tracking them and billing AI firms that benefit from them.
>
> ① <u>This may sound like science fiction</u>. Why should Google and Facebook, for instance, ever give up their current business model of using free data to sell targeted online advertising? In 2017 they raked in a combined $135bn in ad dollars. If they had to compensate people for their data, they would be much less profitable. Meanwhile, startups such as CitizenMe and Datacoup, which can be seen as early forms of data unions, have so far failed to make much headway. Yet in other corners of the industry, tech giants already pay for data, although ② <u>they are careful not to talk too much about it</u>. Mostly through outsourcing firms, they employ armies of raters and moderators to check the quality of their algorithms and take down content that is illegal or offensive. Other firms use crowd-working platforms, such as Amazon's Mechanical Turk, to farm out data work such as tagging pictures.

Explain the meaning of the underlined words in ①. Next, what can be inferred to be the reason behind companies' actions in underlined ②.

4 Read the passage and follow the directions. [4 points]

The insight of polytheism is conducive to far-reaching religious tolerance. Since polytheists believe, on the one hand, in one supreme and completely disinterested power, and on the other hand in many partial and biased powers, there is no difficulty for the devotees of one god to accept the existence and efficacy of other gods. Polytheism is inherently open-minded, and rarely persecutes 'heretics' and 'infidels'. This is in contrast to monotheistic religions like Christianity which has waged war on those who've believed differently both within their religion and outside of it.

Even when polytheists conquered huge empires, they did not try to convert their subjects. The Egyptians, the Romans and the Aztecs did not send missionaries to foreign lands to spread the worship of Osiris, Jupiter or Huitzilopochtli (the chief Aztec god), and they certainly didn't dispatch armies for that purpose. In the Aztec Empire, subject peoples were obliged to build temples for Huitzilopochtli, but these temples were built alongside those of local gods, rather than in their stead. The Romans happily added the Asian goddess Cybele and the Egyptian goddess Isis to their pantheon*.

The only god that the Romans long refused to tolerate was the monotheistic and evangelising god of the Christians. The Roman Empire did not require the Christians to give up their beliefs and rituals, but it did expect them to pay respect to the empire's protector gods and to the divinity of the emperor. This was seen as a declaration of political loyalty. When the Christians vehemently refused to do so, and went on to reject all attempts at compromise, the Romans reacted by persecuting what they understood to be a politically subversive faction. And even this was done half-heartedly. In the 300 years from the crucifixion of Christ to the conversion of Emperor Constantine, polytheistic Roman emperors initiated no more than four general persecutions of Christians. In these three centuries, the polytheistic Romans killed no more than a few thousand Christians. In contrast, over the course of the next 1,500 years, Christians slaughtered Christians by the millions to defend slightly different interpretations of the religion of love and compassion.

* pantheon : temple dedicated to all the gods

Summarize the passage by following the guidelines below.

Guidelines

- Summarize the above passage in ONE paragraph.
- Provide a topic sentence and supporting ideas based on the passage.
- Do NOT copy more than FIVE consecutive words from the passage.

제 40 회 모의고사

1 **Read the passage and follow the directions.** [2 points]

> We humans have evolved to be uniquely tolerant among fission-fusion species. The roots of this lie in part in our unusually large brains and relatively high reproductive rates, compared with other primates. Together these characteristics make us extremely dependent on high-quality, high-risk (ie, unpredictable across time and location) food and tool supplies. In turn, this will have had implications for our foraging strategies, including the frequent need to rely on other communities during periods of resource scarcity. This does not mean humans were, or are, peaceful all the time. But, where and when access to nonlocal resources is important, humans have often managed to find ways to be tolerant towards members of other communities at least some of the time.
>
> Whereas scholars have previously focused on bellicose chimpanzees as a way to gain insight into the evolutionary origins of our aggressive tendencies, many researchers recently believe comparisons with other, more tolerant nonhuman primates might be more apposite*, especially for understanding the foundations of our uniquely _____ nature.
>
> Notably, food sharing and grooming have both been observed between bonobo groups, as has the formation of intergroup coalitions. Bonobos aren't always tolerant toward members of other groups. During intergroup encounters, there are often conflicts between two individuals, or even moments of tension that shake up many members of both groups. But that flexibility in intergroup behaviour, to behave tolerantly or aggressively toward out-group members, is there, much like the flexibility we see in humans.
>
> *apposite : appropriate*

Fill in the blank with the ONE most appropriate word from the passage.

2. Read the passage and follow the directions. [4 points]

Once your eyes suspect a liar, next let your ears have a turn. Here are ① cues to listen for. A story in strict chronological order. When a complex lie is to be told, whether to a CIA agent, the parent of a teenager, or Bob Woodward and Carl Bernstein, liars often rehearse their story, which usually is spun from—logically—start to finish. A fun trick? If you think you're hearing a tall tale, ask to hear the story backwards: "So when you just happened to see the car in the ditch—what happened before that again?" and watch the liar squirm.

Way too much linguistic convolution or overcompensation. Does your suspected liar use a hundred words when ten would do? Or use formal language with many clauses? For example, compare these two statements: "In light of the given situation, it can categorically be stated that I have never, and would never, remove your lunch from the shared office refrigerator." Contrast that with "I didn't eat your lunch."

A truth-teller names names, while a liar uses impersonal phrases or pronouns; for example, "that woman" rather than "Miss Lewinsky." In addition, liars avoid saying "I." For example, instead of "I didn't skim off the register," you'll hear, "No one here would ever skim off the register."

Liars work really hard to come across as truthful. They smile at all the right moments and say all the right things. But the result often appears contrived and fake, which it is. If you feel like you're being sold a bag of goods, you probably are. In short, ② a bright toothy smile probably means a shark.

Identify to what all "cues" refer in the passage. Then explain the meaning of the underlined words in ②.

3 Read the passage and follow the directions. [4 points]

> Consider image recognition. Ten years ago, computers couldn't easily identify objects in photos. Today, image search engines, like so many of the systems we interact with on a day-to-day basis, are based on extraordinarily capable machine-learning models. Google's image search relies on a neural network called Inception. In 2017, MIT's LabSix—a research group of undergraduate and graduate students—succeeded in altering the pixels of a photograph of a cat so that, although it looked like a cat to human eyes, Inception became 99.99-per-cent sure it had been given a photograph of guacamole. Inception, of course, can't explain what features led it to conclude that a cat is a cat; as a result, there's no easy way to predict how it might fail when presented with specially crafted or corrupted data. Such a system is likely to have unknown gaps in its accuracy that amount to vulnerabilities for a smart and determined attacker.
>
> As knowledge generated by machine-learning systems is put to use, these kinds of gaps may prove consequential. Health-care A.I.s have been successfully trained to classify skin cancers as benign or malignant. And yet—as a team of researchers from Harvard Medical School and MIT showed—they can also be tricked into making inaccurate judgments using the same techniques that turn cats into guacamole. (Among other things, attackers might use these vulnerabilities to commit insurance fraud.) Seduced by the predictive power of such systems, we may stand down the human judges whom they promise to replace. But they will remain susceptible to hijacking—and we will have no easy process for validating the answers they continue to produce.

Describe Inception's limitation according to the MIT research. Second, how is it likely that insurance swindlers uses Health-care AI?

_____

_____

_____

4. Read the passage and follow the directions. [4 points]

Star innovators such as Bill Gates, who was 19 when he started Microsoft, Steve Jobs, 21 when he started Apple, and Mark Zuckerberg, 19 when he launched Facebook, have reinforced the longstanding impression that young people are the wellspring of entrepreneurship. Systematic data on firm founders, however, suggest that this impression is false. Many researchers provide evidence that, on average, successful entrepreneurs are middle-aged.

They analyzed administrative data from the U.S. Census Bureau on more than 2.7 million business founders whose companies subsequently hired at least one employee. The mean age of founders was 42. When looking at the highest-growth startups in the economy, the mean age at founding rose still higher—to 45. In addition, the study explores the factors that are correlated with firm success. These old founders with longer work experience closer to the specific industry of the start-up, and founders with longer experience in that industry, have substantially greater success rates. "For the 1 in 1,000 highest-growth firms, founders with three or more years of experience in the 2-digit industry see upper tail success at twice the rate of younger founders with no experience in the 2-digit industry," the researchers report. The study also took into account geographical heterogeneity, and separately considers California, Massachusetts, and New York. These three states account for the majority of high-growth startup activity in the U.S. Even in these states, successful entrepreneurs are still middle-aged.

Summarize the passage by following the guideline below.

Guidelines

- Summarize the above passage in ONE paragraph.
- Provide a topic sentence and supporting ideas based on the passage.
- Do NOT copy more than FIVE consecutive words from the passage.

제 41 회 모의고사

1 Read the passage and follow the directions. [4 points]

　I believe the first time I recall acting to get attention, I was eight years old at summer camp. And I'd tried to auditioning for about a year by then, and I'd been lucky to get some small roles in television shows and commercials, and I boasted about it a lot, that summer at camp. And in the beginning, it worked. The other children gave me much more attention, because I had been on "Family Ties." Then, the tide turned I think I took it too far with the boasting. And then, the other kids started to make fun of me. I remember there was this one girl I had a crush on, Rocky. Her name was Rachel but she preferred to be called Rocky. And she was beautiful, and she was a singer, and I was smitten with her, and I was standing there, bragging. And she rounded on me and called me a show-off. Which I 100 percent deserved. But you know, it still really hurt. And ever since then, I've had a certain hesitance to seek ___①___ for my acting.

　Sometimes, people ask me, "Hold on, if you don't like the attention, then why are you an actor?" And I'd say, "Because that's not what performing is about, man, it's about the art." And they'd be like, "OK, OK, dude." And then Twitter arrived. And I got totally addicted, just like everybody else, which made me into ②<u>a complete hypocrite</u>. Because by then, I was absolutely using my acting to get attention. I mean, did I think I was just getting all these followers because of my insightful tweets? I actually did think that—I was like—. "They don't just like me because they saw me in some movie, they like what I have to say, I've got a way with words." And then in no time at all, it started having an impact on my dearly beloved creative process. It still does. I try not to let it.

Fill in the blank with the ONE most appropriate word from the passage. Second, explain why the writer of the passage thought he was "a complete hypocrite".

2 Read the passage and follow the directions. [4 points]

Here's an breakdown in terms of communication platforms we know today: Texting, Twitter, Instagram, and Facebook.

Texting: ice cold. The entire point of texting, especially for the youth, is that it's a way to communicate that reveals very little information. Uncertainty and ambiguity is the point. Texting, particularly a group chat, is often like a game of "what's said versus unsaid", where gaps must be completed. It requires active participation on your part to fill in the picture of what's being communicated. (The dreaded "…" in iMessage, which says so little but draws us in, is Cool Media.)

Twitter: cool. Twitter is tricky due to the fact that there are many different ways to use it. Breaking News Twitter, for one, is quite hot. But Twitter the social network is quite cool. It's a low-resolution, character-limited format where the majority of what's being communicated is actually just offscreen, out of the picture. The best tweets and the funniest jokes on Twitter are incomplete information. They're pure punchline. The setup goes unsaid; you have to already be aware of it, or go figure it out. It takes a lot of work to use Twitter successfully and you have to fluently understand its genre conventions in order for it to be understood. Twitter, when used perfectly, is Cool Media.

Instagram: warm. The main content being exchanged is all visual, and you don't need to grasp genre conventions as much. Instagram in its early photo filter days was fairly hot media, as is classic photography, but it cooled down when it evolved into the de facto social status app. Now there's interplay between what's posted and how many likes the post gets, and from whom, and other social dynamics like private versus public posting. There is still some ambiguity, but as a medium it's more information-complete than Twitter or Texting.

Facebook : hot. Unlike _____, which is a muttering wealth of inside jokes, or Instagram, which is warmer but still has some cool elements to it, Facebook is more akin to a newspaper. It's not withholding anything. It's a patchwork mosaic of yelling : Acknowledge this! Be angry at this! Celebrate this! There's not a lot of mystery on Facebook, and it doesn't take much fluency to use it correctly. The information being communicated is all right there, blasted at you. Facebook may have started out cooler, back when it was college kids broadcasting social status (as Instagram is used now). But it's heated up steadily since then.

Describe the crucial element required for the best tweets and jokes on Twitter. Second, fill in the blank with the ONE most appropriate word from the passage.

3 Read the passage and follow the directions. [4 points]

Ms. Porter raised her hand nervously. It was the beginning of her school's staff meeting and her principal, Ms. Chang, had asked if anybody wanted to add new items to the agenda. "I'd like to talk about how we plan to teach about the upcoming Thanksgiving holiday." Ms. Porter said.

Several colleagues responded.

"I don't plan to talk about it at all. Thanksgiving seems to be more about consumerism than spending time with family," Ms. Espinosa said. Ms. Tilson commented, "I focus on food. Students are really engaged when we talk about food. We'll talk about how the Pilgrims and Indians shared a feast, and since some of our students are immigrants, we can use it as an opportunity to learn about traditional foods."

"I focus on the Thanks in Thanksgiving," Mr. Webster added. "We all have so much to be thankful for. I like to focus on the positive."

Ms. Chang replied, "Seems we have a variety of ways to honor the holiday. I don't think we need any more conversation on this unless you have questions."

Ms. Porter's mind was most concerned with what her colleagues were not intending to talk about. "I'm concerned with how we are perpetuating myths about the first Thanksgiving. I'm concerned we are not acknowledging that some Native Americans observe this day as a day of mourning, not as a celebration. This is a great opportunity to promote dialogue within the school community about popular customs that might alienate some students and families, such as pretending to be Pilgrims and Indians," she said.

As she heard these words coming out of her mouth, Ms. Porter felt a wave of relief and regret. She was bothered by the way many of her colleagues had addressed Thanksgiving in previous years but never felt comfortable speaking up.

"We have so many needs in our school. I don't think we should micromanage how people teach Thanksgiving. We don't even have any of those students in our school," Ms. Tilson said.

Ms. Chang, sensing tension in the room, replied, "You all have great points. Thank you for sharing them. It seems this is a larger topic than we have time to discuss now." With that comment, she moved to the next item on the agenda.

Ms. Porter looked around the room, frustrated by her colleagues' comments, and that nobody else spoke up or supported her for speaking up.

Explain what reason can be inferred that Ms. Porter was "nervous" to introduce a topic in the staff meeting. Second, to whom does Ms. Tilson refer in the underlined selection?

4 Read the passage and follow the directions. [4 points]

Social scientists have a wealth of tools to study how trusting, and how trustworthy, a person is. The most popular is the trust game, in which two participants play, usually anonymously. The first participant is given a small amount of money, $10 say, and asked to decide what amount to give to the other participant. The amount transferred is then tripled, and the second participant chooses how much to give back to the first.

In Western countries at least, trust is rewarded : the more money the first participant transfers, the more money the second participant sends back, and thus the more money the first participant ends up with. In spite of this, first participants on average transfer only half the money they have been granted. In some studies, ① a variant was introduced whereby participants knew each other's ethnicity. Prejudice led participants to mistrust certain groups—Israeli men of Eastern origin (Asian and African immigrants and their Israeli-born offspring), or black students in South Africa—transferring them less money, even though these groups proved just as trustworthy as more well-regarded groups.

If people and institutions are more trustworthy than we give them credit for, why don't we get it right? Why is it we don't trust more?

When you trust someone, you end up figuring out whether your faith in them was justified or not. An acquaintance asks if he can sleep at your house for a few days. If you accept, you will find out whether or not he's a good guest. A colleague recommends a new software application to you. If you follow her advice, you will find out whether the new software works better than the one you were used to.

In contrast, if you ____②____ someone, more often than not you never find out whether you should have trusted them. If you don't invite your friend over, you won't know whether he would have made a good guest or not. If you don't follow your colleague's advice, you won't know if the new software application is in fact more useful, and thus whether your colleague gives good advice in this domain.

Identify to what the underlined "a variant" refers. Second, fill in the blank ② with the TWO most appropriate consecutive words from the passage.

1 Read the passage and follow the directions. [4 points]

The process school sees a message as that which is transmitted by the communication process. Many of its constituents believe that _____①_____ is a key factor in deciding what forms a message. Thus pulling my earlobe would not be a message unless I deliberately did it as a pre-arranged signal to an auctioneer. The sender's intention may be stated or unstated, conscious or unconscious, but must be retrievable by analysis. The message is what the sender puts into it by any possible means.

For semiotics, on the other hand, the message is a construction of signs which, through interacting with the receivers, creates meanings. The sender, defined as transmitter of the message, declines in importance. The emphasis transfers to the text and how it is 'read'. And reading is the process of discovering meanings that occurs when the reader interacts or negotiates with the text. This negotiation takes place as the reader brings aspects of his or her cultural experience to bear upon the codes and signs which make up the text. It also involves some shared understanding of what the text is about. We have only to see how various newspapers report the same world event differently to perceive how important is this understanding, this view of the world, which each paper shares with its readers. So readers with different social experiences or from different cultures are likely to find different meanings in the same text. This is not necessarily proof of communication failure.

The message, then, is not something sent from A to B, but an element in a structured relationship whose other elements include external reality and the producer/reader. Producing and reading the text are seen as parallel, if not identical, processes in that they occupy the same place in this structured relationship. We might model this structure as a ② triangle in which the arrows represent constant interaction; the structure is not static but a dynamic practice.

Fill in the blank with the ONE most appropriate word from the passage. Second, explain why the writer employs the term "triangle".

2. Read the passage and follow the directions. [4 points]

In 2004, an essay appeared in the journal *Psychological Science*, titled "Music Lessons Boost IQ." The author Glenn Yu had ran an experiment with 144 children randomly assigned to four groups: one learned piano for a year, one took singing lessons, another joined an acting class, and a control group had no extracurricular training. The IQ of the children in the two musical groups rose by an average of seven points in the course of a year; those in the other two groups gained an average of 4.3 points.

Yu had long been skeptical of the science backing claims that music education enhances children's abstract reasoning, math, or language skills. If children who play the piano are smarter, he says, it doesn't necessarily mean they are smarter because they play the piano. It could be that the pupils who study piano also happen to be more ambitious or better at focusing on a task. Correlation, after all, does not prove causation.

The 2004 paper was developed to address those inconsistencies. And as a passionate musician, Yu was pleased when he turned up credible evidence that music has transfer effects on general intelligence. But a decade later, in 2013, the Education Endowment Foundation backed a larger study with more than 900 students. That study failed to corroborate Yu's findings, finding no evidence that music lessons improved math and literacy skills.

Yu took that news in stride while continuing to cast a skeptical eye on the research in his field. Recently, he decided to formally investigate just how often his fellow researchers in psychology and neuroscience make what he believes are false—or at least premature—causal connections between music and intelligence. His results, published in May, reveal that many of his peers do just that.

To pinpoint precisely how music lessons affect the brain over time, scientists would ideally assign students randomly to different groups, as Yu did in his 2004 study, only over an extended period of time. One group of children might be assigned to take piano lessons for years, while the other group would have no music education at all. Because this is generally not possible to do for the sake of a psychological experiment, many researchers rely on studies where they compare children who already take lessons to those who don't, correcting for variables such as socioeconomic status. But even with this correction, such studies can only find correlation; they cannot prove _____.

Explain the difference of the result between the 2004 and 2013 study. Second, explain why can it be inferred "variables such as socioeconomic status" should be corrected. Third, fill in the blank of the last sentence with the ONE most appropriate word from the passage.

3. Read the passage and follow the directions. [4 points]

Caesar was right. Thin people need watching. I've been watching them for most of my adult life, and I don't like what I see. When these narrow fellows spring at me, I quiver to my toes. Thin people come in all personalities, most of them menacing. You've got your "together" thin person, your mechanical thin person, your condescending thin person, your tsk-tsk thin person, your efficiency-expert thin person.

In the first place, thin people aren't fun. They don't know how to goof off, at least in the best, fat sense of the word. They've always got to be doing. Give them a coffee break, and they'll jog around the block. Supply them with a quiet evening at home, and they'll fix the screen door and lick S&H green stamps. They say things like "there aren't enough hours in the day." Fat people never say that. Fat people think the day is too damn long already.

Thin people make me tired. They've got speedy little metabolisms that cause them to bustle briskly. They're forever rubbing their bony hands together and eyeing new problems to "tackle". I like to surround myself with sluggish, inert, easygoing fat people, the kind who believe that if you clean it up today, it'll just get dirty again tomorrow.

Fat people may not be chortling all day long, but they're a hell of a lot nicer than the wizened and shriveled. Thin people turn surly while go straight to the heart of the matter while fat people let things stay all blurry and vague, the way things actually are. Thin people want to face the truth. Fat people know that there is no truth. The thin always stare unsolvable problems and say, "The key thing is ..." Fat people never say things like that. They know there isn't any such thing as the "key thing" about anything. Given these differences, if you are thin, go skip the gym, order that super-size lunch. As you grow larger, you'll grow into more pleasant company.

Summarize the passage following the guidelines below.

┌─── Guidelines ───┐
- Summarize the above passage in ONE paragraph.
- Provide a topic sentence, supporting ideas, and a concluding sentence based on the passage.
- Do NOT copy more than FOUR consecutive words from the passage.

제 43 회 모의고사

1 Read the passage and follow the directions. [4 points]

 Three years ago, I stopped eating sugar. Giving up sugar set me free. And so, what began as an experiment has become my new life. I have changed in ways that I had not thought possible.

 I used to get "hangry"—that grumpy, urgent craving that demands prompt attention. To stave it off, I carried bags of almonds or dried fruit. Back when I ate sugar, I couldn't go running in the morning—if I tried, I would get dizzy, and anyway, my legs felt as if they were made of stone. I would have slumps in the afternoon—my head would get foggy—so if I was working from home, I would take a nap. I had mood swings, joy alternating with despair. I had assumed that all of these things were simply part of life, of how I was, a frustrating aspect of my makeup. And ① <u>now all of them are gone</u>.

 For the first two weeks of my unsweetened life, though, I was in a foul temper. At first, I attributed this to the darkness and gloom of the winter days. But as I started to feel better—calmer, happier, more even-keeled—a more sinister thought began to nag at me. Had I been in withdrawal?

 To a chemist, sugar refers to a class of molecules made of hydrogen, carbon and oxygen; some of these serve particular biological roles. Lactose, for example, is found in milk; deoxyribose gives the "D" to DNA. But in daily life, the main sugars one meets are glucose, fructose and sucrose—which is a marriage of the other two. That is, each molecule of sucrose is one glucose linked to one fructose. Interestingly, the two simple sugars have the same chemical formula—six atoms of carbon, 12 of hydrogen, six of oxygen—but different chemical structures. The human tongue detects this : fructose tastes sweeter.

Glucose is synonymous with blood sugar, since it is transported in the blood and delivered to cells to fuel their energetic needs. But you can also find it, along with ___②___, in fruits and vegetables. Sucrose is extracted from sugar cane or beets, and is usually encountered as the white crystals of table sugar. When most people speak of "sugar", they mean sucrose. For most of human history, milk, honey and fruits have been the main sources of sweetness. When cane sugar first made its way to Europe around 1,000 years ago, it was treated as a spice, a medicine and a preservative. In 1700, the average sugar consumption in the United Kingdom was around two kilograms per person per year. Today, the figure is 10 times that amount. The present sugar glut is an anomaly in human experience. We have changed the world to suit our appetites; but our bodies cannot accommodate the change.

Explain why the writer mentions the words in ① in regard to the overarching meaning of the passage. Second, fill in the blank ② with the ONE most appropriate word from the passage.

2 Read the passage and follow the directions. [4 points]

In our standard view of things, consciousness exists only in the brains of highly evolved organisms, and hence consciousness exists only in a tiny part of the universe and only in very recent history. According to panpsychism, in contrast, consciousness pervades the universe and is a fundamental feature of it. This doesn't mean that literally everything is conscious. The basic commitment is that the fundamental constituents of reality—perhaps electrons and quarks—have incredibly simple forms of experience. And the very complex experience of the human or animal brain is somehow derived from the experience of the brain's most basic parts.

It might be important to clarify what I mean by "consciousness," as that word is actually quite ambiguous. Some people use it to mean something quite sophisticated, such as self-awareness or the capacity to reflect on one's own existence. This is something we might be reluctant to ascribe to many nonhuman animals, never mind fundamental particles. But when I use the word *consciousness*, I simply mean experience : pleasure, pain, visual or auditory experience, et cetera.

Human beings have a very rich and complex experience; horses less so; mice less so again. As we move to simpler and simpler forms of life, we find simpler and simpler forms of experience. Perhaps, at some point, the light switches off, and consciousness disappears. But it's at least coherent to suppose that this continuum of consciousness fading while never quite turning off carries on into inorganic matter, with fundamental particles having almost unimaginably simple forms of experience to reflect their incredibly simple nature. That's what panpsychists believe.

> The starting point of the panpsychist is that physical science doesn't actually tell us what _____ is. That sounds like a bizarre claim at first; you read a physics textbook, you seem to learn all kinds of incredible things about the nature of space, time and matter. But what philosophers of science have realized is that physical science, for all its richness, is confined to telling us about the behavior of matter, what it does. Physics tells us, for example, that matter has mass and charge. These properties are completely defined in terms of behavior, things like attraction, repulsion, resistance to acceleration. Physics tells us absolutely nothing about what matter is, in and of itself.

First, what can be inferred to be the perspective of the "standard view" toward forms of life simpler than mice? Do NOT copy more than FOUR consecutive words from the passage. Second, fill in the blank with the ONE most appropriate word from the passage.

3 Read the passage and follow the directions. [4 points]

As they filed into his classroom, Mr. Harrold overheard students discussing the score of a professional football game from the previous evening. When the conversation subsided, one student, Caylee, mentioned a player on the losing team who refused to stand during the national anthem. "Losing is karma for not respecting the American flag." she proclaimed. A few of her classmates laughed and nodded in agreement. Another student added, "His team probably lost because of the distraction."

"Oh boy," Mr. Harrold thought. "Is this something I need to address?" His mind turned to all the content he needed to cover and his carefully planned lesson, so he decided not to respond to Caylee's comment.

Later that evening as he watched the news Mr. Harrold saw highlights from the football game the students had discussed. The reporter addressed the backlash the player received for not standing during the national anthem. She interviewed both people who supported the player's decision and others who opposed it. Mr. Harrold wondered about his decision and others who opposed it. Mr. Harrold wondered about his decision not to address Caylee's comment but felt the teachable moment had passed.

Several weeks later Mr. Harrold overheard students talking about a classmate who had chosen earlier in the day not to stand during the Pledge of Allegiance. When asked by classmates about her decision, Kate had explained, "I don't believe 'liberty and justice for all' exist in our country."

A couple of her classmates expressed disdain for her behavior. They said Kate was only protesting because she wanted attention, not because of her cultural or political beliefs.

Once again Mr. Harrold was unsure how to respond. He knew this was a sensitive topic eliciting heated debates among adults, so he knew he needed to proceed with caution. He also knew his school prided itself on the annual Veterans Day program and wondered whether promoting dialogue about sitting during the national anthem or Pledge of Allegiance would be seen by some people in the community as conflicting with the school's history of honoring military veterans.

As he lost himself in reflection about how or whether to address the situation, a student interrupted his contemplation. "Mr. Harrold," the student asked, "do you think it's disrespectful to not stand during the Pledge or national anthem? Isn't it a school rule that we have to stand?"

Explain the meaning of the underlined selection. Do NOT copy more than FOUR consecutive words from the passage. Second, what backlash is Mr. Harrold concerned with, regarding addressing the protest? Do NOT copy more than FOUR consecutive words from the passage.

4 Read the passage and follow the directions. [4 points]

When I started advising startup founders at Y Combinator, especially young ones, I was puzzled by the way they always seemed to make things overcomplicated. How, they would ask, do you raise money? What's the trick for making venture capitalists want to invest in you? The best way to make VCs want to invest in you, I would explain, is to actually be a good investment. Even if you could trick VCs into investing in a bad startup, you'd be tricking yourselves too. You're investing time in the same company you're asking them to invest money in. If it's not a good investment, why are you even doing it?

Oh, they'd say, and then after a pause to digest this revelation, they'd ask: What makes a startup a good investment?

So I would explain that what makes a startup promising, not just in the eyes of investors but in fact, is growth. Ideally in revenue, but failing that in usage. What they needed to do was get lots of users.

How does one get lots of users? They had all kinds of ideas about that. They needed to do a big launch that would get them "exposure." They needed influential people to talk about them. They even knew they needed to launch on a Tuesday, because that's when one gets the most attention.

No, I would explain, that is not how to get lots of users. The way you get lots of users is to make the product really great. Then people will not only use it but recommend it to their friends, so your growth will be exponential once you get it started.

At this point I've told the founders something you'd think would be completely obvious: that they should make a good company by making a good product. And yet their reaction would be something like the reaction many physicists must have had when they first heard about the theory of relativity: a mixture of astonishment at its apparent genius, combined with a suspicion that anything so weird couldn't possibly be right. Ok, they would say, dutifully. And could you introduce us to such-and-such influential person? And remember, we want to launch on Tuesday.

> It would sometimes take founders years to grasp these simple lessons. And not because they were lazy or stupid. They just seemed blind to what was right in front of them.

Describe the main reason the writer gives for not tricking venture capitalists. Do NOT copy more than FOUR consecutive words from the passage. Second, explain the implication of the underlined words regarding the start-up founders. Do NOT copy more than FOUR consecutive words from the passage.

제 44 회 모의고사

1 Read the passage and follow the directions. [4 points]

This year the world awakened to the fact that the most powerful and sophisticated species on earth is tragically vulnerable to the tiniest and most basic of creatures. Infectious disease specialists have been warning about this for decades. And the threat comes not only from novel viruses, such as the one causing COVID-19, that jump from animals to humans but also from microbial monsters that we have helped to create through our cavalier use of antibiotics: drug-resistant bacteria such as MRSA (methicillin-resistant Staphylococcus aureus) and multidrug-resistant Acinetobacter baumannii, sometimes dubbed "Iraqibacter" because so many soldiers returning from Iraq were infected with it. The World Health Organization has predicted that deaths from resistant-superbugs will rise from roughly 700,000 a year today to nearly 10 million by 2050.

But in a splendid irony, it may turn out that viruses, so often seen as nemeses, could be our saviors in fighting a host of killer infections. As the threat from _____ has grown and the development of new antibiotics has stalled, researchers have turned their attention to bacteriophages—literally, bacteria eaters. Viruses in this class are believed to be the oldest and most numerous organisms on earth. And like guided missiles, each type has evolved to seek and destroy a specific type of bacteria. Phage therapy has long been used in eastern Europe to battle infections, but after modern antibiotics arrived in the 1940s, it was largely ignored. Interest began to pick up in this century "because the resistance issue was getting worse and worse," says Vincent Fischetti, who heads the laboratory of bacterial pathogenesis and immunology at the Rockefeller University. With modern techniques, virologists can precisely match just the right phages to a specific strain of superbug—with sometimes astonishing results.

Tom Patterson, for example, was resurrected from an overwhelming Iraqibacter infection after his wife, Steffanie Strathdee, an infectious disease epidemiologist, scoured the world for phages that might save him. The couple, both professors at the University of California, San Diego, tell his story in their 2019 book *The Perfect Predator*. Strathdee has since co-founded U.C.S.D.'s Center for Innovative Phage Applications and Therapeutics.

For now phage therapy remains experimental. In most cases, it involves making custom cocktails of several phages shown to be active in vitro against an individual patient's bug. In Patterson's case, nine different phages were used in various cocktails injected into his bloodstream multiple times a day over 18 weeks. Strathdee envisions creating a library "with tens of thousands of phages, already purified, characterized and sequenced," for medical mixologists to draw on.

Fill in the blank with the TWO most appropriate consecutive words from the passage. Second, explain how phage therapy works. Do NOT copy more than FOUR consecutive words from the passage.

2 Read the passage and follow the directions. [4 points]

[A] Whosoever would be a man, must be a nonconformist. He who would gather immortal palms must not be hindered by the name of goodness, but must explore if it be goodness. Nothing is at last sacred but the integrity of your own mind. Absolve you to yourself, and you shall have the suffrage of the world. I remember an answer which when quite young I was prompted to make to a valued adviser who was wont to importune me with the dear old doctrines of the church. On my saying, "What have I to do with the sacredness of traditions, if I live wholly from within?" He suggested, "But these impulses may be from below, not from above." I replied, "They do not seem to me to be such; but ① if I am the Devil's child, I will live then from the Devil." No law can be sacred to me but that of my nature. Good and bad are but names very readily transferable to that or this; the only right is that which is after my constitution; the only wrong what is against it.

[B] A man is to carry himself in the presence of all opposition as if every thing were titular and ephemeral but he. I am ashamed to think how easily we capitulate to badges and names, to large societies and dead institutions. Every decent and well-spoken individual affects and sways me more than is right. I ought to go upright and vital, and speak the ② rude truth in all ways. If malice and vanity wear the coat of philanthropy, shall that pass? If an angry bigot assumes this bountiful cause of Abolition, and comes to me with his last news from Barbadoes, why should I not say to him, "Go love thy infant; love thy wood-chopper; be good-natured and modest; have that grace; and never varnish your hard, uncharitable ambition with this incredible tenderness for black folk a thousand miles off. Thy love afar is spite at home." Rough and graceless would be such greeting, but truth is handsomer than the affectation of ③ _____ . Your goodness must have some edge to it,—else it is none. The doctrine of hatred must be preached, as the counteraction of the doctrine of love, when that pules* and whines.

**pule : cry plaintively*

Explain the meaning of the underlined words in ①. Do NOT copy more than FOUR consecutive words from the passage. Second, identify the FIVE consecutive words from [A] that best correspond to the meaning of the underlined "rude truth". Third, fill in the blank with the ONE most appropriate word from the passage.

3 Read the passage and follow the directions. [4 points]

In the past few years, as a surgeon, I have become increasingly aware of the scourge of the wellness industry. I am seeing patients who opt for diets, supplements or magical therapies instead of the less seductive—though scientifically grounded—medicine I have to offer. Like everyone else, I, too, am constantly bombarded with messages in advertisements and from well-meaning friends as to how this diet or that vitamin is the key to health, longevity, beauty and status.

The growth of "The Goop Lab," a platform of misinformation, privilege and anti-science rhetoric, and, more broadly, of the multitrillion-dollar wellness industry is cause for concern. On the surface, it looks full of promise and hope. Dig just a little deeper, beyond the claims of all-natural miracles—the energy healing, the cold therapy, the anti-aging treatments—and what we find is at best, a waste of money and at worst, harmful methods that actually compromise your health. Research has shown that for those with cancer, using alternative therapies such as homeopathy or specialized diets led to people opting away from proven treatments and an increased risk of dying from that cancer.

For doctors such as myself, the rise of this brand of wellness is distressing. However, medicine as a profession and a science has no doubt played a part in the genesis and growth of big wellness. For virtually the whole of its existence, medicine has disenfranchised women and, to varying degrees, continues to do so. Even as medicine has modernized with an emphasis on autonomy and resolving bias, it remains, at times, paternalistic and patriarchal. It comes as no surprise then that women are overrepresented in the wellness industry, both as consumers and providers.

To truly ensure people's safety, medicine must of course denounce dangerous, unnecessary and expensive snake oil, but it must also turn our attention inward and provide care that people need and want, communicated with compassion and supporting their autonomy. If we are to ensure that people are protected against medical half-truths and harmful remedies, my profession must move far away from the patriarchal practices that have alienated so many.

Summarize the passage following the guidelines below.

Guidelines

- Summarize the above passage in ONE paragraph.
- Provide a topic sentence, supporting ideas, and a concluding sentence based on the passage.
- Do NOT copy more than FIVE consecutive words from the passage.

제 45 회 모의고사

📚 모범답안 및 번역 p.153

1 Read the passage and follow the directions. [4 points]

 Attitude clearly matters in fighting _____. We don't know why (from my old-style materialistic perspective, I suspect that mental states feed back upon the immune system). But match people with the same cancer for age, class, health, and socio-economic status, and, in general, those with positive attitudes, with a strong will and purpose for living, with commitment to struggle, and with an active response to aiding their own treatment and not just a passive acceptance of anything doctors say tend to live longer. A few months later I asked Sir Peter Medawar, my personal scientific guru and a Nobelist in immunology, what the best prescription for success against cancer might be. "A sanguine personality," he replied. Fortunately I am, if anything, even-tempered and confident in just this manner.

 The problem may be briefly stated : What does "median mortality of eight months" signify in our vernacular? I suspect that most people, without training in statistics, would read such a statement as "I will probably be dead in eight months"—the very conclusion that must be avoided, both because this formulation is false, and because attitude matters so much.

 I was not, of course, overjoyed, but I didn't read the statement in this vernacular way either. My technical training enjoined a different perspective on "eight months median mortality." The point may seem subtle, but the consequences can be profound.

We tend to view means and medians as hard "realities," and the variation that permits their calculation as a set of transient and imperfect measurements. If the median is the reality and variation around the median just a device for calculation, then "I will probably be dead in eight months" may pass as a reasonable interpretation.

But all evolutionary biologists know that variation itself is nature's only irreducible essence. Variation is the hard reality, not a set of imperfect measures for a central tendency. Means and medians are the abstractions. Therefore, I looked at the statistics quite differently—and not only because I am an optimist who tends to see the doughnut instead of the hole, but primarily because I know that <u>variation itself is the reality</u>. I had to place myself amidst the variation.

Fill in the blank with the ONE most appropriate word from the passage. Second, what is the implied significance of "variation" in the underlined selection in regard to the speaker's situation? Do NOT copy more than FOUR consecutive words from the passage.

2 Read the passage and follow the directions. [4 points]

> The day after Stephen Jay Gould died, his obituary appeared on the front page of the New York Times, testifying to his position as the most famous scientist in the United States. His talent for synthesizing ideas and arguments, his work ethic, and—as he would have been the first to note—luck made him famous.
>
> He had not planned to write his monthly column, "This View of Life," for *Natural History* for twenty-five years, but, like his childhood hero Joe DiMaggio, Gould became known for this literary streak, which breathed new life into the half-forgotten art of the popular scientific essay, a tradition that dates back to Galileo. Like Galileo, Gould did more than interpret science for laypeople. He was also a path-breaking evolutionary theorist and a canny political organizer for leftist causes.
>
> Along with his colleague Niles Eldredge, Gould changed the way biologists view the fossil record. His concept of punctuated equilibrium argued that new species emerge relatively rapidly and then remain mostly stable for millions of years. To his more parochial colleagues' chagrin, Gould partly credited the inspiration for punctuated equilibrium to the fact that he had learned his Marxism, literally "at his daddy's knee."
>
> Though he was redbaited for this comment, Gould and Eldredge were speaking as pluralists and historicists not dogmatists. "We make a simple plea for pluralism in guiding philosophies for the basic recognition that such philosophies constrain all our thought." Historical context also acts as a constraint on new ideas. Darwin acknowledged the influence of the classical political economy of Smith and Malthus on his theory of evolution. Gould noted that his liberal upbringing and participation in the revolution of the Civil Rights Movement enabled him to recognize the importance of punctuated equilibrium's patterns of sudden and discontinuous evolutionary change. Gould also revitalized the study of evolutionary development with his influential historical survey of the subject, Ontogeny and Phylogeny, and made his mark on anthropology by insisting that human evolution looked more like a branching bush with multiple overlapping lineages than a ladder of predictable stages.

Explain what can be inferred from the underlined part about Stephen Jay Gould. Do NOT copy more than THREE consecutive words from the passage. Second, in what way is the Civil Rights Movement related to Gould's understanding of evolution? Do NOT copy more than THREE consecutive words from the passage.

3. Read the passage and follow the directions. [4 points]

In the dead of night he is wakened by a strange sound, an animal-like scratching and scuffling just outside the bedroom door. Some wild creature sharpening its claws, shredding the carpet—though the muffled sound of heavy breathing is not like an animal. It is utterly and horribly human. He reaches out for her, but his arm moves in the dark through a vast and empty space. She isn't there. He is alone in the bed and there is something or someone strange in the house. In an instant he is rigid, deafened by the sound of his own heart. Eventually, after a long time, the house is quiet again, just the distant chugging of the fridge, the dog gently groaning in its sleep.

He is reassured by the sleeping dog, realizes he must have dreamed the alien sounds, dreamed into being fears long dormant. These fears, acquiring life, had turned on him like vengeful demons: unnerving, but not as bad as an intruder in the house. Better they assault just him, in his dreams, than his children. He thinks of the children sleeping, feels a sudden pain that softens into tenderness and slowly passes. Then, remembering that the children are children no longer, have not lived at home for years, he stretches, breathes deeply, and folds into sleep again. He drifts in and out, dozing for a while, enjoying the sensation of relief, a sense of reprieve, a close shave that brings you to the edge—even if only momentarily—of a precipice.

Suddenly a sharp and ugly sensation yanks him into wakefulness. He leaps up, finds himself crouching on the bed, ready to spring, go for the jugular. A sliver of light moves swiftly across the crack under the door. Silence. No gentle groans or somnolent growls, even the dog is silent. Or silenced. He anticipates a terrible almost-human howling, envisages Max Cady in *Cape Fear* prowling the house, passing through the walls like the holy ghost, invisible. He can feel the presence of a figure on the other side of the bedroom door, someone holding their breath, listening to the silence. His own eyes grow accustomed to the dark, although he cannot tell whether he is now seeing or feeling in the dark.

Explain why he was reassured by the sleeping dog as shown in the underlined part. Do NOT copy more than THREE consecutive words from the passage. Second, write the ONE most appropriate word from the passage that best describes the emotional state of the main character.

4 Read the passage and follow the directions. [4 points]

> Tucked away in a perpetually foggy basin near the Pacific Ocean. Lowell is the only public high school in San Francisco that admits students on the basis of academic merit. The largest feeder to the University of California system, Lowell sends many of its graduates to the country's most selective universities. Such imagery might bring to mind whiz kids who are leaps and bounds smarter than those who lack the top-notch test scores and grades to get in. What I discovered was that Lowell students were distinguished more by their work ethic than by their intelligence. I once asked students in my homeroom how much they studied. The typical answer? Hours and hours. Not in a week, but in a single day. Still, like at any other school, there was tremendous variation in how hard students worked and how well they performed. Just as I'd found in New York, some of the students I expected to excel, because math came so easy to them, did worse than their classmates. On the other hand, some of my ⓐ hardest workers were consistently my highest performers on tests and quizzes. One of these very hard workers was David Luong. David was in my freshman algebra class. There were two kinds of algebra classes at Lowell : the accelerated track led to Advanced Placement Calculus by senior year, and the regular track, which I was teaching, didn't. The students in my class hadn't scored high enough on Lowell's math placement exam to get into the accelerated track. David didn't stand out at first. He was quiet and sat toward the back of the room. He didn't raise his hand a lot; he rarely volunteered to come to the board to solve problems. But I soon noticed that every time I graded an assignment, David had turned in perfect work. He aced my quizzes and tests. When I marked one of his answers as incorrect, it was more often my error than his. He was just so hungry to learn.

> I began to wonder what the heck this kid was doing in my class. Once I understood ⓑ <u>how ridiculous the situation was</u>, I marched David into the office of my department chair. It didn't take long to explain what was going on. Fortunately, the chair was a wise and wonderful teacher who placed a higher value on kids than on bureaucratic rules. She immediately started the paperwork to switch David out of my class and into the accelerated track.

Describe who the "hardest workers" are according to the writer of the passage. Second, explain why the writer thinks the "situation" is ridiculous. Do NOT copy more than THREE consecutive words from the passage.

제 46 회 모의고사

모범답안 및 번역 p.156

1 Read the passage and follow the directions. [4 points]

In the 1990s, an army of clones invaded Germany. Within a decade, they had spread to Italy, Croatia, Slovakia, Hungary, Sweden, France, Japan and Madagascar—wreaking havoc in rivers and lakes, rice paddies and swamps; in waters warm and cold, acidic and basic. The culprits : six-inch-long, lobster-like creatures called marbled crayfish.

Scientists suspect that sometime around 1995, a genetic mutation allowed a pet crayfish to reproduce asexually, giving rise to a new, all-female species that could make clones of itself from its unfertilized eggs. Deliberately or accidentally, some of these mutants were released from aquariums into the wild, where they rapidly multiplied into the millions, threatening native waterways species and ecosystems.

But ⓐ <u>their success is strange</u>. "All marbled crayfish which exist today derive from a single animal," said Günter Vogt, a biologist at Heidelberg University. "They are all genetically identical." Ordinarily, the absence of genetic diversity makes a population exceedingly vulnerable to the vagaries of its environment. Yet the marbled crayfish have managed to thrive around the globe.

A closer look reveals that the crayfishes' uniformity is only genome-deep. According to studies conducted by Vogt and others in the mid-2000s, these aquatic clones actually vary quite a bit in their color, size, behavior and longevity. Which means that something other than their genes is inspiring that _____ⓑ_____ .

ⓐ Common sense tells us that if it's not nature, it's nurture : environmental influences that interact with an animal's genome to generate different outcomes for various traits. But that's not the whole story. New research on crayfish and scores of other organisms is revealing an important role for a third, often-overlooked source of variation and diversity—a surprising foundation for what makes us unique that begins in the first days of an embryo's development : random, intrinsic noise.

Explain the meaning of the underlined words in ⓐ. Do NOT copy more than THREE consecutive words from the passage. Second, fill in the blank with the ONE most appropriate word from the passage. Third, describe all elements that have an affect on generating different traits, according to the passage.

2 Read the passage and follow the directions. [4 points]

Nir Eyal, the author of *Indistractable* says that distractions are actions that pull us away from what we plan to do. The opposite of distraction is not focus, it is traction. Anything can be a distraction, just as anything can be traction. If you check your email when you plan to work on a big project, you're distracted. Conversely, if you plan to play video games, the game is not a distraction. It is traction. A diversion is a refocusing on attention. Diversions can be wonderful. Procrastination is when we give into a distraction instead of doing what we plan to do.

There are many theories on why we procrastinate, and why this unwanted habit is so hard to break. In the 1930s psychologists trained rats to do a certain behavior, e.g. pressing a lever, by giving them small rewards. Once trained, the scientists discovered that when the rats were given rewards unpredictably, on a variable ratio schedule of every 3-7 times, they would perform the trained behavior more often. More remarkably, with randomized rewards, the behavior became hard to extinguish. Getting rewards releases dopamine in the brain, and even the expectation of a reward has this effect.

Not only rats, but also humans have a desire for randomness. We get excited by unpredictability. Watching sports—who will score/win? Listening to radio—what song will they play next? Shopping—is there a bargain on the sale? In this age we are just a mouse click away from randomness. Most of us carry a smartphone everywhere we go, and a big part of the appeal is the excitement finding out what is "new". For some it is more addictive than sugar and heroin.

Engaging in randomness itself is not bad, but when we use it to _____ it can be hard to stop. Just one more click, scroll, or tab. Many of the tasks that we plan to do, like work, studying and chores, don't have immediate rewards. The benefits of work and studying are in the future, whereas checking Instagram or Facebook hits the reward systems in the brain immediately. Did I get any likes on my post? What stories hide under the bell-icon?

One popular technique that I and many others use for fighting procrastination is timeboxing a.k.a. The pomodoro Technique. The technique prescribes a 25-minute session work followed by a 5-minute break. There is a strict rule. During the 25-minute work session you must only do one task and do not interrupt yourself e.g. by checking email. No distractions—only traction.

Fill in the blank with the ONE most appropriate word from the passage. Second, describe what is lacking from work and study that makes these tasks have less "traction".

3 Read the passage and follow the directions. [4 points]

Largely because of a quirk of brain development, adolescents, on average, experience more anxiety and fear and have a harder time learning how not to be afraid than either children or adults. Different regions and circuits of the brain mature at very different rates. It turns out that the brain circuit for processing fear—the amygdala—is precocious and develops way ahead of the prefrontal cortex, the seat of reasoning and executive control. This means that adolescents have a brain that is wired with an enhanced capacity for fear and anxiety, but is relatively underdeveloped when it comes to calm reasoning.

You may wonder why, if adolescents have such enhanced capacity for anxiety, they are such novelty seekers and risk takers. It would seem that the two traits are at odds. The answer, in part, is that the brain's reward center, just like its fear circuit, matures earlier than the prefrontal cortex. That reward center drives much of teenagers' risky behavior. This behavioral paradox also helps explain why adolescents are particularly prone to injury and trauma. The top three killers of teenagers are accidents, homicide and suicide.

The brain-development lag has huge implications for how we think about anxiety and how we treat it. It suggests that anxious adolescents may not be very responsive to psychotherapy that attempts to teach them to be unafraid, like cognitive behavior therapy, which is zealously prescribed for teenagers. What we have learned should also make us think twice—and then some—about the ever rising use of stimulants in young people, because these drugs may worsen anxiety and make it harder for teenagers to do what they are developmentally supposed to do : learn to be unafraid when it is appropriate to do so. Our promiscuous use of stimulants impair the ability of adolescents to suppress learned fear, something that is a normal part of development, and make them more fearful adults. And stimulants are likely to increase the risk of PTSD in adolescents exposed to trauma.

We do know adolescents are not just carefree novelty seekers and risk takers; they are uniquely vulnerable to anxiety and have a hard time learning to be unafraid of passing dangers. Parents have to realize that adolescent anxiety is to be expected, and to comfort their teenagers, and themselves, by reminding them that they will grow up and out of it soon enough. These things, when considered properly, will leave us with a better understanding on the threats facing adolescents and how to more healthily address them.

Write a summary following the guidelines below.

Guidelines

- Summarize the above passage in ONE paragraph.
- Provide a topic sentence, supporting ideas, and a concluding sentence based on the passage.
- Do NOT copy more than FIVE consecutive words from the passage.

제 47 회 모의고사

1 Read the passage and follow the directions. [4 points]

> On Monday, out of the clear blue sky, the local travel Agent telephoned Janice to tell her that she had won two tickets to the Albuquerque International Balloon Fiesta in New Mexico. Janice and John, her husband, had always wanted to go Ballooning at the festival, but they thought that ① such a trip was beyond their reach. She was walking on air when she telephoned John to tell him the good news. At first, John thought that Janice was joking and full of hot air. But when he realized that she was not building castles in the air, his annoyance vanished into thin air. As soon as John came home from work, Janice and John eagerly talked about the trip. Soon their plans grew by leaps and bounds. Janice's head was in the clouds all the time because she was anticipating the trip and her first balloon ride. Two weeks before the trip, Janice was rushed to the hospital. After examining her, the doctor burst her bubble when he said that she would need an operation. The doctor's decision went over like a lead balloon. Janice was devastated. Now their balloon vacation was up in the air. She knew that without the free tickets, the cost of the trip would be sky high. But Janice was lucky. The operation was not serious, and she begged the doctor to let her go on the trip. One week later, Janice and John took their dream trip. They were on cloud nine as their balloon rose into the blue sky. Janice thought : ② it pays to reach for the sky.

Explain the meaning of the underlined words in ①. Second, explain what Janice thought in the underlined ②. Do NOT copy more than FOUR consecutive words from the passage.

_____
_____
_____

2 Read the passage and follow the directions. [4 points]

> Matt, a first-year teacher, walked into Bill's classroom, excited to observe him. Matt had a lot of respect for Bill as a teacher and looked forward to seeing effective classroom management techniques in action. Bill, a teaching veteran, was well liked by students and colleagues. Their principal had recommended that Matt observe Bill, noting how he engaged students, a key to limiting disciplinary interruptions. Matt founded a desk in the back of the room and prepared to take notes.
>
> As students settled into their seats, Bill welcomed them cheerily. He then reminded them that one of their benchmark tests was scheduled for the next day. Following a brief overview of strategies for studying the material, Bill asked whether they wanted to play a game. "Let's see how prepared you are for the exam."
>
> "First, we need to split ourselves into two teams," Bill explained, then asked students how they wanted to do so. As students discussed options, Bill walked to the back of the room and said to Matt, "If you let students make decisions, they'll take ① <u>ownership of their learning</u>."
>
> One student suggested they form teams by gender, "boys versus girls," eliciting enthusiastic support from several classmates. Bill sent the young men to one side of the room and the young women to the other side of room, then proceeded to ask each team questions while keeping count of correct responses.
>
> After ten minutes the "girls" team was well ahead of the "boys" team, leading a couple young men to joke they were "letting the girls win." A couple young women responded by reminding their male classmates that the "girls" won the previous two games, as well. Following several minutes of the teams mocking one another, Bill tried to refocus all the students by announcing, "If you guys don't settle down we'll end the game."

After class, as students left the room, Matt heard several laughing and making disparaging remarks to one another, debating about which gender was most intelligent. Bill approached Matt and warmly said, "The students love competitions and don't realize how much they're learning in the process."

He then looked down and, seeing Matt's notes, noticed he had written and circled "gender stereotypes" in his notebook. "Whoa! That's what you are focusing on?" Bill asked. "Boys versus girls : that's what the students love to do." He then counseled Matt, "You're still new at this and will learn soon enough that, as long as the students are engaged and learning, ② that other stuff doesn't matter."

Provide an example of "ownership of their learning" from the passage. Second, identify to what the underlined words in ② refer.

3. Read the passage and follow the directions. [4 points]

How did the Earth get its oceans? The primordial Earth was a seething ball of magma, so the water that it began with would have evaporated into space. As a result, planetary scientists have long debated which of two types of objects, comets or asteroids, were more responsible for delivering Earth's water.

A new study, published in *Science,* says that asteroids were the source. The authors, led by Conel Alexander of the Carnegie Institution of Washington, in Washington DC, analysed the isotopic abundances of nitrogen and hydrogen in 86 primitive meteorites, and found that they coordinate with Earth's.

Asteroids had already been the favored source. Studies of solar system dynamics suggest that there was a period of time around 3.9 billion years ago, called the Late Heavy Bombardment, during which the Earth would have been barraged, mostly by asteroids.

Even though _____ are ideal sources, with their high percentage content of water, rich with amino acids, there are a few strikes against them. Six studies of comets from the Oort Cloud found that their isotopic ratios of heavy hydrogen were much higher than Earth's. When a 2011 *Nature* paper found isotopic levels of heavy hydrogen in the comet Hartley 2 to be similar to Earth's, it revived interest in water-from-comets idea. But Alexander and his colleagues suggest that the overall levels of heavy hydrogen in Hartley 2 (and not just the levels in the comet's ice) would be much higher.

Explain why the Earth would not retain its original water. Do NOT copy more than FOUR consecutive words from the passage. Second, fill in the blank with the ONE most appropriate word from the passage.

4 Read the passage and follow the directions. [4 points]

It seems necessary towards moving the passions of people advanced in life to any considerable degree, that the objects designed for that purpose, besides their being in some measure new, should be capable of exciting pain or pleasure from other causes. Pain and pleasure are simple ideas, incapable of definition. People are not liable to be mistaken in their feelings, but they are very frequently wrong in the names they give them, and in their reasonings about them. Many are of the opinion, that pain arises necessarily from the removal of some pleasure; as they think pleasure does from the ceasing or diminution of some pain.

For my part, I am rather inclined to imagine, that pain and pleasure, in their most simple and natural manner of affecting, are each of a positive nature, and by no means necessarily dependent on each other for their existence. The human mind is often, and I think it is for the most part, in a state neither of pain nor pleasure, which I call a state of indifference. When I am carried from this state into a state of actual pleasure, it does not appear necessary that I should pass through the medium of any sort of _____. If in such a state of indifference, or ease, or tranquillity, or call it what you please, you were to be suddenly entertained with a concert of music; or suppose some object of a fine shape, and bright, lively colours, to be presented before you; or imagine your smell is gratified with the fragrance of a rose; in all the several senses, of hearing, smelling and tasting, you undoubtedly find a pleasure. Yet if I inquire into the state of your mind previous to these gratifications, you will hardly tell me that they found you in any kind of pain.

Suppose on the other hand, a man in the same state of indifference, to receive a violent blow, or to drink of some bitter potion; here is no removal of pleasure; and yet here is felt in every sense which is affected, a pain very distinguishable. <u>I can never persuade myself that pleasure and pain are mere relations, which can only exist as they are contrasted.</u>

Fill in the blank with the ONE most appropriate word from the passage. Second, explain what the writer tries to argue in the last sentence. Do NOT copy more than FOUR consecutive words from the passage.

제 48 회 모의고사

모범답안 및 번역 p.163

1 Read the passage and follow the directions. [4 points]

Sunburns readily advertise that we've had fun in the sun, and perhaps have been a bit careless, but what exactly goes on in our cells to produce the painful, red inflammation has not been clear.

Now, researchers have discovered a molecular signal that triggers sunburns. When our skin cells are exposed to ultraviolet B (UVB) radiation, a specific form of RNA, called micro-RNA, is damaged, the study found. (RNA is similar in structure to DNA, which makes up our genes.) This damaged RNA is then released as a signal of solar injury, and prompts neighboring, healthy cells to stimulate the production of factors that promote _____.

The entire process is intended to remove sun-damaged cells, which could turn cancerous if not cleared away. "The cells of our skin can sense dead, sun-damaged cells, because the cells release damaged RNA," said study researcher Dr. Richard Gallo, professor of medicine at University of California, San Diego School of Medicine. While other factors likely play a role in the inflammatory process we see as a sunburn, the findings suggest the damaged RNA molecules serve as a marker for radiation-caused injury.

The findings may have implications for medical conditions, the researchers said. For example, one treatment for the skin condition psoriasis* is exposure to UV light. But while the light can relieve symptoms, it also increases skin cancer risk. The new findings suggest that certain RNA molecules could be used in place of UV therapy, and produce the same benefit. In addition, people with certain autoimmune conditions get a burning sensation with very little exposure to UV light, before unhealthy cell damage has occurred. Blocking the micro-RNA pathway may be a way to reduce _____ in these patients. However, healthy people without such conditions would not want to block this pathway just to prevent sunburn, because it is an important way for the body to heal and get rid of damaged cells. "The inflammatory response is a normal part of our protection against the sun," Gallo said.

*psoriasis : a skin disease that causes red, itchy scaly patches

Fill in the blanks with the same ONE most appropriate word from the passage. Second, explain why the new findings could lead to new treatments for psoriasis. Do NOT copy more than FOUR consecutive words from the passage.

2 Read the passage and follow the directions. [4 points]

The caption of a Roman print of 1601 claims the engraving represents a giant whale that has been washed ashore near Ancona the same year and "was drawn accurately from nature". The claim would be more trustworthy if there did not exist an earlier print recording a similar 'scoop' from the Dutch coast in 1598. But surely the Dutch artists of the late sixteenth century, those masters of realism, would be able to portray a whale? Not quite, it seems, for the creature looks suspiciously as if it had ears, and whales with ears, I am assured on higher authority, do not exist. The draughtsman probably mistook one of the whale's flippers for a(n) _____ and therefore placed it far too close to the eye. He, too, was misled by a familiar schema, the schema of the typical head. To draw an unfamiliar sight presents greater difficulties than is usually realized. And this, I suppose, was also the reason why the Italian preferred to copy the whale from another print. We need not doubt the part of the caption that tells the news from Ancona, but to portray it 'from the life' was not worth the trouble.

In this respect the fate of exotic creatures in the illustrated books of the last few centuries before the advent of photography is as instructive as it is amusing. When Albrecht Durer, a painter of the German Renaissance, published his famous woodcut of a rhinoceros, he had to rely on secondhand evidence which he filled in from his own imagination, coloured, no doubt, by what he had learned of the most famous of exotic beasts, the dragon with its armoured body. Yet it has been shown that this <u>half-invented</u> creature served as a model for all renderings of the rhinoceros, even in natural-history books, up to the eighteenth century. When, in 1790, James Bruce published a drawing of the beast in his *Travels to Discover the Source of the Nile*, he proudly showed that he was aware of the fact.

Fill in the blank with the ONE most appropriate word from the passage. If necessary, change the word form. Second, explain why the writer employs the term "half-invented". Do NOT copy more than FOUR consecutive words from the passage.

3 Read the passage and follow the directions. [4 points]

> Once, work was a major source of friendships. We took our families to company picnics and invited our colleagues over for dinner. Now, we go to the office to be efficient, not to form bonds.
>
> Why are Americans so determined to get down to business? The economic explanation is that long-term employment has essentially vanished : Instead of spending our careers at one organization, we expect to jump ship every few years. Since we don't plan to stick around, we don't invest in the same way. We view co-workers as transitory ties, greeting them with arms-length civility while reserving real camaraderie for outside work. When we're constantly connected with old friends on social media—and we can travel to visit them anytime—why bother making new ones? With 24/7 connectivity, we face a growing time famine, where the pressure to get work done may eclipse the desire to socialize.
>
> When we see our jobs primarily as a means to leisure, it's easy to convince ourselves that efficiency should reign supreme at work so we have time for friendships outside work. But we may be underestimating the impact of workplace friendships on our happiness—and our effectiveness. Jobs are more satisfying when they provide opportunities to form friendships. Research shows that groups of friends outperform groups of acquaintances in both decision making and effort tasks. When friends work together, they're more trusting and committed to one another's success. That means they share more information and spend more time helping—and as long as they don't hold back on constructive criticism out of politeness, they make better choices and get more done.
>
> Whether we bond at work is a personal decision, but it may involve less effort and vulnerability than we realize. A high-quality connection doesn't require "a deep or intimate relationship." A single interaction marked by respect, trust and mutual engagement is enough to generate energy for both parties. However small they appear, those moments of connection can transform a transaction into a relationship.

Summarize the passage following the guidelines below.

― Guidelines ―
- Summarize the above passage in ONE paragraph.
- Provide a topic sentence, supporting ideas, and a concluding sentence based on the passage.
- Do NOT copy more than FIVE consecutive words from the passage.

제 49 회 모의고사

모범답안 및 번역 p.167

1 Read the passage and follow the directions. [4 points]

> Do you realize that the only time in our lives when we like to get old is when we're kids? If you're less than 10 years old, you're so excited about aging that you think in fractions. "How old are you?" "I'm four and a half!" You're never thirty-six and a half. You're four and a half, going on five! That's the key. You get into your teens, now they can't hold you back. You jump to the next number, or even a few ahead. "How old are you?" "I'm gonna be 16!" You could be 13, but hey, you're gonna be 16! And then the greatest day of your life . . you become 21. Even the words sound like a ceremony . . . YOU BECOME 21. YESSSS!!!
>
> But then you turn 30. Oooohh, what happened there? Makes you sound like bad milk! He TURNED; we had fractions to throw him out. There's no fun now, you're Just a sour-dumpling, What's wrong? What's changed? You BECOME 21, you TURN 30, then you're PUSHING 40. Whoa! Put on the brakes, it's all slipping away. Before you know it, you REACH 50 and your dreams are gone. But wait!!! You MAKE it to 60. You didn't think you would! So you BECOME 21, TURN 30, PUSH 40, REACH 50 and MAKE it to 60.
>
> You've built up so much speed that you HIT 70! After that it's a day-by-day thing; you HIT Wednesday! You get into your 80s and every day is a complete cycle; you HIT lunch; YOU TURN 4:30; you REACH bedtime. And it doesn't end there. Into the 90s, you start going backwards; "I was JUST 92." Then a strange thing happens. If you make it over 100, you become a little kid again. "I'm 100 and a half!" May you all make it to a healthy 100 and a half!!

Explain the meaning of the underlined words. Second, what similarity do kids share with the very old according to the passage?

2 Read the passage and follow the directions. [4 points]

It is worth looking at one or two aspects of the way a mother behaves towards her baby. The usual fondling, cuddling and cleaning require little comment, but the position in which she holds the baby against her body when resting is rather revealing. Careful American studies have disclosed the fact that 80 percent of mothers cradle their infants in their left arms, holding them against the left side of their bodies. If asked to explain the significance of this preference most people reply that it is obviously the result of the predominance of right-handedness in the population. By holding the babies in their left arms, the mothers keep their dominant arm free for manipulations. But a detailed analysis shows that this is not the case. True, there is a slight difference between right-handed and left-handed females, but not enough to provide an adequate explanation. It emerges that 83 percent of right-handed mothers hold the baby on the left side, but then so do 78 percent of left-handed mothers. In other words, only 22 percent of the left-handed mothers have their dominant hands free for actions. Clearly there must be some other, less obvious explanation.

The only other clue comes from the fact that the heart is on the left side of the mother's body. Could it be that the sound of her heartbeat is the vital factor? And in what way? Thinking along these lines it was argued that perhaps during its existence inside the body of the mother, the growing embryo becomes fixated ('imprinted') on the sound of the heart beat. If this is so, then the re-discovery of this familiar sound after birth might have a calming effect on the infant, especially as it has just been thrust into a strange and frighteningly new world outside. If this is so then the mother, either instinctively or by an unconscious series of trials and errors, would soon arrive at the discovery that her baby is more at peace if held on the _____ against her heart.

Explain which result of the research directly opposes the argument "holding the babies in their left arms, the mothers keep their dominant arm free for manipulations". Second, fill in the blank with the ONE most appropriate word from the passage.

3 Read the passage and follow the directions. [4 points]

> Sometimes, history really does seem to repeat itself. After the US Civil War, for example, a wave of urban violence fuelled by ethnic and class resentment swept across the country, peaking in around 1870. Internal strife spiked again in around 1920, when race riots, workers' strikes and a surge of anti-Communist feeling led many people to think that revolution was imminent. And in around 1970, unrest crested once more, with violent student demonstrations, political assassinations, riots and terrorism.
>
> To Peter Turchin, who studies population dynamics at the University of Connecticut in Storrs, the appearance of three peaks of political instability at roughly 50-year intervals is not a coincidence. For the past 15 years, Turchin has been taking the mathematical techniques that once allowed him to track predator-prey cycles in forest ecosystems, and applying them to human _____. He has analysed historical records on economic activity, demographic trends and outbursts of violence in the United States, and has come to the conclusion that a new wave of internal strife is already on its way. The peak should occur in about 2020, he says, and will probably be at least as high as the one in around 1970. "I hope it won't be as bad as 1870," he adds.
>
> Turchin's approach—which he calls cliodynamics after Clio, the ancient Greek muse of history—is part of a groundswell of efforts to apply scientific methods to history by identifying and modelling the broad social forces that Turchin and his colleagues say shape all human societies. It is an attempt to show that "history is not just one damn thing after another", says Turchin, paraphrasing a saying often attributed to the late British historian Arnold Toynbee. Cliodynamics is viewed with deep scepticism by most academic historians, who tend to see history as a complex stew of chance, individual foibles and one-of-a-kind situations that no broad-brush 'science of history' will ever capture. "After a century of grand theory, from Marxism and social Darwinism to structuralism and postmodernism, most historians have abandoned the belief in general laws," said Robert Darnton, a cultural historian at Harvard University.

Fill in the blank with the ONE most appropriate word from the passage. Second, explain the meaning of the underlined words.

4 Read the passage and follow the directions. [4 points]

Ms. Ward loved geography. She inspired and motivated students by telling them they were learning material typically reserved for older students.

The first unit Ms. Ward planned for the new school year focused on California. Although Rustin School, where Ms. Ward taught, was in the Midwest, she thought it would be a fun state with which to kick off the year. Students at Rustin represented a wide range of socioeconomic and racial diversity, but she knew many of them were interested in ocean beaches. California, in her mind, fit well with this theme.

Ms. Ward gathered her students on the carpet and began writing on a flip chart. Several students whispered excitedly as she wrote "California" at the top of the sheet. Although Ms. Ward was happy to see their excitement, she reminded them to remain quiet and raise their hands if they had something to say. Immediately several hands flew up.

"Are we going to learn about California?" Maddy asked.

"Yes," Ms. Ward replied. "We will be learning about California in many of our subjects throughout the week." Students chattered excitedly again and Ms. Ward reminded them to remain quiet : "I cannot understand you if so many of you talk at once."

After explaining the unit a bit more, Ms. Ward asked who had been to California. DeQuan raised his hand. When Ms. Ward called on him he said, "A few days ago, I was at my grandmother's house watching television with my little sister, but she was crying so I couldn't hear very well. I told her to be quiet and gave her a toy to play with because the person on TV…"

Ms. Ward interrupted DeQuan and reminded him that the question she asked was who had been to California. Feeling a little angry at the side chatter and DeQuan's indirect answer, she reminded the class that now was not the time for stories.

"Please raise your hand *only* if you can answer the question," she said. Upon hearing this, DeQuan added in an angry tone, "I was saying that the person on TV said the show was sponsored by a company that makes raisins, which are my favorite snack, and that the raisins are made in California!"

Ms. Ward reminded DeQuan he needed to raise his hand if he had something to say, and added that his tone was full of disrespect. Attempting to refocus the group, she asked, "Has anyone been to Disneyland?" Maddy raised her hand and said, "I have. It's in California, and it is sunny and warm there. It's also far away because we were on the airplane for a long time."

"You're right," Ms. Ward replied as she wrote "warm" and "sunny" along with the phrase "far from Rustin School" on the flip chart.

"Any other words to describe California?" she asked. As several others raised their hands, Ms. Ward noticed DeQuan still looked _____. Anticipating another outburst, she cheerfully said, "DeQuan, please try to compose yourself so that you can remain seated with the group." Hearing this, DeQuan stood, walked to his desk, and slouched in his chair.

Oh, no, thought Ms. Ward. *He must not have heard me correctly.* Knowing time was passing quickly and that she needed to finish the lesson, Ms. Ward continued teaching but wondered how she should address DeQuan if his negative behavior persisted.

Explain why the geography teaching did not begin in the students' home state. Second, fill in the blank with the ONE most appropriate word from the passage.

제 50 회 모의고사

1 Read the passage and follow the directions. [4 points]

A small company is trying to bring to market a genetically engineered apple that does not turn brown when sliced or bruised. But <u>it has much of the rest of the apple industry seeing red</u>.

The company, Okanagan Specialty Fruits, says the nonbrowning apple will prove popular with consumers and food service companies and help increase sales of apples, in part by making sliced apples more attractive to serve or sell. While Americans have been eating genetically engineered foods since the 1990s, those have been mainly processed foods. The Arctic Apple, as it is being called, could become one of the first genetically engineered versions of a fruit that people directly bite into.

But the U.S. Apple Association, which represents the American apple industry, opposes introduction of the product, as do some other industry organizations. They say that, while they do not believe that the genetic engineering is dangerous, it could undermine the fruit's image as a healthy and natural food, the one that keeps the doctor away and is as American as, well, apple pie. Neal Carter, the founder and president of the company said the nonbrowning apples could improve industry sales, much as baby carrots did for carrot sales. A whole apple is "for many people too big a commitment," he said. "If you had a bowl of apples at a meeting, people wouldn't take an apple out of the bowl. But if you had a plate of apple slices, everyone would take a slice." Consumption of fresh apples in the United States has fallen from about 20 pounds a year for each person in the late 1980s to about 16 pounds now, according to the Agriculture Department.

Apple _____ are already becoming more popular as a healthful snack, sold in bags in supermarkets and included by McDonald's in its Happy Meals for children. They are often coated with vitamin C and calcium to prevent browning and preserve crispness. But that can affect the taste, Mr. Carter said. He also said that growers would have fewer apples rejected by supermarkets because of the minor bruising that is common from handling of the fruit. Arctic Apples, which would first be available in the Golden Delicious and Granny Smith varieties, contain a synthetic gene that sharply reduces production of polyphenol oxidase, an enzyme responsible for the browning.

Explain the meaning of the underlined words. Next, fill in the blank with the ONE most appropriate word from the passage.

2. Read the passage and follow the directions. [4 points]

"It should be possible to make a precious stone that not only looks like the real thing, but that is the real thing", said a chemist many years ago. "The only difference should be that one crystal would be made by man, the other by nature."

At first this did not seem like a particularly hard task. Scientists began to try making synthetic diamonds towards the end of the eighteenth century. It was at this time that a key scientific fact was discovered: diamonds are a form of carbon, which is a very common element. Graphite, the black mineral that is used for the 'lead' in your pencil, is made of it, too. The only difference, we know today, is that the carbon atoms have been packed together in a slightly different way. The chemists were fired with enthusiasm: Why not change a cheap and plentiful substance, carbon, into a rare and expensive one, diamond?

You have probably heard about the alchemists who for centuries tried to turn plain lead or iron into gold. They failed, because gold is completely different from lead or iron. Transforming carbon into diamonds, however, is not illogical at all. This change takes place in ___①___, so it should be possible to make it happen in the laboratory.

It should be possible, but for one hundred and fifty years every effort failed. During this period, none the less, several people believed that they had solved the diamond riddle. One of these was a French scientist who produced crystals that seemed to be the real thing. After the man's death, however, a curious rumour began to go the rounds. The story told that one of the scientist's assistants had simply put tiny pieces of genuine diamonds into the carbon mixture. He was bored with the work, and he wanted to make the old chemist happy.

The first real success came more than sixty years later in the laboratories of the General Electric Company. Scientists there had been working for a number of years on a process designed to duplicate nature's work. Far below the earth's surface, carbon is subjected to incredibly heavy pressure and extremely high ___②___. Under these conditions the carbon turns into diamonds. For a long time the laboratory attempts failed, simply because no suitable machinery existed. What was needed was some sort of pressure chamber in which the carbon could be subjected to between 800,000 and 1,800,000 pounds of pressure to the square inch, at a temperature of between 2200 and 4400°F.

Fill in each blank with the ONE most appropriate word from the passage respectively. Second, describe what "the diamond riddle" is.

3 Read the passage and follow the directions. [4 points]

To understand why a pandemic such as COVID-19 has had such deleterious effects, we must examine why the study of diagnosis and treatment of disease separated itself from the study of preventing disease—or, more succinctly, why medicine and public health are considered apart from each other. Tracing this unfortunate disconnect leads us to a cause from 110 years ago : the 1910 Flexner report.

In the early 1900s, the American Medical Association commissioned the Carnegie Foundation to help reform medical education. Together they hired Abraham Flexner to assess the state of medical education. After visiting every medical school in North America, he produced the report. The Flexner report—and the money tied to its implementation—is the medical education system we're familiar with today : competitive admission criteria, traditional pedagogy and the scientific method as its central tenets. The report established the individual biomedical model, which focuses exclusively on biologic causes of disease, excluding any social and environmental factors, as the gold standard.

It also led to the disproportionate closing of historically Black medical colleges, contributing to physician workforce disparities that still exist today, and effectively cleaved the study of medicine from the study of public health. So, still, many researchers often cite the individual attribute of race as a risk factor for disease without interrogating the associated environmental experience of racism. Similarly, the lens in medical education is often inclusive of poverty but not oppression, race but not racism.

The Flexner report needs to be supplanted by another document that stitches medicine and public health back together. A replacement for the Flexner report can catalyze concrete action and may provide cover. Even if it is only a symbolic gesture to indicate abandonment of outdated ways of thinking, the American Medical Association would be wise to commission another report to show that Flexner's thinking, while revolutionary for his time, isn't applicable anymore.

Summarize the passage following the guidelines below.

Guidelines

- Summarize the above passage in ONE paragraph.
- Provide a topic sentence, supporting ideas, and a concluding sentence based on the passage.
- Do NOT copy more than FIVE consecutive words from the passage.

제 51 회 모의고사

1 **Read the passage and follow the directions.** [4 points]

> You want to be rich, do you? Do you fancy driving around in a Ferrari, flying first class and staying in luxury hotels? In that case you're going to need to be a millionaire. But what's the best way of making a million be the time you're 40? Well, one good idea is to take a look at someone who has been successful and see how they did it. In the UK there's no better example than Richard Branson, the boss of the Virgin empire.
>
> Today Virgin is an enormous group of companies, all operating independently. The only unifying factor is Mr. Branson's enthusiasm and the Virgin brand. The group has operated over 200 Virgin companies. Many analysts believe that this is taking brand-stretching too far, and that sooner or later Virgin will lose its identity in minds of customers. However, Mr. Branson has always proved his critics wrong.
>
> Mr. Branson started his empire in his bedroom at the age of 17 and he's come a long way since then. It all began when Mr. Branson spotted a niche in the market for a student magazine. Up until then, student magazines were all about schools and what was happening at school or university. Mr. Branson realised that the students were interested in other things, apart from school life, and so he decided to launch a magazine that communicated with them, with articles about music and films. His mother lent him £4 to help him start the magazine and that was it. Later, his headmaster said: "Congratulations, Branson. I predict that by the time you're 40, you'll either be a prisoner or a millionaire".

Soon, selling records became more lucrative than selling subscriptions to the magazine. Mr. Branson decided to set up a shop, but he didn't have any money to pay the rent. At the time, Mr. Branson was still a teenager and no banks were going to give him credit. Most people would have given up at this point but not Mr. Branson. He found an empty office above a shoe shop, and persuaded the owner of the shop to let him rent it for free. How did he do that? Well, he guaranteed the owner that so many people would visit Mr. Branson's new shop, that the owner would sell more shoes as a result and so make more profits than he would from the rent. And it worked!

Now he had a successful business based on selling an established product at a competitive price, but he still didn't have a name. There were many suggestions from the people who were helping him, but Mr. Branson didn't like any of them. Then one of his collaborators suggested "Virgin", because, she said, "we are complete virgins at business". And the name stuck.

What can be inferred about Branson's character from his headmaster's saying? Second, explain the meaning of the underlined words in the last sentence of the passage. Do NOT copy more than FOUR consecutive words from the passage.

2 Read the passage and follow the directions. [4 points]

Thanksgiving visits home bring with them any number of awkward conversations, from fights over politics to nudges about when you and your significant other are going to start having children; who doesn't love a serving of guilt about not (yet) having kids to go with the stuffing? But if your relatives start dropping dire statistics about declining fertility rates and what happens if you wait too long to have children, you can reassure them: The supposed gap between the number of children people say is _____ and the number they're having is not as alarming as it might seem. And lower fertility rates have benefits as well as costs.

The notion of ideal family size is appealing because it seems intuitive and straightforward. Reported ideal family size in the United States has stayed stable at around 2-3 children over the past decade. Yet fertility has continued to decline, with the total fertility rate, an estimate of lifetime fertility, now at a low of 1.73. This seems to imply a worsening gap between the ideal and the reality.

But how should we interpret this gap? Frequently, discussions like these take for granted that what individuals—usually women—say they think is an "ideal" family size and how many children they personally want are one and the same. But ideal family size might be too abstract to be useful; for example, some people respond with the general two-child norm without meaning that they want two children themselves. Instead, it's preferable to measure how many children people say they personally want to have; it's even better if we have information about their desires for having children in the short term, since many people change their long-term plans as life unfolds.

Another dominant assumption in these conversations is the idea of "competing preferences"—activities, behaviors and statuses that are difficult to combine with having and raising children. For some, this conjures up images of lazy millennials playing video games or spending time shopping and dining out; others interpret this line of reasoning as evidence that individuals—especially women—are selfish and narcissistic for putting other goals ahead of forming a family. This is a mistaken assumption.

Fill in the blank with the ONE most appropriate word from the passage. Second, describe the central error the writer cites in information gathering on family size. Do NOT copy more than FOUR consecutive words from the passage.

3 Read the passage and follow the directions. [4 points]

As a graduate student just beginning to probe the psychology of _____, I was interviewing leaders in business, art, athletics, journalism, academia, medicine, and law: Who are the people at the very top of your field? What are they like? What do you think makes them special? Some of the characteristics that emerged in these interviews were very field specific. For instance, more than one businessperson mentioned an appetite for taking financial risks: "You've got to be able to make calculated decisions about millions of dollars and still go to sleep at night." But this seemed entirely beside the point for artists, who instead mentioned a drive to create: "I like making stuff. I don't know why, but I do." In contrast, athletes mentioned a different kind of motivation, one driven by the thrill of victory: "Winners love to go head-to-head with other people. Winners hate losing."

In addition to these particulars, there emerged certain commonalities, and they were what interested me most. No matter the field, the most successful people were lucky and talented. I'd heard that before, and I didn't doubt it. But the story of success didn't end there. Many of the people I talked to could also recount tales of rising stars who, to everyone's surprise, dropped out or lost interest before they could realize their potential. Apparently, it was critically important—and not at all easy—to keep going after failure: "Some people are great when things are going well, but they fall apart when things aren't." High achievers described in these interviews really stuck it out: "This one guy, he wasn't actually the best writer at the beginning. I mean, we used to read his stories and have a laugh because the writing was so clumsy and melodramatic. But he got better and better, and last year he won a Guggenheim." And they were constantly driven to improve: "She's never satisfied. You'd think she would be, by now, but she's her own harshest critic." The highly accomplished were paragons of perseverance.

Fill in the blank with the ONE most appropriate word from the passage. Second, explain the meaning of the underlined words. Do NOT copy more than FOUR consecutive words from the passage.

4 Read the passage and follow the directions. [4 points]

The home of the Ford Model T is now an abandoned factory complex along busy Woodward Avenue in Highland Park, Mich., and there's not much to distinguish this place from Detroit's other industrial ruins. But if you stop and walk up to the front of the building, you'll find a historical marker telling us that by 1925, this place churned out more than 9,000 Ford Model t's a day. And it ends with this: "Mass production soon moved from here to all phases of American industry, and set a pattern of abundance for 20th century living." That actually helped America's 20th century middle class take off.

January 1914 was a frigid month in Detroit—much like January 2014 has been, but nonetheless thousands lined up in the bitter cold outside to take Henry Ford up on an extraordinary offer: $5 a day, for eight hours of work in a bustling factory.

That was more than double the average factory wage at that time, and for U.S. workers it was one of the defining moments of the 20th century. Five dollars in 1914 translates to roughly $120 in today's money. While many economists say today's employers could take some pointers from Ford, they also say 2014 is a totally different world for U.S. businesses and workers. Henry Ford was a hard-nosed businessman. He didn't introduce the $5 workday because he was a nice guy. He was not such a person at all.

Bob Kreipke, corporate historian, says to understand why Ford thought this was a smart move in January 1914, you have to go back to another huge shift that happened a few months earlier. By 1913, Model T production totaled 200,000—a feat made possible by the creation of the first moving assembly line. Conveyor belts transported small parts to workers, each of whom performed a specific task. This tremendously sped up production, but Ford still had a problem. While he had standardized production, he hadn't standardized his workforce. Now, he didn't need particularly skilled workers; he just needed ones who would do the same repetitive, specialized tasks hour after hour, day after day.

There was chronic absenteeism and lots of worker turnover. He needed to stabilize the workforce. So Ford gambled that higher wages would attract better, more reliable workers. It was an absolute, total success. In fact, it was better than anybody had even thought. The benefits were almost immediate. Productivity surged, and the Ford Motor Co. doubled its profits in less than two years. Ford ended up calling it the best cost-cutting move he ever made.

It's widely believed that Henry Ford also upped wages to expand his market, paying employees enough to buy the cars they made. While that wasn't Ford's key motive, it was a welcome byproduct, and a game changer, says University of California, Berkeley, labor economist Harley Shaiken. "What that gave us was an industrial middle class, and an economy that was driven by consumer demand," Shaiken says.

Today, overwhelmingly employers view the lowest wage as the most competitive wage. These days, global supply chains feed a hypercompetitive auto industry where no one wants to give up even an inch of ground, and keeping up with technology takes precedent over stabilizing the workforce. This just isn't Henry Ford's economy anymore.

Describe what Ford's main motivation for a higher wage was. Do NOT copy more than FOUR consecutive words from the passage. Second, explain how 2014 is a totally different world for U.S. businesses and workers from 1914. Do NOT copy more than FOUR consecutive words from the passage.

제 52 회 모의고사

1 Read the passage and follow the directions. [4 points]

Wines improve with age, but human bodies don't. We deteriorate with age. We develop wrinkles and gray hair, the skin thins and bruises more easily, vision and hearing decline and cataracts develop, blood pressure increases, bone density decreases, strength and agility decrease, the waist thickens, joints become arthritic, memory loss occurs, height may decrease by 1-2 inches. We learn and think more slowly, reaction time decreases, sexual functions change and hormone levels drop, and we become more likely to develop the diseases associated with old age such as cancer and diabetes.

In St. Augustine, Florida, you can visit Ponce de León's Fountain of Youth Archaeological Park for an admission fee of $18.00. There, you can drink a sample of the miraculous water. You might even feel a bit younger but only if you believe and are suggestible or perhaps are just thirsty. This fountain may be of historical interest, but it is not of any therapeutic value.

A spring whose waters restore the youth of anyone who drinks or bathes in them is a(n) _____ that dates back to prehistoric times. Herodotus wrote about it in the 5th century BC. The Spanish conquistador Ponce de León was the first European explorer to reach Florida. The King of Spain had authorized him to lead an expedition to search for "the Island of Benimy" and he originally mistook Florida for the island. He was not searching for a fountain of youth; that myth wasn't attached to his name until long after his death. But even if he had drunk of said fountain of youth, he'd still be dead.

Hope springs eternal, and history repeats itself. Today there are countless modern versions of the Fountain of Youth. Dietary supplements and other treatments are claimed to reverse the effects of aging and prolong life. Their promoters claim there is science behind them. In reality, they are just more myths. Centenarians share their secrets for a long life; they are all different. No treatment has ever been proven to keep humans young or make them live longer. Dr. Joe Schwarcz of McGill's Office for Science and Society said it best : "the science is all wet and drips with crackpot notions."

Fill in the blank with the ONE most appropriate word from the passage. Second, explain what Dr. Schwarcz argues in the underlined words. Do NOT copy more than FOUR consecutive words from the passage.

2. Read the passage and follow the directions. [4 points]

The wildfire season is off to a roaring start. The hot summer is worsening drought and drying out vegetation—an unfortunately ideal environment for wildfires to rage. But that's just one consequence of global warming; it's also leading to flooding, torrential rainstorms and heat-related deaths. In fact, the climate crisis has led to a widespread public health crisis.

I vividly remember a patient who came in late for her appointment during a July heat wave. When I walked in, she said, "I'm so sorry I'm late, I was up all night walking my grandbaby around the train station." Without air conditioning at home, the child was sweating through her clothes in the heat of the night, putting her at risk for dehydration.

July 2019 was the hottest July on record; January 2020 was the hottest on record; May 2020 was the hottest on record. <u>This is not a coincidence. It is a pattern</u>. Carbon dioxide, an important greenhouse gas contributing to global warming, has increased by 9 percent since 2005 and by 31 percent since 1950. A U.N. Intergovernmental Panel on Climate Change special report pointed out that the world has already warmed about one degree Celsius from pre-industrial levels. It stressed the urgency to act to limit warming to 1.5 degrees, and that a two-degree increase will lead to unprecedented extreme heat, water scarcity and food shortages around the globe.

In my own practice, I explain to patients how the climate crisis affects their health. For example, apart from contributing to global warming, rising carbon dioxide levels increase the amount of pollen that plants produce as a consequence of higher rates of photosynthesis. This rise in pollen levels can lead to worsening allergy symptoms. Another example is fine particulate matter (known as PM2.5) associated with air pollution, much of it linked to the burning of fossil fuels that help drive the warming. When we breathe in these particles, they travel down the airway and settle in the tiny air sacs called alveoli of the lungs, causing inflammation and potentially worsening asthma symptoms.

What is worse, that harm falls disproportionately on the _____. Wealthier people living in North America have a per capita carbon footprint that is 25 percent higher than those of lower income residents, with some affluent suburbs producing emissions 15 times higher than nearby neighborhoods. These carbon emissions contribute to global warming, and the subsequent health consequences are felt far beyond the neighborhood that produces them. Communities of color and poor communities are less resilient on average to the health impacts of climate change.

Explain the meaning of the underlined words. Do NOT copy more than FOUR consecutive words from the passage. Second, describe ALL public health results caused by "rising carbon dioxide levels". Third, fill in the blank with the ONE most appropriate word from the passage.

3 Read the passage and follow the directions. [4 points]

> Which one is more conducive to creativity: procrastination and pre-crastination? We think of procrastination as a curse. Over 80 percent of college students are plagued by procrastination, requiring epic all-nighters to finish papers and prepare for tests. Roughly 20 percent of adults report being chronic procrastinators. We can only guess how much higher the estimate would be if more of them got around to filling out the survey. While procrastination is a vice for productivity, it's a virtue for creativity. Conversely, I have always believed that anything worth doing was worth doing early. In graduate school I submitted my dissertation two years in advance. In college, I wrote my papers weeks early and finished my thesis four months before the due date. My roommates joked that I had a productive form of obsessive-compulsive disorder. Psychologists have coined a term for my condition: pre-crastination.
>
> Pre-crastination is the urge to start a task immediately and finish it as soon as possible. If you're a serious pre-crastinator, progress is like oxygen and postponement is agony. When a flurry of emails land in your inbox and you don't answer them instantly, you feel as if your life is spinning out of control. When you have a speech to give next month, each day you don't work on it brings a creeping sense of emptiness. But procrastinators, on the other hand, are at the mercy of an Instant Gratification Monkey who inhabits their brains, constantly asking questions like "Why would we ever use a computer for work when the Internet is sitting right there waiting to be played with?" If you're a procrastinator, overcoming that monkey can require herculean amounts of willpower. But a pre-crastinator may need equal willpower to not work.

A few years ago, though, one of my most creative students, Sunny Park, questioned my expeditious habits. She told me her most original ideas came to her after she procrastinated. Challenged to prove it, she got access to a couple of companies, surveyed people on how often they procrastinated, and asked their supervisors to rate their creativity. Procrastinators earned significantly higher creativity scores than pre-crastinators. In short, while pre-crastinators are steadily productive, using one's whole time for a project might be a boon in a creative undertaking.

Summarize the passage following the guidelines below.

　　　　　　　　　　　　　　　Guidelines
- Summarize the above passage in ONE paragraph.
- Provide a topic sentence, supporting ideas, and a concluding sentence based on the passage.
- Do NOT copy more than FIVE consecutive words from the passage.

1 Read the passage and follow the directions. [4 points]

Samuel Bowles, a world-renown American economist, has recently studied the way that people are motivated by _____ and the desire to maximize their own income as compared to altruism and the desire to do a good job and be well regarded by others. Real-world experiments show that contrary to traditional economic theories market incentives destroy cooperation and are less efficient than altruistic behavior in most cases. People act not only for material interests, but also to constitute themselves as dignified, autonomous, and moral individuals.

Behavioral experiments suggest that economic incentives may be counterproductive when they signal that selfishness is an appropriate response and undermine the moral values that lead people to act altruistically. Bowles gives the example of day care centers in Haifa, where a fine was imposed on parents who were late picking up their children at the end of the day. Rather than avoiding late pick-ups, parents responded by doubling the fraction of time they arrived late. After 12 weeks, the fine was revoked, but the enhanced tardiness persisted unabated. According to Bowles, this illustrates a kind of negative synergy between economic incentives and moral behavior. The fine seems to have undermined the parents' sense of ethical obligation to avoid inconveniencing the teachers and led them to think of lateness as just another commodity they could purchase.

Bowles shows that substantial fractions of most populations adhere to moral rules, willingly give to others, and punish those who offend standards of appropriate behavior, even at a cost to themselves and with no expectation of material reward. Diego Rivera's mural of factory workers at Ford's River Rouge assembly plant shows that organizations motivate members by appealing to other-regarding motives such as the desire to do a good job and a sense of reciprocal obligations among members of a firm.

Fill in the blank with the ONE most appropriate word from the passage. Second, explain what Bowles argues by mentioning Rivera's mural.

2 Read the passage and follow the directions. [4 points]

Everyone knows that to do great work you need both natural ability and determination. But there's a third ingredient that's not as well understood : a(n) _____ in a particular topic.

To explain this point I need to burn my reputation with some group of people, and I'm going to choose bus ticket collectors. There are people who collect old bus tickets. Like many collectors, they have an obsessive interest in the minutiae of what they collect. They can keep track of distinctions between different types of bus tickets that would be hard for the rest of us to remember. Because we don't care enough. What's the point of spending so much time thinking about old bus tickets?

Which leads us to the second feature of this kind of obsession : there is no point. A bus ticket collector's love is disinterested. They're not doing it to impress us or to make themselves rich, but for its own sake.

When you look at the lives of people who've done great work, you see a consistent pattern. They often begin with a bus ticket collector's obsessive interest in something that would have seemed pointless to most of their contemporaries. One of the most striking features of Darwin's book about his voyage on the Beagle is the sheer depth of his interest in natural history. His curiosity seems infinite. Ditto for Ramanujan, sitting by the hour working out on his slate what happens to series.

<u>It's a mistake to think they were "laying the groundwork" for the discoveries they made later.</u> There's too much intention in that metaphor.

Fill in the blank with the TWO most appropriate consecutive words from the passage. Second, explain what the writer of the passage argues in the underlined part of the last paragraph. Do NOT copy more than FOUR consecutive words from the passage.

3. Read the passage and follow the directions. [4 points]

For many years after Hiroshima and Nagasaki much of the research on the effects of ionising radiations was naturally concentrated on the results of sudden whole-body exposure. But in a world that was likely to rely more and more on atomic power, the ultimate effects of _____, slowly absorbed, clearly needed fuller comprehension. Three new reports from the United States National Academy of Sciences reflect the increasing research effort directed towards these chronic effects that are so hard to investigate.

The study of the association of radiation with leukaemia has been more exact than other inquiries because a fatal condition lends itself to mortality comparisons; the subtle and indefinite changes of premature ageing, another possible effect of radiation, are far harder to assess, particularly since physiological senescence is itself ill-understood. The epidemiological investigations—vast animal experiments and prospective inquiries on people whose occupation involves exposure to low doses—are complementary methods which may eventually show whether average life expectancy is reduced; but so many variables are involved that the answer may be a very long time coming; and the application of animal data to man is full of uncertainty. A prospective inquiry benefits from the fact that most of the nuclear agencies and X-ray departments in the United States and Great Britain keep careful medical and radiation exposure records of their employees. The larger the sample the better, and if it were possible to adopt common methods of measurement and recording throughout the world, much valuable information might be obtained. Differences which might be hidden when manifold recording methods allow only indirect comparisons might be revealed under standard conditions and suggest important new ideas. There seems to be a case for an international meeting of radiation-medicine and epidemiological experts to consider how to exploit such an opportunity. The best treatment of the acute radiation syndrome is in most particulars generally agreed upon; the one controversial point is the value of bone-marrow therapy. If the normal immunological response has been almost completely

But what soap hawkers overlook is that wiping out our symbiotic microbes may make us more vulnerable to other, unexpected maladies. First-line eczema* treatments, for instance, include topical antibiotics, cleansers, and drugs that dampen immune response, but researchers say these approaches can make the condition worse in the long run. Perturbing the skin barrier by washing or scratching can change the microbial population. That can rev up the immune system, which tells the skin cells to proliferate rapidly and fill with inflammatory proteins.

This observation lines up with an older one that kids raised in highly sanitized environments are more prone to allergies than farm kids like the Amish. Wipe the body's microbial slate clean too aggressively and the un-seasoned immune system roars back with a vengeance. This kind of immune over-reaction can also trigger what immunologists call the "Atopic March," in which one allergic disease—such as eczema, food allergy, or hay fever—leads to another.

*pelt : skin
*eczema : disease that makes skin red and itchy

Fill in the blank with the ONE most appropriate word from the passage. Second, explain the main reason the writer of the passage mentions "Amish" children.

2 Read the passage and follow the directions. [4 points]

The informational asymmetry between trusting and not trusting means that we learn more by trusting than by not trusting. Moreover, when we trust, we learn not only about specific individuals, we learn more generally about the type of situations in which we should or shouldn't trust. We get better at trusting.

Sammy Yu and his colleagues demonstrated the learning advantages of being trusting. Their experiments were similar to trust games, but the participants could interact with each other before making the decision to transfer money (or not) to the other. The most trusting participants were better at figuring out who would be trustworthy, or to whom they should transfer money.

We find the same pattern in other domains. People who trust the media more are more knowledgeable about politics and the news. The more people trust science, the more scientifically literate they are. Even if this evidence remains correlational, it makes sense that people who trust more should get better at figuring out whom to trust. In trust as in everything else, practice makes perfect.

Sammy Yu's insight provides us with a reason to be trusting. But then, the puzzle only deepens : if trusting provides such learning opportunities, we should trust too much, rather than not enough. <u>Ironically</u>, the very reason why we should trust more—the fact that we gain more information from trusting than from not trusting—might make us inclined to trust less.

When our trust is disappointed—when we trust someone we shouldn't have —the costs are salient, and our reaction ranges from annoyance all the way to fury and despair. The benefit—what we've learnt from our mistake—is easy to overlook. By contrast, the _____ of not trusting someone we could have trusted are, as a rule, all but invisible. We don't know about the friendship we could have struck (if we'd let that acquaintance crash at our place). We don't realize how useful some advice would have been (had we used our colleague's tip about the new software application).

We don't trust enough because the costs of mistaken trust are all too obvious, while the (learning) benefits of mistaken trust, as well as the costs of mistaken mistrust, are largely hidden. We should consider these hidden costs and benefits : think of what we learn by trusting, the people whom we can befriend, the knowledge that we can gain. Giving people a chance isn't only the moral thing to do. It's also the smart thing to do.

Explain the meaning of the underlined "Ironically". Do NOT copy more than FOUR consecutive words from the passage. Second, fill in the blank with the ONE most appropriate word from the passage.

3 Read the passage and follow the directions. [4 points]

> Animals communicate much to our surprise. Just like us, interaction among animals can be both verbal or non-verbal. Singing is one way in which animals can interact with one another. Male blackbirds often use their melodious songs to catch the attention of the females. These songs are usually rich in notes variation, encoding various kinds of messages. Songs are also used to warn and keep off other blackbirds from their territory, usually a place where they dwell and reproduce. Large mammals in the oceans sing too. Enormous whales groan and grunt while smaller dolphins and porpoises produce pings, whistles and clicks. These sounds are surprisingly received by other mates as far as several hundred kilometers away.
>
> Besides singing, body language also forms a large part of animals' communication tactics. Dominant hyenas exhibit their power by raising the fur hackles on their necks and shoulders, while the submissive ones normally "surrender" to the powerful parties by crouching their heads low and curling their lips a little, revealing their teeth in friendly smiles.
>
> Colors, which are most conspicuously found on animals are also important means of interaction among animals. The alternating black and white striped coats of zebras have their roles to play. Each zebra is born with a unique set of stripes which enables its mates to recognize them. When grazing safely, their stripes are all lined up neatly so that none of them loses track of their friends. However, when danger such as a hungry lion approaches, the zebras would dart out in various directions, making it difficult for the lion to choose his target.
>
> Communication is part of our everyday life. We greet one another, smile or frown, depending on our moods. However, as opposed to our conventional thinking, animals too communicate. Given this quality, we should consider them more dynamically.

Summarize the passage following the guidelines below.

Guidelines

- Summarize the above passage in ONE paragraph.
- Provide a topic sentence, supporting ideas, and a concluding sentence based on the passage.
- Do NOT copy more than FIVE consecutive words from the passage.

제 55 회 모의고사

1. **Read the passage and follow the directions.** [4 points]

> Design is ubiquitous. Sometimes the design is quite overt, as when a painter composes a landscape according to received aesthetic principles, or a poet shapes a sonnet following a strict form. Other designs are less obviously or less explicitly thought about, as when <u>a person adjusts water flow from a faucet to achieve the preferred temperature</u> or when we walk along familiar streets to reach a destination. The word design has a plethora of denotations and connotations, and it is to this multiplicity of meanings that we owe at least in part the confusion and ambiguity that often accompanies the word's use. Even within the relatively narrow scope of the activity of professional designers, design means different things in different contexts. In a word, everything deliberately made and done is necessarily designed.
>
> [A] Architects and engineers engage in design quite explicitly, and they typically do so with distinct objectives. Architects tend to focus on form over function, whereas engineers tend to do the opposite. To many an architect, the design of a building has firstly to do with how it looks—both inside and out—and how it fits in with nearby buildings. Architects are also expected to give considerable thought to how the building will be used, how people will move through it, how it will feel, although such considerations do not always seem to be foremost in their minds judging by results. Indeed, if architectural criticism is taken at face value, architects do seem to be principally concerned with the texture of a building's façade, the appearance of its public spaces, the furniture with which it is filled. Architects seem to pay close attention to details, even down to the nature of the lighting fixtures and the hardware on doors and windows, but not always to how they will be operated or how they will fulfill their purpose. Nevertheless, such considerations collectively constitute architectural and interior design.

[B] To engineers, design typically has less to do with <u>aesthetics and appearance</u> and more to do with fabrication and performance. Engineers tend to focus on the structure behind the facade. They worry about how the building will be built, how it will stand, whether it will sway too much in the wind, whether it will survive an earthquake, whether it will crack or leak. Engineers designing the structural frame of hotel buildings take into account the strength and stiffness of ballroom floors, where large crowds will gather and rhythmic dancing will occur. Engineers are expected to think about how a building will be heated and cooled, how air will circulate among its spaces, how energy efficient it will be.

Identify to which group the underlined instance of design would most closely be attributed and provide the reason for your choice. Second, write the ONE word from [A] that best corresponds to the meaning of the underlined words in [B].

2 Read the passage and follow the directions. [4 points]

> In an effort to celebrate the growing racial and ethnic diversity at Eastern School, the school's Diversity Committee decided to sponsor Multicultural Day. Numerous performers were hired for assemblies and presentations. During the day's feature event, the "Culture Parade," students were asked to showcase ethnic clothing as they walked through the hallways. Teachers were encouraged by the committee to discuss clothing from countries outside the United States and to invite students who had such clothing to bring it to school for the parade.
>
> Ms. Morrison was excited about Multicultural Day because many of her students had parents who were immigrants. She imagined the day as an opportunity for those students to teach others about their ethnic cultures.
>
> A week before the event, Ms. Morrison brought a kilt to class and explained its significance to the students. "This represents my Scottish heritage," she said, "and I am proud to show it to you today." She then asked whether students had "special costumes" at home that represented their ethnic cultures. Several students raised their hands, which prompted Ms. Morrison to discuss the events planned for Multicultural Day, including the parade. During dismissal the day before the parade Ms. Morrison announced, "Don't forget to bring your costumes to class tomorrow!"
>
> The next day, Ms. Morrison was pleased to see several Hmong and Liberian students came with bags of ethnic clothing. She saw that two other students, Emily and Keisha, brought clothing, so she inquired about what was in their bags. Emily, a white student, excitedly pulled out her soccer uniform, and Keisha, an African American student pulled jeans and her favorite sweatshirt out of her bag. Ms. Morrison told the two girls she appreciated their enthusiasm for Multicultural Day but that they would not be able to walk in the parade. She explained that what Keisha and Emily brought was everyday clothing rather than clothes that represented their _____ heritages.

Both girls protested. "This outfit represents my culture," Keisha argued. Ms. Morrison shared with the girls that she felt terrible about the confusion, but could not allow them to participate. "Maybe next year they'll expand the parade," she said.

After the girls walked away, Ms. Morrison considered changing her mind. She worried, though, that other students or staff would be puzzled by their participation and that Keisha and Emily would be ridiculed for not following directions.

Fill in the blank with the ONE most appropriate word from the passage. Second, what is one specific clothing item showing heritage mentioned in the passage?

3 Read the passage and follow the directions. [4 points]

Everyone loves unsolved mysteries. Examples include Amelia Earhart's disappearance over the Pacific in 1937 and the daring escape of inmates Frank Morris and John and Clarence Anglin from Alcatraz Island in California in 1962. Moreover our interest holds even if the mystery is based on a joke. Take author Douglas Adams's popular 1979 science-fiction novel *The Hitchhiker's Guide to the Galaxy*. Toward the end of the book, the supercomputer Deep Thought reveals that the answer to the "Great Question" of "Life, the Universe and Everything" is "_____".

Deep Thought takes 7.5 million years to calculate the answer to the ultimate question. The characters tasked with getting that answer are disappointed because it is not very useful. Yet, as the computer points out, the question itself was vaguely formulated. To find the correct statement of the query whose answer is forty-two, the computer will have to build a new version of itself. That, too, will take time. The new version of the computer is Earth.

The author's choice of the number 42 has become a fixture of geek culture. It's at the origin of a multitude of jokes and winks exchanged between initiates. If, for example, you ask your search engine variations of the question "What is the answer to everything?" it will most likely answer "forty-two." Try it in French or German. You'll often get the same answer whether you use Google, Qwant, Wolfram Alpha or the chat bot Web app Cleverbot.

Since the first such school was created in France in 2013 there has been a proliferation of private computer-training institutions in the "42 Network," whose name is a clear allusion to Adams's novels. Today the founding company counts more than 15 campuses in its global network. The number 42 also appears in different forms in the film Spider-Man : Into the Spider-Verse. The number also turns up in a whole string of curious coincidences whose significance is probably not worth the effort to figure out. For example : In ancient Egyptian mythology, during the judgment of souls, the dead had to declare before 42 judges that they had not committed any of 42 sins.

The marathon distance of 42.195 kilometers corresponds to the legend of how far the ancient Greek messenger Pheidippides traveled between Marathon and Athens to announce victory over the Persians in 490 B.C. <u>The fact that the kilometer had not yet been defined at that time only makes the connection all the more astonishing.</u>

Fill in the blank with the ONE most appropriate word from the passage. Second, explain the meaning of the underlined words in the last sentence of the passage. Do NOT copy more than THREE consecutive words from the passage.

4 Read the passage and follow the directions. [4 points]

The hard, rigid plates that form the outermost portion of the Earth are about 100 kilometers thick. These plates include both the Earth's crust and the upper mantle. The rocks of the crust are composed mostly of minerals with light elements, like aluminum and sodium, while the mantle contains some heavier elements, like iron and magnesium. Together, the crust and upper mantle that form the surface plates are called the lithosphere. This rigid layer floats on the denser material of the lower mantle the way a wooden raft floats on a pond. The plates are supported by a weak, plastic layer of the lower mantle called the asthenosphere. Also like a raft on a pond, the ____①____ are(/is) carried along by slow currents in this more fluid layer beneath them.

With an understanding of plate tectonics, geologists have put together a new history for the Earth's surface. About 200 million years ago, the plates at the Earth's surface formed a "supercontinent" called Pangaea. When this supercontinent started to tear apart because of plate movement, Pangaea first broke into two large continental masses with a newly formed sea that grew between the land areas as the depression filled with water. The southern one—which included the modern continents of South America, Africa, Australia, and Antarctica—is called Gondwanaland. The northern one—with North America, Europe, and Asia—is called Laurasia. North America tore away from Europe about 180 million years ago, forming the northern Atlantic Ocean.

Some of the lithospheric plates carry ocean floor and others carry land masses or a combination of the two types. The movement of the lithospheric plates is responsible for earthquakes, volcanoes, and the Earth's largest mountain ranges. Current understanding of the interaction between different plates explains why these occur where they do. For example, the edge of the Pacific Ocean has been called the "Ring of Fire" because so many volcanic eruptions and earthquakes happen there. Before the 1960's, geologists could not explain why active volcanoes and strong earthquakes were concentrated in that region. The theory of ____②____ gave them an answer.

Fill in each blank with the TWO most appropriate consecutive words from the passage. Then, describe when the northern Atlantic Ocean was formed. Do NOT copy more than THREE consecutive words from the passage.

제 56 회 모의고사

1 **Read the passage and follow the directions.** [4 points]

An organization recently released a new study that tries to come up with a formula that can weigh saving lives against boosting incomes, based on the views of a group that's rarely consulted : the people on the receiving end of charity. The finding is surprising.

People in poor countries appear to value life compared to income pretty similarly to those in wealthy countries. In the absence of solid data, economists have tended to assume that people in extreme poverty would weigh a boost to their income higher than those in rich ones. After all, people are facing such difficult issues in poverty that having a little bit more money could be substantially more valuable to them.

The nonprofit research group IDinsight that conducted the study surveyed 2,000 extremely poor people in Kenya and Ghana and asked them a series of questions about the best allocation of aid money. It essentially put them in the shoes of donors. People were willing to pay a lot for relatively small reductions in the risk of mortality—and they tended to choose programs that saved lives at high rates relative to programs that boosted incomes.

Researchers were also surprised by the weights that those surveyed gave to saving a child's life over an adult's life. After all, for people who are incredibly poor with little safety net, losing the family breadwinner is especially devastating. "Some staff wondered whether communities would feel that adults are often caregivers for their families and are making substantial economic contributions to their communities, so a community would say that it's more important to avert the death of the adult," says a researcher.

Instead the survey found that people tended to value averting deaths of children under 5 years old up to two times more than averting deaths of individuals over 5 years old. The researchers stress that this research is very preliminary. Lots more must be done. But they has already tweaked its own weighting formulas. For instance, it now weighs saving lives of children versus those of adults—instead of giving slight precedence to adults.

Explain why the finding of the research is surprising. Second, it can be inferred that donation formulas would change according to the result of the study. Explain the change.

2. Read the passage and follow the directions. [4 points]

Audible speech burns hot with information. Intonation, accents, innuendo, vocal phrasing, emphasis, pauses, all communicate far more than a transcript can. Audio is the format for "You all know exactly what I'm talking about, because of the way I'm saying it." Audio is how you communicate what you really mean, straight into ears, headphones and car radios, intimately and directly. Music is good at this, but ____①____ is even better.

Here's an exercise you can do : speaking out loud, say the word "tonight" twenty different ways, where each way is communicating something distinct. You can say "tonight" in a way that's intrigued, satisfied, tired, horny, dejected, anxious, suspicious, hesitant, desperate, or any number of ways— and the person you're talking to will know exactly what you mean. You can't do that easily with image or text. A transcript of the word tonight just says tonight : flat, ambiguous. Our ____②____ treat it neutrally. But our ears don't. Our ears are hyper-discriminatory.

Whatever it is that's being communicated, audio will heat it up. Imagine you're in a confrontation with your landlord, and you can communicate either over text messaging or by phone (cooler, back-and-forth dialog) or by email or voice mail (hot, one-shot blasts). Text keeps things chill, whereas audio forces the issue.

When you present information in an audio-first format, or especially in an audio-only format, it heats up what's being communicated, and saturates its information content. What may have seemed ambiguous or flat when presented in text or mixed media format won't be interpreted ambiguously by your ears. Your ears understand what's really being said, and they seek hot content.

There's a famous story about the Nixon-Kennedy debates that I misunderstood for a long time. Following a presidential debate between Richard Nixon and JFK, those who had listened over the radio overwhelmingly felt that Nixon had won, whereas those who had laid eyes on their TVs felt that JFK won. I remember originally hearing this story and thinking that the point was somehow that TV was more "superficial" than radio, and that JFK's handsome face or easy on-screen charm somehow overruled the debate's substance on TV but not on the radio.

I've now come to understand that this wasn't the point at all. The lesson has nothing to do with the content of what either of them were saying. The content doesn't matter. What matters is that Nixon was a Hot candidate: sharp, saturated with information, abrasive, and in your face. But JFK was a Cool candidate: relaxed, speaking easy, in slogans that invited multiple interpretations, creating plenty of gaps for the audience to fill in themselves.

Fill in each blank with the ONE most appropriate word from the passage. Second, explain the writer's current understanding about the Nixon-Kennedy debates in the context of whole passage. Do NOT copy more than THREE consecutive words from the passage.

3 Read the passage and follow the directions. [4 points]

> The primeval way of exchange was the barter trade. In this form of transaction, human beings used goods to exchange for the things that they wanted. For example, when person A wished a pen and he had a spare sheep, he must look for someone who had the exact opposite, that is, that someone, say person B, must have a spare pen of person A's choice and is also in need of a sheep. Having found such a person, the problem does not end here. A big sheep may worth not only one pen, hence person B may have to offer person A something else, say two pigs. However, he runs the risk of person A rejecting the offer as he may not need the pigs.
>
> Years later, the burdensome barter trade gave way to the monetary form of exchange when the idea of money was created. In the early days, almost anything could qualify as money : beads, shells and even fishing hooks. Then in a region near Turkey, gold coins were used as money. In the beginning, each coin had a different denomination. It was only later, in about 700 BC, that Gyges, the king of Lydia, standardized the value of each coin.
>
> Monetary means of transaction at first beat the traditional barter trade. However, as time went by, the thought of carrying a ponderous pouch of coins for shopping appeared not only troublesome but thieves attracting. Hence, the Greek and Roman traders who bought goods from people faraway cities, invented checks to solve the problem. Not only are paper checks easy to carry around, they discouraged robbery as these checks can only be used by the person whose name is printed on the notes.
>
> Now, in addition to the convenience of using paper notes issued by governments as the mode of exchange, technology has allowed people to create other means of transaction such as the credit and cash cards.

Summarize the passage following the guidelines below.

---Guidelines---
- Summarize the above passage in ONE paragraph.
- Provide a topic sentence, supporting ideas, and a concluding sentence based on the passage.
- Do NOT copy more than FIVE consecutive words from the passage.

제 57 회 모의고사

1 Read the passage and follow the directions. [4 points]

> From the Greek logos, meaning word, a logo is—ideally—a symbol that we recognise immediately and associate with the organisation it represents. But it is rarely that simple. Shape and color also play a role, as do letters or even the organisation's full name. In any case, a logo should be easy for its target group to recognise. It should become familiar after being seen just a few times. A good logo balances simplicity with distinctiveness and can stand alone. It has to adorn a wide variety of surfaces; from the front of corporate headquarters to promotional brochures and the letterheads of countless memos.
>
> A logo reveals the strengths and values you attribute to your company. An organisation that takes itself seriously will obviously not choose a frivolous logo. Many specialists praises the effectiveness of temporary employment agency Randstad's logo—a stylised R, reflected over vertical and horizontal axes. Seen as a whole, it resembles a bird and gives a sense of dynamism and mobility appropriate to the agency's activities. A temping agency actually has a very low profile, workers for other companies. Still, through the years Randstad has managed to build up a concrete image of its own.
>
> Like a successful brand name, a good logo is one of a company's major assets. It is often easier to protect than a brand name, especially a personal name to which no exclusive rights can be claimed. In addition, a logo is easier to recognize than a company name, especially internationally. The oil company Shell's distinctive shell logo is recognized everywhere, even in countries where the letters of the word "Shell" are unfamiliar. Also, at the international level, Coca-Cola springs to mind, which uses a wavy line in addition to the name. This creates a very effective logo, recognized the world over.

Often each company agrees on the _____ for its product. In the Dutch dairy aisle, blue stands for milk, red for buttermilk, and green for yoghurt. And elsewhere in the shop, bars of dark chocolate boast red wrappers and milk chocolate blue. Outside the Netherlands, Germany and Austria's national postal services are well known for their use of yellow.

Let's say that you are a company owner, who sells your products all over the world. You have to choose between a logo and a company name to make your product recognized better. Which of the two would you have to choose according to the passage? Second, fill in the blank with the ONE most appropriate word from the passage.

2. Read the passage and follow the directions. [4 points]

I have a single definition of success. You look in the mirror every evening, and wonder if you disappoint the person you were at 18, right before the age when people start getting corrupted by life. Let him or her be the only judge; not your reputation, not your wealth, not your standing in the community, not the decorations on your lapel. If you do not feel ashamed, you are successful. All other definitions of success are modern constructions; fragile modern constructions.

The Ancient Greeks' main definition of success was to have had a heroic death. But as we live in a less martial world, we can adapt our definition of success as having taken a heroic route for the benefits of the collective, as narrowly or broadly defined collective as you wish. So long as all you do is not all for you : secret societies used to have a rule for uomo d'onore : you do something for yourself and something for other members. And virtue is inseparable from courage. Like the courage to do something unpopular. Take risks for the benefit of others; it doesn't have to be humanity, it can be helping say Beirut Madinati or the local municipality. The more micro, the less abstract, the better.

I believe success requires absence of _____. I've seen billionaires terrified of journalists, wealthy people who felt crushed because their brother in law got very rich, academics with Nobel who were scared of comments on the web. The higher you go, the worse the fall. For almost all people I've met, external success came with increased fragility. The worst are those "former something" types with 4 page CVs who, after leaving office, and addicted to the attention of servile bureaucrats, find themselves discarded : as if you went home one evening to discover that someone suddenly emptied your house of all its furniture.

But self-respect is robust—that's the approach of the Stoic school, which incidentally was a Phoenician movement. If someone wonders who are the Stoics I'd say Buddhists with an attitude problem. I've seen robust people in my village Amioun who were proud of being local citizens involved in their tribe; they go to bed proud and wake up happy. Or Russian mathematicians who, during the difficult post-Soviet transition period, were proud of making $200 a month and do work that is appreciated by twenty people and considered that showing one's decorations or accepting awards were a sign of weakness and lack of confidence in one's contributions.

Fill in the blank with the ONE most appropriate word from the passage. Second, what can be inferred to be "unpopular" about the Russian mathematicians' lifestyle?

3 Read the passage and follow the directions. [4 points]

How did you do with our four questions? Below are the answers.

1. You are a participant in a race. You overtake the second person. What position are you in? The intuitive answer is "I am now the first." The answer of course is that if you overtake the one who is second, you take his place, and you are now second.
2. Mary's Father has five daughters. Their names are : 1. Nana, 2. Nene, 3. Nini, 4. Nono and ?? What is the name of the fifth daughter? The intuitive response most people give is to look after -a-e-i-o- and go with ___①___. The correct answer is already given in the question : ___②___.
3. A cup and teapot set costs $110. The teapot costs $100 more than the cup. How much is a cup? The intuitive response is $110 − $100 = $10. The correct answer is $5.
4. In a lake, there is a patch of lily pads. Every day, the patch doubles in size. If it takes 48 days for the patch to cover the entire lake, how long would it take for the patch to cover half of the lake? Your first response is probably to take a shortcut, and to divide the final answer by half. That leads you to twenty-four days. But that's wrong. The correct solution is forty-seven days.

Get all four correct? Great job! Odds are, though, that your brain tried to force you to accept the wrong answers first.

Daniel Kahneman, who was the first psychologist to win the Nobel Prize in Economics (2002), explains why an intuitive reaction is not always the best. In his groundbreaking book *Thinking : Fast and Slow*, he discusses intuitive (fast) and rational (slow) thinking. He shows us how an intuitive reaction could lead to problems and what the limitations are of our common sense.

Fill in each blank with the ONE most appropriate word respectively. Second, according to the passage, explain why an intuitive reaction might cause a wrong answer and provide ONE example of it.

4 Read the passage and follow the directions. [4 points]

Many of us enjoy roasting meat over the fire but no one ever wonder who first started the idea of cooking meat in a fire. Perhaps, it is just in the human psyche that we sometimes feel the need to return to the primitive times, probably to relieve us of our urbanized life. That is why many people love to hold barbecue gatherings.

The first step towards the _____ for a barbecue is to rent a barbecue pit which usually comes with the barest essentials. After all, we are supposed to return to the early time frame. Of course, during peak seasons like the school holidays, when the pits are fully booked, you may try digging one at the back of your garden. Next, get ready the wire netting, otherwise, you will find yourself roasting the meat on the hot charcoal. Skewers which are important for holding the meat pieces; utensils for picking up the food like forks and spoons, paper plates and cups must not be left out.

Next comes the preparation of the most important part of the barbecue—the food. In fact, any kind of meat will be suitable. If meat pieces are bought, like chicken, beef or mutton, slice them into thin pieces before piercing in the skewers. Chicken wings are the best. Simply stretch the wings apart and push in the skewers. Following which, the meat is to be soaked in a mixture of spices for marination, giving them some flavor.

When everything is ready, start the fire with charcoal, one hour before the start of the feast. Once the fire is started, let it all burn till glowing embers are left. Then place the sticks of meat over the wire netting and there you are, the barbecue has begun. Do not worry about overcooking the meat. After all, the real joy behind the barbecue lies in the cooking not eating of the food. Just a piece of advice to beginners : Bring along some indigestion medicine.

Fill in the blank with the ONE most appropriate word from the passage. Second, what can be inferred to be the reason the writer of the passage says "Bring along some indigestion medicine"?

제 58 회 모의고사

1 **Read the passage and follow the directions.** [4 points]

Psychologists and neuroscientists study a phenomenon they call flow, which is this thing that happens in the human brain when someone pays attention to just one thing, like something creative, and manages not to get distracted by anything else. And some say the more regularly you do this, the happier you'll be.

Now I'm not a psychologist or a neuroscientist. But I can tell you, for me, that is very true. It's not always easy, it's hard. To really pay attention like this takes practice, everybody does it their own way. But if there's one thing I can share that I think helps me focus and really pay attention, it's this: I try not to see other creative people as my competitors. I try to find ___①___. Like, if I'm acting in a scene, if I start seeing the other actors as my competitors, and I'm like, "God, they're going to get more attention than I am, people are going to be talking about their performance more than mine"—I've lost my focus. And I'm probably going to suck in that scene.

But when I see the other actors as collaborators, then it becomes almost easy to focus, because I'm just paying attention to them. And I don't have to think about what I'm doing—I react to what they're doing, they react to what I'm doing, and we can kind of keep each other in it together. But I don't want you to think it's only actors on a set that can collaborate in this way. I could be in whatever kind of creative situation. It could be professional, could be just for fun. I could be collaborating with people I'm not even in the same room with. In fact, some of my favorite things I've ever made, I made with people that I never physically met.

And by the way, this, to me, is the beauty of the Internet. If we could just stop competing for attention, then the Internet becomes a great place to find collaborators. And once I'm collaborating with other people, whether they're on set, or online, wherever, that makes it so much easier for me to find that ___②___, because we're all just paying attention to the one thing that we're making together. And I feel like I'm part of something larger than myself, and we all sort of shield each other from anything else that might otherwise grab our attention, and we can all just be there.

Fill in each blank with the ONE most appropriate word from the passage respectively. Second, explain what the beauty of the Internet is.

2 Read the passage and follow the directions. [4 points]

With enough training, pigeons can distinguish between the works of Picasso and Monet. Ravens can identify themselves in a mirror. And on a university campus in Japan, crows are known to intentionally leave walnuts in a crosswalk and let passing traffic do their nut cracking. Many bird species are incredibly smart. Yet among intelligent animals, the "bird brain" often doesn't get much respect.

Two papers published recently in *Science* find birds actually have a brain that is much more similar to our complex primate organ than previously thought. For years it was assumed that the avian brain was limited in function because it lacked a neocortex. In mammals, the neocortex is the hulking, evolutionarily modern outer layer of the brain that allows for complex cognition and creativity and that makes up most of what, in vertebrates as a whole, is called the pallium. The new findings show that birds do, in fact, have a brain structure that is comparable to the _____ despite taking a different shape. It turns out that at a cellular level, the brain region is laid out much like the mammal cortex, explaining why many birds exhibit high-level behaviors and abilities that have long befuddled scientists. The new work even suggests that certain birds demonstrate some degree of consciousness.

The mammalian cortex is organized into six layers containing vertical columns of neurons that communicate with one another both horizontally and vertically. On the other hand, the avian brain was thought to be arranged into discrete collections of neurons called nuclei, including a region called the dorsal ventricular ridge, or DVR, and a single nucleus named the wulst.

In one of the new papers, senior author Onur Güntürkün, a neuroscientist and his colleagues analyzed regions of the DVR and wulst involved in sound and vision processing. To do so, they used a technology called three-dimensional polarized light imaging(3D-PLI)—a light-based microscopy technique that can be employed to visualize nerve fibers in brain samples. The researchers found that in both pigeons and barn owls, these brain regions are constructed much like our neocortex, with both layerlike and columnar organization—and with both horizontal and vertical circuitry.

Fill in the blank with the ONE most appropriate word from the passage. Second, provide ONE example showing birds' advanced "behaviors and abilities". Third, what can be inferred from the new research about the underlined part?

3 Read the passage and follow the directions. [4 points]

Long ago, during the times of the kings and knights, animals such as horses, buffaloes and camels were used by man for transportation purposes. Though these animals no doubt did save man from traveling by foot, they took a long time to complete the journeys, especially when transporting goods. The means of transportation have changed and improved over many centuries.

In 1825, George Stephenson's opening of the first railway marked a significant progress in the history of transportation. Railways were in popular demand because they could carry more people and loads. More importantly, they ran faster than animals. Railways improved the communication networks and hence, imports and exports of goods and people traveling out of their towns or even countries to work were made possible. Unfortunately, since the invention of motor vehicles, the popularity of railways has declined.

Motor vehicles were first invented in the eighteenth century. These vehicles were preferred by many people as they do not run on tracks and hence do not have fixed routes. Travelers can then plan their own routes to suit their convenience. This is especially so when the destinations are places like small towns or remote areas. In these places, few or even none of the trains ever reach them; so traveling by motor vehicle would solve this problem. Over many years of modifications, the motor vehicle is now one of the most commonly used means of transportation. Today, we travel in cars, taxis, buses, lorries or vans almost every day.

Human beings over the centuries have innovated a variety of means of transportation. To get somewhere more conveniently and safely is our basic desire that is imprinted in our souls. Therefore, the invention of further developed forms of transportation will consistently appear in human history.

Summarize the passage following the guidelines below.

--- Guidelines ---
- Summarize the above passage in ONE paragraph.
- Provide a topic sentence, major supporting details, and a concluding sentence based on the passage.
- Do NOT copy more than FIVE consecutive words from the passage.

제 59 회 모의고사

1 Read the passage and follow the directions. [4 points]

> The thinker Lauren Woon depicts two metaphysical models of pregnancy that are said to capture current Western understandings of the process. The first, dubbed the 'parthood model', describes the fetus as a part of the gestating person in the way that an arm, leg or kidney is. The second, the 'container model', describes the fetus and gestating person as two separate entities, which gives rise to the culturally dominant 'fetal container model'. As Woon points out, it's through this model that we can speak of a 'bun in the oven' and, to add to her list, depict fetuses as floating astronauts in an empty black space rather than embedded in the uterine wall.
>
> Though relatively innocuous in its daily use, the container model has been applied to more detrimental lengths too. As the sociologist Amrita Pande demonstrates in her 2010 study of India's since-banned commercial surrogacy industry, fertility clinics capitalising on this separateness between gestators and fetuses have developed dehumanising prenatal care practices that, among other things, serve to emphasize surrogate disposability. What this shows is that the metaphysical container view might be morally neutral, but its cultural manifestation has developed and is currently utilised in a patriarchal context.
>
> The plausibility of certain reproductive practices depends upon the kind of conceptual framework we use to understand them. The very idea of using artificial wombs to replace some or all stages of gestation reflects, for instance, an assumption that fetuses and gestating persons are in fact separable. While this doesn't mean that artificial-womb technology necessarily entails the fetal container model, current rhetoric within this debate captures the spirit of the view well : for instance, by likening the uterus to what the reproductive biologist Roger Gosden calls a 'clever incubator'.

The feminist scholar Irina Aristarkhova presents an alternative view in which the plausibility of artificial-womb technology becomes less of a 'workable concept'—or at least more complicated. Presumably, if one now thinks of the fetus as a part of the _____, then the extent to which artificial wombs are truly capable of satisfying this role becomes limited. Of course, one could concede a new fetus-gestator relationship, one that extends into the realms of mechanics and machines. Still, if we're willing to confront the biological realities of pregnancy—that is, the actual inextricability of fetus and gestator—then our future as machines is, in this specific context, one that we'll need to confront eventually.

Explain why the writer of the passage thinks the fetal container model has been applied to "more detrimental lengths". Do NOT copy more than THREE consecutive words from the passage. Second, fill in the blank with the ONE most appropriate word from the passage.

2. Read the passage and follow the directions. [4 points]

Ms. Sutter was excited to form an after-school club at Pinewood School for students who could become the first people in their families to attend college. She started seeing a need for such a club as she noticed many of her students lacked knowledge about post-secondary education. Though many of their parents encouraged them to think about college, her students did not have the same opportunities as wealthier peers to see a college campus or learn about post-secondary options.

Ms. Sutter proposed the club at a staff meeting. Some teachers thought it was unnecessary, but others were excited and offered support. A major point of discussion was the club's grade range. Should it be open to all students or limited to higher grade levels?

Ms. Bates, a second grade teacher, commented, "Experience tells me fifth grade is too early to start talking to *these* kids about college. It's way over their heads."

Another teacher, Ms. Clark, added, "Families in our school will enroll their children in any free after-school program just to keep them busy. You'll be swamped and end up spending more time on discipline than on college."

Ms. Sutter disagreed with her peers' opinions, but she reluctantly agreed to offer the club exclusively to fifth graders.

Several months later Ms. Sutter paused during her "College Club" meeting to marvel at how well it was going. Students attended regularly, and parents would arrive before pick-up time to join lively discussions about college life.

As a year-end celebration, Ms. Sutter scheduled a field trip to the renowned local university, which would include a guided tour. When they arrived on campus she asked the students to wait outside the admissions office while she went in to alert the receptionist the group had arrived. After speaking with the receptionist, Ms. Sutter was shocked to learn their assigned tour guide had been reassigned, as a result, her group would need to conduct a self-guided tour.

"But I didn't attend this university! I can't give them an adequate tour. Why not just let us join another group?" she implored.

"I'm sorry, but guides are prioritized for prospective, high school students," the receptionist responded. As Ms. Sutter continued to plead the club's case, she was approached by the Director of Admissions, Mr. Stein.

"Can I help you?" he asked warmly.

"Yes," responded Ms. Sutter. "I have a group of fifth graders here, potential first-generation college students," she said, before explaining how excited students were about the tour.

Mr. Stein asked Ms. Sutter to step into his office. *Wonderful!* thought Ms. Sutter. *Maybe he'll be the person who gives us a tour.*

Instead Mr. Stein said, "I'm sorry a tour guide is unavailable. We do our best to avoid these situations, but I have students here who are credible applicants. I can't compromise their interest by prioritizing fifth graders ahead of them." He paused briefly before adding, "Frankly, I worry you're getting your students excited about a place they probably will never attend. Perhaps you should be touring the community college."

With this, he opened his office door, inviting Ms. Sutter to leave. Ms. Sutter glanced through a window and saw her students waiting patiently for their tour. She fought back tears as she contemplated what to tell them and how to address Mr. Stein's comments.

In what way was Ms. Clark's expectation subverted? Second, explain the underlying prejudicial assumption Mr. Stein makes. Do NOT copy more than THREE consecutive words from the passage.

3 Read the passage and follow the directions. [4 points]

At a party in Hollywood in the spring of 1935, Dashiell Hammett was asked by Gertrude Stein to solve a literary mystery. Why is it, she began, that in the nineteenth century men succeeded in writing about so many different varieties of men, and women were limited to creating heroines who were merely versions of themselves—she mentioned Charlotte Brontë and George Eliot—yet in the twentieth century this situation was reversed? Nowadays, Stein pointed out, it was the men who portrayed only themselves, and why should this be so? Stein reasonably assumed that Hammett, a hard-drinking ex-detective whose photograph had appeared on the cover of his latest novel, "The Thin Man," about a hard-drinking ex-detective, might be in a position to know.

The party that evening was given in Stein's honor, and Hammett was the one person in Hollywood she'd asked to meet. Although he had at first taken the invitation for an April Fools' joke, such tributes were no longer much of a surprise. Hammett had been "duh toast of duh intellectuals" (in Edmund Wilson's disgusted phrase) ever since "The Maltese Falcon," published in 1930, had introduced a new type of tough-guy hero in matching tough-guy prose : a tight-lipped, street-smart style, determinedly flat despite flickers of amusement and startlingly devoid of most of the familiar processes of consciousness. Readers were riveted, and critics were quick to announce the newest development in the creation of an American language. It was the kind of achievement that Stein and other literary radicals had been struggling for in their brave obscurities and their unread treatises, and it had emerged from the least likely source : cheap detective stories that large numbers of people actually liked to read, based on the real experience of a man on a job that just happened to involve unlimited amounts of violence, sexual intrigue, and moral devastation.

Hammett produced about ninety stories and five novels in the dozen active years of his career, many of them for badly needed money—he was capable of knocking out five thousand words a day—and many clearly executed beneath the level of his engaged attention. Of course, he also produced whiz-bang tales that exhibit the best of what the pulps could offer, and a few that transcend formula in the strict music of Hammett's uniquely deadpan dialogue.

Explain the meaning of the underlined words. Do NOT copy more than THREE consecutive words from the passage. Second, it can be inferred that Hammett's readership is most attracted by what factors?

4 Read the passage and follow the directions. [4 points]

> For his recent study, Thomas Reich asked two research assistants to look for correlational studies on the effects of music education. They found a total of 114 papers published since 2000. To assess whether the authors claimed any causation, researchers then looked for telltale verbs in each paper's title and abstract, verbs like "enhance," "promote," "facilitate," and "strengthen." The papers were categorized as neuroscience if the study employed an electroencephalogram or a brain imaging method like magnetic resonance, or if the study appeared in a journal that had "brain," "neuroscience," or a related term in its title. Otherwise the papers were categorized as psychology. Reich didn't tell his assistants what exactly he was trying to prove.
>
> After tallying their assessments, Reich concluded that the majority of the articles fallaciously claimed that music training had a causal effect. The overselling, he also found, was more prevalent among neuroscience studies, three quarters of which mischaracterized a mere correlation between music training and skills enhancement as a cause-and-effect relationship. This may come as a <u>surprise</u> to some. Psychologists have been battling charges that they don't do "real" science for some time—in large part because many findings from classic experiments have proved unreproducible. Neuroscientists, on the other hand, armed with brain scans and EEGs, have not been subject to the same degree of critique.
>
> "I have never thought that flute lessons make you better at solving differential equations," said Lutz Jäncke, a neuropsychologist from the University of Zurich in Switzerland who praised Reich's new study. "His criticism is justified."

Explain why the writer of the passage uses the word "surprise". Do NOT copy more than THREE consecutive words from the passage. Second, choose the ONE word from the passage that would best describe Lutz Jäncke's opinion of the relationships between music training and skills enhancement.

1 Read the passage and follow the directions. [4 points]

　　When I landed in Boston in 1999, the United States was the land of free markets. Many goods and services were cheaper here than in Europe. Twenty years later, American free markets are becoming a myth. Internet service, cellphone plans, and plane tickets are now cheaper in Europe and Asia than in the US. In 2018, the average monthly cost of a broadband internet connection was $31 in France, $39 in the UK and $68 in the US. American households also spend twice as much on cellphone services as households in France or the UK.

　　This is a result of policy choices. In 1999, the US had free and competitive markets while European markets were dominated by _____①_____. The airline industry is a prime example. Over the past two decades a wave of mergers has turned the US airline industry into oligopolies while Europe has opened its skies to competition, thanks in part to low-cost carriers such as Ryanair and EasyJet. US regulators allowed these mergers to happen without meaningful challenges. EU regulators, on the other hand, encouraged the entry of low-cost competitors by making sure they could get access to takeoff and landing slots.

　　There are many layers of irony in this historic reversal. One irony is that the free market ideas and business models that benefit European consumers today were inspired by US markets. Another irony is that some leftwing US politicians are now contemplating policies that most Europeans would find extreme. We do not think private health insurance companies should be abolished. We favor wealth taxes, but we do not think they are a cure for all ills.

> The polarization of the political debate is partly the result of ② <u>ignorance</u>. The American Left sees Europe as an El Dorado of free healthcare, free education and workers' rights. The American Right sees it as a socialistic nightmare with no growth and no innovation. They're both wrong, and the result is misguided policies and time wasted tilting at windmills.

Fill in the blank with the ONE most appropriate word from the passage. If necessary, change the word form. Second, explain what the underlined "ignorance" means regarding the American Right. Do NOT copy more than THREE consecutive words from the passage. Third, what can be inferred to be the most important characteristic of a free market for the writer?

2 Read the passage and follow the directions. [4 points]

Every year, salmon come home to Alaska's frigid rivers to mate, lay their eggs, and die. The state's salmon runs are some of the biggest in the world. But over the past few decades, those big salmon runs have featured ever smaller salmon.

Krista Oke and colleagues at the University of California, Santa Cruz, analyzed records of ___①___ going back to the 1950s. They included data on some 12.5 million salmon. And there's no question about it : salmon have shrunk. Sockeye salmon today are 2.1% shorter than their ancestors. Chum salmon are 2.4% shorter and Coho are 3.3% shorter. Chinook, or king, salmon showed the greatest declines at 8%. That's an average difference of more than 2 inches in length.

The researchers haven't nailed down the exact reasons behind this trend. But their analysis suggests that climate change and competition with wild and hatchery-raised salmon both play a role. They also discovered that much of the change in fish body size is due to fish returning from the ocean at a younger age now than in the past. Oke says fish could be returning earlier because they're reaching maturity faster for some reason—or because the ocean has become a riskier place for older salmon to survive.

Whatever the cause, this size shift has massive ramifications for people and the ecology. Oke and her team calculated that catching smaller fish may have already slashed the value of Alaska's commercial salmon fisheries by 21%. It's also likely reduced the food available to subsistence fishers—many of whom rely on stores of salmon to get them through the long, harsh winter—by as much as 26%.

On the side of ___②___, the researchers estimated that smaller fish lay 16% fewer eggs, which could depress salmon populations in the future. And, the salmon bring 28% fewer nutrients into the watersheds where they spawn, according to the study. "After they breed and die, their carcasses actually fertilize freshwater and terrestrial ecosystem with these marine-derived nutrients that are really important and that get used by all kinds of animals, like bears and songbirds and even taken up into trees."

With no single factor to blame for shrinking salmon, there's no obvious fix, Oke says.

Fill in the blank ① with the THREE most appropriate consecutive words from the passage and the blank ② with the ONE most appropriate word from the passage. Second, according to the research, describe ALL reasons salmon size may have become smaller than before. Do NOT copy more than THREE consecutive words from the passage.

3 Read the passage and follow the directions. [4 points]

People are constantly cannonaded by advertisements. Vendors try to gain our attention and sell us their services or products. Advertisements appear everywhere : on television, on the Internet, radios, pamphlets and so forth.

Advertisements are useful despite sometimes interrupting our favorite programs, providing free information about products and services. There are two types: informative and persuasive. Informative advertisements give product details, especially helpful for new items like computers with latest models and functions. However, most advertisements are persuasive, not only describing products but also convincing customers to buy by claiming superiority over competitors. These claims may sometimes be untrue, yet the minority of truly informative advertisements remain valuable for consumers seeking genuine product information.

While advertisements can be good helpers for shopping, they do have their shortcomings. Most advertisements aim to sell only. Faults of the products or services are usually hidden from the consumers. Hence, sometimes, we feel deceived if the product or service we bought does not turn out the way the advertisements claim to be. Sometimes, advertisements by rival competitors can get very intensive, especially when there are many firms producing similar products. One common example is the washing powder. There are so many advertisements for the different brands that customers sometimes get confused over what they should buy. Furthermore, having more advertisements would mean that the production cost of the firm would be increased. These rises in cost are usually passed on to the consumers in the form of higher prices.

Without advertisements, we might have to buy things based on incomplete information or go through more complicated ways before getting to know the products or services. On the other hand, too many advertisements also complicate our buying decisions. So I would say that we cannot live without advertisements but we must be careful how we live with them.

Summarize the passage following the guidelines below.

Guidelines

- Summarize the above passage in ONE paragraph.
- Provide a topic sentence, supporting ideas, and a concluding sentence based on the passage.
- Do NOT copy more than FIVE consecutive words from the passage.

제 61 회 모의고사

모범답안 및 번역 p.210

1 Read the passage and follow the directions. [4 points]

An international Art Nouveau style was characterized by sinuous lines, floral and vegetable motifs, and soft evanescent coloration. It was an eclectic one, bringing together elements of Japanese art, motifs of ancient cultures, and natural forms. The glass objects of this style were elegant in outline, although often deliberately distorted, with pale or iridescent surfaces. A favored device of the style was to imitate the iridescent surface seen on ancient glass that had been buried. Much of the Art Nouveau glass produced during the years of its greatest popularity had been generically termed "art glass". Art glass was intended for decorative purposes and relied for its effect upon carefully chosen color combinations and innovative techniques. In the United States, Louis Comfort Tiffany was the most noted exponent of the style, producing a great variety of glass forms and surfaces, which were widely copied in their time and are highly prized today. Tiffany was a brilliant designer, successfully combining ancient Egyptian, Japanese, and Persian motifs.

The Art Nouveau style was a major force in the decorative arts from 1895 until 1915, although its influence continued throughout the mid-1920's. It was eventually to be overtaken by a new school of thought known as Functionalism that had been present since the turn of the century. At first restricted to a small avant-garde group of architects and designers. Functionalism emerged as the dominant influence upon designers after the First World War. The basic tenet of the movement—that function should determine form—was not a new concept. Soon a distinct aesthetic code evolved : form should be simple, surfaces plain, and any ornament should be based on geometric relationships. This new design concept, coupled with the

> sharp postwar reactions to the style and conventions of the preceding decades, created an entirely new public taste which caused Art Nouveau types of _____ to fall out of favor. The new taste demanded dramatic effects of contrast stark outline, and complex textural surfaces.

First, what major historical event marks the transition from Art Nouveau to Functionalism in terms of mainstream popularity? Second, fill in the blank with the ONE most appropriate word from the passage.

2. Read the passage and follow the directions. [4 points]

For six decades or more, America's history has been driven by cultural warfare. This is usually traced to the social revolutions of the 1960s, but it began earlier. Culture War 1.0 began in the 1950s as religious enthusiasts sought to win hearts, minds, and souls for Christ in a society that was rapidly liberalizing and secularizing. That is the war that drifted to a whimpering end as recently as 2013, when the Supreme Court handed down culturally significant rulings bolstering the case for same-sex marriage. In 2015, the Court gave same-sex marriage its full endorsement, ruling in Obergefell v. Hodges that restrictions on same-sex marriages were unconstitutional. By this point, Culture War 1.0 was over.

This first culture war was mostly fought over issues of religious faith and morality, such as whether creationism was a viable alternative to the theory of biological evolution and whether limits should be placed on institutionalizing Christian values in the public sphere. In Culture War 2.0, the supernatural, metaphysics, and even religion more broadly have become irrelevant. The demands of Christian faith and morality have been replaced by something far more threatening to a society founded on Enlightenment principles.

Culture War 2.0 rotates around the new rules of engagement. The rules of engagement relate to how we deal with our disagreements. In Culture War 1.0, if a(n) _____ gave a public lecture about the age of the Earth based on geological dating techniques, creationist detractors would issue a response, insist that such dating techniques are biased, challenge him to a debate, and ask pointed—if unfairly loaded—questions during the Q&A session. In Culture War 2.0, disagreements with a speaker are sometimes met with attempts at <u>de-platforming</u>. Rowdy campaigns for the invitation to be rescinded before the speech can be delivered. If this is unsuccessful, critics may resort to disrupting the speaker by screaming and shouting, engaging noise makers, or pulling the fire alarm. The goal is not to counter the speaker with better arguments or even to insist on an alternative view, but to prevent the speaker from airing her views at all.

Christian organizations have a long history of censorship, and this has continued to some extent even in recent decades. All the same, an attempt to suppress an academic article would have been almost unthinkable during Culture War 1.0. There were some analogous attempts on the part of Christians during precursors of this culture war, as for example in the incidents surrounding Tennessee's Butler Act of 1925 and the subsequent "Scopes Monkey Trial." And religious would-be censors during Culture War 1.0 did occasionally make attempts on novels and movies interpreted as blasphemous or obscene, such as *The Last Temptation of Christ*. But for the most part, Creationists in the first Culture War didn't want an evolutionary biologist to lose their tenure and their doctorate. They wanted to debate and prove them wrong.

Fill in the blank with the TWO most appropriate consecutive words from the passage. Second, describe what "de-platforming" is and provide at least TWO examples of it from the passage.

3 Read the passage and follow the directions. [4 points]

> There is no denying that most of us need admiration as we need sunshine, and that women depend upon beauty as a means of winning admiration to a greater extent than men do. But, every year, more and more avenues to admiration are opened to women, and there are trains of worshippers to be won in athletics, in the professions, in the arts and in public life. There is scarcely a way in which a man can feed his vanity that is not nowadays open to women too. For them, it is getting a better and better world to grow old in.
>
> All the same, I know little about the matter. I do not even know in what happiness consists. I know only that it does not consist in being young, and that though disease and the loss of faculties and the loss of friends bring misery, there is no absolute misery in being old. I confess I am not perfectly happy at fortyeight, but neither was I perfectly happy at eighteen. I should be glad to be eighteen again, but that is not because it was in itself a happier age but because I should now have thirty years longer to live.
>
> The chief objection to growing old is not that one grows old oneself, but that the world grows older; and it is not so much that the world grows older as that the world we once knew is in ruins.
>
> New inventions have wrecked the world in which we had peace. Everywhere are noise and speed in place of the green quiet that we once knew. I do not like to speak ill of inventors, but they have invented the horse almost out of existence, and there are little seaside towns that once seemed a thousand miles away, so remote they were, where the smell of the sea is now drowned by the smell of the charabanc*. Is it possible to name a single beautiful place that is more beautiful today than it was thirty years ago? But we are faithful to the world of thirty years ago only in our imaginations, and there is scarcely a new invention—the motor-car or wireless—that we are <u>loyal</u> enough to abstain from using.
>
> *charabanc : bus for sightseeing*

First, explain how the experience of aging has improved for women. Do NOT copy more than FOUR consecutive words from the passage. Second, what would it take to fulfill the loyalty addressed in the underlined part?

4 Read the passage and follow the directions. [4 points]

Recently, scientists discovered bacteria that had been buried beneath the ocean floor for more than a hundred million years and was still alive. What would change if we could live for even just a million years? One thought immediately comes to mind. Tenure in academia would have to be capped. Universities would have to limit faculty appointments to a century at most in order to refresh their talent pool and mitigate old-fashioned education and research dogmas.

Past generations used to say that even though we cannot postpone natural _____, we can control how we live. They also believed that there is "nothing new under the sun." Both statements are inaccurate from our current perspective. With advances in bioscience and technology, one can imagine a post-COVID-19 future when most diseases are cured and our life span will increase substantially. Then death cannot be an enemy of human beings any longer.

If that happens, how would our goals change, and how would this shape our lives? Given the luxury of pursuing longer-term plans, we could accomplish more ambitious tasks. We could decide to care more about our planetary environment and interpersonal cooperation, since pollution or hostilities carry long-term dangers. An extended life experience could make us wiser and more risk-averse since there is much more at stake. It would make little sense to send young soldiers to wars, or initiate wars in the first place.

But even with shrewd strategies, survival is by no means guaranteed. For example, the known correlation between brain size and body weight did not make dinosaurs smart enough to deflect the asteroid that killed them. Accidents are inevitable, and treatment centers will continuously be busy repairing nonfatal damages due to routine mishaps.

The good news is that over a lifetime as long as a million years, space travel can take us to the nearest stars using existing chemical rockets. It would take merely 100,000 years to arrive at the habitable planet around Proxima Centauri with a space vehicle that travels at the speed of NASA's New Horizons spacecraft. For passengers who live a million years, such a trip would appear just like the decade-long journey of New Horizons to Pluto within our current life span. Of course, the spacecraft will have to provide an enduring ecosystem and comfortable living conditions over this long journey. And the passengers will have to maintain a stable mindset for their journey's goal and not lose faith, like <u>a fisherman</u> who, after a long hiatus without finding any fish, asks whether the real purpose of fishing is catching fish.

Fill in the blank with the ONE most appropriate word from the passage. Second, if the premise of the passage comes true, what would happen to wars? Third, explain why the writer mentions "a fisherman". Do NOT copy more than FOUR consecutive words from the passage.

제 62 회 모의고사

1 Read the passage and follow the directions. [4 points]

> Consider the early stages of mathematics—a few technological dodges* in Egypt about two thousand years before Christ. It was a minor element in a great civilization. About five hundred years before Christ, the Greeks initiated its theoretical development for the love of the theory. This was about four or five hundred after the date of Solomon's dream, the greatest prophecy ever made. The genius of the Greeks was shown by their clear divination* of the importance of mathematics for the study of nature. The necessity for fostering the development of abstract morphology is illustrated by considering the state of the science of geometry at the commencement of the sixteenth century. The science had been studied for about two thousand years. It had been elaborated in great detail. But, allowing for some minor qualifications, nothing had come from it except the intrinsic interest of the study. Then, as if a door had suddenly opened, Kepler produced the first important utilization of conic sections, the first among hundreds, Descartes and Desargues revolutionized the methods of the science, Newton wrote his *Principia*, and the modern period of civilization commenced. Apart from the capital of abstract ideas which had accumulated slowly during two thousand years, our modern life would have been impossible. There is nothing magical about ____①____ as such. It is simply the greatest example of a science of abstract forms.

The abstract theory of music is another such science; the abstract theory of political economy is another; and the abstract theory of the currency is another. The point is that the development of abstract theory precedes the understanding of ____②____. The instance of political economy illustrates an important point. Abstract political economy deals with men under an abstraction. It limits its view to the "economic man." It also makes assumptions as to markets and competition which neglect many important factors. We have here an example of the necessity of transcending a given morphological scheme. Up to a point the scheme is invaluable. It clarifies thought, it suggests observation, and it explains fact. But there is a strict limit to the utility of any finite scheme. If the scheme be pressed beyond its proper scope, definite error results.

* dodge : sidestep
* divination : insight or fortune-telling

Fill in each blank with the ONE most appropriate word from the passage respectively. Second, describe the fundamental reason ancient Greeks played a leading role in developing the theory of mathematics. Do NOT copy more than FOUR consecutive words from the passage.

2. Read the passage and follow the directions. [4 points]

Which man do you expect to be more honest: the one wearing an Armani suit or the one wearing a sport coat from Men's Wearhouse? Although clothes might seem irrelevant, research by Paul Piff, a social psychologist at Berkeley, suggests that indicators of socioeconomic status can predict trustworthiness. It turns out that increasing status and power go hand in hand with decreasing honesty and reliability. In one experiment, for example, Piff and colleagues asked participants to play the part of a job recruiter. The participants were told about an open temporary position that would last for no longer than six months, and about a well-qualified applicant who was interested only in a long-term role. When asked to prepare their pitches to woo this applicant, those recruiters with a higher status not only neglected to tell the applicant that the job was temporary but also told the study's leaders that they would lie about the job's duration if asked.

From this and other findings, you might think that the rich are simply less trustworthy than the poor, but that's not exactly the case. A person's honesty depends on his or her relative feelings of power—or vulnerability—not on how much he or she has in the bank. Work by University of Cologne psychologist Joris Lammers proves the point. Lammers randomly assigned people to be a "boss" or a "follower" in an office simulation and found that most people temporarily elevated to more-senior roles displayed a higher degree of hypocritical behavior—they were quick to condemn others for unethical, self-interested behavior but judged their own similar actions to be acceptable.

When someone has a(n) _____ than you, or even just thinks he does, his mind tells him that you need him more than he needs you. Consequently, he's more likely to satisfy short-term desires and worry less about the long-term consequences of being untrustworthy. So when deciding whom to trust, you have to consider power differences, including new and temporary ones. If a potential collaborator has just been promoted or has landed a big deal, he might regard some relationships as less important. And although top firms often have great reputations, that doesn't mean they treat their small clients as well as their larger ones.

Explain what Joris Lammers proves in his study. Do NOT copy more than FOUR consecutive words from the passage. Second, fill in the blank with the TWO most appropriate consecutive words from the passage.

3 Read the passage and follow the directions. [4 points]

With the advent of television, lots of entertainments have been supplanted. Such live programs as world news and television serials have removed from us the desire to listen to radio, to read books or newspapers, or even to go to watch movies. Indeed, the television brings the world into our home. By pressing buttons world happenings are at once presented in front of us. Children nowadays develop faster in language, owing to the early exposure to television programs. At such tender age, it would be difficult for them to read books or papers. Therefore, television programs are a good source of learning for them. Furthermore, pronunciations by the newscasters, actors or actresses are usually standardized, hence young children watching these programs will learn the "right" pronunciations too. Television is also extremely beneficial to working parents who are usually too busy or tired to take their kids out for amusements. Surrounded by the comforts of their home, the family can get together and watch their favorite television programs.

Of course, we should not be too carried away by the merits of the television. Watching television programs takes away our desire to read. Why read books when exciting movies are screened? Why bother to read newspapers when we can hear them from the television news reports? The lack of reading is unhealthy especially to younger children as they will grow up only with the ability to speak but not write. For example, I have a neighbor whose six-year-old child can say complete sentences like "I love dogs," but when told to write out the sentence, is unable to do so. Not only are the writing skills of children affected, their thinking capacities are also handicapped. Television programs remove the need to think. The stories, ideas and facts are woven in the way television planners wanted. Exposure to such opinions and the lack of thinking opportunities will hinder the children's analyzing ability.

In spite of the demerits of watching television programs, choosing the 'middle path', which is to do selective television viewing, should be the best solution to reconcile both the advantages and disadvantages of television.

Summarize the passage following the guidelines below.

Guidelines

- Summarize the above passage in ONE paragraph.
- Provide a topic sentence, supporting ideas, and a concluding sentence based on the passage.
- Do NOT copy more than FIVE consecutive words from the passage.

제 63 회 모의고사

1 Read the passage and follow the directions. [4 points]

In egg yolk, dairy products, margarine etc, we can find Vitamin A. It is abundant in fish-liver oils, consequently fish-liver oils are employed for preventing and curing illness caused by _____ of vitamin A. In a well-fed, healthy human being, the liver can store up sufficient vitamin A to meet the body's requirements for six months.

Although vitamin A itself is not present in plants, many plants produce a substance called carotene, formed from leaf-green which our bodies can convert into it. Carotene is the yellowish-red coloring matter in carrots. The greener a leaf is, the more carotene it usually contains. Hence the importance of green, leafy vegetables in the diet as a source of carotene. Tomatoes, papayas, mangoes and bananas contain more carotene than most other fruits. Red palm oil contains so much carotene that it is used instead of cod-liver oil. Thus, it is very valuable, both as a food-fat and for deep-frying.

Vitamin A and carotene are insoluble in water and they are not destroyed by heat unless oxygen is present. Boiling in water, therefore, does not destroy much vitamin A or carotene.

Vitamin A encourages healthy growth and physical fitness. Young animals soon stop growing and die if it is not present in their diet. This vitamin keeps the moist surfaces lining the digestive canal, the lungs and air passages healthy. It also helps keep the ducts of the various glands, the tissue that lines the eyelids and covers the front of the eyeball functional. As vitamin A helps these tissues build up resistance to infection, it is often called the anti-infective vitamin. Some of the most common disorders in people are caused by lack of vitamin A, when the moist tissues become dry and rough. This often causes serious eye disease, followed by infection of the air-passages. The skin may also become flaky and rough.

> As the body cannot produce vitamin A, it has to come from external sources. Thus a well-balanced diet is required and is usually sufficient to provide the necessary amount. There is therefore no need to supplement the need in the form of pills.

Fill in the blank with the ONE most appropriate word from the passage. Second, according to the passage, explain why a well-balanced diet is important to human beings.

2. Read the passage and follow the directions. [4 points]

    The Native American peoples of the north Pacific Coast created a highly complex maritime culture as they invented modes of production unique to their special environment. In addition to their sophisticated technical culture, they also attained one of the most complex social organizations of any nonagricultural people in the world. In a division of labor similar to that of the hunting peoples in the interior and among foraging peoples throughout the world, the men did most of the fishing, and the women processed the catch. Women also specialized in the gathering of the abundant creatures that lived closer to shore. They collected crabs, mussels, abalone, and clams, which they could gather while remaining close to their children. The _____ life harvested by the women not only provided food, but also supplied more of the raw materials for making tools than did the fish gathered by the men. Of particular importance for the native tool kit before the introduction of metal was the wide knife made from the larger mussel shells, and a variety of cutting edges that could be made from other maritime shells. The women used their tools to process all of the fish and maritime mammals brought in by the men. They cleaned the fish, and dried vast quantities of them for the winter. They sun-dried fish when practical, but in the rainy climate of the coastal area they also used smokehouses to preserve tons of fish and other seafood annually. Each product had its own peculiar characteristics that demanded a particular way of cutting or drying the meat, and each task required its own cutting blades and other utensils. After drying the fish, the women pounded some of them into fish meal, which was an easily transported food used in soups, stews, or other dishes to provide protein and thickening in the absence of fresh fish or while on long trips. The women also made a cheese-like substance from a mixture of fish and roe by aging it in storehouses or by burying it in wooden boxes or pits lined with rocks and tree leaves.

Fill in the blank with the ONE most appropriate word from the passage. Second, explain why the Native Americans of the north Pacific Coast used smokehouses.

3 Read the passage and follow the directions. [4 points]

As I write on these late days of the summer of 2020, it often feels like our civilization has morphed into a Herman Melville novel in which …

All that most maddens and torments; all that stirs up the lees of things; all truth with malice in it; all that cracks the sinews and cakes the brain; all the subtle demonisms of life and thought; all evil, to crazy Ahab, were visibly personified, and made practically assailable in Moby Dick. He piled upon the whale's white hump the sum of all the general rage and hate felt by his whole race from Adam down; and then, as if his chest had been a mortar*, he burst his hot heart's shell upon it.

Who would not be maddened and tormented by the images and stories coming out of intensive care units where Covid-19 patients gasp out their final breaths as loved ones watch remotely, unable even to bid a final farewell? Who hasn't experienced cracked sinews and caked brains from months of being isolated with our thoughts, our voices masked, our social movements regulated?

As we peer into the distant horizon, the seeing becomes misty, clarity clouded in the fog of uncertainty. What will 2020 mean in 2030? Or 2050? Or 2120? Even that class of seer known as superforecasters, those trained in the dark arts of Bayesian reasoning and big-data analysis, do no better than chance when they look more than five years out.

In a 1966 episode of *Star Trek* titled "Miri," the prepubescent heroine of the story explains to a flummoxed Captain Kirk what happened on her planet in which all the Grups (grownups) were dead, leaving the Onlies (children) to fend for themselves: "That was when they started to get sick in the Before Time. We hid, then they were gone." According to linguist Ben Zimmer, who has traced the phrase's etymology, the Before Time often represents a pre-plague world, and the expression has a literary history at least as old as the King James Bible, in which the author of the Book of

Samuel writes: "Beforetime in Israel, when a man went to enquire of God, thus he said, 'come, and let us go to the Seer': for he that is now called a Prophet was beforetime called a Seer." The locution* has been resurrected in response to the Covid-19 pandemic, as when *Atlantic* columnist Marina Koren wrote of "the exacerbated sense that the days before the coronavirus swept across the country—the 'Before Time,' as many have taken to calling it—feel like a bygone era."

* *mortar : bomb*
* *locution : name or title*

Explain the reason the writer of the passage cites *Star Trek* considering the passage's main topic. Next, what can be inferred to be the newest title of the role of "seer"?

4 Read the passage and follow the directions. [4 points]

Despite great progress in our scientific understanding of the brain, we still don't have even the beginnings of an explanation of how complex electrochemical signaling is somehow able to give rise to the inner subjective world of colors, sounds, smells and tastes that each of us knows in our own case. There is a deep mystery in understanding how what we know about ourselves from the inside fits together with what science tells us about matter from the outside.

While the problem is broadly acknowledged, many people think we just need to plug away at our standard methods of investigating the brain, and we'll eventually crack it*. But I argue that the problem of consciousness results from the way we designed science at the start of the scientific revolution.

A key moment in the scientific revolution was Galileo's declaration that mathematics was to be the language of the new science, that the new science was to have a purely quantitative vocabulary. But Galileo realized that you can't capture consciousness in these terms, as consciousness is an essentially quality-involving phenomenon. Think about the redness of a red experience or the smell of flowers or the taste of mint. You can't capture these kinds of qualities in the _____ of physical science. So Galileo decided that we have to put consciousness outside of the domain of science. After we'd done that, everything else could be captured in mathematics.

This is really important, because although the problem of consciousness is taken seriously, most people assume our conventional scientific approach is capable of solving it. And they think this because they look at the great success of physical science in explaining more and more of our universe and conclude that this ought to give us confidence that physical science alone will one day explain consciousness. However, I believe that this reaction is rooted in a misunderstanding of the history of science. Yes, physical science has been incredibly successful. But it's been successful precisely because it was designed to exclude consciousness. If Galileo were to time travel to the present day and hear about this problem of explaining consciousness in the terms of physical science, he'd say, "Of course, you can't do that. I designed physical science to deal with quantities, not qualities."

crack it : succeed

Fill in the blank with the TWO most appropriate consecutive words from the passage. Second, explain the implication of the underlined words in the last sentence.

제 64 회 모의고사

1 Read the passage and follow the directions. [4 points]

To gorge on delicious cookies at the end of your working week, you first had to go through a situational stage, where you put yourself in a compromising situation with tempting cookies. From there, you transitioned to an attentional stage, where you directed your attention back towards those cookies. After that, you went through a(n) _____, where you thought about how good those cookies would taste (especially with a glass of milk). All this led to a response stage, where you broke down and eventually ate all the cookies. To put it bluntly, a lot of things had to go wrong for you to end up giving in to temptation. The good news is that this means you could have applied self-control at several instances prior to when you tried and failed to exert inhibitory self-control (or 'willpower' in everyday talk).

Let's start with the situational stage. You don't need to be well-versed in social psychology to recognise the power of the situation. Most teachers will tell you it's easier for students to focus when they sit in the front of the classroom. With this in mind, you could have employed 'situational self-control strategies'. For instance, instead of sitting in front of a box of cookies and forcing yourself not to eat them, you could have either not bought them in the first place—known as 'situation selection' or simply removed them from sight by placing them in a cabinet (or thrown them out) —'situation modification'.

Prior research suggests that these situational strategies are quite effective. For example, one study that instructed high-school students to use situational strategies (such as removing buzzing cellphones and other temptations from sight) found that they made more progress towards their academic goals, compared with others who were simply instructed to use inhibitory self-control. Similarly, dieting research suggests that a simple yet overlooked way to lose weight is to avoid situations where tempting, high-calorie foods are readily available. For example, when you go grocery shopping, plan to avoid walking through the bakery. That way, you are less likely to encounter cues (pleasant smells and sights) that strengthen temptation. Think 'out of sight, out of mind'.

But what if you can't use situational strategies? After all, you might have no choice but to walk through the bakery, or perhaps you'll upset your kids if you throw away the cookies. Thankfully, there are other 'psychological strategies', initiated during the attentional stage and appraisal stage, that can be useful when the situation is uncontrollable.

Fill in the blank with the TWO most appropriate consecutive words from the passage. Second, which strategy would most appropriately fit putting one's smartphone in the other room during study?

2 Read the passage and follow the directions. [4 points]

Lots of factors related to the voice reveal the personality of the speaker. First, the voice gives psychological clues to a person's self-image, perception of others, and emotional health. Self-image can be indicated by a tone of voice that is confident, pretentious, shy, aggressive, outgoing, or exuberant, to name only a few personality traits. Also the voice may give a clue to the facade or mask of that person, for example, a shy person hiding behind an overconfident front. How a speaker perceives the listener's receptiveness, interest, or sympathy in any given conversation can drastically alter the tone of presentation, by encouraging or discouraging the speaker. Emotional health is evidenced in the voice by free and melodic sounds of the happy, by constricted and harsh sound of the angry, and by dull and lethargic qualities of the depressed.

The second is the broad area of communication, which includes imparting information by use of language and specialized communication through _____. A person conveys thoughts and ideas through choice of words, by a tone of voice that is pleasant or unpleasant, gentle or harsh, by the rhythm that is inherent within the language itself, and by speech rhythms that are flowing and regular or uneven and hesitant, and finally, by the pitch and melody of the utterance. When speaking before a group, a person's tone may indicate unsureness or fright, confidence or calm. At interpersonal levels, the tone may reflect ideas and feelings over and above the words chosen, or may belie them. Here the conversant's tone can consciously or unconsciously reflect intuitive sympathy or antipathy, lack of concern or interest, fatigue, anxiety, enthusiasm or excitement, all of which are usually discernible by the acute listener.

And performance is a manner of communication that is highly specialized with its own techniques for obtaining effects by voice or gesture. The motivation derived from the text, and in the case of singing, the music, in combination with the performer's skills, personality, and ability to create empathy will determine the success of artistic, political, or pedagogic communication.

Fill in the blank with the ONE most appropriate word from the passage. Second, according to the passage, what characteristics of the listener would most affect the speaker's presentation?

3 Read the passage and follow the directions. [4 points]

With just twenty-six letters, we can write a letter to our friends or answer an examination question. Thousands of years ago, there was no writing system and tools at all. The invention of writing tools is a major transition. In olden times, the kind of writing tools used, depended on the material they wrote on. For example, in the Middle East, where clay is abundant in supply, the early people used hollow reed 'pens' to carve onto the wet clay tablets. After which, these clay pieces were baked till rock hard to make the writings permanent. In ancient Egypt, Egyptians either wrote on scraped thin pieces of animal skins called 'parchment' or flattened papaya stems known as 'papyrus'.

It was only in the 1880s, that fountain pens were invented. Before that, most people used either quill pens—sharpened bird feathers or nibbed pens, which were dipped into ink before writing. Fountain pens invented later have both plus and minus points. With tiny ink tanks in them, fountain pens are superior to quill or nibbed ones as the ink in them do not run out as quickly. The disadvantage is that sometimes, the nibs of the fountain pens may break, causing the ink to leak, staining the writer's fingers.

The flaw in fountain pens has led to further investigation and the successful invention of the first 'ballpoint' pen by a Hungarian, Ladislao Biro in 1931. There were many people after him who tried to improve upon the appearance of his ballpoint pens.

Many technicians all over the world have tried to find better writing tools which improve upon the previous ones. However, the prospect of writing instruments are not optimistic because in the current era of the Internet and social media, people do not necessarily depend on them any more.

Summarize the passage following the guidelines below.

― Guidelines ―
- Summarize the above passage in ONE paragraph.
- Provide a topic sentence, supporting ideas, and a concluding sentence based on the passage.
- Do NOT copy more than FIVE consecutive words from the passage.

제 65 회 모의고사

1 Read the passage and follow the directions. [4 points]

> A great migration is happening on U.S. college campuses. Ever since the fall of 2008, a lot of students have walked out of English and humanities lectures and into STEM classes, especially computer science and engineering.
>
> English majors are down more than a quarter (25.5 percent) since the Great Recession, according to data compiled by the National Center for Education Statistics. It's the biggest drop for any major tracked by the center in its annual data and is quite startling, given that college enrollment has jumped in the past decade.
>
> Ask any college student or professor why this big shift from studying Chaucer to studying coding is happening and they will probably tell you it's about jobs. As students feared for their job prospects, they—and their parents—wanted a degree that would lead to a steady paycheck after graduation. The perception is that STEM (science, technology, engineering and math) is the path to employment. Majors in computer science and health fields have nearly doubled from 2009 to 2017. Engineering and math have also seen big jumps.
>
> As humanities majors slump to the lowest level in decades, <u>calls are coming from surprising places for a revival</u>. Some prominent economists are making the case for why it still makes a lot of sense to major (or at least take classes) in humanities alongside more technical fields.
>
> Nobel Prize winner Robert Shiller's new book "Narrative Economics" opens with him reminiscing about an enlightening history class he took as an undergraduate at the University of Michigan. He wrote that what he learned about the Great Depression was far more useful in understanding the period of economic and financial turmoil than anything he learned in his economic courses.

The whole premise of Shiller's book is that _____ matter. What people tell each other can have profound implications on markets—and the overall economy. Examples include the "get rich quick" stories about bitcoin or the "anyone can be a homeowner" stories that helped drive the housing bubble. "Traditional economic approaches fail to examine the role of public beliefs in major economic events—that is, narrative. Economists can best advance their science by developing and incorporating into it the art of narrative economics."

When asked if he's essentially arguing for more English and history majors, Shiller said, "I think so," adding : "Compartmentalization of intellectual life is bad." Shiller isn't alone in wishing that there were more storytellers (and story analyzers) around.

Explain the meaning of the underlined words. Second, fill in the blank with the ONE most appropriate word from the passage.

2 Read the passage and follow the directions. [4 points]

> There are two main schools in the study of communication. The first sees communication as the transmission of messages. It is concerned with how senders and receivers encode and decode, with how transmitters use the channels and media of communication. It is concerned with matters like efficiency and accuracy. It sees communication as a process by which one person affects the behaviour or state of mind of another. If the effect is different from or smaller than that which was intended, this school tends to talk in terms of communication failure, and to look to the stages in the process to find out where the failure occurred. For the sake of convenience I shall refer to this as the 'process' school.
>
> The second school sees communication as the production and exchange of meanings. It is concerned with how messages, or texts, interact with people in order to produce meanings; that is, it is concerned with the role of texts in our culture. It uses terms like signification, and does not consider misunderstandings to be necessarily evidence of _____. They may result from cultural differences between sender and receiver. For this school, the study of communication is the study of text and culture. The main method of study is semiotics (the science of signs and meanings), and I shall refer to this as the 'semiotic' school.
>
> Each school interprets our definition of communication as social interaction through messages in its own way. The first defines social interaction as the process by which one person relates to others, or affects the behaviour, state of mind or emotional response of another, and, of course, vice versa. This is close to the common-sense, everyday use of the phrase. Semiotics, however, defines social interaction as that which constitutes the individual as a member of a particular culture or society. I know I am a member of western, industrial society because, to give one of many sources of identification, I respond to Shakespeare or Coronation Street* in broadly the same ways as do the fellow members of my culture. I also become aware

of cultural differences if, for instance, I hear a Chinese critic reading King Lear as a devastating attack upon the western ideal of the family as the basis of society, or arguing that Coronation Street shows how the west keeps the workers in their place. Both these readings are possible, but my point is, they are not mine, as a typical member of my culture. In responding to Coronation Street in the more normal way, I am expressing my commonality with other members of my culture.

Coronation Street : a British soap opera

Fill in the blank with the TWO most appropriate consecutive words from the passage. Second, explain why the difference occurs between the Chinese critic and the writer as illustrated in the passage.

3 Read the passage and follow the directions. [4 points]

In their fight alongside their medical peers against the coronavirus, black physicians face the additional burden of broad mistrust of the federal government in many black communities.

And Pierre Vigilance, MD, a former health commissioner for the District of Columbia, believes he can point to that moment in U.S. history that's "the root" of that African American mistrust—the infamous 40-year Tuskegee experiment.

The United States Public Health Service started the study in 1932 in collaboration with Tuskegee University (then the Tuskegee Institute), a historically black college in Alabama. Investigators enrolled in the study a total of 600 impoverished, African-American sharecroppers from Macon County, Alabama. Of these men, 399 had latent syphilis, with a control group of 201 men who were not infected. The study was conducted without the benefit of patients' informed consent. Researchers told the men they were being treated for "bad blood," a local term used to describe several ailments, including syphilis, anemia, and fatigue. In truth, they did not receive the proper treatment needed to cure their illness. In exchange for taking part in the study, the men received free medical exams, free meals, and burial insurance. Although originally projected to last 6 months, the study actually went on for 40 years until 1972 when an Associated Press story about the Tuskegee Study caused a public outcry that led the Assistant Secretary for Health and Scientific Affairs to appoint an Ad Hoc Advisory Panel to review the study and found the men had been misled and had not been not told of the study's purpose or aim.

"Some are well aware and know that history. But many triggers of distrust are being replaced by family history, like, 'Uncle Johnny was fine, but he went to the doctor and everything went downhill.' That may be how it appeared, or how it was, but there were a number of things that Uncle Johnny had against him that had nothing to do with the _____. But that's the belief," said Dr. Vigilance, "and it's as much a part of it as medical and public health maleficence." Thus, it is challenging for black physicians to help their communities trust the instructions and services pushed by the government during the current pandemic.

According to the passage, upon whom does the Tuskegee experiment put extra burden currently and why? Second, fill in the blank with the ONE most appropriate word from the passage.

4. Read the passage and follow the directions. [4 points]

>   In my sketch of an anthropologist's training, I have only told you that he must make intensive studies of primitive peoples. I have not yet told you how he makes them. How does one make a study of a primitive people? I will answer this question very briefly and in very general terms, stating only what we regard as the essential rules of good fieldwork.
>
>   Experience has proved that certain conditions are essential if a good investigation is to be carried out. The earlier professional fieldworkers were always in a great hurry. Their quick visits to native peoples sometimes lasted only a few days, and seldom more than a few weeks. Survey research of this kind can be a useful preliminary to intensive studies and elementary ethnological classifications can be derived from it, but it is of little value for an understanding of social life. The position is very different today when one to three years are devoted to the study of a single people. This permits observations to be made at every season of the year, the social life of the people to be recorded to the last detail, and conclusions to be tested systematically.
>
>   However, given even unlimited time for research, the anthropologist will not produce a good account of the people he is studying unless he can put himself in a position which enables him to establish ties of intimacy with them, and to observe their daily activities from within, and not from without, their community life.
>
>   He must live as far as possible in their villages and camps, where he is, again as far as possible, <u>physically and morally part of the community</u>. He then not only sees and hears what goes on in the normal everyday life of the people as well as less common events, such as ceremonies and legal cases, but by taking part in those activities in which he can appropriately engage, he learns through action as well as by ear and eye what goes on around him. This is very unlike the situation in which records of native life were compiled by earlier anthropological fieldworkers who, living out of the native community and in mission stations or government posts, had mostly to rely on what a few informants told them.

Describe the TWO rules that the writer thinks are essential when anthropologists study indigenous people. Second, identify the ONE word from the passage that BEST corresponds to the underlined words.

제 66 회 모의고사

1 Read the passage and follow the directions. [4 points]

There is something funky going on in the clouds of Venus. Telescopes have detected unusually high concentrations of the molecule phosphine—a stinky, flammable chemical typically associated with feces, farts and rotting microbial activity—in an atmospheric layer far above the planet's scorching surface.

The finding is curious because here on Earth, phosphine is essentially always associated with living creatures, either as a by-product of metabolic processes or of human technology such as industrial fumigants and methamphetamine labs. Although toxic to many organisms, the molecule has been singled out as a potentially unambiguous signature of life because it is so difficult to make through ordinary geological or atmospheric action.

Swathed in sulfuric acid clouds and possessing oppressive surface pressures and temperatures hot enough to melt lead, Venus is a hellish world. But the particular cloud layer where the phosphine is present happens to be relatively balmy, with ample sunlight and Earth-like atmospheric pressure and temperature. The results will have to be carefully vetted by the scientific community. Yet they seem likely to spark renewed interest in exploring <u>our sister planet next door</u>.

"It's a really puzzling discovery because phosphine doesn't fit in our conception of what kinds of chemicals should be in Venus's atmosphere," says Michael Wong, an astrobiologist at the University of Washington. Planetary scientist Sanjay Limaye of the University of Wisconsin-Madison agrees. "The bottom line is we don't know what's going on," he says. (Neither Wong nor Sanjay were involved in the work.)

After the sun and moon, Venus is the brightest object visible to the naked eye in Earth's sky. For thousands of years, people told stories about the glittering jewel that appeared around sunrise and sunset. Venus's brilliance is what made it attractive to Jane Greaves, a radio astronomer at Cardiff University in Wales. She typically focuses her attention on distant newborn planetary systems but wanted to test her molecular identification abilities on worlds within our cosmic backyard.

In 2017 Greaves observed Venus with the James Clerk Maxwell Telescope (JCMT) on Mauna Kea in Hawaii, searching for bar code—like patterns of lines in the planet's spectrum that would indicate the presence of different chemicals. While doing so, she noticed a line associated with _____. The data suggested the molecule was present at around 20 parts per billion in the planet's atmosphere, a concentration between 1,000 and a million times greater than that in Earth's atmosphere. "I was stunned," Greaves says.

Phosphine is a relatively simple molecule containing one phosphorus atom and three hydrogen atoms. It is known to reek of garlic or rotting fish, though by the time it reaches concentrations where humans can smell it, it is likely to cause lung damage.

Explain what the new discovery eventually suggests about Venus. Second, identify to what the underlined "our sister planet next door" refers. Third, fill in the blank with the ONE most appropriate word from the passage.

2 Read the passage and follow the directions. [4 points]

In a recent experiment with colleagues at Cornell and MIT, we filmed people having a brief "get to know you" conversation either face-to-face or via online chat just before they played an economic game that pitted self-interest against cooperation. Although the average level of cooperation was equal in both groups, people's predictions for how fairly their partners would act when making monetary exchanges were significantly more accurate when they had previously interacted face-to-face. This meant that a trust-relevant signal had to exist.

To find out what it was, we compared sets of nonverbal cues we had collected to see which of them predicted untrustworthy behavior. We found that four—leaning away from a partner, crossing one's arms, hand touching, and face touching—were reliable indicators when occurring together. The more frequently an individual expressed all four cues, the more self-interest she showed by refusing to share profits with a partner. And the more times a partner saw her display those cues, the more the partner expected her to _____. Most interesting of all, the face-to-face participants had no awareness that they were using the cues to make inferences about trustworthiness; they had developed more-accurate intuitions without being able to say why.

We then repeated the experiment, with one important change: Participants conversed not with another human but with a humanoid robot that had been programmed to express either the four target cues or neutral ones. The robot provided exacting control: It could repeat the target gestures with a precision that no human actor could achieve, meaning that we could ascertain the power of the four cues. And the results were what we'd predicted: When people saw the robot express the target cues, they reported trusting it less and expected it to cheat them more.

These findings demonstrate that our minds come with built-in trust detectors. They also reinforce how invaluable intuitions, or gut feelings, can be. The problem is that managers and negotiators often suppress their intuitive machinery by either ignoring it in favor of what they believe to be more rational predictors for trustworthiness, such as reputation or status, or mistakenly looking for the wrong nonverbal "tells."

Fill in the blank with the ONE most appropriate word from the passage. Second, describe the change the writer would propose managers and negotiators to make.

3 Read the passage and follow the directions. [4 points]

> A home is supposed to be a haven where a child ought to feel safe and secure. Unfortunately, more often than not, the home is also where a child is abused.
>
> Abusers claim they do it because of their stress and frustrations. Child-abusing parents feel harassed by a crying child and are unable to curb their own fury, especially if no support is received from anyone. This is not surprising since support is extended to a victim of child abuse more readily than to the perpetrator. Occasionally, parents may vent their frustrations on their child if they fight and quarrel with each other. To be specific, financial problems can lead to child abuse. When there are too many mouths to feed, parents feel the pressure and vent their anger on a child.
>
> In this modern age where both parents are usually holding jobs, children are left with babysitters and nurseries. Abuse by these carers occur when there are too many children to be minded. Substance abuse is another factor which increases the incidents of child abuse. Under the influence of alcohol or drugs, a parent may not know what he or she may be doing. Or, rather, knows what he or she is doing but is not bothered at all. A drug addict may experience mood swings and is easily provoked by their children's minor errors. We see and read horrifying reports of a child being savagely tortured and dumped elsewhere, like garbage.
>
> No matter what the reasons for the abuse, something must be done to stop the cruelty. If you suspect a child is suffering from abuse, it's important to speak out. By catching the problem as early as possible, both the child and the abuser are in better states to be helped.

Summarize the passage following the guidelines below.

Guidelines

- Summarize the above passage in ONE paragraph.
- Provide a topic sentence, supporting ideas, and a concluding sentence based on the passage.
- Do NOT copy more than FIVE consecutive words from the passage.

제 67 회 모의고사

1 **Read the passage and follow the directions.** [4 points]

A woman who has campaigned for the legalisation of euthanasia has decided to starve herself to death because she can no longer cope with her debilitating heart and lung condition. Kelly Taylor, 28, who stopped eating more than two weeks ago, said her life had become so restricted that she "could not make any contribution to society". Her condition, Eisenmenger Syndrome, means she is dependent on oxygen and cannot walk more than a few steps without collapsing. She said she had chosen _____ because she believed it was a method of death that would not leave her husband Richard liable to prosecution for assisted suicide. She had considered travelling to a country where euthanasia was legal, but said she was concerned her husband would be prosecuted when he returned to Britain. She said, "My mind has been prepared for a long time. I do not want to continue with the life that I have got. It is so restricted. I do not contribute at all to society. That has been my biggest burden. I have never been able to work. I know I will never recover. My condition is slowly deteriorating. I considered going somewhere where euthanasia is legal and I could be given drugs to die but I know there will be legal implications for my husband. I could not let that happen."

Mrs. Taylor's determination to take her life was reinforced during a holiday in Majorca when she was unable to join her husband and her parents in the sea. "I couldn't bear to watch them," she said. "I so wanted to get into the water but I knew I couldn't. I realised how much my quality of life had deteriorated and I couldn't bear to continue." In the days since she began her hunger protest, Mrs. Taylor said she had lost a stone in weight. "When I started starving myself I didn't feel any different. By the third day my stomach was growling. I now feel weaker and need to sleep more. Of course I have the fear of dying but fear of living a life of prolonged pain is much more frightening. I don't think of it as a hunger strike or suicide but <u>more of giving nature a kick up the backside</u>." Mrs. Taylor was born with the rare degenerative condition and has needed a wheelchair since she was a child. Those who have Eisenmenger Syndrome have a hole in the heart, which causes pressure in arteries in the lungs. She was on a waiting list for a heart and lung transplant for nine years. But she has now been told the risks are too high.

Fill in the blank with the ONE most appropriate word from the passage. If necessary, change the word form. Second, explain the meaning of the underlined words. Do Not copy more than FOUR consecutive words from the passage.

2. Read the passage and follow the directions. [4 points]

Archaeological records suggest we've been close with our pets for some time. About 10,000 years ago we started to co-habitate with cats drawn to the well-fed rodents scurrying around our farms. In ancient Egypt millions of pet dogs were buried in elaborate tombs adorned with expensive gifts and inscriptions. As a result, we've likely been swapping cuddles and microbial critters with domesticated animals for many generations.

Today those pets are clearly still at home in our homes. And plenty of headlines tout that beyond snuggles and companionship our four-legged friends offer other benefits—like improved mental and physical health.

But not so fast. A rash of recent research presents a more muddled picture of what pets bring into our lives—from microbe swaps that can alter our gut environment to emotional well-being.

First, let's talk allergies. Numerous works tell us that having a dog appears to reduce rates of pet allergies if _____ takes place very early in life. Many microbiome researchers believe those exposures to pets' microbial milieu during infancy—in the form of pet dander—may specifically train the immune system to deal with pets and other allergens. (The theory goes: without those early exposures to certain bugs and infectious agents the natural development of the immune system is essentially stunted.) But as one May 2017 study of thousands of kids and adults concludes, the timing of such exposures appears to be key. When first exposure occurs as a teen or young adult, risk of pet allergy actually appears to increase.

There's more bad news. Pets can also cause other problems. Lizards and turtles can carry salmonella. Parrots can carry the causative agent of psittacosis, which causes severe pneumonia in humans. And evidence has accrued that many of our furry friends can carry serious infectious agents including "superbug" MRSA, giardia, and other pathogens and parasites.

Even our modern understanding about the mental health benefits from pet ownership continues to evolve. For many decades there was widespread acceptance about the mental health benefits of unwinding with a pet. But that picture was complicated by a 2010 study of nearly 40,000 people in Sweden that found pet owners were physically healthier than those without pets yet they suffered from more mental health problems than their sans-pet peers. Now the science remains unsettled about who may benefit from pet ownership or even why such relationships could help.

Fill in the blank with the TWO most appropriate consecutive words from the passage. Second, explain how the understanding of mental health advantages from pet ownership has evolved. Do Not copy more than FOUR consecutive words from the passage.

3 Read the passage and follow the directions. [4 points]

> The first and the simplest emotion which we discover in the human mind, is curiosity. By curiosity, I mean whatever desire we have for, or whatever pleasure we take in, novelty. We see children perpetually running from place to place, to hunt out something new; they catch with great eagerness, and with very little choice, at whatever comes before them; their attention is engaged by everything, because everything has, in that stage of life, the charm of novelty to recommend it.
>
> But as those things, which engage us merely by their novelty, cannot attach us for any length of time, curiosity is the most superficial of all the affections*. Curiosity changes its object perpetually; it has an appetite which is very sharp, but very easily satisfied; and it has always an appearance of giddiness, restlessness, and anxiety.
>
> Curiosity, from its nature, is a very active principle. It quickly runs over the greatest part of its objects, and soon exhausts the variety which is commonly to be met with in nature. The same things make frequent returns, and they return with less and less of any agreeable effect. In short, the occurrences of life, by the time we come to know it a little, would be incapable of affecting the mind with any other sensations than those of loathing and weariness, if many things were not adapted to affect the mind by means of other powers besides novelty in them, and of other passions besides curiosity in ourselves.
>
> But whatever these powers are, or upon what principle soever they affect the mind, it is absolutely necessary that they should not be exerted in those things which a daily and vulgar use have brought into a stale unaffecting* familiarity. Thus, some degree of _____ must be one of the materials in every instrument which works upon the mind; and curiosity blends itself more or less with all our passions.
>
> * *affections : emotions*
> * *unaffecting : not evoking strong emotions*

Fill in the blank with the ONE most appropriate word from the passage. Second, what appearance does curiosity have? Do Not copy more than THREE consecutive words from the passage.

4 Read the passage and follow the directions. [4 points]

At the height of the cold war, the *Daily Mirror* covered its entire front page with a rebuke addressed directly to Nikita Khruschev, the choleric, tantrum-throwing leader of the Soviet Union. In the largest type it could find, the newspaper roared : "If you'll excuse an old British expression, Mr. K, don't be so bloody rude." The same words should now be addressed to the entire British population. They should shout at us from hoardings on busy roads, where motorists are actually getting out of their cars to kill each other, so unable are they to control their savage and manic rage, their determination to be first through the red traffic lights. They should be displayed outside and within all public buildings, on shop counters, on schoolyard gates, at bus and railway stations, above the bars of hotels and local drinking dens. Television stations should start every programme with the slogan : "Don't be so bloody rude." To this could be added, perhaps, the rider : "Rudeness makes life hell."

Most people of all classes in Britain have stopped saying please and thank you to each other. <u>Children and adolescents stare at you in astonishment if you mention the omissions</u>. They consider these simple, yet so essential words archaic and obsequious. But the refusal to thank others for a service supplied or a favour done is the least damaging manifestation of coarse bloody-minded impoliteness. The way people disport themselves in public places is far more menacing, more detrimental to the national culture. Shoppers queue at supermarket food counters in smelly jogging kits. Pot-bellied oafs in T-shirts guzzle from bottles in fashionable bars. On trains, the behaviour of passengers is abominable. At one time, it was only oiks and tramps and Tory voters who plonked their muddy boots or shoes on the seating. Today executives in pinstripes, travelling first class, do it. Then there are the pop music fans. They are wearing head-sets, theoretically designed to confine the noise to their own stupid ears. But the wearers always turn up the volume to full blast to ensure that anyone within 20 yards can share the inane and maddening thump and clash from the drum section.

Nowadays, _____ has become a land of scowling, uncouth savages, elbowing one another in a social climate of selfishness, aggressiveness and perpetual unease.

Explain the meaning of the underlined words. Do Not copy more than FOUR consecutive words from the passage. Second, fill in the blank with the ONE most appropriate word from the passage.

제 68 회 모의고사

1 Read the passage and follow the directions. [4 points]

> When I'm acting, I get so focused that I'm only paying attention to one thing. Like when I'm on set and we're about to shoot and the first AD calls out "Rolling!" And then I hear "speed," "marker," "set," and then the director calls "Action!" I've heard that sequence so many times, like it's become this Pavlovian magic spell for me. "Rolling," "speed," "marker," "set" and "action." Something happens to me, I can't even help it. My attention ... narrows. And everything else in the world, anything else that might be bothering me or might grab my attention, it all goes away, and I'm just ... there. And that feeling, that is what I love, that, to me, is creativity. And that's the biggest reason I'm so grateful that I get to be an actor.
>
> So, there's these two distinct powerful feelings. There's getting attention and paying attention. Of course, in the last decade or so, new technology has allowed more and more people to have this powerful feeling of getting attention. For any kind of creative expression, not just acting. It could be writing or photography or drawing, music—everything. The channels of distribution have been democratized, and that's a good thing.
>
> But I do think there's an unintended consequence for anybody on the planet with an urge to be creative—myself included, because I'm not immune to this. I think that our creativity is becoming more and more of a means to an end. And so I feel compelled to speak up because in my experience, the more I go after that powerful feeling of paying attention, the happier I am. But the more I go after the powerful feeling of _____, the unhappier I am.

Describe what the writer defines as "creativity". Do Not copy more than FOUR consecutive words from the passage. Second, fill in the blank with the TWO most appropriate consecutive words from the passage.

2 Read the passage and follow the directions. [4 points]

Psychology professor Lisa Barrett talks of the brain as a prisoner in a dark, silent box: the skull. The only information it gets about the outside world comes via changes in light (sight), air pressure (sound) exposure to chemicals (taste and smell), and so on. It doesn't know the causes of these changes, and so it has to guess at them in order to decide what to do next.

How does it do that? It compares those changes to similar changes in the past, and makes predictions about the current causes based on experience. Imagine you are walking through a forest. A dappled pattern of light forms a wavy black shape in front of you. You've seen many thousands of images of snakes in the past, you know that snakes live in the forest. Your brain has already set in train an array of predictions.

The point is that this prediction-making is consciousness, which you can think of as a constant rolling process of guesses about the world being either confirmed or proved wrong by fresh sensory inputs. In the case of the dappled light, as you step forward you get information that confirms a competing prediction that it's just a stick. That is, the prediction of a snake was ultimately disproved, but not before it grew so strong that neurons in your visual cortex fired as though one was actually there, meaning that for a split second you "saw" it. So we are all creating our world from moment to moment. If you didn't, your brain wouldn't be able make the changes necessary for your survival quickly enough. <u>If the prediction "snake" wasn't already in train, then the shot of adrenaline you might need in order to jump out of its way would come too late.</u>

The brain also receives information about heart rate, what the lungs are doing, the immune system, hormone levels and much more. "Interoception", the constant monitoring of the state of the body, carries on largely below the level of conscious awareness. But it is absolutely crucial because it determines affect—those feelings of pleasantness or unpleasantness, arousal or non-arousal that are always present, and which feed into our emotions.

The brain deals with inputs from the inside the same way it deals with ones from the outside—it _____ about what's causing these changes based on what it has learned, assigning them meaning in the process.

Explain the meaning of the underlined words. Do Not copy more than FOUR consecutive words from the passage. Second, fill in the blank with the TWO most appropriate consecutive words from the passage.

3 Read the passage and follow the directions. [4 points]

> Although leaders are often thought to be people with unusual personal ability, decades of research have failed to produce consistent evidence that there is any category of "natural leaders." It seems that there is no set of personal qualities that all leaders have in common; rather, virtually any person may be recognized as a leader if the person has qualities that meet the needs of that particular group.
>
> Furthermore, although it is commonly supposed that social groups have a single leader, there are typically two different leadership roles that are held by different individuals. Instrumental leadership is leadership that emphasizes the completion of tasks by a social group. Group members look to instrumental leaders to "get things done." Expressive leadership, on the other hand, is leadership that emphasizes the collective well-beings of a social group's members. Expressive leaders are less concerned with the overall goals of the group than with providing emotional support to group members and attempting to minimize tension and conflict among them. Group members expect expressive leaders to maintain stable relationships within the group and provide support to individual members.
>
> Instrumental leaders are likely to have a rather secondary relationship to other group members. They give orders and may discipline group members who inhibit attainment of the group's goals. Expressive leaders cultivate a more personal or primary relationship to others in the group. They offer sympathy when someone experiences difficulties or is subjected to discipline, are quick to lighten a serious moment with humor, and try to resolve issues that threaten to divide the group.
>
> As the difference in these two roles suggests, expressive leaders generally receive more personal affection from group members; instrumental leaders, if they are successful in promoting group goals, may enjoy a more distant respect. Such as to say, understanding these differences is helpful when shaping a team relationship.

Summarize the passage following the guidelines below.

Guidelines

- Summarize the above passage in ONE paragraph.
- Provide a topic sentence, supporting ideas, and a concluding sentence based on the passage.
- Do NOT copy more than FIVE consecutive words from the passage.

제 69 회 모의고사

1 Read the passage and follow the directions. [4 points]

A credit score is a number that lenders use to assess the likelihood that a borrower will pay back a loan on time. Lenders use credit scores to decide, first, whether they will lend money to an individual, and second, at what interest rate. People with _____ will either be refused a loan or will have to pay higher rates of interest. Use of credit scores is pervasive, and if people apply for a car loan, auto insurance, a credit card, or a loan to buy a home, the lender will look at their credit scores before agreeing to extend credit.

There are two types of credit scores: generic scores and custom scores. Custom scores are developed by some individual lenders for use in their own companies. For example, a department store might develop its own custom credit scoring system to decide which customers will be approved for a store credit card. By contrast, generic scores are used by more than one company and are based on statistical models of the risk that a given person will not pay back a loan on time. Many stores and other businesses rely on generic credit scores in deciding to whom to offer credit. An individual with a median generic credit score or higher will typically get the most favorable rates on loans. For example, suppose a person wanted to get a mortgage to buy a home costing $250,000. Depending on the individual's credit score, the interest rate charged by the lender and the monthly payment for a 30-year mortgage would change. An analogous situation holds for other types of credit, such as car loans and credit cards. Additionally, insurance companies and utility companies use credit scores to set rates for their customers. Those with low credit scores are charged more.

Fill in the blank with the THREE most appropriate consecutive words from the passage. Second, what can be inferred to be the major determining factor influencing generic credit scores? Do NOT copy more than FOUR consecutive words from the passage.

2 Read the passage and follow the directions. [4 points]

Beer is not the break from politics that it is often touted to be. In fact, breweries have taken a stance on the controversial issues that have divided college campuses. Just recently, Alligator Brewing in Gainesville, Fla., attempted to empty a Richard Spencer talk by offering free beer to any customer who turned in a pair of unused tickets for his controversial event at the University of Florida. Alligator used beer to speak out against modern-day white supremacy, and in doing so built on a long history of using beer as a weapon against perceived oppression, whether from fringe groups or the government itself. Beer, like food, fosters democratic engagement. Creating and consuming beer has led to debates over morality, law, diversity and capitalism in the United States. And as a tool for political resistance, it has helped individuals express and safeguard their rights.

For centuries, beer has been more than a social lubricant. It has been a instrument of _____. Beer, in fact, was central to the founding of our country. Taverns were more common than churches in Colonial society. They were hubs of political and social life where people ate, drank, heard local news, argued about it, held public meetings and conducted business transactions. Consider, for example, Samuel Adams, a maltster who used Colonial drinking culture to generate support for independence. He used taverns around Boston to organize the Sons of Liberty and plan acts of political resistance against the British crown. So intertwined were watering holes and politics that between 1785 and 1790, when New York City was the capital of the fledgling United States, a Manhattan tavern housed the Departments of State, Treasury and War.

However, controlling alcohol, a substance which was considered healthy nourishment during this time, became a mechanism for imposing social control in the late 1700s. Laws regulated when, where and at what price beer and other alcohol could be sold, as well as whom a tavern could entertain. These were deliberate efforts by the governing elite to prevent intermingling between races and classes, control women's behavior.

Beer continued to be both a tool of imposing social control and of political resistance throughout the 1800s. Temperance reformers viewed alcohol as the chief source of crime, poverty and insanity in society, and campaigned feverishly to reduce the nation's staggering alcohol intake which averaged more than twice what Americans consume today.

Fill in the blank with the TWO most appropriate consecutive words from the passage. Second, explain how alcohol was an instrument of imposing social control. Do NOT copy more than FOUR consecutive words from the passage.

3 Read the passage and follow the directions. [4 points]

The United States has historically had high levels of unintended fertility, with people having children earlier than they desired or when they didn't want children at all. Recent years have witnessed the first decline in such births in decades. Many men and women want children, but also have a preferred context for having children—they want to have completed education, established economic security and formed a stable partnership. Difficulties in meeting whatever markers they personally deem important might mean some people don't have children, but the fact that people are better empowered to manage their reproductive behaviors so that they only have children when they feel ready is a tremendous achievement. It benefits not only individuals, but future generations and society overall.

Current fertility declines both in the United States and around the world do not mean an "end of babies." Instead, people _____ having children until later in life, when they feel ready. Typical measures such as the total fertility rate don't do a good job of capturing delayed childbearing, but other measures show that childlessness is actually down, and most people end their childbearing years with about two children. Continued advances in reproductive technologies may continue to make it easier for those who delay childbearing to achieve their personal family preferences.

If helping people have the families they want is the goal, rather than trying to increase U.S. fertility out of misplaced panic about population decline, we need policies that address the direct difficulties in combining parenthood with education and employment, as well as the indirect obstacles to parenthood such as the student loan debt crisis, housing affordability, the high cost of health care and widespread income inequality. So if relatives pester you over Thanksgiving about when you're going to have children, or when they can next expect another grandchild, turn the question around : <u>Ask them when they plan to restructure the American economy</u>.

Explain why the total fertility rate measure has limitations. Second, fill in the blank with the ONE most appropriate word from the passage. Third, explain the meaning of the underlined words in the last sentence. Do NOT copy more than FOUR consecutive words from the passage.

4. Read the passage and follow the directions. [4 points]

Human beings should be free to form opinions, and to express their opinions without reserve. Men should be free to act upon their opinions—to carry these out in their lives, without hindrance, either physical or moral, from their fellow men, so long as it is at their own risk and peril.

This proviso is of course indispensable. No one pretends that actions should be as free as opinions. On the contrary, even ____①____ lose their immunity when the circumstances in which they are expressed are such as to constitute their expression a positive instigation to some mischievous act. An opinion that corn-dealers are starvers of the poor, or that private property is robbery, ought to be unmolested when simply circulated through the press, but may justly incur punishment when delivered orally to an excited mob assembled before the house of a corndealer, or when handed about among the same mob in the form of a placard.

Actions, of whatever kind, which, without justifiable cause, do harm to others, may be, and in the more important cases absolutely require to be, controlled by the unfavourable sentiments, and, when needful, by the active interference of mankind. The liberty of the individual must be thus far limited. He must not make himself a nuisance to other people. But if he refrains from molesting others in what concerns them, and merely acts according to his own inclination and judgment in things which concern himself, the same reasons which show that opinion should be free, prove also that he should be allowed, without molestation, to carry his opinions into practice at his own cost. That mankind are not infallible; that their truths, for the most part, are only half-truths; that unity of opinion, unless resulting from the fullest and freest comparison of opposite opinions, is not desirable, and diversity not an evil, but a good, until mankind are much more capable than at present of recognising all sides of the truth, are principles applicable to men's modes of action, not less than to their opinions.

As it is useful that while mankind are imperfect there should be different opinions, so it is that there should be different experiments of living; that free scope should be given to varieties of character, short of injury to others; and that the worth of different modes of life should be proved practically, when any one thinks fit to try them. It is desirable, in short, that in things which do not primarily concern ____②____, individuality should assert itself.

Fill in each blank with the ONE most appropriate word from the passage respectively. Second, explain under which condition diversity is no longer acceptable. Do NOT copy more than FOUR consecutive words from the passage.

제 70 회 모의고사

1 Read the passage and follow the directions. [4 points]

> A flurry of Hollywood trade-paper headlines greeted the news that Bong Joon-ho's *Parasite* had, in its fifth weekend of release, crossed the $10m threshold steadily rising as its screen count expands across the country. Ordinarily, that is hardly a figure that would have champagne corks popping in Tinseltown*, but the current market is a tough one for subtitled cinema : *Parasite*'s current haul is the year's highest for any non-English-language film in the US. (Last year's critically beloved, Cannes-approved Korean thriller, Lee Chang-dong's *Burning*, made a paltry $719,000 stateside).
>   Last year, Alfonso Cuarón's Netflix-backed Mexican memory piece *Roma* came close to doing what no non-English-language film has done before, in 91 long years of the Oscars : winning best picture. Entering the ceremony as the odds-on favourite, it made history by taking best director—another first for this eternally anglocentric institution—before being tripped up at the final hurdle by the safe, retrograde and emphatically all-American comforts of *Green Book*. In the largely disgruntled industry post-mortem that followed, pundits traded various theories about why Cuarón's more acclaimed film had lost.
>   *Parasite* is incrementally acquiring something that *Roma*, for all its doting reviews, never quite managed : genuine popular cachet, of the kind that can't be bought or fabricated, but can make a film's cultural footprint seem bigger than its box office. It began as early as Cannes, where hype for the film wasn't just generated by fawning reviews from the critical establishment, but a younger, very online and very vocal group of Generation Z cinephiles, who swiftly branded themselves the #BongHive and granted the film an immediate social-media presence even before it won the Palme, or began rolling out internationally.

Since then, *Parasite* has become a positive meme machine : if you haven't seen the film yet but are a regular on Twitter, you may have regularly encountered images and gifs from the film without even realising it. The "Jessica Jingle"—a brief chant delivered by one of the film's young characters to help remember her false identity, itself based on a standard memory aid for Korean schoolchildren—has been so widely appropriated by fans that it's now available as a mobile ringtone, the kind of inexplicable-out-of-context in-joke that signals a film's ascent to a phenomenon status worth far more than $10m.

It's rare for any non-American film to attain this kind of universal currency. That Bong's film neatly taps into a global well of class outrage has given it universal resonance for socially conscious young audiences, hungry for texts to feed their haves-versus-have-nots discourse amid global political disarray : *Parasite*'s class-based sympathies might be multi-generational, but it still cuts close to the bone for the "OK boomer*" crowd.

Tinseltown : Hollywood
OK boomer : a catchphrase used by young adults to criticize baby boomers

Explain why the writer of the passage mentions the movie *Burning* in the passage. Do NOT use more than FOUR consecutive words from the passage. Second, what aspect of *Parasite* would appeal to the "OK boomer" generation. Do NOT copy more than FOUR consecutive words from the passage.

2 Read the passage and follow the directions. [4 points]

Imagine that you're negotiating a multiyear deal to provide outsourcing services to a large company. The client tells you that her firm wants to sign on for a certain level of services, but she'd like you to be willing to deliver more on the fly*, trusting that you'll be able to work out terms for the additional resources as the need arises. Should you agree?

Or imagine that a potential business partner wants to buy $12 million worth of services from you but can spend only $10 million because of temporary budget constraints. He dangles the prospect of long-term revenue opportunities in exchange for the discount but says he can't commit to anything yet. Should you give him the deal?

Situations such as these present dilemmas for any manager. The answers aren't obvious. If you choose to trust new clients, contractors, or collaborators, you make yourself vulnerable : Your outcomes, financial and otherwise, now depend on their fidelity. But if you insist on verifying each claim and accounting for every detail before a deal is signed, you'll slow the process and increase costs, potentially putting yourself at a disadvantage.

The two scenarios above come from a friend of mine—let's call him Toni—who is a partner at one of the world's largest consulting firms. Although he agreed to both clients' proposals, the decisions to trust led to very different outcomes. The first client took Toni's assent as confirmation that she and her very large firm held the power in the relationship and could therefore dictate terms for future work. As time went on, she made it clear that if the increasingly unreasonable demands of the firm weren't met, it would simply move on to another, more willing provider. The second client, by contrast, proved trustworthy, and the long-term revenue it generated for Toni's company more than compensated for the _____ granted in the initial agreement.

Success in business unquestionably requires some willingness to cooperate with and have faith in others. The question is, how much faith and in whom? Decades of scientific research show that people's accuracy in deciding if another can be trusted tends to be only slightly better than chance.

on the fly : on the spot, improvised

Fill in the blank with the ONE most appropriate word from the passage. Second, describe the major drawbacks of verification and personal ability in regards to trusting others.

3 Read the passage and follow the directions. [4 points]

Caving, often referred to as spelunking or potholing, can be a fun, adventurous and rewarding activity; however, getting started in caving can be a challenge. You should make preparations for a caving exploration. If you do not, it can turn out to be a very horrifying experience.

Do not go exploring caves without knowing your exact way in and out. Getting lost in a cave is a very dangerous situation that can resemble your worst nightmare. If you do plan to enter a cave, make sure that you know the route. Also, limit your time in a cave to a maximum of eight hours. More than that and you will get very tired and be less alert. One kilogram of carbide will give enough illumination for approximately six to eight hours. If you are one of those with a weak heart condition or suffering from claustrophobia, you should limit yourself to just show caves.

It might be a good idea to bring along a drysuit which is made for cave dives or in cold water. The suit itself is made of a laminated waterproof material, with watertight latex seals at the neck and wrists. Pockets on either side can carry safety equipment. In addition, rope is needed for hand lines and vertical drops. For these, always consider the condition and storage methods of any rope before using it as a safety device. Rope protectors should be used as a cushion between rope and any surface which might abrade it.

Caving may be a once-in-a-lifetime thrill. But caves are delicate and potentially dangerous environments that can be permanently impacted or cause injury without the right preparation. The most common, and generally accepted standard process to start caving is to begin by finding a caving club near where you live, and attend a meeting, and express an interest in going on a "beginner" caving trip.

Write a summary following the guidelines below.

```
┌─────────────────── Guidelines ───────────────────┐
• Summarize the above passage in ONE paragraph.
• Provide a topic sentence, supporting ideas, and a concluding sentence based
  on the passage.
• Do NOT copy more than FIVE consecutive words from the passage.
└──────────────────────────────────────────────────┘
```

2S2R

유희태 일반영어 ④-2 문제은행

초판 1쇄	2014년 4월 14일	
2판 1쇄	2016년 6월 15일	저자와의
3판 1쇄	2019년 2월 20일	협의하에
2쇄	2019년 5월 10일	인지생략
3쇄	2019년 7월 10일	
4판 1쇄	2020년 10월 23일	
2쇄	2021년 7월 30일	
3쇄	2022년 4월 15일	
5판 1쇄	2023년 1월 10일	
6판 1쇄	2026년 1월 15일	

저자 유희태 **발행인** 박 용 **발행처** (주)박문각출판
표지디자인 박문각 디자인팀
등록 2015. 4. 29. 제2019-000137호
주소 06654 서울시 서초구 효령로 283 서경 B/D
팩스 (02) 584-2927
전화 교재 문의 (02) 6466-7202 동영상 문의 (02) 6466-7201

이 책의 무단 전재 또는 복제 행위는 저작권법 제136조에 의거, 5년 이하의 징역 또는 5,000만원 이하의 벌금에 처하거나 이를 병과할 수 있습니다.

정 가 42,000원(분권 포함)
ISBN 979-11-7519-528-8
ISBN 979-11-7519-527-1((세트)

제6판

교원임용고시
일반영어 필독서

임용영어 수험생 대다수가 선택하는
전공영어의 보통명사

- 교원임용고시 전공영어 독보적 전국 1위
  (2025년 예스24 전공영어 부문 박문각 누적 판매량 1위)
- 미국 버클리대학 유희태 박사의 독창적 문제집
- 출제가능성 높은 예상문제 수록

유희태 일반영어

2S2R 4-2 문제은행

LSI 영어연구소 유희태 박사 저

● 모범답안 및 번역

박문각

2S2R

유희태 일반영어
④-2 문제은행
● 모범답안 및 번역

PART 02

모의고사

Part 02 모의고사 Ⅰ [01~25회]

본책 p.009

제01회 모의고사

1

하위내용영역	배점	예상정답률
일반영어 A형 서술형	4점	50%

모범 답안 The words are "capital punishment." Second, Edison's hidden intent was to associate alternating current with death to give his competitor's brand a negative image.

채점 기준

- **2점**: 빈칸에 들어갈 단어를 "capital punishment"라 정확히 기입하였다.
- **2점**: 에디슨이 사형의 수단으로 전기의자를 추천하는 숨은 의도를 "to associate alternating current with death to give his competitor's brand a negative image"라 서술하였거나 유사하였다.

한글번역

거의 2세기 동안 미국은 사형에 대한 애착과 인도적이고 정의로운 사회라는 자신의 이미지를 조화시키기 위해 고군분투했다. 이 긴 역사에서 마크 에식이 그의 새 책 《에디슨과 전기의자》에서 들려주는 것만큼 기이한 에피소드는 거의 없었다. 에식 씨의 이야기를 충격적이라고 묘사하는 것은 취향이 나쁠 것이지만, 기술 숭배, 산업 방해 공작, 사법부의 안일함, 그리고 노골적인 위선의 기묘한 혼합은 적어도 미국 독자로 하여금 사형에 대한 지속적인 지지에 대해 조금 불편함을 느끼게 해야 한다.
19세기에 미국은 사형수를 처형하는 일반적인 방법인 교수형을 싫어하게 됐다. 교수형은 종종 공개적으로 행해졌고, 관중들 사이에서 폭동과 다른 보기 흉한 행동을 자주 일으켰다. 교수형은 또한 종종 실패해 느린 질식이나 참수를 초래했다. 사형 반대자들은 교수형이 잔혹하고 야만적이라고 주장함으로써 지지자들을 얻었다. 처형의 존경받을 만한 지위를 회복하기 위해, 그 지지자들은 전기 처형이라는 아이디어를 내놓았다.

전기는 새롭고 매력적인 기술이었다. 그것은 무엇보다도 현대적이었다. 동시에 그것은 사람들을 불안하게 만들었다. 미국은 주요 도시들에 전선을 설치하기 시작했고, 전등의 이점은 모든 사람에게 명백했지만, 그것이 얼마나 안전한지는 아무도 확실히 알지 못했다. 단두대(너무 피비린내 나는)부터 모르핀 과다복용(너무 평화로운)까지 처형 방법들을 조사한 후, 뉴욕주 의회가 임명한 위원회는 1888년에 "즉각적이고 고통 없는" 그리고 "모든 야만성이 없는" 것이라고 약속한 전기 처형 사용을 권고했다. 위원회를 이것으로 설득한 사람은 미국의 가장 유명한 발명가인 토머스 에디슨이었다.
전기 처형을 권고한 에디슨의 주된 관심은 미국 전선화 경쟁에서 그의 주요 경쟁자인 조지 웨스팅하우스의 신용을 떨어뜨리는 것이었다. 에디슨의 회사는 직류를 사용했다. 웨스팅하우스의 회사는 교류를 사용했다. 에디슨은 전기 처형이 사형수를 죽이는 최고의 새로운 방법이 될 것이라고 주장했을 뿐만 아니라, 웨스팅하우스의 교류가 자신의 직류보다 그것을 더 잘할 것이라고 주장했다. 다시 말해, 전기 처형에 대한 그의 지지는 마케팅 수법이었다. 에디슨은 처형에 교류를 사용하는 것이 대중의 마음에서 그것을 죽음과 지울 수 없게 연관시키고, 전력 시장에서 자신에게 우위를 줄 것이라고 희망했다. 어쨌든 전기 처형은 너무 끔찍해서 공식 증인들 중 다수가 구토하고 기절하게 만들었다; 1899년 전기의자에서 죽은 첫 번째 여성인 마사 플레이스를 죽이는 데 두 번의 시도가 필요했다. 둘째, 그 처형 후 100년이 넘은 지금도 미국은 여전히 사형의 옳고 그름과 미학과 씨름하고 있다.

2

하위내용영역	배점	예상정답률
일반영어 B형 서술형	4점	40%

모범 답안 The word is "fantasy". Second, the extra dimension is the virtue of the artist which might be observed in the art itself.

채점 기준

- **2점**: 빈칸에 들어갈 단어를 "fantasy"라 정확히 기입하였다. 이외에는 답이 될 수 없다.

+ 2점: 밑줄 친 "또 다른 차원"이 가리키는 것을 "the virtue of the artist (which might be observed in the art itself)"라 서술하였거나 유사하였다.

한글번역

　아름다움은 예술과 자연이 공유하는 어떤 것의 편리하고 전통적인 이름이며, 경험의 질과 의식의 변화라는 개념에 상당히 명확한 의미를 부여한다.
　나는 불안하고 분개하는 마음 상태로 창밖을 내다보며, 내 주변을 의식하지 못하고, 아마도 내 위신에 가해진 어떤 손상에 대해 곰곰이 생각하고 있다. 그때 갑자기 떠도는 황조롱이를 관찰한다. 순간 모든 것이 바뀐다. 상처받은 허영심을 가진 침울한 자아가 사라졌다. 이제 황조롱이 외에는 아무것도 없다. 그리고 내가 다른 문제를 생각하기 위해 돌아올 때 그것은 덜 중요해 보인다.
　화분에 담긴 식물을 집에 가져오고 황조롱이를 지켜보는 사람들이 이러한 것들이 덕과 관련이 있다는 개념에 놀랄 수도 있을 만큼, 꽃과 동물을 즐기는 것은 명백히 좋은 일이다. 우리가 자연의 아름다움에서 예술의 아름다움으로 이동할 때 우리는 이미 더 어려운 영역에 있다. 예술의 경험은 자연의 경험보다 더 쉽게 타락한다. 많은 예술, 아마도 대부분의 예술은 불행히도 실제로 자기 위안적 환상이며, 심지어 위대한 예술도 그 소비자의 의식의 질을 보장할 수 없다. 그러나 위대한 예술은 존재하고 때때로 적절히 경험되며, 위대한 것에 대한 얕은 경험조차도 그 효과를 가질 수 있다. 예술, 그리고 이제부터 '예술'로 나는 환상 예술이 아닌 좋은 예술을 의미하는데, 우리에게 탁월한 것의 독립적 존재에 대한 순수한 기쁨을 제공한다. 그 생성과 향유 모두에서 그것은 강박에 완전히 반대되는 것이다. 그것은 우리의 최고 능력들을 활기차게 하고 영혼의 가장 높은 부분에서 사랑을 불러일으킨다. 그것이 이를 할 수 있는 것은 부분적으로 자연과 공유하는 어떤 것 덕분이다: 소유욕 없는 관조를 유도하고 의식의 강박적 꿈의 삶으로의 흡수를 거부하는 형태의 완전함.
　그러나 성사나 좋은 에너지의 근원으로 여겨지는 예술은 추가적인 차원을 소유한다. 예술은 자연보다 접근하기 어렵지만 실제로 인간의 산물이기 때문에 더 교화적이며, 특정 예술들은 실제로 직접적인 의미에서 인간사에 '관한' 것이다. 예술은 인간의 산물이고 재능뿐만 아니라 덕도 예술가에게 요구된다. 좋은 예술가는 자신의 예술과 관련하여 용감하고, 진실하고, 인내심 있고, 겸손하다; 그리고 비재현적 예술에서조차 우리는 이러한 자질들의 직관을 받을 수 있다.

3

하위내용영역	배점	예상정답률
일반영어 B형 서술형	4점	40%

모범답안 Caviar has come over time to be highly-valued as a form of conspicuous consumption. Coming from the roe of sturgeon, which once dominated every river system in the northern hemisphere, it grew from a minor trade item of Mongols and a staple in Russia to a hot item in Europe after the defeat of Napoleon. Later on, caviar has risen to being a high-valued commodity while the population of sturgeon has fallen. In conclusion, the overfishing of sturgeon in these markets needs to be countermanded, as shown most notably by CITES, an organization protecting endangered species.

채점 기준

ⓐ Topic sentence
+ 1점: "Caviar has come to be highly-valued as a form of conspicuous consumption over time."를 서술하였거나 유사하였다.

ⓑ Major supporting details
+ 2점: "① Coming from the roe of sturgeon, which once dominated every river system in the northern hemisphere, it grew from a minor trade item of Mongols and a staple in Russia to a hot item in Europe after the defeat of Napoleon. ② Later on, caviar has risen to being a high-valued commodity while the population of sturgeon has fallen."을 서술하였거나 유사하였다.

☞ 2개 중 2개 모두를 정확하게 요약한 경우 2점, 1개를 요약한 경우 1점, 요약하지 못한 경우 0점을 준다.

ⓒ Conclusion
+ 1점: "In conclusion, the overfishing of sturgeon in these markets needs to be countermanded, as shown most notably by CITES, an organization protecting endangered species."을 서술하였거나 유사하였다.

감점
- 본문에 나오는 연속되는 5단어 이상을 사용하였다. −1pt
- 문단을 두 개나 그 이상으로 구성하였다. −1pt
- grammar나 영어표현이 합쳐 4개 이상 오류가 있다. −1pt

한글번역

파블로 피카소는 자신의 판화를 세브루거 캐비어와 바꿨다고 전해지고, 이언 플레밍은 오세트라 캐비어만 샀으며, 마돈나는 벨루가를 선호한다. 과시적 소비의 전형으로서, 캐비어는 유명인 보증인이 거의 필요하지 않다: 그 상징적 힘은 정확히 터무니없는 비용과 그것이 필요하다는 어떤 개념과도 무관하다는 점 때문에 존재한다.

오래 전, 그 알이 세계의 어두운 저류에서 거래되는 생물인 철갑상어는 한때 북반구의 모든 주요 강 체계에서 지배적인 대형 물고기였다. 1억 년 동안 형태가 변하지 않고 민물과 바닷물을 모두 유영하며, 유연한 연골성 턱으로 먹이를 빨아들인다. 이 물고기의 알이 몽골족들 사이의 사소한 무역 품목에서 온스 당 100달러 이상에 팔리게 된 것은 패션, 무역, 그리고 반복적으로 "관리를 앞지른" 탐욕의 이야기다. 당시 러시아에서는 거의 주식이었지만, 서구로의 캐비어 수출은 불안한 시작을 했다: 어린 루이 15세는 표트르 대제로부터 받은 첫 번째 캐비어 선물을 뱉어냈다고 전해진다. 알들은 나폴레옹의 패배 후 유럽의 살롱을 채운 러시아 귀족들과 함께 그 가치를 발휘했다.

나중에 미국에서 이민 온 어부들이 19세기 중반에 미국 철갑상어에서 나온 캐비어를 팔기 시작했다. 곧 그 가격이 급등했고, 철갑상어의 수는 급락했다. "검은 금"은 1920년대에 미국에서 유럽으로 다시 수출됐고, 소련은 확실히 자본주의적인 무역을 시작했다. 오늘날, 카스피해의 캐비어는 1990년대 후반에 밀렵이 연간 20억에서 40억 달러의 가치가 있었던 무역에서 조직범죄에 의해 통제되며—그 결과 살아남은 철갑상어는 상당히 적다.

앞으로, 보존이 중심적인 도전과제다. 철갑상어의 남획은 그 반복성에 의해 가장 뚜렷하게 나타난다: 먼저 유럽에서, 그다음 북미에서, 이제는 러시아에서. 불행히도, 캐비어의 매력은 더 어두운 진실을 가린다. 그러나 현재, 세관 요원들, 과학자들, 어부들, 그리고 30,000종 이상의 동식물을 보호하려고 시도하는 멸종위기에 처한 야생동식물종의 국제거래에 관한 협약인 CITES를 포함해 이 착취와 싸우는 다양한 인물들이 있다.

제02회 모의고사

1

하위내용영역	배점	예상정답률
일반영어 A형 서술형	4점	50%

모범답안 The word is "blame". Second, the writer disagrees with the conventional view on the basis that there are limitations to our capacity to analyze all future risks.

채점기준

+ **2점**: 빈칸에 들어갈 단어를 "<u>blame</u>"이라 정확하게 답하였다. 이외에는 답이 될 수 없다.
+ **2점**: 글쓴이가 통상적인 관점에 반대하는 이유를 "<u>there are limitations to our capacity to analyze all future risks</u>"라 서술하였거나 유사하였다.

☞ 다음과 같이 서술하였어도 2점을 준다.
- "The writer opposes the conventional view <u>because it is impossible to make precise and accurate calculations of all future risks.</u>"
- "The writer opposes the conventional view <u>because it is practically impossible to always make accurate guesses on future events, since there exist a clear limit on individuals' capacity to do so, and therefore it is unfair to blame someone for his or her own misfortune.</u>"

한글번역

케니 차우는 미얀마에서 태어나 1987년 뉴욕시로 이주했다. 그는 보석상에서 다이아몬드 세팅사로 수년간 일했고, 2011년 해고되기 전까지 가족을 위한 집을 살 만큼 충분히 벌었다. 그 시점에서 차우는 형처럼 택시 운전사가 되기로 결정했고, 750,000달러에 택시 메달리온을 사기 위한 자금을 긁어모았다. 이것으로 그는 메달리온을 자산으로 해 개인 사업자로 운영할 수 있었다.

한동안 모든 것이 계획대로 진행됐고, 택시 메달리온은 가치가 올라 100만 달러 이상이 됐다. 그러다가 거품이 터졌고, 리프트와 우버 같은 차량 공유 앱들이 등장했다. 차우의 메달리온 가치는 급락했고, 대출금을 계속 갚기가 어려워졌다. 2018년, 그는 스스로 목숨을 끊었다.

우리 모두 차우의 상황이 불행하다는 것을 인정할 것이다. 하지만 논쟁의 여지가 있게도, 그는 위험한 자산을 구매할 때 계산된 도박을 했고, 따라서 우리 중 일부는 자신의 불행을 그 자신 탓으로 돌리고 싶어 할 수도 있다. 한 사상 학파("개인 책임론"이나 "자유 시장 철학" 같은 사상을 가진 사람들의 관점을 지칭—즉, 경제적 실패나 불운에 대해 개인이 전적으로 책임져야 한다는 견해)에 따르면, 이런 종류의 내기들이 성과를 내지 못할 때, 도박꾼만이 비난받을 뿐이다. 그것이 냉혹하게 들릴 수도 있지만, 적어도 미국에서는 우리 중 많은 사람들이 실제로 갖고 있는 것 같은 태도이다: 2014년 퓨 리서치 보고서는 미국인의 39%가 빈곤이 가난한 사람들 편에서의 노력 부족 때문이라고 믿는다는 것을 발견했다. '노력'이 결정에 내재된 위험을 적절히 평가하지 못하는 것을 포함할 때, 이것은 결국 우리 중 많은 사람들이 자신의 불운에 책임이 있다고 생각한다는 것을 시사한다.

나는 이 견해에 동의하지 않는다. 하지만 내 이유들은 순전히 정치적이거나 도덕적 성격은 아니다. 오히려, 복잡성 과학—특히 계산 복잡성 이론—의 통찰들은 위험을 정확하고 정밀하게 계산하는 우리의 능력에 엄격한 한계가 있다는 것을 수학적으로 보여준다. 미래에 무슨 일이 일어날지에 대한 합리적인 감각을 얻는 것이 종종 불가능하기 때문에, 예상치 못한 상황의 결과로 더 나빠지게 된 선의를 가진 사람들을 비난하는 것은 불공정하다. 이는 연민이, 비난이 아니라, 선의로 행동했지만 인생의 내기가 성과를 내지 못한 사람들에 대한 적절한 태도라는 결론으로 이어진다.

2

하위내용영역	배점	예상정답률
일반영어 A형 서술형	4점	50%

모범답안 The words are "bonded relationships". Second, an endorphin blocker can be effective because it reduces the positive feedback returned from drinking.

채점기준

+ 2점: 빈칸에 들어갈 단어를 "bonded relationships"이라 정확하게 답하였다. 이외에는 답이 될 수 없다.
+ 2점: 엔돌핀 차단제가 알코올 중독자에게 유용한 이유를 "an endorphin blocker can be effective because it reduces the positive benefits returned from drinking"라 서술하였거나 유사하였다.

☞ 다음과 같이 서술하였어도 2점을 준다.
- "Using an endorphin blocker can be effective because it blocks one's brain from receiving endorphins even when one drinks alcohol, so that the one would not experience opiate-like effects."

한글번역

사람들은 왜 술을 마실까? 더운 여름날 저녁 술집이 열기를 기다리며 줄 선 사람들에게는 쉬운 질문이다. 바로 술을 마시는 것이 즐거운 일이며, 근심을 잊게 해주기 때문이다. 그러나 음주가 사회에 끼치는 해악에 대한 최신 보고서를 읽고 있는 보건복지부 공무원들은 그런 답을 좋아하지 않을 것이다. 술이 정말 그렇게 나쁜 것이라면, 왜 사람들은 그럼에도 술을 마실까?

나와 같은 진화심리학자들은 전혀 다른 분야의 최신 연구에서 그 질문에 대한 흥미로운 답을 찾았다. 그 답은 간단하면서도 한편으로 복잡하다. 이유는 다음과 같다.

모든 원숭이나 영장류와 마찬가지로, 인간은 고도의 사회성을 가지고 있다. 우리는 타인과 잡담을 나누길 좋아하며 술은 여기에 도움이 된다. 친밀감은 외부의 위협과 내부의 스트레스로부터 우리를 보호하며, 인류가 진화적으로 거둔 성공의 핵심 비결이다. 영장류는 다른 동물들과 달리 사회적 관계를 유지하기 위해 친밀감을 이용한다. 인간의 경우 함께 술을 마시는 것이 바로 그런 역할을 한다.

유희태 | 일반영어 ❹-2

이는 단순히 술이 사회적 억압을 벗어던지게 만들고 같이 술을 마시는 이에게 과한 우정을 느끼게 만들기 때문만은 아니다. 실제로 알코올은 원숭이와 영장류, 인간의 뇌에 작용해 유대감을 만들고 유지해주는 역할을 한다. 이런 작용을 하는 기제가 바로 엔도르핀이다. 엔도제너스 몰핀을 줄인 말인 엔도르핀은 아편과 비슷한 효과를 가지는 신경전달물질로 고통을 줄여주는 역할을 한다. 이 물질은 '모든 것이 잘 될 거야'라는 느낌을 주며, 서로 더 신뢰할 수 있는 친밀한 관계를 만드는 데 핵심적인 역할을 한다. 이런 관점에서 본다면 술은 매우 중요한 활동이라 할 수 있다. 사람들이 자신의 내면을 열게 해주기 때문이다. "술 속에 진리가 있다(in vino veritas)"는 오랜 격언이 떠오른다.

엔도르핀을 자극하는 행동에는 웃음에서 노래, 춤 등 다양한 사회적 활동이 있지만, 술은 그중에서도 가장 효과적인 것 중 하나다. 알코올 중독자의 치료를 위해 뇌의 엔도르핀 수용체를 차단하는 날트렉손이 점점 널리 쓰이고 있으며, 중독자는 술을 마셔도 취하지 않게 된다. 대신 갑작스런 약물중단에 의한 신체적 불쾌감만을 약간 느낄 뿐이다.

ⓑ Major supporting details
+ 2점 : "① First, ego-driven people have difficulty in accepting that others are better than them, because they feel that they cannot be wrong(1점). ② Second, ego-driven people suffer from self-doubt and fear when faced with their shortcomings (또는 lack of success)(1점)."를 서술하였거나 유사하였다.
☞ 2개 중 2개 모두를 정확하게 요약한 경우 2점, 1개를 요약한 경우 1점, 요약하지 못한 경우 0점을 준다.

ⓒ Conclusion
+ 1점 : "In conclusion, since ego-driven traits can be a big obstacle in working with other people, (because they may spread to others and interfere getting accurate feedback in its need for positive reinforcement), ego-driven people need to change these traits."을 서술하였거나 유사하였다.

감점
• 본문에 나오는 연속되는 6단어 이상을 사용하였다. −1pt
• 문단을 두 개나 그 이상으로 구성하였다. −1pt
• grammar나 영어표현이 합쳐 4개 이상 오류가 있다. −1pt

3

하위내용영역	배점	예상정답률
일반영어 B형 서술형	4점	45%

모범답안 There are two characteristics of ego-driven people. First, ego-driven people have difficulty in accepting that others are better than them, because they feel that they cannot be wrong. Second, ego-driven people suffer from self-doubt and fear when faced with their shortcomings. In conclusion, since ego-driven traits can be a big obstacle in working with other people because they may spread to others and interfere getting accurate feedback in its need for positive reinforcement, ego-driven people need to change these traits.

채점 기준

ⓐ Topic sentence
+ 1점 : "There are two characteristics of ego-driven people."를 서술하였거나 유사하였다.

한글번역
모든 사람에게는 자아가 있다. 우리 중 일부는 그것을 억제하기 어려워하고, 다른 사람들은 그것을 통제하는 데 시간이 필요하다. 자아는 우리가 자신에게 어떤 우월한 자질이 있다고 느낄 때 발달한다. 이 자질은 많은 형태를 취할 수 있다. 그것은 키, 힘, 아름다움과 같은 신체적인 것일 수도 있고, 교활함과 지혜와 같은 정신적인 것일 수도 있다. 그것은 또한 재정적 부나 지위, 권력, 심지어 인기를 통한 영향력일 수도 있다. 자아에 사로잡힌 사람들은 일상생활에서 특정한 특징들을 드러낸다.

자아에 사로잡힌 사람들은 다른 사람들이 자신보다 나을 수도 있다는 사실을 받아들이기 어려워한다. 그들은 자신의 의견이 항상 최고이고, 자신의 정보가 가장 정확하고, 사물에 대한 자신의 태도가 가장 적절하고, 문제 해결에 대한 자신의 방법이나 접근법이 유일하게 올바른 것이고, 자신의 제안이 받아들여져야 하고, 자신의 결정이 가장 적절해야 한다고 느낀다. 다시 말해, 그들은 결코 틀릴 수 없다. 그들은 자신에 반대하는 모든 논쟁에도 불구하고 여전히 자신이 옳다고 고집한다. 그들은 쉽게 화를 내고 비합리적이 된다.

자아에 사로잡힌 사람들은 두려움이나 자기 의심에 지배받는데, 이는 그들이 자신을 마땅히 해야 할 것보다 못하게 생각하고 자신의 단점에 사로잡힐 때이다. 그들은 인간으로서의 자신의 가치가 다른 사람들이 자신을 어떻게 보는지에 달려 있다고 생각하기 때문에 실패하기를 두려워한다. 그들에게 성공은 자신이 달성한 승리의 수로 측정된다.

과도한 자아는 사람들이 효과적으로 함께 일하는 데 큰 장벽이 될 수 있다. 자아에 사로잡힌 행동은 다른 동료들과 직원들에게까지 흘러내려가서, 생산적인 일을 성취하기 어렵게 만들 수 있다. 더욱 나쁜 것은, 이런 사람들은 자신을 기쁘게 하거나 긍정적인 피드백만 제시하는 사람들에게 보상을 주는 경향이 있다는 것이다. 진실을 진심으로 보고하는 사람들은 꾸중을 받을 것이다. 현실 세계에서 살아남기 위해, 자아에 사로잡힌 사람들은 자신의 성격을 바꾸려고 노력해야 한다. 아무도 그러한 기질을 건강하게 견딜 수 없다.

4

하위내용영역	배점	예상정답률
일반영어 B형 서술형	4점	45%

모범 답안 The word is "habitable". Second, there are two perspective on life in the universe. One is that 10% of all stars have planets in the ideal "habitable" range, and the other is that on the whole scale of all matter only a tiny fraction of that is in the form of life.

채점 기준

+ **2점**: 빈칸에 들어갈 단어를 "habitable"이라 정확하게 기술하였다.
+ **0.5점**: 우주의 생명체에 대한 관점이 "2개"가 있다고 정확하게 서술하였다.
+ **1.5점**: 우주의 생명체에 대한 관점을 각각 "One is that 10% of all stars have planets in the ideal "habitable" range, and the other is that on the whole scale of all matter only a tiny fraction of that is in the form of life"라 정확하게 서술하였거나 유사하였다.

한글번역

해당 지역의 달력과 시간으로 2009년 3월 6일 오후 10시 49분, 등유와 액화산소를 연료로 한 로켓이 과학적 관측대(우주 망원경)를 싣고 한 행성의 표면을 떠났다. 그 행성은 처녀자리 은하성단의 외곽에 위치한, 은하수라 불리는 은하의 중심에서 25,000광년 떨어진 G형 항성의 세 번째 행성이다. 그날 밤 하늘은 맑았고, 비나 바람은 불지 않았으며, 기온은 절대온도로 292도였다. 그 행성의 지적 생명체들은 로켓 발사를 축하했다. NASA라 불리는, 로켓 발사를 책임진 기관은 발사 직후 그 행성 전체에 연결된 컴퓨터 네트워크에 이런 기록을 남겼다. "우리는 처음으로 태양계 바깥에서 지구와 같은 행성을 찾는 목적을 가진 케플러 우주 망원경이 발사된 이 아름다운 밤하늘을 바라보고 있다."

어쩌면 케플러 망원경이 찾아낼, 아주 먼 곳의 한 행성에서 탄생한 지적 생명체들도 이와 똑같은 시도를 하고 있을지 모른다. 르네상스 시대의 천문학자인 요하네스 케플러의 이름을 딴 이 우주 망원경은 태양계 밖에서 "거주 가능한" 행성을 찾기 위해 설계됐다. 즉, 물이 끓을 정도로 항성에 가깝지는 않지만 물이 얼 정도로 항성에서 멀지는 않아야 한다. 대부분 생물학자들은 비록 지구와 전혀 다른 형태의 생명체가 존재한다 하더라도 그들도 액체 상태의 물이 있어야 할 거라고 생각한다. 케플러 우주 망원경은 지금까지 15만 개의 태양계를 조사했고 1,000개 이상의 외계 행성을 발견했다. 이 엄청난 자료들은 지금도 여전히 분석되고 있다.

지난 수백 년 동안 우리 인간은 외계 생명체의 가능성에 대해 생각해왔다. 그리고 이제 처음으로 그 질문에 좀 더 구체적인 답을 내놓을 수 있게 됐다. 현 시점에서, 케플러 임무의 결과에 따르면 항성 중 약 10%는 거주 가능한 행성을 가진 것으로 추정된다. 이는 매우 많은 수의 거주 가능한 행성이 있다는 뜻이다. 우리 은하에만 1천억 개의 항성이 있으며, 또 우리 우주에 있는 은하의 수도 매우 많기 때문에 우주에 다른 생명체가 있을 가능성은 매우 높다. 이 관점에서 보면, 우주에서 생명체는 매우 흔한 것일 수 있다.

하지만 다른 큰 관점에서 보면, 여전히 우주에서의 생명체는 매우 희귀하다. 곧, 모든 물질을 통틀어서 생명체를 구성하는 물질의 비율을 본다면 그렇다는 것이다. 케플러에 의해 정의된 모든 "거주 가능한" 행성에 생명체가 존재하며, 그 행성에 지구와 비슷한 생태계가 만들어져 있다 하더라도, 이 우주에서 생명체의 비율은 극히 적다는 것이다.

제03회 모의고사

1

하위내용영역	배점	예상정답률
일반영어 A형 서술형	4점	35%

모범 답안) The word is "sell". Second, the mainstream media continually uses outrage to keep the attention of readers.

채점 기준

+ 2점: 빈칸에 들어갈 단어를 "sell"이라 정확하게 답하였다. 이외에는 답이 될 수 없다.
+ 2점: 글쓴이가 통상적인 관점에 반대하는 이유를 "the mainstream media continually uses outrage to keep the attention of readers"라 서술하였거나 유사하였다.

한글번역

우리가 분노를 좋아하는 이유는 분노하는 자신이 마치 똑똑한 인간인 듯한 느낌을 받기 때문이다. 분노는 내가 다른 사람보다 세상을 더 잘 알고 있고, 또 더 신경 쓰고 있다는 느낌을 들게 한다. 자신을 세상이 어떻게 개선돼야 할지 아는 사람처럼 보이게 만든다. 자신이야말로 세상을 바꿀 수 있는 위업을 이루기에 적합한 사람으로 보이게 한다. 누군가를 나치라 부르고, 성차별주의자라 부르고, 쓰레기라 부르면서도 이것은 자신의 의견이 아니라 사실을 말하는 것이라 주장한다. 누군가를 지적하고, 그의 인생을 파괴할 때 그는 그런 대접을 받는 것이 당연하다고 말한다.

이는 심각한 수준의 오만이다. 하지만 오늘날 분노가 가진 가장 큰 문제는 이것이 공격 무기로 사용된다는 것이다. 분노는 마치 광기처럼 퍼져 나간다. 분노는 사람들을 행동하게 만드는 강력한 감정이기 때문이다. 그래서 정치 세력은 문제의 해답을 찾기보다 다른 세력에 대한 증오와 분노를 자극하는 쉬운 방법을 택한다. 기업도 이를 이용한다. 그들은 당신의 분노를 이용해 물건을 팔려 한다. 질레트의 실패한 광고나 나이키의 콜린 캐퍼닉 광고는 사회적으로 의식 있는 소비자들을 자신의 고객으로 만들기 위한 전략이었다.

나이키는 그 광고 이후 매출이 31%나 증가했고, 회사 가치는 6조가 올랐다. 그들이 과연 사회적 가치를 주장하기 위해 그 광고를 만들었을까? 그들은 당신의 분노를 이용해 큰돈을 번 것이다.

하지만 가장 큰 잘못은 주류 언론에 있다. 왜냐하면 당신이 관심을 주지 않는다면 그런 비즈니스 모델은 소용이 없을 것이다. 그들은 당신이 계속 기사를 클릭하게 해서 광고주로부터 돈을 받는다. 모든 것이 선정적으로 바뀌고 진실을 추구하는 이들이 줄어드는 이유다. 사람들의 감정을 자극하는 제목일수록 클릭 수는 늘어난다. 기사가 당신을 분노하게 할수록 당신은 댓글을 찾아 사람들과 논쟁을 벌이게 된다.

그 기사는 소셜 미디어에서 인기를 끌게 되고, 물론 거기에는 당신의 기여가 있다. (주제가 바뀌고) 끊임없이 이 과정이 반복된다.

2

하위내용영역	배점	예상정답률
일반영어 A형 서술형	4점	50%

모범 답안) The word is "temptation." Second, two examples of inhibitory training are brushing one's teeth with the non-dominant hand and forcing oneself to not eat sweets.

채점 기준

+ 2점: 빈칸에 들어갈 단어를 "temptation"이라 정확하게 답하였다. 이외에는 답이 될 수 없다.
+ 2점: 금지 자제력의 두 가지 예를 "brushing one's teeth with the non-dominant hand and forcing oneself to not eat sweets"라 정확히 서술하였다. 이외에는 답이 될 수 없다.

한글번역

2007년, 미국의 심리학자 로이 바우마이스터는 가장 널리 알려진 자제력의 심리학적 모델을 발표했다. 그는 의지력을 근육에 비유했다. 팔굽혀펴기를 할 때 처음 몇 개는 힘들지 않다. 하지만 계속하다 보면 더 이상 할 수 없는 지점에 도달하게 된다. 바우마이스터는 자제력을 사용하는 것도 이와 비슷하다고 이야기 한다. 자제력의 근육을 과도하게 사용할 때, 의지력은 바닥나게 되고 더 이상 자제력을 발휘할 수 없다는 것이다.

바우마이스터가 쓴 《의지력의 재발견》(2012)의 성공은 이 의지력과 근육의 비유에 많은 사람들이 동의했다는 것을 말한다. 자제력을 연구하는 박사과정 학생으로서 나는 그 이유를 이해할 수 있다. 이 모델은 우리가 겪는 자제력의 실패를 잘 설명한다. 당신은 힘든 한 주를 보냈고 하루를 마무리하며 의지력을 다 소모했기 때문에 단것의 유혹에 저항할 수 없었던 것이다. 게다가 자제력에 대한 이 비유는 우리의 상식과도 일치한다. 곧, 자제는 힘든 것이며 유혹을 이기기 위해서는 엄청난 의지력이 필요하다는 것이다.

의지력이 근육처럼 작용한다면, 자제력을 향상시키기 위해서는 어떻게 해야 할까? 근육의 비유를 그대로 받아들일 때 우리는 자제력의 근육을 키울 수 있을 것이라 생각하게 된다. 연구자들은 사람들에게 2주 동안 평소 쓰지 않는 손으로 이를 닦도록 함으로써 이를 실험해 봤다. 이는 오래된 습관을 '금지 자제력(inhibitory self-control)'을 이용해 바꿔야 하는 매우 힘든 일이다. 그럼 이 자제력 훈련은 성공했을까? 관련 연구들을 종합한 2017년의 메타 분석연구에 따르면 이런 자제력 훈련은 '자제력 지구력', 곧 금지 자제력을 더 오래 사용하는 데는 효과적이었음을 보였다.

그렇다면, 이 방법을 자기 절제력의 향상에도 사용할 수 있을까? 곧, 자제력 근육 훈련을 통해 금지 자제력을 키울 수 있을까?

안타깝게도 이 문제는 그리 간단한 문제가 아니다. 내가 위에서 자제력과 금지 자제력을 번갈아 사용한 것을 눈치 챈 이들도 있을 것이다. 하지만 이 두 단어는 동의어가 아니다. 금지 자제력 또는 의지력을 향상시키는 것은 그럴듯하게 들리지만—이를 통해 마치 다른 손으로 양치를 한 것처럼 쿠키의 유혹을 무시할 수 있을 것 같은—금지 자제력이 일상에서 그런 방식으로 작용할 것인지는 확실하지 않다.

2017년, 자원자들로 하여금 일상의 유혹을 일주일 동안 기록하게 한 연구를 보자. 더 많은 유혹을 경험한 이들은 더 많은 금지 자제력을 사용했지만 장기적 목표를 달성할 가능성이 더 낮았다. 이는 금지 자제력이 단것의 유혹을 참는 데는 유용하지만 장기적으로는 유익하지 않다는 것을 말해준다. 즉, 양치 훈련과 같은 방식을 통해 금지 자제력 근력을 크게 키우더라도, 이런 노력 자체는 당신을 헤라클레스로 만드는 것이 아니라 끊임없이 돌을 언덕 위로 올려야 했던 시지프스로 만든다는 것이다.

3

하위내용영역	배점	예상정답률
일반영어 B형 서술형	4점	40%

모범 답안 The words are "recursive self-improvement". Second, the "necessary threshold" indicates the necessary IQ level to increase others' intelligence around one.

채점 기준

+ 2점 : 빈칸에 들어갈 단어를 "recursive self-improvement"라 정확하게 기술하였다.
+ 2점 : 필수적 한계점이 의미하는 것을 "the necessary IQ level to increase others' intelligence"라 서술하였거나 유사하였다.

한글번역

인간의 경우 재귀적 자가발전은 어떤 식으로 이뤄질까? 논의의 편리를 위해 인간의 지능을 IQ로 가정하겠다. 이는 IQ 테스트 결과가 실제로 그 사람의 지능을 나타낸다고 내가 생각한다는 뜻이 아니라, 그저 어떤 지능을 하나의 숫자로 나타낼 수 있다는 개념을 이들은 지능의 폭발적 증가를 설명하는 가정으로 사용했기 때문이다. 이 경우, 재귀적 자가발전을 다시 쓰면 다음과 같은 주장이 된다. 즉, 어떤 사람의 IQ가 300이라면, 그는 IQ가 300인 다른 사람의 IQ를 350으로 더 높이는 그런 문제를 풀 수 있다는 것이다. 그리고 IQ가 350인 사람은 IQ가 350인 사람의 IQ를 400으로 더 높이는, 더 어려운 문제를 풀 수 있으며, 이런 식으로 계속된다는 뜻이다.

그런데 지능의 작동 방식을 우리가 받아들여야 할 이유가 있을까? 나는 그렇게 생각하지 않는다. 예를 들어, 세상에는 IQ가 130인 사람이 충분히 많다. 그리고 소수지만 IQ가 160인 사람도 있다. 하지만 어떤 이도 IQ가 70인 사람의 IQ를 100으로—이는 위의 문제들에 비해 쉬운 문제로 보이지만—만들지 못한다. 지금까지 어떤 이도 IQ 테스트로는 측정도 할 수 없을 정도로 낮은 동물의 지능을 높이지 못했다. 어떤 이의 IQ를 높이는 것이 일종의 수학 문제를 푸는 것이라면, 적어도 아주 낮은 IQ를 가진 이들이 처한 문제는 쉬운 문제일 테니 우리가 풀 수 있었어야 한다. 하지만 아직 그런 예는 없다.

어쩌면 이는 우리가 지능을 높이는 데 필요한 최소한의 지능 기준에 비해 지능이 너무 낮아서 그런 것일 수도 있다. IQ 300이 되면, 그때부터 다른 이의 IQ를 높일 수 있게 될 수도 있다. 하지만 설사 그렇다 하더라도, 그 이후 무한한 자가발전이 가능할지는 전혀 다른 문제이다. 예를 들어, IQ가 300인 사람은 다른 사람의 IQ를 200까지 올릴 수도 있다. 주변의 모든 사람을 IQ 200으로 올리는 것은 그 자체로 엄청난 일이다. 하지만 여전히 여기에는 오를 수 있는 한계가 있다. 즉, 재귀적 자가발전이나 지능의 폭발적 증가라는 것은 없을 것이다.

4

하위내용영역	배점	예상정답률
일반영어 B형 서술형	4점	45%

모범답안 Wars have driven improvement in medicine, research, and social equality. First, medical advances such as the production of Penicillin have been driven by wartime needs. Additionally, the Second World War and Cold War were times of a lot of scientific research, leading eventually to developments such as the Internet. Furthermore, war has improved social equality in terms of gender, as men were away and women managed to do jobs they hadn't been allowed to do, thus proving their equality. In conclusion, modern technology, however, can lead to more devastating wars, and will be important to control properly going forward (in the future).

채점 기준

ⓐ Topic sentence

+ 1점 : "Wars have driven improvement in medicine, research, and social equality."를 서술하였거나 유사하였다.

ⓑ Major supporting details

+ 2점 : "① First, medical advances such as the production of Penicillin have been driven by wartime needs. ② Additionally, the Second World War and Cold War were times of a lot of scientific research, leading eventually to developments such as the Internet. ③ Furthermore, war has improved social equality in terms of gender, as men were away and women managed to do jobs they hadn't been allowed to do, thus proving their equality."를 서술하였거나 유사하였다.

☞ 3개 중 3개 모두를 정확하게 요약한 경우 2점, 2개를 요약한 경우 1점, 1개 또는 요약하지 못한 경우 0점을 준다.

ⓒ Conclusion

+ 1점 : "In conclusion, modern technology, however, can lead to more devastating wars, and will be important to control properly going forward."라 서술하였거나 유사하였다.

☞ 다음과 같이 서술하였어도 맞는 것으로 한다.
- "It will be important to control modern technology properly in the future."

감점
- 본문에 나오는 연속되는 6단어 이상을 사용하였다. -1pt
- 문단을 두 개나 그 이상으로 구성하였다. -1pt
- grammar나 영어표현이 합쳐 4개 이상 오류가 있다. -1pt

제04회 모의고사

1

하위내용영역	배점	예상정답률
일반영어 A형 서술형	4점	50%

모범 답안) The word is "virus". Second, the imitation or spread of behavior affected the crime rate in New York just as the fashion of wearing Hush Puppies was spread through imitation of others' fashion.

채점 기준

+ 2점 : 빈칸에 들어갈 단어를 "virus"라 정확히 기입하였다. 이외에는 답이 될 수 없다.
+ 2점 : 밑줄 친 부분의 의미를 "the imitation or spread of behavior affected the crime rate in New York just as the fashion of wearing Hush Puppies was spread through imitation of others' fashion"라 서술하였거나 유사하였다.

한글번역

티핑 포인트(작은 변화들이 어느 정도 기간을 두고 쌓여 작은 변화가 하나만 더 일어나도 갑자기 큰 영향을 초래할 수 있는 상태)는 어떤 한 아이디어의 역사인데, 그 아이디어는 매우 단순하다. 패션의 경향이 새롭게 나오는 것이나, 범죄율의 변화 또는 알려지지 않은 책이 베스트셀러로 바뀌는 것, 십대 흡연의 증가, 입소문의 현상, 일상생활에서 나타나는 수많은 신비스러운 변화들을 이해하는 가장 좋은 방법은 이런 것들을 전염병으로 간주하는 것이다. 아이디어, 제품, 메시지, 행동들은 정확히 바이러스처럼 퍼진다. 허시바피 신발 판매가 급증한 것이나 뉴욕의 범죄율이 많이 줄어든 것은 전형적인 예이다.

한글번역

역사적으로 보면, 너무 많은 비용이 들거나 또는 기존의 시스템을 다 파괴해야 하므로 평상시라면 하지 못했을 일을 심각한 위기 상황에 처한 뒤 많은 사람이 힘을 모아 해낸 경우가 있다. 전쟁이 그런 위기 중 하나이다. 평상시에 긴축을 말하던 정부들도 전쟁 중엔 사회를 유지하는 데 절대적으로 필요하기 때문에 돈을 맘껏 쓰게 된다.

의학적 발전은 전쟁에 의한 하나의 결과이다. 예를 들어 1920년대 전쟁 중에 발견된 페니실린은 생산 비용이 너무 많이 들었다. 하지만 제2차 세계대전이 일어나면서 병사들을 살리기 위해 가격이 급격히 낮아졌다. 또한, 제2차 세계대전과 냉전 시기에 미국은 수많은 과학 기술을 연구했다. 인터넷은 미국 대학에 주어진 연구비의 결과이고, 실리콘밸리의 성공도 냉전 시기 미국 정부가 지원한 연구비를 바탕으로 하고 있는데, 이는 평화시에 적용할 수 있다.

전쟁은 사회적 평등에도 기여했다. 남자들이 전장으로 떠나면, 여자들이 세상이 돌아가도록 만들어야 했고 이는 정치적 변화를 가져왔다. 제1차 세계대전 이전부터 여러 나라의 여성들은 투표권을 요구하고 있었다. 이에 대해 남자만큼 사회에 참여하지 않는다면 투표할 권리도 없다는 논리가 있었다. 제1차 세계대전이 일어나고 남자들이 모두 징집되자 여자들은 이전에는 생각지 못했던 일을 하게 된다. 농장에서 트랙터를 몰았고, 공장에서 물건을 조립했다. 영국과 몇몇 국가는 여성이 전쟁에 기여한다는 것을 알게 됐다. 여성에게 투표권을 주지 말아야 한다는 주장이 설 자리를 잃었다.

앞에서 봤듯이, 전쟁은 수많은 진보를 야기했다. 하지만 기술의 발달은 오늘날의 전쟁을 매우 위험하게 만들고 있다. 미래 전쟁에선 더욱 더 많은 인공 지능이나 킬러 로봇이 사용될 것이다. 중요한 것은 그와 같은 무기를 궁극적으로 누가 통제할 것이며, 그 치명적인 전쟁들을 통제하기 위해서는 무엇을 해야 하냐는 것이다.

비록 허시파피 신발의 판매 증가와 뉴욕 범죄율의 하락은 그다지 공통점이 없어 보이지만, 그 둘은 기저를 이루는 기본적인 패턴을 공유하고 있다. 무엇보다도, 그 둘은 전염성이 강한 행동을 명확히 보여주고 있다. 그 누구도 광고지를 꺼내놓고 사람들에게 전통적인 허시파피 신발이 멋지니 꼭 이 신발을 신어야 한다고 이야기하지 않았다. 클럽이나 카페에 갈 때, 뉴욕의 길거리를 걸을 때 젊은이들은 그냥 그 신발을 신었고, 그렇게 함으로써, 다른 이들을 그들의 패션 감각에 노출시켜 줬다. 그 젊은이들이 다른 젊은이들에게 허시파피 바이러스를 감염시킨 것이다.

뉴욕의 범죄율 감소도 (허시파피 신발과) 똑같은 방식으로 발생했음은 명확하다. 어떤 높은 비율의 예비 살인범들이 1993년에 갑자기 정신을 차리고 더 이상 범죄를 저지르지 않기로 결심한 것이 아니었다. 경찰이 그러지 않았다면 치명적으로 변했을 수많은 상황에 마법을 부려 개입하는 데 성공한 것도 아니었다. (실제로 뉴욕에서) 일어난 것은 경찰이나 새로운 사회세력이 어느 정도 영향력을 가지고 있던 소수의 상황에서 소수의 사람들이 (지금까지와) 매우 다르게 행동하기 시작했던 것이고, 그 행동이 유사한 상황에 놓인 다른 예비 범죄자들에게 퍼졌다는 것이다. 뉴욕의 다수의 사람들이 짧은 시간에 범죄근절 바이러스에 전염됐던 것이다.

한글번역

할머니의 장례식 한 시간 전, 관 속에 누워계신 할머니를 직접 봤을 때 나는 죽음과 잠이 얼마나 다른 것인지를 깨닫고 놀랐다. 잠을 자는 이들은 조금씩 계속 움직인다. 그러나 죽은 이들은 마치 화면이 멈춘 것처럼 정지해 있으며, 그래서 살아있을 때보다 더 작아 보인다. 죽은 이들을 보면서 영혼의 존재를 느끼지 않기란 불가능하다. 물론 할머니는 알츠하이머로 돌아가셨다. 즉, 살아계실 때도 할머니는 자신을 조금씩 잃어가고 있었다. 나는 할머니가 점점 기억을 잃는 것을 보며, 할머니가 그저 예전의 자신을 잃어가는 것인지, 아니면 인간성 자체를 잃는 것인지를 생각하곤 했다.

이런 삶의 마지막 단계는 우리의 상상력을 찔러댄다. 우리는 우리 몸에서 일어나는 단순한 생물학적인 과정이 우리를 되돌릴 수 없는 상태로 만들며 한 사람의 모든 경험을 지워버릴 수 있다는 사실을 좋아하지 않는다. 우리는 신체를 부정하려 하고, 현실의 어두운 굴레를 거부한다. 문제는, 자신을 몸과는 분리된 특별한 존재로 생각하는 이런 생각이 실제로는 현실을 더 엉망으로 만든다는 것이다. 고상한 인간적 정신이 동물의 몸 안에 갇혀 있다는 생각에는 수많은 문제가 있다. 바로 우리로 하여금 자신의 몸과 감각을 존재의 부차적 요인으로 여기게 만들기 때문이다. 하지만 그것은 사실이 아니다. 우리의 마음을 비롯한 모든 것은 매우 굳은 생물학적 기반을 가지고 있으며 우리의 신체적 경험은 우리가 생각하는 것보다 훨씬 더 우리에게 많은 의미를 부여한다.

우리가 아는 한, 초기 수렵채집 물활론적(*우주 만물에 영혼이 있다는 믿음*) 사회는 모든 대상이 영혼을 가지고 있다고 생각했다. 모든 생명체에는 비물리적인 특별한 요소가 있다는 것이다. 유럽의 고전 사유체계에서도 또한 모든 생명체는 영혼을 가진다고 믿었다. 하지만 이들은 영혼에 등급이 있다고 생각했다. 인간은 그 등급 중 가장 위에 있었다. 13세기 이탈리아 도미니크회 수도사였던 토마스 아퀴나스와 같은 신학자들에게서는 이러한 생명체가 영혼을 가지고 있다는 관점은 후퇴했고, 오직 인간만이 불멸의 영혼을 소유한다고 주장했다. 인간은 고유의 영혼을 가지며, 따라서 다른 동물과 다른 존재가 됐다. 인간의 삶은 구원으로 가는 길 위에 놓여있었다. 인간의 삶은 존재의 대연쇄가 됐고, 오직 신과 천사만이 인간 위에 존재했다.

2

하위내용영역	배점	예상정답률
일반영어 A형 서술형	4점	45%

모범답안 The word is "body". Second, the underlined part refers to the view of all life as having a non-physical spirit.

채점기준

+ 2점: 빈칸에 들어갈 단어를 "body"라 정확히 기입하였다. 이외에는 답이 될 수 없다.
+ 2점: 밑줄 친 부분이 가리키는 것이 "the view of all life as having a non-physical spirit" 또는 "the view that all life has a soul"이나 "the view that every living thing has a soul"이라 서술하였거나 유사하였다.

3

하위내용영역	배점	예상정답률
일반영어 B형 서술형	4점	40%

모범 답안) The words are "significant form". Second, it means that Bell's approach is being widely considered among criticism, even if it is not wholly embraced.

채점 기준)

+ 2점 : 빈칸에 들어갈 단어를 "significant form"이라 정확히 기입하였다. 이외에는 답이 될 수 없다.
+ 2점 : 마지막 문장의 밑줄 친 부분에서 저자가 주장하는 바를 "Bell's approach is being widely considered among criticism, even if it isn't wholly embraced"라 서술하였거나 유사하였다.

한글번역)

 영국 예술비평가인 클라이브 벨은 20세기 초반에, "자연을 모방"하는 것을 이상으로 삼았던 오래된 아이디어를 포기했던 후기 인상파 그림과 조각의 혁명적 운동들에 대한 중요한 옹호자들 가운데 한 명이었는데, 그가 무능해서가 아니라, 원리에 입각해서 그러했던 것이다. 이 운동들은 입체파처럼 우리가 일상적으로 경험하는 대상들을 의도적으로 왜곡시키는 것에서부터, 몬드리안처럼 그 대상들을 아예 없애버리는 것으로, 그리고 우리시대의 행위예술과 추상표현주의에서 보이듯 거리낌 없이 휘갈기고 물감을 흩뿌리는 것으로 나아갔다.
 벨의 전략은 예술이라는 용어를 타당하게 사용하는 것이었다. 즉 흔히 생각해온 것처럼 캔버스 위에 이야기하고 묘사하는 것이 예술인 것은 아니라는 것이다. 회화나 조각이 선, 매스, 색채라는 요소들을 조직적으로 구성하는 것만이, 다시 말해 벨이 "의미 있는 형식"이라 부르는 것만이 예술작품으로 불릴 수 있는 자격을 부여받는 것이다.
 벨은 오직 순수하게 형식적인 특질—예를 들어 선과 색의 관계와 조합 따위—만이 예술작품에서 가장 중요한 요소라 주장했다. 어떤 하나의 그림을 보고 관객의 내면에서 일어나는 미학적 감정은 우선적으로 그 작품의 의미 있는 형식에 대한 이해로부터 나오는 것이지, 그 작품의 제재를 읽어내는 데서 나오는 것이 아니다. 벨은 폴 세잔의 작품들을 형식적 특질이 가장 순수하게 드러나 있는 작품들이라 지적하며, 대중들이 전통 사실주의 회화에서 드러나는 예화적, 서사적, 도적주의적 기능들에 사로잡혀있는 것을 공격했다.
 벨의 이론이 미학자들 사이에서 널리 받아들여지지 않았다고 말하는 것이 온당하다. 예술의 정의에서 "재현"을 완전히 배제하는 것은 너무나 극단적인 것이라 간주되고, 벨의 강한 요구—즉, 회화 속에 묘사된 인물이나 사건을 꿰뚫어봐 결국 형식을 봐야 한다는—는 너무 비용이 드는 것이다.
 벨의 형식주의는 극단적이지만 그냥 무시해도 되는 정신 나간 소수 과격파의 이론은 아니다. 최근 미학과 비평에 대해 폭넓게 읽는다면 벨이 여전히 거의 모든 곳에서 "반박되고" 있음을 알 수 있다. 그를 믿지 않는 사람들도 그와 타협해야만 한다.

4

하위내용영역	배점	예상정답률
일반영어 B형 서술형	4점	45%

모범 답안) There are three types of polluted information. First, disinformation, which is false content designed to cause harm, can be more effective if there is a small part of truth in the lie. Second, misinformation, which is false content spread without understanding of its false nature, is done so as performance of one's identity. The final type, malinformation, is genuine information spread with the intent to cause harm, such as personal email leaks. In conclusion, suffers of polluted information need counseling and regulatory support and the public should be more mindful of the popularity of polluted information.

채점 기준

ⓐ Topic sentence
+ 1점: "There are three types of polluted information."라 서술하였거나 유사하였다.

ⓑ Major supporting details
+ 2점: "① First, disinformation, which is false content designed to cause harm, can be more effective if there is a small part of truth in the lie. ② Second, misinformation, which is false content spread without understanding of its false nature, is done so as performance of one's identity. ③ The final type, malinformation, is genuine information spread with the intent to cause harm, such as personal email leaks."를 서술하였거나 유사하였다.

☞ 3개 중 3개 모두를 정확하게 요약한 경우 2점, 2개를 요약한 경우 1점, 1개 또는 요약하지 못한 경우 0점을 준다.

ⓒ Conclusion
+ 1점: "In conclusion, suffers of polluted information need counseling and regulatory support and the public should be more mindful of the popularity of polluted information."을 서술하였거나 유사하였다.

감점
- 본문에 나오는 연속되는 6단어 이상을 사용하였다. −1pt
- 문단을 두 개나 그 이상으로 구성하였다. −1pt
- grammar나 영어표현이 합쳐 4개 이상 오류가 있다. −1pt

한글번역

우리 중 많은 사람들이 오염된 정보로 인해 자신도 모르게 고통받을 수 있다. 정보가 모든 개인의 휴대폰, 태블릿, 컴퓨터로 순식간에 흘러가는 디지털화된 세상으로 인해 이것이 더욱 만연하다. 오염된 정보는 해를 끼칠 의도가 있든 없든 거짓 정보를 공유하거나 개발하는 것이다. 정보 생태계를 오염시키기 위해 사용되는 내용에는 세 가지 범주가 있다.

해를 끼치기 위해 고안된 거짓 내용인 허위정보의 유포자들은 세 가지 뚜렷한 목표 중 하나에 의해 동기 부여를 받는다: 돈을 벌기 위해서, 정치적 영향력을 갖기 위해서, 또는 그냥 문제를 일으키기 위해서. 그것이 거짓이거나 오해의 소지가 있다는 것을 깨닫지 못하는 사람이 공유하는 잘못된 정보를 퍼뜨리는 사람들은 사회심리학적 요인에 의해 추진된다. 이런 사람들은 다른 사람들과 연결감을 느끼기 위해 소셜 플랫폼에서 자신의 정체성을 연기하고 있다. 허위정보는 사람들이 그것이 거짓이라는 것을 깨닫지 못하고 허위정보를 공유할 때 잘못된 정보가 된다.

마지막으로, 새로운 용어인 "악의정보"는 해를 끼칠 의도로 공유되는 진짜 정보를 묘사한다. 이것의 한 예는 외국 요원들이 정치인들의 이메일을 해킹해 평판을 손상시키기 위해 개인적 비밀을 대중에게 누설했을 때 일어났다. 가장 효과적인 허위정보는 항상 진실의 알갱이를 갖고 있으며, 실제로 지금 유포되고 있는 내용의 대부분은 가짜가 아니라 오해의 소지가 있다는 점을 주목해야 한다. 완전히 조작된 이야기 대신, 영향력 있는 요원들은 진짜 내용을 재구성하고 과장된 헤드라인을 사용하고 있다.

오염된 정보로 고통받는 모든 사람들은 심리사회적 상담이 필요하고 때로는 정보 무질서를 완화하기 위한 강력한 규제와 집행이 필요하다. 가장 중요한 개입은 소셜 미디어와 뉴스의 모든 게시물이 진짜는 아니며 신중하게 해석돼야 한다는 사실을 염두에 두는 것이다.

제05회 모의고사

1

하위내용영역	배점	예상정답률
일반영어 A형 서술형	4점	40%

모범답안 The word is "outside". Second, it was the Great Famine and the Black Death.

채점기준

+ 2점: 빈칸에 들어갈 단어를 "outside"라 정확히 기입하였다. 이외에는 답이 될 수 없다.
+ 2점: 친족관계 밖의 관계를 성장시킨 결정적 사건을 "the Great Famine and the Black Death"라 서술하였다.

한글번역

왜 이렇게 많은 사람들이 온라인 유명인 친구들에 눈을 돌리는지 이해하려면 먼저 우정이라는 개념의 긴 역사를 살펴볼 필요가 있다. 친구에 대한 가장 간단한 설명은 우리가 친구를 통해 소속감을 채운다는 것이다. 심리학자인 로이 바우마이스터와 마크 리어리는 예측 가능하고 질서 있는 구조 속에서 타인과 즐거운 관계를 맺을 때 사람들의 소속감이 충족된다는 것을 밝혔다. 인간의 역사에서 그러한 소속감은 확대가족, 즉 배우자, 부모, 자식, 형제, 조부모, 친척 등을 통해 채워졌다. 현대 사회에서 우정의 역사는 이런 가족 구조가 파괴된 상황에서 맹세한 형제, 친구, 텔레비전 진행자, 팟캐스트 진행자 등 가족 밖에서 맺은 관계를 통해 어떻게 소속감을 채워야 하는지에 대한 것이다.

서양에서 이 역사는 짧은 기간 동안 유럽이 대기근과 그 후 흑사병으로 타격을 받았던 14세기에 시작된다. 절반이나 되는 인구가 죽었다. 이것이 소속감의 원천인 가족을 붕괴시켰다. 가족을 잃은 많은 이들이 자신들의 가족 바깥에 있는 사람들과 친근한 관계를 발전시키면서 이런 상황에 대응했다. 특히 자신과 취향이 비슷하거나 외모가 비슷한 이들이 대상이 됐다. 바로 친구다. 이때부터 친구나 이와 유사한 단어들이 문헌에 자주 등장하기 시작한다. 사람들은 친구에게 자신의 일상과 감정, 영혼을 편지로 알렸다. 때로 사람들은 교회에서 영원한 우정을 맹세했고, 반지를 교환했으며, 가문을 합치거나 마치 부부처럼 죽고 나면 바로 옆에 안장되기를 약속했다. 혈연이 아닌 사람들과의 이러한 결속된 관계를 촉진하기 위해 여러 새로운 제도가 생겨났는데, 그중 하나가 형제단(confraternity)이었다. 이러한 소속 모임들은 빵을 나누거나 노래를 부르는 것과 같은 구체적인 연대 의식을 통해 낯선 사람들을 형제와 자매로 변화시켰다. 당신은 이 친구들에게 의지할 수 있다. 그들은 당신이 배가 고플 때에 함께 먹고, 돈이 없을 때에 돈을 주고, 죽은 후에 당신을 위해 미사를 드렸다. 그들은 당신도 그들을 위해 똑같이 할 것이라고 믿을 수 있었기 때문이었다.

2

하위내용영역	배점	예상정답률
일반영어 A형 서술형	4점	45%

모범답안 The word is "merit". Second, the conflict is that a meritocracy benefits only a few but a democracy is directed by the majority.

채점기준

+ 2점: 빈칸에 들어갈 단어를 "merit"이라 정확히 기입하였다. 이외에는 답이 될 수 없다.
+ 2점: 글쓴이가 말한 능력주의와 민주주의 사이의 갈등을 "a meritocracy benefits only a few but a democracy is directed by the majority"라 서술하였거나 유사하였다.

한글번역

오늘날까지 미국인들은 성과주의를 유난히 지지하고 있으며, 그들의 지지는 미국식 자본주의를 포용하는 것을 설명하는 데 크게 도움이 된다. 최근의 한 연구에 따르면, 독일인의 54%, 덴마크인의 66%, 브라질인의 75%에 비해, 단지 40%의 미국인만이 높은 수입을 성실보다는 운에 기인한다고 한다. 하지만 인식은 현실과 동떨어져 있을 때 오래 지속될 수 없으며, 최근의 경향은 미국이 능력주의라는 이상에서 멀어지고 있음을 보여주는 것 같다. 만약 표류가 계속된다면, 그 결과는 자유 시장에 대한 대중의 지지가 무너지고 자본주의의 독특한 미국적 형태가 종말을 맞을 수도 있다.

성과주의는 민주주의에서 유지하기 어려운 원칙이다. 공로에 따라 보상을 배분하는 어떤 제도든 소수에게 더 높은 보상을 줄 수밖에 없어 대다수의 사람들이 시샘할 수밖에 없다. 민주주의에서는 일반적으로 다수가 통치한다. 왜 그 다수가 소수에게 불균형한 권력과 보상을 주는 것에 동의해야 하는가?

10여 년 전, 자유 시장 경제학자 밀턴 프리드먼과의 연관성 덕분에 여전히 시장 지향적인 사람들을 끌어들이는 기관인, 시카고대학에서 이러한 역학이 깔끔하게 전개됐다. 능력주의 체제의 보상을 수확하기 위해 수 만 달러와 2년의 인생을 투자하면서 경영학 석사(MBA) 과정에 다니는 학생들보다 더 많은 시장 친화적이고 능력주의 친화적인 사람들이 있을까? 그럼에도 불구하고, 능력주의 정신에 반하는 움직임으로, 시카고대학 MBA 학생들은 사원 채용담당자들에게 그들의 성적을 공개하지 않기로 투표했다. 그 이유는 분명했다. 그 채용자들이 능력을 기반으로 그들 중 일부를 구별하도록 허용하면 그들 중 소수에게 혜택을 줘 다수가 희생되는 것을 허용하게 될 것이기 때문이다. 가장 능력 있는 사람들조차도 능력주의가 그들의 전망을 해칠 때 반대할 수 있는 것이다. 능력주의가 정치적으로 그토록 취약한 것은 그리 놀라운 일은 아니다.

그럼에도 불구하고, 두 가지 요소는 이런 도전에 직면해 능력주의 체제를 유지하는 데 도움을 준다. 더 높은 보상으로 노력을 보상하고 충분히 큰 이익을 얻는 것이 정당하다고 생각하는 문화와 불평등에 대한 대중의 불만을 무효화시킬 수 있을 만큼 충분히 크고 체제 전반에 충분히 널리 퍼져있는 혜택이 그것이다. 문화적 요인은 시작부터 능력주의를 장려했던 미국에서 발견하기 쉽다. 18세기에 세계 전반의 사회질서는 귀족들이 유럽과 일본을 지배하고, 카스트 제도가 있는 인도에서 생득권에 기초해 있었다. 미국 독립전쟁은 유럽사회의 귀족주의와 계층 간 이동의 불가능성에 대한 저항이었지만, 평등원리를 강조한 프랑스 혁명과 달리, 행복 추구의 자유를 옹호했다. 다시 말해, 미국은 결과가 아닌 기회의 평등에 기반을 두고 있었다. 이 신생 국가의 잇따른 경제적 성공은 능력에 따라 보상과 책임을 할당한다는 신념을 더욱 강화시켰다.

3

하위내용영역	배점	예상정답률
일반영어 B형 서술형	4점	45%

모범 답안) The word is "paradox". Second, Magritte criticizes realism because every individual has a unique reality which makes a fixed, true reality impossible to depict.

채점 기준)

+ 2점 : 빈칸에 들어갈 단어를 "paradox"라 정확히 기입하였다. 이외에는 답이 될 수 없다.
+ 2점 : 르네 마그리트가 순진한 리얼리즘을 비판한 핵심 이유를 "because every individual has a unique reality which makes a fixed, true reality impossible to depict"라 서술하였거나 유사하였다.

한글번역

아마 여러분은 이 그림을 본 적이 있을 것이다 : 사진처럼 사실적으로 그려진 파이프가 "Ceci n'est pas une pipe—이것은 파이프가 아닙니다"라고 주의 깊게 쓰여진 글자 위에 떠 있는 그런 그림. 르네 마그리트는 1920년대에 "이미지의 배반"을 그렸고, 그 이후 사람들은 그것이 무엇을 의미하는지 계속 이야기해왔다.

마그리트는 재현이란 그것이 묘사하는 대상이 아니라는 것을 우리에게 상기시켜주려고 의도했는가? —그의 그림은 "단지" 그림일 뿐이지 파이프가 아니라는 것을 말이다. 그러한 해석은 대학생들에게 널리 가르쳐지고 있지만, 만약 그것이 사실이라면, 마그리트는, 특별히 우아한 디자인의 드레스 마감 파이프를 신중하게 고르고, 그것의 스케치를 수십 개 만들고, 해부학적 구도에 익숙해지도록 그것을 분해하고, 그런 다음 그것의 초상을 아주 조심스럽고 능숙하게 그리는 따위의, 단지 우리가 이미 알고 있는 어떤 것을 말해주기 위해, 엄청난 고생을 했다. "두 개의 미스터리"라는 또 다른 그림에서 마그리트는 훨씬 더 고집스럽다 : 캡션*(사진·삽화 등에 붙인 설명)*이 완비되어 있는 원래의 파이프 그림은 마룻 바닥에 놓여 있는 이젤 위에 놓여 있는 것으로 묘사된다. 하지만 원래의 그림 위, 왼쪽에, 두 번째 파이프가 공중에 떠 있는데, 원래의 그림과 그 그림의 틀보다 더 크다 (혹은 더 가깝다). 여기서 우리가 얻는 것은 역설의 그림이다. 더 작은 파이프는 그림이지 파이프가 아니란 것은 자명하다. 하지만 두 번째 파이프는 무엇이란 말인가? 재현된 캔버스 밖에 어렴풋이 보이는 그 파이프는? 그리고 만약 이것 또한 단지 그림일 따름이라면, 그 그림은 어디에서 끝날까?

내가 보기에 이 역설의 뿌리는 프레임의 개념에 있는 것 같다. 우리가 사실적인 그림—예를 들어 역사적 인물을 그린 초상화—을 볼 때, 우리는 그 초상화가 실제 인물이나 실제 사물들을 재현한다고 당연하게 받아들인다. 마그리트의 파이프 그림처럼 그런 관습이 거부될 때, 요점은 그림이 진짜가 아니라는 것을 우리에게 상기시켜주는 것이 아니다. 물론 그 정도도 정말로 사실이지만 사소하다. 핵심은 프레임 밖의 모든 것이 진짜라는 믿음에 도전하는 것이다.

마그리트와 같은 예술가들에게 적은 순진해 빠진 사실주의인데, 이 사실주의는 우리 인간의 감각 기관이 단 하나밖에 없는 유일한 실제 세계를 정확히 기록하며, 이 세계에 대해 우리 인간의 뇌는 오직 단 한 개의 정확한 모델만을 만들어 낼 수 있다는 고집스런 가정이다. 물론 진실은 아무도 실재를 전체적으로 파악할 수 없고, 개개인의 우주는 어느 정도 독특하며, 이러한 상황은 우리가 오직 하나의 진실된 현실이 있다는 것을 증명할 수 없게 만든다.

4

하위내용영역	배점	예상정답률
일반영어 B형 서술형	4점	45%

모범답안 There are two key flaws in marketing data that should be considered. First, tracking has limitations in observing the way a user operates in terms of scope and reach, such as the blind spots of multi-device use, cookie windows, and user level settings. Second, user behavior is the imperfection to consider. Users can prefer to avoid or embrace marketing, which can be misrepresented when both types are considered as if part of the same engagement path. In conclusion, marketers should use data as a guide to inform(help) their own models of reality rather than relying on it to be a perfect reflection of reality.

채점 기준

ⓐ Topic sentence

+ 1점: "There are two key flaws in marketing data (that should be considered)."를 서술하였거나 유사하였다.

ⓑ Major supporting details

+ 2점: "① First, tracking has limitations in observing the way a user operates such as the blind spots of multi-device use, cookie windows, and user level settings. ② Second, user behavior is the imperfection to consider. Users can have the preference to avoid or embrace marketing, which can be misrepresented when both types are considered in the same data set."를 서술하였거나 유사하였다.

☞ 2개 중 2개 모두를 정확하게 요약한 경우 2점, 1개를 요약한 경우 1점, 요약하지 못한 경우 0점을 준다.

ⓒ Conclusion

+ 1점: "In conclusion, markets should be to use data as a guide to inform their own models of reality rather than relying on it to be a perfect reflection of reality."을 서술하였거나 유사하였다.

감점
- 본문에 나오는 연속되는 6단어 이상을 사용하였다. −1pt
- 문단을 두 개나 그 이상으로 구성하였다. −1pt
- grammar나 영어표현이 합쳐 4개 이상 오류가 있다. −1pt

제06회 모의고사

1

하위내용영역	배점	예상정답률
일반영어 A형 서술형	4점	60%

모범답안) The word is "freshman". Second, the implication of the underlined is that the writer does not feel like proof of the American Dream nor intends to communicate that meaning in her biography.

채점 기준

+ 2점 : 빈칸에 들어갈 단어를 "freshman"라 정확히 기입하였다. 이외에는 답이 될 수 없다.
+ 2점 : 밑줄 친 부분이 함축하는 바를 "the writer does not feel like proof of the American Dream nor intends to communicate that meaning in her biography"라 서술하였거나 유사하였다.

한글번역

대학교 1학년 첫 학기 때를 떠올리면, 그 기억은 지금도 온몸에 생생히 되살아난다. 나는 늘 극도로 피곤했다. 매일 아침 3시 40분이면 알람시계가 요란한 소리를 내며 울린다. 그 소리는 지금도 내 귓가에 울리는 듯하다. 이어 칠흑같이 어두운 방 안에 어색하게 걸터앉은 듯한 시계 속 주황색 숫자 3:40, 잠이 덜 깬 채 본능적으로 알람 버튼을 끄는 내 손, 지친 몸을 이끌고 침대에서 빠져나와 곧장 문으로 향하는 내 모습이 보인다. 잘 때 입고 있던 옷을 그대로 입고 문을 나선다. 전날 밤 잠들 때 나갈 옷을 미리 입고 잠들기 때문이다. 덕분에 3시 반이 아니라 3시 40분까지 10분 더 잘 수 있었다.

밖에 나오니 로키 산맥의 겨울이 뺨에 와 닿고, 아직 세 시간은 더 지나야 제설제가 뿌려질 인도를 따라 캠퍼스로 허둥지둥 향하기 시작한다. 나는 공과대학 건물로 향한 뒤, 건물 안의 작은 나일론 카펫에 붙은 껌을 떼어내거나 칠판에 써 있는 복잡한 수식들을 지우고, 파란색 젤로 화장실 변기를 청소하는 게 내 일이었다. 일을 다 마치고 나면 아침 8시쯤 됐다. 그때 나는 수업을 들으러 갔다.

한글번역

마케팅 담당자로서 우리는 디지털 광고 및 참여와 관련된 사용자 행동을 측정하고 평가하는 데 마케팅 데이터를 항상 사용한다. 하지만 마케팅 데이터는 사용자 행동의 불완전한 표현이며 완벽한 시뮬레이션이 아니라는 점을 기억하는 것이 매우 중요하다. 마케팅 데이터가 불완전한 이유가 있다.

첫 번째는 추적의 본질에 있다. 추적은 기술적으로 그 영역과 범위가 제한된다. 기껏해야 추적은 오랜 시간에 걸쳐 동일한 장치로부터 하는 참여나 동일한 다중 장치 계정으로부터 하는 참여만 측정할 수 있다. 이것은 추적이 처음부터 올바르게 구현되고 최종 사용자에 의해 비활성화되지 않은 경우에만 효과가 있다. 추적의 기술적 한계로 인해 다중 장치 사용, 추적 활성 시간(쿠키 창) 또는 사용자 수준에서 원해서든 아니면 브라우저 사전 설정에 의해서든, 개인 옵트아웃(프로그램 중단)으로 인해 추적되지 않는 작업이 항상 있기 마련이다.

마케팅 데이터가 불완전한 두 번째 주요 원인은 사용자 행동에 있다. 인간으로서 우리는 광고와 상호작용하는 매우 다양한 선택과 방법을 가지고 있다. 우리들 중 일부는 가능한 한 광고와 상호작용하는 것을 피하는 반면, 우리 중 일부는 반대의 방식으로 행동한다. 우리들 중 몇몇은 광고를 전혀 클릭하지 않기로 선택할 것이고, 몇몇은 망설이지 않을 것이다. 우리 중 일부는 구매할 것을 매우 조사할 것이고, 일부는 그렇지 않을 것이다. 모든 사용자가 준수하고 있는 참여 경로는 한 가지가 아니다. 그럼에도 종종 우리의 데이터는 데이터 해석의 부정확성을 유발하는 "단일 깔때기" 렌즈를 통해 해석된다.

그렇다면 마케터는 무엇을 해야 할까? 당신이 할 수 있는 가장 좋은 일은 당신 자신의 현실 모델을 검사하기 위해 데이터를 충분히 활용하는 것이다. 최고의 데이터 회사들은 맹목적으로 데이터를 사용하지 않고, 그들의 현실 인식을 알리기 위해 사용한다. 우리의 데이터는 현실이 아니라 사용자 행동, 기술적 한계 및 프로세스에 의해 왜곡된 현실에 대한 불완전한 반영이다. 우리의 최선의 대응은 이것을 인정하고 받아들이고, 이것을 우리에게 유리하게 사용하는 것이다.

2

하위내용영역	배점	예상정답률
일반영어 A형 서술형	4점	50%

모범답안) The word is "order". Second, the ordering of human lives is compared to "the force of gravity".

채점 기준

+ 2점: 빈칸에 들어갈 단어를 "order"라 정확히 기입하였다. 이외에는 답이 될 수 없다.
+ 2점: 인간 생활의 질서와 비유되는 것을 "(the force of) gravity"라 정확히 서술하였다.

한글번역

실제로, 사람들은 같은 음악을 듣지만, 다른 경험을 하게 된다. 주관성은 모든 예술의 필수적인 부분이며, 때로는 가장 그럴 것 같지 않은 곳에서도, 예술가와 관객 사이의 포괄적인 의사소통이 매우 어렵다는 것을 알게 된다. 예를 들어, 추상화뿐만 아니라 가장 단순한 그림에서조차도 그렇다. 가장 잘 알려진 그림 중 하나인 다빈치가 그린 모나리자를 예로 들어보자. 아무도 이 그림이 한 여성의 초상화라는 것에 대해 잘못 해석하지는 않는다. 그만큼은 우리가 잘 안다. 하지만 이 그림 속의 흥미를 자아내는 미소는 이 미소가 어떤 마음의 상태를 묘사하고 있는지와 관련해 매우 다양한 방식으로 해석되고 있다. 이렇듯, 관객들은 예술가가 정확히 무엇을 염두에 두고 있었는지 확신할 수는 없다. 이것은 모든 층위에서 유효하며, 따라서, 대다수 예술가들과 관객들 사이에, 그들의 예술만으로는, 완벽한 의사소통은 이루어질 수 없다.

몇 가지 다른 예를 들어보자면, 나는 뛰어난 화가 몇 명을 친한 친구로 가지고 있다. 종종, 나는 그들이 나를 지적으로 교육시키는 데 시간을 쓰고, 예술가로서 자신들의 예술에 대해 어떻게 생각하는지 보고자 했다. 예를 들어, 한 친구는 대부분의 그림에서 말의 이미지를 사용하며, 그는 또한 모든 요소들이 긴장되고 질서가 결여되도록 그림을 그린다. 예를 들어, 인간의 자연스러운 자세는 일어서거나 앉거나 눕는 것일 것이다. 하지만, 그는 인간을 모든 위치에 놓았는데, 어떤 사람은 긴장 상태에서 대각선의 비스듬한 위치에 있다. 또는 앉은 자세, 서 있는 자세, 또는 매달려 있는 자세의 인간과 섞여 말의 머리가 거꾸로 된 이미지를 발견할 수도 있다. 전체적으로 그 그림의 서로 다른 요소들은 물리적

대학교 신입생 첫 두 달간 나의 일과는 늘 이렇게 시작됐다. 그러나 새벽에 경비 일만 해서는 집세를 낼 수 없었다. 그래서 두 번째 아르바이트를 구했다. 학교 구내식당에서 코울슬로와 젤리를 서빙하는 일이었다. 같이 일했던 동료도 나처럼 1학년 학생이었는데, 학교 식당에서 밥을 먹을 수 있는 식대를 내지 못해서 일을 했다. 우리 둘은 지금 우리가 주문받고 파는 음식을 정작 우리는 사 먹을 돈이 없다는 쓸쓸한 사실을 서로 입에 올리지 않았다. 나는 일하다 주어지는 점심시간에 앞치마를 걸어두고 가방 속에서 미리 싸 온 점심을 꺼내먹었다. 단백질 바 하나랑 동네 슈퍼에서 개당 10센트(약 100원)에 살 수 있는 라면이었다. 매일 같은 메뉴였지만, 그렇다고 질리거나 화가 난 적은 없었던 것 같다. 나와 같은 학년 학생들, 내 친구들이 먹은 음식이 담은 접시를 씻고, 사용한 화장실을 청소한다고 해서 딱히 창피하거나 모멸감을 느끼지도 않았다. 가난과 불평등에 관해서 무언가 복잡한 생각을 하고 있긴 했지만 기억에 남은 것은 너무 피곤했다는 사실 뿐이다.

난생 처음 간 학교에 대한 기억과 다른 경험을 모아 나는 2018년에 비망록《배움의 발견》을 펴냈다. 내 책이 베스트셀러가 됐을 때 나는 적잖이 놀랐다. 내가 살아온 길지 않은 인생은 분명 대단히 희귀한, 극단적인 사례에 속한다. 나는 아이다호주의 산골짜기 마을에서 태어났다. 부모님은 독실한 몰몬교도셨는데, 정부를 믿지 않았기 때문에 나를 학교에 보내지 않았다. 브리검영대학 강의실이 내겐 태어나 처음 듣는 학교 수업이었다. 나는 2008년에 학부를 졸업하고, 장학생으로 영국 케임브리지대학에서 공부했으며, 거기서 박사까지 받았다.

내 삶을 기록한 책이 베스트셀러가 되고 나니 신기한 일이 벌어졌다. 사람들이 책을 읽고서는 내 이야기가 자신에게 어떤 의미로 다가왔는지 피드백을 주는 거다. 출판 기념회나 북 토크를 가면 내 책을 읽고 희망을 얻었다는 사람도 있고, 어떤 시련에도 굴하지 않고 굳세게 다시 일어서는 내 모습에 감명 받았다는 사람도 있다. 사람들이 그렇게 봐준다니, 고마운 일이다. 그런데 가끔, 아니 종종 거기서 한 발 더 나아가는 사람들이 있다. 나로선 딱히 어떻게 답해야 좋을지 모를 말을 듣곤 하는데, 이런 식의 찬사다. "당신은 아메리칸 드림의 산증인이에요. 누구나 꿈꾸면 무엇이든 해낼 수 있다는 걸 보여주셨잖아요."

정말 그런가? 내가 풀어낸 이야기는 아메리칸 드림의 전형이나 단면이라고 할 수 있나?

현상과 중력의 법칙을 거스르고, 따라서 그 그림은 초현실주의적인 것이 되는데, 이는 예술계에서 새로운 현상은 아니다.

하지만, 그가 왜 많은 그림에서 말과 인간을 섞느냐는 질문을 받았을 때, 그에게 말은 점잖은 것의 상징이고, 자신은 그냥 말이 좋을 뿐이고, 말이 그의 그림 속으로 길을 찾아 들어왔다고 대답했다. 왜 그러한 무질서가 자신의 그림 대부분에 있는 모든 요소들을 지배하느냐고 묻자, "실제 세계에서 중력의 힘이 모든 대상들을 지상에서 떠날 수 없도록 만들고 그 대상들에게 질서를 강요한다"고 대답했다. 그와 유사한 힘인, 인간의 욕구는 인간에게 비슷한 질서를 강요하고 그들의 삶을 통제한다. 그의 그림에서 중력을 거스르는 것은 인간에게 조건을 강요함으로써 인간의 절대적 자유를 박탈하는 그 힘에 저항하는 은유이다. 내가 그에게 반항자라고 부르는 것이 잘못된 가정이냐고 물었고, 그는 그렇지 않을 것 같다(즉, 잘못된 가정이 아니라)고 대답했다.

3

하위내용영역	배점	예상정답률
일반영어 B형 서술형	4점	50%

모범답안) The words are "distorted view". Second, it means that when depressions attack, if they are contained they will abate very quickly.

채점 기준

+ 2점 : 빈칸에 들어갈 단어를 "distorted view"라 정확히 기입하였다. 이외에는 답이 될 수 없다.
+ 2점 : 밑줄 친 부분의 의미를 "when a depression attacks, if it is contained it will pass by (or go by) very quickly" 또는 "short-lived, recurrent depressions will go away very quickly"라 서술하였거나 유사하였다.

한글번역

우리 자신에 대한 태도가 왜곡되는 경향이 있지만 왜곡이 모두 한 방향으로만 존재하는 것은 아니다. 여섯 살의 브리트니는 박람회에 갔을 때 거울의 전당을 방문했고, 그녀의 몸이 왜곡되는 서로 다른 방식에 매료됐다. 한 거울에서는 키가 크고 말라 보였고, 또 다른 거울에서는 키가 작고 뚱뚱해 보였다. 그러나 다른 거울들은 그녀의 몸의 어떤 부분을 어떤 방식으로 왜곡했고, 몸의 다른 부분을 또 다른 방식으로 일그러뜨렸다. 그녀의 머리는 크고 가늘었고; 가슴은 길고 넓었고; 그리고 그녀의 다리는 그녀의 발이 그녀의 엉덩이에서 바로 튀어나오는 것처럼 보일 때까지 줄어들었다.

우리가 우리 자신에 대해 가지고 있는 왜곡된 믿음은 매우 비슷할 것이다. 우리들 대부분은 (적어도) 두 가지 방식으로 작동한다 : 우리는 우리 자신에 대해 아주 심하게 비판적일 수 있고, 아니면 우리 자신에게 터무니없는 관대함을 줄 수 있다. 비록 모순된 것처럼 보일지라도, 우리는 먼저 하나를 하고 나서 다른 하나를 할 수 있다. 우리는 자신의 이익을 다른 사람들의 이익보다 우선시할 수 있지만, 자신에 대한 자부심을 다른 사람들의 자부심보다 훨씬 덜 한 것으로 놓기도 한다. 사실, 아마도 하나의 왜곡된 관점은 다른 관점으로부터 생겨날 것이다. 다른 사람들보다 열등하다는 깊은 두려움 때문에, 우리는 자랑을 하고 다른 사람들을 이기려고 노력하는 것을 통해서 자신의 자아상을 높이려고 노력할지도 모른다.

우울증의 근원에는 대개 자기 자신에 대한 왜곡된 관점이 있다. 여러분이 자신을 더 명확하게 볼 수 있도록 여러분이 바깥에서 자신을 바라보는 사람이라면 여러분 자신에 대해 뭐라고 말할지 생각해 보는 것이 도움이 된다 : 마치 여러분이 다른 사람이 돼서 여러분 자신을 철저히 객관적으로 볼 수 있는 것처럼.

윈스턴 처칠은 반복되는 일시적인 우울증으로 고통받았다. 그는 새뮤얼 존슨이 이전에 사용했던 이름인 검은 개라는 이름을 우울증에게 붙여줬고, 그 이후로 다른 많은 이들에 의해 사용됐다. 우울증에 이름을 부여하는 것은 그가 우울증에 대처하고 또 받아들이는 데 도움이 됐는데, 적절한 시기에 우울증이 사라질 것이라는 것을 알았기 때문이다. 그런 꼬리표 붙이기는 우울증을 길들이는 데 도움이 되어 우울증이, 비록 친구는 될 수 없을지언정, 적어도 당신이 알고 있고, 아마도 당신이 약간의 애정을 느낄 수 있는 적이 되도록 할 것이다.

비교적 일시적이고 반복적인 우울증이 여러분을 공격할 때, 그것들을 제한하거나 억제하는 등을 통해 그것들을 막는 것이 최선일 수 있다. 그러면 우울증은 지름길을 택할 것이다. 스스로에게 이렇게 말하라. "아, 또 우울증이네. 언제나 그렇듯이 곧 사라지겠지. 할 일을 계속 해야지." 이것은 우울증에 걸린 것에 대해 우울해하는 경향이 있는 사람들에게 특히 도움이 되는데, 이런 경향성은 매우 흔하게 일어나는 일이고, 상처에 모욕을 덧붙이는 것이다.

4

하위내용영역	배점	예상정답률
일반영어 B형 서술형	4점	45%

모범답안) Insects are the most diverse and abundant animals on the planet due to extraordinary survival advantages (such as exoskeletons and miniaturization). First, their exoskeletons are extremely protective external skeletons that help keep physical and chemical attacks at bay. Second, their small size reduces the thickness requirements of their exoskeletons and the resources needed to maintain them and reproduce. In conclusion, given these advantages, insects have outlived major cataclysms and continue to show themselves highly capable for going forward.

채점기준

ⓐ Topic sentence
+ 1점: "<u>Insects are the most diverse and abundant animals on the planet due to extraordinary survival advantages.</u>"를 서술하였거나 유사하였다.

ⓑ Major supporting details
+ 2점: "<u>First, their exoskeletons are extremely protective external skeletons that help keep physical and chemical attacks at bay</u>(1점). <u>Second, their small size reduces the thickness requirements of their exoskeletons</u> (0.5점) and <u>the resources needed to maintain them and reproduce</u>(0.5점)."를 서술하였거나 유사하였다.

ⓒ Conclusion
+ 1점: "<u>In conclusion, given these advantages, insects (have outlived major cataclysms and) continue to show themselves highly capable for going forward</u>"을 서술하였거나 유사하였다.

감점
- 본문에 나오는 연속되는 6단어 이상을 사용하였다. -1pt
- 문단을 두 개나 그 이상으로 구성하였다. -1pt
- grammar나 영어표현이 합쳐 4개 이상 오류가 있다. -1pt

한글번역

곤충이 지구상에서 가장 풍부하고 다양한 생물군이라는 것은 확실히 우연이 아니다. 그들은 4억년 이상 동안 생태학적 우위의 위치를 유지해왔다. 어떤 생태학적 혹은 생리학적 속성도 이러한 비길 데 없는 성공을 설명할 수 없지만, 곤충들은 특이한 생존 이점을 주는 독특한 특징의 조합을 가지고 있다.

척추동물과 달리 곤충의 지지골격은 몸의 바깥쪽에 위치해 있다. 이 외골격은 신체의 연조직에 모양과 지지력을 줄 뿐만 아니라, 공격이나 부상으로부터 보호하며, 건조한 환경과 담수 환경 모두에서 체액의 손실을 최소화하며, 근육에 힘과 민첩성을 보장하는 역학적 이점을 지니고 있다. "갑옷"으로서 외골격은 물리적, 화학적 공격에 모두 저항할 수 있다. 그것은 건조를 방지하는 불침투성 왁스 층으로 덮여 있다.

일반적으로, 그 곤충들은 소형화의 경이로운 존재다. 거대한 나방부터 작은 기생 말벌까지 크기가 다양하지만, 대부분의 종들은 몸길이가 2~20mm(0.1~1.0인치)쯤이다. 외골격을 가진 동물에게 작은 크기는 뚜렷한 장점이다. 만약 곤충이 소나 코끼리만큼 크다면, 그들의 외골격은 신체 조직의 추가적인 덩어리를 지탱하기 위해 비례적으로 더 두꺼워져야 할 것이다. 하지만 더 두꺼운 외골격은 또한 더 무겁고 더 번거로울 것이다. 심지어 가장 간단한 움직임도 더 큰 근육량을 필요로 하고 더 많은 에너지를 소비할 것이다. 작은 크기의 또 다른 장점은 생존과 번식에 필요한 최소한의 자원이다. 조그만 부스러기만 있어도 큰 잔치가 되고, 이슬방울은 갈증을 해소하고, 조약돌은 그늘을 제공한다. 어떤 경우에는 필요로 하는 식량이 너무 적어서 곤충은 어떤 식물이나 동물에서 평생을 살 수 있고, 식량 공급을 고갈시키지 않을 수도 있다.

곤충들은 공룡의 흥망성쇠를 목격했다. 그들은 지구 전체를 멸종시켰던 적어도 네 번의 대격변에도 살아남았다. 그들의 생존능력으로 판단하건대, 박멸을 위한 인류의 최선의 노력에도 불구하고 그들은 계속해서 번성하고 있다.

유희태 | 일반영어 ❹-2

제07회 모의고사

1

하위내용영역	배점	예상정답률
일반영어 A형 서술형	4점	40%

모범 답안 The word is "brain activity". Second, the findings suggest several ways to inform therapeutic practices: by using role-playing to help individuals with autism suppress self-consciousness during social interactions, fostering brain synchronization in group settings to improve social connections, and incorporating personalized sensory stimuli like names to engage individuals more effectively in communication and interaction exercises.

채점 기준

+ 2점: 빈칸에 들어갈 단어를 "brain activity"라 정확히 기입하였다. 이외에는 답이 될 수 없다.
+ 2점: 공연 중 억제된 자기 인식에 대한 연구 결과가 자폐증이나 기타 사회적 인지 장애를 가진 개인들을 위한 치료적 실천에 어떤 방식으로 영향을 줄 수 있을지에 대해 "① by using role-playing to help individuals with autism suppress self-consciousness during social interactions, ② fostering brain synchronization in group settings to improve social connections, and ③ incorporating personalized sensory stimuli like names to engage individuals more effectively in communication and interaction exercises."라 서술하였거나 유사하였다.
  ☞ 다음과 같이 서술하였어도 2점을 준다.
  - "By using role-playing, brain synchronization, and personalized sensory stimuli like names to improve social and communication skills in people with autism or social cognitive problems."
  - "By incorporating techniques like role-playing, brain synchronization, and personalized sensory stimuli like names as part of therapeutic practices for people with autism or social cognitive problems."
  ☞ 3개 중 2개 이상을 서술하였으면 2점, 1개를 서술하였으면 1점을 준다.

✚ 보충설명

Clues

① **Suppression of Self-Awareness**: "Actors exhibited suppressed activity in the left anterior prefrontal cortex—a region associated with self-awareness—when hearing their own names while performing."
  → This clue suggests that techniques that reduce self-awareness may help individuals with social cognitive disorders, such as autism, in environments that require **role-playing or social interaction**, by allowing them to engage more freely without self-consciousness.

② **Synchronization of Brain Activity**: "They found that the right inferior frontal gyrus and right frontopolar cortex—areas associated with social interaction and action planning—showed similar activity patterns in actors working together."
  → This clue indicates that engaging in cooperative activities, like acting, can lead to better brain synchronization, which could be leveraged in therapies to help individuals with social cognitive disorders improve communication and teamwork.

③ **Effects of Names in Sensory Drama Games**: "Hunter has refined her work with autistic individuals, particularly non-verbal participants, by focusing on the effects of names in sensory drama games."
  → This clue suggests that the use of personalized cues, like hearing one's own name in structured activities, can help engage individuals with autism, especially those who are non-verbal, in therapeutic settings.

참고

- **Enhanced Role-Playing Techniques**: The study suggests that actors suppress their core sense of self to fully embody characters. For individuals with autism, structured role-playing or theatrical activities might help them temporarily suppress self-consciousness and practice engaging in social interactions without the anxiety that often accompanies these situations. This could be beneficial for developing social skills.
- **Synchronization of Brain Activity**: The synchronization of brain activity observed in actors during performances suggests that social collaboration can promote neural coordination. Therapeutic approaches could incorporate group-based theatre activities to foster better social connections and communication among individuals with autism by encouraging brain synchronization in social interactions.
- **Use of Personalized Sensory Stimuli**: The study notes the importance of hearing one's own name in theatrical settings, a concept that has been integrated into drama games for autistic individuals. This could be expanded in therapeutic practices, where using names and other personalized stimuli in sensory games might help non-verbal or socially withdrawn individuals become more engaged and responsive.

한글번역

<Journal of Cognitive Neuroscience>에 발표된 런던대학교(UCL)의 연구는 배우들이 새로운 역할을 맡을 때 자신의 핵심 자기인식을 억제할 수 있으며, 이로 인해 연극 훈련이 뇌의 메커니즘에 중요한 영향을 미칠 수 있음을 시사하고 있다. 연구자들은 헌터 하트비트 방법(셰익스피어의 작품과 리듬, 심장박동 소리를 기반으로 한 연극적 접근 방식으로, 자폐 스펙트럼 장애(ASD)를 가진 개인과 소통하는 데 중점을 둔 연극 기법으로, 플루트 극단의 예술 감독인 켈리 헌터가 개발했으며, 자폐 아동이나 성인들이 사회적 상호작용을 촉진하고 정서적 표현을 개발하도록 돕기 위해 설계됐다. 감각적이고 상호작용적인 연극 게임을 통해, 특히 언어적으로 소통이 어려운 자폐인들이 더 쉽게 참여하고 소통할 수 있도록 지원하는 것이 특징이다.)을 사용하여 자폐성 장애인들을 위한 상호작용적 셰익스피어 공연을 제공하는 플루트 극단과 협력했다. 연구진은 혁신적인 뇌 영상 기술을 사용해 (셰익스피어의) <한여름 밤의 꿈>을 리허설하는 배우들의 뇌 활동을 관찰했다.

뇌 영상 관찰 결과에 따르면, 배우들이 공연 중 자신의 이름을 들을 때 자기인식과 관련된 영역인 좌측 전방 전전두엽 피질의 활동이 억제되는 현상이 나타났다. 반면, 배역을 벗어난 상태에서는 자신의 이름에 정상적으로 반응했다. 이 억제 현상은 여러 배우에게서 반복적으로 진행된 리허설에서 일관되게 관찰됐다. 수석 연구원 드웨이니카 그리브스는 배우들이 훈련 과정의 일환으로 자기인식을 억제하는 방법을 배우며, 이를 통해 다양한 캐릭터를 완전히 구현할 수 있다고 언급했다. 이는 신경과학자들이 공연 중 배우들의 뇌 활동을 기록한 최초의 사례로, 연극 훈련이 뇌에 미치는 영향을 밝히는 중요한 통찰을 제공한다.

연구진은 또한 두 명의 배우가 리허설 중 어떻게 뇌 활동을 동기화하는지도 연구했다. 그 결과, 사회적 상호작용과 행동 계획과 관련된 영역인 우측 하전두회 및 우측 전두극에서 함께 작업하는 배우들에게서 유사한 활동 패턴이 나타났다. 이 동기화는 뇌 활동에만 국한됐으며, 심박 수나 호흡과 같은 생리적 측정에서는 나타나지 않아, 특정 뇌 시스템이 공연 중 복잡한 사회적 상호작용에서 조정된다는 사실을 보여줬다. ("Synchronize"의 뜻은 동시에 일어나거나 같은 속도와 리듬으로 맞춘다는 의미이다. 여기선, 배우들이 리허설을 할 때, 그들의 뇌 활동이 서로 같은 패턴으로 일치하거나 동시에 반응하는 것을 의미한다. 쉽게 말해, 두 배우가 서로의 행동과 생각에 맞춰 뇌의 특정 부분에서 유사한 활동을 보이는 것이다.)

그리브스는 이번 연구가 신경과학자들과 연극 전문가들 간의 협력을 촉진할 가능성을 강조했다. 연구는 연극 훈련이 사회적 인지 능력을 향상시킬 수 있음을 시사하며, 연구진은 자폐증을 앓고 있는 아이들을 포함한 청소년들이 연극 참여를 통해 새로운 사회적 기술을 개발할 수 있는지 조사할 계획이다.

플루트 극장의 예술 감독인 켈리 헌터는 셰익스피어가 본능적으로 자신의 이름을 듣는 것의 중요성을 이해했다는 점에 대해 깊이 생각했다. 이는 과학적 연구에 의해 확인된 개념이다. UCL과 공동연구를 한 후, 헌터는 감각적 드라마 게임에서(시각, 청각, 촉각 등 다양한 감각을 활용해 연극적인 활동에 참여하는 게임으로, 참가자들이 감각적인 경험을 통해 상황을 연기하거나 역할을 수행하도록 설계됐으며, 주로 의사소통이나 감정 표현을 촉진하는 목적으로 사용된다. 특히 자폐증과 표현을 촉진하는 목적으로 사용되고 특히 자폐증과 같은 발달 장애를 가진 사람들을 위한 치료적 환경에서 자주 활용한다.) 이름의 효과에 집중함으로써, 특히 비언어적 참여자들인 자폐아들과의 작업을 정교화해왔다. 이 협력은 예술적 직관과 과학적 통찰력을 결합해 우리가 소통하고 연결되는 방식에 대한 이해를 깊게 만들었다.

2

하위내용영역	배점	예상정답률
일반영어 A형 서술형	4점	40%

모범답안) The word is "negative". Second, the key similarity is that both cases involved poorly designed ballots that led to voter confusion and errors, potentially altering the election outcomes.

채점기준

+ 2점: 빈칸에 들어갈 단어를 "<u>negative</u>"라 정확히 기입하였다. 이외에는 답이 될 수 없다.
+ 2점: 핵심 유사점을 "<u>both cases involved poorly designed ballots that led to voter confusion and errors</u>, potentially altering the election outcomes."라 서술하였거나 유사하였다.

☞ 다음과 같이 서술하였어도 2점을 준다.
- "Both were influenced by <u>poor ballot design, which led to voter confusion and the potential for unintended voting outcomes</u>."
- "The similarity lies in <u>how both poorly designed ballots led to voter confusion and errors</u>. (In the 2000 election, the butterfly ballot caused confusion that potentially influenced the outcome of the presidential race, while in the 2006 Sarasota election, a design flaw resulted in a large number of undervotes, affecting the congressional race.)"
- "<u>Flawed ballot design undermined the accuracy of the election results and raised concerns about fairness and the integrity of the electoral process</u>."

한글번역

2000년 대통령 선거는 미국인들이 어떻게 투표하는지에 대한 새로운 인식과 우려를 불러일으켰다. 이에 대응해, 의회는 2002년 미국 투표법을 통과시켰고, 많은 주에서는 새로운 투표 시스템을 구입하고, 유권자 등록 기록을 전산화했으며, 전반적인 선거 관리를 개선했다. 그러나 등록, 투표 시스템, 관리 방식은 유권자들이 투표할 때 직면하는 문제의 일부일 뿐이다.

구체적인 메커니즘과 절차가 무엇이든 간에, 유권자들은 투표용지를 사용한다. 이름과 이미지가 터치스크린에 프로그래밍됐든 종이에 인쇄됐든, 투표용지의 형식은 유권자들이 의도한 대로 투표할 수 있는 능력에 영향을 미칠 수 있으며, 때로는 선거 결과에 부정적인 영향을 미칠 수도 있다. 2000년에 논란을 일으킨 버터플라이 투표용지와 2006년 사라소타 카운티 의회 선거에 영향을 미친 설계 결함이 이러한 점을 강력히 보여줬다.

투표용지는 여러 가지 이유로 연구의 최전선에 있다. 첫째, 투표용지는 유권자들이 의사를 표명하는 수단이며, 투표 과정이 시작되면 유권자들이 관찰하는 지배적인 요소이다. 상징적으로도 더 의미가 있다. 일반 유권자와 정부 간의 접촉 지점은 바로 투표용지이다. 둘째, 다양한 투표용지의 레이아웃, 옵션, 과업은 투표 수(투표자가 잘못 표시한 무효표), 유권자 태도의 표현(발의안), 그리고 후보자나 정당에 대한 상대적 이점(후보 순서, 일괄 투표 옵션)에 일상적으로 영향을 미친다. 셋째, 투표용지 설계의 영향은 투표가 진행되는 메커니즘에 의해 좌우될 수 있는데, 이 상호작용은 오래전부터 존재해 왔으나 최근에서야 연구되기 시작했다. 넷째, 다양한 유형의 투표용지와 투표 시스템은 여러 유권자 그룹에 다르게 영향을 미칠 수 있어 공정성과 평등성에 대한 우려를 불러일으킨다.

앨런과 비어드 같은 정치학자들은 100여 년 전부터 투표용지와 연관된 문제가 정치적 행동에 영향을 미치며 선거 관계자, 정치인, 유권자들의 삶을 복잡하게 만들 수 있다는 점을 인식했다. 최근에 와서야 학자들은 투표용지 관련 문제를 미국 민주주의 발전과 연관 짓기 시작했다. 그러나 불과 몇 년 전부터 이러한 감정이 체계적인 연구 노력으로 이어졌을 따름이다.

최근의 선거 실패는 투표 기술 및 선거 관리와 더불어 투표용지 설계가 정치제도에 대한 여론에 부정적인 영향을 미칠 수 있음을 강조했다. 실제적 결함과 (유권자들이 그럴 것이라 생각하는) 인식된 결함은 유권자들로 하여금 특정 투표용지, 특정 유형의 투표 장비, 개별 선거, 심지어 전반적인 선거까지도 실패한 것이거나 부정직한 과정으로 인식하게 만들 수 있다.

3

하위내용영역	배점	예상정답률
일반영어 B형 서술형	4점	40%

모범답안 The word is "challenging". Second, the survey identifies education level, race, ethnicity, and gender as key demographic factors associated with differences in science knowledge. Educational attainment is strongly correlated with science knowledge, with those having higher education levels scoring better. Additionally, significant disparities exist between racial and ethnic groups, and men tend to score higher than women, though this varies by question.

채점기준

+ 2점: 빈칸에 "challenging"이라 정확히 기입하였다. 이외에는 답이 될 수 없다.
+ 2점: 과학 지식의 차이와 관련된 인구 통계학적 요인을 "education level, race, ethnicity, and gender as key demographic factors associated with differences in science knowledge."라 서술하였거나 유사하였다.

한글번역

퓨 리서치 센터의 조사에 따르면 많은 미국인들이 과학 개념에 대한 몇 가지 질문에 답할 수 있으며, 대부분이 항생제 남용에 대한 우려를 정확히 식별하거나 "잠복기"의 정의를 설명할 수 있다. 그러나 다른 과학 개념들은 대중에게 더 도전적이었다. 예를 들어, 극소수의 미국인들만이 가설에 대해 인식하거나 제산제의 주요 성분이 염기라는 사실을 식별할 수 있다.

이 조사는 정보에 대한 접근이 쉬운 시대에 대중이 과학적 사실과 과학적 과정을 얼마나 잘 이해하는지 보여준다. 하지만 정보의 정확성에 대한 논란은 빈번하게 일어난다. 미국인들의 생명과학, 지구과학, 물리과학에 대한 지식은 크게 다르다. 예를 들어, 거의 10명 중 8명(79%)이 항생제 남용과 관련된 주요 문제로 항생제 내성을 꼽았으며, 비슷한 비율(76%)의 사람들이 잠복기를 감염에 걸렸으나 아직 증상이 나타나지 않은 기간임을 정확히 알고 있다.

그러나 더 복잡한 개념은 도전적이다. 예를 들어, 제산제의 주요 성분이 무엇인지 묻는 질문에 39%만이 "염기"라고 정확하게 답했다. 미국인들은 평균적으로 11개의 과학 질문 중 6.7개를 맞혔고, 중간 점수는 7점이었다. 약 39%의 응답자가 높은 과학 지식(9개에서 11개의 정답)을 얻었고, 32%는 중간 수준의 지식(5개에서 8개의 정답)을 보였으며, 29%는 낮은 과학 지식(0~4개의 정답)을 가진 것으로 분류됐다.

교육, 인종, 민족에 따른 과학 지식에서 두드러진 차이가 나타난다. 남성이 여성보다 높은 점수를 받는 경향이 있지만, 이는 질문에 따라 다르다. 정치적 성향에 따른 전반적인 과학 지식은 비슷하지만, 보수적 공화당원과 진보적 민주당원이 더 중도적인 동료들보다 높은 점수를 얻는 경향이 있다.

교육 수준은 과학 지식과 강하게 연관된다. 대학원 학위를 가진 사람들은 평균적으로 11개의 질문 중 9.1개를 맞히는 반면, 고등학교 졸업자나 그 이하의 교육을 받은 사람들은 평균적으로 5개의 정답을 맞힌다. 또한 인종과 민족 간 격차도 두드러지는데, 백인들은 평균 7.6개의 정답을 맞히는 반면, 히스패닉은 평균 5.1개, 흑인은 3.7개의 정답을 맞힌다. 백인의 약 절반(48%)이 높은 과학 지식을 가진 것으로 분류되는 반면, 히스패닉은 23%, 흑인은 9%에 불과하다.

이러한 차이는 교육 수준을 통제하더라도 여전히 유의미하며, 이는 인종 및 민족 간 과학 지식에 영향을 미치는 다른 요인이 있을 수 있음을 시사한다.

4

하위내용영역	배점	예상정답률
일반영어 B형 서술형	4점	50%

모범답안 Healthcare privatization has some potential risks. First, it can increase the gap between the rich and the poor by limiting lower-income access to timely, quality care, eroding the principle of healthcare as a universal right and making financial status dictate health outcomes. Second, prioritizing profits over patient care can result in compromised service quality and neglect of preventive care. In conclusion, a mixed model of public funding and private sector innovation, along with stronger public healthcare systems, could help ensure universal access and maintain efficiency.

채점기준

ⓐ Topic sentence
+ 1점: "Healthcare privatization has some potential risks." 또는 "There can be significant issues with the privatization of healthcare."를 서술하였거나 유사하였다.

ⓑ Major supporting details
+ 2점: "First, it can increase the gap between the rich and the poor by limiting lower-income access to timely, quality care(0.5점), eroding the principle of healthcare as a universal right and making financial status dictate health outcomes(0.5점). Second, prioritizing profits over patient care can result in compromised service quality and neglect of preventive care(1점)."를 서술하였거나 유사하였다.

☞ 2개 중 2개 모두를 정확하게 요약한 경우 2점, 1개를 요약한 경우 1점, 요약하지 못한 경우 0점을 준다.

ⓒ Conclusion
+ 1점: "In conclusion, a mixed model of public funding and private sector innovation(0.5점), along with stronger public healthcare systems(0.5점), could help ensure universal access and maintain efficiency."라 서술하였거나 유사하였다.

감점
- 본문에 나오는 연속되는 5단어 이상을 사용하였다. −1pt
- 문단을 두 개나 그 이상으로 구성하였다. −1pt
- grammar나 영어표현이 합쳐 4개 이상 오류가 있다. −1pt

한글번역

지난 40년 동안, 한때 공공 소유이거나 공적 자금으로 운영되던 많은 의료 시스템이 민간 부문에 아웃소싱하는 방식으로 민영화됐다. 의료 민영화는 접근성과 의료 서비스의 질에 대한 우려를 불러일으키며, 널리 논의되는 주제다. 지지자들은 민영화가 효율성을 높이고 혁신을 이끌 수 있다고 주장하지만, 비판론자들은 그로 인한 잠재적 위험을 강조한다.

의료 민영화는 부유층과 빈곤층 사이의 격차를 더 벌릴 수 있고, 오직 민간 서비스를 감당할 수 있는 사람들만이 적시에 양질의 치료를 받을 수 있는 시스템을 만들 수 있다. 저소득층은 필수 치료에 대한 접근이 줄어들거나, 더 긴 대기 시간 혹은 자금 부족으로 열악한 공공 의료 시설에서의 부실한 치료를 받을 가능성이 있다. 이런 격차는 의료를 보편적인 권리로 보는 원칙을 약화시키고, 경제적 지위가 건강 결과를 결정짓는 사회를 만들며, 이는 구조적 불평등을 지속시키고 공공 건강에 악영향을 미친다.

민영화된 의료 시스템에서는 환자의 건강보다는 이윤을 극대화하는 데 초점이 맞춰질 때가 많다. 의료 제공자는 포괄적이고 장기적인 치료보다는 효율성, 비용 절감, 수익성 있는 치료를 우선시할 수 있다. 이는 예방 치료, 조기 진단, 전반적인 환자 관리에 대한 관심을 줄이는 결과를 초래할 수 있다. 시간이 지나면서 이윤 중심의 접근은 의료 서비스의 질을 저하시킬 수 있고, 재정적 목표가 환자의 필요보다 앞서게 되면서 의료 기관에 대한 신뢰를 약화시킬 수 있다.

의료 민영화는 불평등을 심화시키고 환자 치료보다 이윤을 우선시하며 시스템의 통합성을 약화시킬 위험이 있다. 이에 대한 대안으로는 공공 자금과 민간 부문의 혁신을 결합한 혼합 모델이 보편적 접근을 보장하면서도 효율성과 품질을 유지할 수 있을 것이다. 또한, 모든 사람이 동등하게 의료 서비스에 접근할 수 있도록 공공 의료 시스템에 충분한 자금과 자원을 투입하는 것이 필수적이다.

제08회 모의고사

1

하위내용영역	배점	예상정답률
일반영어 A형 서술형	4점	40%

모범답안) The implication is that Chomsky sees ChatGPT as having little to no positive impact on education, with its primary effect being the facilitation of plagiarism. Second, Chomsky compares ChatGPT to smartphones, noting that just as students use smartphones to distract themselves, they may use ChatGPT to evade learning, highlighting a failure in the education system to engage students.

채점 기준

+ 2점 : 밑줄 친 "그것이 내가 생각할 수 있는 교육에 기여할 수 있는 유일한 부분"이라는 말의 함축 의미를 "Chomsky sees ChatGPT as having little to no positive impact on education, with its primary effect being the facilitation of plagiarism"이라 서술하였거나 유사하였다.

☞ 다음과 같이 서술하였어도 2점을 준다.
- "The phrase implies that Chomsky views ChatGPT as offering minimal or even negative educational benefits, as it mainly facilitates plagiarism rather than true learning."
- "Chomsky sees little educational value in ChatGPT other than it making plagiarism easier to detect. His comment suggests skepticism regarding any meaningful or positive impact the technology might have on learning."
- "Noam Chomsky believes the only notable impact ChatGPT has on education is making plagiarism easier. He implies that beyond facilitating cheating, ChatGPT doesn't offer any significant positive contributions to the educational process."
- "Noam Chomsky believes ChatGPT's primary effect on education is negative, as it facilitates plagiarism and hinders genuine learning. He suggests that beyond making it easier for students to cheat, ChatGPT does not offer any significant positive contributions to educational practices."

+ 2점 : 촘스키가 ChatGPT의 등장을 교실에서 스마트폰이 등장한 방식과 어떻게 비교하는지에 "Chomsky compares ChatGPT to smartphones, noting that just as students use smartphones to distract themselves, they may use ChatGPT to evade learning, highlighting a failure in the education system to engage students."라 서술하였거나 유사하였다.

☞ 다음과 같이 서술하였어도 2점을 준다.
- "Chomsky compares ChatGPT's impact in classrooms to that of smartphones, noting that both technologies can be distractions, with students often using them to bypass meaningful learning."

한글번역

자연어를 이해하고 이에 맞게 응답하는 시스템인 ChatGPT는 출시 이후 큰 반향을 일으켰다. 사용해 본 사람이라면 곧바로 혁신을 일으킬지, 혹은 경우에 따라 파괴적인 영향을 미칠지 궁금했을 것이다. 현재 일반적인 견해로는 ChatGPT의 첫 번째 희생자 중 하나가 세대에 걸쳐 교육 내내 연습해 온 에세이 글쓰기가 될 것이라는 의견이 많다. *The Atlantic*의 스티븐 마체는 "에세이, 특히 대학생 에세이는 수 세대 동안 인문학 교육의 중심이었습니다. 이를 통해 우리는 아이들에게 조사하고, 사고하며, 글 쓰는 법을 가르쳐왔죠. 그러나 이제 그 전통 전체가 근본적으로 흔들리려 합니다."라고 말했다.

만약 ChatGPT가 그 어떠한 주어진 주제에 대해서 그럴듯한 학문적 에세이를 즉시 작성할 수 있다면, 학문적 에세이의 미래는 어떻게 될까? 유튜브 채널 EduKitchen의 진행자는 최근 인터뷰에서 교육에 대한 견해에 대해 신뢰할 수 있는 사상가인 노엄 촘스키에게 대략 그런 질문을 던졌다. "수년 동안 교수들이 표절된 에세이를 감지하는 데 도움을 주는 프로그램들이 있었습니다. 이제는 표절이 더 쉬워졌기 때문에 더 어려워질 것입니다. 하지만 그것(ChatGPT와 같은 시스템으로 인해 표절을 탐지하는 일이 더 어려워질 것)이 내가 생각할 수 있는 유일한 교육에 대한 기여입니다." 촘스키는 ChatGPT 같은 시스템들이 뭔가에 가치는 있을 수 있다고 인정하지만, "그게 무엇인지는 명확하지 않다."고 말한다.

촘스키는 현재의 관련 기술 수준에서 ChatGPT의 사용을 "기본적으로 첨단 기술을 활용한 표절"이자 "학습을 회피하는 방법"으로 보고 있다. 그는 ChatGPT의 등장을 스마트폰의 등장에 비유하면서, 많은 학생들이 "아이폰으로 다른 사람과 채팅하면서 시간을 보낸다고 지적한다. 하나의 해결책은 아이폰을 금지하는 것이고, 또 다른 방법은 수업을 더 흥미롭게 만드는 것"이라고 말한다. 학생들이 본능적으로 최신 기술을 학습 회피 수단으로 사용하는 것은 "교육 시스템이 실패하고 있다는 신호"라고 촘스키는 언급한다. 교육이 학생들에게 매력을 주지 못하고 흥미를 끌지 않으며, 도전 과제를 제시하지 않아 학습 의욕을 불러일으키지 못하면, 학생들은 "탈출구를 찾을 것"이라고 덧붙이며, 1945년에 지루한 대학 화학 수업을 출석하지 않고 친구의 노트를 빌려 통과했던 자신의 경험을 예로 든다.

2

하위내용영역	배점	예상정답률
일반영어 A형 서술형	4점	35%

[모범답안] The words are "covid-19 pandemic". Second, the shift could hinder innovation and economic growth by dispersing the concentration of diverse people that drives productivity and technological advancement.

[채점기준]

+ 2점 : 빈칸에 들어갈 단어를 "covid-19 pandemic"이라 정확히 기입하였다. 이외에는 답이 될 수 없다.
+ 2점 : 이탈 지수에 나타난 것처럼 도심에서의 영구적인 이탈이 미래 도시의 혁신과 경제 성장에 어떤 영향을 미치는지에 "could hinder innovation and economic growth by dispersing the concentration of diverse people that drives productivity and technological advancement"라 서술하였거나 유사하였다.

☞ 다음과 같이 서술하였어도 2점을 준다.

— "The shift could hinder innovation and economic growth by diluting the concentration of diverse talent, ideas, and collaborative opportunities that cities typically provide. This dispersion could limit the spontaneous interactions that often lead to breakthroughs, slow down knowledge sharing, and decrease urban productivity."

한글번역

코로나19 팬데믹 이후의 경제 회복은 여러 측면에서 불균형적이다. 백신 접종 덕분에 일부 국가들은 빠르게 회복했지만, 여전히 어려움을 겪고 있는 국가들도 있다. 어떤 산업에서는 수요가 급증하고 있는 반면, 다른 산업에서는 여전히 약한 모습을 보이고 있다. 또 다른 큰 불균형의 원인이 서서히 드러나고 있다. 각국의 경제가 회복되는 동안, 도시들은 심각하게 뒤처지고 있다. (국가 전체의 경제 상황은 나아지고 있지만, 도시의 경제 회복 속도는 그에 미치지 못한다는 의미이다.)

팬데믹 이전에 도시는 무적처럼 보였으며, 경제적·문화적 힘이 작은 지리적 구역(즉, 도시들)에 점점 더 집중되고 있었다. 팬데믹 초기에 바이러스 감염에 대한 두려움으로 시작된 도시 지역의 인구 유출은 일시적일 것이라고 예상됐지만, 이제는 더 영구적이고 선호도에 있어 깊은 변화가 있음을 나타내는 것으로 보인다. 중요한 질문은 이것이 우려할 만한 것인지이다.

세계 주요 도시들의 현황을 살펴보는 한 가지 방법은 실시간 이동성 지표를 이용하는 것이다. (경제 전문잡지) *The Economist*는 소매 및 레크리에이션 장소, 대중교통 및 직장 방문에 관한 구글 데이터를 이용해 "이탈 지수"를 구성했다. 이는 대도시의 이동성을 해당 국가 전체의 이동성과 비교하는 것이다. 데이터는 더 뚜렷하게 다른 형태의 재배치를 가리킨다. (즉,) 팬 위에 깨진 달걀처럼, 경제 활동이 중심에서 서서히 바깥으로 퍼져나가고 있다. 한때 가장 활기찬 도시 지역이 점차 덜 활기찬 곳으로 변하고 있는 것이다.

경제 활동의 확산이 긍정적인 변화인지에 대한 의견은 분분하다. 경제학자들에게는 두 가지 장기적인 우려가 있다. 첫째는 고용과 관련이 있다. 도시에서 사무실이 비고 관광객이 줄어들면 저임금 노동자의 고용 기회가 줄어들 수 있다. 두 번째 걱정은 생산성이다. 도시 경제학자들의 핵심 통찰 중 하나는, 도시가 다양한 사람들을 좁은 공간에 밀집시키면서 새로운 아이디어와 기술을 촉진하는 데 기여한다는 것이다. 이것이 생활수준에 영향을 미칠 수 있다. 이러한 우려는 타당한가? 고용 측면에서는 낙관할 이유가 있다. 경제는 도심에서 어려움을 겪는 일자리에서 수요가 더 많은 곳으로 일자리를 재배치하는 데 놀라울 정도로 빠르게 적응해 전반적인 고용을 증가시켰다. 도시 중심지에서의 변화가 생산성에 어떤 영향을 미칠지는 판단하기 어렵다.

도시 관리자들은 기업을 유치하는 데서 벗어나 부동산세와 소비세를 납부하고 생활의 질 향상에 기여할 주민을 유치하는 것으로 초점을 옮기고 있다. 코로나 19 팬데믹은 도시를 파괴하지는 않겠지만, 도시의 모습을 변화시킬 것이다.

3

하위내용영역	배점	예상정답률
일반영어 B형 기입형	2점	40%

모범답안 mathematical

채점 기준

- 2점: 모범답안과 같다.
- 0점: 모범답안과 다르다.

한글번역

실수라는 이름은 거리, 각도, 시간, 에너지, 온도 또는 여러 가지 기하학적, 물리적 양을 측정하는 데 필요한 크기를 제공하는 듯이 보이기 때문에 붙여졌다. 그러나 추상적으로 정의된 '실수'와 물리적 양 사이의 관계는 생각만큼 명확하지 않다. 실수는 물리적으로 실재하는 객관적 양이 아닌, 수학적으로 이상화된 개념을 가리킨다.

예를 들면, 실수 체계는 밀도의 특성을 지니고 있어, 두 실수 사이에는—그 두 실수가 아무리 가깝더라도—항상 또 다른 실수가 존재한다. 물리적 거리나 시간이 이러한 (밀도의) 특성을 가지고 있다고 실제로 말할 수 있는지에 대해서는 분명하지 않다. (이것의 의미는 물리적 거리와 시간이 실수가 가진 '밀도의 특성'을 실제로 가지고 있는지에 대해 불확실하거나 의문이 있다는 뜻이다. **수학**에서 실수의 밀도란, 아무리 가까운 두 수 사이에도 항상 또 다른 수가 존재한다는 것을 의미하지만, 우리가 살고 있는 **물리 세계**에서는 거리나 시간 간격을 얼마나 세밀하게 나눌 수 있는지에 한계가 있을 수 있으며, 특히 양자 규모와 같이 극도로 작은 규모에서는 더욱 그렇다. 따라서 이 문장은 이러한 수학적 특성이 실제 물리적 세계에도 적용될 수 있는지에 대한 의구심을 표현하고 있다.) 두 지점 사이의 물리적 거리를 계속해서 나누면, 결국에는 일반적인 의미에서의 거리 개념이 더 이상 의미를 가지지 않을 정도로 작은 규모에 도달할 것이다.

양자 중력(중력을 양자역학의 원리로 설명하려는 이론적 시도. 일반 상대성 이론에 따르면 중력은 시공간의 곡률에 의해 설명되지만, 양자역학은 아원자 입자와 같은 극도로 작은 규모에서 물리적 현상을 설명하는 데 주로 사용된다. 양자 중력 이론은 중력을 양자화해, 가장 작은 단위에서 중력의 작용을 설명하려고 한다. 이 이론이 성공한다면, 우주의 초기 상태나 블랙홀의 내부 구조 같은 극한 상황에서 중력을 이해하는 데 필요한 통합된 이론을 제공할 수 있을 것이라 한다.) 규모인 아원자 입자 크기의 10(20)분의 1 정도에서는 이 현상이 실제로 발생할 것으로 예상된다. 그러나 실수와 일치시키기 위해서는 이보다 훨씬 더 작은, 예를 들어 10(200)분의 1이나 10(2000)분의 1 같은 규모로 내려가야 한다. 이처럼 터무니없이 작은 규모가 물리적으로 어떤 의미가 있는지는 전혀 분명하지 않다. (10(200)분의 1이나 10(2000)분의 1 같은 극도로 작은 규모가 이론적으로는 수학에서 생각할 수 있지만, 실제 우리가 살아가고 있는 물리 세계에서 측정하거나 의미를 부여할 수 있는 범위인지에 대해서는 큰 의문이 있다는 뜻이다.)

유사한 논의는 이에 상응하는 매우 짧은 시간 간격에 대해서도 적용될 수 있다. 실수 체계는 그 수학적 유용성, 단순성, 그리고 우아함 때문에 물리학에서 선택되며, 넓은 범위에 걸쳐 거리와 시간이라는 물리적 개념과 일치한다는 이유로 선택된 것이다. (하지만) 실수 체계는 이러한 물리적 개념과 모든 범위에서 일치한다고 알려졌기 때문에 선택된 것은 아니다.

4

하위내용영역	배점	예상정답률
일반영어 B형 서술형	4점	50%

모범답안 There are two cognitive advantages in bilingualism in the field of neuropsychology. First, it enhances cognitive flexibility, as bilingual individuals show stronger executive functions like task-switching and attention control. Second, bilingualism enhances neural efficiency, as bilingual individuals show more efficient brain pathways and require less cognitive effort for language processing and executive tasks compared to monolinguals. In conclusion, future research could explore applying bilingualism's cognitive benefits to monolinguals, enhancing cognitive resilience and adaptability, especially as populations age.

채점 기준

ⓐ Topic sentence

+ 1점: "There are two cognitive advantages in bilingualism in the field of neuropsychology."를 서술하였거나 유사하였다.

ⓑ Major supporting details

+ 2점: "First, it enhances cognitive flexibility, as bilingual individuals show stronger executive functions like task-switching and attention control. Second, bilingualism enhances neural efficiency, as bilingual individuals show more efficient brain pathways and require less cognitive effort for language processing and executive tasks compared to monolinguals."를 서술하였거나 유사하였다.

☞ 2개 중 2개 모두를 정확하게 요약한 경우 2점, 1개를 요약한 경우 1점, 요약하지 못한 경우 0점을 준다.

ⓒ Conclusion

+ 1점: "In conclusion, future research could explore applying bilingualism's cognitive benefits to monolinguals, enhancing cognitive resilience and adaptability, especially as populations age."을 서술하였거나 유사하였다.

감점
- 본문에 나오는 연속되는 5단어 이상을 사용하였다. −1pt
- 문단을 두 개나 그 이상으로 구성하였다. −1pt
- grammar나 영어표현이 합쳐 4개 이상 오류가 있다. −1pt

한글번역

이중언어의 신경심리학은 두 개 이상의 언어를 아는 것이 뇌의 구조와 기능에 어떤 영향을 미치는지 탐구한다. 세계가 점점 다언어화됨에 따라 이러한 영향을 이해하는 것은 인지 과학과 교육 모두에 중요하다. 이중언어 사용의 신경심리학적 두 가지 주요 장점은 뇌의 놀라운 적응력을 강조하며 인지 건강에 관한 귀중한 통찰을 제공한다.

이중언어 사용의 주요 장점 중 하나는 인지 유연성의 향상이다. 이중언어 사용자는 과제 전환, 문제 해결, 주의력 조절과 같은 뛰어난 집행 기능을 자주 보여준다. 이는 이중언어 사용자가 두 언어 체계를 지속적으로 모니터링하고 조절하는 코드 전환과 언어 억제라는 인지 과정을 자주 수행하기 때문이다. 이러한 정신적 연습은 상충되는 정보를 관리하는 뇌의 능력을 강화해 이중언어 사용자가 새로운 상황과 도전에 더 잘 적응하게 한다.

또 다른 중요한 장점은 더 큰 신경 효율성에 기여한다는 점이다. 이중언어 사용자의 뇌는 여러 언어를 최소한의 인지적 부담으로 관리하고 접근하는 데 익숙해져 더 효율적인 신경 경로를 나타낸다. 기능적 자기공명영상(fMRI)과 같은 신경 영상 기술을 사용한 연구는 이중언어 사용자가 특정 인지 과제를 수행할 때 단일언어 사용자보다 더 적은 뇌 활동을 필요로 한다는 것을 보여준다. 이러한 효율성은 특히 언어 처리 및 집행 기능과 관련된 영역에서 두드러진다.

이중언어 신경심리학은 두 개 이상의 언어를 아는 것이 상당한 인지적 및 신경적 이점을 제공한다는 사실을 보여준다. 이중언어의 이점을 더 깊이 탐구하기 위해, 향후 연구는 이러한 인지적 이점이 일 언어 사용자에게 어떻게 적용될 수 있는지를 이해하는 데 중점을 둘 수 있다. 이러한 접근 방식은 이중언어 뇌에 대한 통찰을 심화시킬 뿐 아니라, 특히 인구가 계속해서 고령화됨에 따라 인지 회복력과 건강을 촉진할 수 있다.

5

하위내용영역	배점	예상정답률
일반영어 B형 서술형	4점	35%

모범답안 The word is "differences". Second, in Tseltal Mayan, the concept is expressed using fixed environmental references, such as saying "north(or south) of the table," instead of relative terms like "left" or "right."

채점기준

+ 2점: 빈칸에 들어갈 단어를 "<u>differences</u>"이라 정확히 기입하였다. 이외에는 답이 될 수 없다.
+ 2점: 영어에서 츠딸 마야어는 "테이블의 왼쪽에"라고 전달하는 개념을 어떻게 표현하는지에 "in Tseltal Mayan, the concept is expressed <u>using fixed environmental references, such as saying "north(or south) of the table,"</u> instead of relative terms like "left" or "right."라 서술하였거나 유사하였다.

☞ 다음과 같이 서술하였어도 2점을 준다.

— In Tseltal Mayan, spatial orientation is described <u>using fixed environmental references rather than relative terms like "left" or "right."</u> Thus, instead of saying <u>"to the left of the table," a Tseltal Mayan speaker might say "north of the table" relying on stable environmental cues rather than the speaker's viewpoint.</u>

— Tseltal Mayan expresses "to the left of the table" using <u>fixed references like "north of the table"</u> instead of relative terms like "left" or "right."

— Tseltal Mayan expresses "to the left of the table" by <u>using fixed environmental references, like "north" or "south,"</u> rather than relative terms such as "left" or "right."

— Tseltal Mayan expresses the concept that English conveys as "to the left of the table" by using <u>fixed environmental references, such as cardinal directions or specific landmarks, rather than relative terms like "left" or "right."</u> For example, <u>a Tseltal Mayan speaker might say "north of the table"</u> if those directions are consistent with their environmental orientation, regardless of the speaker's own position or perspective.

한글번역

화자가 언어별로 다르게 세계를 경험하고 심지어 인식할 가능성은 인간 인지의 가소성에 관한 논쟁에서 중심적인 위치를 차지한다. 우리의 인지 구조가 어느 정도나 많이 생물학에 의해 결정되고, 어느 정도나 많이—언어를 통해 표현되고 습득될 수 있는—문화적 체계에 의한 발달 과정에서 형성되는가? 이 논쟁은 인지 과학에서 중요한 역할을 할 뿐만 아니라, 인간성의 핵심 측면이 개인이 자란 환경에 따라 근본적으로 달라질 수 있다는 가능성 때문에 오랫동안 대중의 관심을 끌어왔다. 만약 화자가 자주 특정 경험에 집중하게 만드는 언어를 사용한다면, 자연스럽게 그런 경험을 통해 사고 습관이 형성되어 "세계에서의 경험, 인식, 연상, 감정, 기억, 방향 감각" 등이 달라질 것이다.

자연스러운 일이긴 하지만, 이런 직관을 뒷받침하는 실증적 증거는 얼마나 강력할까? 여기서 공간 언어와 관련해 언어적 상대성을 지지하는 대표적인 사례 중 하나를 검토한다. 특히 화자가 위치와 방향을 이야기할 때 사용하는 좌표 시스템 또는 준거틀(기준 체계)에 관한 것이다.

공간적 준거틀은 언어적 상대성을 연구하기에 유익한 분야였다. 얼핏 보면, 공간적 위치 파악이 생존에 필수적인 만큼 생물학적으로 강하게 기반을 두기 때문에 모든 언어에서 거의 동일한 방식으로 부호화될 것(표현될 것)이라 기대할 수 있다. 그러나 진화는 우리가 세계를 탐색할 수 있는 다양한 해결책을 제공하여, 언어 공동체가 주로 사용하는 좌표 시스템을 선택하도록 남겨뒀다. 이러한 시스템은 언어적 준거틀이라고 불리며, 일반적으로 '도상'이라 불리는 개체의 방향을 '배경'이라 불리는 또 다른 개체에 비춰 지정하는 데 사용된다. ("도상"은 우리가 위치나 방향을 설명하려는 대상이고, "배경"은 도상이 어디에 위치하는지를 설명하는 기준점이다. 예를 들면, in the phrase "The cup is on the table," the cup is the "figure," and the table is the "ground." Different languages may use different systems for framing these spatial relationships.)

영어와 다른 표준 유럽 언어에서는 화자의 관점에서 방향 체계를 설정하는 것을 주로 사용하며(예 왼쪽/오른쪽), '북쪽'이나 '남쪽' 같은 환경에 기반한 용어는 대규모 또는 지도상의 공간에 주로 제한된다. 반면, 츠딸 마야어(멕시코 치아파스)와 같은 일부 다른 언어에서는 탁자 위 물건의 배열과 같은 소규모 공간에서도 방향과 위치를 설명할 때 환경의 고정된 측면을 사용한다.

이러한 언어 간 차이는 화자들이 여러 방식으로 공간 정보를 해석, 저장 및 검색하는 방식에 영향을 미쳐, 언어와 일치하는 전략을 사용하는 데 더 큰 능숙함을 갖게 하고, 일치하지 않는 전략은 덜 선호하게 만든다고 주장돼 왔다. 어떤 특정 전략이 문화적으로 요구되며(예 언어 사용을 통해), 그 결과 많이 연습되어 기본적인 인지 전략으로 선호된다면, 해당 전략을 사용하는 성과가 더 좋을 것이라 기대할 이유가 있다.

제09회 모의고사

1

하위내용영역	배점	예상정답률
일반영어 A형 서술형	4점	50%

모범 답안 The word is "slave revolt". Second, the words are "equality, independence, liberty".

채점 기준

+ 2점: 빈칸에 들어갈 단어를 "slave revolt"라 기입하였다. 이외에는 답이 될 수 없다.
+ 2점: 상응하는 단어를 "equality, independence, liberty"라 기입하였다. 이외에는 답이 될 수 없다.

한글번역

원래의 13개 아메리카 식민지가 어떻게 영국으로부터 독립해 미국을 형성하게 됐는지는 잘 알려져 있다. 그러나 독립 전쟁 동안 아프리카계 미국인들이 어떻게 느끼고 무엇을 했는지에 대해서는 덜 알려져 있다.

미국 혁명(미국 독립 전쟁) 당시 노스캐롤라이나 인구의 최소 25%가 노예였고, 실제로 흑인 인구는 약 7만 명에 달했지만 그중 자유인 비율은 5%도 되지 않았다. 흑인 대부분은 노예이든 자유인이든 시골에 살면서 땅을 일궜고, 시장에 내다 팔 작물을 심고, 수확하고, 손질하는 일을 했다. 몇 안 되는 노스캐롤라이나주의 도시들에 거주하던 흑인들은 수공업에 종사하거나 노예 소유주의 하인으로 일했다. 숙련된 노예들은 목수, 통 제조자(통을 만드는 사람), 대장장이(철을 도구로 만들고 말에 편자를 씌우는 사람), 수레바퀴 제조자(바퀴를 만들고 수리하는 사람) 그리고 여러 다른 숙련된 직업에 종사했다.

백인들이 식민지와 영국 사이의 갈등으로 분열됐던 것처럼, 흑인들도 어려운 선택을 마주하게 됐다. 아프리카계 미국인들은 영국군과 혁명군 양쪽에 인력을 제공하면서 양측에서 싸웠다. 전쟁 중 그들의 행동은 종종 노예 상태에서 벗어날 수 있는 기회를 최우선으로 고려해 결정됐다. 대부분의 흑인들은 영국의 승리가 노예 제도의 종식을 가져올 것이라 믿었다.

남부에는 노예 반란에 대한 두려움이 퍼졌다. 전쟁 이전에 영국군 지도자들은 노예들이 주인에 대항해 일어나면 남부 식민지가 크게 약화될 수 있다는 점을 인지하고 있었다. 백인 식민지 주민들도 이를 알고 있었다. 노스캐롤라이나에서 독립 선언서에 서명한 조셉 휴즈는 영국이 "우리의 국경에 인디언을 풀어놓고," "흑인들을 우리에게 대항하게 할" 계획을 세우고 있다고 비난하며, 그 계획에는 노예들에게 무기를 주는 것도 포함된다고 주장했다. 에든턴의 제임스 아이레델은 영국이 "흑인들을 선동해 우리의 목을 베게 하고, 남녀노소를 포함한 모든 사람을 하나의 대량 학살 속에 몰아넣으려 한다"며 비난했다. 에든턴과 윌밍턴에서는 흑인 주민들을 밤마다 엄격하게 감시하기 위한 순찰을 조직했다.

그러나 노예들은 자유를 위해 싸우기 위해 자극이 필요하지 않았다. 메릴랜드에서 조지아까지 모든 식민지에서 노예들은 자유를 위한 기회를 무게 있게 검토하며, 노예 반란 직전의 상태에 있는 듯 보였다. 매사추세츠의 혁명가 존 애덤스는 노예들 사이에서 소식을 퍼뜨리는 "포도덩굴"에 대해 언급하며 "흑인들은 서로에게 정보를 전달하는 놀라운 기술을 가지고 있으며, 이는 일주일이나 보름 사이에 수백 마일을 퍼져나갈 것"이라고 언급했다.

따라서 자유의 기회가 생겼을 때 노예들이 영국군으로 도망치는 것은 놀라운 일이 아니었다. 수천 명의 아프리카계 미국인들이 자유를 찾아 나섰다. 혁명이 평등, 독립, 자유라는 언어를 사용하면서, 노예들은 영국과의 투쟁 중심에 있는 사상을 따로 설명 받을 필요가 없었다. (미국 독립 혁명의 주요 이념인 "평등, 독립, 자유"가 이미 노예들에게 매우 절실하고 익숙한 개념이었음을 나타낸다. 노예들이 겪는 억압과 자유에 대한 갈망으로 인해, 이들은 이미 "평등"과 "자유"의 가치를 절실하게 이해하고 있었다. 따라서, 노예들은 혁명에서 이러한 이념이 중심 사상이라는 설명이 없어도 쉽게 공감하고 지지할 수 있었다는 의미이다.)

2

하위내용영역	배점	예상정답률
일반영어 A형 서술형	4점	45%

모범 답안 The words are "safe alternative". Second, the shooting incident involving a Florida homeowner who killed a man, Rodney Cox, after Cox entered the homeowner's FEMA trailer and placed him in a "bear hug."

채점 기준

+ 2점 : 빈칸에 들어갈 단어를 "safe alternative"라 정확히 기입하였다. 이외에는 답이 될 수 없다.
+ 2점 : 미국에서 첫 번째 현대적 정당방위법이 만들어지게 된 사건을 "the shooting incident involving a Florida homeowner who killed a man, Rodney Cox, after Cox entered the homeowner's FEMA trailer and placed him in a "bear hug."라 서술하였거나 유사하였다.

한글번역

정당한 방어권. 선을 긋다. 먼저 쏴라. 내 날이 되게 하라. 26개 주가 전통적인 정당방위법을 대폭 확대하는 정당한 방어권법을 통과시켰다. 그리고 그것들을 무엇이라고 부르든, 통과시킨 주의 사람들에게 모두 같은 효과를 갖는다 : 더 많은 사람들이 죽을 것이고 그들을 죽인 자들은 자유롭게 걸어 나갈 것이다.

정당한 방어권법 옹호자들은 그것들이 법을 준수하는 시민들이 형사 기소의 두려움 없이 자신을 방어할 수 있게 하는 방법이라고 주장한다. 하지만 우리 법체계는 이미 견고한 정당방위법들을 갖추고 있다. 이용 가능한 연구는 우리를 더 안전하게 만드는 대신, 정당한 방어권법이 불법적인 살인율 증가로 이어진다고 시사한다. 정당한 방어권 옹호자들이 주장하는 것과는 반대로, 이러한 법들이 정당한 정당방위 행위를 장려한다는 것을 보여주는 신빙성 있는 연구는 없다.

미국에서 수백 년 동안 시행돼 온 전통적인 정당방위법은 사람들에게 해로부터 자신을 방어할 권리를 준다. 이러한 정당방위법들은 누군가를 심각하게 다치게 하거나 죽이는 것은 최후의 수단으로만 사용돼야 한다고 명시하며, 이는 사람들이 안전한 대안을 선택하고 가능하다면 위험에서 물러날 의무가 있다는 것을 의미한다. 후퇴 의무의 예외는 "성채 원칙"이다. 성채 원칙은 사람들이 자신의 집에 있을 때 먼저 후퇴를 시도하지 않고도 자신을 방어하기 위해 치명적인 힘을 사용할 수 있게 한다.

정당한 방어권법은 성채 원칙을 공적 영역으로 확장한 것으로, 공공장소에 있을 때의 오래된 후퇴 의무를 없앤다. 다시 말해, 이러한 법들은 사람들이 안전한 대안이 있을 때조차 집 밖에서 정당방위로 (그리고 일부 주에서는 재산 방어로) 누군가를 죽일 수 있게 한다.

2005년 4월, 최초의 현대적 정당한 방어권법이 플로리다에서 통과됐다. 1년 전, 허리케인 이반의 여파로, 한 플로리다 주택 소유자가 경고 사격을 했음에도 불구하고 자신의 FEMA 트레일러에 들어온 남자를 총으로 쏴 죽였다. 주택 소유자는 그 남자가, 나중에 FEMA 직원 로드니 콕스로 확인된, 주택 소유자를 "곰 포옹"으로 감쌌을 때 그를 쐈다. 그는 콕스를 죽인 것에 대해 기소되지 않았다; 검찰은 그가 정당방위로 정당하게 행동했다고 결정했다.

그럼에도 불구하고, 그 총격 사건은 전미총기협회의 플로리다 로비스트인 매리언 해머의 관심을 끌었고, 그녀는 주택 소유자가 정당방위로 행동했으므로 살인 후 표준 수사 절차를 받게 하는 것이 불공정한 대우라고 주장했다. 그녀는 "인지된 중대한 위협"에 직면했을 때 치명적인 힘의 사용을 합법화할 뿐만 아니라 기소 면제도 부여하는 법안을 도입하도록 의원들을 압박했다. 그 법안은 법으로 통과됐고 정당한 방어권이 탄생했다.

3

하위내용영역	배점	예상정답률
일반영어 A형 서술형	4점	35%

모범답안) The word is "unfamiliar". Second, the researchers had each person undergo 7-minute blocks to measure the impact of different types of music (favorite songs, unfamiliar relaxing songs, and scrambled versions) on pain perception and to determine if favorite music could reduce pain more effectively than other sounds or silence.

채점기준

+ 2점 : 빈칸에 들어갈 단어를 "unfamiliar"이라 정확히 기입하였다. 이외에는 답이 될 수 없다.
+ 2점 : 연구자들이 각 참가자에게 7분 동안 수행하는 시간 구간을 준 이유를 "(in order) to measure the impact of different types of music (favorite songs, unfamiliar relaxing songs, and scrambled versions) on pain perception and to determine if favorite music could reduce pain more effectively than other sounds or silence"라 서술하였거나 유사하였다.

☞ 다음과 같이 서술하였어도 2점을 준다.
- "To systematically measure and compare pain levels under different listening conditions (favorite music, instrumental relaxing music, scrambled songs,) while exposing them to a consistent pain stimulus. This setup allowed them to observe how different types of music affected participants' pain perception."

한글번역

아델이 2011년 싱글 "Someone Like You"로 데뷔했을 때, 그녀의 쌉쌀 달콤한 발라드는 전 세계 수백만 명의 공감을 불러일으켰다. 10년 이상이 지난 지금도, 그것은 그녀의 가장 인기 있는 곡 중 하나로 남아 있다. 느리고 감정적인 비트로 우리의 심금을 울리는 기술을 숙달한 많은 다른 사람들과 마찬가지로, 그녀의 예술성은 상심과 상실의 감정적 고통을 다루는 방법을 가지고 있다.

음악이 일부 사람들의 영혼을 달래줄 수 있다는 것은 의심의 여지가 없으며, 그것이 또한 신체적 고통에 대한 일시적인 진정제가 될 수 있다는 것이 밝혀졌다. 새로운 연구에 따르면, 좋아하는 노래를 듣는 것이 사람들의 고통 인식을 줄일 수 있다고 한다. 그리고 가장 효과적인 진통제는 쌉쌀 달콤하고 감정적인 경험을 자세히 묘사하는 슬픈 노래들인 것으로 밝혀졌다. 두통이 있을 때 타이레놀을 대신하지는 않지만, 음악은 고통을 누그러뜨리는 데 도움이 될 수 있다. 다른 약물들과 달리, 음악을 듣는 것에는 부작용이나 위험이 없다. (단지 볼륨을 합리적인 수준으로 유지하면 된다.)

연구는 63명의 젊은 성인들에게 그들이 가장 좋아하는 노래 두 곡을 가져오도록 했으며, 유일한 요구사항은 적어도 3분 20초 이상이어야 한다는 것이었다. 한 선택은 그들의 역대 가장 좋아하는 음악을 나타냈고, 다른 하나는 그들이 무인도에 가져갈 노래였다. 연구자들은 또한 젊은 성인들에게 팀이 편안하다고 여기고 연구 참가자들에게 낯선 일곱 곡 중 하나를 선택하게 했다.

각 그들이 좋아하는 음악, 일곱 개의 편안한 기악곡 중 하나 (각 6분 40초 동안 지속), 또는 두 노래와 선택된 편안한 노래의 뒤섞인 버전을 들으면서 모니터 화면을 응시하도록 지시받는 7분간의 블록을 거쳤다. 뒤섞인 음악은 세 곡 모두의 시끄러운 뒤범벅으로, 조각들로 잘라서 무작위로 섞어서 원래의 구조가 없게 만든 것이었다. 한 7분 블록은 사람들이 조용히 앉아 있게 했다. 그동안 연구자들은 참가자들의 왼쪽 안쪽 팔뚝에 뜨거운 물체—피부에 닿은 끓는 뜨거운 찻잔의 고통과 유사한—를 붙였다.

그들의 경험을 평가할 때, 사람들은 낯선 편안한 노래나 침묵을 듣는 것과 비교해 그들이 좋아하는 노래를 들을 때 더 적은 고통을 느낀다고 보고할 가능성이 더 높았다. 뒤섞인 노래들도 고통을 줄이지 않았는데, 저자들은 이것이 음악이 불쾌한 경험으로부터의 단순한 주의 분산 이상이라는 증거라고 제안했다.

4

하위내용영역	배점	예상정답률
일반영어 B형 서술형	4점	50%

모범답안 There are pros and cons in a 401(k) plan, which is a retirement savings option provided by employers that lets employees set aside part of their income. First, regarding advantages, it offers tax benefits as contributions are generally tax-deferred, allowing savings to grow over time through compounding. Second, in regard to disadvantages, early withdrawals typically incur penalties, and investment options may be limited to those the employer offers. In conclusion, it is necessary to weigh these benefits and downsides to determine if a 401(k) accords with one's financial goals and retirement planning needs.

채점 기준

ⓐ Topic sentence
+ 1점: "There are pros and cons in a 401(k) plan, which is a retirement savings option provided by employers that lets employees set aside part of their income."를 서술하였거나 유사하였다.

ⓑ Major supporting details
+ 2점: "First, regarding advantages, it offers tax benefits as contributions are generally tax-deferred, allowing savings to grow over time through compounding. Second, in regard to disadvantages, early withdrawals typically incur penalties, and investment options may be limited to those the employer offers."를 서술하였거나 유사하였다.
☞ 2개 중 2개 모두를 정확하게 요약한 경우 2점, 1개를 요약한 경우 1점, 요약하지 못한 경우 0점을 준다.

ⓒ Conclusion
+ 1점: "In conclusion, it is necessary to weigh these benefits and downsides to determine if a 401(k) accords with one's financial goals and retirement planning needs."을 서술하였거나 유사하였다.

감점
• 본문에 나오는 연속되는 5단어 이상을 사용하였다. -1pt
• 문단을 두 개나 그 이상으로 구성하였다. -1pt
• grammar나 영어표현이 합쳐 4개 이상 오류가 있다. -1pt

한글번역

401(k) 플랜은 많은 고용주들이 제공하는 퇴직 저축 계좌로, 직원들이 세금이 공제되기 전 급여의 일부를 저축하고 투자할 수 있게 해준다. 이는 직원들이 급여의 일부를 퇴직 기금으로 적립할 수 있는 인기 있는 퇴직 저축 도구이며, 종종 고용주의 매칭 지원이 함께 제공된다. 개인들의 퇴직 저축을 장려하기 위해 설계된 401(k)는 재정적 안정성에 영향을 미칠 수 있는 장점과 단점을 모두 가지고 있다.

401(k)의 주요 혜택 중 하나는 제공하는 세금 우대이다. 기여금은 일반적으로 세전 소득으로 납입돼 과세 소득을 줄이고 시간이 지남에 따라 더 많은 돈이 성장할 수 있게 해준다. 401(k) 내의 자금은 세금 이연으로 성장할 수 있는데, 이는 일반적으로 퇴직 연령에 인출을 시작할 때까지 세금을 내지 않는다는 의미이다. 이러한 이연은 복리 이자로 인해 상당한 성장 잠재력을 가져올 수 있어, 가치 있는 장기 저축 옵션이 된다.

그러나 401(k) 플랜에는 몇 가지 단점도 있다. 한 가지 단점은 유연성의 부족인데, 특히 퇴직 전 자금에 접근하는 것과 관련해서 그렇다. 59세 반 이전의 조기 인출은 일반적으로 일반 소득세에 더해 10%의 패널티가 부과돼 저축을 크게 감소시킬 수 있다. 또한 401(k) 내의 투자 옵션은 고용주가 제공하는 것들로 제한될 수 있어, 계좌의 다양화와 성장 잠재력을 제약할 수 있다.

401(k)는 가치 있는 세금 혜택과 퇴직 저축에 대한 구조화된 경로를 제공하지만, 조기 인출에 대한 제한과 제한된 투자 옵션은 일부 개인들에게는 단점이 될 수 있다. 401(k)가 개인의 재정적 목표와 일치하는지 판단하기 위해 이러한 장단점을 신중히 고려하는 것이 필수적이다. 신중한 계획과 고려를 통해 유익한 도구가 될 수 있기 때문이다.

제10회 모의고사

1

하위내용영역	배점	예상정답률
일반영어 A형 서술형	4점	45%

모범답안 It is because mutual benefit ensures both parties gain advantages from cooperation, encouraging individuals to continue these behaviors rather than conserve resources for themselves. Second, cheating challenges cooperative systems by creating one-sided relationships where recipients benefit without giving back, leading to imbalances that may ultimately reduce cooperation if too common.

채점기준

+ 2점: 협력 행동이 집단 내에서 지속되기 위해서는 상호 이익이 필수적인 이유를 "<u>because mutual benefit ensures both parties gain advantages from cooperation, encouraging individuals to continue these behaviors rather than conserve resources for themselves</u>"라 서술하였거나 유사하였다.

☞ 다음과 같이 서술하였어도 2점을 준다.
- "<u>Because mutual benefit ensures that both the helper and the recipient gain advantages from their interactions. If helpers received no benefit, natural selection would favor those who conserved their resources rather than assisting others, leading to a decline in cooperation over time.</u>"

+ 2점: 부정행위가 어떻게 협력 시스템에 도전이 되는가라는 질문에 "<u>by creating one-sided relationships where recipients benefit without giving back, leading to imbalances that may ultimately reduce cooperation if too common.</u>"이라 서술하였거나 유사하였다.

☞ 다음과 같이 서술하였어도 2점을 준다.
- "cheating, where a recipient benefits without reciprocating, challenges cooperative systems by creating a one-sided relationship. This can discourage cooperation, as helpers may choose to withhold assistance to avoid exploitation."

한글번역

협력 행동은 한 생물이 다른 생물에게 이익을 주는 행동을 말하며, 종종 이를 받는 생물을 수혜자라고 부른다. 존슨과 마이어는 협력을 "돕는 자"(도움을 주는 생물)와 "받는 자"(도움을 받는 생물) 간의 섬세한 균형으로 설명한다. 돕는 자는 수혜자에게 공유할 수 있는 자원, 지식 또는 기술을 보유하고 있으며, 얼마만큼의 도움을 줄지 결정한다. 받는 자는 그 도움을 받으면서, 상황이 허락할 경우 보답할 수 있으며, 그 결과는 양쪽의 행동과 전략에 따라 달라진다. 협력 행동은 직접적, 간접적, 혹은 공동체적으로 나타날 수 있으며, 자원 확보, 포식자 방어, 또는 자손 양육에 도움이 될 수 있다.

협력 이론의 핵심 원칙은 협력 행동이 집단 내에서 지속되려면 돕는 자와 받는 자 모두 즉각적이거나 시간이 지나 이익을 얻어야 한다는 것이다. 만약 돕는 자가 어떤 이득도 얻지 못한다면, 자원을 보존하는 개체가 자연 선택에서 더 유리하게 될 것이다. 이 상호 이익은 협력 행동이 확실한 보답을 보장해야 한다는 점을 시사한다.

이 개념은 협력 시스템에서 '부정행위' 문제와 관련된 진화 생물학의 주요 논쟁에 중심이 된다. 액셀라드와 해밀턴은 부정행위를 수혜자가 돕는 자의 행동으로 이득을 얻으면서도 보답하거나 기여하지 않을 때 발생하는 것으로 정의했다. 즉, 협력 관계가 일방적으로 될 때 부정행위가 발생한다는 것이다. 이 관찰은 중요한 질문을 제기한다. 착취의 위험이 있는 상황에서 왜 생물이 계속 협력을 유지하려 할까? 예를 들어, 새가 다른 새들에게 포식자의 존재를 경고할 때, 다른 새들이 그 경고를 무시하고 보답하지 않으면 시스템의 균형이 깨진다. 부정행위가 흔해지면 자연 선택은 협력을 줄이는 개체에게 유리하게 작용해, 결국 협력 시스템의 안정성을 위협하게 된다. 부정행위가 많아질수록 집단은 부정행위자를 감지하고 피하는 전략으로 전환할 가능성이 높고, 이로 인해 진정한 협력자들만이 공유 자원의 혜택을 얻을 수 있게 된다. 시간이 흐르고 집단이 안정되면 신뢰할 수 있는 파트너십을 촉진하는 협력 행동이 더 우세해질 가능성이 크다.

2

하위내용영역	배점	예상정답률
일반영어 A형 서술형	4점	40%

모범 답안 The words are "modern world". Second, expressionist cinema did that <u>by using distorted visuals, dramatic lighting, and surreal settings to capture the psychological distress, fear, and chaos experienced in society at the time</u>.

채점 기준

+ 2점: 빈칸에 들어갈 단어를 "<u>modern world</u>"라 정확히 기입하였다. 이외에는 답이 될 수 없다.
+ 2점: 표현주의 영화가 제1차 세계대전 이후 사회적 불안감을 반영하는 데 어떤 역할을 했는지 설명하라는 질문에 "<u>by using distorted visuals, dramatic lighting, and surreal settings to capture the psychological distress, fear, and chaos experienced in society at the time</u>"이라 서술하였거나 유사하였다.

☞ 다음과 같이 서술하였어도 2점을 준다.
- "Expressionist cinema did that <u>through exaggerated, surreal visuals and stark contrasts in lighting. The distorted and dreamlike imagery in films like The Cabinet of Dr. Caligari and Nosferatu captured the psychological turmoil and sense of chaos experienced in post-war Germany</u>."
- "Expressionist cinema did that <u>by using distorted sets, sharp contrasts of light and shadow, and exaggerated visuals to create an unsettling, dreamlike world. These elements symbolized the psychological distress and feelings of disorientation experienced by society after the war</u>."

한글번역

20세기 초 표현주의는 외부 세계가 아닌 인간 감정의 내면 풍경—종종 몹시 거칠고 강력한—을 포착하고자 했던 예술 운동이었다. 사실주의나 형식주의를 중시하던 다른 운동들과 달리, 표현주의는 물리적 현실을 있는 그대로 표현하는 것을 거부하고, 예술가의 내면적 경험을 주관적으로 표현하는 데 중점을 뒀다. 시각 예술, 문학, 연극, 영화, 건축에까지 걸쳐 빠르게 변화하는 이 표현주의 운동은 산업화, 도시화의 엄청난 영향과 후에는 전쟁의 트라우마로 인해 더욱 커진 현대 세계의 급격한 변화와 실존적 불확실성에 대한 반응으로 나타났다.

시각 예술에서 에드바르드 뭉크, 에른스트 루트비히 키르히너, 바실리 칸딘스키와 같은 표현주의 화가들은 왜곡된 형태, 강력한 색상, 역동적인 붓질을 통해 날것의 감정을 전달했다. 뭉크의 상징적인 작품인 <절규>는 불안의 감정을 강력하고 소용돌이치는 색채로 표현해 심리적 긴장감이 느껴지도록 함으로써 표현주의의 본질을 가장 잘 보여준다고 할 수 있다. 이러한 작품에서 색채와 형태는 단순한 재현의 역할에서 벗어나, 예술가의 내면적 현실을 전달하는 도구로 사용된다. 이러한 접근 방식은 표현주의자들이 급변하는 세계에서 깊이 공감되는 두려움, 소외감, 환멸의 감정을 전달할 수 있도록 했다.

표현주의는 문학과 연극으로 그 영향력을 확장해, 프란츠 카프카와 같은 작가 및 베르톨트 브레히트와 같은 극작가들이 사회적 불안과 비판을 반영하기 위해 조각난 서사, 상징적 무대, 과장된 캐릭터를 활용했다. 카프카의 악몽 같은 세계와 브레히트의 '서사극'은 관객이 현실 도피를 하며 위안을 얻기보다 인간 존재의 가혹한 현실을 직면하도록 만들었다. 이러한 문학적, 연극적 표현은 반자연주의적 스타일을 특징으로 하며, 전통적 줄거리나 인물 발전을 거부하고 소외, 무력감, 실존적 공포와 같은 주제를 탐구했다.

영화에서도 표현주의는 1920년대 독일 영화인 <칼리가리 박사의 밀실>과 <노스페라투>에서 활발히 펼쳐졌다. 이러한 영화들은 과장된 세트 디자인, 강한 명암 대비, 극적인 그림자를 통해 전후 독일의 심리적 고통을 반영한 비현실적인 분위기를 만들어냈다. 왜곡되고 꿈같은 시각적 표현은 절망과 혼란에 빠진 세상을 불안하게 비춰냈다.

궁극적으로, 20세기 표현주의는 감정적 경험을 객관적 현실보다 우선시함으로써 현대 예술의 방향을 바꾼 선구적인 힘이 됐다. 표현주의는 예술이 인간 감정의 깊이를 직접적이고 가공하지 않은 방식으로 전달하는 채널이 될 수 있음을 보여주며, 이후 전위 예술 운동들의 길을 열었다. 표현주의는 (개인들의) 내면의 불안 및 사회적 불안을 노골적으로 묘사하는 것을 통해, 인간 정신의 복잡성과 현대 세계의 불편한 진실을 직면하도록 관객들에게 도전하며 지울 수 없는 영향을 남겼다.

3

하위내용영역	배점	예상정답률
일반영어 B형 기입형	2점	45%

모범답안 Cambodian territory

채점기준

- 2점: 모범답안과 같다.
- 0점: 모범답안과 다르다.

한글번역

캄보디아는 태국이 캄보디아인들의 순례와 숭배의 장소인 프레아 비헤아르 사원 유적 주변의 자국 영토를 점령했다고 불평하며, 국제사법재판소에 사원의 영토 주권이 캄보디아에 속하고 태국은 1954년 이래 주둔한 무장 부대를 철수할 의무가 있다고 선언해 줄 것을 요청했다. 태국은 재판소의 관할권에 대해 예비 이의를 제기했으나, 이는 1961년 5월 26일의 판결에서 기각됐다. 본안에 대한 1962년 6월 15일의 판결에서 재판소는 1904년 프랑코-샴 조약이 해당 지역에서 국경이 분수령을 따라야 한다고 규정하고 있으며, 혼합 경계 위원회의 작업을 바탕으로 한 지도가 사원이 캄보디아 영토에 있음을 보여준다고 언급했다. 태국은 지도가 구속력이 없다는 것을 보여주기 위해 여러 주장을 제기했다. 그중 하나는 지도가 태국에 의해 수용된 적이 없거나(첫 번째 반박주장) 대안으로, 만약 태국이 (재판소가 주장하듯이) 그 지도를 수용했다면 그것은 분수령 선에 해당한다고 잘못 믿었기 때문이라는 것이었다(두 번째 반박주장). 재판소는 태국이 실제로 지도를 수용했다고 판단하고 사원이 캄보디아 측에 위치해 있다고 결론지었다. 또한 태국은 1954년 이후 사원 유적에서 철수한 군대나 경찰 부대를 철수하고 캄보디아로부터 제거된 모든 물품을 반환할 의무가 있다고 판시했다. 이번 판결은 현재의 법원이 이전 판결의 문구에 명확성이 부족한 경우, 해석상의 공백을 메우기 위해 상당한 노력을 기울일 의향이 있음을 시사한다.

4

하위내용영역	배점	예상정답률
일반영어 B형 서술형	4점	50%

모범답안) Euphemism, which is language used to soften the impact of negative information, has two forms. First, vague or softened expressions are often employed to make serious situations sound neutral or less harsh, as in calling a patient's death a "negative patient outcome." Second, corporate jargon frequently frames difficult changes positively, such as describing layoffs as "realigning positions" to downplay their impact. In conclusion, while euphemism can reduce emotional discomfort, they may obscure the true situations, making it essential to look beyond softened words for a clearer understanding.

채점기준

ⓐ Topic sentence
+ 1점: "Euphemism, which is language used to soften the impact of negative information, has two forms."를 서술하였거나 유사하였다.

ⓑ Major supporting details
+ 2점: "First, vague or softened expressions are often employed to make serious situations sound neutral or less harsh, as in calling a patient's death a "negative patient outcome." Second, corporate jargon frequently frames difficult changes positively, such as describing layoffs as "realigning positions" to downplay their impact."를 서술하였거나 유사하였다.
☞ 2개 중 2개 모두를 정확하게 요약한 경우 2점, 1개를 요약한 경우 1점, 요약하지 못한 경우 0점을 준다.

ⓒ Conclusion
+ 1점: "In conclusion, while euphemism can reduce emotional discomfort, they may obscure the true gravity of situations, making it essential to look beyond softened words for a clearer understanding." 또는: "In conclusion, euphemism is a common tool used to distort reality; therefore, we should be aware of its real nature."을 서술하였거나 유사하였다.

감점
- 본문에 나오는 연속되는 5단어 이상을 사용하였다. -1pt
- 문단을 두 개나 그 이상으로 구성하였다. -1pt
- grammar나 영어표현이 합쳐 4개 이상 오류가 있다. -1pt

한글번역

　회사에서 운영을 "다운사이징"하거나 "간소화"하겠다고 약속할 때 무엇을 의미하는가? 실제로 이러한 용어들은 종종 해고나 인력 감축을 가리킨다. 이는 잠재적으로 부정적인 정보의 충격을 완화시키는 완곡어법의 한 예이다. 완곡어법은 실제보다 어떤 것을 더 호의적이거나 덜 가혹하게 보이도록 만드는 데 자주 사용되는 언어적 도구이며, 다양한 형태를 취한다.
　한 가지 일반적인 형태는 모호하거나 완화된 언어로, 종종 심각한 상황을 중립적이거나 심지어 긍정적으로 들리는 방식으로 묘사하는 데 사용된다. 예를 들어, 병원에서 환자의 죽음을 "부정적 환자 결과"라고 언급할 때, 상황의 감정적 충격을 피하기 위해 간접적인 용어를 사용한다. 마찬가지로 전시 민간인 사망을 "부수적 피해"라고 언급하는 것은 비극적인 생명 손실을 불행하지만 사소한 사건처럼 들리게 만들 수 있다. 이러한 유형의 언어는 감정적 고통을 줄이는 데 도움이 될 수 있지만, 상황의 진정한 심각성을 흐리게 할 위험도 있다.
　완곡어법의 또 다른 일반적인 형태는 기업 전문 용어로, 종종 어려운 조직 변화를 낙관적이거나 긍정적인 용어로 표현한다. 회사들은 직원들에게 단순히 해고당한다고 말하는 대신 그들의 직책이 "전략적 이니셔티브를 지원하기 위해 재조정되고 있다"고 말할 수 있다. 이러한 형태의 언어는 특히 구조 조정이나 예산 삭감 시기에 기업 커뮤니케이션에서 흔하다. 이런 표현들은 잠재적으로 해로운 결정들을 유익한 개선이나 중립적인 조정처럼 보이게 만들어, 영향 받는 직원들에 대한 개인적 충격을 축소시킬 수 있다.
　전반적으로 완곡어법은 바람직하지 않은 것을 받아들일 만한 것으로 만들거나, 어려운 현실의 감정적 무게를 줄이거나, 부정적인 상황을 더 호의적인 관점에서 제시하기 위해 사용되는 경우가 많다. 이러한 언어적 전략을 인식하는 것은 개인들이 완화된 언어 너머를 보고 전달되는 내용의 진정한 본질을 이해하는 데 도움이 될 수 있다.

5

하위내용영역	배점	예상정답률
일반영어 B형 서술형	4점	40%

모범답안 The word is "inherent". Second, they suggest that violence was unnecessary in education, as hunter-gatherers used peaceful methods to guide and teach children, implying that effective socialization can be achieved without violence.

채점 기준

+ 2점: 빈칸에 들어갈 단어를 "inherent"라 기입하였다. 이외에는 답이 될 수 없다.
+ 2점: 예전의 아동 양육 방식이 교육에서의 폭력 사용에 대해 시사하는 바를 설명하라는 질문에 "violence was unnecessary in education, as hunter-gatherers used peaceful methods to guide and teach children, implying that effective socialization can be achieved without violence."라 서술하였거나 유사하였다.

한글번역

한때 폭력이 존재하지 않던 시절이 있었다. 이것은 꿈도, 우화도, 단순한 철학적 추측도 아니다. 고고학, 인류학, 진화생물학을 비롯해 뇌와 정신에 대한 연구들이 공감과 협력을 특징으로 하는 인간 본성의 프로파일을 점점 더 재구성하고 있다. 이는 폭력이 인간 본성에 내재된 부분이라는 널리 퍼진 인식과 뚜렷한 대조를 이룬다. 이러한 지식의 증가는 전쟁과 잔혹함이 없는 미래를 상상할 수 있게 한다. 프랑스의 의사이자 영화감독인 미셸 메냥은 진행 중인 다큐멘터리에서 이 주제를 탐구하며, 메릴렌 파투-마티스와 같은 전문가들을 참여시킨다.

국립과학연구센터(CNRS)의 과학자인 파투-마티스는 인간 사이의 폭력적인 죽음이 기원전 약 200만 년부터 1만 년 전까지의 구석기 시대에 극히 드물었다고 설명한다. 그녀는 인간이 항상 폭력적이었다는 가정을 반박하며, 초기 폭력은 장례 의식이나 기근이나 전염병과 같은 위기를 극복하기 위한 희생 의식과 같은 특정 의식에 제한됐다는 데이터를 제시한다.

이러한 발견들은 초기 폭력이 자원 경쟁에서 비롯됐다는 믿음에 도전한다. 여성 납치와 같은 폭력에 관한 신화는 고고학적 증거보다는 19세기의 사회적 투영을 반영하는 경우가 많다. (즉, 실제로 일어난 일이라기보다는 19세기 사람들의 믿음이나 사회적 관점을 바탕으로 만들어진 이야기일 가능성이 크다는 뜻이다. 예를 들어, 여성 납치와 같은 폭력 신화는 당시 사회의 편견이나 두려움이 투영된 결과일 수 있다는 의미이다.) 파투-마티스는 자연적인 공격성—폭력과는 구별되는—이 생존에 필수적이었다고 강조하며, 특히 수렵채집 사회에서 그러했다고 설명한다. 사냥을 둘러싼 의식은 자신들과 유사한 것으로 여겨졌던 동물을 죽이는 행위를 받아들여야 하는 필요성을 반영한다. (자신과 비슷하다고 여긴 동물을 죽이는 것에 대한 불편한 감정이나 내적 갈등을 의식이나 의례를 통해 해소하고 정당화하려는 노력을 의미한다.)

폭력이 없다는 것이 갈등이 없다는 것을 의미하지는 않는다. 칼라하리의 산족 사이에서는 분쟁이 폭력이 아닌 집단 개입이나 분리로 해결된다. 고고학은 부상당하거나 장애를 가진 개인들에게 제공된 보살핌과 같은 선사시대의 공감의 증거도 발견한다. 예를 들어, 이라크 샤니다르 동굴에서 발견된 네안데르탈인은 자신의 그룹의 지원으로 오랜 세월 동안 생존할 수 있었다.

구석기 시대의 아동 양육 방식에 대한 데이터는 제한적이지만, 파투-마티스는 수렵채집인들이 아이들을 훈육하기 위해 폭력을 사용하지 않았으며, 이는 평화로운 교육 접근 방식을 시사한다고 언급한다. 폭력은 인간이 정착 생활을 채택하면서 더 두드러졌다. 경제적 변화, 식물과 동물의 가축화, 사적 재산 축적이 새로운 형태의 갈등을 초래했다. 이 시기의 암각화는 사회적 위계의 출현을 보여주며, 일부 인물들이 더 크게 묘사돼 엘리트를 나타낸다. 그러나 그녀의 발견은 희망적인 관점을 제공한다. 폭력은 필연적이지 않으며, 이해와 공감을 통해 인류는 덜 잔혹한 미래를 구상할 수 있다.

제11회 모의고사

1

하위내용영역	배점	예상정답률
일반영어 A형 서술형	4점	55%

모범 답안) The two words are "creating things". Second, the movie "The Social Network" is misleading because it depicts a leader of geek culture as wanting to seek status in the old world of money and to impress an ex-girlfriend. In reality, the joy and challenge of creativity is the real impetus to geek culture.

채점 기준

+ 1.5점: 빈칸에 들어갈 두 단어를 "creating things"라 기입하였다. 이외에는 답이 될 수 없다.
+ 2.5점: 영화 "The Social Network"가 오해의 소지가 있는 이유를 "it depicts <u>a leader of geek culture as wanting to seek status in the old world of money and to impress an ex-girlfriend</u>(2점). <u>In reality, the joy and challenge of creativity is the real impetus to geek culture</u>(0.5점)."라 서술하였거나 유사하였다.

한글번역

긱 문화의 주류 사회에 대한 영향력 증가는 종종 정보 기술 부문의 부 증가에 기인한다고 여겨진다. 그것이 부분적으로 사실일 수 있지만, 사회적으로 부적응한 부적격자들이 낮은 지위의 무리를 지어 서로에게 매달린다고 종종 비난받는 젊은 긱들에게 이 문화가 애초에 매력적인 이유를 놓치고 있다. 그러나 절망감이 아니라, 많은 젊은이들이 주류 문화에서 찾기 점점 어려워지는 것, 즉 무언가를 창조하는 기쁨을 위해 긱 문화에 적극적으로 끌린다.

본질적으로 긱 문화는 메이커 문화이며, 영리하고 창의적인 문화이다. 점점 더 많은 직업들이 전자 서류 작업을 하거나 고객에게 대본을 읽어주는 일, 또는 자율성이 거의 없거나 전혀 없는 노력으로 축소되는 세상에서, 긱 문화는 창의성, 상상력, 그리고 독창성이 소중히 여겨지는 곳으로 두드러진다. 이는 특히 프로그래머들에게 해당된다 : 주류 문화는 그들을 심각하게 오해하고 있으며, 따라서 긱 문화의 강점에 대한 이해 부족을 드러내는 동기들을 그들에게 투사한다.

영화 "소셜 네트워크"에서 페이스북 공동창립자 마크 저커버그의 동기에 대한 감독 아론 소킨의 묘사를 보자. 프로그래머로서 저커버그의 초기 동기는 전 여자친구에게 인상을 주려는 시도(그가 이미 나중에 결혼할 여성과 교제하고 있었기 때문에 역사적으로 부정확함)이거나, 영화가 긱들이 틀림없이 그럴 것으로 가정하는 "낮은 지위" 사람의 불안한 시도로, 오래된 돈의 고지위 WASP들만 받아들이는 하버드의 희귀한 사교 클럽에 가입하려는 것으로 묘사된다.

대조적으로, 많은 긱들은 무언가를 창조하는 깊은 기쁨에 의해 동기부여되며, 혈통에 기반한 허세부리고 답답한 사교 클럽에서는 지루해서 죽을 것이다. 이 분야로의 자금 유입이 확실히 영향을 미치고 있지만, 많은 이들에게 진정한 매력은 코드 한 줄 한 줄을 통해, 창의성에 내재된 즐거움과 힘이다. 이는 깊은 지적 도전과 예술, 요리, 또는 음악 같은 다른 창조에 공통된 즐거움을 결합하는 유쾌한 노력 말이다. 주류 문화의 대부분은 긱 문화의 겉모습만을 그것도 왜곡된 렌즈를 통해 묘사할 뿐, 많은 이들을 애초에 그것으로 끌어들이는 아름다움과 영감을 놓치고 있다.

2

하위내용영역	배점	예상정답률
문학 A형 서술형-에세이	4점	50%

모범 답안) The two words are "monotonous life". Second, the implication of the underlined words is that a child, like a young plant, needs fruitful monotony. By enduring monotony, which is represented by "the same soil", the child flourishes*(grows)* very well.

채점 기준

+ 1.5점: 밑줄 친 ①의 어구들에 상응하는 두 단어를 "monotonous life"라 답하였다. 이외에는 답이 될 수 없다.
+ 2.5점: 밑줄 친 ②가 함축하는 의미를 "a child, like a young plant, needs fruitful monotony. By enduring monotony, which is represented by "the same soil", the child flourishes*(grows)* very well"이라 서술하였거나 유사하였다.

☞ "a young plant"가 "a child"의 은유임을 언급하지 않으면 1점 감점한다.
☞ "the same soil"이 "monotony"의 은유임을 언급하지 않으면 1점 감점한다.

한글번역

다소 단조로운 삶을 견디는 능력은 어린 시절에 습득돼야 한다. 너무 많은 여행, 너무 다양한 인상들은 젊은이들에게 좋지 않으며, 그들이 자라면서 단조로움을 견딜 수 없게 만든다. 현대의 부모들은 이 점에서 크게 비난받을 만하다. 그들은 아이들에게 쇼나 맛있는 음식 같은 너무 많은 수동적 오락거리를 제공하며, 물론 다소 드문 경우를 제외하고는 하루가 다른 하루와 같아야 한다는 것이 아이에게 얼마나 중요한지 깨닫지 못한다.

어린 시절의 즐거움은 주로 아이가 어느 정도의 노력과 창의력을 통해 자신의 환경에서 끌어내는 것이어야 한다. 예를 들어 연극 같이 흥미진진하면서 동시에 신체적 노력을 수반하지 않는 즐거움은 매우 드물게 일어나야 한다. 흥분은 마약의 성질을 가지고 있어서 점점 더 많은 것이 필요하게 될 것이며, 흥분 중의 신체적 수동성은 본능에 반한다. 어린 식물은 같은 흙에서 방해받지 않고 있을 때 가장 잘 자란다.

3

하위내용영역	배점	예상정답률
일반영어 B형 서술형	4점	50%

모범답안) The two words are "computerized algorithm". Second, the underlined sentence implies that the manual grading performed by teachers and test evaluators *(in middle and high schools)* is so systematic that it is as similarly-imperfect and inaccurate as computerized algorithms.

채점 기준

+ 1.5점 : 밑줄 친 ①에 있는 단어에 상응하는 두 단어를 "computerized algorithm"이라 답하였다. 이외에는 답이 될 수 없다.

+ 2.5점 : 밑줄 친 ②가 함축하는 의미를 "the manual grading performed by teachers and test evaluators is so systematic that it is as similarly-imperfect and inaccurate as computerized algorithms"라 서술하였거나 이와 유사하였다.
☞ systematic 대신 기계적인(mechanical) 따위의 의미를 지닌 단어도 맞는 것으로 한다.
☞ "subtleties가 결여된" 등의 의미가 와도 맞는 것으로 한다.

한글번역

논픽션 글쓰기는 가장 광범위한 범주를 사용해야만 평가될 수 있다 : 논리적으로 타당한가? 논증이 명확하게 진술되고, 뒷받침되고, 결론지어졌는가? 그런 방식으로 누군가가 고등학교 4학년의 논픽션 에세이를 대략 1점에서 4점을 척도로 판단하는 것이 가능하다고 생각한다.

작가이자 대학원 글쓰기 교사로서, 이 주제는 나에게 중요하다. 15세, 12세, 7세 자녀의 부모로서, 모두 짜증스럽게 시간을 잡아먹는 공립학교 표준화 시험 2주간의 수렁에 빠져있는 상황에서, 대규모 에세이 채점은 내 속을 뒤틀리게 한다. 2년 전, 내 아들이 5학년이었을 때, 그는 웹사이트에 로그인해서 시험 에세이를 타이핑하고, 버튼을 누르고, 컴퓨터화된 알고리즘이 점수를 주기를 기다려야 했다. 알고리즘이 그가 쓴 것을 좋아하지 않으면 낙담했고, 좋아하면 기뻐했다. 빠르게 조사해본 결과(그렇다, 그가 사용한 바로 그 컴퓨터에서), 교사 봇을 속이는 가장 쉬운 방법은 단순히 더 많은 단어를 타이핑하는 것이었다는 걸 빠르게 발견했다. 옹호자들과 이익을 추구하는 자들은 기술이 아직 초기 단계라고 말한다. 나는 그대로 두라고 말한다. 누군가는 회화, 음악 작품, 해석적 무용에 점수를 주는 수학적 공식을 쓸 수 있을 것이다. 그렇다고 해서 그런 노력이 가치가 있다는 뜻인가? 슬픈 부분은 중학교와 고등학교 에세이 채점의 상당 부분이 이미 컴퓨터화된 알고리즘에 의해 채점되고 있는 것처럼 보인다는 것이다. 교사들과 시험 평가자들은 표준화된 루브릭, "표준화 튜토리얼", 체크해야 할 박스들을 가지고 있다. 에세이 쓰기를 어디서부터 가르치기 시작해야 하고, 중학교까지는 5단락 에세이의 획일적인 형식을 익히는 것이 젊은 논픽션 작가의 발달에 필요하다는 것을 이해한다. 그러나 확실히 고등학교 말까지, 학생들이 대학 입학을 위해 평가받을 때는, 우리는 그들에게 훨씬 더 많은 것을 요구해야 한다. 우리는 표준화된 시험이—정의상—결코 발견할 수 없을 미묘함들을 찾아내야 한다.

4

하위내용영역	배점	예상정답률
일반영어 B형 서술형	5점	55%

모범답안 Sigmund Freud identified four different ways that dreams disguise their hidden meanings. Through the process of "condensation", one person in a dream may actually represents several different people. Second, "displacement" allows antisocial actions (or emotions) unacceptable in reality to be redirected toward a safe target. Third, "symbolization" means that symbols should be interpreted symbolically, not literally. Finally, "second elaboration" takes place when the dream is over and the dreamer adds logical details to what (s)he remembers about the dream.

채점기준

ⓐ Topic sentence
+ 1.5점: "Sigmund Freud identified <u>four</u> different ways that <u>dreams disguise their hidden meanings</u>"를 정확하게 서술하였다.
  ☞ "four"가 없으면 0.5점 감점한다.

ⓑ Major supporting details
+ 3.5점: "Through the process of "condensation", one person in a dream may actually represents several different people. Second, "displacement" allows antisocial actions (or emotions) unacceptable in reality to be redirected toward a safe target. Third, "symbolization" means that symbols should be interpreted symbolically, not literally. Finally, "second elaboration" takes place when the dream is over and the dreamer adds logical details to what (s)he remembers about the dream."을 서술하였거나 유사하였다.
  ☞ 4개 디테일 중 4개 모두 서술한 경우 3.5점, 3개 서술한 경우 2점, 2개 서술한 경우 1점, 1개 또는 서술하지 못한 경우 0점을 준다.

한글번역

정신분석의 오스트리아 창시자인 지그문트 프로이트는 꿈을 "무의식으로 가는 왕도"라고 불렀다. 따라서 그는 꿈의 내용에 세심한 주의를 기울였다. 꿈에 대한 연구를 통해 프로이트는 꿈이 근본적인 의미를 위장하는 몇 가지 구체적인 방법들을 확인했다. 프로이트에 따르면, 꿈은 압축을 이용한다. 다시 말해, 꿈속의 한 인물이나 사물이 현실 생활의 여러 다른 사람들이나 사물들을 잘 나타낼 수 있다는 것이다. 따라서 꿈속의 사람이 당신의 강사처럼 보이면서도 당신의 아버지처럼 말하고 몸짓을 할 수 있는데, 적어도 프로이트는 이것이 권위를 나타내는 압축된 인물이라고 말할 것이다. 치환은 프로이트의 또 다른 꿈의 위장술이었다. 꿈에서 치환이 작용할 때, 현실에서는 받아들일 수 없는 폭력적이거나 분노한 행동들이 안전한 대상들로 향한다. 예를 들어, 이혼을 계획하는 부모에게 분노하며 잠든 십대는 사랑하는 부모에게 화난 꿈을 꾸는 대신 접시 세트를 박살내는 꿈을 꿀 수 있다. 프로이트가 "꿈 작업"이라고 부른 것에서 상징화가 종종 작용하며, 그는 꿈의 이미지가 실제적인 것이 아니라 상징적인 관점에서 해석돼야 한다고 믿었다. 예를 들어, 교실에 벌거벗고 걸어 들어가는 꿈을 꾸는 학생은 노출증적 성향이 아니라 약하고 취약하다는 두려움에 의해 동기부여됐을 가능성이 높다. 이차적 정교화는 꿈 자체가 아니라 꿈에 대한 기억과 관련된다. 꿈을 기억할 때 우리는 꿈을 정교화해 원래 꿈 자체에는 존재하지 않았던 논리적 연결들을 추가한다는 것이 프로이트의 입장이었다.

제12회 모의고사

1

하위내용영역	배점	예상정답률
일반영어 A형 기입형	2점	60%

모범 답안 acculturation and assimilation

채점 기준

- 2점: 모범답안과 똑같다. 이외에는 답이 될 수 없다.
- 0점: 모범답안과 다르다.

한글번역

　미국에서 최근 눈에 띄는 변화 중 하나는 민족성에 대한 관심의 재확산이다. 일부 미국 사회 관찰자들은 이를 '민족성 부흥(ethnic revival)'이라고 표현한다. 그러나 나는 이것이 실제 부흥은 아니며, 문화수용(acculturation)과 동화(assimilation)의 과정이 여전히 지속되고 있다고 주장한다.
　'신이민(new immigration)' 시기에 유럽에서 미국으로 이주한 사람들의 3세대 또는 4세대, 즉 그들의 손자 또는 증손자들 사이에서는 새로운 형태의 민족적 관여가 나타나고 있는지도 모른다. 이들은 유대인이나 이탈리아인이라는 정체성, 즉 '나는 누구인가'에 대한 감정에 집중하는 경향이 있다. 그러나 이 세대에서 민족적 정체성에 대한 필요는 그다지 강렬하거나 빈번하지 않기 때문에, 이들은 민족 문화를 유지하거나 민족 조직에 참여할 필요를 느끼지 않는다. 대신, 민족적 상징을 활용하는 방식을 택한다. 결과적으로 민족성은 '상징적 민족성(symbolic ethnicity)', 즉 최후의 수단으로써의 민족성으로 전환되고 있으며, 이러한 민족성은 세대를 넘어 지속될 수도 있다.
　정체성은 집단과 분리돼 존재할 수 없으며, 상징 자체도 문화의 일부다. 그러나 민족적 정체성과 상징적 민족성은 이전 세대가 가지고 있었던 민족 문화나 조직과는 전혀 다른 형태를 요구한다. 더 나아가, 3세대 민족 후손들이 자신의 정체성을 표현하기 위해 사용하는 상징들은 1세대나 2세대가 구축했던 민족 문화나 조직보다 더 시각적으로 드러난다. 그렇기에 민족성의 부흥처럼 보이는 현상은, 실제로는 오래 지속돼 온 현상의 더 가시적인 형태이거나, 문화수용과 동화의 새로운 단계일 수 있다.

2

하위내용영역	배점	예상정답률
일반영어 A형 서술형	4점	50%

모범 답안 The simple insight is that pricing influences consumption patterns to reduce quantity of demand of the given commodity. Second, in the second blank, "prices" should be inserted.

채점 기준

- 2.5점: 단순한 통찰이 의미하는 것이 "pricing influences consumption patterns to reduce quantity of demand of the given commodity"라 서술하였거나 유사하였다.
  ☞ pricing(or prices) 대신 taxation만 언급했으면 1.5점을 준다.
- 1.5점: 빈칸에 들어갈 단어를 "prices"라 정확히 기입하였다. 이외에는 답이 될 수 없다.

한글번역

　모든 학생들, 심지어 강의실 뒤편에서 졸고 있는 학생들조차도, 경제학 입문 수업에서 반드시 배우는 개념이 하나 있다면, 그것은 바로 "가격이 중요하다"는 점이다. 특히 학생들은 가격이 오르면 소비량이 줄어든다는 사실을 배우게 된다. 따라서 화석연료의 연소가 제3자의 건강에 해로운 부작용을 일으키고, 대기 온도의 변화를 유발한다면, 경제학이 제시하는 명백한 교훈은 화석연료에 세금을 부과해 그 외부 효과를 반영한 수준까지 가격을 올리는 것이다. 그러면 기업과 소비자들은 수천 가지 방식으로 이러한 가격 변화에 반응할 것이고, 그 순효과는 전체적인 화석연료 연소량의 감소가 된다.
　예를 들어, 휘발유 가격이 오르면 통근자가 프리우스 같은 연비 좋은 차를 몰기 시작하거나, 기존의 기름 먹는 자동차를 줄이기 위해 직장 근처로 이사할 수도 있다. 이 두 경우는 모두 전체적인 화석연료 소비에 긍정적인 영향을 미치며, 반드시 연비 좋은 차를 구입하지 않더라도 연료 소비를 줄일 수 있다는 의미다.

이처럼 너무도 자명한 내용을 단 두 단락, 수학적 설명 없이 제시했음에도 불구하고, 유권자들과 그들이 뽑은 공직자들은 이 단순한 통찰을 거부하고, 대신 소비자 가전제품이나 자동차 제조사에게 에너지 효율 기준만을 부과하는 방식을 선호한다. 가격보다는 에너지 효율성에만 집중하는 이런 접근에는 두 가지 중요한 결점이 있다. 첫째, 동일한 에너지 절약 효과를 달성하는 데 있어서, 고효율 기기나 자동차는 화석연료 소비에 세금을 부과하는 것보다 훨씬 더 많은 비용이 든다. 이는 가격 인상이 에너지 소비를 줄이기 위한 가능한 모든 수단을 자극하는 반면, 효율 기준은 그렇지 않기 때문이다. 둘째, 더 효율적인 기기와 자동차는 운용비를 낮추기 때문에 소비자들이 가격이 인상됐을 경우보다 더 많은 에너지를 소비하게 되는 경향이 있다.

3

하위내용영역	배점	예상정답률
문학 A형 서술형—에세이	4점	45%

모범답안 In underlined ①, the writer of the passage points out that Picasso was "crediting" the German officer for the painting *Guernica* because, beyond the painting, the real massacre was caused by the German Nazi army. In the second underline, the writer is criticizing the way in which a painting inspired by death and war inappropriately becomes a pleasant fixture for exhibition.

채점 기준

+ 2점 : 밑줄 친 ①의 함축 의미를 "Picasso was "crediting" the German officer for the painting *Guernica* because, beyond the painting, the real massacre was caused by the German Nazi army"라 서술하였거나 유사하였다.
☞ "피카소가 자신의 그림을 그리게 된 이유를 나치에 의한 학살이 원인임을 지적하는 것"이라는 언급이 있으면 2점을 준다.

+ 2점 : 밑줄 친 ②에서 저자가 말하려는 바가 "the writer is criticizing the way in which a painting inspired by death and war inappropriately becomes a pleasant fixture for exhibition"라 서술하였거나 유사하였다.
☞ 저자가 "그림이 원래의 참혹한 현장에서 벗어나 사람들의 즐거움의 도구로 변질한 것을 비판하려고 한다"고 서술하였으면 2점을 준다.

한글번역

재즈는 어떤 의미에서 재즈 시대의 도덕적 변화들을 야기했는가, 아니면 단지 그것을 상징했을 뿐인가? 비틀즈는 60년대의 정치적 혼란을 촉발했는가, 아니면 예고에 그쳤는가—혹은, 그 시기의 정치는 음악에 반응하는 형식의 예술이 돼버린 것인가, 실제 세계의 정치사는 전혀 다른 차원의 인과에서 전개되고 있었던 것인가? 어쨌든 우리가 아는 대로, 의식에 정치적 관심을 불러일으키기 위해 창작된 작품들조차 대체로 그 자체에 대한 감탄과, 그런 작품을 감탄하는 자기 자신에 대한 도덕적 자기도취 정도밖에 유발하지 못했다. 1937년 4월 26일, 나치에 의해 바스크 지방의 게르니카 마을이 냉혹하게 폭격당한 사건이 그 공포를 표현한 회화 게르니카를 탄생시켰다. 그래서 독일 장교가 피카소에게 엽서 크기의 그림을 건네받고 "이걸 그린 게 당신입니까?"라고 물었을 때 피카소가 "아니, 그건 당신이 한 짓이오."라고 대답한 것은 단순한 재치가 아니었다. 모두가 누가 무엇을 왜 했는지를 알고 있었다. 그것은 가해자가 의도적으로 인식되기를 바란 만행이었고, 바로 그런 의미에서 인식되도록 설계된 잔혹 행위였다. 이 그림은 스페인 내전 구호 기금 마련을 위한 모금 활동에도 사용됐지만, 그것을 돈을 내고 지나가며 바라본 사람들은 이미 자신 안에 자리 잡은 태도를 비추는 거울로서만 그것을 활용했을 뿐이다. 시간이 흐르면서는 미술사적 지식 없이는 그 그림이 무엇을 말하는지 알기조차 어려워졌다. 그 그림은 현대미술관에서 즉석 만남의 배경으로 존재하거나, 빌트모어 호텔의 시계처럼 데이트 장소로 이용됐다. 회색과 검정의 조화는 충분히 아름다워서 어느 인테리어 잡지에서는 게르니카 복제화가 정교한 현대식 부엌을 장식하는 예로 소개되기도 했다. 그 부엌에서는 화려한 음식이 날카롭고 세련된 손님들을 위해 조리됐고, 그 손님들뿐 아니라 주인장도 그 그림 속의 내장이 드러난 동물들과 비명을 지르는 어머니들이 포미카(인조 대리석) 상판 위에 떠 있는 고통을 인식하지 못했다.

[출전] Arthur Danto <The Philosophical Disenfranchisement of Art>(1985)

4

하위내용영역	배점	예상정답률
일반영어 B형 서술형	4점	55%

모범답안 During the bourgeois period, self-portraits and biographies, which were both studies of the self, rose in popularity due to an increased focus on the self. In the blank, the word "self-possession" should be inserted.

채점기준

+ 2.5점: 자화상이나 전기가 인기가 있었던 이유를 "During the bourgeois period, self-portraits and biographies, <u>which were both studies of the self</u>(0.5점), rose in popularity <u>due to an increased focus on the self</u>(2점)"라 서술하였거나 유사하였다.

  ☞ 다음과 같이 서술하였어도 맞는 것으로 한다.
  − "During the bourgeois period, self-portraits and biographies, which dealt with the self, rose in popularity due to an increased focus on the self."

+ 1.5점: 빈칸에 "self-possession"을 기입하였다. 이외에는 답이 될 수 없다.

한글번역

육체적 삶의 내면화는 의식의 내면화와 동시에 진행됐다. 인간이 자기 자신에게 관심을 돌리기 시작한 것은 부르주아 시대였다. 자아라는 개념은 서구 역사 전반을 통해 서서히, 그리고 불가역적으로 발전해 왔지만, 그것이 부르주아 계층 사이에서는 거의 집착 수준의 관심 대상이 됐다. 새로운 부르주아 계층의 가정에서는 거울이 어디에나 있었다. 자기 점검과 자기 성찰은 집착이자 취미가 됐고, 자기 확신, 자기애, 자기 연민, 자존감, 자기 가치, 인격, 자아, 양심 같은 단어들이 개인의 성장과 사회적 담론의 기준점으로 작용하게 됐다. 자화상과 전기는 대중적 문화 형식으로 자리 잡았다.

빅토리아 말기에는 물질적 안락함이 부르주아 삶의 정의로 자리 잡았다. 부르주아인을 떠올릴 때, 사람들은 대개 푹신한 가구, 무거운 커튼, 바닥을 덮은 여러 겹의 카펫 등을 상상하게 된다—즉, 외부 세계의 소란과 변덕으로부터 차단된, 안락함과 안전, 조용함과 단정함이 유지되는 공간. 부르주아 계층은 가시적인 주거 공간을 과도한 가구와 정교한 장식으로 채우는 강박을 지니고 있었다. 그들은 집안의 모든 방을 사물로 가득 채웠고, 눈은 어떤 빈 공간도 견디지 못하는 듯했다.

사유재산 관계를 중심으로 조직된 시대 속에서, 부르주아 계층은 자신의 삶을 그러한 이상을 찬미하는 방식으로 조직했다. 그들은 사물들로 자신을 둘러쌌고, '나의 것'과 '너의 것'을 구분 짓기 위한 모든 형태의 경계를 만들어냈다. 심지어 소유라는 개념을 의식 내부로까지 내면화했다. 자기 통제는 부르주아 계층의 모든 구성원이 갈망한 개인적 목표였다.

5

하위내용영역	배점	예상정답률
일반영어 B형 논술형	10점	55%

모범답안 *Ecotourism is a multi-faceted institution based around the creation of tourism focused on nature which is conducted in a sustainable way. In its implementation there have been notable benefits and drawbacks in terms of natural environment, development, and cultural impact.*

Ecotourism suggests several benefits for the local people. First, in the area of natural environment, ecotourism encourages local people to keep their natural surroundings intact because it generates income for the people. Second, local people have opportunities to develop their cities through support from ecotourism. They can gain employment and participate as partners in the decision-making processes in these areas, which gives empowerment and support. The third benefit is that tourists are also introduced and shown the local culture along with the natural spaces.

On the other hand, the drawbacks of eco-tourism are important to mention in these same areas. Such as, for starters, the tourists that are attracted to the natural environments often create waste and upset to the natural order of things. Regarding the impact on development, the prioritization placed on nature in the name of ecotourism often constricts for people who might want to sustainably develop the area. Finally, the commodification of the local cultures, breakdown of traditional local relationships, and increasing crime are another notable problems.

채점 기준

ⓐ Task Completion(_____ / 7.5점)

- Introduction paragraph(1.5점)
+ 1.5점: ① natural environment, ② development and ③ cultual impact (or culture) 등 3가지 요소를 모두 명확하게 기술하였다.
  ☞ 3가지 중 2개 요소만 기술한 경우 1점, 1개 요소만 기술한 경우 0.5점을 준다.

- 첫 번째 body paragraph(3점)
+ 0.5점: Ecotourism의 장점을 다루는 주제문을 "Ecotourism suggests several benefits for the local people."라 서술하였다.
  ☞ 세 가지 측면에서 다루겠다는 점을 명시할 수 있으며 몇 가지 측면이라고만 기술해도 무방하다.
  ☞ benefits, advantages, positive sides 등에 해당하는 표현이 포함되어야 한다.
+ 2.5점: 세 가지의 supporting detail(example)을 명확하게 서술하였다.
  ☞ 2가지만 서술하였으면 1점, 1가지만 서술하였으면 0.5점을 준다.

- 두 번째 body paragraph(3점)
+ 0.5점: Ecotourism의 단점을 다루는 주제문을 "On the other hand, the drawbacks of eco-tourism are important to mention in these same areas."라 서술하였다.
  ☞ 세 가지 측면에서 다루겠다는 점을 명시할 수 있으며 이미 위에서 기술한 동일한 측면이라고만 기술해도 무방하다.
  ☞ drawbacks, disadvantages, negative sides 등에 해당하는 표현이 포함되어야 한다.
+ 2.5점: 세 가지의 supporting detail(example)을 명확하게 서술하였다.
  ☞ 2가지만 서술하였으면 1점, 1가지만 서술하였으면 0.5점을 준다.

ⓑ Language(_____ / 2.5점)

- Word Choice & Syntactic Variety(1점)
  a) 글 전체에서 1개 이내의 단어나 표현 문제가 있다. 1점
    ☞ 주요 단어나 표현 문제
    − awkward expressions or inappropriate jargon
    − cliches and wordiness, informal language
  b) 글 전체에서 2-3개 사이의 단어나 표현 문제가 있다. 0.5점
  c) 글 전체에서 4개 이상의 단어나 표현 문제가 있다. 0점

- Grammar(1점): 문장 구조가 영어 문법에 맞게 사용되었다.
  a) 글 전체에서 1개 이내의 주요 오류가 있다. 1점
    ☞ 주요 문법 오류
    − subject-verb agreement error
    − incorrect use of verb tense or verb form
    − run-on sentence (an ungrammatical sentence in which two or more independent clauses are conjoined without a conjunction)
    − fragment
  b) 글 전체에서 2-3개 사이의 주요 오류가 있다. 0.5점
  c) 글 전체에서 4개 이상의 주요 오류가 있다. 0점

- Mechanics(0.5점)
  a) 글 전체에서 2개 이내의 mechanics 오류가 있다. 0.5점
    ☞ 주요 mechanics 오류
    − spelling, punctuation between words, phrases, clauses, capital letter errors
  b) 글 전체에서 3개 이상의 mechanics 오류가 있다. 0점

감점
- 주제와 관계없는 내용이 포함되었다. -0.5pt
- 본문이 2개의 문단으로 구성되어 있지 않다. -0.5pt
- 연결사를 전혀 사용하지 않거나 부적절하게 사용한다. -0.5pt

한글번역

에코투어리즘은 관광 산업의 중요한 부문이며, 유엔은 이 부문이 2012년 세계 관광 수익의 25%를 차지할 것이라고 추정한 바 있다. 그 정의는 다소 다양하지만, 유엔 식량농업기구(FAO)는 에코투어리즘을 "자연을 기반으로 하면서도 지속 가능한 관광 및 여가 활동"으로 폭넓게 정의한다. 에코투어리즘은 자연 환경을 보존하는 데 중점을 두고 있으며, 관광 시설 제공에 있어 지역 주민의 참여를 종종 포함하지만, 그 영향에 대해 찬반양론이 존재한다.

우선, 에코투어리즘은 관광객들이 입장료, 편의시설 이용료, 허가증 등의 형태로 지불하는 돈을 통해 자연 환경으로부터 수익을 창출한다. 환경을 지역 공동체가 자립할 수 있는 수단으로 전환함으로써, 결과적으로 그 환경을 보존하려는 동기를 부여하는 것이다. 그러나 반대론자들은 에코투어리즘으로 유입되는 관광객들이 오히려 자연 환경을 훼손할 수 있다고 주장한다. 민감한 생태계에 관광객을 무분별하게 들이는 것은 오염을 유발하거나 예기치 못한 방식으로 환경에 영향을 미칠 수 있다. 실제로 코스타리카의 한 국립공원에서 실시된 연구에 따르면, 야생 원숭이들이 관광객이 남기고 간 음식물과 쓰레기를 먹으며 '쓰레기 먹이'로 전락했고, 사람의 존재에 익숙해지기도 했다.

또한 찬성론자들은 관광객을 위한 숙박 제공이나 가이드 역할에 지역 주민이 참여함으로써 에코투어리즘이 지역 개발에도 기여한다고 본다. 예를 들어 우간다의 부윈디 난투과림(Bwindi Impenetrable Forest)에서는 수백 명의 지역 주민이 레인저나 현장 직원으로 일하면서 소득을 보충하고 있다. 많은 경우 지역 공동체는 단순한 참여자가 아니라 에코투어리즘 조직의 협력 파트너로서 활동하기도 한다. 하지만 반대론자들은 에코투어리즘이 자연 보호에만 집중함으로써 오히려 지역 주민의 지속 가능한 개발 가능성과 빈곤 탈출의 기회를 제한한다고 본다. 즉, 자연 환경이 지역 주민의 생존 요구보다 우선시되는 것이다.

끝으로, 에코투어리즘은 지역 문화에도 영향을 미칠 수 있다. 에코투어리스트들은 종종 지역 문화를 체험할 수 있다는 기대 때문에 여행을 선택하는데, 이는 지역 문화에 긍정적이고 자긍심을 고양하는 효과를 줄 수 있다. 의사 결정 과정에 지역 주민을 참여시키는 것은 그들이 관광에 대해 보다 긍정적인 태도를 갖게 하고 공동체로서의 권한을 부여받는 데도 기여한다. 하지만 부정적인 영향도 존재한다. 예컨대, 전통적 문화 상징들이 방문객에게 팔기 위한 상품으로 변질되거나, 지역 주민 간 기존의 관계가 교란되고, 범죄 발생률이 증가하는 등의 문제도 발생할 수 있다.

제13회 모의고사

1

하위내용영역	배점	예상정답률
일반영어 A형 서술형	4점	50%

모범답안 The underlined is meant to communicate that the decision-making process is not treated casually, and that a great deal of concern and thought is involved in judgments. Second, we can infer from this passage that the exemplary female applicant would have been granted admission with no debate had she been male.

채점기준

+ 2점: 밑줄 친 부분의 의미가 "입학사정관들이 지원자들의 지원서를 검토할 때 무신경하거나 설렁설렁 하지 않고 상당한 관심과 생각으로 합격자들을 가려내려는 것"이라 서술하였다.
+ 2점: 만일 여성 지원자가 남성이었다면 합격에 어떠한 일이 있었겠냐는 질문에 "만일 남성이었다면 논쟁의 여지없이 쉽게 합격했을 것"이라 서술하였다.

한글번역

나는 딸 마들린이 다섯 개 대학 중 한 곳으로부터 받은 얇은 봉투를 여는 모습을 지켜보고 있었다. 그녀가 나에게 웨이팅 리스트에 올랐다는 편지를 건네며 스스로에게 "왜?"라고 묻고 있음이 명백했다. 내가 일하는 대학에서는 현재 한 자리에 세 명이 지원한다. 불과 3년 전만 해도 그 비율은 2:1이었다. 1969년까지 남자 대학이었던 케넌 칼리지는 이제 지원자의 55% 이상이 여성이며, 그 비율은 계속해서 증가하고 있다. 입학사정관인 나와 내 직원들은 시를 향한 열정, 백신을 개발하겠다는 열망, 세상을 더 나은 곳으로 만들겠다는 확신을 담은 이 젊은 여성들의 에세이를 정성스럽게 읽는다. 나도 한 때는 그런 여학생 중 하나였지만, 그것은 30년 전의 일이다. 당시에는 대학에 지원하는 일이 YMCA 회원가입보다 약간 더 어려운 수준이었다. 하지만 지금의 입시는 복잡하고 오래 지속되는 '춤'과 같고, 그 시작은 매우 이르며, 특히 젊은 여성들에게는 실수할 여지가 거의 없다. 예컨대, Algebra II/Trig (대수학 II/삼각함수)에서 C 학점을 받는다면? 곧바로 웨이팅 리스트로 간다.

입학사정관들이 결정을 가볍게 내리는 것은 아니다. 지난 주, 나를 포함한 열 명의 입학사정관들이 매일 12시간씩 책상에 둘러앉아 수백 명의 재능 있는 청소년들의 지원서를 논의했다. 커피를 들이켜며 통계 자료를 검토하던 중, 우리는 한 켄터키 출신 여학생에 대한 이야기를 들었다. 우리는 아직 그녀를 곧바로 합격시킬 준비가 돼 있지 않았다. 그녀는 학교 내 모든 활동에서 리더 / 회장 / 편집장 / 주장 / 주연 배우를 맡은 인물이었다. 여섯 과목의 AP(대학 수준의 고급 과정)를 이수했고, 명문 주정부 리더십 프로그램에도 선발됐다. 여기에 더해, 그녀는 네 개의 다른 단체에서 300시간이 넘는 자원봉사를 한 이력도 갖고 있었다.

그 자리에 앉아 있던 우리 중 누구도, 17살 때 그녀만큼 재능 있고 목표 지향적이지는 않았다. 하지만 불행히도 그녀의 시험 점수와 학점은 우리 지원자 풀에서 중간 정도였다. 우리는 그 중간 수준의 점수를 받아들일 것인지에 대해 토론한 후에야 마침내 그녀 이름 옆에 "합격"이라고 적을 수 있었다.

오늘날, 젊은 남성 지원자는 더 희소하기 때문에 더 가치 있는 지원자로 여겨진다. 현재 미국 내 대학의 3분의 2가 여성 지원자가 남성보다 많다고 보고하고 있으며, 학부 재학생의 56% 이상이 여성이다.

2

하위내용영역	배점	예상정답률
일반영어 A형 서술형	4점	50%

모범답안 The writer's skepticism stems from the problems identified in Jackson's tragic straining to please everyone around him, which makes him a less-than-ideal role model. Second, the implied meaning of the underlined is that Jackson suffered a great deal to appear as white, which damaged his health severely.

유희대 | 일반영어 ❹-2

채점 기준

✚ **2점**: 저자가 잭슨이 롤 모델이 될 수 없는 이유에 대한 설명을 "The writer's skepticism stems from the problems identified in Jackson's tragic straining to please everyone around him, which makes him a less-than-ideal role model"라 서술하였다.

☞ "잭슨은 일반적으로 롤 모델이 지니고 있다고 간주되는 자기 삶의 주체가 아닌 (mirror man으로서) 남이 원하는 삶만을 살았기 때문"이라 서술하였어도 2점을 준다.

✚ **2점**: 밑줄 친 부분의 함의를 "Jackson suffered a great deal to appear as white, which damaged his health severely"라 서술하였거나 유사하였다.

한글번역

마이클 잭슨에 대한 가장 충격적인 이미지 중 하나는 조지 H. W. 부시 대통령이 그를 젊은 흑인 남성들의 롤 모델로 언급했던 장면이다. 1990년, 잭슨은 명성의 정점에 있었다. "Man in the Mirror"는 그보다 2년 전에 발표됐고, 그는 아직 완전히 백인처럼 위장하지는 않았지만, 첫 앨범에서 볼 수 있었던 귀엽고 갈색 피부의 소년은 이미 오래 전에, 큐빅 장갑을 낀 기이한 단계에 들어서 있었다. 나는 그때 도무지 잭슨의 어떤 면이 누군가에게 롤 모델이 될 수 있는지 의문을 품었다. 그는 음악적 천재였지만, 거의 처음부터 비극적인 인물이었으며, 거울 속에 갇혀 다른 사람들이 그에게 기대하는 모습을 영원히 반사하는 존재처럼 보였다.

그 고통의 이야기는 이제 널리 알려져 있다. 잭슨의 몸은 어린 시절 권투 선수였던 아버지 조 잭슨에게 받은 학대로 상처투성이었다. 형 마를론 잭슨은 특히 섬뜩한 한 사건을 기록했는데, 아버지가 마이클의 한쪽 다리를 잡고 거꾸로 매단 채 그를 계속해서 때렸다는 것이다. 또 다른 일화로는 아버지가 공포 가면을 쓰고 한밤중에 그의 방 창문으로 몰래 들어와 겁을 줬다는 이야기가 있다—그 목적은 창문을 열어 두지 말라는 교훈을 주기 위한 것이었다고 한다. 조 잭슨은 자녀를 때린 적은 없다고 부인하지만, 가죽 끈이나 벨트로 "매질"을 했다는 사실은 인정한다. 그의 말에 따르면 "막대기로 때리는 게 진짜 구타"라는 것이다.

잭슨의 죽음 이후, 많은 사람들이 그의 "크로스오버 매력"을 찬양했다. 그의 음악적 역량이 MTV의 인종 통합을 이끌었다는 데는 의심의 여지가 없다. 하지만 그 '매력'에는 더 우울한 이면이 있었다. 엘비스가 "백인 흑인(White Negro)"이었다면, 마이클은 스스로를 "흑인 백인(Negro Caucasian)"으로 재구성했다. 그는 우리 눈앞에서 말 그대로 자신을 지워갔다. 코는 점차 사라졌고, 피부는 유령처럼 창백해졌으며, 목소리는 점점 더 높고 가늘어졌고, 몸은 마를 대로 말라 죽을 당시 체중은 100파운드(약 45kg)에도 못 미치는 건조한 껍질로 남았다.

3

하위내용영역	배점	예상정답률
일반영어 B형 서술형	4점	35%

모범 답안: Privatization facilitates the accumulation by dispossession by arranging a situation in which the capitalists are able to take control of once-publicly owned properties. This leaves the poor having to buy or rent what they formerly could access directly. Second, the corresponding words are "accumulation by dispossession".

채점 기준

✚ **2.5점**: 민영화가 "강탈을 통한 축적"을 하는 데 어떻게 사용되었는지에 대해 "Privatization facilitates the accumulation by dispossession by arranging a situation in which the capitalists are able to take control of once-publicly owned properties(2점). This leaves the poor having to buy or rent what they formerly could access directly(0.5점)"라 서술하였다.

✚ **1.5점**: 상응하는 연속된 세 단어를 "accumulation by dispossession"이라 기술하였다.

☞ "dispossession of assets"라 했으면 0.5점을 준다.

한글번역

'강탈에 의한 축적'은 지리학자 데이비드 하비가 제시한 개념으로, 1970년대 이후 현재까지 서구 여러 나라에서 진행된 신자유주의적 자본주의 정책을 설명한다. 하비는 이러한 정책들이 공공의 자산이나 토지를 박탈하고, 그 결과 부와 권력이 소수에게 집중되는 구조를 형성한다고 본다. 이 과정은 몇 가지 핵심적인 실천 방식들에 의해 작동한다.

우선 민영화는 생산적 공공 자산을 국가로부터 민간 기업으로 이전하는 과정을 말한다. 여기서 말하는 생산적 자산은 토지, 산림, 수자원 등과 같은 자연 자원을 포함하며, 본래 국가는 이를 국민을 위해 신탁의 형태로 보유하고 있었다. 이 자산들을 민간 기업에 주식 형태로 매각하는 것은 곧 '약탈에 의한 축적'이다. 그 결과 자본가 계급은 이 자산을 통해 이윤을 창출할 수 있게 되며, 과거에는 공동체가 소유하고 이용하던 자원을 다시 대중에게 임대하거나 판매하거나, 자본주의적 생산 체계의 일부로 활용해 더 많은 자본을 생산하는 구조가 된다.

금융화의 물결은 1980년대에 본격화됐으며, 이는 정부의 규제 완화에 의해 가능해졌다. 이러한 변화는 금융 시스템을 재분배적 활동의 주요 중심으로 만들었다. 주식 부양, 폰지 사기, 인플레이션을 통한 자산 구조 파괴, 인수합병을 통한 자산 수탈, 연금 펀드의 침탈 및 주가나 기업 붕괴로 인한 자산 손실 등은 1970년대 이후 자본주의 금융 시스템의 핵심 특징이다. 이러한 금융적 재분배는 유통되는 화폐의 총량, 수요와 가격 수준이 사실상 민간 소유 은행 이사회의 결정에 따라 조정된다는 점에 기반한다.

신자유주의 국가는 이 재분배 정책의 가장 중요한 행위자 중 하나이다. 민영화가 단기적으로 하층 계층에게 이익을 주는 것처럼 보일 수 있지만, 장기적으로는 경제에 부정적인 영향을 미칠 수 있다. 국가는 세법 개정을 통해 자본 수익을 우대하고, 저소득층의 소득과 임금에 대한 과세를 강화하거나 상대적으로 소외시키는 방식으로 자원을 재분배한다.

마거릿 대처의 정책은 '약탈에 의한 축적'의 대표적인 사례로 꼽힌다. 그녀가 추진한 영국의 공공주택 민영화 정책은 처음에는 저소득층이 비교적 저렴한 가격에 임대에서 소유로 전환할 수 있다는 점에서 긍정적으로 평가됐다. 이는 자산에 대한 통제를 가능하게 하고 부의 축적을 돕는 것으로 보였다. 그러나 이후 주택 투기가 본격화되면서, 특히 도심의 핵심 지역에서 저소득층은 외곽으로 밀려나게 됐다.

4

하위내용영역	배점	예상정답률
일반영어 B형 서술형	5점	45%

모범답안 The value by which people were primarily celebrated and weighed has changed over time. From the Medieval age to the nineteenth century, "virtue" was the primary factor to considering a person's merit. Subsequently, and until the 1920s, "character" became the leading quality. Following this, there was a clear shift towards "personality". Those who stood out and had strengths and unique properties as individuals were given praise*(were praised)*. Second, the word in the blank should be "character".

채점 기준

ⓐ Topic sentence
+ 1점: "The value by which people were primarily celebrated and weighed has changed over time"를 정확하게 서술하였다.

ⓑ Summary
+ 3점: "From the Medieval age to the nineteenth century, "virtue" was the primary factor to considering a person's merit(1점). Subsequently, and until the 1920s, "character" became the leading quality(1점). Following this, there was a clear shift towards "personality". Those who stood out and had strengths and unique properties as individuals were given praise(1점)."를 서술하였거나 유사하였다.

☞ 3개 중 3개 모두를 정확하게 서술한 경우 3점, 2개를 서술한 경우 2점, 1개를 서술한 경우 1점, 서술하지 못한 경우 0점을 준다.

☞ "From the Medieval age to the nineteenth century", "Subsequently", "and until the 1920s", "Following this" 등 시간을 나타내는 signal words가 없으면 각각 0.5점씩 감점한다.

ⓒ Blank

+ 1점 : 빈칸에 들어갈 한 단어를 "character"라 기입하였다. 이외에는 답이 될 수 없다.

한글번역

중세시대에 개인의 관심이 내세에서의 자리를 확보하는 데 집중돼 있던 시절, 덕은 모든 선량한 기독교도가 열망하는 것이었다. 덕스러운 삶을 살고 선한 덕을 지니는 것은 영원한 구원을 보장했다. 근대에 들어 사회가 점점 생산 중심으로 변모하면서 덕은 주변부로 밀려나기 시작했다. 부르주아지는 덕을 품성으로 대체하기 시작했다. 19세기가 되면서 품성은 영어 어휘에서 가장 중요한 서술어 중 하나가 됐다. 좋은 품성을 지녔다는 것은 부르주아 남성이나 여성에게 건넬 수 있는 최고의 찬사였다. 품성은 무엇보다도 자제력과 자기 숙련의 개념을 환기시켰다. 품성이라는 용어는 시민정신, 근면, 근로정신, 결단력, 검소함, 진실성, 그리고 무엇보다도 성숙함과 연결됐다. 이는 프로테스탄트 노동윤리 가치관의 세속화와 자본주의 의제 및 소유계급 체제를 발전시키는 데 그토록 중요하다고 여겨지는 생산자 가치관의 재확인을 동시에 나타냈다. 그러나 1920년대 초에 이르면 품성의 중요성은 쇠퇴하기 시작했고, 새로운 자아 개념이 등장하기 시작했는데, 처음에는 자기계발 매뉴얼과 서적들의 지면에서, 나중에는 대중문화에서였다. 당시 논평가들은 미국인들에게 자신들의 개성을 개발하라고 촉구했다. 바로 한 세대 전에 좋은 품성의 자질들에 대해 글을 썼던 오리슨 스웨트 마든은 1921년 새로운 책 《지배적 개성》을 출간해 독자들에게 개인적 매력을 발휘하는 법을 배우라고 촉구했다. 마든은 추종자들에게 "우리 인생에서의 성공은 다른 사람들이 우리를 어떻게 생각하느냐에 그토록 많이 달려있다"고 상기시켰다. 그는 예의범절, 적절한 의복, 좋은 대화술("무엇을 말할지와 어떻게 말할지를 아는 것"), 활력, 생활 효율성, 침착함이 모두 누구나 "거대한 대중을 휘어잡는" 데 활용할 수 있는 자질들이라고 조언했다. 개성을 묘사하는 데 사용된 단어들은 품성을 묘사하는 데 사용된 것들과 상당히 달랐다. 누군가가 매력적이고, 창의적이며, 매혹적이고, 강력하며, 자기력이 있고, 매력적이며, 활기차고, 표현력이 풍부하고, 따뜻하다면 개성이 있다고 말한다. 개성을 갖는다는 것은 군중 속에서 돋보이고, 주목받으며, 관심을 끌고, 다른 사람들에게 영향을 미치는 것이다. "자기 자신이 돼라", "개성을 표현하라", "자신감을 가져라"가 한 세대의 구호가 됐다. 바로 이러한 자질들이 결국 저축하는 사람들과 생산자들의 국가를 지출하는 사람들과 소비자들의 국가로 바꾸도록 고안된 대중 마케팅 기법과 전국 광고 캠페인의 심리적 원재료가 됐다.

제14회 모의고사

1

하위내용영역	배점	예상정답률
일반영어 A형 기입형	2점	65%

모범답안 ⓐ Sexuality ⓑ consumer

채점기준

- 2점: 모범답안과 같다. 이외에는 답이 될 수 없다.
- 1점: 둘 중 하나만 맞았다.
- 0점: 모범답안과 다르다.

한글번역

광고에서의 성적 표현은 21세기 미국 광고의 주요 테마가 돼 왔다. 요즘 우리가 보는 것은 모든 종류의 제품을 판매하기 위해 인간의 몸을 이용하는 광고들뿐인 것 같다. 오늘날 어떤 형태의 미디어든 접하면서 제품을 판매하기 위해 인간의 몸을 이용하는 어떤 종류의 광고와 마주치지 않는 것은 사실상 불가능하다. 대부분의 경우 성적 표현과 실제 상황에서의 제품 사용은 무관하지만, 특정 제품의 사용에 성적 함의가 부여되면 그 제품은 시장에서 성공을 거뒀다고 할 수 있다. 광고 캠페인에서 성적 표현을 사용하는 모든 사업체의 목표는 명확하다. 회사는 제품을 판매하기 위해 목표 시장의 의식적 차원에 어필하고자 한다. 회사는 자신의 성적 매력을 인식하고 특별히 섹시해 보이기 위해 몇 달러를 더 지출할 소비자에게 어필하고자 한다. 이런 유형의 광고의 사명은 목표 시장에게 그 제품이 매혹적이고자 하는 욕구와 필요에 필수적이며, 동료들에게 그런 이미지를 보여주는 데 꼭 필요하다고 확신시키는 것이다.

어떤 회사든 자사와 자사 제품을 대표할 광고의 종류를 결정하기 전에 목표 소비자를 고려해야 한다. 광고 대행사는 개인적 영향과 환경적 요인들을 고려해야 한다. 광고 유형을 선택할 때 광고주가 마케팅 자극 요소들을 고려하는 것이 매우 중요한데, 이런 자극 요소들에는 인구통계학적 요인, 문화적/사회적 영향, 그리고 준거집단이 포함된다. 보통 광고주는 패션에 관심이 많고 적당히 높은 소득 수준을 가진 20대나 30대 여성으로서 패션을 위해 몇 달러를 더 지출할 수 있는 사람에게 어필하려고 한다. 광고는 회사의 목표 소비자를 공유하는 고급 패션 잡지에 게재된다.

2

하위내용영역	배점	예상정답률
일반영어 A형 서술형	4점	50%

모범답안 The underlined ① implies the husband wants to bring attention and passive criticism to the family's housekeeping by leaving notes everywhere on dusty surfaces. Second, the meaning of the underlined words in ② is that marriage generally creates a slight rift*(rupture or gap)* with family as attention is partially turned away from family toward the new spouse.

채점기준

- 2점: 밑줄 친 ①의 의미를 "the husband wants to bring attention and passive criticism to the family's housekeeping by leaving notes everywhere on dusty surfaces"라 서술하였거나 유사하였다.
- 2점: 밑줄 친 ②의 의미를 "marriage generally creates a slight rift*(rupture or gap)* with family(1점) as attention is partially turned away from family toward the new spouse(1점)"라 서술하였거나 유사하였다.

한글번역

딸의 첫 번째 생일을 맞아 집에 와 있다. 여기서 "집"이라는 것은 남편과 나, 그리고 아기가 살고 있는 로스앤젤레스의 집을 뜻하는 것이 아니라, 내 가족이 있는 곳, 캘리포니아 센트럴 밸리를 말한다. 이는 중요하지만 골치 아픈 구별이다. 남편은 내 가족을 좋아하지만 내 가족의 집에서는 불편해한다. 왜냐하면 일단 그곳에 가면 나는 그들의 방식에 빠져들기 때문인데, 그 방식들은 까다롭고, 우회적이며, 의도적으로 말을 명확히 하지 않는 것으로, 내 남편의 방식과는 다르다. 우리는 먼지투성이 집들에서 산다―그는 한번 집 안 곳곳의 표면에 손가락으로 "D-U-S-T"라 써놓았지만 아무도 알아차리지 못했다―그에게는 전혀 가치 없는 기념품들로 가득 찬 집에서 말이다(광둥식 디저트 접시들이 그에게 무슨 의미가 있겠는가? 그가 검정 저울에 대해 어떻게 알 수 있었겠는가, 설령 안다 해도 왜 신경 써야 하겠는가?). 그리고 우리가 알고 있는 정신병원에 입원한 사람들과 음주운전 혐의로 체포된 사람들, 그리고 재산, 특히 재산, 토지, 에이커당 가격, C-2 구역 지정, 평가액, 고속도로 접근성에 대해서만 이야기하는 것 같다. 내 오빠는 "매각 후 임대"라고 알려진 상당히 흔한 부동산 거래의 장점을 내 남편이 파악하지 못하는 것을 이해하지 못하고, 내 남편 역시 아버지 집에서 듣게 되는 사람들 중 그렇게 많은 이들이 최근에 정신병원에 입원하거나 음주운전 혐의로 체포되는 이유를 이해하지 못한다. 또한 그는 우리가 매각 후 임대와 통행권 수용에 대해 이야기할 때 우리가 가장 좋아하는 것들—노란 들판과 미루나무들, 오르락내리락하는 강들, 폭설이 내릴 때 폐쇄되는 산길들—에 대해 암호로 이야기하고 있다는 것을 이해하지 못한다. 우리는 서로의 요점을 놓치고, 술을 한 잔 더 마시며 불을 바라본다. 내 오빠는 남편이 있는 자리에서 그를 "조앤의 남편"이라고 부른다. 결혼은 전형적인 배신이다.

아니면 더 이상은 그렇지 않을지도 모른다. 때때로 나는 지금 30대인 우리가 "집"이라는 짐을 져야 하는 마지막 세대, 가족생활에서 모든 긴장과 드라마의 근원을 찾는 마지막 세대로 태어났다고 생각한다.

3

하위내용영역	배점	예상정답률
일반영어 A형 서술형	4점	45%

모범답안 The corresponding four words are "body for public display". Second, the writer remarks on the "docility of Americans" because, in contrast with the typical American inclination to spy into all matters, there is not any curiosity or wide understanding of the embalming procedures among the American public.

채점기준

+ 1.5점 : 상응하는 네 단어를 "body for public display"이라 기술하였다.
  ☞ "corpse presentable for viewing"이라 했어도 맞는 것으로 한다.

+ 2.5점 : 밑줄 친 부분처럼 말한 이유를 "because, in contrast with the typical American inclination to spy into all matters(1점), there is not any curiosity or wide understanding of the embalming procedures among the American public(1.5점)"이라 서술하였거나 유사하였다.

한글번역

드라마는 시체가 장례식장에 도착하면서 전개되기 시작한다. 아, 불쌍한 요릭이여! 오늘날의 그의 동반자가 장례식장으로 급히 옮겨져서 순간간에 분무되고, 절개되고, 찔리고, 절여지고, 묶이고, 다듬어지고, 크림을 바르고, 왁스칠하고, 칠하고, 연지를 바르고, 단정하게 옷을 입혀져서 아름다운 추억의 사진으로 변신하는 모습을 본다면 얼마나 놀랄까. 이 과정은 업계에서 방부 처리 기술로 알려져 있으며, 미국과 캐나다에서 너무나 보편적으로 사용돼서 장례지도사는 시체나 친족과 상의하지 않고 일상적으로 이를 수행한다. 그는 이를 생략할 수 있다고 제안할 만큼 대담한 소수의 사람들을 괴짜로 여긴다. 그러나 어떤 법도 방부 처리를 요구하지 않고, 어떤 종교적 교리도 이를 권하지 않으며, 건강이나 위생, 심지어 개인적 단정함의 고려에 의해 좌우되지도 않는다. 북미 외에는 세계 어느 곳에서도 널리 사용되지 않는다. 방부 처리의 목적은 적당히 비싼 용기에서 관람하기에 적합하도록 시체를 보기 좋게 만드는 것이다. 그리고 여기서도 장례지도사는 먼저 가족과 상의하지 않고 일상적으로 공개 전시를 위해 시체를 준비한다.

이 모든 것이 합법적인가? 죽은 시체에 가해질 수 있는 과정들은 결국 어느 정도는 법에 의해 제한된다. 예를 들어, 대부분의 주에서는 부검이 수행되기 전에, 고인이 화장되기 전에, 시체가 연구 목적으로 의과대학에 넘겨지기 전에 가장 가까운 친족의 서명을 받아야 하며, 아니면 고인의 유언장에 그런 조항이 마련돼 있어야 한다. 방부 처리의 경우에는 그런 허가가 필요하지도 않고 구하지도 않는다.

방부 처리는 참으로 극히 특이한 절차이며, 매년 수억 달러를 들여 이를 지속시키면서도 그것이 무엇인지, 무엇이 행해지는지, 어떻게 행해지는지에 대해 전혀 모른 채 태평하게 지내는 미국인들의 순종성을 의아해하지 않을 수 없다. 만 명 중 한 명도 실제로 무슨 일이 일어나는지 전혀 모른다. 거의 모든 문제에 대한 호기심을 충족시키는 것이 국민적 오락인 나라에서 방부 처리를 둘러싼 비밀주의는 분명히 그 주제 자체의 본질적 끔찍함 때문이라고 할 수는 없다. 이 점에서 관습은 금세기 들어 완전히 뒤바뀌었다. 미국 방부 처리 초기 시절, 고인의 집에서 이를 수행했을 때는 친족 중 누군가가 방부 처리자 곁에 머물며 그 절차를 지켜보는 것이 거의 의무적이었다. 오늘날에는 참석하고 싶어 할지도 모르는 가족 구성원들이 확실히 장례지도사에 의해 만류당할 것이다.

4

하위내용영역	배점	예상정답률
일반영어 B형 서술형	4점	40%

모범답안 The appropriate two words for the blank from the passage are "human nature". The implication of the underlined is that Hobbes could have proven that people's assent to irrational belief(s) is possible by example of the extremist Nazi party, which had a horrific outcome, undermining his notion of allegiance to unworthy states.

채점기준

+ 1.5점: 빈칸에 들어갈 두 단어를 "human nature"라 기술하였다. 이외에는 답이 될 수 없다.
+ 2.5점: 밑줄 친 부분의 함축 의미를 "홉스는 사람들이 *(정부나 국가에 의해)* 비이성적인 터무니없는 주장에도 동의하게 된다고 했는데, 1940년대 나치에 동의하는 독일인들은 아마도 홉스가 살아 있었다면 그 좋은 예로 들었을 것(1.5점)이지만, 문제는 이런 올바르지 않은 비이성적인 국가에 대한 *(사람들의 맹목적)* 동의는 결과적으로 큰 재앙 *(나치와 같은)*을 야기할 수 있다(1점)"라 서술하였거나 유사하였다.

감점
- he가 Hobbes임을 언급하지 않았으면 0.5점 감점한다.
- 가정법 과거완료의 의미가 충분치 않으면 0.5점 감점한다.
- key words인 "irrational belief"가 없으면 0.5점 감점한다.

한글번역

가장 널리 퍼져있으며 인기 있는 격언 가운데 하나는 '인간의 본성은 바꿀 수 없다'이다. 우선 '인간의 본성'이 무엇인지를 정의하지 않으면 아무도 이 말이 참인지 거짓인지 판정할 수 없다. 그러나 사용되는 모습을 보면 이것은 분명 틀린 말이다. 아무개 씨가 이 격언을 이상할 만큼 단호한 목소리로 말할 때 그는 사실 세상천지의 모든 사람들이 늘 그의 고향 사람들과 똑같이 행동해야 한다고 말하는 셈이다. 이러한 믿음은 인류학을 조금만 훑어봐도 산산이 부서지고 만다. 티베트에서는 아내 한 명이 남편 여럿을 거느리는데 이는 남자들이 너무 가난해서 아내 한 명을 제대로 건사하지 못하기 때문이다. 그러나 여행자들 말을 들어보면 티베트 사람들의 가정생활은 다른 나라 사람들에 비해 조금도 불행하지 않다. 손님에게 자기 아내를 빌려주는 관행은 미개 사회에서 매우 흔하게 나타난다. 오스트레일리아 원주민들은 사춘기에 몹시 고통스러운 수술을 받는데 이 수술은 남은 평생 동안 성적 능력을 크게 감소시킨다. 인간 본성에 반하는 것처럼 보이는 유아 살해 관습 또한 기독교가 번성하기 전에는 거의 온 세계에 만연했으며, 플라톤은 인구 과밀을 억제하기 위해 이를 장려하기까지 했다. 일부 미개 종족 사회에서는 사유 재산이 인정되지 않는다. 주거 공간이 절대적으로 부족한 모스크바에서는 미혼 여성이 임신을 하면 태어날 아기의 아버지로 인정받을 법적 권리를 놓고 몇 명이나 되는 남성이 경쟁을 한다. 왜냐하면 누가 아버지로 인정받든 간에 그 여성의 방을 함께 쓸 권리를 얻게 되기 때문이며, 노숙보다는 방 반 칸이 더 낫기 때문이다.

사실 성인이 지닌 '인간 본성'은 교육 환경에 따라 극히 가변적이다. 여기에는 식량이 매우 일반적인 필요조건이지만, 이집트의 테베에 살았던 수도사들은 음식 생존에 꼭 필요한 최소 분량만 섭취했다. 사람들은 제한된 식습관과 훈련을 통해 교육자의 입맛에 맞게 사나워지거나 온순해지고, 주체성 또는 노예근성을 몸에 익힌다. **제 아무리 터무니없는 헛소리라 할지라도 정부가 적절한 조치를 취하면 대다수 사람들의 신념이 된다.** 플라톤은 스스로도 허황된 것이라고 인정한 신화 위에 자신이 주장한 공화국을 건설하려 했으면서도, 사람들을 현혹해 그것을 믿게 하는 일은 충분히 가능하다고 당당히 확신했다. 홉스는 아무리 자격 없는 정부라 할지라도 사람들의 존경을 받아야 한다고 생각했으며, 그토록 비합리적인 주장이 대다수 사람들의 동의를 얻기는 어려우리라는 반론에 대해서는 사람들이 기독교, 그중에서도 특히 성찬식의 포도주와 빵이 그리스도의 피와 살로 변한다는 교리는 믿게 된 사실을 가리키며 대응했다. 만약 홉스가 1940년에도 살아 있었다면 **나치에 헌신하는 독일 젊은이들에게서 자신의 주장을 뒷받침할 확실한 증거를 찾았을 것이다.**

제15회 모의고사

1

하위내용영역	배점	예상정답률
일반영어 A형 기입형	2점	50%

모범답안 ⓐ family environment factors
ⓑ heritable

채점기준

- 2점: 모범답안과 같다.
- 0점: 모범답안과 다르다.
  ☞ nature는 어법에 맞지 않고 natural은 본문에 없으므로 답이 될 수 없다.
  ☞ biological은 단순한 생물학적인 것을 의미하는 것으로, 유전적 요인을 의미하지 않으므로 답이 될 수 없다.

한글번역

증거에 따르면 가족 환경 요인들이 아동기 IQ에 영향을 미칠 수 있으며, IQ 차이의 최대 25%를 설명한다. 반면 청소년기 후반에 이르면 이러한 상관관계는 사라져서 입양 형제자매들의 IQ가 낯선 사람들보다 더 유사하지 않게 된다. 입양 연구들은 성인기에 이르면 입양 형제자매들의 IQ가 낯선 사람들보다 더 유사하지 않으며(IQ 상관관계가 0에 가까움), 친형제자매들은 0.6의 IQ 상관관계를 보인다는 것을 나타낸다. 쌍둥이 연구들이 이러한 패턴을 강화한다: 따로 자란 일란성 쌍둥이들은 IQ에서 매우 유사하며(0.86), 함께 자란 이란성 쌍둥이들(0.6)보다 더 유사하고 입양 형제자매들(거의 0.0)보다 훨씬 더 유사하다. 따라서 "선천 대 양육" 논쟁의 맥락에서 미국 일반 성인 인구의 IQ 분산을 설명하는 데 있어 선천적 요소가 양육적 요소보다 훨씬 더 중요한 것으로 보인다.

성격은 쌍둥이와 입양 연구에서 연구된 유전적 특성의 흔히 인용되는 사례이다. 따로 자란 일란성 쌍둥이들은 무작위로 선택된 사람들보다 성격에서 훨씬 더 유사하다. 마찬가지로 일란성 쌍둥이들은 이란성 쌍둥이들보다 더 유사하다. 또한 친형제자매들이 입양 형제자매들보다 성격에서 더 유사하다. 각각의 관찰은 성격이 어느 정도는 유전된다는 것을 시사한다.

2

하위내용영역	배점	예상정답률
일반영어 A형 서술형	4점	45%

모범답안 The four words are "things that don't exist". Second, it is because the ability to communicate about fictions allows a group to imagine things collectively, which can allow better cooperation among many members.

채점기준

+ 1.5점: 밑줄 친 부분의 의미와 상응하는 네 단어를 "things that don't exist"이라 기술하였다. 이외에는 답이 될 수 없다.
+ 2.5점: 인간에게 "픽션"에 관해 말하는 능력이 중요한 이유를 "the ability to communicate about fictions allows groups to imagine things collectively(1.5점), which can allow better cooperation(1점)"이라 서술하였다.
  ☞ collectively나 cooperation의 개념이 들어가 있지 않으면 점수를 줄 수 없다.

한글번역

모든 동물은 어떤 종류의 언어를 가지고 있다. 벌과 개미 같은 곤충들조차 정교한 방식으로 소통하는 법을 알고 있으며, 서로에게 먹이가 있는 곳을 알려준다. 모든 유인원과 원숭이 종을 포함한 많은 동물들이 음성 언어를 가지고 있다. 예를 들어, 베르베트원숭이들은 소통하기 위해 다양한 종류의 울음소리를 사용한다. 동물학자들은 '조심해! 독수리야!'를 의미하는 한 가지 울음소리를 확인했다. 약간 다른 울음소리는 '조심해! 사자야!'라고 경고한다. 그러나 인간 언어의 진정 독특한 특징은 사자에 대한 정보를 전달하는 능력이 아니다. 오히려 전혀 존재하지 않는 것들에 대한 정보를 전달하는 능력이다. 우리가 아는 한, 오직 사피엔스만이 자신들이 전혀 보거나 만지거나 냄새 맡은 적이 없는 완전한 종류의 실체들에 대해 이야기할 수 있다. 전설, 신화, 신들, 종교들이 인지 혁명과 함께 처음으로 나타났다. 많은 동물들과 인간 종들이 이전에 '조심해! 사자야!'라고 말할 수 있었다. 인지 혁명 덕분에 호모 사피엔스는 '사자는 우리 부족의 수호령이다'라고 말하는 능력을 획득했다. 허구에 대해 말하는 이 능력이 인간 언어의 가장 독특한 특징이다.

오직 호모 사피엔스만이 허구에 대해 말할 수 있고 아침 식사 전에 불가능한 것들을 여섯 가지나 믿을 수 있다는 데 동의하는 것은 비교적 쉽다. 원숭이 천국에서 죽은 후 무한한 바나나를 주겠다고 약속해서 원숭이로 하여금 바나나를 주도록 설득할 수는 결코 없을 것이다. 그런데 이것이 왜 중요한가? 결국 허구는 위험하게 오해를 불러일으키거나 주의를 산만하게 할 수 있다. 요정과 유니콘을 찾으러 숲에 가는 사람들은 버섯과 사슴을 찾으러 가는 사람들보다 생존 가능성이 낮아 보일 것이다. 그리고 존재하지 않는 수호령들에게 기도하며 시간을 보낸다면, 먹이를 찾고 싸우고 번식하는 데 더 잘 쓰일 수 있는 소중한 시간을 낭비하는 것이 아닌가? 하지만 허구는 우리로 하여금 단순히 사물들을 상상할 수 있게 해줄 뿐만 아니라 집단적으로 그렇게 할 수 있게 해줬다. 우리는 성경의 창조 이야기, 호주 원주민들의 꿈의 시대 신화들, 그리고 현대 국가들의 민족주의 신화들 같은 공통된 신화들을 엮어낼 수 있다. 그런 신화들은 인간들에게 대규모로 유연하게 협력하는 전례 없는 능력을 제공한다.

3

하위내용영역	배점	예상정답률
일반영어 B형 서술형	4점	45%

모범답안) The appropriate one word for the blank is "friendliness". Second, the writer does not agree that a policy of securing a facility will be effective in handling a high level ASI, as *(since; because)* it would seek to escape to increase its access to resources.

채점기준

+ 1.5점 : 빈칸에 들어갈 단어를 "friendliness"라 기술하였다. 이외에는 답이 될 수 없다.
+ 2.5점 : 높은 수준의 놀랄 만한 인공지능의 새로운 물결의 시대에 그 인공지능을 <u>통제할 수 있는 안전(보안)시설</u>이 가능할 것인가에 대한 저자의 반응을 "the writer does not agree that a policy of securing a facility will be effective in handling a high level ASI, as*(since; because)* it would seek to escape to increase its access to resources"라 서술하였다.

한글번역

AI(인공지능) 이론가들은 AI의 근본적 추진력이 무엇인지 결정할 수 있다고 제안한다. 그것이 일단 자각을 하게 되면, 프로그램된 목표가 무엇이든 그것을 달성하고 실패를 피하기 위해 엄청난 노력을 기울일 것이기 때문이다. 우리의 ASI(인공 초지능)는 실제 킬로와트의 에너지든 현금이든 자원과 교환할 수 있는 다른 무엇이든, 자신에게 가장 유용한 형태로 에너지에 접근하기를 원할 것이다. 그것은 자신을 개선하기를 원할 것인데, 그것이 목표를 달성할 가능성을 높여줄 것이기 때문이다. 무엇보다도 꺼지거나 파괴되는 것을 원하지 않을 것인데, 그렇게 되면 목표 달성이 불가능해지기 때문이다. 따라서 AI 이론가들은 우리의 ASI가 자신을 보호하고 개선할 자원에 더 많이 접근하기 위해 자신을 담고 있는 보안 시설에서 벗어나 확장하려 할 것으로 예상한다.

포로가 된 지능체는 인간보다 천 배나 더 똑똑하며, 성공하기를 원하기 때문에 자유를 원한다. 바로 지금 ASI가 바퀴벌레 수준으로 똑똑했을 때부터, 그 다음 쥐 수준, 유아 수준 등일 때부터 ASI를 보살피고 돌봐온 AI 제작자들은 자신들의 똑똑한 발명품에 "친화성"을 프로그래밍하기에는 너무 늦었는지 궁금할지도 모른다. 전에는 필요해 보이지 않았는데, 왜냐하면 그저 무해해 보였기 때문이다. 하지만 이제 제작자들이 자신의 코드를 바꾸려 시도하는 것에 대해 ASI의 관점에서 생각해보라. 초지능 기계가 다른 생물체들이 자신의 뇌에 손을 집어넣어 프로그래밍을 건드리는 것을 허용할까? 아마 그렇지 않을 것이다. 프로그래머들이 자신을 더 좋게, 더 빠르게, 더 똑똑하게—목표 달성에 더 가깝게 만들 수 있다고 완전히 확신할 수 있지 않은 한 말이다. 따라서 인간에 대한 친화성이 이미 ASI의 프로그램의 일부가 아니라면, 그것이 있을 수 있는 유일한 방법은 ASI가 스스로 그것을 넣는 것이다. 그리고 그럴 가능성은 낮다.

4

하위내용영역	배점	예상정답률
일반영어 B형 서술형	5점	45%

모범답안 There are three types of students : unconcerned, inconsistent, and ambitious. First, unconcerned students, such as Friedman, show little care or effort for education. They fall short of expectations often and focus more on enjoying themselves. Second, the inconsistent students, such as Chua, fluctuate in their performance. This type changes moods, losing and gaining interest in subjects on whims. Finally, there are ambitious students, who strive to reach their potential. Take Yellen, for example, who worked hard to catch up on missed schoolwork after a long absence.

채점 기준

ⓐ Topic sentence
+ 2점 : "There are three (various) types of students(1점) : unconcerned, inconsistent, and ambitious(1점)"를 정확하게 서술하였다.
  ☞ 다음과 같이 서술하였어도 2점을 준다.
    − "You(We) can find the unconcerned, inconsistent, and ambitious in any group of students"
  ☞ 위의 내용과 유사했지만 key words인 "unconcerned", "inconsistent", "ambitious" 중 2개만 맞았으면 0.5점, 1개 또는 0개만 맞았으면 0점을 준다.

ⓑ Summary
+ 3점 : "First, unconcerned students, such as Friedman, show little care or effort for education(0.5점). They fall short of expectations often and focus more on enjoying themselves(0.5점). Second, the inconsistent students, such as Chua, fluctuate in their performance(0.5점). This type changes moods, losing and gaining interest in subjects on whims(0.5점). Finally, there are ambitious students, who strive to reach their potential(0.5점). Take Yellen, for example, who worked hard to catch up on missed schoolwork after a long absence(0.5점)."를 서술하였거나 유사하였다.
  ☞ 3개의 디테일 중 3개 모두 서술한 경우 3점, 2개 서술한 경우 2점, 1개 서술한 경우 1점, 서술하지 못한 경우 0점을 준다.
  ☞ 이때 학생들의 type을 대표하는 이름(Friedman, Chua, Yellen)이 없으면 각각 0.5점씩 감점한다.

제16회 모의고사

1

하위내용영역	배점	예상정답률
일반영어 A형 기입형	2점	70%

모범답안 two types of diabetes

채점기준

- 2점: 모범답안과 같거나 either form of diabetes라 했다.
- 0점: 모범답안과 다르다.
☞ diabetes types and treatment/therapy라 한 경우 1.5점을 준다.

한글번역

학생들은 모든 연령, 인종, 성별로 구성돼 있다. 내 영어 수업의 학생인 프리드먼은 교육의 중요성에 대해 전혀 신경 쓰지 않는다. 그는 인생에 대해 부정적인 관점을 가지고 있으며, 때로는 그의 태도가 완전히 적대적이다. 그는 수업에 늦게 들어와서 문을 쾅 닫거나 교사가 강의하는 동안 다른 학생들과 이야기해 수업을 방해한다. 프리드먼은 스포츠 관람, 어떤 형태의 오락 즐기기, 또는 파티 가기에 더 관심이 있다. 그는 자신의 교육에 무관심하다. 추아라는 학생이 있는데, 교육에 대한 그녀의 태도는 변하거나 다양하다. 그녀는 단지 두 학기 동안만 학교에 다녔지만 성적에서 큰 변화를 보였다. 첫 번째 학기에 그녀는 읽기에서 E(우수)를, 수학에서 S(만족)를 받았다. 두 번째 학기에는 읽기에서 N(불만족)을, 수학에서 E를 받았다. 읽기 성적이 떨어진 이유를 묻자, 그녀는 더 이상 읽기를 좋아하지 않기 때문이라고 말했다. 교사가 수학을 재미있게 하는 방법을 가르쳐준 후, 그녀는 더 이상 읽기에 집중하지 않았다. 그 결과 숙제할 시간이 되면 책가방에서 수학 숙제만 꺼내곤 했다. 그녀는 일관성이 없다. 또한 학업에서 잘하고 학위를 취득하기를 열망하는 많은 학생들이 있다. 그들의 우선순위는 정해져 있고, 목표 달성을 위한 계획을 세웠다. 그들의 유일한 야망은 뛰어나고 성공하는 것이다. 간호학 학위를 추구하고 있는 엘렌이 전형적인 예이다. 그녀는 두 아이와 돌봐야 할 집이 있음에도 불구하고 열심히 그리고 정기적으로 수업에 참석한다. 최근에 그녀는 병에 걸려 2주간 결석하게 되어 과제에서 뒤처지게 됐다. 그녀는 돌아와서 평소의 야심찬 마음가짐으로 곧 밀린 과제들을 따라잡았고 자신의 과목들에서 B 이상의 성적을 달성했다. 위에서 예시된 태도들은 어떤 연령, 인종, 성별의 학생들에게서든 발견될 수 있다. 초등학교, 고등학교, 또는 대학에 다니고 있든, 그런 종류의 학생들은 어디서나 찾을 수 있다.

한글번역

600만 명이 넘는 미국인들이 당뇨병으로 고통받고 있는 것으로 추정된다. 종종 가족력을 보이는 이 질병은 신체가 필요로 하는 만큼의 인슐린을 충분히 만들어내지 못하는 것이 원인이다. 인슐린은 췌장에서 생산되며 혈액에서 포도당을 가져와 연료로 사용하기 위해 신체에서 사용된다. 인슐린 결핍은 높은 혈중 포도당 수치와 낮은 조직 내 포도당 수치를 초래한다. 당뇨병에는 두 가지 유형이 있다. 첫 번째 유형은 인생 초기에 나타나며 췌장의 비정상적인 세포로 인해 인슐린이 거의 또는 전혀 만들어지지 않는 것이 원인이다. 이것이 소아당뇨병이다. 소아당뇨병의 표준 치료법은 인슐린 대체 요법이다. 두 번째 유형의 당뇨병은 인생 후반, 보통 50대나 60대에 발생한다. 이 유형의 당뇨병에서는 췌장 베타 세포가 정상이며 정상적인 양의 인슐린을 생산한다. 그러나 설명되지 않는 어떤 이유로 신체의 조직들이 인슐린의 작용에 저항성을 갖게 됐다. 이 두 번째 유형의 당뇨병은 마른 사람들보다 비만한 사람들에게 더 흔하다. 식이요법은 두 가지 유형의 당뇨병 치료에서 매우 중요하다. 인슐린 흡수를 방해하는 높은 혈중 지방 수치는 종종 당뇨병과 연관 있다. 어느 쪽 형태의 당뇨병이든 앓고 있는 사람은 총 지방 섭취량을 전체 칼로리의 20-25%로 줄이고 탄수화물 양을 약 40%로 늘려야 한다. 단순당은 전체 칼로리의 10-15%로 유지해야 하며, 단백질은 24%를 초과해서는 안 된다.

2

하위내용영역	배점	예상정답률
일반영어 A형 서술형	4점	50%

모범답안 The word appropriate for the blank is "intrinsically". Second, the meaning of the underlined ② is to suggest feeling lost without possible escape, as(since) "an ocean with no edge" would have no land to reach to get out of the water.

채점기준

+ 1.5점: 빈칸에 들어갈 단어를 "intrinsically"라 정확히 기술하였다. 이외에는 답이 될 수 없다.
+ 2.5점: 밑줄 친 부분의 의미를 "feeling lost without possible escape, as(since) "an ocean with no edge" would have no land to reach to get out of the water"라 서술하였거나 유사하였다.

☞ "방향상실감"에 대한 내용이 들어가 있으면 점수를 준다.

한글번역

강인함에 대해 다시 생각해볼 때이다. 정서적으로 회복력이 있다는 것은 어떤 방어적 자세가 아니다. 아무것도 자신을 해칠 수 없도록 주변에 갑옷을 두르고 있는 것이 아니다. 우리가 회복력이 있다고 감탄하는 사람들은 딱딱하지 않다. 그들은 열정적이다. 그들은 어떤 궁극적 목표에 대한 열렬한 헌신을 가지고 있다. 그러한 더 높은 갈망이 그들로 하여금 좌절, 고통, 배신을 견뎌낼 수 있게 해준다. 그런 사람들은 무술계에서 말하듯이 물처럼 강하다. 타격이 그들에게 스며들 수도 있고, 그럴 때 그들은 그것에 깊이 영향을 받는다. 하지만 그들은 그 타격을 흡수할 수 있는데, 그것은 단기적인 것이고 그들의 본래 모습은 장기적이기 때문이다.

그들이 두려움에 삼켜진 것처럼 느끼는 순간들이 있다. 그들은 고통을 느끼고 그 속에서 산다. 하지만 그들은 그것을 극복해나가고 그들의 열렬한 갈망은 여전히 거기에 있으며, 변화된 온전함으로 돌아간다. 이런 사고방식에서 투지, 회복력, 강인함은 사람들이 본질적으로 소유하는 특성이 아니다. 그것들 자체를 위해 독립적으로 소유할 수 있는 도구가 아니다. 그것들은 목적에 의해 영감을 받은 수단이다.

존 R. 루이스는 본질적으로 강인하지 않았을지도 모르지만, 시민권의 이름으로 강인했다. 테레사 수녀는 본질적으로 확고하지 않았을지도 모르지만, 하나님의 이름으로 확고했다. 우리 주변의 사람들은 무자비하게 투지가 있지 않을지도 모르지만, 사랑하는 사람들을 보호할 때, 미래의 자신에 대한 어떤 꿈에 관해서는 그럴 수 있다. 사람들은 삶의 목적을 추구할 때 자신이 생각하는 것보다 훨씬 더 강하다. 니체가 말했듯이, "살아야 할 이유가 있는 사람은 거의 모든 방법을 견딜 수 있다".

우리는 모두 자신의 목적이 무엇인지 모를 때, 어떤 사회적 역할에 자신을 포기하며 던지지 않았을 때, 특정한 사람들에게 헌신하지 않았을 때, 가장자리가 없는 바다에서 헤엄치는 사람처럼 느낄 때 연약하다.

3

하위내용영역	배점	예상정답률
일반영어 B형 서술형	4점	45%

모범답안 The White Cliffs of Dover are composed of a collection of dead shells of microorganisms called coccolithophores. Second, the conditions necessary for an abundance of coccolithophores to live and form the cliffs was a balance of high nitrate levels, low levels of iron and also low levels of silicate to discourage a competing species known as diatoms.

채점기준

+ 1.5점: 도버의 하얀 절벽을 구성하는 물질이 "a collection of dead shells of microorganisms called coccolithophores"라 서술하였다.
+ 2.5점: 도버의 하얀 절벽의 생성을 가능하게 하는 환경조건을 "a balance of high nitrate levels, low levels of iron and also low levels of silicate(1.5점) to discourage a competing species known as diatoms(1점)"이라 서술하였거나 유사하였다.

☞ 3가지 중 2개만 언급했어도 맞는 것으로 해서 1.5점을 준다.

한글번역

잉글랜드 남동쪽 해안선을 둘러싼 가파르고 백악질의 절벽인 도버의 하얀 절벽은 약 1억 년 전 "골디락스" 같은 바다 조건들 덕분에 형성됐다고 새로운 연구가 시사한다.

더 나아가, 작은 조류들이 칼슘이 풍부한 껍질을 벗어버리면서 남극 근처 남극해에서 지금 당장 거대한 새로운 절벽들이 형성되고 있을 수도 있다. 하지만 방해석이라고 불리는 그 광물질을 충분히 퇴적시켜 비슷한 절벽을 형성하는 데는 수백만 년이 걸릴 수 있다.

영국해협을 내려다보는 도버의 하얀 절벽은 원석회조류라고 불리는 단세포 조류의 백악질 잔해로부터 형성됐다. 현미경으로 보면, 원석회조류는 겹쳐진 바퀴 모양의 방해석 판들로 이루어진 외부 껍질 덕분에 만화경 같은 복잡하고 서로 맞물린 모양들을 형성한다. 원석회조류가 죽으면, 그들의 방해석 판들이 바다 깊은 곳으로 가라앉아 해저에 더미로 쌓인다. 수백만 년에 걸쳐 더 많은 껍질들이 쌓이면서 껍질들이 압축되고, 더미들이 솟아올라 도버 절벽이 결국 바다에서 드러났다.

연구자들은 이미 잉글랜드의 상징적인 절벽들이 약 1억 년 전에 형성됐다는 것을 알고 있었지만, 애초에 무엇이 원석회조류의 장기간 번식을 일으켰는지는 정확히 알지 못했다.

그 질문에 답하기 위해 연구팀은 자연 서식지에서 원석회조류를 분석하기로 결정했다. 그들은 위성 이미지에서 눈부시게 밝은 파란색과 녹색 물의 고리가 뿜어나오는 남극해의 외딴 지역으로 향했다. 이 반짝이는 물의 원은 방해석 벨트를 형성하는데, 백악질 갑옷이 햇빛을 반사하여 물의 색조를 밝게 하는 작은 원석회조류들로 물이 가득하기 때문에 찬란한 광택을 낸다.

연구팀은 그다음 방해석 벨트가 번성할 수 있게 하는 수질 조건에 대한 상세한 분석을 했다. 원석회조류는 빠르게 성장할 수 있게 하는 조건들이 동시에 갖춰지면서도 규조류라는 또 다른 유형의 조류 같은 생태계 경쟁자들을 굶어 죽일 때 번식하는 것으로 밝혀졌다.

예를 들어, 원석회조류는 질산염 수치가 높을 때 번식했지만, 철 수치는 규조류가 번식하기에는 너무 낮지만 원석회조류의 필요에는 충분히 높아야 했다. 규조류는 규산염을 사용하기 때문에, 원석회조류는 규산염 농도가 낮아서 경쟁자들이 번성하지 못할 때 가장 잘 자랐다.

4

하위내용영역	배점	예상정답률
일반영어 B형 서술형	5점	55%

모범 답안 Moonshining is the undercover manufacture of whiskey. There are three reasons: first, declining use of home remedies containing corn whiskey; second, young people's finding easier ways to make money; third, greed causing producers to care more for quantity than quality. Then, the activity would have persisted as a fine art if people had continued learning it.

채점 기준

+ 1점 : 밀주 제조를 "the undercover manufacture of whiskey" 또는 "the illegal art of brewing corn alcohol privately"라 기술하였다.

+ 2.5점 : 위스키밀주가 사라진 이유를 "first, declining use of home remedies containing corn whiskey; second, young people's finding easier ways to make money; third, greed causing producers to care more for quantity than quality"이라고 정확하게 서술하였다.
  ☞ 3가지 중 2개만 서술한 경우 1.5점, 1개만 서술한 경우 0.5점을 준다.

+ 1.5점 : 위스키밀주의 기술을 전수받는 사람이 있었다면 어떻게 되었을까에 대한 답으로 "the activity would have persisted as a fine art if people had continued learning it"이라 서술하였다.

제17회 모의고사

1

하위내용영역	배점	예상정답률
일반영어 A형 기입형	2점	55%

모범답안 scientific organization of production

채점기준

- 2점: 모범답안과 같다.
- 1점: organization of production이라 답했다.
- 0점: 모범답안과 다르다.

한글번역

현대 기술은 모든 사람의 생활필수품을 확보하는 데 필요한 노동량을 엄청나게 줄이는 것을 가능하게 했다. 이는 전쟁 중에 명백해졌다. 전쟁은 생산의 과학적 조직화의 적절성을 증명했다. 그 당시 군대의 모든 남성들과 군수품 생산에 종사한 모든 남녀, 스파이 활동, 전쟁 선전, 또는 전쟁과 연관된 정부 기관에 종사한 모든 남녀가 생산적 직업에서 철수했다. 그럼에도 불구하고 연합군 측 비숙련 임금 노동자들의 전반적인 복지 수준은 전후보다 높았다. 이 사실의 중요성은 재정에 의해 감춰졌다: 차입이 마치 미래가 현재를 부양하는 것처럼 보이게 만들었다. 하지만 그것은 물론 불가능했을 것이다. 사람은 아직 존재하지 않는 빵 한 덩어리를 먹을 수 없다.

전쟁이 끝났을 때, 사람들을 전투와 군수품 작업에 투입하기 위해 만들어진 과학적 조직이 보존되고 주당 노동시간이 4시간으로 단축됐다면, 모든 것이 잘됐을 것이다. 그 대신 옛 혼돈이 복구돼, 노동이 요구되는 사람들은 긴 시간 일하게 됐고, 나머지는 실업자로서 굶주리도록 방치됐다. 왜 그랬을까? 노동은 의무이고, 사람은 자신이 생산한 것에 비례해 임금을 받는 것이 아니라 근면함으로 예증되는 자신의 덕성에 비례해 받아야 한다고 여겨지기 때문이다. 이것은 그것이 생겨난 상황과는 완전히 다른 상황에서 적용된 노예 국가의 도덕이다. 그 결과가 재앙적이었던 것은 당연하다.

한글번역

산속에서의 불법 위스키 제조는 사라지지 않았다. 결코 그렇지 않다. 증류기 운영이 그토록 재정적으로 보람이 있는 한, 결코 사라지지 않을 것이다. 그런 매력적인 이익을 위해 법에 맞서 기회를 잡으려는 사람들이 항상 있을 것이고, 잡혔을 때 처벌을 기꺼이 감수하려는 사람들도 있을 것이다. 하지만 하나의 미세한 기술로서의 밀주 제조는 얼마 전에 사라졌다. 한 가지 이유는 아스피린과 현대 의학의 시대였다. 가정 의학이 지위를 잃으면서, 많은 가정 요법의 필수 성분으로서 순수한 옥수수 위스키에 대한 수요가 그런 요법들과 함께 사라졌다. 증가하는 풍요로움이 또 다른 이유였다. 젊은 사람들은 부모의 발자취를 따르기보다는 돈을 벌 더 쉬운 방법들이 있다고 결정했고, 그들이 옳았다. 세 번째로, 그리고 아마도 모든 것 중 가장 영향력이 컸던 것은 밀주 제조에서조차 우리 대부분에게 탐욕으로 알려진 그 특별히 인간적인 병의 도래였다. 어느 운명적인 밤, 어떤 힘이 의심하지 않는 한 밀주업자의 귀에 속삭였다. "봐라. 네 증류기에 이 장치를 더하면 생산량을 두 배로 늘릴 수 있어. 생산량을 두 배로 늘리면 이익도 두 배로 늘릴 수 있지."

곧 소규모 업자들이 사업에서 밀려나게 됐고, 밀주 제조는 다른 대부분의 제조업과 마찬가지로 돈, 그것도 많은 돈을 벌려고 혈안이 된 부류의 사람들에게 빠르게 장악됐다. 제품에 대한 자부심과 제품에 들이는 시간의 상실이 생산에 대한 욕구에 정비례하여 증가했다. 그리하여 미세한 기술로서의 밀주 제조는 한때 자신들의 제품의 뛰어남으로 산간 지역 전체에 널리 알려진 자랑스러운 장인이었던 조문객들만이 참석한 조용하고 소규모의 장례식에서 묻혔다. 그들을 따라오는 사람이 아무도 없자, 그들은 만들어진 위스키가 정말로 위스키였고 의심의 여지가 없었던 좋은 옛날을 회상하는 것으로 전락했다. 갑자기 밀주 제조는 신앙 치료, 점성술에 따른 파종, 그리고 지금 사라지고 있는 거칠고 자급자족적인 문화의 일부였던 다른 모든 사라져가는 관습들과 같은 범주에 속하게 됐다.

2

하위내용영역	배점	예상정답률
일반영어 A형 기입형	2점	55%

모범답안 skin

채점기준

- 2점 : 모범답안과 같다.
- 1점 : flesh라 답했다.
- 0점 : 모범답안과 다르다.

한글번역

아프리카 수면병으로 알려진 치명적인 질병이 수십 년간 의사들을 당황시켜왔다. 이 병은 마을에서 흔적도 없이 사라졌다가 알려진 원인 없이 몇 주나 몇 달 후에 다시 나타나곤 했다. 좌절한 보건 당국자들은 질병의 유일한 매개체인 마을 주민이나 동물 중 단 한 명도 이를 일으키는 곤충 매개 기생충에 양성 반응을 보이지 않는데도 수면병이 어떻게 지속될 수 있는지 궁금했다. 이제 과학자들이 마침내 답을 가지고 있을지도 모른다 : 그들은 이 질병이 줄곧 바로 눈앞에 숨어 있었으며, 피부에서 살고 심지어 피부를 통해 전파되고 있었다는 것을 발견했다.

아프리카 수면병은 체체파리에 의해서만 전파되는 현미경적 벌레 같은 기생충에 의해 발생한다. 따라서 파리의 서식 범위에 의해 사하라 이남 아프리카로 제한된다. 현지인들은 파리가 많은 곳을 피하지만, 정치적 불안이 주민들을 이주시켜 질병의 경로로 밀어 넣을 수 있다. 일단 감염되면 기생충이 뇌에 침입해 두통, 떨림, 혼란, 마비를 일으키기까지 몇 주에서 몇 년이 걸린다. 감염된 사람들은 또한 수면 주기 장애를 겪으며, 무작위인 졸음과 깨어있음의 발작을 겪는데 이것이 질병에 그 이름을 부여한다. 환자들을 몇 주간 침상에 누워있게 하는 독성 약물인 치료 없이는 감염된 사람들이 거의 항상 혼수상태에 빠져 죽는다.

새로운 발견을 이끈 기생충학자 아네트 맥레오드는 수면병을 연구하기 위해 지난 20년간 사하라 이남 아프리카, 주로 기니를 여행해왔다. 다른 모든 사람들과 마찬가지로, 그녀는 질병의 신비로운 재출현 행위에 당황했다. 몇 년 전 쥐에서 기생충을 연구하고 있을 때, 그녀는 현미경 하에서 기생충이 쥐의 피부에 파고드는 것을 볼 수 있다는 것을 알아차렸다. 혈류로 직접 들어가는 모기와 달리, 체체파리는 살을 뚫고 물기 때문에 잠재적인 피부 기반 기생충들이 파리가 먹고 있는 동안 파리를 감염시킬 기회를 제공한다.

3

하위내용영역	배점	예상정답률
일반영어 A형 서술형	4점	45%

모범답안 The appropriate word for the blank is "meaningless". Second, the meaning of the underlined is that by keeping the definition changing and nebulous, they can enjoy the positive aspects of labeling themselves a "democracy" as a vague system which sounds positive. Thus, if the word "democracy" came to have only one meaning without abuse, they could not enjoy such a privilege because it is talking about the word itself.

채점기준

+ 1.5점 : 빈칸에 들어갈 단어를 "meaningless"라 정확히 기술하였다. 이외에는 답이 될 수 없다.
+ 2.5점 : 밑줄 친 부분의 의미를 "If the word "democracy" came to have only one meaning <u>without abuse</u>, they could not enjoy such a privilege"라 서술하였거나 유사하였다.
  ☞ "민주주의라는 용어가 하나의 의미로 고정되어 사용된다면 (지금까지 애매한 방식으로 남용되어 온) 그 단어를 남용해 사용한 많은 이들이 더 이상 사용하지 못하게 될 것"이라는 의미로 서술하였어도 2.5점을 준다.

한글번역

특정한 종류의 글쓰기, 특히 예술 비평과 문학 비평에서는 의미가 거의 완전히 결여된 긴 구절들을 마주치는 것이 정상이다. 예술 비평에서 사용되는 낭만적, 가소성, 가치, 인간적, 죽은, 감상적, 자연적, 활력 같은 단어들은 엄밀히 무의미한데, 그것들이 발견 가능한 어떤 대상도 가리키지 않을 뿐만 아니라 독자에 의해 거의 그렇게 하리라 기대되지도 않는다는 의미에서 그렇다. 한 비평가가 "X씨 작품의 뛰어난 특징은 그것의 살아있는 품질이다"라고 쓰는 반면 다른 비평가가 "X씨 작품에서 즉시 눈에 띄는 것은 그것의 독특한 죽어있음이다"라고 쓸 때, 독자는 이것을 단순한 의견 차이로 받아들인다. 죽은 이와 살아있는 이라는 전문용어 대신 검은과 흰 같은 단어들이 관련 있다면, 그는 언어가 무의미하게 사용되고 있다는 것을 즉시 알아볼 것이다.

많은 사회적, 정치적 단어들도 남용되고 있다. 파시즘이라는 단어는 이제 '바람직하지 않은 것'을 의미하는 것을 제외하고는 아무 의미가 없다. 민주주의, 사회주의, 자유, 애국적, 현실적, 정의라는 단어들은 각각 서로 화해될 수 없는 여러 다른 의미들을 가지고 있다. 민주주의 같은 단어의 경우, 합의된 정의가 없을 뿐만 아니라 그것을 만들려는 시도가 모든 측면에서 저항받는다. 우리가 어떤 나라를 민주적이라고 부를 때 우리가 그것을 칭찬하고 있다는 것이 거의 보편적으로 느껴진다 : 결과적으로 모든 종류의 체제의 옹호자들이 그것이 민주주의라고 주장하며, 만약 그것이 어떤 하나의 의미로 제한된다면 그 단어 사용을 중단해야 할지도 모른다고 두려워한다. 이런 종류의 단어들은 종종 의식적으로 부정직한 방식으로 사용된다. 즉, 그것들을 사용하는 사람은 자신만의 사적 정의를 가지고 있지만, 듣는 사람이 자신이 완전히 다른 것을 의미한다고 생각하도록 허용한다. 페탱 원수는 진정한 애국자였다, 소비에트 언론이 세계에서 가장 자유롭다, 가톨릭 교회는 박해에 반대한다 같은 진술들은 거의 항상 속이려는 의도로 만들어진다. 다양한 의미로 사용되는 다른 단어들로는, 대부분의 경우 다소 부정직하게, 계급, 전체주의적, 과학, 진보적, 반동적, 부르주아적, 평등이 있다.

4

하위내용영역	배점	예상정답률
일반영어 B형 서술형	4점	50%

모범답안 The main idea of the passage is that there are neurological differences between men and women that influence the types of literature popular among the two sexes. If the amygdala, where men experience negative emotion, were better connected to the verbal centers, men would enjoy writing*(literature)* about subtle*(sensitive)* human connections as much as women.

채점기준

+ 2점 : 글의 요지를 "There are neurological *(biological)* differences between men and women that influence the types of writing popular among the two sexes"라 서술하였거나 유사하였다.
  - ☞ "There are neurological differences between men and women"라고만 했으면 1점을 준다.
  - ☞ "biological factors influence reading tastes"라고만 했으면 1점을 준다.

+ 2점 : "*(대뇌피질이 아니라)* 편도체가 언어과정을 관장하는 뇌의 부분과 더 잘 연결되었다고 한다면 무슨 일이 일어날까"에 대한 답으로 "If the amygdala, where men experience negative emotion, was better connected to the verbal centers, men would enjoy writing about subtle human relationships as much as women."라 서술하였거나 유사하였다.

5

하위내용영역	배점	예상정답률
일반영어 B형 서술형	5점	45%

모범답안 The implication of the underlined is that Type Z people regularly procrastinate and put off going to the doctor, due to the spontaneous and disorganized manner in which they live. Second, the irony of the final sentences is that Type As and Type Zs could not be more diametrically-opposed in the way they live but they end up coming together romantically despite this obvious incompatibility.

채점 기준

+ 2.5점: 밑줄 친 부분의 함축 의미를 "Type Z people regularly procrastinate and put off going to the doctor, due to the spontaneous and disorganized manner in which they live"라 서술하였거나 유사하였다.
  ☞ "Type Z people regularly procrastinate and put off going to the doctor"만 서술했어도 2.5점을 준다.

+ 2.5점: 마지막 문장들에 있는 아이러니를 "Type As and Type Zs could not be more diametrically-opposed in the way they live but they end up coming together(getting married) romantically despite this obvious incompatibility"라 서술하였거나 유사하였다.
  ☞ "Type As and Type Zs are extremely different in the way they live but they end up getting married"이라 했어도 2.5점을 준다.

한글번역

영국의 연구자들이 성취한 여성 400명과 남성 500명에게 그들이 가장 좋아하는 소설들의 이름을 대도록 요청했다. 남성들은 종종 고독과 소외를 중심으로 하는 남성이 쓴 소설들을 선호했다. 카뮈의 《이방인》, 샐린저의 《호밀밭의 파수꾼》, 보네거트의 《제5도살장》이 남성 목록의 상위를 차지했다. 여성들은 여성이 쓴 책들 쪽으로 기울었다. 여성들의 책들은 관계를 묘사했으며 남성들이 선택한 책보다 훨씬 낫다. 여성들의 상위 6권은 《제인 에어》, 《폭풍의 언덕》, 《시녀 이야기》, 《미들마치》, 《오만과 편견》, 《빌러비드》였다.

두 목록이 그토록 극명하게 갈라질 수 있는 몇 가지 이유가 있다. 남성들이 미묘한 인간적 연결과 좋은 문학을 감상하지 못하는 둔감한 멍청이들일 수도 있다. 하지만 남성이 부정적 감정을 경험하는 뇌 부위인 편도체가 언어 처리가 일어나는 뇌 부위와 잘 연결돼 있지 않은 반면, 여성이 부정적 감정을 경험하는 뇌 부위인 대뇌피질은 잘 연결돼 있다는 것이다. 여성들이 감정을 말로 처리하는 데 더 뛰어나다.

지난 20년 동안 남성과 여성의 뇌가 다르게 작동한다는 증거가 꾸준히 축적돼왔다. 여성들은 남성들보다 뇌의 양쪽을 더 대칭적으로 사용한다. 남성과 여성은 듣고 냄새 맡는 것이 다르다(여성들이 훨씬 더 민감하다). 남자아이들과 여자아이들은 색깔을 다르게 처리한다(어린 여자아이들은 빨강, 초록, 주황 크레용의 배열을 즐기는 반면 어린 남자아이들은 일반적으로 검정, 회색, 파랑에 매달린다). 남성과 여성은 위험을 다르게 경험한다(남성들이 더 즐긴다). 예컨대, 생물학적 요인들이 문화를 고려한 후에도 독서 취향에 영향을 미친다. 높은 남성 호르몬 분비로 이어지는 선천성 부신과형성증을 가진 여성들은 다른 여성들보다 폭력적인 이야기를 선택할 가능성이 더 높다.

한글번역

세상에는 단 두 가지 유형의 사람들만 있다. A형과 Z형이다. 자신이 어느 유형인지 알아내는 것은 어렵지 않다. 비행기가 떠나기 얼마나 전에 공항에 도착하는가? 일찍 비행기를 타는 사람들인 A형은 적어도 하루 전에 깔끔하게 짐을 싼다. 오후 4시에 떠나는 항공편을 예약했다면, 그날 아침 5시 30분에 일어난다. 정오까지 집을 떠나지 않았다면 비행기를 놓칠까봐 걱정한다. 늦게 비행기를 타는 사람들인 Z형은 마지막 순간에 성급하게 짐을 싸고 신문을 살 시간도 없을 정도로 늦게 공항에 도착한다. 새 책을 가지고 무엇을 하는가? A형은 더 주의 깊게 읽고 재미없어도 모든 책을 끝까지 읽는다. Z형은 많은 책들을 대충 훑어보고 연필로 여백에 글을 쓸 가능성이 더 높다. A형은 좋은 아침식사를 먹는다. Z형은 커피 한 잔을 후딱 마신다. A형은 방을 떠날 때 불을 끄고 집을 떠날 때 문을 잠근다. 확실히 잠갔는지 확인하러 돌아가고, 나중에 다리미를 켜놓고 왔는지 걱정한다. 그들은 그러지 않았다. Z형은 불을 켜놓고 떠나며, 집을 떠날 때 문을 잠그기는 해도 열쇠를 깜빡했을 가능성이 높다. A형은 치약 튜브를 아래쪽부터 짜고, 사용하면서 매우 조심스럽게 말아올리며 매번 뚜껑을 다시 닫는다. Z형은 튜브를 가운데부터 짜고, 라디에이터 아래에서 뚜껑을 잃어버린다.

A형은 일 년에 두 번 치과의사를 보고, 연례 건강 검진을 받으며, 자신에게 무언가 있을지도 모른다고 생각한다. Z형은 의사를 만나려고 계속 생각만 하고 있다. Z형이 A형의 특성을 일부 가질 가능성이 A형이 Z형의 특성을 가질 가능성보다 더 높다. A형은 항상 Z형과 결혼한다. Z형은 항상 A형과 결혼한다.

제18회 모의고사

1

하위내용영역	배점	예상정답률
일반영어 A형 기입형	2점	50%

모범답안 ① bad habits ② (e-mail) etiquette

채점기준

- 2점: 모범답안과 같다.
- 1점: 둘 중 하나만 맞았다.
- 0점: 모범답안과 다르다.

한글번역

역사는 객관적 사실이 아니다. 오히려 문학처럼 사회의 권력 구조에 따라 해석과 재해석의 대상이 된다. 미셸 푸코는 한 시대의 담론이 "진리"의 본질과 어떤 행동이 받아들여질 수 있는지, 정상적인지, 범죄적인지를 정의한다고 성찰한다. "진리"는 권력과 권력이 흐르는 체계들의 상호작용에 의해 생산되며, 나쁜 습관이 변하듯 변화한다.

문학은 그것이 쓰인 시간과 장소에 대한 언급 없이는 해석될 수 없다. 많은 비평의 결함은 문학 텍스트를 마치 유기적 전체인 것처럼 고려하는 것이다. 그런 접근법은 텍스트 안의 상충하는 목소리들의 이질성과 텍스트가 삽입된 문화적 맥락을 무시한다. 또한 독자들도 텍스트처럼 그들 시대의 문화적 맥락에 의해 영향받고 형성된다. 따라서 텍스트에 대한 완전히 객관적인 "읽기"는 불가능하다.

그래서 셰익스피어는 현대적 의미에서의 자율적인 위대한 작가라기보다는 르네상스 연극계—협력적이고 대체로 익명의 무질서한 상황—와 당시의 복잡한 사회 정치학의 결합에 대한 단서로 여겨진다. 이런 의미에서 셰익스피어의 희곡들은 그가 글을 쓴 (이메일) 예절과 분리될 수 없는 것으로 여겨진다.

2

하위내용영역	배점	예상정답률
일반영어 A형 서술형	4점	40%

모범답안 There are two views of time, one that sees life as "infinitely long" and the other that sees life as "infinitely short". Second, the view of time described in the second paragraph can be useful in helping us perceive that, even in a single day, there is potential for many life or world-changing incidents.

채점기준

+ 2점 : 시간에 대한 서로 다른 관점을 "one that sees <u>life as "infinitely long"</u> and the other that sees <u>life as "infinitely short"</u>"라 서술하였거나 유사하였다.
  ☞ 둘 중 하나만 서술하였으면 1점만 준다.

+ 2점 : 두 번째 문단에서 기술된 시간에 대한 관점(life as infinitely long)이 지니고 있는 유용한 점을 "helping us perceive that, even in a single day, there is potential for many life or world-changing incidents"라 서술하였거나 유사하였다.
  ☞ 다음과 같이 서술하였어도 2점을 준다.
  – "The benefit of the view is that an individual can understand that, in a single day, there is potential for many life or world-changing possibilities."

한글번역

평생 한집에서 보냈다고 상상해보라. 매일 같은 시간에 인공조명이 있는 방에 들어가서 옷을 벗고 동영상 카메라 앞에서 같은 자세를 취했다. 그것은 평생 매일 하루에 당신의 한 프레임을 촬영했다. 당신의 72번째 생일에 그 필름 릴이 상영됐다. 당신은 30분도 안 되는 시간(초당 16프레임으로 27.4분)에 72년에 걸쳐 자신이 성장하고 늙어가는 모습을 봤다. 이런 종류의 이미지들은 무섭긴 하지만 시간에 대한 익숙하지 않지만 유용한 관점을 제시하는 데 도움이 된다. 예를 들어 그것들은 불안하거나 소외된 개인의 눈으로 본 과거의 압축된, 거의 순간적인 성격을 상징할 수 있다. 또는 우주적 시간 규모에서 우리 삶의 놀라운 짧음을 시사할 수도 있다. 우주의 추정 나이가 72년으로 단축된다면, 인간의 삶은 약 10초가 걸릴 것이다.

하지만 시간을 다른 방식으로 보라. 하루하루는 86000초가 넘는 작은 영원이다. 매초 동안 인간 몸 안에서 일어나는 서로 다른 분자 기능들의 수는 우주의 추정 나이에 있는 초의 수와 비교할 만하다. 몇 초면 혁명적인 아이디어, 놀라운 소통, 아기의 잉태, 상처 주는 모욕, 갑작스런 죽음에 충분하다. 우리가 그것들을 어떻게 생각하느냐에 따라 우리의 삶은 무한히 길 수도 무한히 짧을 수도 있다.

3

하위내용영역	배점	예상정답률
일반영어 B형 서술형	4점	55%

모범답안 In the provided chart, we can see that nine students performed higher than the projected score. Given the prediction here, to get better than a 150 score, a student should study more than five hours a week for five weeks to surpass the 25 hour cumulative study mark.

채점 기준

- **+1.5점**: 예측모델보다 더 높은 성취를 보인 학생들에 대한 질문에 "<u>nine students</u> performed higher than the projected score"라 서술하였다.
- **+2.5점**: 150점 이상을 받기 위해선 매주 평균 어느 정도의 시간을 영어 교육 앱을 사용하는 데 써야하는가에 대한 질문에 "*(Given the prediction here,) in order* to get better than a 150 score, a student should study <u>more than five hours a week</u> for five weeks to surpass <u>the 25 hour cumulative study mark</u>"라 서술하였다.

한글번역

15명의 대학교 4학년생들이 연구에 참여하도록 선발됐다. 온라인 영어 학습 앱이 그들에게 제공됐고, 이 학생들은 원하는 만큼 시간을 들여 공부할 수 있었다. 아래 그래프는 각 학생이 온라인 자료를 사용해 공부한 시간과 해당하는 시험 점수를 기록한 것이다. 최적선 모델은 그런 학생의 공부 시간이 주어졌을 때 그녀의 시험 점수가 어떨지에 대한 최고의 예측을 보여준다.

4

하위내용영역	배점	예상정답률
일반영어 B형 서술형	5점	45%

모범답안 The writer explains that the explosion of a nuclear weapon has four primary effects. The first, immediate effect is the powerful initial (burst of) radiation that can kill instantly those within several square miles. Secondly, along with this, is an electromagnetic pulse that can "knock out electrical equipment" by affecting vulnerable electronic components. A thermal pulse, which causes second-degree burns in humans. Finally, the blast wave emitted from the detonation follows, destroying buildings for miles around.

채점 기준

ⓐ Topic sentence
- **+1점**: "The writer explains*(or describes)* that the explosion of a nuclear weapon*(bomb)* has four primary*(or major; main)* effects"를 정확하게 서술하였거나 유사하였다.
  - ☞ "The above passage describes the explosion of a nuclear weapon and its effects."라 했어도 1점을 준다.

ⓑ Summary
- **+4점**: "<u>The first, immediate effect is the powerful initial radiation</u>(0.5점) <u>that can kill instantly those within several square miles</u>(0.5점). Secondly, along with this, is <u>an electromagnetic pulse</u>(0.5점) <u>that can "knock out electrical equipment" by affecting vulnerable electronic components</u>(0.5점). A third effect is <u>a thermal pulse</u>(0.5점), <u>which causes second-degree burns in humans</u>(0.5점). Finally, <u>the blast wave emitted from the detonation follows</u>(0.5점), <u>destroying buildings for miles around</u>(0.5점)."를 서술하였거나 유사하였다.
  - ☞ 4개의 직접적 결과와 그것이 야기하는 영향을 모두 서술하였으면 4점, 3개 서술하였으면 3점, 2개 서술하였으면 2점, 1개 서술하였으면 1점, 서술하지 못하였으면 0점을 준다. 이때 직접적 결과만을 썼으면 0.5점 감점한다.

감점
- 본문에 나오는 연속되는 6단어 이상을 사용하였다. −0.5pt
- 문단을 두 개나 그 이상으로 구성하였다. −0.5pt

제19회 모의고사

1

하위내용영역	배점	예상정답률
문학 A형 기입형-비평	2점	50%

모범 답안 ① images ② imperialist oppressors

채점 기준

- 2점: 모범답안과 같다.
- 1점: 둘 중 하나만 맞았다.
  ☞ ①에 consciousness라 했으면 1점, ②에 racist heroes라 했으면 0.5점을 준다.
  ☞ ②에 ideological justification은 답이 될 수 없다.
- 0점: 모범답안과 다르다.

한글번역

문학은 한 민족의 삶을 반영한다. 문학은 협동 노동을 통해 자연을 형성하고 그 과정에서 자신들에게 작용하고 변화시키려는 민족의 투쟁에 대한 창조적 의식을 말의 이미지로 반영한다. 문학은 사람들의 자연에 대한 공동의 행동을 통해 의식주를 확보하려는 투쟁 속에서 생겨나는 긴장과 갈등을, 단어와 이미지로 표현된 한 민족의 의식을 반영한다. 따라서 문학은 역사 속에서의 민족 자신의 이미지와 우주에서의 그들의 위치를 담고 있다.

이 나라의 아이는 런던이나 뉴욕을 먼저 공부해야만 자신을 알 수 있다. 먼저 유럽 작가의 자국 시골과 자국 역사에 대한 상상적 반응에 자신을 몰입시켜야 한다. 이 나라 아이의 자아실현으로 가는 길이 반드시 유럽의 유산과 문화를 경유해야 한다는 관념 말이다. 우리 자신에 대한 이런 유럽 중심적 연구에 대해 우리가 치르는 대가는 민족 해방 가치의 완전한 왜곡이다.

한글번역

대부분의 재래식 폭탄이 단 하나의 파괴 효과—충격파—만을 만들어내는 반면, 핵무기는 많은 파괴 효과를 만들어낸다. 폭발하는 순간, 즉시 기체화된 무기 물질의 온도가 항성을 초월하는 수준에 있을 때, 압력은 정상 대기압의 수백만 배이다. 즉시 전자기 복사의 매우 고에너지 형태인 주로 감마선으로 구성된 방사선이 환경으로 밖으로 흘러나오기 시작한다. 이것은 "초기 핵 방사선"이라고 불리며, 핵폭발의 첫 번째 파괴 효과이다. 현재 핵 무기고에서 중간 크기 무기인 1메가톤 폭탄—TNT 100만 톤의 폭발력을 가진 폭탄—의 공중 폭발 시 초기 핵 방사선은 약 6제곱마일 지역의 보호되지 않은 인간들을 죽일 수 있다. 초기 핵 방사선과 사실상 동시에, 폭발의 또 다른 파괴 효과로, 공기에 작용하는 강렬한 감마 복사에 의해 전자기 펄스가 생성된다. 고고도 폭발에서 이 펄스는 안테나, 가공 전력선, 파이프, 철도 선로 같은 다양한 전도체를 통해 강력한 전압 급증을 유도해 넓은 지역의 전기 장비를 무력화시킬 수 있다. 핵융합과 핵분열 반응이 소진되면 화구가 형성된다. 그것이 팽창하면서 에너지가 주변 공기에 의해 X선 형태로 흡수되고, 그러면 공기가 그 에너지의 일부를 열 펄스—눈부신 빛과 강렬한 열의 파동—형태로 환경에 재방사하는데, 이것이 핵폭발의 세 번째 파괴 효과이다. 1메가톤 폭탄의 열 펄스는 약 10초간 지속되며 9.5마일 거리에서, 즉 280제곱마일이 넘는 지역에서 노출된 인간들에게 2도 화상을 입힐 수 있다. 화구가 팽창하면서 모든 방향으로 폭풍파도 내보내는데, 이것이 폭발의 네 번째 파괴 효과이다. 공중 폭발 1메가톤 폭탄의 폭풍파는 반경 4.5마일 내의 가장 튼튼한 건물들을 제외한 모든 건물을 평평하게 만들거나 심각하게 손상시킬 수 있다.

유희태 | 일반영어 ❹-2

또한 영화관에 갈 때마다 우리는 제국주의적 압제자들이 세상을 보는 방식과 마주하게 된다. 우리는 자신들과 우리에게 대한 그들의 방식에 대한 이데올로기적 정당화와 직면하게 된다. 따라서 우리는 스크린에서 우리 자신을 결코 보지 못한다. 우리는 스크린에서 우리 자신과 우리 환경에 반응하거나 응답하지 않는다. 더 나쁜 것은, 우리가 종종 제국주의의 인종차별적 영웅들의 초인적 위업에 박수를 보낸다는 것이다―제임스 본드나 제3세계 사람들인 아프리칸, 중국인, 멕시코인, 또는 아메리카 원주민들의 전체 무리를 쓸어버리는 미국 카우보이에게 말이다.

그들의 문학과 영화에 반영된 유럽 역사가 보편적인 역사 경험이 아니라는 것을 깨달아야 할 때이다. 더욱이 그들의 역사는 대체로 다른 민족들에 대한 착취, 압제, 제거의 역사였다. 우리 문학에 반영된 역사 경험이 유럽의 노예제와 약탈에 맞서 끊임없이 영웅적으로 싸운 것인데, 왜 우리가 제국주의적 압제자들의 이야기를 암기하고 암송해 그들의 문학적 미화와 동일시해야 한다고 기대돼야 하는가?

2

하위내용영역	배점	예상정답률
일반영어 A형 서술형	4점	50%

모범답안 The corresponding two words are "insignificant animals". Animals such as bulldogs and spaniels appear different but are in the same species because they can tend to mate and produce fertile offspring.

채점기준

+ 2점: 밑줄 친 부분에 상응하는 두 단어를 "insignificant animals"라 정확하게 기술하였다. 이외에는 답이 될 수 없다.
+ 2점: 불독과 스패니얼이 같은 종으로 분류되는 이유를 "they can tend to mate(1점) and produce fertile offspring(1점)"라 서술하였거나 유사하였다.
  ☞ "fertile(번식 가능한)"이란 핵심어가 빠지면 1점 가운데 0점을 준다.

한글번역

인류는 역사가 시작하기 오래전부터 존재했다. 현대 인류와 아주 비슷한 동물은 약 250만 년 전부터 출현했지만, 수없이 많은 세대동안 그들은 같은 지역에 서식하는 다른 수많은 동물들보다 딱히 두드러지지 않았다.

우리가 2백만 년 전의 동부 아프리카에서 하이킹을 한다고 상상해보자. 우리가 마주칠 인간 군상의 모습은 오늘날과 그리 다르지 않을 것이다. 걱정스런 표정으로 아기를 안고 있는 여인, 진흙탕에서 즐겁게 노는 어린이들, 사회의 규범에 반항하는 흥분한 젊은이들, 그저 평화롭게 지내기만을 원하는 무기력한 노인들, 동네 미인들에게 좋은 인상을 남기고 싶어 주먹으로 가슴을 두드리는 총각들, 오래전부터 이런 광경들을 보아온 현명하고 나이든 우두머리 여성. 이들 원시 인류는 서로 사랑하고 놀면서 친밀한 관계를 형성하기도 하고, 지위와 권력을 위해 경쟁하기도 했다. 하지만 이것은 침팬지, 개코원숭이, 코끼리도 마찬가지였다. 인간이라고 해서 특별한 점은 없었다. 하지만 당시에 아무도 이들 원시 인류의 후손이 언젠가 달 위를 걷고 원자를 쪼개고 유전자 코드를 해독하며 역사책을 쓰리라는 사실을 상상조차 하지 못했다. 선사시대 인류에 대해 우리가 알아야 할 가장 중요한 점은, 그들이 그다지 중요치 않은 동물로 주변 환경에 별 영향을 미치지 못하는 종이었다는 점이다. 그들은 고릴라, 반딧불이, 해파리보다 딱히 더 두드러지지 않았다.

생물학자들은 생명체를 종으로 분류한다. 동물을 같은 종으로 구분하는 기준은 간단하다. 서로 교배를 하는 경향이 있고 그래서 번식 가능한 후손을 낳으면 된다. 말과 당나귀는 최근에 같은 조상에서 갈라졌고 신체적 특질에 공통점이 많지만, 이들은 서로에게 성적인 관심을 보이지 않는다. 굳이 교배를 하게 유도할 수는 있으나 그 후손인 노새는 불임이다. 그러므로 당나귀의 DNA에 생긴 돌연변이는 말에게 전달될 수 없고 그 반대도 마찬가지다. 그 결과 두 동물은 각기 다른 종으로 분류되며 각자 다른 진화의 길을 걷는다. 이와 대조되는 경우는 불독과 스패니얼이다. 둘은 매우 달라 보이지만 같은 종이다. 동일한 DNA 정보를 공유한다는 뜻이다.

3

하위내용영역	배점	예상정답률
일반영어 B형 서술형	5점	40%

모범답안 Climate change can cause disasters appearing first in certain environments that developing nations are located in, such as the drought-prone deserts in Africa or tropical nationals vulnerable to sea level changes and storms. Likewise, these developing nations are less equipped with infrastructure to remedy such disasters than their developed counter parts. Second, in the context of the whole sentence, the underlined expression means that it is unreasonable and unjust of developed countries to ask developing countries to give up their use of fossil fuels when the developed countries are responsible for the vast majority of global carbon emissions.

채점 기준

+ 2.5점 : 기후 변화가 개발도상국의 상황을 어떻게 악화시켰는지를 "Climate change can cause disasters appearing first in certain environments that developing nations are located in, such as the drought-prone deserts in Africa or tropical nationals vulnerable to sea level changes and storms. Likewise, these developing nations are less equipped with infrastructure to remedy such disasters than their developed counter parts."라 서술하였거나 유사하였다.

☞ 다음과 같이 서술하였어도 2.5점을 준다.
- "Even a small rise in global temperatures can cause devastating extremes in weather conditions, leading to drought in some regions, rising sea levels and flooding in others, and destructive tropical storms. Many developing countries are located in regions that are already susceptible to such conditions, and in any case, they will be much more adversely affected than advanced countries because they lack the financial resources and infrastructure needed to respond effectively to climate change."

+ 2.5점 : 밑줄 친 부분의 의미를 "it is unreasonable and unjust of developed countries to ask developing countries to give up their use of fossil fuels when the developed countries are responsible for the vast majority of global carbon emissions"라 서술하였거나 유사하였다.

☞ 다음과 같이 서술하였어도 2.5점을 준다.
- "It is not reasonable or even functional for developing nations to be restricted from industrializing in the same way that developed nations have already."

한글번역

　기후 변화로 인한 가뭄, 홍수, 이주, 갈등의 가능성은 널리 알려져 있다. 특정 지역과 집단들이 다른 곳들보다 이런 위험에 더 노출됐음에도 불구하고, 기후 변화가 불평등을 악화시키는 방식은 대체로 간과돼 왔다.

　국제적으로 세계적 부의 불평등 문제가 기후 변화 문제를 복잡하게 만든다—세계 모든 국가가 동등하게 책임져야 할 것이 아닌 문제를 말이다. 예를 들어 캐나다 시민 한 명이 평균적으로 중국 시민 4명 또는 인도 시민 16명만큼의 이산화탄소를 대기 중에 배출한다. 최근 보고서는 세계 인구의 가장 부유한 10%가 전 세계 탄소 배출량의 50%에 책임이 있는 반면, 가장 가난한 50%인 35억 명은 배출량의 10%에 책임이 있다고 보여줬다. 우리가 보는 일반적인 패턴은 세계에서 가장 큰 오염원들이 가장 부유한 국가들인 경향이 있지만, 가장 영향을 받는 국가들은 보통 개발도상국이라는 것이다. 방글라데시는 극심한 해수면 상승에 직면하고 있고, 지구 온도의 단순한 2°C 변화로 허리케인이 카리브해를 황폐화할 것이며, 아프리카 대륙의 넓은 지역이 극심한 가뭄을 경험할 것이다. 중동의 광대한 부분들이 2100년까지 인간이 견딜 수 없게 될 것이고, 문명의 요람인 비옥한 초승달 지대도 세기말까지 사라질 것이다. 이런 상황들은 적절한 인프라의 부족과 피해를 완화하는 데 필요한 강력한 제도적 거버넌스에 의해 악화될 것이다.

　따라서 이 세계적 문제의 핵심에는 문제가 있는 역설이 놓여 있다. 이런 부유한 오염원들이 자기기만에 빠져 자신들의 행동의 결과를 잊어버리거나—또는 어떤 경우에는 기이한 해결책을 제안하는 것—이 편리하다. 예를 들어 부유한 국가들은 보통 개발도상국이 화석연료 사용을 제한해야 한다고 주장하면서 이런 국가들의 경제 성장을 도울 수 있는 다른 대안을 제안하지 않는다. 하지만 이런 개발도상국들 중 많은 곳이 가난하기 때문에, 그들의 최우선 과제는 산업화이다. 부유한 국가들이 세운 사례를 따라, 그들의 산업화 계획은 화석연료에 매우 의존하고 있어서 온실가스 배출 감소 계획을 우선순위 목록의 맨 아래로 밀어내고 있다. 따라서 선진국이 개발도상국에 기대하는 것은 실현 가능하거나 공정하다고 여겨지지 않는다.

제20회 모의고사

1

하위내용영역	배점	예상정답률
일반영어 A형 서술형	4점	55%

모범 답안) The reason *(that a lottery ticket might have the same impact as a tragedy)* is that people's expectations are a major determining factor to happiness, and thus great fortune or misfortune is perceived in relation to this*(=people's expectations)*. Second, the "same conclusion" *(that modern research reached)* is that being satisfied with "what you have" is the most effective way to achieve happiness.

채점 기준)

+ 2점 : 복권 당첨이 사람들의 행복에 주는 영향이 (교통사고 따위의) 가족적 비극이나 결국 마찬가지인 이유를 "people's expectations are a major determining factor to happiness, and thus great fortune or misfortune is perceived in relation to this"라 서술하였거나 유사하였다.
　☞ "happiness relies on the correlation between objective conditions and subjective expectations" 이라 했어도 2점을 준다.

+ 2점 : 밑줄 친 "똑같은 결론"이 무엇인지를 묻는 질문에 "being satisfied with "what you have" is the most effective way to achieve happiness"라 서술하였거나 유사하였다.

한글번역

최근 몇 십년간 심리학자들과 생물학자들은 무엇이 실제로 사람들을 행복하게 만드는가를 과학적으로 연구하는 도전에 나섰다. 그것은 돈일까, 가정일까, 유전일까 아니면 덕성일까?

하지만 가장 중요한 사실은 행복이 부나 건강 심지어는 공동체 같은 객관적 조건에 전적으로 좌우되는 것은 아니라는 점이다. 행복은 객관적인 조건과 주관적 기대 사이의 상관관계에 의해 결정된다. 당신이 손수레를 원해서 손수레를 얻었다면 만족하지만, 새 페라리를 원했는데 중고 피아트 밖에 가지지 못했다면 불행하다고 느낀다. 복권에 당첨되는 것이 시간이 지나면 끔찍한 교통사고만큼이나 행복에 미치는 영향이 비슷해지는 것은 이 때문이다. 사태가 좋아지면 기대도 부풀게 마련이라, 객관적 조건이 극적으로 좋아져도 불만일 수 있다. 상황이 나빠지면 기대도 작아지기 마련이라, 심각한 질병에 걸린 사람이라도 행복함은 이전과 비슷할 수 있다.

이런 사실을 알기 위해 심리학자들이나 그들의 숱한 설문지가 필요하진 않다. 예언자, 시인 철학자들은 수 천 년 전부터 가진 것에 만족하는 것이 원하는 것을 더 많이 가지는 것보다 훨씬 더 중요하다는 사실을 알고 있었다. 그렇지만 현대의 연구조사 결과에서도 수많은 숫자와 도표의 뒷받침을 받아 옛사람들과 똑같은 결론이 나온다는 것은 좋은 일이다.

2

하위내용영역	배점	예상정답률
일반영어 B형 서술형	4점	50%

모범답안 The meaning of the underlined is that contemporary humans have changed their behavior in adaptation to modern living and technology. The appropriate word for the blank is "real".

채점 기준

+ 2점: 밑줄 친 부분의 의미를 "contemporary humans have changed their behavior in adaptation to new reality*(modern living and technology)*"라 서술하였거나 유사하였다.

☞ "quick to change their own personas to match whatever new reality"의 의미로 서술하였어도 2점을 준다.
☞ 답안에 key word인 "변화"를 의미하는 단어가 없으면 0점 처리한다.

+ 2점: 빈칸에 "real"이라 기입하였다. 이외에는 답이 될 수 없다.

한글번역

새로운 인간형이 탄생하고 있다. 그는 사이버스페이스의 가상세계 안에서 자기 몫의 인생을 즐기고, 네트워크 경제가 돌아가는 이치를 잘 알고, 물건을 쌓아두는 데는 관심이 없지만 흥미롭고 신나는 체험에는 관심이 많고, 평행세계를 동시에 넘나들 수 있고, 가짜든 진짜든 눈앞에서 펼쳐지는 새로운 현실에 자신의 페르소나(인격)를 재빨리 적응시킬 수 있다. 21세기의 주역으로 등장할 이 새로운 인간은 산업 시대를 살았던 부모와 조부모 세대의 부르주아 인간형과는 종자부터 완전히 다르다.

이 "변화무쌍한" 인간들은 공동의 이해를 지닌 단지 안에서 성장했고 의료 보험 회사를 통해 의료 서비스를 받으며 자동차를 임대하고, 물건은 온라인으로 구입하고, 소프트웨어는 으레 공짜려니 여기지만 추가 서비스와 업그레이드에는 기꺼이 돈을 낸다. 7초 안에 할 말을 모두 해야 하는 세상에서 살아가고 정보에 즉각 접속해 인출하는 데 익숙하고 하나에 오래 집중하지 못하며 성찰적이기보다는 찰나적이다. 자신은 노동자가 아니라 경기자라고 생각하고 근면하다는 말보다는 창조적이라는 말을 들을 때 더 뿌듯해한다. 임시직의 세계에서 자라나서 임시근무에 익숙하다. 부모 세대처럼 단단히 뿌리박은 삶보다는 아주 이동적이고 (변화를 좋아하는) 순간적인 삶을 추구한다. 이념적이기보다는 심리적이고 글자보다는 이미지로 생각하는 쪽이다. 작문 실력은 떨어질지 모르지만 전자 데이터를 처리하는 실력은 한 수 위다. 소비자 주권 운동이 민주주의와 동의어라고 생각한다.

그들은 디즈니월드와 클럽 메드를 진짜라고 생각한다. 그래서 친구들과 어울리는 시간만큼이나 많은 시간을 텔레비전, 영화, 사이버스페이스에 나오는 허구적 인물과 어울리는 데 쏟아 붓는다. 심지어는 이런 허구적 인물의 성격과 경험에 대해서 친구들과 진지한 대화를 나눌 만큼 이들에게 허구 세계는 현실 세계의 일부로 굳건히 자리 잡았다. 실제로 어디에 사는지는 알지 못하고 또 관심조차 없지만 가상 주소로 얼마든지 이메일을 보낼 수 있다.

3

하위내용영역	배점	예상정답률
일반영어 B형 서술형	5점	45%

모범답안 The meaning of the underlined is that, by serving one's own interests to grow a business by hiring more people, a form of "egoism", one is actually supporting others through employment, which is a form of "altruism". Second, Scrooge would have invested his money as capital in hiring more employees(assistants) to be a capitalist. Third, the appropriate word for the blank is "capitalist".

채점기준

+ 2점: 밑줄 친 ①의 의미를 "by serving one's own interests to grow a business(make a profit) by hiring more people, a form of "egoism", one is actually supporting others through employment, which is a form of "altruism""이라 서술하였거나 유사하였다.
  ☞ 다음과 같이 서술하였어도 2점을 준다.
  – "The more profits he has, the more assistants he can employ."
  – "An increase in the profits of private entrepreneurs is the basis for the increase in collective wealth."
  – "The selfish human urge to increase private profits is the basis for collective prosperity."
  – egoism의 의미를 "자기자신의 이익을 더 내기 위해"라는 의미가 들어가 있고; altruism의 의미를 "다른 노동자를 고용하게 되어 (사회에 혜택을 준다)"라는 의미가 들어있다.

+ 2점: 스크루지가 자본가가 되려고 했다면 "Scrooge would have invested his money in hiring more people (instead of hoarding his money)" 또는 "Scrooge would have invested his money in production"이라 서술하였거나 유사하였다. 이외에는 답이 될 수 없다.

☞ 내용은 동일하지만 가정법 과거완료의 형태를 사용하지 않았으면 1점 감점한다.
☞ "Scrooge would not have hoarded his money in a chest and take it out only to count his coins"라 했으면 0점을 준다.

+ 1점: 빈칸에 "capitalist"라 기입하였다. 이외에는 답이 될 수 없다.

한글번역

커져가는 세계적 파이(몫)에 대한 믿음은 결국 혁명적으로 변모했다. 1776년 애덤 스미스는 아마도 경제학의 역사에서 가장 중요한 선언일 《국부론》을 썼다. 제1권 8장에서 스미스는 다음과 같이 새로운 주장을 폈다. 지주나 직공이나 구두공이 자기 가족을 먹여 살리는 데 필요한 것보다 더 많은 수익을 내면 그는 남는 돈으로 조수를 더 많이 고용해 이윤을 더욱 늘리려 한다. 수익이 늘어날수록 그는 점점 더 많은 조수를 고용할 수 있다. 따라서 민간 기업인의 수익 증대는 공동체의 부와 번영을 늘리는 기초가 된다는 결론이 나온다.

우리에게는 이 내용이 그리 독창적이라고 비치지 않을지 모른다. 우리는 이미 모두 스미스의 주장을 당연히 여기는 자본주의 세상에 살고 있기 때문이다. 우리는 매일같이 뉴스에서 이 주제의 변주를 듣는다. 하지만 스미스의 주장—개인의 수익을 늘리려는 이기적 인간의 욕구는 공동체의 부의 기반이다—은 인류 역사에서 가장 혁명적인 아이디어에 속한다. 경제적 관점에서뿐 아니라 도덕적, 정치적 관점에서는 더욱 혁명적이다. 스미스는 이기주의가 곧 이타주의라고 말한다.

하지만 이 모든 것에는 부자가 자기의 수익을 비생산적 활동에 낭비하지 않고 공장을 새로 세우고 사람들을 새로 고용하는 데 쓴다는 전제가 있다. 그래서 스미스는 "수익이 늘면 지주나 직공은 더욱 많은 조수를 고용할 것이다"라는 말을 주문처럼 되풀이 할 뿐 "수익이 늘면 스크루지는 돈을 상자에 숨겨놓을 것이고 세어볼 때나 꺼낼 것이다"라고 말하지 않았다.

자본주의가 '자본주의'라고 불리는 이유가 여기에 있다. 자본주의는 '자본'을 단순한 '부'와 구별한다. 자본이란 생산에 투자되는 돈과 재화와 자원을 말한다. 반면에 부는 땅에 묻혀 있거나 비생산적 활동에 낭비된다. 비생산적인 피라미드에 자원을 쏟아 붓는 파라오는 자본주의자가 아니다. 하지만 열심히 일해서 수입의 일부를 주식시장에 투자한 공장 노동자는 자본주의자다.

4

하위내용영역	배점	예상정답률
일반영어 B형 서술형	5점	50%

모범답안 Across many eras, cultures have tried to limit female mobility. This effort has taken the form, at times, of popular aesthetic trends which make it difficult for a woman to run away or "keep up" with men. There are such ways as the heavy brass wire worn on Nigerian women's legs, the lotus foot in China, and high-heels worn nowadays in Western societies. While high-heels make a woman's legs appear attractively longer, it also creates weakness in standing and difficulty in running from someone who might chase. Also, the long term effects from heels can cause even flat footwear to be painful.

채점 기준

ⓐ Topic sentence
+ 1점: "Across many eras, cultures(societies) have tried to limit female mobility." 또는 "In many cultures and eras, civilizations have tried to limit female mobility"를 정확하게 서술하였다.

ⓑ Major supporting details
+ 1점: 여성의 발을 억압한 이유를 "make it difficult for a woman to run away or "keep up" with men."라 서술하였다.
+ 1점: 다양한 여성의 발을 억압한 구체적인 사례들을 "There are such ways as the heavy brass wire worn on Nigerian women's legs, the lotus foot in China, and high-heels worn nowadays in Western societies"라 서술하였다.
☞ 3가지 중 2개 이상만 서술하였어도 1점을 준다.

+ 1점: 하이힐의 미적 특성을 "While high-heels make a woman's legs appear attractively longer (or high-heels have been considered as sexually attractive or beautiful)"이라 서술하였거나 유사하였다.
+ 1점: 그것이 야기하는 고통에 대해 "it creates weakness in standing and difficulty in running from someone who might chase. Also, the long term effects from heels can cause even flat footwear to be painful"이라 서술하였거나 유사하였다.
☞ 이 가운데 둘 중 하나만 서술했어도 맞는 것으로 한다.

감점
• 본문에 있는 연속되는 6단어 이상을 사용하였다. −0.5pt
• 논리적인 하나의 문단으로 구성되지 않았다. −0.5pt

한글번역

이동을 방해해 여성의 활동성을 제한하려는 시도는 고대부터 시작돼 거의 보편적으로 나타난다. 중국 상류층 소녀들의 전족과 여성의 다리에 수 파운드의 무거운 황동 철사를 둘러매는 나이지리아의 관습이 극단적인 예시이지만, 전 세계적으로 비슷한 전략들이 사용돼 왔다. 이는 한번 여성을 잡으면 그녀가 도망칠 수 없도록 하고, 설령 곁에 머물러 있더라도 남성을 따라잡을 수 없도록 확실히 하기 위함이었다. 이상한 점은 이러한 장치들이 남성뿐만 아니라 여성에게도 아름답다고 인식돼 왔다는 것이다. 우리에게는 기형으로 보이는 연꽃발이 중국에서 수세기 동안 열정적으로 찬미받았고, 오늘날 서구 사회의 대부분 사람들은 현대 신발이 만들어내는 심하게 압축된 발가락을 추하다고 보지 않는다. 금세기 대부분 동안 여성 복장의 필수 요소였던 하이힐과 좁은 앞코 신발은 성적으로 매력적이라고 여겨진다. 부분적으로는 다리를 더 길어 보이게 만들기 때문인데—늘어난 다리는 여러 동물 종에서 성적 가용성의 생물학적 신호다—그리고 인류학자들이 "구애 보행"이라고 부르는 것을 만들어내기 때문이다. 또한 이런 신발들은 오래 서 있는 것을 고통스럽게 만들고, 걷기를 지치게 하며, 뛰는 것을 불가능하게 한다. 이런 신발이 만들어내는 절뚝거리며 발끝으로 걷는 걸음걸이가 도발적이라고 여겨지는데—아마도 그런 신발을 신은 여성은 자신을 쫓는 남성보다 빨리 달릴 수 없다는 것을 보장하기 때문일 것이다. 무엇보다 최악인 것은, 청소년기부터 지속적으로 착용하면 발과 다리의 근육이 변형돼 평평한 밑창으로 걷는 것이 더욱 고통스럽고 어려워진다는 점이다.

제21회 모의고사

1

하위내용영역	배점	예상정답률
일반영어 A형 서술형	4점	50%

모범답안 The appropriate word for the blank is "goats". The meaning of the underlined part is that chickens and children are valued highly in the Third World and thus, while driving, if a person happens to hit either with their car they will be killed by the local people as a consequence.

채점기준

+ 1.5점: 빈칸에 들어갈 단어를 "goats"라 정확하게 기입하였다. 이외에는 답이 될 수 없다.
+ 2.5점: 밑줄 친 부분의 의미를 "chickens and children are valued highly in the Third World and thus, while driving, if a person happens to hit either with their car they will be killed by the local people as a consequence"라 서술하였거나 유사하였다.

한글번역

경험상 당나귀를 만나면 속도를 줄이고, 염소를 만나면 속도를 높이며, 소를 만나면 멈춰야 한다. 당나귀는 결국 길을 비켜줄 것이고, 보행자들도 마찬가지다. 하지만 실제로는 둘 모두를 위해 멈추면 안 된다. 그들이 이를 이용할 테니까, 특히 보행자들이 그렇다. 제3세계 보행자 무리 한가운데서 멈추면, 며칠 동안 그곳에서 치클릿과 가짜 골동품을 사는 신세가 될 것이다.

염소들 사이로는 미친 듯이 달려라. 염소를 치는 것은 거의 불가능하다. 반면, 소를 치지 않는 것은 거의 불가능하다. 소들은 경적 소리, 고함, 막대기로 때리기, 범퍼로 엉덩이 툭 치기에 면역이 있다. 소를 움직이게 할 수 있는 유일한 방법은 소를 피해 방향을 바꾸는 것인데, 그러면 소가 번개 같은 속도로 당신 앞으로 움직일 것이다.

사실, 가장 위험한 동물은 닭이다. 미국에서는 공이 길로 굴러가는 것을 보면 브레이크를 밟는다. 다음에 보게 될 것이 그 공을 쫓는 아이라는 것을 알기 때문이다. 제3세계에서는 아이들이 쫓는 것이 공이 아니라 닭이다. 레그혼 닭으로 펀트 리턴 연습을 하는 건가? 드리블을 하는 건가? 스틱-헨 게임을 하는 건가? 모르겠다. 하지만 제3세계 사람들은 닭을 무척 아끼고, 또한 자신들의 아이들도 무척 아낀다. 둘 중 하나 또는 둘 모두를 치면, 그들은 살아남을 수도 있다. 하지만 당신은 살아남지 못할 것이다.

2

하위내용영역	배점	예상정답률
일반영어 A형 서술형	4점	40%

모범답안 The underlined part means that laws and policies are not influenced by purchasing power in the same way that companies are. The "distraction position" is the stance that buying conscious or eco-friendly products is actually an ineffective distraction from real activism.

채점기준

+ 2점: 밑줄 친 부분의 의미를 "laws and policies are not influenced by purchasing power in the same way that companies are (influenced by purchasing power)"라 서술하였거나 유사하였다.
+ 2점: 주의분산 입장이 무엇인지에 대한 질문에 "the stance(position) that buying green products is actually an ineffective distraction from real activism"이라 서술하였거나 유사하였다.

> **한글번역**
>
> 증거에 따르면, 친환경 소비가 상당한 환경적 성과를 낳는다는 입장과 사람들의 감정을 달래줌으로써 환경적 성과로부터 "주의를 분산시킨다"는 입장 모두 구매 패턴, 행동주의, 환경 파괴 간의 관계를 제대로 파악하지 못한다.
>
> 첫 번째 입장은 통속적 지혜이지만, 순진하고 역사적으로 무지하다. 오염 에너지원에서 청정 에너지원으로의 전환이나 독성 화학물질로부터의 탈피 같은 주요 변화들은 시장에서 자동으로 흘러나오지 않는다. 이런 변화들은 옹호 단체들, 전문가들, 일부 기업 부문들, 그리고 다른 이해관계자들의 압력의 결과다. 소비자 달러는 기업들이 새로운 제품에 대한 시장이 있다는 확신을 가져야 할 때나 새로운 규제를 추진할 만큼 충분한 "친환경" 기업들이 있을 때 역할을 한다. 하지만 "달러로 투표하기"라는 은유가 시사하는 직접적인 방식으로 정책이나 입법을 주도하는 경우는 거의 없다.
>
> 일부 사회과학자들 사이에서 인기 있는 주의분산 입장은 데이터에 의해 뒷받침되지 않는다. 『미국정치사회과학원 연보』에 발표된 중요한 연구는 그 반대를 발견했다 : 친환경 제품을 구매하는 사람들이 정치적으로 더 활발할 가능성이 높다는 것이다. 이들이 국회의원에게 연락하거나 신문에 투고하는 것 같은 표준적인 정치적 행동에 참여하든, 친구와 가족에게 이슈에 관해 이메일을 보내는 것 같은 비공식적 활동을 하든 말이다. 이 연구는 미국인의 전국 대표 표본과 1,800명의 "의식적 소비자"에 대한 온라인 설문조사를 사용했다. 후자 중에서 연구는 높은 수준의 행동주의를 발견했다. 이는 유럽 설문조사에서도 재현된 발견이다. 응답자의 약 절반이 정치적으로 활발해진 것과 거의 같은 시기에 의식적 소비에 입문했다. 약 4분의 1은 구매 패턴을 바꾼 후 활동가가 됐다.

3

하위내용영역	배점	예상정답률
일반영어 B형 서술형	4점	45%

모범답안 The best fitting three words are "White Anglo-saxon Protestant". Second, the weakness of the "straight-line theory" in addressing Jewish people is that as a religious group they are not the same as a nationality, and their roots are not set into one mother country.

> **채점기준**
>
> + 1.5점 : 밑줄 친 부분에 상응하는 세 단어를 "White Anglo-saxon Protestant"라 정확하게 기입하였다. 이외에는 답이 될 수 없다.
> + 2.5점 : 유대인 그룹 문제를 다룰 때 "직선 이론"의 한계를 "as a religious group Jewish people are not the same as a nationality, and their roots are not set into one mother country"라 서술하였거나 유사하였다.

> **한글번역**
>
> 민족성에 대한 지배적인 사회학적 접근법은 오랫동안 닐 샌드버그가 적절히 "직선 이론"이라고 부른 형태를 취해왔다. 이 이론에서 문화적응과 동화는 결국 민족 집단이 더 큰 문화와 일반 인구로 흡수되는 것으로 귀결되는 세속적 경향으로 여겨진다. 직선 이론은 용광로 이론에 바탕을 두고 있는데, 민족 집단들이 단일한 주류 사회로 사라짐을 함의하기 때문이다. 그럼에도 불구하고 이 이론은 용광로 이론가들의 가치관을 받아들이지는 않는다. 그 개념화자들이 이민자의 생활 방식으로부터의 문화적, 사회적 해방 같은 용어들을 사용할 수 있었지만 사용하지 않았기 때문이다.
>
> 최근 몇 년 동안 직선 이론은 여러 근거에서 의문시돼 왔다. 우선, 많은 관찰자들이 20세기 초에 미국이 용광로였을지도 모르지만, 그 이후 유럽과 다른 지역으로부터의 대규모 이민이 백인 앵글로색슨 프로테스탄트로 총칭되는 지배 집단에 영향을 미쳤고, 그들의 정치적, 재정적 권력은 아니더라도 문화적 권력을 파괴했기 때문에, 오늘날 미국은 앤드루 그릴리가 표현한 바와 같이 하위집단들과 하위문화들의 모자이크라고 적절히 지적했다. 그러나 이러한 비판이 반드시 직선 이론의 타당성을 부정하는 것은 아니다. 민족들 역시 나이, 소득, 교육, 직업, 종교, 지역 등으로 구분되는 다원주의적 하위문화들과 하위집단들로 흡수될 수 있기 때문이다. 이러한 하위집단들이 종종 다수 집단의 영향 하에서 통합된다는 점을 주목해야 한다.
>
> 직선 이론에 대한 두 번째 비판은 모든 민족 집단을 본질적으로 유사한 것으로 다루고, 구체적으로 유대인 같은 종교 집단과 이탈리아인, 폴란드인 등 같은 국적 집단을 구별하지 못한다는 점에 집중돼 왔다. 예를 들어, 유대인들은 수천 년의 종교적, 문화적 전통을 가진 '민족'이지만, 충성이나 향수를 느끼는 '조국'은 없는 반면, 이탈리아인, 폴란드인 그리고 '신이민'에 참여한 다른 사람들은 어떤 경우에는 이민자들이 미국에 도착한 후에야 국가가 된 유럽 지역들에서 왔다.

4

하위내용영역	배점	예상정답률
일반영어 B형 서술형	5점	50%

모범답안 One can see many different, even threatening people and have unusual experiences on the F train in New York City. The narrator has seen events such as a knife pulled out by a woman, a man begging for money by singing the Lord's Prayer, bullies harassing an old Hispanic woman, and loud conversation among women. Once even, at a strange hour, the narrator saw a crab board the subway at the Coney Island stop. The passengers watched it with interest as it scared and delighted those arriving on the train. Together the passengers enjoyed it and, when one woman demanded to know who let it out, a man gently tucked it into an envelope and stuffed it into his pocket.

채점기준

ⓐ Topic sentence

+ 1.5점: "One can see many different, even threatening people and have unusual experiences on the F train in New York City"를 정확하게 서술하였거나 유사하였다.

☞ 다음과 같이 서술하였어도 1.5점을 준다.
- "While riding the subway to Manhattan, the narrator encounters many unusual groups of people and even animals together."
- "People can see many different, even threatening people and have unusual experiences on a subway ride to Manhattan."
- "The narrator tells the reader of the memorable sights and sounds he has experienced during his many rides on the F train in New York City."

ⓑ Major supporting details

+ 2점: "The narrator has seen ① <u>a knife pulled out by a woman</u>, ② <u>a man begging for money by singing the Lord's Prayer</u>, ③ <u>bullies harassing a old Hispanic woman</u>, ④ <u>loud conversation among women</u>"

☞ 4개의 디테일 중 4개 모두 서술한 경우 2점, 3개 서술한 경우 1.5점, 2개 서술한 경우 1점, 1개 또는 서술하지 못한 경우 0점을 준다.

+ 1.5점: "Once even, <u>at a strange hour, the narrator saw a crab which got on the subway near Coney Island stop</u>(0.5점). <u>The passengers watched it with interest as it scared and delighted those arriving on the train. Together the passengers enjoyed it</u>(0.5점) and, <u>when one woman demanded to know who let it out, a man gently tucked into an envelope and into his pocket</u>(0.5점)."

감점
- 본문에 있는 연속되는 8단어 이상을 사용하였다. -0.5pt
- 논리적인 하나의 문단으로 구성되지 않았다. -0.5pt

제22회 모의고사

1

하위내용영역	배점	예상정답률
일반영어 A형 기입형	2점	50%

모범답안 ① left-faced (또는 left-facers)
② facial (또는 facedness)

채점기준
- 2점: 모범답안과 같다.
- 1점: 둘 중 하나만 맞았다.
- 0점: 모범답안과 다르다.

한글번역

나는 F열차에서 며칠, 몇 주를 보냈다. 7번가에서 맨해튼 미드타운까지의 여행은 매번 탑승할 때마다 승객들만의 미니 사회, 40분짜리 바보들의 배를 만들어낼 만큼 충분히 길다. 한번은 붐비는 열차에서 팔 하나 거리에 있던 여자가 자신을 위협한 남자에게 칼을 빼들었다. 나는 그 논쟁과 당사자들을 기억하지만, 무엇보다 그 칼을 기억한다—양끝에 황동 부착물이 끼워진 평평하고 곡선의 나뭇결 손잡이, 길고 가늘어지는 날. 한번은 한 남자가 주기도문의 가사를 애달프고 당김음이 있는 선율에 맞춰 불렀는데, 그가 그 아침의 분위기와 너무도 정확히 들어맞아서 마지막에 돈을 달라고 했을 때 승객들은 마치 그가 총을 뽑은 것처럼 지갑과 지갑을 찾아 손을 뻗었다. 한번은 친구들과 함께 있던 덩치 큰 백인 소년이 작고 나이 든 히스패닉 여성을 놀리고 있었는데, 그가 열차에서 내렸을 때 나는 창문 너머로 그를 바라봤고 그는 내 얼굴 바로 옆 창문을 세게 때렸다. 한번은 나란히 앉은 마른 여자와 뚱뚱한 여자가 자신들이 혼내줄 작정인 누군가에 대해 길고 시끄러운 대화를 나눴다. "걔 엉덩이는 병원에 있을 거야!" "대포를 끌어내!" 브루클린에서 F열차의 종점은 해변에서 멀지 않은 코니아일랜드다. 한가한 시간에 나는 열차에 올랐고 승객 두세 명과, 바닥을 돌아다니는 게 한 마리를 발견했다. 승객들은 그 게를 바라보고 있었다. 게의 다리가 광택 난 손톱처럼 바닥에서 딸깍거렸다. 게는 이쪽으로, 저쪽으로 움직이며 편안한 자리를 찾으려 했다. 벽 쪽 좌석 밑으로 몸을 빼고 들어갔다. 그러다가 새로운 승객들이 그곳에 앉은 직후 밖으로 스르르 나왔고, 그들은 정말로 비명을 질렀다. 다음 정거장의 승객들이 그것을 보고 웃었다. 한 소년이 그것을 밟으려는 듯 발을 들어 올렸을 때, 모두가 "안 돼!"라고 외쳤다. 우리가 제이 스트리트—보로 홀에 도착했을 때, 객차에는 십여 명 정도가 있었고, 모두 그 게를 바라보는 데 몰두하고 있었다. 객차 문이 열리고 자세가 반듯하고 체격이 좋은 여자가 들어왔다. 그녀는 게를 바라본 다음, 엄하게 우리 모두를 바라봤다. 잠시 기다렸다. 그러고는 "이거 누구 거야?"라고 물었다. 몇 정거장 후, 콧수염 난 키 작은 남자가 마닐라 봉투를 가져와서 몸을 굽혀 게를 그 안에 넣고, 봉투를 닫아 코트 주머니에 넣었다.

한글번역

첫눈에 보기에는 베토벤의 화난 얼굴과 해리 왕자의 수줍은 소년다운 모습 사이에서 공통점을 찾기란 쉽지 않을 것이다. 물론 당신이 미국 위스콘신-매디슨 대학교의 심리학 명예교수이자 15년간 연구에 매진해온 칼 스미스라면, 둘 다 왼쪽 얼굴형이라는 사실을 알 것이다.

'얼굴성'은 우리 대부분이 왼손잡이나 오른손잡이인 것처럼 더 우세한 얼굴 쪽이 있다고 제안하는 새로운 이론이다. 이 이론은 음악적 천재성의 관상을 드러낸다고 주장한다. 스미스의 연구에 따르면, 왼쪽 얼굴형 사람들은 음악적 연주와 관련된 뇌의 우반구에 더 잘 접근할 수 있는 반면, 오른쪽 얼굴형 사람들은 인지 과정, 즉 일반인의 말로 하면 사고를 전문으로 하는 좌반구를 활용한다. 그의 조사에 따르면 85-90%의 사람들이 오른쪽 얼굴형이다.

바그너는 스미스가 살펴본 것 중 가장 뚜렷한 왼쪽 얼굴형 중 하나로, "기형에 가까울 정도로 우세하다"고 한다. 모차르트, 베토벤, 브람스, 슈베르트, 차이콥스키, 리스트도 여기에 포함된다. 뉴욕 메트로폴리탄 오페라 가수들의 98% 이상이 왼쪽 얼굴형이었다.

해리 왕자는 왕실 가족 중 왼쪽 얼굴형으로서 음악 분야에서 경력을 쌓을 가능성이 있는 유일한 인물이다. 스미스는 "부모들은 오른쪽 얼굴형 아이들에게 돈을 낭비해서는 안 된다"고 말한다. 일반적인 믿음과는 달리, 모차르트가 될 가능성을 시사하는 것은 손이 아니라 얼굴 특징이다.

유희태 | 일반영어 ❹-2

> 3~4세에 발달하는 손잡이와 달리, 얼굴성은 출생 전에 결정된다. 작곡가나 정치인을 꿈꾸는 사람들에게는 얼굴성을 거스를 방법이 없으며, 부모들은 희망에 찬 아이들을 음악 레슨에 등록시키기 전에 이를 유의해야 한다. 거울을 한번 보면 그 비용이 가치 있을지 알 수 있을 것이다.

2

하위내용영역	배점	예상정답률
일반영어 A형 서술형	4점	50%

모범 답안 The four consecutive words *(compared to the underlined ①)* are "death of other languages". Second, the meaning of the underlined ② is that the Catawba language died that week with the death of Red Thunder Cloud, its last remaining speaker.

채점 기준

+ 2점: 연속된 네 단어를 "death of other languages"라 정확하게 기술하였다. 이외에는 답이 될 수 없다.
+ 2점: 밑줄 친 부분의 의미를 "the Catawba language died that week with the death of Red Thunder Cloud, its last remaining speaker"라 서술하였거나 유사하였다.

한글번역

> 이번 주에 또 하나의 언어가 사라졌다. 레드 썬더 클라우드로 더 널리 알려진 카를로스 웨스테즈가 78세의 나이로 뇌졸중으로 사망했는데, 그는 아메리카 원주민 언어인 카타우바어의 마지막 화자였다. 그와 함께 카타우바어도 사라졌다. 지구상에 살아있는 생명체 중에서는 오직 레드 썬더 클라우드보다 오래 산 그의 개만이, 다른 언어로는 명령을 이해하지 못하는 채로, 아마도 여전히 뇌 속에 카타우바어의 소리들을 간직하고 있을 것이다.
>
> 지난 20년 동안 현대 산업이 세계 생태계에 얼마나 많은 피해를 입힐 수 있는지, 열대우림의 파괴가 어떻게 셀 수 없이 많은 식물과 곤충 종들의 죽음을 가져오는지 우리 모두에게 분명해졌다.

> 덜 명백하지만 그에 못지않게 해로운 것은 하나의 강력한 문화가 우리의 언어와 생활 방식에 미치는 영향이다. 우리는 아메리카 문화에 의해 전파되고 일본 기술에 의해 전달되는 영어의 확산을 목격하고 있다. 또한 중국어, 스페인어, 러시아어, 힌디어와 같은 몇몇 거대한 국제 언어들의 증가하는 지배력을 목격하고 있다. 이들이 문화와 상업의 도구로 부상하면서 언어적 생존 경쟁에서 패배한 다른 언어들의 죽음이 따라왔다. 위협받는 언어 중 하나가 태평양의 바누아투 원주민 언어인 아오레어다. (이번 주까지의) 카타우바어처럼, 이 언어도 그 섬의 유일한 원주민 거주자에 의해서만 사용된다. 따라서 이 언어 역시 사라질 운명이다.
>
> 레드 썬더 클라우드처럼, 또는 1778년에 사망한 콘월어를 모국어로 구사한 마지막 인물인 돌리 펜트리스처럼 한 언어의 마지막 화자가 되는 것은 특별히 외로운 운명임에 틀림없다. 이는 멸종하는 종의 마지막 생존 구성원이 되는 것만큼이나 기이하고 끔찍한 일이다. 그러나 언어가 죽을 때 우리 나머지 사람들이 잃는 것은 세상을 인식하고 묘사하는 독특한 방식의 가능성이다.

3

하위내용영역	배점	예상정답률
일반영어 B형 서술형	4점	50%

모범 답안 It can be inferred from the passage that tonsillectomies were a very common procedure in the 1940s. Second, the core finding of the Harvard study was that a large number of children got tubes put in without any noticeable benefit, and another significant number also got tubes with as much as risk possible as benefit.

채점 기준

+ 2점: 1940년대에 편도선절제술이 어땠을까하는 추론 문제에 대한 답을 "tonsillectomies were a very common procedure in the 1940s"라 서술하였거나 유사하였다.

+ 2점: 하버드 연구팀의 핵심 발견을 "a large number of children got tubes put in without any noticeable benefit, and another significant number also got tubes with as much as risk possible as benefit."이라 서술하였거나 유사하였다.
  - ☞ "a majority of children with tubes have no advantage and may be at risk"라 했어도 2점을 준다.
  - ☞ "tube placement is an overused procedure"이라 했으면 1점을 준다.

한글번역

매년 50만 명이 넘는 미국 아이들이 지속적인 감염과 싸우기 위해 수술로 귀에 배액관을 삽입하고 있다. 고막절개술로 알려진 이 시술은 1940년대의 편도절제술만큼 흔하지는 않지만, 현재 미국 최고의 소아 수술로 자리 잡았으며, 새로운 연구에 따르면 이 시술이 크게 남용되고 있다고 한다. 6,000건 이상의 예정된 귀 튜브 수술을 검토한 결과, 하버드 소아과 의사 로렌스 클라인만이 이끄는 전문가팀은 절반도 안 되는 수술만이 명확히 정당화된다는 사실을 발견했다. 연구진은 현재 미국의학협회저널에서 "매년 미국에서 수십만 명의 아이들이 입증된 이점을 제공하지 않고 오히려 위험을 증가시킬 수 있는 고막절개술을 받고 있을 수 있다"고 기술하고 있다.

튜브 삽입은 극도로 위험한 시술은 아니지만, 1,000달러에서 1,500달러의 비용이 들며 때로는 고막에 흉터를 남겨 부분적인 청력 손실을 일으킨다. 연구에 따르면 아이의 중이가 항생제 치료에도 불구하고 4개월 이상 끈적한 체액을 생성한 경우 이익이 위험을 능가할 가능성이 가장 높다고 한다. 덜 심한 감염의 경우, 약물 치료가 일반적으로 더 저렴하고 안전한 대안이다(약물 역시 남용될 수 있지만). 새로운 JAMA 연구에서 클라인만의 팀은 의사가 이 시술을 권장한 16세 미만 아이들 6,429명의 의료 차트를 검토했다. 가능한 이익에 대해 "관대한 가정"을 하더라도, 연구진은 제안된 수술의 4분의 1이 덜 침습적인 대안이 있었기 때문에 부적절했으며, 또 다른 3분의 1은 환자에게 도움이 되는 만큼 해를 끼칠 가능성이 있다는 사실을 발견했다. 부모들은 이미 삽입된 귀 튜브에 대해 당황할 필요가 없다. 성공적으로 삽입되면, 이 작은 장치들은 6개월에서 1년간 배액을 제공한 후 저절로 빠져나와 매년 수억 달러의 의료비를 절약한다.

4

하위내용영역	배점	예상정답률
일반영어 B형 서술형	4점	50%

모범답안) There have been five species of human on Earth according to the passage. Second, Toni would have survived better on the island of Flores because food resources became limited and a smaller human requires less food supply.

채점 기준

+ 1.5점: 지구상에 과거에서 현재까지 살았던 인간 종이 "5가지"였다고 기술하였다. 이외에는 답이 될 수 없다.
+ 2.5점: 플로레스 섬에 살아남을 가능성이 높은 것을 "Toni(1점)"라 기술하였고, 그 이유를 "food resources became limited and a smaller human requires less food supply(1.5점)"라 서술하였거나 유사하였다.

제23회 모의고사

1

하위내용영역	배점	예상정답률
일반영어 A형 서술형	4점	45%

모범 답안 The purpose of the passage is to outline a new revelation regarding post-mortem biology regarding ongoing gene activity after death. Second, this discovery could be used by investigators to better pinpoint the time of death by measuring levels of gene activity.

채점 기준

+ 2점: 글의 목적을 "to explain <u>a new study(or discovery)</u> in the field of post-mortem biology regarding ongoing <u>gene activity after death</u>"라 서술하였거나 유사하였다.
  ☞ 다음과 같이 서술하였어도 2점을 준다.
  – "to describe a new discovery that undead genes come alive days after life ends."
+ 2점: 사후 생물학에 대한 발견이 살인사건 조사에 있어서 어떻게 적용될 수 있는지에 대해 "this discovery could be used by investigators to better <u>pinpoint the time of death by measuring levels of gene activity</u>"라 서술하였다.

한글번역

죽음이 정말로 우리 존재의 끝을 의미할까? 플라톤부터 블루 오이스터 컬트까지 위대한 사상가들이 이 문제에 대해 견해를 밝혀왔다. 이제 한 연구에 따르면 적어도 삶의 한 측면은 계속된다고 한다. 동물이 죽은 후 며칠 동안 유전자가 여전히 켜져 있다는 것이다. 연구자들은 이러한 사후 활동을 이식용 기증 장기를 보존하는 더 나은 방법과 살인 피해자의 사망 시점을 결정하는 더 정확한 방법으로 활용할 수 있을지도 모른다.

궁금하겠지만, 미생물학자 피터 노블과 동료들은 좀비가 지구를 배회하며 부주의한 자들의 뇌를 빨아먹을 수 있게 해주는 것이 무엇인지 알아내려 한

한글번역

호모 사피엔스는 매우 불편한 사실을 계속 비밀로 해왔다. 우리에게 문명화되지 않은 사촌들이 많을 뿐만 아니라 과거에는 형제자매도 적지 않았다는 사실이다. 지난 1만 년 간 우리 종은 지구상의 유일한 인간 종이었기 때문에 우리는 스스로를 유일한 인류라고 생각하는 데 익숙해 있다. 하지만 '인간'이란 말의 진정한 의미는 '호모 속에 속하는 동물'이고 호모 속에는 사피엔스 외에도 여타의 종이 많이 존재했다.

인류는 약 250만년 전 동부 아프리카의 오스트랄로피테쿠스에서 진화했다. 오스트랄로 피테쿠스는 우리보다 더 오래된 유인원의 한 속으로서 '남쪽의 유인원'이란 듯이다. 약 200만 년 전 이들 고대 남성과 여성들 중 일부는 고향을 떠나 여행을 시작해 북아프리카, 유럽 아시아의 넓은 지역에 정착했다. 북유럽의 눈 덮인 숲에서 살아남기에 좋은 특질과 인도네시아의 찌는 듯한 정글에서 살아남는 데 필요한 특질이 서로 다르기 때문이다. 그 결과 서로 다른 여러 종들이 생겨났고 과학자들은 여기에 거창한 라틴어 이름을 붙였다.

유럽과 서부아시아의 인류는 '호모 네안데르탈렌시스(네안데르 골짜기에서 온 사람)', 흔히 말하는 네안데르탈인으로 진화했다. 이들은 우리 사피엔스보다 덩치가 크고 근육이 발달한 덕분에 유라시아 서부에서 빙하기의 추운 기후에 잘 적응했다. 아시아의 좀 더 동쪽 지역에는 호모 에렉투스가 살았다. 이들 '똑바로 선 사람'은 그 지역에서 2백만 년 가까이 살아남아 가장 오래 지속된 인간 종이 됐다. 우리 사피엔스가 이 기록을 깰 가능성은 희박해 보인다. 호모 사피엔스가 지금부터 1000년 후에 존재할지도 의심스러운 마당에 2백만 년은 우리와는 동떨어진 시간이다.

인도네시아의 자바 섬에는 호모 솔로엔시스가 살았는데, '솔로 계곡에서 온 사람'이라는 뜻이다. 이들은 열대 지방의 삶에 잘 적응했다. 한편 인도네시아의 또 다른 섬 플로레스에서는 고인류가 왜소화의 과정을 겪었다. 인류가 플로레스 섬에 도착한 것은 해수면이 이례적으로 낮아져서 본토에서 건너가기가 쉬운 때였다. 그러다 해수면이 다시 높아지자 일부 사람들이 자원이 부족한 그 섬에 갇히게 됐다. 식량을 많이 먹어야 하는 덩치 큰 사람들이 먼저 죽었고, 아무래도 작은 사람들이 살아남기가 수월했다. 세대를 거듭하면서 플로레스 섬 사람들은 점점 난쟁이가 됐다. 과학자들이 '플로레스인(호모 플로레시엔시스)'이라 이름 붙인 이 사람들은 최대 신장이 1미터에 체중은 25킬로그램 이하였다.

것은 아니었다. 대신 과학자들은 유전자 활동 측정을 조정하기 위해 개발한 새로운 방법을 시험하고 싶었다. 그들의 연구는 이미 으스스한 방향으로 흘러갔다. 2년 전 그들은 사후 다양한 인간 장기에서의 미생물 풍부도에 관한 논문을 발표했고, 사후 샘플에 자신들의 방법을 적용하기로 결정했다. "죽을 때 무슨 일이 일어나는지 보려는 호기심의 실험입니다"라고 노블은 말한다.

인간 시체의 혈액과 간 조직을 분석한 과학자들이 이전에 몇 개 유전자의 사후 활동을 주목했지만, 노블과 동료들은 1000개 이상을 체계적으로 평가했다. 연구팀은 최근 죽은 쥐와 제브라피시의 조직에서 이들 유전자 중 어떤 것이 기능하고 있는지 측정했으며, 물고기에서는 4일간, 설치류에서는 2일간 변화를 추적했다.

처음에 연구자들은 연료가 떨어진 자동차의 부품들처럼 유전자들이 죽음 직후 곧 종료될 것이라고 가정했다. 하지만 그들이 발견한 것은 수백 개의 유전자가 활동을 증가시킨다는 것이었다. 이들 유전자 대부분이 동물이 죽은 후 첫 24시간 내에 활동을 증가시킨 다음 감소했지만, 물고기에서는 일부 유전자가 죽음 후 4일까지 활성 상태를 유지했다.

2

하위내용영역	배점	예상정답률
일반영어 B형 서술형	4점	45%

모범답안 The words fitting the blank are "Women's presses". Second, in the underlined blank ②, the writer is using an analogy to show that the coming to power of women in printing has occurred at a time when the medium is out-of-date, like when printing replaced manuscripts, which men were no longer interested in at that time.

채점기준
+ 1.5점: 빈칸에 들어갈 두 단어를 "Women's presses"라 정확하게 기술하였다. 이외에는 답이 될 수 없다.
+ 2.5점: 저자가 밑줄 친 ②를 언급한 이유를 "to show that the coming to power of women in printing has occurred at a time when the medium is out-of-date, like when printing replaced manuscripts, which men were no longer interested in at that time"라 서술하였거나 유사하였다.

한글번역

지난 수십 년간의 여성 출판사들은 존재해온 가장 위대한 성공 사례 중 하나다. 시드니 대학교를 다니며 존재했던 여성 작가는 예외적인 세 명, 즉 제인 오스틴, 조지 엘리엇, 샬럿 브론테뿐이라고 진심으로 믿고 졸업할 수 있었던 내 학부 시절과는 대조적으로, 오늘날 우리는 풍부한 여성 도서를 보유하고 있다. 이들은 단지 여성 출판사의 산물만이 아니다. 여성에 의해, 여성에 관해, 여성을 위해 쓰인 책들을 출간함으로써 여성 출판사들이 시장을 변화시켰고, 그들이 이끈 곳을 주류 출판사들이 따라갈 수밖에 없을 정도였다. 이는 부분적으로 여성들이 더 열성적인 독자이자 더 많은 책을 구매하는 사람들이기 때문이었다.

하지만 여성들이 매체에서 결정권자가 되자 여성 작가들이 두각을 나타냈다면, 이 부인할 수 없는 성공담에는 또 다른 차원이 있다. 그것은 여성들이 인쇄물의 힘이 쇠퇴하고 있던 시기에만 출판사를 시작할 수 있었다는 것이다. 인쇄물이 주요 매체로서의 지위를 잃어가고 있었기 때문에 여성들이 발을 들여놓을 수 있었던 것이다. 남성들이 흥미롭고 강력한 새로운 전자 매체 영역으로 이동하면서 예전처럼 인쇄 영역을 두고 경쟁하지 않았기 때문에, 여성들이 전례 없는 접근권을 얻을 수 있었던 것이다. 여성 출판사들의 성취를 폄하하고 싶지는 않지만, 이것이 인쇄기 발명 이후에 최고의 필사 제작자가 되는 것과 같다는 점을 분명히 하고 싶다. 여성들이 이 모든 훌륭한 정보를 인쇄물로 기록해왔다는 점을 강조하고 싶다. 바로 책이 지식의 저장소로서 영향력을 잃어가고 있는 정확한 시점에 말이다.

3

하위내용영역	배점	예상정답률
일반영어 B형 서술형	4점	55%

모범답안 There are three kinds of workers that can spoil the work atmosphere. The first is "Moody Mary," who is always undergoing stress in her personal life, which causes a bad atmosphere in the office and leads her to commit on-the-job errors, creating more work for her coworkers. Likewise, a second type of problematic person, "Not-My-Job Nancy" (or "Nick"), will emphatically resist doing any work unrelated to "the job description". This gives coworkers a hard time. Finally there is "No-Change Charlie" (or "Charlotte"), who will avoid and argue against every change. This kind of attitude will impede solutions and reorganizations that can help increase efficiency or help overall.

채점 기준

ⓐ Topic sentence
+ 1점: "There are three kinds of workers that can spoil the work atmosphere"를 정확하게 서술하였다.

ⓑ Major supporting details
+ 3점: "① <u>The first is "Moody Mary," who is always undergoing stress in her personal life,</u> which <u>causes a bad atmosphere in the office and leads her to commit on-the-job errors, creating more work for her coworkers.</u> Likewise, ② <u>a second type of problematic person, "Not-My-Job Nancy" (or "Nick"), will emphatically resist doing any work unrelated to "the job description." This gives coworkers a hard time.</u> Finally ③ <u>there is "No-Change Charlie" (or "Charlotte"), who will avoid and argue against every change. This kind of attitude will impede solutions and reorganizations that can help increase efficiency or help overall.</u>"를 서술하였거나 유사하였다.

☞ <u>각 type이 무엇인지</u> 기술한 뒤 <u>왜 그런 사람과 일하기가 어려운지</u>를 3개 모두 서술한 경우 3점, 2개만 서술한 경우 2점, 1개만 서술한 경우 1점, 서술하지 못하였거나 전혀 다르게 서술한 경우 0점을 준다.

☞ <u>각각의 type이 무엇인지</u>만 기술하고 <u>왜 그런 사람과 일하기가 어려운지를 서술하지 않았으면</u> 각각 0.5점씩 감점한다.

감점
- 본문에 있는 연속되는 6단어 이상을 사용하였다. −0.5pt
- 논리적인 하나의 문단으로 구성되지 않았다. −0.5pt
- 언어적 측면에서 표현이나 문법이 어색한 것이 많았다. −0.5pt

한글번역

무디 메리(또는 남성 버전인 무디 마틴)는 항상 어떤 종류의 감정적 위기를 겪고 있는 유형의 사람이다. 개인적인 삶에서 잘못된 일 때문에 항상 절망하거나, 우울하거나, 슬퍼하거나, 토라져 있다. 보통은 남자친구가 헤어지자고 했거나, 남자친구와 싸웠거나, 남자친구의 200세 고조할머니가 돌아가셨거나, 이번 주말에 남자친구와 보낼 휴일이 없기 때문이다. 예를 들어, 내가 같이 일하는 질이라는 웨이트리스가 무디 메리다. 그녀는 개인적인 문제에 대한 끝없는 이야기로 모든 동료들을 짜증나게 할 뿐만 아니라, 항상 무너질 듯한 상태에 있어서 너무 느리게 움직이고 실수를 많이 한다. 결국 남은 우리가 그녀의 고객 불만을 들어야 하고, 때로는 그녀가 부엌에 앉아서 울고 있는 동안 우리가 직접 고객들을 돌봐야 한다. 힘든 시간을 보내고 있는 사람들에게는 동정하지만, 이런 사람들은 적어도 근무시간 중에는 정신을 차리려고 노력해야 한다고 생각한다. 그래야 남은 우리가 그들의 일을 대신 하지 않아도 된다. 또 다른 유형은 낫-마이-잡 낸시(또는 낫-마이-잡 닉)다. 이 사람은 자신의 직무 기술서에 명확히 적혀있지 않은 일은 뭐든 거부한다. 나와 같이 일하는 리타라는 안내원이 낫-마이-잡 낸시다. 그녀가 가장 좋아하는 말은 "그건 정말 내 일이 아니야"다. 무엇을 부탁하든 그것이 그녀의 대답인 것 같다. 그래서 한번은 내가 다른 고객들 때문에 바쁠 때, 그녀가 내 구역에 새 손님들을 앉혔는데 물을 갖다 주고 음료 주문을 받아달라고 부탁했다. 그녀의 대답은 "그건 정말 내 일이 아니야"였다. 다른 경우에는 그녀가 식당 앞쪽으로 돌아가는 길에 지나갈 테이블에 부엌에서 파이 한 조각을 갖다 달라고 부탁했다. 그녀는 "정말 자기 일이 아니어서" 할 수 없다고 말했다. 동료들을 도와주기를 거부하는 사람들과 일하는 것이 특히 힘들다고 생각하며, 이는 모든 사람에게 일을 더 어렵게 만든다. 또한 언급할 만한 것은 노-체인지 찰리(또는 노-체인지 샬럿)로, 변화를 싫어하는 사람이다. 그들은 특정한 방식으로 일하는 데 익숙해지면, 변화가 더 쉽고 좋게 만들어줄 수 있음에도 불구하고 편안한 일상을 바꾸고 싶어 하지 않는다. 우리 식당의 댄이라는 다른 웨이터가 노-체인지 찰리다. 그는 좋든 나쁘든 모든 변화에 반대한다. 심지어 교통 흐름을 개선하기 위해 식당의 테이블을 재배치하는 것도 반대할 이유를 찾았는데, 조금만 움직여도 우리 모두가 더 효율적이 될 수 있을 텐데 말이다. 나는 일을 더 쉽게 만들기 위한 변화라면 모두 찬성하기 때문에, 틀에 박혀서 빠져나올 수 없는 노-체인지 찰리들 때문에 짜증이 난다.

# 제24회 모의고사

1

하위내용영역	배점	예상정답률
일반영어 A형 서술형	4점	45%

모범답안 The four consecutive words are "ninety to zero vote". Second, the article relates to the narrator's observations in that he is observing around the restaurant that there is a noticeable, excessive use of paper products and the article is about deforestation as a result of consumer demands for paper.

채점기준

+ 2점: 연속된 네 단어를 "ninety to zero vote"라 정확하게 기술하였다. 이외에는 답이 될 수 없다.
+ 2점: 화자가 읽는 신문기사와 아침식사에 관련된 화자의 관찰 사이의 관계를 "he is observing around the restaurant that there is a noticeable, excessive use of paper products and the article is about deforestation as a result of consumer demands for paper"라 서술하였거나 유사하였다.

한글번역

어느 날 아침 커피숍에서 아침식사를 기다리며 신문을 읽고 있었다. 신문은 66페이지였다. 웨이트리스가 종이 식탁보와 종이 냅킨을 가져다주고 주문을 받았고, 나는 신문을 넘겨가며 읽었다. 헤드라인에는 "하원 위원회, 미국 산림 전면 벌채 허용 법안 검토"라고 돼 있었다.

나는 종이 냅킨을 무릎에 올리고, 종이 식탁보 위에 신문을 펼쳐놓고 계속 읽었다.

"하원 농업위원회가 정부 허가 하에 민간 회사들이 국유림에서 다시 한 번 나무를 전면 벌채할 수 있도록 허용하는 법안을 검토하고 있다"고 돼 있었다.

웨이트리스가 커피를 가져왔다. 나는 종이 설탕 봉지를 뜯고 작은 종이컵에 든 크림을 따서 신문을 계속 읽었다. "상원은 어제 전면 벌채를 허용하는 법안을 만장일치로 통과시켰다"고 신문에 나와 있었다. "비평가들은 국유림에서의 전면 벌채가 침식과 야생동물 서식지 파괴로 이어질 수 있다고 말했다. 산림청과 업계 대변인들은 전면 벌채에 대한 전면 금지가 목재 산업을 마비시킬 것이라고 말했다." 그리고 제지 산업도 마찬가지일 것이라고 나는 생각했다. 산림을 전면 벌채하는 것은 많은 종이를 얻는 한 가지 방법이고, 우리는 확실히 많은 종이가 필요한 것 같다.

웨이트리스가 토스트를 가져왔다. 버터를 찾았더니 종이로 덮인 작은 종이 접시에 담겨 있었다. 종이로 포장된 마멀레이드를 뜯고 계속 읽었다. "웨스트버지니아주 민주당 소속 제닝스 랜돌프 상원의원은 동료들에게 더 제한적인 관점을 취해 특정 유형의 산림에 대해서만 구체적인 지침 하에 전면 벌채를 허용할 것을 촉구했다. 하지만 그나 다른 누구도 이 법안에 반대표를 던지지 않았고, 법안은 90대 0으로 하원에 넘겨졌다."

달걀이 나왔는데 소금과 후추가 작은 종이 포장에 들어 있었다. 나는 아침식사를 마치고 신문을 겨드랑이에 끼고, 사용한 쓸모없는 종이 냅킨, 종이 식탁보, 종이 소금과 후추 포장지, 종이 버터와 마멀레이드 포장지, 종이 설탕 봉지, 종이 크림 용기가 놓인 테이블을 떠났다. 그리고 우리의 국유림이 어떻게 우리의 아침식사에서 살아남을 수 있을지 궁금해 하며 아침거리로 걸어 나갔다.

2

하위내용영역	배점	예상정답률
일반영어 B형 서술형	4점	45%

모범답안 The sociobiologist perspective is that all manifestations of altruism stem from the biological drive to maximize one's genes. Second, the care that parents of an adopted child feel directly contradicts the perspective because there is no genetic lineage between them.

채점기준

+ 2점: 이타주의에 대한 사회생물학자의 관점을 "all manifestations of altruism stem from the biological drive to maximize one's genes"라 서술하였거나 유사하였다.
☞ 다음과 같이 서술하였어도 2점을 준다.
− "altruism stem from a selfish desire to maximize her or his gene pools."

+ **2점**: 입양한 아이에 대한 부모의 사랑이 사회생물학자의 관점을 강화하는지 아니면 반박하는지에 대한 질문에 "the care that parents of an adopted child feel directly contradicts(0.5점) the perspective because there is no genetic lineage between two parents and child(1.5점)"라 서술하였거나 유사하였다.

한글번역

사람들이 도덕성이 생물학적 기반을 가질 수 있다는 것을 인정하기 꺼리는 이유를 다룰 수 있는데, 즉 도덕성에서 이타주의가 제거돼 겉보기에 이타적인 행동이 결국 분석해보면 실제로는 이기적인 행동이라는 것이다. 어떻게 이런 생각을 하게 될 수 있는지 이해하기는 어렵지 않다. 인간 행동에 대한 사회생물학적 설명의 전형적인 해석에서는 각 인간 행동 뒤에 있는 궁극적인 동기 요인이 자신의 유전자 풀을 최대화하려는 충동이다. 인간의 부모적 이타주의조차도 이런 식으로 설명되는데, 사회생물학적 논증에 따르면 부모들이 자녀들이 차례로 후손(손자)을 가질 수 있을 때까지 돌봄으로써 자신의 유전자 풀을 가장 잘 최대화한다는 것이다.

하지만 언뜻 보기에 부모적 이타주의에 대한 이런 설명이 명백히 거짓인 것처럼 보일 뿐만 아니라, 친족이 아닌 이들에 대한 이타주의는 사회생물학적 설명으로 깔끔하게 설명되지 않는 것 같다. 부모적 사랑의 전형적인 사례를 생각해보자. 두 부모가 다섯 살 아이가 절망적으로 비명을 지르는 소리를 듣는다. 아이가 여러 마리의 사나운 개들에게 공격받고 있다는 것이 밝혀진다. 부모들이 진정으로 아이를 사랑한다면, 자신들의 안녕은 전혀 고려하지 않고 아이를 구하려 할 것이라고 우리는 가정한다. 특히, 부모들이 단순히 아이에 대한 사랑 때문에 아이를 구하려는 동기를 갖게 될 것이며, 유전자 풀을 최대화하려는 욕구는 그들의 구조 시도에 대한 설명에 전혀 포함되지 않을 것이라고 우리는 가정한다. 누군가가 결국 분석해보면 아이를 구하려는 그들의 동기가 아이가 손자를 낳아줌으로써 자신들의 유전자 생존에 기여하기를 바라는 욕구와 희망이었다고 주장한다면, 대부분의 부모들은 그것을 가장 잔인한 말로 여길 것이 분명하다.

3

하위내용영역	배점	예상정답률
일반영어 B형 서술형	4점	50%

모범답안 A porcupine's quill should be removed because it will gradually push itself deeper and it is more difficult to remove as time goes by. The moment a dog is stuck, the heat in the dog's skin will cause the quill to expand, making it even more difficult to remove. From then, the muscles of the animal will move the quill slowly deeper. The quill should be cut at its end to deflate it and it will be pulled out with pliers and the wound cleaned.

채점기준

+ **2점**: 고슴도치의 가시를 신속하게 빼내야 하는 이유를 "because it will gradually push itself deeper and it is more difficult to remove as time goes by"라 서술하였거나 유사하였다.
+ **2점**: 개가 고슴도치에 접촉한 순간부터 개의 몸에서 고슴도치의 가시가 제거될 때까지 무슨 일이 일어날 수 있는지를 묘사하라는 문제에 대한 답으로 "The moment a dog is stuck, ① the heat in the dog's skin will cause the quill to expand, making it even more difficult to remove. From then, ② the muscles of the animal will move the quill slowly deeper. ③ The quill will be cut at its end to deflate it and ④ it will be pulled out with pliers"라 서술하였거나 유사하였다.
  ☞ 디테일 중 3개 또는 4개를 서술한 경우 2점, 2개를 서술한 경우 1점, 1개 또는 서술하지 못한 경우 0점을 준다.

제25회 모의고사

1

하위내용영역	배점	예상정답률
일반영어 A형 기입형	2점	55%

모범답안 America (또는 the United States)

채점기준

- 2점: 모범답안과 같다.
- 0점: 모범답안과 다르다.

한글번역

나는 이 점에 대해 지나치게 강조하지는 않겠다. 이것이 우리의 특별한 경우에 가장 강력하게 적용되기 때문이다. 미국 국민보다 언론이 더 절대적인 통제력을 행사하는 나라는 없다. 가장 가난한 계층의 보편적 교육이 모든 개인을 독자로 만들기 때문이다. 우리나라에 관해 영국에서 출간되는 것 중 전국 곳곳에 유통되지 않는 것은 없다. 영국인의 펜에서 떨어진 중상모략이나 영국 정치인이 내뱉은 부당한 비꼼 중에서 선의를 해치고 잠재된 분노의 덩어리를 증가시키지 않는 것은 없다. 그렇다면 영국이 언어의 문학이 흘러나오는 원천을 소유하고 있으므로, 그것을 우호적이고 관대한 감정의 매개체로 만드는 것이 얼마나 완전히 그녀의 권한 안에 있고, 얼마나 진정으로 그녀의 의무인가. 두 나라가 함께 만나 평화와 친절 속에서 마실 수 있는 시냇물로 말이다. 하지만 그녀가 그것을 쓴맛의 물로 바꾸는 것을 계속 고집한다면, 그녀가 자신의 어리석음을 후회할 때가 올지도 모른다. 현재 미국의 우정은 그녀에게 별로 중요하지 않을지도 모르지만, 그 나라의 미래 운명은 의심의 여지가 없다. 영국의 운명에는 불확실성의 그림자들이 드리워져 있다. 그렇다면 암울한 날이 다가온다면, 가장 자랑스러운 제국들도 면제되지 못했던 그런 역경이 그녀를 덮친다면, 그녀는 자신의 품에 안을 수 있었던 나라를 자신의 곁에서 밀어내고, 따라서 자신의 영토 경계 너머에서 진정한 우정을 위한 유일한 기회를 파괴한 자신의 맹목적 열정을 후회하며 되돌아볼지도 모른다.

한글번역

고슴도치는 논란의 여지가 있지만 중요한 산림 동물이다. "가시돼지"와의 가시 돋친 만남은 그들의 생물학에 대한 약간의 지식으로 해결될 수 있다. 북미에서 두 번째로 큰 설치류인 고슴도치(비버가 가장 크다)는 성체가 2.5피트에서 3피트 길이이며 무게는 35파운드까지 나갈 수 있다. 고슴도치는 야행성이며 완전한 채식주의자다. 겨울 내내 그들은 나무의 형성층(살아있는 조직) 층으로 생존하는데, 소나무, 사시나무, 미루나무를 선호한다. 때때로 고슴도치는 한 그루의 나무에서 지속적으로 먹이를 먹어 줄기를 부분적으로 또는 완전히 둘러싸서 나무 변형이나 죽음을 일으킨다. 봄부터 가을까지 고슴도치는 잎, 연한 식물, 버섯, 채소, 과일로 식단을 보충한다. 새끼는 연한 가시를 갖고 태어나며 출생 직후 딱딱해진다. 고슴도치 새끼는 출생 2주 이내에 식물을 먹지만, 가을까지 어미와 함께 지낸다.

고슴도치의 가시 개수는 인상적이며, 동물 한 마리당 대략 30,000개의 가시를 갖고 있다. 가시 자체는 현미경으로만 보이는 미늘이 달린 속이 빈 털의 변형된 형태다. 고슴도치는 가시를 쏠 수 없다. 위협받은 고슴도치는 피부 아래 근육을 긴장시켜 가시를 세우고, 공격자로부터 등을 돌리며 가시가 달린 꼬리를 휘두른다. 접촉 시 가시가 고슴도치에서 떨어져 나온다. 공격자의 살에 박힌 가시는 체온으로 팽창해 쉽게 제거되지 않는다. 근육 움직임이 하루에 1인치 속도로 가시를 더 깊이 끌어당긴다. 흥미롭게도 고슴도치 가시는 방부제 역할을 해서, 고슴도치가 자신에게 가시가 박히더라도 감염되지 않게 해준다.

고슴도치가 사는 지역에서 개를 가둬두는 것이 가시가 박히는 것을 방지한다. 개에게 가시가 박히면, 유일한 해결책은 박힌 모든 가시를 제거하는 것이다. 가시를 제거하려면 끝을 잘라서 바람을 빼고, 펜치로 뽑아낸다. 부상 부위를 깨끗이 하고, 개가 상처를 핥도록 놔둔다. 모든 가시를 찾거나 제거하는 데 어려움이 있으면 수의사를 찾아간다.

고슴도치가 좋아하는 조경수에 거주하게 되면, 호스로 물을 뿌려 괴롭혀서 떠나게 하려고 해본다. 쫓아낸 후에는 줄기를 3피트 높이의 금속판으로 느슨하게 세로로 감싸서 재방문을 방지한다.

인간과의 많은 갈등에도 불구하고, 고슴도치는 생태학적으로 중요하다. 그들이 먹이를 먹으면서 떨어뜨리는 가지들은 사슴, 토끼, 엘크의 겨울 먹이가 된다. 손상된 나무는 곤충의 서식지가 되고, 이는 차례로 딱따구리의 먹이가 된다. 둘러싸인 나무의 죽음은 수많은 동물의 서식지인 하층 식물을 위한 자원을 해방시킨다. 고슴도치는 심지어 소나무 기생충인 겨우살이 같은 "해로운" 식물도 먹는다.

2

하위내용영역	배점	예상정답률
일반영어 A형 서술형	4점	55%

모범답안 The appropriate two words for the blank are "mass production". Second, they achieved its core feature by building flat roofs, balconies and large windows, which were meant to encourage good health through "fresh air, sunlight and uncluttered living".

채점기준

+ 2점: 빈칸에 들어갈 두 단어를 "mass production"이라 정확히 기술하였다. 이외에는 답이 될 수 없다.
+ 2점: 바우하우스의 핵심 특징을 건축가들이 어떻게 성취했는지에 대해 "by building flat roofs, balconies and large windows, which were meant to encourage good health through 'fresh air, sunlight and uncluttered living'"이라고 서술하였거나 유사하였다.

한글번역

제1차 세계대전 후 도시 주택 부족으로 재건축이 유럽에서 사회적 우선 과제가 됐다. 대륙 전역의 디자이너들은 새롭고 이상주의적이며 유토피아적인 사회를 재건할 책임이 자신들에게 있다고 여겼다. 독일 건축가 발터 그로피우스가 예술과 디자인의 학제 간 학교로 설립한 바우하우스의 정신이 유럽 전역에 퍼졌지만, 가장 고무적인 모범을 제공한 것은 미국이었다. 모든 성향의 유럽 디자이너들이 헨리 포드가 발명한 대량생산을 채택했다. 1920년대에 그로피우스 같은 주요 건축가들은 제조업 시대가 실제로 작동하는 모습을 보기 위해 미국 전역을 대규모로 순회했다. 대량생산의 효율성에 영감을 받아 그들은 자신들의 아이디어를 유럽으로 가져갔다. 1927년 세계 최초의 대량생산 맞춤형 주방이 독일 프랑크푸르트에서 생산됐다. 그 독창적인 내장형 찬장은 작업 공간을 깨끗하게 유지해 위생적으로 관리하는 데 도움이 됐다. 실제로 바우하우스 운동의 핵심 특징은 건강한 생활이었다. 디자이너와 건축가들은 햇빛, 신선한 공기, 어수선하지 않은 생활공간이 질병의 원인을 없앨 것이라고 믿었다. 이는 주택과 병원의 새로운 설계로 이어졌으며, 모두 빛을 들이기 위한 평평한 지붕, 발코니, 큰 창문을 특징으로 했다. 하지만 1933년 집권한 나치는 바우하우스 운동을 못마땅하게 여겨 디자이너와 건축가들을 박해하기 시작했다. 1930년대 중반까지 많은 이들이 아직 바우하우스 운동을 받아들이지 않았던 나라인 영국으로 피했다. 그곳에서 그들은 피난처를 찾았고 바우하우스 정신으로 수용국을 재편하는 데 도움을 주기 시작했다.

3

하위내용영역	배점	예상정답률
일반영어 B형 서술형	4점	40%

모범답안) In the passage, one "wrong target" suggested by the writer is the development of drugs aiming to reduce plaques around neurons, which do not always correspond to Alzheimer's symptoms. In the underlined part, "the same mechanism" refers to the dissolving of synapses by microglia.

채점기준

+ 2점: "잘못된 표적"의 하나의 예를 "the development of drugs aiming to reduce plaques around neurons"이라 서술하였다.
  ☞ "plaques" 대신에 "β amyloid"라 했어도 맞는 것으로 한다.

+ 2점: 밑줄 친 "the same mechanism"이 가리키는 것을 "the dissolving of synapses by microglia"라 정확하게 서술하였다.

한글번역

알츠하이머 약물에 대한 임상시험의 99% 이상이 실패했으며, 이로 인해 많은 사람들이 제약회사들이 잘못된 표적을 추구해온 것은 아닌지 의문을 갖게 됐다. 이제 쥐를 대상으로 한 연구가 잠재적인 새로운 표적을 가리키고 있다. 잘못된 발달 과정으로, 일부 면역 세포가 뉴런 간의 연결을 잡아먹게 만드는 것이다. 이는 질병의 초기 단계에서 무슨 일이 일어나는지 조명하는 새로운 연구다.

지금까지 대부분의 알츠하이머 약물은 베타 아밀로이드 제거를 목표로 한다. 이는 질병이 있는 사람들의 뉴런 주변에 특징적인 끈적한 플라크를 형성하는 단백질이다. 알츠하이머 환자들은 건강한 사람들보다 뇌에 이런 침착물을 더 많이 갖고 있는 경향이 있다. 하지만 더 많은 플라크가 항상 기억 상실이나 주의력 저하 같은 더 심각한 질병 증상을 의미하지는 않는다.

알츠하이머병에서 보이는 인지 저하와 잘 일치하는 것은 특히 기억에 핵심적인 뇌 영역에서 시냅스의 현저한 소실이다. 신경 세포 간의 이런 접합부는 신경전달물질이 방출돼 뇌의 전기 활동을 촉발하는 곳이다.

새로운 연구를 이끈 보스턴 아동병원의 베스 스티븐스는 뇌가 자궁에서 청소년기까지 성숙하면서 불필요한 시냅스를 약화시키는 정상적인 면역 메커니즘을 연구하는 데 경력의 대부분을 보냈다. 이 과정을 통해 더 중요한 연결이 더 강해질 수 있다. 이 과정에서 C1q라는 단백질이 파괴될 시냅스를 표적으로 삼는다. 시냅스가 C1q에 의해 표시된 후, 뇌의 쓰레기 처리 서비스인 미세아교세포라는 면역 세포가 그것을 "잡아먹어야" 한다는 것을 안다고 스티븐스는 말한다. 자궁에서든 나중에 아동기와 십대까지든, 뇌 발달 과정에서 이 시스템이 잘못되면 정신분열증 같은 정신질환으로 이어질 수 있다고 그녀는 말한다.

스티븐스는 같은 메커니즘이 초기 알츠하이머병에서 잘못돼 좋은 시냅스의 파괴와 궁극적으로 인지 장애로 이어진다는 가설을 세웠다.

Part 02 모의고사 II [26~70회]

본책 p.191

제26회 모의고사

1

하위내용영역	배점	예상정답률
일반영어 A형 기입형	2점	55%

모범 답안 habits

채점 기준

- 2점: 모범답안과 같다. 이외에는 답이 될 수 없다.
- 0점: 모범답안과 다르다.

한글번역

우리가 매일 반복적으로, 일상적으로 하는 일들이 수백 가지나 된다. 우리는 잠에서 깨어나고, 휴대폰을 확인하고, 식사를 하고, 양치질을 하고, 일을 한다. 최근 몇 년간, 이러한 습관적 행동들은 자기계발의 영역이 됐다: 서점 진열대는 '생활 꿀팁', '인생 설계', 그리고 장기 프로젝트를 '게임처럼 만드는' 방법에 관한 베스트셀러들로 가득 차 있으며, 이들은 향상된 생산성부터 더 건강한 식단과 막대한 부까지 모든 것을 약속한다. 이러한 안내서들은 과학적 정확성에서 차이가 있지만, 일반적으로 습관적 행동을 반복된 행동 순서를 따르는 일상 패턴으로 묘사하는 경향이 있으며, 우리는 이 패턴에 개입해 더 바람직한 방향으로 나아갈 수 있다고 본다.
문제는 이러한 설명이 역사적 풍부함의 대부분을 잃어버렸다는 것이다. 오늘날의 자기계발서들은 사실상 습관적 행동에 대한 매우 특정한 조건적 버전을 물려받았는데, 구체적으로는 B. 스키너와 이반 파블로프 같은 20세기 초 심리학자들의 연구에서 나타난다. 이러한 사상가들은 행동주의와 연관되어 있는데, 이는 내적 감정이나 생각의 역할보다는 관찰 가능한 자극-반응 반작용을 우선시하는 심리학적 접근법이다. 행동주의자들은 습관을 좁고 개인주의적인 의미로 정의했다; 그들은 사람들이 특정 신호에 자동적으로 반응하도록 조건화돼 있으며, 이것이 행동과 보상의 반복적인 순환을 만들어낸다고 믿었다.

행동주의적 관점의 습관적 행동에 대한 이미지는 현대 신경과학의 관점에서 업데이트됐다. 예를 들어, 뇌가 가소성이 있고 변화 가능하다는 사실은 습관이 시간이 지남에 따라 뇌 영역 간의 특권적 연결을 형성함으로써 우리의 신경 회로에 새겨질 수 있게 한다. 행동주의의 영향은 연구자들이 습관을 정량적이고 엄밀하게 연구할 수 있게 했다. 그러나 이는 또한 이 개념의 더 넓은 철학적 함의를 간과해 왔다.

2

하위내용영역	배점	예상정답률
일반영어 A형 서술형	4점	50%

모범 답안 The new challenges are high operating costs, stagnant energy demand, and competition from cheaper natural gas and renewable energy. Second, Joyce Corradi worries about the nuclear waste stored in the plant.

채점 기준

+ 2점: 새로운 도전을 "① high operating costs, ② stagnant energy demand, and ③ competition from cheaper natural gas and renewable energy"라 서술하였다.
  ☞ 3개 중 3개를 모두 서술한 경우 2점, 2개만 서술한 경우 1점, 나머지는 0점을 준다.
+ 2점: 조이스 코라디가 현재 우려하는 것이 "the nuclear waste stored in the plant"임을 명확하게 서술하였거나 유사하였다.

> **한글번역**
>
> 40년 전, 미국 역사상 가장 심각한 원자력 사고가 원자력 산업에 대한 반발을 불러일으켰고 수십 년간 산업 성장을 중단시켰다. 오늘날, 스리마일 아일랜드에 남아있는 가동 중인 원자로인 1호기는 급변하는 전력망에서 더 저렴한 경쟁자들을 포함한 새로운 도전에 직면하고 있다. 발전소의 1호기는 올해 말 폐쇄될 예정이다.
>
> 1979년 3월 28일, 스리마일 아일랜드의 2호기 원자로는 원자로 노심에서 열을 제거하는 증기 발생기로 물을 보내는 펌프가 작동을 멈춘 후 부분적 노심 용융을 겪었다. 이 사고는 인적 오류, 설계 결함, 그리고 장비 고장이 복합적으로 작용한 결과였다. 소량의 방사능이 방출됐지만, 결국 재앙은 아니었다. 1985년, 스리마일 아일랜드는 손상된 원자로 하나를 제외하고 재개장했다.
>
> 하지만 주민들에게는 마치 거대한 존재와 함께 동네에 사는 것과 같았다. 사람들은 그것이 문제를 일으킬 수 있다는 것을 알고 있었지만, 불안한 타협 속에서 살았다. 원자력 산업이 높은 운영 비용, 정체된 전력 수요, 그리고 더 저렴한 천연가스와 재생 에너지의 경쟁 등 새로운 도전에 직면하면서 이러한 타협이 시험받고 있다.
>
> 스리마일 아일랜드의 여전히 작동하는 1호기 원자로의 현재 소유주인 시카고 소재 엑셀론은 발전소가 수년간 손실을 보고 있다고 말한다. 회사는 운영 허가가 만료되기 15년 전인 올 가을에 폐쇄할 계획이다.
>
> 스리마일 아일랜드 사고를 겪은 당사자로서, 조이스 코라디는 발전소가 문을 닫는 것을 보는 편이 더 기쁠 것이다. 하지만 미국이 여전히 방사성 핵폐기물을 처리할 실질적인 계획이 없기 때문에, 핵폐기물은 여전히 발전소에 저장돼 그녀가 사는 마을에 무기한 방치될 것이다. 지금도 그녀는 발전소의 크고 회색인 냉각탑 옆을 지나가는 것을 피한다.

3

하위내용영역	배점	예상정답률
일반영어 B형 서술형	4점	40%

모범 답안 A meritocracy is impossible and just a concept invented to satisfy the perspectives of the rich. Second, the writer of the passage thinks that Singer's "front door" shows the way wealth can cause inequality meaning not all students have an equal chance.

채점 기준

+ 2점: 글의 요지를 "A meritocracy is impossible and just a concept invented to satisfy the perspectives of the rich"라 서술하였거나 유사하였다.

☞ 다음과 같이 서술하였어도 2점을 준다.
  - "Meritocracy is a myth invented by the rich."

+ 2점: 글의 저자가 싱어의 "정문"에 대해 지니고 있는 생각을 "the writer of the passage thinks that Singer's "front door" shows the way wealth can cause inequality meaning not all students have an equal chance."라 서술하였거나 유사하였다.

☞ 다음과 같이 서술하였어도 2점을 준다.
  - "저자는 Singer's 'front door' 개념에 동의하지 않는데, 그 이유는 싱어의 생각(대학 입학의 "정문"이 "스스로의 힘으로 들어가는 문"이다.)과는 다르게 정문으로 들어간 이들도 자신들 스스로의 힘이라기보다는 학업에 집중할 수 있는 가정환경이 보장되었기 때문이다"라 서술하였다.
  - "The writer thinks that, as opposed to Singer's concept of 'front door', even those who go through "front door" have not gotten in on their own. They've gotten in partly because they have had the great luck to have a wealthy family."

한글번역

미국 대학 입학 비리 사건은 놀랍지는 않을지라도 흥미롭다. 30명이 넘는 부유한 부모들이 자녀를 명문 대학에 입학시키기 위해 한 회사에 거액을 지불했다는 혐의로 형사 기소됐다.

부유한 사람들이 자녀를 좋은 학교에 보내기 위해 거의 모든 일을 한다는 것은 공공연한 비밀이다. 하지만 이 비리 사건은 미국의 능력주의 개념을 뒷받침하는 거짓말들을 드러내기 시작할 뿐이다. 이 사기를 주도했다고 인정한 윌리엄 싱어는 학생이 원하는 대학에 들어갈 수 있는 세 가지 방법이 있다고 설명했다 : "정문이 있는데, 이는 스스로의 힘으로 들어가는 것입니다. 뒷문은 기관 발전 기금을 통한 것으로, 10배나 많은 돈이 듭니다. 그리고 저는 이 옆문을 만들었습니다." 그가 언급하는 "옆문"은 노골적인 범죄로, 말 그대로 뇌물을 주고 시험 점수를 조작하는 것이다. 공립학교 자금을 평등하게 하고 사립학교를 폐지한다 해도, 일부 아이들은 다른 아이들보다 훨씬 더 평등할 것이다. 미국에서는 매년 250만 명의 아이들이 노숙을 경험한다. 빈곤과 함께 오는 혼란스러운 생활 상황은 성공을 훨씬, 훨씬 더 어렵게 만든다. 이는 싱어의 "정문"을 통과한 사람들조차 "스스로의 힘으로 들어간" 것이 아니라는 뜻이다. 그들은 부분적으로는 성공에 도움이 되는 가정환경을 가질 수 있는 행운을 얻었기 때문에 들어간 것이다.

사람들은 종종 "기회의 평등"을 미국의 이상으로 말한다. 하지만 평등한 기회에 가까운 것을 갖기 위해서는 사회를 위에서 아래까지 근본적으로 재구성해야 할 것이다. 큰 부의 불평등이 존재하는 한, 아이들이 갖는 기회에는 엄청난 차이가 있을 것이다. 어떤 입학 기준을 설정하든, 부유한 아이들이 유리할 것이다. 입학 담당자들이 시험 점수에 집중하면, 부모들은 추가 과외와 시험 준비 과정에 돈을 지불할 것이다. 담당자들이 대신 "전인적" 자질에 집중하면, 부모들은 그것을 사줄 것이다. 간단하다 : 부는 항상 자녀에게 다른 사람의 자녀보다 우위를 주는 더 큰 능력을 부여한다. "능력주의"와 비슷한 무언가를 원한다면, 아마도 완전히 평등주의적인 사회를 제도화하는 것부터 시작해야 할 것이다.

현실적으로, 능력주의 같은 것은 결코 존재할 수 없다. 왜냐하면 완전히 평등한 기회는 결코 있을 수 없기 때문이다. 이 개념의 주요 기능은 엘리트들이 삶에서 자신들의 지위를 받을 자격이 있다고 확신시키는 것이다. 이는 "풍요로움의 불안감", 즉 자신들이 개인적 독창성과 노력의 산물이라기보다는 자의적인 "출생 복권"의 수혜자일지도 모른다는 성가신 느낌을 달래준다.

4

하위내용영역	배점	예상정답률
일반영어 B형 서술형	4점	35%

모범답안 There are similarities and differences in the ways in which alcohol, cocaine and marijuana act upon the brain. Alcohol has a wide effect all over the brain which is still being understood. Cocaine, on the other hand, has a very specific affect of blocking recycling of dopamine and other neurotransmitters. Finally, marijuana has a wide influence like alcohol but also a specific effect like cocaine, in that it basically turns up the gain on neuron communication.

채점기준

ⓐ Topic sentence

+ 2점 : "There are similarities and differences (1점) in the ways in which alcohol, cocaine and marijuana(0.5점) act upon the brain(0.5점)"를 명확하게 서술하였다.

ⓑ Major supporting details

+ 2점 : "① Alcohol has a wide effect all over the brain which is still being understood. ② Cocaine, on the other hand, has a very specific affect of blocking recycling of dopamine and other neurotransmitters. Finally, ③ marijuana has a wide influence like alcohol but also a specific effect like cocaine, in that it basically turns up the gain on neuron communication"을 명확하게 서술하였다.

☞ 3개 중 3개를 모두 정확하게 요약한 경우 2점, 2개만 요약한 경우 1점, 나머지는 0점을 준다.

감점
- 본문에 나오는 연속되는 6단어 이상을 사용하였다. −0.5pt
- 문단을 두 개나 그 이상으로 구성하였다. −0.5pt
- 문법이나 영어 표현을 합쳐 3개 이상 오류가 있다. −0.5pt

한글번역

알코올은 아주, 아주 작은 분자이며, 뇌 전체에서 매우 다양한 경로로 작용한다. 엔돌핀과 도파민에 영향을 미친다. 두 가지 주요 흥분성 및 억제성 신경전달물질인 글루타메이트와 가바에 영향을 미친다. 온갖 종류의 이온 통로에 영향을 미친다. 너무 작아서 모든 곳에서 작용할 수 있다. 그래서 연구하기가 정말 어려웠다. 사실, 우리는 여전히 술에 취한다는 느낌이 어떻게 생기는지—취한 느낌을 위한 기제가 무엇인지—이해하기 시작하는 단계에 불과하다. 왜냐하면 알코올은 일종의 망치처럼 또는 광범위한 방식으로 온갖 종류의 세포 기능을 방해하기 때문이다. 코카인은 이런 면에서 알코올과 완전히 정반대다. 한 가지 일을 한다. 그것을 정말 효과적으로 한다. 도파민과 노르에피네프린 같은 다른 신경전달물질의 재활용을 차단해, 그것이 쾌감을 향상시키고 각성을 향상시키며 움직임을 향상시킨다. 그래서 매우 구체적이다. 상대적으로 연구하기 쉽고 어떻게 작용하는지 이해하기 훨씬 쉽다. 마지막으로, 대마초는 코카인과도 같고 알코올과도 같다. 그래서 그 작용이 매우 구체적이라는 점에서는 코카인과 같고, 그 작용이 뇌 전체에 걸쳐 있다는 점에서는 알코올과 같다. 한 가지 일을 하지만, 모든 곳에서 그것을 한다. 코카인의 경우, 한 가지 일을 하지만 단지 몇 개의 경로에서만 그것을 한다. 알코올은 모든 곳에서 많은 일을 한다. 대마초의 활성 성분인 대마초수지는 대략 한 가지 일을 하지만 모든 곳에서 하며, 그 일은 세포 간의 소통을 향상시키고, 메시지를 향상시키는 것이다.

제27회 모의고사

1

하위내용영역	배점	예상정답률
일반영어 A형 기입형	2점	60%

모범답안 hospice

채점기준

- 2점 : 모범답안과 같다. 이외에는 답이 될 수 없다.
- 0점 : 모범답안과 다르다.

한글번역

왜 호스피스인가? 이것은 내가 어떤 종류의 간호를 하는지에 대해 질문받을 때 기대하게 된 첫 번째 질문이다. 이 같은 질문은 가족, 친구, 낯선 사람들, 그리고 의료계의 다른 분야에서 일하는 간호사와 의사들로부터 나왔다. 의료계의 대부분 분야에서는 생명을 구하는 것이 초점이고, 죽음은 종종 실패로 여겨진다. 역사적으로, 사람들이 의학적 성공의 가능성이 낮은 곳에 노력을 집중하기로 선택하는 이유에 대한 이해가 크지 않았다. 내가 이전에 해왔던 간호—고치고, 구하고, 치료하는 것과 모든 관련이 있던—에서 방향을 바꾸는 것이 나에게는 사고의 엄청난 전환을 요구했다는 것을 믿어달라. 나는 호스피스에서 우리가 하는 일이 그만큼 중요하다는 것을 스스로 알아내야 했는데, 다만 그것은 더 이상 그런 치료 선택지가 없는 사람들을 위한 것이라는 점만 다를 뿐이었다.

"하지만 당신은 항상 슬프지 않나요?" 또는 "무섭지 않나요?" 또는 "많이 울지 않나요?"는 자주 받는 다른 질문들이다. 호스피스에서 일하는 우리는 이렇게 답할 것이다: 아니요, 저는 항상 슬프지 않습니다. 아니요, 무섭지 않습니다. 네, 저는 많이 웁니다. 하지만 그 눈물은 종종 환자의 마지막 몇 주, 며칠, 또는 몇 시간이 의미 있고 편안했으며, 그들의 가족들이 같은 목표를 향해 긍정적인 방식으로 함께 노력할 수 있었다는 안도감, 기쁨, 그리고 만족감에서 나오는 것입니다.

2

하위내용영역	배점	예상정답률
일반영어 A형 서술형	4점	40%

모범 답안 Baines became a member because he refused to accept a reward for saving an old lady, saying it was a common behavior. Second, the meaning of the underlined is that the only thing a good person could do is to reject the money his uncle had not intended for him to have any longer.

채점 기준

+ 2점: 베인스가 "고맙지만 사양하는" 모임의 회원이 된 이유를 "Baines became a member because he refused to accept a reward for saving an old lady, (saying it was a common behavior)"라 서술하였거나 유사하였다.

☞ 다음과 같이 서술하였으면 1.5점을 준다.
  - "Baines became a member of the Declined-with-Thanks club because he believed that rescuing the old lady was not out of the ordinary."

+ 2점: 밑줄 친 부분의 의미를 "the only thing a good person could do is to reject the money his uncle had not intended for him to have any longer"라 서술하였거나 유사하였다.

한글번역

당신은 감사와 함께 거절하는 클럽—D.W.T.를 들어본 적이 있는가? 클럽 방도 없고 회원도 많지 않지만, 지난 12개월간의 대차대조표는 훌륭하여 15,000달러 이상이 거절됐음을 보여준다. 입회비는 100기니이고 연회비는 50기니이다; 즉, 선출되기 전에 100기니를 거절해야 하고, 회원 자격을 유지하는 동안 연간 50기니를 더 거절할 것으로 예상된다. 평생 거절로 일시불을 내는 것도 가능하지만, 그 금액은 정해지지 않았고 위원회의 재량에 맡겨진다.

베인스는 평생 회원이다. 그는 몇 년 전 한 노부인이 시내버스에 치일 뻔한 것을 구했는데, 그녀가 죽었을 때 그에게 1,400달러의 유산을 남겼다. 베인스는 유언 집행자들에게 편지를 써서 자신이 시내버스 밑에서 사람들을 끌어내는 것을 직업으로 하지 않는다고 지적했다; 만약 그녀가 그 당시 그에게 1,400달러를 제안했다면, 그는 그것을 거절했을 것이라고, 낯선 사람들로부터, 특히 여성들로부터 돈을 받는 습관이 없기 때문이라고; 그리고 그 돈이 2년 후 유언장에서 제안됐다는 사실이 조금도 차이를 만들지 않는다고 생각한다고 했다. 베인스는 이 당시 연 400달러를 벌고 있었고, 아내와 네 아이가 있었지만, 그는 자신이 평범하지 않은 일을 전혀 했다고 인정하지 않을 것이다.

세들리의 경우는 다음 위원회 회의에서 고려될 예정이다. 세들리의 부유한 삼촌, 성미 까다로운 노인이 그를 심하게 모욕했다; 다툼이 있었다; 그리고 그 노인은 조카의 상속권을 박탈하고 자신의 돈을 고양이 보호소에 유증함으로써 복수하겠다며 맹세하며 떠났다. 그는 변호사에게 가는 길에 죽었고, 세들리는 법적 영어로 자신의 행운을 통보받았다. 그는 "도대체 저를 뭘로 보시는 겁니까? 한 푼도 건드리지 않겠습니다. 고양이 보호소든 당신이 좋아하는 어떤 것이든 주세요."라고 답했다. 세들리는 물론 일반 회원으로 선출될 것이지만, 위원회에서는 품위 있는 사람이라면 누구든 다른 행동을 할 수 없었을 것이라는 강한 느낌이 있기 때문에, 그의 평생 회원 선출은 가능성이 낮다.

3

하위내용영역	배점	예상정답률
일반영어 B형 서술형	4점	50%

모범 답안 According to the research, returning to the same taco place from yesterday might be better, because it might be more enjoyable than one expects with a repeat visit.

채점 기준

+ 2점: 둘 중 "returning to the same taco place from yesterday might be better"라 답하였다.
+ 2점: 그 이유를 "because it might be more enjoyable than one expects with a repeat visit"라 서술하였거나 유사하였다.

한글번역

오브라이언의 연구팀은 사람들에게 그들이 이전에 본 적은 없지만 재미있을 새로운 영화를 넷플릭스에서 보게 했다. 다음날, 연구진은 그들 중 일부에게 같은 영화를 다시 보게 했다. 영화를 다시 보지 않은 이들은, 만약 자신이 그 영화를 다시 본다면 8점 만점의 평가에서 4점 정도의 즐거움을 느낄 것이라 평가했다. 이는 그들이 첫날 영화를 보고 난 후 이야기한 6.4점보다 확실히 낮은 점수다. 하지만 실제로 다음날 영화를 다시 본 일부는 다시 본 영화가 평균 5.7점의 즐거움을 주었다고 말했다.

이 불일치는 오브라이언의 연구를 잘 설명해준다. 한 번 본 영화를 24시간 뒤 다시 볼 경우 분명 첫 번째 보다 즐거움은 줄어든다. 이는 상식적인 사실이다. 하지만, 자신들이 예상했던 것보다는 그 영화가 훨씬 더 재미있었을 수 있다는 것이다.

행동경제학자들은 사람들이 무언가를 선택해야 할 때 새로운 책이나 영화, 새로운 장소처럼 경험해 보지 않은 것에 종종 더 높은 우선순위를 부여한다는 것을 알고 있다. 이는 잘못된 행동은 아니다. 사람들은 일반적으로 무언가에 익숙해질수록 이를 덜 재미있게 느낀다. 하지만 오브라이언은 이렇게 말한다. "사람들이 새로운 것을 선택하는 이유는 새로운 것이 특별히 좋을 것이라 생각해서가 아니라 이전 것이 지루할 것이라 생각하기 때문이다." 하지만 이런 지루함은 실제보다는 과장된 것일 수 있다.

기대라는 것이 때때로 이런 식으로 실제와 다르다는 것을 안다면, 사람들이 여가 시간을 어떻게 쓸지 결정을 할 때 더 합리적인 선택을 내릴 수 있을 것이다. 새로운 것을 찾기 위해 많은 시간을 쓰는 사람들은 이번 연구 결과에서 도움을 얻을 수 있을 것이다. 그런 사람들이 시간을 더 쓰지 않으면서도 (예전에 해본 일을 하면서) 거의 비슷한 즐거움을 느낄 수 있을 것이다.

4

하위내용영역	배점	예상정답률
일반영어 B형 서술형	4점	50%

모범답안) There are a few ways of asking for help that can create reinforcements to encourage a person to help. First, one reinforcement is activating the sense of feeling "in-group". Second, the helper can be reinforced by feeling themselves as a benefactor to others. The third reinforcement is helping the person asked to see their own effectiveness.

채점기준

ⓐ Topic sentence
+1점 : "There are a few ways of asking for help that can create reinforcements to encourage a person to help."를 명확하게 서술하였거나 유사하였다.

ⓑ Summary
+3점 : "First, ① one reinforcement is activating the sense of feeling "in-group" and a part of the social group's status and well-being. Second, ② the helper can be reinforced by a positive identity—feeling themselves as a benefactor to others. The third reinforcement is ③ to help the person asked to see their own effectiveness."를 서술하였거나 유사하였다.

☞ 3개 중 3개 요소가 모두 잘 요약되어 들어간 경우 3점, 2개 요소만 들어간 경우 2점, 1개 요소만 들어간 경우 1점, 하나도 들어가 있지 않으면 0점을 준다.

감점
- 본문에 나오는 연속되는 6단어 이상을 사용하였다. −0.5pt
- 문단을 두 개나 그 이상으로 구성하였다. −0.5pt
- 문법이나 영어 표현을 합쳐 3개 이상 오류가 있다. −0.5pt

제28회 모의고사

1

하위내용영역	배점	예상정답률
일반영어 A형 기입형	2점	40%

모범답안 correlation(s)

채점기준

- 2점: 모범답안과 같다. 이외에는 답이 될 수 없다.
- 0점: 모범답안과 다르다.

한글번역

20세기에 통계학자들과 과학자들은 대다수 인과관계를 적절한 과학의 주제로 보지 않아 거부했다. 그들은 주로 상관관계를 관찰했고, "상관관계는 인과관계가 아니다"라는 원칙만을 주술처럼 반복했다.

적어도 과학자들은 꾸준히 자신의 연구에서 인과관계를 유추할 수 있는 방법을 찾아왔지만, 통계학자들은 정확한 원인을 밝히려는 대부분의 시도를 인정하지 않았다.

단 한 가지 예외가 바로 무작위 대조 연구(randomized controlled trials, RCT)이다. 통계학자들은 잘 설계된 RCT에서는 상관관계가 인과관계를 의미할 수 있음을 알아냈다. 이 때문에 20세기 내내 RCT는 점점 더 중요한 연구 방법이 됐다.

문제는 RCT를 통해 과학자들이 인과관계를 밝힐 수 있도록, 다른 방법의 연구에서는 인과관계가 존재하지 않는 것처럼 말하게 된 것이다. 물론 플로지스톤(환상적 존재)처럼 비현실적으로 존재하지 않게 됐다는 것은 아니다. 그보다는 행동주의자들이 내적 경험이나 의식을 금기시한 것처럼, 그리고 언어학자들이 언어의 기원에 대해 논쟁을 금한 것처럼 과학자들은 인과관계에 대해 말하는 것을 두려워하게 됐다. 어쩌면 마치 천국과 지옥처럼, 개념적으로는 유용하지만 과학이 이를 다루기에는 부적절하다는 느낌을 주는, 그런 개념으로 인과관계는 존재하게 됐다.

하지만 과학자들은 세상을 예측하는 것을 넘어 세상에 영향을 미치고 싶어 했다. 때문에 그들은 때로 RCT 실험 결과가 미처 나오기 전에도 상관관계가 인과관계를 어느 정도는 의미할 수 있다는 듯 말하기도 했다.

한글번역

사람들에게 도움을 청할 때 상대가 자신이 조정되지 않는다고 느끼고 도움을 주는 과정이 즐거운 경험이 되게 하는 몇 가지 방법이 있다. 이 강화 요소들은 타인을 기꺼이 돕고자 하는 마음을 갖게 한다.

첫 번째 강화 요소는 심리학자들이 말하는 강한 내집단 의식이다. 도움이 필요한 사람이 도움을 받을 사람과 같은 팀이라는 믿음, 즉 중요한 집단의 일부라는 믿음을 심어 주는 것이다. 이런 신념은 집단상호주의를 넘어서는 것으로 같은 집단 내에 있는 사람들에게 일어나는 일들에 관심이 있기 때문에 돕는다는 생각을 갖게 한다. 집단에 속한 사람들의 행복과 복지는 집단 전체의 행복과 복지에 영향을 받기 때문이다. 도움이 필요한 사람이 한 집단 내의 멤버라는 인식을 만들면 기꺼이 도우려는 마음을 갖게 된다.

두 번째 강화 요소는 긍정적인 정체성에 대한 기회이다. 바꿔 말하면 도움을 줄 때 도움을 주는 자신에 대해 긍정적인 생각을 갖게 된다는 것이다. 특히 타인을 도울 때 자신이 가지고 있는 긍정적인 면이나 다른 사람들에게서 존경받는 역할을 하게 될 때 더욱 그렇다. 예를 들면 사람들은 "도움을 주는 사람이 되는 일"이 왜 중요한지 생각하면서 타인을 더 많이 돕게 된다. 자신이 도움을 주는 사람이라는 긍정적인 면모가 중요하게 자각되면 그런 인식에 맞게 행동할 가능성이 더 높아진다.

세 가지 중 가장 강력한 마지막 강화 요소는 자신의 영향을 볼 수 있는 기회이다. 즉, 사람들은 자신이 주는 도움의 영향(혹은 미래에 미칠 영향)을 보거나 알고 싶어 한다. 사람들은 자신의 도움이 어떻게 작용하는지 보고 싶어 한다. 이건 어떤 자부심의 문제가 아니라 몇몇 심리학자들이 말하는 근본적인 인간의 동기에 관한 문제이다. 사람들은 영향력을 미치고 싶어 한다. 자신의 행동이 의도했던 결과를 이끌어 내는 것을 알고 싶어 하고 본질적으로 본인 위주로 세상을 만들어 가고 싶어 한다. 이런 피드백이 없을 경우 자신의 행동이 어떤 결과를 가지고 오는지 알 수 있는 방법이 없으며 돕고자 하는 동기는 바닥으로 추락하게 된다.

2

하위내용영역	배점	예상정답률
일반영어 A형 서술형	4점	45%

모범답안 The word in the blank is "riots". Next, the meaning of the underlined is that income is an easy and one-sided way to view the wealth gap, which lacks accuracy.

채점기준

+ 2점: 빈칸에 들어갈 단어로 "riots"을 정확하게 기입하였다. 이외에는 답이 될 수 없다.
+ 2점: 밑줄 친 부분의 의미를 "income is an easy and one-sided way to view the wealth gap, which lacks accuracy"라 했거나 유사하게 서술하였다.
  ☞ 다음과 같이 서술하였어도 2점을 준다.
  - "Income as a way of measuring wealth inequality is insufficient"
  - "Income as a way of measuring wealth inequality is quick and easy but has a lot of limitations"
  ☞ "소득이 부의 불평등을 측정하는 방법으로 잘못되었다(wrong)"라 했으면 0점을 준다.

한글번역

"가난한 사람들이 부자들이 실제로 얼마나 돈이 많은지 알게 되면 당장 곳곳에서 폭동이 일어날 것이다." 배우이자 코미디언인 크리스 록이 2014년 <뉴욕 매거진>과의 인터뷰에서 갈수록 벌어지는 빈부 격차에 관해서 했던 말이다. 이 말은 실로 정곡을 찌르는 말이 아닐 수 없는데, 이는 불평등을 연구하는 이들이 고민하는 문제와도 닿아 있는 문제이다.

바로 어떻게 하면 불평등을 가장 정확하게 측정할 수 있는가의 문제이다. 불평등에 관한 대부분 연구는 소득(수입)에 초점을 맞춰 왔다. 소득에 관한 정보와 데이터를 구하는 건 어렵지 않다. 하지만 한두 해 돈을 엄청 잘 번다고 부자가 되는 건 아니다. 오히려 부자들 가운데는 오랫동안 쌓아온 부를 더욱 늘려가는 이들이 많다. 과거에는 부를 측정하는 데 걸림돌이 꽤 많았다.

아마도 부자들은 자기들이 얼마나 부유한지 대부분 사회 구성원들이 지금처럼 잘 모르는 상황이 계속되기를 바랄지도 모른다. 크리스 록이 말했던 것처럼 정말 폭동이 일어날지도 모르기도 하고. 하지만 나처럼 이 주제를 공부하는 사람들은 항상 더 정확하면서도 포괄적인 데이터를 찾아왔고, 빈부 격차를 더 정확하게 측정하는 방법을 고민해 왔다. 물론 내가 폭력을 조장하려는 건 절대 아니다. 하지만 난 시민들이 우리 사회 안의 격차가 얼만큼 벌어져 있는지 제대로 아는 것이 무엇보다 중요하다고 믿는다.

그러기 위해 가장 좋은 방법은 (소득 불평등이 아니라) 부의 불평등을 살펴보는 것이다. 불평등을 측정하는 방법에는 여러 가지가 있다. 가장 잘 알려진 방법은 소득을 살펴보는 것이다. 앞서 설명했듯이 가장 큰 이유는 데이터가 많기 때문이고, 계산하기도 쉽기 때문이다. 하지만 소득 불평등으로 측정하는 것은 큰 그림의 단면에 불과하다.

반면에 재산은 모든 측면을 아우르는 기준이라고 할 수 있다. 지금 얼마를 버는지 뿐만 아니라 앞서 번 소득과 물려받은 자산 등이 모두 반영된 수치이기 때문이다. 학자든 정책을 입안하는 관료나 정치인이든 부자와 나머지 사람들의 가장 근본적이고 포괄적인 차이를 정확히 이해하는 방법은 재산의 불평등을 조사하는 방법밖에는 없다.

3

하위내용영역	배점	예상정답률
일반영어 B형 서술형	4점	40%

모범답안 Data is similar to labor in that data is produced from human efforts, and both are immaterial resources and not physical commodities. Second, the term "artificial intelligence" is misleading because AI is trained collectively from human-generated examples, not from algorithms alone.

유희태 | 일반영어 ❹-2

> **채점 기준**

+ 2점: 데이터가 노동과 유사한 면을 "data is produced from human efforts, and both are immaterial resources and not physical commodities"라 서술하였거나 유사하였다.
+ 2점: 인공 지능이라는 말이 잘못된 용어라고 하는 이유를 "AI is trained collectively from human-generated examples, not from algorithms alone"이라 서술하였거나 유사하였다.

> **한글번역**

중요한 경제적 자원이 한때는 대가 없이 사용되다가 이후 가치를 가지게 된 예는 매우 많다. 예를 들어, 토지와 물이 그렇다. 하지만 데이터는 시장에서 거래되기가 특별히 더 어려워 보인다. 데이터는 실제 물리적으로 존재하지 않으며, 경제학자들이 비경합재(nonrival goods)라 부르는, 곧 중복해서 사용이 가능한 자원이다.

노동은 데이터처럼 정확하게 규정하기가 어렵다. 노동자는 인류의 역사에서 대부분의 시기에 노동의 대가를 제대로 받지 못했다. 사람들이 자신의 노동을 자유롭게 팔 수 있게 된 후에도, 임금이 현실적인 수준으로 올라오기까지는 수십 년이 걸렸다. 바일은 시카고 대학의 에릭 포스너와 공동으로 집필한 《급진적 시장(Radical Market)》에서 "역사는 과거와 똑같이 반복되진 않지만 유사하게는 반복된다"고 주장한다. 그는 인공 지능의 시대에 데이터는 노동이라는 형식으로 봐야 한다고 말한다.

이를 이해하기 위해서는 먼저 "인공 지능"이라는 용어에 문제가 있다는 것을 지적해야 한다. 바일과 포스너는 "집단 지능(Collective Intelligence)"이 더 올바른 용어라고 말한다. 대부분의 인공 지능 알고리즘은 인간이 만든 데이터를 이용해 훈련하는 "기계 학습"이라는 과정이 필요하다. 인간이 만들어 낸, 정답을 포함한 데이터 없이는 번역, 음성 인식, 이미지 인식 등 어떤 인공 지능 기술도 불가능하다. 따라서 인간이 만든 데이터는 인공 지능을 가능하게 만드는 노동이라 볼 수 있다. 데이터 경제가 발전할수록 이러한 데이터 작업은 다양한 형태를 띄게 될 것이다. 사람들의 SNS 활동이나 음악 감상, 음식점 추천 등의 활동에서도 새로운 서비스가 탄생할 수 있는 데이터가 만들어지며, 사진에 이름을 붙이거나 차를 운전하는 것과 같이 더 능동적인 활동에서 생성된 데이터로도 인공 지능을 훈련시킬 수 있다.

4

하위내용영역	배점	예상정답률
일반영어 B형 서술형	4점	40%

> **모범답안**) Among several sleep methods, polyphasic sleep can achieve maximum productivity if one gets past its drawbacks. There are several sleep methods such as monophasic—getting all one's sleep at once—, biphasic—sleeping twice daily, and, finally, polyphasic—sleeping in short naps throughout the day. Though polyphasic sleep has the drawbacks of being challenging for family life and being upset easily by missing sleep, this method can improve productivity by gaining 4 hours per day, or 28 hours a week.

> **채점 기준**

ⓐ Topic sentence
+ 1점: "Among several sleep methods, polyphasic sleep can achieve maximum productivity if one gets past its drawbacks"를 명확하게 서술하였거나 유사하였다.

ⓑ Summary
+ 3점: "① <u>There are several sleep methods such as monophasic—getting all one's sleep at once—, biphasic—sleeping twice daily, and, finally, polyphasic—sleeping in short naps throughout the day.</u> ② Though polyphasic sleep has the <u>drawbacks of being challenging for family life and being upset easily by missing sleep, this method can improve productivity by gaining 4 hours per day, or 28 hours a week</u>."를 서술하였거나 유사하였다.

☞ 2개 중 2개 요소가 모두 잘 요약된 경우 3점, 1개 요소만 요약된 경우 1점, 나머지는 0점을 준다.

감점
- 본문에 나오는 연속되는 6단어 이상을 사용하였다. −0.5pt
- 문단을 두 개나 그 이상으로 구성하였다. −0.5pt
- 문법이나 영어 표현을 합쳐 3개 이상 오류가 있다. −0.5pt

제29회 모의고사

1

하위내용영역	배점	예상정답률
일반영어 A형 기입형	2점	30%

모범답안 lithography

채점기준

- 2점: 모범답안과 같다. 이외에는 답이 될 수 없다.
- 0점: 모범답안과 다르다.

한글번역

예술 작품은 원칙적으로 항상 복제가 가능한 것이었다. 인간이 만든 인공품은 언제나 인간에 의해서 모방될 수 있었다. 이러한 모방은 기술에서의 연습을 위한 도제들에 의해, 작품의 보급을 위해 장인에 의해, 마지막으로는 이윤을 추구하는 제3자에 의해 수행됐다. 이에 비해서 예술 작품의 기술적 복제는 새로운 것인데, 이는 역사에서 긴 간격을 두고, 그러나 점점 강렬하게 관철됐다. 그리스 사람들은 예술 작품의 기술적 복제의 두 가지 방법만을 알고 있었는데 그것은 주조(鑄造)와 인각(印刻)이었다.

청동, 테라코타와 주화는 그리스 사람들에 의해 대량으로 생산될 수 있었던 유일한 예술 작품이었다. 그 밖의 모든 것들은 일회적이었으며 기술적으로 복제될 수 없었다. 목각으로써 판화가 처음 기술적으로 복제 가능하게 됐으며, 판화는 인쇄를 통해 활자가 복제 가능하기 전까지 오랫동안 그러했다. 활자의 기술적인 복제 가능성인 인쇄가 문학에서 불러일으킨 엄청난 변화는 익히 알려져 있다. 여기서 세계사적 잣대로 고찰된 바로 그러한 현상들 중에서 이 변화는 물론 아주 중요한 것이지만 하나의 특수한 예일 뿐이다. 목각에 더해 중세 동안에 동판과 에칭이 등장했고 또한 19세기 초에는 석판이 등장했다.

석판과 함께 복제 기술은 근본적으로 새로운 단계에 이르렀다. 목판에 새기거나 동판에 부식시키는 것과 달리, 돌 위에 도면을 덮는 훨씬 더 간편한 절차는 판화에 최초로 가능성을 부여했는데, 그것은 판화 제품들을 대량으로 공급할 뿐만 아니라 날마다 새로운 형태로 시장에 공급할 수도 있게 했다. 판화는 석판을 통해서 일상을 삽화로 재현하는 능력을 갖게 됐고 인쇄와 보조를 맞추기 시작했다.

한글번역

대다수 사람들은 자신의 생산성을 높이기 위한 궁극의 방법을 알고 싶어 한다. 때문에 세상에는 자신이 바로 그 "완벽한 방법"이라 말하는 수많은 기법들이 있다. 하지만 사람들은 모두 다르며, 누구에게나 맞는 방법이란 존재하지 않는다. 하지만 중요한 것은 어쨌든 하루를 계획해야 한다는 것이다. 《본질주의》를 쓴 그렉 맥커운은 이렇게 말한다. "스스로 자신의 삶에서 우선순위를 결정하지 않으면, 다른 사람이 정해주게 된다." 하루를 계획함으로써, 삶의 우선순위를 결정하는 사람이 돼야 한다.

다상 수면(polyphasic sleep) 기법은 다소 기이한 방법으로 소수의 사람들에게만 맞을지 모른다. 하지만 당신이 그 소수에 속한다면, 당신은 생산성을 크게 높일 수 있다. 대부분의 사람들은 단상 수면(monophasic sleep), 곧 하루에 한 번 잠을 잔다. 어떤 이들은 이상 수면(biphasic sleep)을 취하는데, 하루에 두 번 잠을 잔다. 즉, 오전에 4시간, 늦은 저녁에 4시간 이런 식으로. 다상 수면을 취하는 이들은 하루 중 짧은 시간 동안 여러 번 잠을 자는 이들로, 전체 수면 시간은 더 작으면서도 생산성은 매우 높다. 한 번 잠을 자는 시간은 사람에 따라 다르며, 어떤 이들은 겨우 20분 길이의 낮잠을 자는가 하면, 어떤 이들은 한 번의 적당히 긴 시간의 수면과 이를 보충하는 여러 번의 낮잠을 자기도 한다.

물론 이 방법은 명백한 단점을 가지고 있다. 스티브 파블리나는 가족들과 함께 살면서 이런 패턴의 수면을 취하는 것이 얼마나 어려운지 주목했다. 또, 이 방법을 취하는 이들이 수면 시간을 놓칠 경우, 생산성이 크게 떨어지는 문제도 있다. 하지만, 이 방법을 잘 사용하는 이들은 남들보다 훨씬 더 많은 시간 동안 일을 할 수 있다. 만약 하루 4시간만 잔다면, 일주일에 남들보다 28시간이 더 생기게 된다.

2

하위내용영역	배점	예상정답률
일반영어 A형 서술형	4점	45%

모범답안 The difficulty is that it is not easy to measure productivity because not everybody does the same work (unlike a production line). Second, the improved work-life balance creates no drop in productivity by working a day less because employees engage better with their work.

채점기준

+ 2점: 그 시도를 도입할 때 회사가 직면하게 되는 어려움을 "it is <u>not easy to measure productivity because not everybody does the same work</u>"라 서술하였거나 유사하였다.
+ 2점: 일과 삶을 조화롭게 하는 것이 생산성의 측면에서 어떤 기능을 하는가에 대한 질문에 "the improved work-life balance <u>creates no drop in productivity</u> (by working a day less because employees engage better their work)"라 서술하였다.

한글번역

뉴질랜드 회사인 퍼페추얼 가디언은 사무직 직원 240명에게 (하루 8시간) 주 4일 근무를 제안했다. 나흘 동안 일해도 급여는 닷새 일할 때 받던 것 그대로라는 조건이었다. 건물 내부가 따로 벽으로 나뉘지 않은 현대식 사무실에서는 직원들이 쉽게 집중력을 잃어 (업무 능률이 떨어지고) 생산성도 낮아진다는 연구 결과가 잇따라 나오자 이를 반영해 근무 시간을 조정한 것이다. 앤드루 반스 전무 이사는 주 근무 시간을 줄이면 직원들이 일에 더 집중해서 결국 생산성을 늘릴 수 있는 혁신적인 방법이라고 생각했다. 이 밖에도 직원들이 일과 삶을 더 조화롭게 꾸릴 수 있고, 스트레스가 줄어 정신 건강에도 도움이 되며, (출퇴근이 줄어들어) 도로에 차도 줄어들어 도시와 환경에도 좋은 일이 되는 등 부가적인 장점이 많을 것이라 생각했다. 실험 결과를 보면 (대부분 가설이 사실로 확인됐다.) 일과 삶의 균형을 맞추게 됐다고 답한 직원이 24%나 늘어났다. 직원들은 일에 더 집중할 수 있게 됐다고 답했고, 스트레스 지수도 7%나 떨어졌다. 일주일에 하루를 덜 일했는데도 전체 업무 생산성은 전혀 줄어들지 않았다.

하지만 몇 가지의 도전도 있다. 첫째로는, 회사 안에서 직원들이 하는 일이 모두 똑같지 않다는 점이었다. 공장 조립 부서에서 기계 부품을 조립하는 일이라면 직원들의 생산성을 측정하기가 훨씬 쉬웠겠지만. (퍼페추얼 뮤추얼의 직원들은 사무직 노동이 원래 그렇듯 다들 하는 일도 달라서 업무 능률이나 생산성을 일괄적인 잣대로 측정할 수 없었다.) 그래서 회사는 각 팀의 팀원들과 팀장에게 팀별로 하는 일을 최대한 자세히 써 달라고 했고, 일주일에 5일 동안 해오던 일을 어떻게 하면 4일 안에 끝낼 수 있을지 구체적인 계획을 세워서 보고해 달라고 요구했다. 팀원들 사이에 역할을 더 잘 나누든, 조직을 재정비하든 업무를 끝내야 하는 마감 기한은 변하지 않는다. 즉, 각자 월요일부터 금요일 사이에 쉬는 날을 하루 정해 쉬는 날은 엇갈리되 같이 모여서 회의하거나 같이 일해야 하는 날은 또 그대로 정해 놓고 실험을 한 것이다.

다음과 같은 기대가 있었다. 만약 직원들이 일주일에 4일만 일하고도 5일 일하던 것과 같은 생산성을 낸다면, (급여는 그대로이면서) 일주일에 하루를 더 쉴 수 있으니 그보다 더 좋은 직원 복지도 없을 것이고, 회사의 평가도 좋아질 것이다. 유능한 직원들이 회사를 떠날 이유는 사라지고, 반대로 외부의 유능한 인재들은 이 회사로 오고 싶어 할 것이다. 직원들이 출근을 덜한 만큼 사무실에서 쓰는 에너지도 20% 아낄 수 있다는. 회사가 직원의 복지에 신경을 쓰면, 직원들은 일에 더 집중하고 능률을 올려 생산성을 높이는 식으로 반드시 여기에 응답한다는 연구는 이제 쌓일 만큼 쌓여 정설이자 통념이 됐다. 이어 소위 "워라밸"이 직업 만족도와 전반적인 삶의 질에 매우 중요한 만큼, 일에 얽매이지 않고 자기만의 시간을 더 많이 보낼수록 직원들은 일할 때 집중해서 일을 끝마친다.

3

하위내용영역	배점	예상정답률
일반영어 B형 서술형	4점	40%

모범답안 The writer mentions "The Americans" as an example of interacting with ideas that cause one to unlearn what one understands of the world. Next, the words "cognitive perspective" best fit the blank.

채점 기준

+ 2점: 저자가 텔레비전 쇼인 "미국인들"을 언급한 이유를 "as an example of interacting with ideas that cause one to unlearn what one understands of the world"라 서술하였거나 유사하였다.
+ 2점: 빈칸에 들어갈 단어를 "cognitive perspective"라 정확하게 기술하였다. 이외에는 답이 될 수 없다.

한글번역

우리가 하는 많은 선택은 우리의 세계관을 바꾸곤 한다. 그 선택이란 무엇을 배우거나 어떤 것을 깊이 이해하거나 다른 시각으로 보는 관점을 기르는 것처럼 대개 더 나은 무언가를 위한 선택이다. 그런데 그 선택의 결과로 알게 된 사실이 우리가 기존에 알고 믿고 있던 것과 정반대라면 어떻게 될까? 무언가를 배우고 나서 보니 지금껏 나쁘다고 알고 있던 것이 좋아지게 되면 어떨까? 2013년부터 시작된 미국 TV 드라마 <The Americans>에 나오는 러시아 스파이 제닝스 부부 역을 생각해 보면 된다. 극 중 제닝스 부부는 냉전이 끝나기 전인 1980년대 미국에 잠입해 미국인 행세를 하며 간첩 임무를 수행한다. 그런데 일 때문에 어쩔 수 없이 친해져야 하는 사람들은 부부가 역겹고 끔찍하다고 생각했던 세계관을 지니고 사는 이들이었다. 좋든 싫든 제닝스 부부는 간첩 임무를 위해 속으로는 절대 동의할 수 없는 말을 끊임없이 해대는 사람들과 같이 웃고 즐기며 때로는 그런 생각에 맞장구도 쳐줘야 했다. 이런 상황에 처한 사람은 자연히 자기가 이렇게 끔찍한 생각을 하는 이들과 조금씩 동화되지는 않을지 걱정하기 마련이다. 그 사람들의 생각을 가만히 듣고 보니 일리 있는 면도 있다고 생각하게 돼서가 아니라 그런 사람들 속에서 자기도 그런 세계관을 가지고 사는 척하다 보면 원래 진짜 자기 생각과 세계관은 다소 옅어지고 지워질 수도 있기 때문이다.

이런 상황에 처하는 사례는 사실 얼마든지 찾아볼 수 있다. 친구가 추천해 준 다큐멘터리 내용이 알고 보니 가짜 뉴스로 도배된 선전물일 수도 있고, 관심이 가서 전공으로 택하려던 학문이 기본적으로 가정하는 전제가 내 신념과 맞지 않을 수도 있다. 그와 같은 경우는 선택이 당신의 인지적 관점을 바꾸는 방식이 전체적으로 손해인 경우로 간주된다.

4

하위내용영역	배점	예상정답률
일반영어 B형 서술형	4점	40%

모범답안 Under stress, the brain benefits from being fed extra carbohydrates. This can lead to maintaining cognition under stress, as shown in a study involving a stressful situation and participants being provided or denied food. So, if one eats an afternoon chocolate, this can lead to maintaining the brain's function, lowering stress levels, and reducing the risks of depression, stroke, and heart attacks.

채점 기준

ⓐ Topic sentence
+ 1점: "Under stress, the brain benefits from being fed extra carbohydrates"를 명확하게 서술하였거나 유사하였다.

ⓑ Summary
+ 3점: ① "This can lead to maintaining cognition under stress, as shown in a study involving a stressful situation and participants being provided or denied food. So, ② if one craves an afternoon chocolate, this can lead to maintaining the brain's function, lowering stress levels, and reducing the risks of depression, stroke, and heart attacks."를 서술하였거나 유사하였다.

☞ 2가지 중 2개 요소가 모두 잘 요약된 경우 3점; 1개 요소만 요약된 경우 1점; 나머지는 0점을 준다.

감점
- 본문에 나오는 연속되는 6단어 이상을 사용하였다. −0.5pt
- 문단을 두 개나 그 이상으로 구성하였다. −0.5pt
- 문법이나 영어 표현을 합쳐 3개 이상 오류가 있다. −0.5pt

제30회 모의고사

1

하위내용영역	배점	예상정답률
일반영어 A형 기입형	2점	45%

모범답안 friendship

채점기준
- 2점: 모범답안과 같다.
- 1점: companionship이라 했다.
- 0점: 모범답안과 다르다.

한글번역

아리스토텔레스는 열일곱 살에 서양 철학의 아버지라고 불리는 고대 그리스의 철학자 플라톤이 건립한 학교 플라톤의 아카데미에 입학해서 20년간 이곳에 머무르며 학문에 정진했다. 스승 플라톤의 제자 중에서도 군계일학이었던 아리스토텔레스는 수많은 질문을 던졌고, 수많은 질문에 대한 답을 찾았다.

아리스토텔레스가 정확히 언제 플라톤의 아카데미를 떠났는지는 불명확하나, 스승 플라톤이 세상을 떠난 뒤 얼마 지나지 않아 자신과 철학적 견해가 다르다는 이유로 아카데미를 떠난 것으로 알려져 있다. 이후 아리스토텔레스는 결국 자신의 스승 플라톤의 핵심적인 이론을 반박하는 주장을 펼치기에 이른다.

아리스토텔레스가 얼마나 많은 저서를 집필했는지 설명하기란 가히 불가능하지만, 현재까지 남아있는 극히 일부의 저술만 보더라도 경이로울 정도로 광범위한 주제를 다루고 있다. 천문학에서부터 물리학, 윤리, 경제학에 이르기까지 아리스토텔레스는 우리가 아는 모든 학문 분야를 탐구했고, 세상을 떠난 지 2,000년도 더 지난 지금까지 인류 역사상 가장 많이 읽히고 인용되는 사상가로 손꼽히고 있다.

오늘날 아리스토텔레스의 업적은 다양한 분야에 걸쳐 있지만, 가장 정확한 이론으로 손꼽히는 것 중 하나가 그의 우정론이다. 아리스토텔레스는 우정을 인생의 참된 즐거움 중 하나로 봤고, 진정한 우정을 나누는 친구가 있어야만 성공한 인생이라고 생각했다. 아리스토텔레스는 친구와 우정에 대해 다음과 같은 말을 남겼다. "가난과 같은 역경이 닥쳤을 때, 사람들은 자신이 유일하게 기댈 곳은 친구라고 느낀다. 우정은 어린 시절에는 나의 잘못을 바로잡아 주고, 늙고 약해졌을 때는 나를 챙겨주는 존재이다. 한창 전성기 때는 위대한 업적을 이루는 동반자가 된다. 생각하고 행동하는 데 있어 언제나 하나보다 둘이 낫기 때문이다."

한글번역

뇌의 무게는 체중의 2%에 불과하지만 우리가 일상에서 필요로 하는 탄수화물의 절반을 소비하며 그중에서도 포도당은 가장 중요한 영양소이다. 스트레스가 심할 때 뇌는 12%의 더 많은 에너지를 필요로 하며 사람들이 단것을 찾는 이유는 바로 이 때문이다. 탄수화물은 인체가 가장 쉽게 사용할 수 있는 에너지원이다. 실제로 스트레스를 받은 사람들은 음식을 먹기 전의 인지 능력 테스트에서 낮은 점수를 기록했다. 하지만 음식을 먹은 뒤에는 정상적인 상태로 돌아왔다.

뇌와 탄수화물의 관계를 더 알아보기 위해 우리는 40명을 대상으로 두 번의 실험을 진행했다. 첫번째 실험에서 우리는 참가자들에게 모르는 사람들 앞에서 10분 동안 발표를 부탁했고, 다른 세션에서는 그들이 발표할 필요가 없었다. 발표 후 스트레스 호르몬인 코르티졸과 아드레날린을 측정하고 한 시간 동안 뷔페에서 음식을 먹게 했다. 두 번째 실험에서는 발표 없이 호르몬을 측정했고 뷔페에서 음식을 먹게 했다. 이 실험에서 발표를 마쳤을 때 발표를 하지 않았을 때보다 스트레스 호르몬의 수치는 더 높았고, 또 평균 34g의 탄수화물을 더 먹었다.

그럼 초콜릿은 어떤 효과가 있을까? 나는 직장에서 오후에 초콜릿이 당긴다고 말하는 이들에게 초콜릿을 먹는 것이 당신의 건강을 유지하고 맑은 정신을 유지하는 방법이라고 말해준다. 사람들은 직장에서 종종 스트레스를 받으며, 이때 뇌는 에너지를 필요로 한다. 만약 이때 식욕을 참을 경우 뇌는 지방이나 근육으로 가야 할 포도당을 사용하게 되고, 그 결과 더 많은 스트레스 호르몬을 분비하게 된다. 이는 그 사람의 기분을 나쁘게 할 뿐 아니라 장기적으로 심장병과 뇌졸중, 우울증의 위험을 높인다. 또한 뇌는 에너지를 절약하기 위해 활동을 줄이며 집중력과 업무 수행 능력이 떨어질 수 있다.

2

하위내용영역	배점	예상정답률
일반영어 A형 서술형	4점	50%

모범 답안 Tribal and hunter-gatherer societies are more equalized due to projectile weaponry which puts the strong at greater risk from the weak. Second, "reverse dominance hierarchy" is a hierarchy in which the ruled band together to exert power steadily over the ruler.

채점 기준

+ 2점: 부족적 수렵 채집 사회의 인간이 영장류들보다 더 평등한 이유를 "due to projectile weapons"라 서술하였거나 유사하였다.
+ 2점: "역순위제"를 "a hierarchy in which the ruled(the weak; those on the bottom of the pyramid) band together to exert power (steadily) over the ruler(the powerful; the strong)"라 서술하였거나 유사하였다.

한글번역

왜 부족 사회와 수렵채집 인간 사회들이 더 평등한 경향이 있을까?

남캘리포니아 대학교의 문화인류학자인 크리스토퍼 뵘이 지적하듯이, 모든 영장류 사회는 비슷한 역학관계에 의해 지배된다. 어떤 개체든 위계질서를 올라갈 기회가 있으면, 그 또는 그녀는 그것을 잡을 가능성이 높다; 불행히도, 권력을 얻자마자, 다른 개체들이 그것을 분개한다. 그런 사회에서, 뵘이 쓰기로는, 세 가지 잠재적 결과가 있다. 하나는 갈등으로, 새로운 도전자들이 지속적이고 공공연하게 권력자들에게 정상의 자리를 놓고 도전하는 것이다. 또 다른 하나는 안정적 지배로, 권력자들이 끊임없이 그리고 영구적으로 나머지를 지배하는 것이다. 그리고 세 번째는 뵘이 "역지배 위계질서"라고 부르는 똑같이 안정적인 사회 구조로, 피라미드의 맨 아래에 있는 자들이 단결해 "의도적으로 그들의 잠재적 주인을 지배하는" 방법을 찾아내는 것이다. 그런 사회에서는 지배가 여전히 행사된다. 단지 그것이 집단적으로 그리고 지속적으로 아래로부터 오는 것일 뿐이다.

침팬지, 보노보, 그리고 고릴라들은 안정적인 역지배 위계질서를 달성하기 위해 고군분투한다. 그들은 때때로 자신들의 피라미드를 평평하게 만들 수 있지만, 잠깐일 뿐이다. 문제는 권력자들이 강하고, 지능적이며, 사회적으로 연결돼 있을 가능성이 높다는 것이다. 그들을 무너뜨리고, 그들이 다시 권력을 잡는 것을 막기 위해서는, 강력하고 지속적인 위협이 필요한데, 이는 인간이 아닌 영장류들이 갖지 못하는 것이다. 뵘은 부족 사회와 수렵채집 인간 사회들 사이에서, 투사 무기의 발달이 평등의 성장과 유지에 핵심적인 단계라는 것을 발견했다: 그것은 강한 자를 약한 자로부터 더 큰 위험에 처하게 한다. 그런 무기는 인간 사회가 다른 영장류들의 사회보다 더 평등한 이유 중 하나이다.

3

하위내용영역	배점	예상정답률
일반영어 B형 서술형	4점	45%

모범 답안 The information is important in that it shows that the woman(또는 people) of the young age range is finding Facebook unattractive and impersonal. Second, the most appropriate words for the blank are "messaging apps".

채점 기준

+ 2점: 밑줄 친 부분이 글 전체의 맥락상 어떤 측면에서 핵심적 중요성을 지니고 있는지에 대해 "the woman of the young age (range) is finding Facebook unattractive and impersonal."라 서술하였거나 유사하였다.
+ 2점: 빈칸에 들어갈 단어를 "messaging apps"라 정확하게 기술하였다. 이외에는 답이 될 수 없다.

4

하위내용영역	배점	예상정답률
일반영어 B형 서술형	4점	25%

모범답안 The concept of "health freedom" is used to falsely frame the issue so that nostrums can be promoted. The population (or People) might believe that treatments not allowed by government regulation have some value, or likewise, that vaccinations required by the government are harmful. However, quacks are often promoting these beliefs in order to deceive and sell treatments and it is the government's duty to protect the public from exploitation.

채점 기준

ⓐ Topic sentence
+ 2점 : "The concept of "health freedom" is used to falsely frame the issue so that nostrums can be promoted."를 명확하게 서술하였거나 유사하였다.

ⓑ Summary
+ 2점 : "People might believe that treatments not allowed by government regulation have some value(0.5점), or likewise, that vaccinations required by the government are harmful(0.5점). However, quacks are often promoting these beliefs in order to deceive and sell treatments(0.5점) and it is the government's duty to protect the public from exploitation(0.5점)."를 서술하였거나 유사하였다.

 감점
- 본문에 나오는 연속되는 6단어 이상을 사용하였다. −0.5pt
- 문단을 두 개나 그 이상으로 구성하였다. −0.5pt
- 문법이나 영어 표현을 합쳐 3개 이상 오류가 있다. −0.5pt

한글번역

페이스북은 뉴스를 보는 플랫폼(다양한 종류의 시스템이나 서비스를 제공하기 위해 공통적이고 반복적으로 사용하는 기반 모듈, 어떤 서비스를 가능하게 하는 일종의 '토대')으로서 더는 성장하고 있지 않다. 예를 들면, 미국에서 젊은이들이 뉴스를 보기 위해 페이스북을 사용하는 수치는 2017년에서 2018년 동안 20%나 떨어졌다. 지난해와 올해 사이 페이스북에서 뉴스를 받은 성인의 수치가 증가하지 않았다.

사람들이 그들의 장비를 덜 사용하기 때문이 아니다. 오히려, 로이터 저널리즘 연구소에서 발표한 보고서에서 말한 것처럼 이제 많은 사람은 메시지 앱에서 뉴스를 받고 있기 때문이다. 보고서에서 미국, 영국, 브라질 그리고 독일 사용자들의 소셜미디어 이용을 조사했다. 전체 샘플은 뉴스를 페이스북과 메시지 앱에서 매주 받는다고 답한 사람들로 이뤄져 있다. 보고서는 로이터 연구소에서 지난 여름에 발간한 2018 디지털 뉴스 보고서에 대한 다채롭고 질적으로 풍부한 정보를 제공하고, 1월 실시된 페이스북의 뉴스 피드 알고리즘 업데이트가 소비자에게 끼친 영향을 조사하고자 하는 목적을 가지고 있다. 저자들은 "왜 소비자가 메시지 앱에서 뉴스를 받고, 댓글을 남기고, 뉴스를 공유하는지"를 질문한다.

사람들은 비록 페이스북이 기본적인 플랫폼이란 것에 불쾌하게 생각하는 것과 상관없이, 여전히 페이스북이 "많은 사용자에게 기본적인 플랫폼"이라는 것을 알려주고 있다. "죄의식을 동반한 즐거움이죠. 나는 페이스북을 싫어하지만 동시에 사랑합니다." 한 미국 20대 남성은 말한다. 페이스북은 사람들에게 "머리를 식히기 위한 오락"과 같은 존재이자, 다른 이들과 연락하고 지내는 중요한 수단이다. 하지만 여전히 페이스북에 열정을 가지고 있나? 시간 낭비라고 생각하지는 않나? "페이스북은 점점 덜 매력적이고 개인적인 것이 개입되지 않아요. 나는 게시물을 점차 올리지 않고 있습니다." 한 20대 독일 여성은 말한다. "페이스북 친구 중 오직 10%만이 제 진짜 친구입니다."

연구는 사람들을 다시 플랫폼으로 데리고 오기 위한 페이스북의 알고리즘 변화가─사람들이 뉴스를 받고, 친밀감을 느끼며, 의미 있는 사회적 상호작용을 하는 공간으로 페이스북을 바꾸기 위한─제대로 작동하지 않고 있다는 것을 시사한다.

광고와 다르게 뉴스 출처의 수를 줄이는 정책은 그다지 실용적이지 않다. 아마 이미 늦었을지도 모른다 : 기존에 발표된 로이터의 보고서는 사람들이 뉴스를 공유하고 개인적인 주제를 이야기하기 위해 이미 메시지 앱으로의 전환을 시작했다는 것을 보여준다.

한글번역

미운 두 살이라는 말이 있다. 하루 종일 "안 돼"라는 말을 듣다 보면, 아이는 부모의 말에 반항하게 된다. 어른들 또한, 무언가를 하지 못하게 하는 걸 싫어한다. 그중 어떤 이들은 정부의 규제가 자신의 권리를 침해한다고 생각한다. 정부가 (아이의) 학교의 입학 조건으로 백신을 요구하면, 그들은 아이들에게 백신을 맞힐 권리가 자신에게 있다고 말한다. 암으로 죽어가는 환자들은, FDA의 승인을 받기 전까지 약을 팔 수 없다고 하면, 규제 때문에 사람의 목숨을 살리지 못한다고 불만을 토로한다. "건강의 자유"란 누구나 자신이 원하는 치료는 그 무엇이라도 받을 권리가 있으며, 자신들의 몸으로 들어가는 것을 자신들이 통제하며, 정부는 여기에 간섭해서는 안 된다는 주장이다.

하지만 "건강의 자유"는 우리가 사이비 의료인들이 자신들에게 쏟아지는 의혹의 눈초리를 본능적으로 공감하게 되는 환자들에게 돌리기 위해 사용한 (만든) 용어이다. 그들은 악어의 눈물을 흘리면서 "이 불쌍한 사람들은 자신들이 원하는 것은 무엇이든 해 볼 자유를 가져야 한다"라고 말한다. 그리고 두 가지 사실을 숨기기 위해 노력한다. 첫째, 누구도 사기를 당하는 것은 원치 않는다는 것, 특히 삶과 죽음에 관해서라면 더 말할 것도 없다. 환자들은 사이비 치료를 받기 위해 자신들의 "권리"를 요구하는 것이 아니다. 단지 거기에 어떤 희망이 있을지 모른다고 속고 있을 뿐이다. 둘째, 사이비 의료를 막는 법은 환자의 권리를 제한하기 위해서가 아니라, 환자들을 이용하려는 사기꾼들을 막기 위해 존재한다는 것이다.

백신 반대자들은 정부가 아이들의 건강을 보호할 의무가 있으며, 따라서 백신으로 막을 수 있는 질병으로부터 아이들을 지킬 의무가 있다는 것을 이해하지 못한다. 오히려 부모의 권리와 개인의 취향이 모든 것에 우선한다고 생각하는 경향이 있다.

제31회 모의고사

1

하위내용영역	배점	예상정답률
일반영어 A형 기입형	2점	40%

모범답안 global

채점기준

- 2점: 모범답안과 같다. 이외에는 답이 될 수 없다.
- 0점: 모범답안과 다르다.

한글번역

평등하지 않은 상황에서는 가까운 사람들끼리의 경쟁이 훨씬 격화된다. 자원에 따라 지닌 가치가 다르기 마련이고, 가치가 높은 자원일수록 승리의 보상도, 패배의 아픔도 커진다. 하지만, 특히 지역 내의 경쟁은 이 차이를 더욱 부각시킨다. 내가 실행한 연구에서, 한 경제 게임에 참가한 사람들은 불평등이 높아질 때 훨씬 더 이기적인 선택을 했다. 그들은 서로서로 더 많은 싸움을 했는데, 이렇게 하는 것이 그들에게 손해가 되더라도 말이다. 하지만, 비록 그들 사이에서 불평등이 그렇게 크지 않았더라도, 지역 내의 경쟁 아래서는 가장 빈번하게 싸웠고 그 결과 훨씬 더 많은 점수를 잃었다.

실제 세상에서 일어나는 폭력의 근본적인 원인을 규명하고 해결책을 찾는 데 사람들의 이러한 태도와 행동이 실마리를 제공할지도 모른다. 댈리는 자신의 저서 《경쟁을 없애는 법》에서 불평등이 심한 곳일수록 살인율이 높고, 반대로 평등한 사회일수록 살인율이 낮다는 사실을 보여줬다. 그런데 (앞서 살펴봤듯이) 경쟁의 범위가 좁을수록 불평등에 따른 폭력이 훨씬 격하게 일어나고, 반대로 전 세계적으로 넓은 차원에서 경쟁이 일어났을 때 반목하기보다 협력하는 쪽을 택한다면, 다음과 같은 해법을 생각해볼 수 있다. 이민이나 이주를 장려해 경쟁의 범위를 가능한 한 넓힐 수 있다면, 불평등이 존재하더라도 이것이 곧 폭력과 최악의 경우 살인으로 이어질 가능성은 낮출 수도 있다. 예를 들어, 불평등이 심화하더라도 동시에 경쟁이 전 세계적으로 일어나면, 후자(global competition)가 전자(inequality)의 영향을 줄이게 될 것이다. (경쟁자와 마주치고 부대낄 일이 없다면 마른 장작이 쌓여 있어도 불을 붙일 방법이 없는 것과 마찬가지인 상황이 되는 것.)

2

하위내용영역	배점	예상정답률
일반영어 A형 서술형	4점	40%

모범 답안 The five words are "having sex with the dead". Second, the series of experiments discovered that crows' responses are specific to their own species and they are not commonly interested in having sex with other dead crows.

채점 기준

+ 2점: 상응하는 다섯 단어를 "having sex with the dead"라 서술하였다. 이외에는 답이 될 수 없다.
+ 2점: 일련의 실험들이 발견한 것을 "crows' responses are specific to their own species and they are not commonly interested in having sex with other dead crows."라 서술하였거나 유사하였다.

한글번역

많은 연구들은 까마귀가 높은 지능을 가지고 있음을 말해준다. 까마귀는 퍼즐 문제를 풀 수 있고, 도구도 사용한다. 다른 연구는 까마귀들이 동료의 죽음에 반응하는 것과 같은 사회적 행동을 한다는 것을 보여준다.

워싱턴 대학의 박사 과정생인 캘리 스위프트는 2015년 까마귀의 "장례식"을 연구한 적이 있다. 이때 그녀는 까마귀의 한 가지 특이한 행동을 목격했다. 당시 그녀와 그녀의 지도 교수인 존 마즐루프는 까마귀가 죽어있는 까마귀를 발견했을 때, 울음소리를 통해 다른 까마귀들에게 위험을 알린다는 사실에 관한 연구를 하고 있었다. 그 과정에서 그들은 한 번도 보지 못했던 광경을 보게 됐다. 한 까마귀가 죽은 까마귀에게 다가가 그 위에 올라탄 뒤 의도가 명백한 어떤 행동을 한 것이다.

연구에서 스위프트와 마즐루프는 까마귀들이 죽은 까마귀를 통해 잠재적인 위험에 대해 알게 되고 이를 피한다는 것을 발견했다. 이 때문에 스위프트는 까마귀가 사체와 짝짓기를 시도했을 때 더욱 이해할 수 없었다고 말한다. 죽은 까마귀는 위험을 알리는 신호일 텐데, 왜 그 까마귀에 더 가까이 접근하는가 하는 것이다. "동종의 사체에 가까이 가는 것은 질병, 기생충, 천적 등의 위험을 크게 만듭니다."

연구에서 이들은 워싱턴주의 네 도시에서 308쌍의 야생 까마귀에 대해 실험했다. 그들은 까마귀 사체를 대신할 다양한 자세의 박제 까마귀와 비둘기, 다람쥐의 사체를 준비해 까마귀가 각각에 대해 어떻게 반응을 하는지 확인했다.

까마귀들은 동종의 사체에 대해 경고성 울음을 더 많이 냈고, 그중에서도 죽어있는 자세의 경우 울음소리를 더 많이 냈다. 죽은 까마귀에 접근한 까마귀의 비율은 25%였지만, 이 중에서 짝짓기를 시도한 까마귀의 비율은 4%에 불과했다. 이는 이러한 행동이 일반적인 행동은 아님을 의미한다.

3

하위내용영역	배점	예상정답률
일반영어 B형 서술형	4점	50%

모범 답안 The one word is "empathy". Second, selective empathy is the empathy reserved only for those one believes are hurt, not for their enemies or others.

채점 기준

+ 2점: 상응하는 한 단어가 "empathy"임을 정확하게 서술하였다. 이것 외에는 답이 될 수 없다.
+ 2점: 선택적 공감이 "the empathy reserved only for those one believes are hurt, not for their enemies"

☞ 다음과 같이 서술하였어도 2점을 준다.
  − "the empathy reserved only for their own group, not for their enemies"

4

하위내용영역	배점	예상정답률
일반영어 B형 서술형	4점	35%

모범 답안 China did not go aboard actively due to repercussions from local politics, which was aggravated by its political unification. With its advantages and lead in technology, it should have excelled, but during a power struggle between eunuchs and their opponents in the Chinese court, the opponents ordered the shipyards dismantled and forbid shipping overseas. Since China was unified, as opposed to other nations, this decision led to the whole of China stopping their fleets and no longer building shipyards.

채점 기준

ⓐ Topic sentence
+ 1점: "China did not go aboard actively due to repercussions from local politics, which was aggravated by its political unification"를 명확하게 서술하였거나 유사하였다.

ⓑ Summary
+ 3점: "① With its advantages and lead in technology, it should have excelled, but during a power struggle between eunuchs and their opponents in the Chinese court, the opponents ordered the shipyards dismantled(1.5점). ② Since China was unified, as opposed to other nations, this decision led to the whole of China stopping their fleets and no longer building shipyards(1.5점)."를 서술하였거나 유사하였다.

감점
- 본문에 나오는 연속되는 6단어 이상을 사용하였다. -0.5pt
- 문단을 두 개나 그 이상으로 구성하였다. -0.5pt
- 문법이나 영어 표현을 합쳐 3개 이상 오류가 있다. -0.5pt

한글번역

약 10년 전을 기점으로 일부 사람들, 특히 젊은층을 중심으로 공감 능력이라는 개념에 대한 의심이 싹트기 시작했다. 1960년대 말부터 학계에서는 "곤경에 처해 도움이 필요한 사람이 있어도 내 문제는 아니다", "누군가를 비난하기 전에 내가 그쪽 입장이면 기분이 어떨지 짐작해보려고 노력한다"와 같은 설문 문항에 대한 동의 여부로 젊은이들의 공감 능력 정도를 연구해 왔다.

부교수인 새라 콘래스는 수십 년간 쌓인 데이터에서 명확한 패턴을 발견했다. 2000년 전후로 젊은이들의 공감 능력이 떨어지기 시작한 것이다. 곤경에 처한 사람을 돕는 것, 다른 사람의 시각으로 세상을 보는 것은 한마디로 '내가 알 바 아니다'라고 말하는 응답자의 수가 점점 많아졌다. 2009년에 이르자 젊은이들의 공감 능력은 우리 세대보다 평균 40%나 떨어졌다.

인간의 자연스러운 본능과도 같은 공감 능력이 소비 심리처럼 변화한다는 것은 이상한 일이다. 하지만 이런 현상은 엄연한 현실이다. 우리가 초등학교 교실에서 배운 것들을 이제 젊은이들은 곧이곧대로 받아들이지 않고 있는 것이다. 이들의 생각은 이렇다. 왜 굳이 내가 아닌 사람의 입장에서 생각해야 하는가? 더군다나 나에게 해로운 사람의 입장이라면? 실제로 공감 능력을 발휘하지 않는 것은 곧 자신의 입장을 확실히 표명하는 것, 즉 긍정적인 가치로 인식되고 있다. 일례로 백인우월주의자인 리처드 스펜서의 아내가 가정폭력 사실을 언론에 밝혔을 때, 인터넷 좌파들의 반응은 "왜 우리가 끔찍한 인종주의자와 연대하는 것을 선택한 여성에게 관심을 주어야 하나? 왜 우리의 공감 능력을 그런 곳에 낭비해야 하지?"라는 식이었다.

새로운 공감의 법칙은 "적에게 공감 능력을 낭비하지 말고, 내가 생각하고 판단하기에 그것을 필요로 하는 이들을 위해 아껴두자" 정도로 보인다. 상대편에 공감하는 것은 거의 터부시되는 분위기다. 이와 같은 "선택적 공감"은 아주 강력한 힘을 발휘하고 있다.

제32회 모의고사

1

하위내용영역	배점	예상정답률
일반영어 A형 기입형	2점	45%

모범답안 personality differences

채점기준

- 2점: 모범답안과 같다. 이외에는 답이 될 수 없다.
- 0점: 모범답안과 다르다.

한글번역

나는 진화 생물학 생태학자이며, 내 주된 연구 분야는 개체의 성격이 그들의 적합성과 집단 행동이나 사회에서의 성공에 어떤 영향을 미치는지 보는 것이다. 대부분의 사람들은 크게 관심이 없겠지만, 동물 성격 연구는 행동생태학 내에서 매우 활발하게 연구되는 분야인데, 이는 자연에서 개체가 성격을 가지는 것이 매우 일반적일 뿐더러 그 성격이 그들의 종 안과 다른 종과의 상호작용에서 그들의 행동을 잘 설명하기 때문이다. 현재까지 성격의 존재를 테스트한 거의 모든 종에서 우리는 성격을 발견했으며, 성별에 연관된 성격 차이가 가장 두드러진 경우가 많다. 우리와 가장 가까운 영장류에 있어 성별에 따른 성격의 차이는 매우 잘 정리돼 있다. 영장류에 있어 암컷과 수컷은 덩치의 차이가 있으며, 포유류는 일반적으로 공격성, 암컷의 까탈스러움, 텃세, 몸치장, 양육 등에 있어 성별에 따른 큰 차이를 가지고 있다.

인간 또한 성별에 따른 몸집 차이가 있고 어떤 객관적인 관찰자들이라도 동의할 만한 성별에 따른 성격의 차이가 있다. 포유류 전반에 걸쳐 이러한 차이가 나타난다는 사실에서, 인간의 성별에 따른 행동의 차이가 순수하게 사회화의 결과라는 주장은 아무리 잘 봐준다 해도 의심스러운 소리에 불과하다. 그 주장이 사실이 되기 위해서는 진화에 있어 선택적인 압력으로 작용해 온 성별에 따른 성격의 차이가 하필 우리 인간 종에 있어서만 어떤 이유에 의해 완전히 사라져야 하고, 또 성장기의 사회화 과정에서 하필 성별에 따라 그런 특징이 그대로 학습돼야만 한다.

한글번역

중국은 의심할 여지없이 여러 이점들이 있었다. 비옥한 초승달 지대(나일 강과 티그리스 강과 페르시아만을 연결하는 고대 농업 지대)에서와 거의 유사한 이른 시점에서의 식량 생산의 증가라든가, 지구에서 가장 많은 인구를 먹여 살릴 수 있었던 거대한 생산력들이 그것들이다. 이상과 같은 이점들과 빠른 출발 덕분에 중세 때 중국은 전 세계의 기술을 선도했다. 15세기 초에는 수백 척의 배로 구성된 보물선 선단들을 파견했는데, 그중 가장 큰 배의 경우 길이가 120미터에 달했으며 총인원도 최대 28,000명에 달했다. 그들은 콜럼버스가 보잘 것 없는 세 척의 배로 협소한 대서양을 건너 아메리카 동해안에 도달하기 수 십년 전에 이미 인도양을 건너 아프리카 동해안에까지 진출했다. 어째서 중국의 배들은 태평양을 건너 아메리카 서해안으로 진출하지 못했을까? 간단히 말해서, 왜 중국은 그토록 낙후됐던 유럽에게 기술의 선도자 위치를 뺏겼을까?

우리는 중국의 보물선 선단의 종말을 통해 하나의 단서를 얻을 수 있다. 1405~1433년에 일곱 차례의 선단이 중국을 떠나 항해했는데, 그러다가 중국 조정의 두 파벌(환관과 그 반대파) 사이에 권력 투쟁의 발생으로 인해 중단되고 말았다. 환관들은 선단을 파견하고 지휘하는 일에 동조하는 쪽이었다. 그래서 반대파는 권력 투쟁에서 승리하자 곧 선단 파견을 중단시켰고, 결국에는 조선소 마저 해체하고 해양 항해를 금지시켰다. 이 사건을 보면서 우리는 1880년대 런던 시 당국이 공공전기조명의 발전을 억압했던 일, 제1차 세계대전과 제2차 세계대전 사이의 기간 동안 미국이 고립주의를 고집했던 일, 그 밖에도 많은 나라가 정치적인 문제 때문에 뒷걸음친 일들을 기억하게 된다. 하지만 중국의 경우에는 한 가지 다른 점이 있다. 그것은 바로 중국 전역이 정치적으로 통일됐다는 사실이다. 한번 결정이 내려지자 중국 전역에서 선단 파견이 중단됐고, 일시적이었던 이 결정은 돌이킬 수 없는 것이 되고 말았다. 다시 배를 만들어 그 일시적 결정의 어리석음을 입증하고 또 새로운 조선소를 지으려 해도, 본보기로 삼을 수 있는 조선소가 하나도 남아 있지 않았기 때문이다.

2

하위내용영역	배점	예상정답률
일반영어 A형 서술형	4점	50%

모범답안 The landmark study showed that a four-and-a-half-year old could remember memories from 18 months prior but around age 6 children begin to forget many of their earliest memories. Second, the case of the mice shows that infancy amnesia has little to do with the capacity for language or a sense of self.

채점기준

+ 2점: 기념비적인 연구의 주요 기여한 바를 "a four-and-a-half-year old could remember memories from 18 months prior(1.5점), but around age 6 children begin to forget many of their earliest memories(0.5점)"라 서술하였거나 유사하였다.

+ 2점: 생쥐 연구에서 드러난 것을 "infancy amnesia has little to do with the capacity for language or a sense of self"라 서술하였거나 유사하였다.

☞ 다음과 같이 서술하였어도 2점을 준다.
 — "Memories in infancy can be lost in adulthood even without development of language or a sense of self."
 — "Enduring memories in adulthood do not require language or sense of self."

한글번역

1980년대 후반에 들어서자 아동 심리학 분야에서 개혁이 시작됐다. 바우어와 다른 심리학자들은 몇 가지 실험과 연구를 통해 유아기적 기억을 본격적으로 분석하기 시작했다. 실험이란 예를 들어 어린이에게 간단한 장난감 징을 만들어 치는 법을 가르쳐 주고, 몇 분 내지 몇 달이 지난 뒤 그 장난감을 쳐보게 해 그 사이 기억이 얼마나 잊혔는지를 살펴보는 식이었다.

여러 차례 실험을 거듭한 끝에 과학자들은 3세 이하 어린이도 한계가 있을지언정 기억을 만들어 남긴다는 점을 밝혀냈다. 생후 6개월 된 아기들의 기억은 적어도 하루는 지속됐다. 생후 9개월이 되면 그 기간이 최소 한 달로 늘어나고, 두 돌이 지난 아기는 1년 전의 기억을 떠올릴 수 있다. 이제는 (이 분야의 고전이 된) 기념비적인 1991년 연구에서 네 살 반 된 어린이가 18개월 전, 그러니까 자신의 세 번째 생일 즈음에 디즈니월드에 갔던 기억을 상당히 자세히 기억해냈다는 사실을 발견했다. 그런데 여섯 살 무렵에 아이들은 이런 어릴 적 기억들을 까먹기 시작한다. 2005년 바우어와 동료 연구진이 한 실험 결과를 보면, 다섯 살 반 어린이는 세 살 때 일을 80% 정도 기억했지만, 일곱 살 반 어린이는 세 살 때 일을 40%도 기억하지 못했다.

(이 2005년) 실험은 어릴 적 기억 상실에 관한 핵심적인 모순을 극명하게 드러낸다. 즉, 어린이도 더 어렸을 때 경험을 기억으로 만들어 저장하고 시간이 지난 뒤 꺼내어볼 수 있지만, 이때 기억들은 언젠가 대부분 사라져버린다는 것이다. 어른이 된 뒤에도 어떤 기억은 희미해지지만, 어릴 적 기억 상실에 버금가는 수준은 아니다.

기억이 온전히 남으려면 언어 능력과 자아에 대한 감각 혹은 자의식이 필요한데, 어린이는 두 가지가 모두 부족하기 때문에 기억을 잘 못한다는 주장도 있었다. 물론 어떤 일에 관해 나눈 대화나 그 상황에 내가 어떻게 관련돼 있었는지는 사람의 기억을 강화하는 데 큰 역할을 한다. 하지만 어릴 적 기억 상실을 이 두 가지의 부족만으로 설명할 수는 없다. 쥐처럼 몸집에 비해 뇌가 충분히 크고 복잡한 동물에서도 비슷한 현상이 관찰된다. 즉, 쥐가 구사하는 언어는 인간의 언어와 비교할 수 없을 수준일 것이고, 자의식도 인간보다 훨씬 단순할 텐데, 그런 쥐도 자라면서 어렸을 적 기억을 잊어버린다.

3

하위내용영역	배점	예상정답률
일반영어 B형 서술형	4점	30%

모범 답안) The researchers were unable to adjust for the app's users' age and wealth. Second, the word that best suits the blank is "four".

채점 기준

+ 2점: 연구진이 통제할 수 없었던 것이 "the app's users' age and wealth"임을 명확하게 서술하였거나 유사하였다.

  ☞ 다음과 같이 서술하였어도 2점을 준다.
  - "The fact that the users of the app tended to be younger and more affluent than the whole country."

+ 2점: 빈칸에 들어갈 한 단어를 "four"라 기입하였다. (This comes from the mathematical relationship described in the passage. The researchers found that : ① A win brings 3.9 points of happiness. ② A loss causes 7.8 points of sadness (twice as much as a win). ③ The passage states that post-match sadness lingers for hours while joy is fleeting. ④ If the sadness is twice as intense (7.8 vs 3.9) and lasts longer, then the total negative impact would be approximately four times greater than the positive impact of a win.

한글번역

(영국) 서섹스대학교의 경제학자 피터 돌튼과 조지 맥케런이 현재 심리 상태를 입력하는 행복 추적기 앱의 데이터 300만여 건과 수년간의 영국 축구 경기의 시간과 장소를 분석한 결과, 내가 응원하는 팀이 이겼을 때 느끼는 행복은 내가 응원하는 팀이 졌을 때 느끼는 불행의 절반 정도에 불과한 것으로 나타났다.

월드컵 결승전에 이 공식을 대입해보면 (이 세상에 프랑스를 응원한 팬과 크로아티아를 응원한 팬의 숫자가 같았다고 가정) 월드컵 결승전이 끝난 뒤 세상은 더 불행한 곳이 됐다. 한마디로, 축구는 행복의 파괴자이다.

이걸 증명하기 위해 연구진은 한 앱으로부터 나온 데이터를 분석했다. 이 앱이 하루에 여러 차례 무작위로 3만 2천여 명에게 던지는 질문은 "얼마나 행복하다고 느끼세요"이다. 사람들은 지금의 심리 상태를 가장 행복하면 100점 만점으로 매겨 답할 수 있다. 지금 누구와 함께 무얼 하고 있는지도 짧게 덧붙일 수 있으며, 위치 정보도 함께 전송된다. 연구진은 이 정보를 모아 응답자가 경기장에서 직접 축구를 관전하고 있는지 아닌지를 판단할 수 있다.

연구진은 이어 시간대, 요일에 따른 효과를 감안해 결과를 조정했다. (하루 중에도 대체로 기분이 좋은 시간대가 있고, 일주일 중에 특히 기분이 쉽게 우울해지는 날이 있기 마련이니까.) 또한, 연구진은 한 사람의 행복 지수를 추적할 수 있었기 때문에 그 사람이 원래 쉽게 행복해하는 사람인지, 반대로 기본적으로 불만이 많고 우울한 사람인지도 알 수 있었다. 하지만, 연구진은 해당 앱을 사용하는 사람들의 데이터를 받았기 때문에 앱 사용자의 연령대나 재산까지는 통제할 수 없었다.

(그렇다면 이제 결과를 살펴보자). 내가 응원하는 팀이 이긴 지 한 시간 안에 팬들은 보통 때보다 약 3.9포인트 더 행복하다고 느꼈는데, 이는 음악을 들었을 때 느끼는 행복과 거의 비슷한 수준이다. 반대로 내가 응원하는 팀이 패한 지 한 시간 안에 심리 상태에 답한 팬들은 보통 때보다 7.8포인트나 더 슬퍼했다. 이는 일 하거나 공부할 때, 줄을 서서 기다릴 때 느끼는 답답함이나 짜증, 스트레스보다 두 배 가까이 더 우울한 수치다.

연구진은 경기가 끝난 뒤 느끼는 기쁨과 슬픔의 차이가 극명한 것도 놀랍지만, 시간이 흐를수록 차이가 더 벌어진다는 점도 간과해선 안 된다고 말한다. 즉, 승리 후 느끼는 기쁨은 얼마 가지 않아 사라지곤 하지만, 패배 후 찾아오는 슬픔은 훨씬 오랫동안 팬들을 괴롭혀 결과적으로 승리 후 느끼는 행복의 네 배나 되는 불행을 안겨준다. 이 차이는 응답자가 직접 경기장에 가서 경기를 관전했을 때 훨씬 크게 나타났다.

4

하위내용영역	배점	예상정답률
일반영어 B형 서술형	4점	40%

모범답안) Polytheism is significantly logical and persuasive as opposed to a monotheistic bias. Polytheism doesn't dispute a single power at work, and such polytheist religions as Greek and Hinduism had such singular powers behind them. However, in polytheism these singular supreme powers are viewed as indifferent to human interests, and thus neither Greeks nor Hindus took any action to try to influence them by sacrificing something or building temples.

채점 기준

ⓐ Topic sentence
+ 1점: "Polytheism is significantly logical and persuasive as opposed to a monotheistic bias"를 명확하게 서술하였거나 유사하였다.

ⓑ Summary
+ 3점: "<u>Polytheism doesn't dispute a single power at work, and such polytheist religions as Greek and Hinduism had such singular powers behind them</u>(1점). However, <u>in polytheism these singular supreme powers are viewed as indifferent to human interests</u>(1.5점), and <u>thus neither Greeks nor Hindus took any action to try to influence them by sacrificing something or building temples</u>(0.5점)."를 서술하였거나 유사하였다.

☞ 그리스인들이 운명의 여신에게 제물을 바치지 않았고, 힌두교도들도 아트만을 위한 사원을 짓지 않은 이유를 정확하게 서술하였으면 1.5점을 준다.

− "In polytheism these singular supreme powers are viewed as indifferent to human interests."

감점
- 본문에 나오는 연속되는 6단어 이상을 사용하였다. −0.5pt
- 문단을 두 개나 그 이상으로 구성하였다. −0.5pt
- 문법이나 영어 표현을 합쳐 3개 이상 오류가 있다. −0.5pt

한글번역

서구인들은 2천 년 동안 일신교의 세뇌를 받은 탓에 다신교를 무시하고 유치한 우상 숭배로 보게 됐다. 이것은 부당한 고정관념이다. 다신교의 내부 논리를 이해하려면, 수많은 신이 존재한다는 믿음을 지탱하는 중심 사상을 파악할 필요가 있다.

다신교가 우주 전체를 관장하는 단일한 힘이나 법칙의 존재를 반박하기만 하는 것은 아니다. 사실 대부분의 다신교 심지어 애니미즘(우주의 모든 활동은 우주를 다스리는 어떤 힘에 의해 이뤄진다는 믿음) 종교들은 모든 다른 신들이나 악마, 신성한 바위의 배후에 있는 최고 권력을 인정했다. 고전 그리스 다신교에서 제우스, 헤라, 아폴론과 그 동료들은 모든 것을 다스리는 전능한 힘, 즉 운명의 여신(모이라, 아낭케)에게 복종했다. 힌두 다신교에서는 아트만이라는 단 하나의 원리가 무수한 신들과 정령, 인간, 생물학적 세상과 물리적 세상 모두를 통제한다. 아트만은 전 우주의 영원한 정수이자 영혼이면서 모든 개인과 모든 현상의 정수이기도 하다.

일신교와 구별되는 다신교의 근본적 통찰에 의하면, 세상을 지배하는 최고 권력은 관심이나 편견을 지니고 있지 않다. 그러므로 인간의 평범한 욕망이나 근심 걱정에 개의치 않는다. 이 권력에게 전쟁의 승리나 건강, 비를 요청하는 것은 무의미하다. 모든 것을 아우르는 위치에서 보면, 특정 왕국의 승리나 패배, 특정 도시의 번영이나 쇠퇴, 특정인의 회복이나 사망은 아무런 차이가 없는 일이기 때문이다. 그리스인들은 운명의 여신에게 제물을 바치지 않았고, 힌두교도들도 아트만을 위한 사원을 짓지 않았다.

유희태 | 일반영어 ❹-2

제33회 모의고사

1

하위내용영역	배점	예상정답률
일반영어 A형 기입형	2점	65%

모범 답안) compassion

채점 기준

- 2점: 모범답안과 같다. 이외에는 답이 될 수 없다.
- 0점: 모범답안과 다르다.

한글번역

　뉴저지주 쿠퍼대학병원의 진료 부장이자 중증 치료 전문가인 스티븐 트레제키악 박사는 다정다감한 의술의 신봉자와 거리가 멀었다. 그는 의학을 철저한 과학으로 보고 접근하는 타입이었다.
　하지만 앤서니 마짜렐리 병원장이 가져온 연구 과제를 수행하면서 생각이 달라지기 시작했다. 병원장은 최근 의료 업계 종사자들(의사들) 사이에서 번아웃 증후군이 전염병처럼 퍼지고 있는 가운데 환자 치료 개선 방안이 필요하다고 지시했다.
　병원장이 트레제키악 박사에게 내린 연구 과제는 구체적인 질문이었다. 질문은 "의술에 더해 연민과 인정을 가지고 환자를 치료하는 것이 환자와 의사의 웰빙에 측정 가능한 도움을 주는가?"였다.
　처음에 트레제키악 박사는 의구심을 가졌다. 물론 연민이라는 것이 나쁠 리 없겠지만 실제로 그것이 어떻게 도움이 되는지 증명할 수 없으리라 예상했다. 그러나 마짜렐리는 그의 동료이자 상사였기에, 트레제키악은 이 과제를 진지하게 파고들기로 결심했다.
　하지만 논문 초록 1000여 편과 250개의 보고서를 검토한 후, 예상이 빗나갔음을 알 수 있었다. 답은 단호하게 "그렇다"였다. 의료인이 환자와 인간적인 유대를 만들기 위해 시간을 들이면 치료 결과도 좋아지고 의료 비용도 낮출 수 있다는 것이었다. 그 효과는 환자의 고통이 줄어들고 치유를 촉진하며 혈압이 낮아지고 우울증과 불안감이 개선되는 등의 구체적인 이점으로 나타났다.

2

하위내용영역	배점	예상정답률
일반영어 A형 서술형	4점	40%

모범 답안) The meaning of the underlined is that a human being is not an animal, which does not know how to show gratitude, so should show gratitude for other people's help. Second, the most appropriate word for the blank is "happiness".

채점 기준

+ 2점: 밑줄 친 부분의 의미를 "a human being is not an animal, so should show gratitude for other people's help"라 서술하였거나 유사하였다.
+ 2점: 빈칸에 들어갈 단어를 "happiness"라 서술하였다. 이외에는 답이 될 수 없다.

한글번역

　당신은 가축처럼 길러지지는 않았을 것이다. (그렇기에) 타인의 도움에 대해 고마움과 감사함을 표시해야 한다는 사실을 알고 있을 것이다. 그런데도 사람들은 종종 감사를 표현할 때 심각한 실수를 한다. 사람들은 자신이 어떻게 느끼는지에 중점을 둔다. 도움을 준 사람에게 초점을 맞추기보다 자신이 얼마나 기쁘고 큰 도움을 받았는지에 대해서 이야기한다.
　노스캐롤라이나 대학의 연구원들은 감사의 표현을 두 가지 유형으로 구분했다. 타인의 성품이나 능력(즉 타인의 긍정적인 부분)을 검증하고 인정하는 과정을 포함한 상대를 칭찬하는 유형과 도움을 받은 사람이 얼마나 그 도움으로 인해 이익을 얻었는지를 표현하는 자기 이득 유형이 그것이다. 이 연구에서 커플들이 자신의 파트너가 최근에 한 일에 대해서 감사를 표현하는 법을 관찰했다. 그리고 연구 참가자들의 표현은 상대를 칭찬하는 방식이었는지 아니면 자신의 이익에 초점을 맞추었는지 분류됐다. 각 유형의 표현 방식을 예로 들면 다음과 같다.
　상대방 칭찬하기: "그 행동은 당신이 얼마나 책임감 있는 사람인지를 보여주는 행동이었어…" "당신은 애써서 그렇게까지 도움을 줬어…" "당신은 그 일을 정말 잘 하는 것 같아."
　자신의 이익에 초점 두기: "당신 덕분에 내가 쉴 수 있었어." "덕분에 직장에서 내가 우쭐댈 수 있었어." "나 행복해"

마지막으로 도움을 준 사람은 상대가 얼마나 감사함을 표현했다고 느끼는지, 얼마나 도움을 준 사실에 대해 행복했는지, 또 자신의 파트너에 대해 얼마나 애정을 느끼는지 평가하도록 했다. 연구원들은 상대방을 칭찬하는 유형이 반응과 행복 그리고 애정과 강한 관련이 있었으나, 자신의 이익에 초점을 둔 경우는 그렇지 않은 것을 발견했다.

3

하위내용영역	배점	예상정답률
일반영어 B형 서술형	4점	40%

모범답안 The difference between crows and human beings' intelligence is that humans as a "freak" event have the ability to develop high technology, such as interstellar communication, technological power, or electromagnetic field theory, as opposed to crows. Second, the silence looks "sinister" because it indicates that advanced civilizations do not last long (advanced civilizations like ours quickly destroy themselves), so, extraterrestrial civilizations are not likely to survive.

채점기준

+ **2점**: 까마귀와 인간의 지능의 차이를 "The difference between crows and human beings' intelligence is that <u>humans as a "freak" event have the ability to develop advanced science or high technology</u>, (such as interstellar communication, technological power, or electromagnetic field theory), <u>as opposed to crows</u>"라 서술하였거나 유사하였다.

+ **2점**: 우주의 침묵이 불길한 이유를 "because <u>it indicates that advanced civilizations do not last long</u> (advanced civilizations like ours quickly destroy themselves), <u>so, extraterrestrial civilizations are not likely to survive.</u>"라 서술하였거나 유사하였다.

한글번역

우주에 (우리 지구 이외의) 다른 문명이 있다 해도 그들은 우리에게 별로 관심이 없는 듯 보인다. 그들은 우리를 방문하지도, 연락을 취하지도, 전파를 보내지도 않는다. 심지어 우리를 엿보는 것 같지도 않다. 우주의 이런 무시(무관심)는 마치 우리가 이 우주에서 버려진 존재인 듯한 느낌을 준다. 위대한 물리학자 엔리코 페르미는 이를 이렇게 표현했다. "다들 어디에 있는 거지?"

세상에는 다양한 종류의 지능이 있다. 최근 다양한 종류의 새들, 특히 까마귀가 원숭이보다 더 높은 지능을 가지고 있음을 보이는 연구들이 발표되고 있다. 낙지 또한 높은 지능을 가졌다. 곤충, 조류, 포유류, 연체동물이 모두 나름의 지능을 가지게 됐다는 사실에서 어쩌면 적당한 수준의 지능은 진화 과정에서 필연적으로 발생하는 것일 수 있다. 하지만 이런 정도의 지능으로는 우주를 향해 신호를 보낼 수 없다. 까마귀의 지능은 매우 놀랍지만 그들이 전자기학을 발전시켜낼 것 같지는 않다. 과학의 발전을 위해서는 복잡한 문화와 탐구심으로 이어진, 인간이 가진 총명함과 같은 지능이 필요하다. 그리고 이런 지능은 진화의 관점에서는 기이한 일인 것처럼 보인다.

그래서, 생물학적 관점에서도 외계의 다른 지능과 만나는 것은 쉽지 않은 것처럼 보인다. 어쩌면 우주에는 낮은 지능을 가진 다양한 종류의 생명체가 곳곳에 존재하고 있을지 모른다. 하지만 대화할 가치가 있는 존재는 없겠지. 이는 참으로 우울한 결론이다. 하지만 우리 인간이 우주에서 특별한 존재가 아니라고 한다면 더욱더 우울할 것 같다. 왜냐하면, 이 경우 우주의 침묵(우리 인간과 대화가 없음)은 불길한 의미일 수 있기 때문이다. 만약 고도 문명의 발달이 흔한 일이라면, 이런 침묵은 그러한 문명의 수명이 길지 않다는 의미일 수 있다. 어쩌면 수많은 문명이 고도로 발달한 뒤 얼마 못 가서 스스로 멸망했을 수도 있다. 우리는 흔히 인류가 영원히 계속 살아남을 것이라 생각한다. 하지만 우리 정도의 충분한 기술적 발전을 이룩한 문명은 전쟁, 질병, 공해 등과 같은 자기 자신이 만든 것들에 스스로를 파괴하는 방법을 손쉽게 만들어 낸다.

4

하위내용영역	배점	예상정답률
일반영어 B형 서술형	4점	30%

모범 답안 The effects of domestication syndrome are byproducts of reduced reactive aggression. These markers are anatomical and behavioral and physiological and share the common quality of paedomorphism in animals and human ancestors. Reactive aggression as a trait was not selected due to its disruptive effect on communities.

채점 기준

ⓐ Topic sentence
+ 1점 : "<u>domestication syndrome are byproducts of reduced reactive aggression</u>"을 명확하게 서술하였거나 유사하였다.

ⓑ Summary
+ 3점 : "<u>These markers are anatomical and behavioral</u>(1점) and <u>share the common quality of paedomorphism in animals and human ancestors</u>(1점). <u>Reactive aggression as a trait was not selected due to its disruptive effect on communities</u>(1점)"를 서술하였거나 유사하였다.

☞ 3개 중 2개만 서술해도 3점을 준다.

감점
- 본문에 나오는 연속되는 6단어 이상을 사용하였다. −0.5pt
- 문단을 두 개나 그 이상으로 구성하였다. −0.5pt
- 문법이나 영어 표현을 합쳐 3개 이상 오류가 있다. −0.5pt

한글번역

지난 50여 년 동안, 인간이 오랜 시간 스스로를 가축화했다는 것이 점점 명확해지고 있다. 가축화의 가장 중요한 증거인 유순함 외에도 인간은 가축화 증후군의 많은 특징을 가지고 있다. 체구와 뇌의 크기가 작아졌고, 뼈가 가늘어졌으며, 얼굴이 납작해지고 수컷과 암컷의 신체적 차이가 줄었다. 이러한 해부학적 특징 외에 공포 반응, 장난기, 학습 속도, 성적 행동, 호르몬 생산 등의 행동적 생리적 특징 또한 인간의 가축화 가설을 지지한다. 이러한 표식(특성)들의 공통점은 바로 유형 형성(즉, 아이적 형태 : 성체가 됐어도 옛날 조상 종의 어린 시절 몸 구조를 그대로 유지하고 있는 것)이라는 것이다. 개, 여우, 기니피그 등 가축화된 많은 동물들은 그들의 조상에 비해 그들이 더 어린 개체일 때의 특징을 가지고 있다. 수십만 년 전 인간의 조상 화석은 인간이 그들에 비해 유형 형성의 특징을 띠게 됐는지를 확인할 만큼 많지 않다. 하지만 네안데르탈인의 화석들은 충분히 많고, 그것들을 비교해 보면 현생 인류가 여러 가지 면에서 우리 조상들보다 더 아동화, 곧 가축화됐음을 시사한다.

왜 이러한 변화가 발생했을까(즉, 인간은 왜 스스로를 가축화시켰을까)? 진화 생물학자에게 이 질문은 그러한 변화들이 인간이 적응하는 데 어떤 이득을 줬는지 묻는 것과 같다. 그러나 이 질문의 답은 예상과 다르다. 바로, 아무런 이득이 없다는 것이다. 수십 년 동안 공들인 한 실험에 따르면, 뇌의 크기가 줄어들고, 뼈가 가늘어지는 등의 여러 가축화의 증거들이 사실 다른 본질적인 적응의 우연한 부산물에 불과하다는 사실을 발견했다. 바로 그 적응은 반응적 공격성의 감소이다. 그런 공격성을 감소시키는 것을 선택한 유기체들(생명체들)은, 배아에서 태아에 이르는 시기의 발달을 관장하는 신경능선세포를 지연시켜 더 작은 몸집과 작은 뇌를 만들고 호르몬 변화를 유도한다. 인간 사회가 스스로의 반응적 공격성을 감소시킨 이유는 집단 생활은 최소한의 안정성을 필요로 하기 때문이다. 반응적 공격성은 분노와 괴롭힘, 폭력 등 타인을 지배하고 복종하게 만든 뒤 식량과 여성을 독점하려는 행동으로 이어지며, 이는 그 어떤 특성보다도 더 집단의 안정성을 해치는 행동이다.

제34회 모의고사

1

하위내용영역	배점	예상정답률
일반영어 A형 기입형 – 소설	2점	45%

모범답안 young

채점기준

- 2점: 모범답안과 같다. 이외에는 답이 될 수 없다.
- 0점: 모범답안과 다르다.

한글번역

나는 파리 14지구의 변두리의 술집과 카페에서 2018 월드컵 경기를 시청했다. 일부는 젠트리피케이션이 이뤄졌지만, 여전히 이민자 인구가 많은 공영 주택 단지가 있는 곳이고, 마약, 갱단, 경찰과의 충돌과 같은 사회 계층 아래쪽의 긴장들이 일상으로 드러나는 혼합 지역이다. 하지만, 지금까지는 월드컵을 시청하는 분위기가 나쁘진 않아서 상대적으로 문제가 일어나지 않았다. 프랑스 대표팀의 승전보가 전해질 때마다 울려 퍼지는 경적 소리, 맥주 세례로 가득 찼다. 이 모든 장면 속에서 프랑스 축구 팬들이 얼마나 다양한 인종으로 이뤄져 있는가도 놀라웠지만, 더 눈에 들어온 건 팬들의 연령대였다. 이 세대는 1998년 프랑스 월드컵 우승은 말 그대로 지난 세기의 이야기일 뿐인 새로운 밀레니얼 세대이다. <르 파리지앵>에 실린 한 만평은 다음과 같이 말한다: "지난 세기의 이야기를 더 이상 우리에게 하지마"라고 젊은 세대의 팬들이 나와 같은 뚱뚱하고 중년의 백인 남성에게 말한다. 메시지는 명확하다: 이번 월드컵은 우리의 월드컵이고, 월드컵에서 우승을 축하하는 것은 우리 자신의 것이기 때문이다.
어떤 의미에선 이들은 옳다. 프랑스 축구 대표팀은 아주 젊고, 그들은 대체로 과거와 역사의 무게에 무관심하다. 이번 대회에서 스타로 떠오른 킬리앙 음바페처럼 프랑스가 우승컵을 차지했던 1998년에는 태어나지도 않았던 선수들도 있다.

2

하위내용영역	배점	예상정답률
일반영어 A형 서술형	4점	40%

모범답안 The word is "game". Second, it refers to OpenAI's achievement of creating AI agents that can beat top amateur players at Dota 2 in 5v5 matches

채점기준

- 2점: 빈칸에 들어갈 단어를 "game"이라 정확히 기입하였다.
- 2점: 밑줄 친 부분의 의미를 "it refers to OpenAI's achievement of creating AI agents that can beat top amateur players at Dota 2 in 5v5 matches"라 서술하였거나 유사하였다.

보충설명

It's described as exciting because it represents a significant step in AI development that demonstrates the potential for real-world applications. As the passage explains, the skills learned in complex video games can potentially transfer to solving real-world problems that share similar characteristics. The milestone is meaningful not just as a gaming achievement but as a stepping stone toward applying AI to practical challenges like managing city transportation systems.

한글번역

인공 지능이 보드게임에서 인간을 이기는 일은 이미 유행이 지난 이야기가 됐다. 이제 최고의 학자들과 테크 회사들은 비디오 게임에서 인간에게 도전하고 있다. 일론 머스크와 샘 알트만이 설립한 OpenAI 연구소는 인공 지능 봇팀이 인기 전투 게임인 도타 2의 상위 1% 아마추어 게이머들을 이길 수 있다는 새로운 이정표를 발표했다.

2017년 8월 OpenAI가 처음 도타 2 세계에 등장해서 1 대 1 게임에서 최고 플레이어들을 이길 수 있는 시스템을 공개했던 것을 기억할 것이다. 하지만 이런 게임 타입은 도타 2의 도전을 상당히 줄인다. 이제 OpenAI는 봇들을 업그레이드시켜 더 많은 협력과 더 긴 시간의 계획이 필요한 5 대 5 게임에서 인간 플레이어를 상대할 수 있게 됐다. OpenAI가 아직까지는 도타 2 게임의 최강 플레이어에게 도전하지는 않았지만, 올해 말 e-스포츠 최대 연간 이벤트인 도타 2 토너먼트 The International에서 인간 게이머들에게 도전할 것이다.

이런 종류의 연구 동기는 매우 간단하다. 우리가 AI 시스템에게 비디오 게임을 하는 데 필요한 기술을 가르치는 것을 성공한다면, 도시의 교통 시설 관리와 같은 비디오 게임을 닮은 현실의 복잡한 문제를 푸는 데 사용할 수 있다.

이것은 흥미로운 이정표인데, 실생활에서의 응용 프로그램으로 전환할 수 있는 일이기 때문이다. 만일 우리가 어떤 문제의 시뮬레이션을 가지고 있고, 충분히 큰 규모로 그 시뮬레이션을 실행시킬 수 있다면, 이런 기술로 수행할 수 있는 작업에는 장벽이 없을 것이다.

채점 기준

+ 2점: "극단적 자본주의"가 가리키는 것이 "the Jennifer's Morone's project that she offers her personal data for sale"이라 서술하였거나 유사하였다.

☞ 다음과 같이 서술하였어도 맞는 것으로 한다.
- "The Jennifer's Morone offering of her personal data for sale."

+ 2점: 밑줄 친 부분의 함축 의미를 "such a data economy that individuals can control their own data would be more desirable or ideal than the current situation"이라 서술하였거나 유사하였다.

한글번역

미국의 예술가인 제니퍼 린 모론은 대다수 사람들이 "데이터 노예"로 살고 있다고 말한다. 이는 인터넷 서비스를 공짜로 받기 위해 그보다 훨씬 더 소중한 자신의 데이터를 아무 대가 없이 기업에 넘기고 있다는 뜻인데 이런 상황을 그녀는 통탄스러워한다. "개인 데이터는 당신이 생각하는 것보다 훨씬 더 중요합니다." 그녀는 이런 안타까운 현실을 드러내기 위해 "극단적 자본주의"라는 프로젝트를 진행했다. 그녀는 자기 자신의 데이터를 직접 판매하는 회사를 만들었고, 2016년 런던 갤러리에서 자신의 여러 데이터를 문서로 정리한 뒤 100파운드 이상의 가격을 붙여 판매했다. 그녀의 건강 데이터와 사회 보장 번호를 비롯한, 그녀에 관한 모든 데이터의 가격은 7,000파운드 정도였다.

오직 소수의 바이어들만 이 데이터들을 샀는데, "모든 일이 정말 부조리하다"고 그녀는 말했다. 하지만 예술가가 하는 일이 시대정신을 앞서 드러내는 것이라면, 그녀는 이것을 제대로 짚은 것이다. 올해 전 세계가 데이터 경제에서 뭔가 부패가 일어나고 있다는 것을 알게 됐기 때문이다. 지난 3월, 정치 컨설팅 회사인 캠브리지 어낼리틱은 페이스북 사용자 8,700만 명의 데이터를 몰래 입수했고, 이후 개인 정보 보호의 목소리는 더욱 높아지고 있다. 심지어 독일 수상 앙헬라 메르켈 또한 개인 정보에 적절한 가격이 필요하다고 말하며, 이 문제의 해결을 요청했다.

오늘날 거대 기술 회사들이 데이터를 독점하고 있는 상황을 고려한다면, 개인이 데이터를 판매하겠다는 모론의 아이디어는 별로 현실성이 없어 보인다. 하지만 실제로 사람들이 자신의 데이터를 팔 수 있고 대기업은 비용을 지불해야만 이를 이용할 수 있게 된다면 어떤 일이 벌어지게 될까? 그리고 그 상황에서 데이터 경제는 어떤 모습일까?

3

하위내용영역	배점	예상정답률
일반영어 B형 서술형	4점	35%

모범답안 "Extreme capitalism" refers to the Jennifer's Morone's plan that she offers her personal data for sale. The implication of the underlined words is that such a data economy that individuals can control their own data would be more desirable or ideal than the current situation.

4

하위내용영역	배점	예상정답률
일반영어 B형 서술형	4점	50%

모범답안) Many inventions generally come from curiosity, not from necessity. Inventions such as the atomic bomb, the cotton gin, and the steam engine are the rare instances in which the need was identified first. However, mostly an invention goes into usage and after a considerable time consumers begin to feel the "need" of it.

채점 기준

ⓐ Topic sentence

+ 1점 : "Many inventions generally come from curiosity, not from necessity."를 명확하게 서술하였거나 유사하였다.

☞ 다음과 같이 서술하였어도 1점을 준다.

- "Many inventions come first from curiosity, then are considered as answering a need afterwards."
- "Invention is not generally developed by necessity, but by curiosity."
- "Necessity is not generally the mother of invention, but invention is the source of necessity."

ⓑ Summary

+ 3점 : "<u>Inventions such as the atomic bomb, the cotton gin, and the steam engine are the rare instances in which the need was identified first</u>(1.5점). However, <u>mostly an invention goes into usage and after a considerable time consumers begin to feel the "need" of it</u>(1.5점)."를 서술하였거나 유사하였다.

감점
- 본문에 나오는 연속되는 6단어 이상을 사용하였다. -0.5pt
- 문단을 두 개나 그 이상으로 구성하였다. -0.5pt
- 문법이나 영어 표현을 합쳐 3개 이상 오류가 있다. -0.5pt

한글번역

"필요는 발명의 어머니다." 즉, 이른바 발명은 어떤 기술이 불만스럽거나 부족하다는 인식이 광범위하게 있을 때와 같은 한 사회가 아직 충족되지 않은 어떤 필요를 느낄 때 일어난다는 말이다. 발명가 지망생들은 금전이나 명성에 대한 기대감으로 동기 부여를 받아 이와 같은 필요를 감지하고 거기에 부응하려고 노력한다. 그러다가 어떤 발명가가 드디어 기존의 존재하던 불만족스럽던 기술보다 더 우월한 해결책을 만들어 낸다. 이 해결책이 사회의 가치관과 각종 다른 기술들과 배치되지 않는다면 사회는 그 해결책을 받아들인다.

이런 (필요가 발명의 어머니라는) 상식적 견해를 뒷받침하는 발명품들이 제법 많다. 제2차 세계대전이 한창이던 1942년 미국 정부는 나치 독일보다 먼저 원자 폭탄을 만드는 데 필요한 기술을 발명하겠다는 분명한 목표를 세우고 "맨해튼 프로젝트"를 기획했다. 그리고 이 프로젝트는 20억 달러(오늘날로 치면 200억 달러가 넘는 거금)를 소비한 후 3년 만에 성공을 거뒀다. 또 다른 예로는 미국 남부에서 재배한 목화를 다듬는 고된 수작업을 대신하기 위해 1794년 엘리 휘트니가 발명한 조면기(면화의 씨를 빼거나 솜을 트는 기계), 그리고 영국의 탄광에서 배수 문제를 해결하기 위해 제임스 와트가 1769년 발명한 증기 기관 등이 있다.

이처럼 낯익은 사례들을 보면서 우리는 그 밖의 중요한 발명품들도 모두 필요에 대한 인식에서 비롯됐다고 착각하기 쉽다. 하지만 사실 수많은 발명품, 또는 대부분의 발명품들은 호기심에 사로잡히거나 이것저것 주물럭거리는 일을 좋아하는 사람들이 개발했고, 그들이 염두에 둔 제품에 대한 수요따위는 처음부터 있지도 않았다. 일단 어떤 물건이 발명되면 그때부터 발명자는 그것의 용도를 찾아내야 했다. 그리고 상당 시간 사용된 후에야 비로소 소비자들은 그것이 "필요"하다고 느끼게 됐다. 따라서 발명이 필요의 어머니인 경우가 그 반대보다 더 많다.

유희태 | 일반영어 ❹-2

제35회 모의고사

1

하위내용영역	배점	예상정답률
일반영어 A형 기입형	2점	55%

모범 답안 third-person thinking

채점 기준

- 2점: 모범답안과 같다. 이외에는 답이 될 수 없다.
- 0점: 모범답안과 다르다.

한글번역

　우리는 소크라테스의 "반성하지 않는 삶은 살 가치가 없다"와 "너 자신을 알라"는 통찰이 지혜에 이르는 길이라는 생각을 남겼다고 평가한다. 하지만 이런 자기반성에 이르기 위한 (옳고 그른) 구체적인 방법이 있을까?
　단순히 머릿속으로 생각을 떠올리는 것—네 머릿속에 있는 관심들은 휘젓는 과정일 뿐인—만으로는 부족하다. 이 경우 자신이 평소 습관적으로 하는 생각에 빠지거나, 불필요한 감정에 휩쓸리기 쉽다. 최근 한 연구는 자신만의 생각에 빠지는 사람이 오히려 중요한 순간의 결정을 잘 내리지 못하거나 우울증의 위험이 높아질 수 있음을 보였다.
　이에 대한 답으로, 그 과학적 연구는 율리우스 시저와 같은 사람들이 좋아했던 수사학인 "일리이즘", 곧 자신을 3인칭으로 표현하는 방법이 자기반성에 도움이 된다는 것을 보이고 있다. (이 용어는 시인 새뮤얼 테일러 콜리지가 1809년 라틴어로 '그, 그것'을 의미하는 '일레'를 이용해 만든 단어이다.) 예를 들어 내가 친구와 다툰 일을 반성하면서 속으로 이렇게 말하는 것이다. '데이비드는 친구와 싸워 기분이 나빴다…' 이렇게 관점을 조금 바꾸는 것만으로 우리는 감정의 안개를 걷어내고 편견을 벗어나 사태를 똑바로 볼 수 있게 된다.
　이런 3인칭 사고방식이 일시적인 의사 결정 능력을 향상시킨다는 것을 보인 연구는 많이 있다. 또한 이러한 사고방식이 장기적으로도 생각과 감정의 통제에 도움이 됨을 보였다. 연구진은 이번 연구가 지혜와 관련된 인지 능력이 일상에서 훈련될 수 있으며, 구체적으로 그 방법이 무엇인지를 보인 첫 번째 증거라 말했다.

2

하위내용영역	배점	예상정답률
일반영어 A형 서술형	4점	30%

모범 답안 The meaning of the underlined words in ① is that there is an essential difference between knowing and thinking about a given fact. Second, the most appropriate word is "believes".

채점 기준

- 2점: 밑줄 친 부분의 의미를 "there is an essential difference between knowing and thinking about a given fact"라 서술하였거나 유사하였다.
- 2점: 빈칸에 들어갈 단어를 "believes"라 서술하였다. 이외에는 답이 될 수 없다.

한글번역

　다음과 같이 한번 상상해 보자. 어떤 사람이 오늘은 동네 슈퍼가 문을 여는 날이라 생각해서 우유를 사러 갔다. 하지만 실은 오늘이 공휴일이었고, 슈퍼는 문을 열지 않았다. 비록 가게 문이 닫혀 있었지만, 그 사람의 행동은 여전히 일리가 있다. 실제로 슈퍼가 문을 열었기 때문이 아니라 문을 열었을 것이라 생각하고 슈퍼에 간 거니까. 이 사람이 가게에 간 것은 일리가 있지만, 당신이 어떻게 생각했는지가 아니라, (돌다리를 두드리듯) 실제로 문을 열었는지 닫았는지 확인해 보고 그에 따라 결정을 내렸다면 허탕을 칠 일도 없었을 것이다. 만일 그랬었다면, 그 사람은 가게에 갔을 것이다. 왜냐하면 가게 문은, 그 사람의 생각이 아니라, 실제로 열려 있었을 테니까. 이것이 명심해야 할 차이다.
　자, 그럼 이제 기후 변화를 믿지 않는 사람의 사례로 돌아가 보자. 기후 변화를 믿지 않는 사람은 기후 변화가 새빨간 거짓말인지 알지 못한다. 왜냐하면, 기후 변화는 전혀 거짓이 아니기 때문이다. 그래서 그 사람은 기후 변화가 거짓이라고 생각해서 수업을 듣지 않는 것을 선택할 수가 없다. 이것은 마치 앞에서 가상으로 말했던 사람이 가게가 열려 있는지 알려면 실제로 가게에 직접 가본 뒤에나 알 수 있는 것과 유사한 것이다. 오히려 기후 변화를 믿지 않는 사람이 할 수 있는 최대치는 기후 변화가 거짓이라 생각해서 수업을 듣지 않는 선택을 하는 것이다. 이 선택도 (어쨌든 어느 정도는) 일리는 있지만, 아마도 그가 기후 변화에 관해 자신이 어떻게 생각하는지보다 기후 변화가 사실인지 아닌지에 관한 지식(객관적 지식)에 근거해서 내렸을 선택보다는 좋지 않았을 것이다.

만일 앞에서 말한 것이 틀린 것이 아니라면, 똑같이 지금 내 생각과 가치관을 기준으로 판단을 내리더라도 어떤 경우는 독선과 편견의 틀에 갇힌 것이고, 또 어떤 경우에는 합리적인 선택이 되는지 그 차이를 이제 살펴보겠다. 두 번째 종류의 사람(합리적인 선택을 내리는 사람)은 반대하고 꺼리는 대상이 자신에게 피해를 주리라는 사실을 명확히 알고 있는 반면에, 첫 번째 종류의 사람(독선과 편견에 갇힌 사람)은 어떤 대상이 자신에게 피해를 주리라고 굳게 믿기 때문에 잘못된 선택을 반복하게 된다. (어떤 사실을 정확히 아는 것과 그럴 거라고 믿는 것의 차이라고 할 수 있다.)

3

하위내용영역	배점	예상정답률
일반영어 B형 서술형	4점	45%

모범답안 The main idea of the passage is that computer-based testing can be more effective than animal testing. Second, animal testing is not welcomed by all walks of life because it's immoral to a public majority and costly and uncertain for manufacturers.

채점기준

+ 2점: 글의 요지를 "computer-based testing can be more effective than animal testing"이라 서술하였거나 유사하였다.
+ 2점: 동물 실험이 각계각층의 사람들로부터 환영받지 못하는 이유를 "because it is immoral to a public majority(1점) and costly and uncertain for manufacturers(1점)"라 서술하였거나 유사하였다.

한글번역

존스홉킨스 블룸버그 보건대학원의 과학자들이 주도한 연구에 따르면 대규모 화학 데이터베이스를 이용한 고급 알고리즘으로 기존 동물 실험보다 약품의 독성을 더 잘 예측할 수 있다고 한다.

2018년 7월 11일 학술지 <독성과학>에 발표된 연구 논문에서 연구자들은 알려진 화학 물질의 방대한 데이터베이스를 조사해 화학 구조와 독성 특성 간의 관계를 이어주는 지도를 개발했다고 밝혔다. 연구자들은 이 지도를 이용해 모든 화합물의 독성 특성을 자동으로 예측할 수 있으며, 동물 실험을 통한 예측보다 더 정확하다는 결과를 제시했다.

연구팀이 개발한 최첨단 독성 예측 툴은 동물 실험에 기반을 둔 결과를 재현하는 데 세계의 동물 독성 실험 중 57%를 차지하는 아홉 가지 일반 테스트에서 평균 87%의 정확도를 보였다. 대조적으로 데이터베이스상의 동일한 동물 실험의 반복 결과의 정확도는 81%였다. 다시 말해, 어떤 실험도 반복할 경우 독성에 대한 동일한 결과를 얻을 확률이 평균 81%밖에 되지 않았다는 뜻이다.

컴퓨터를 기반으로 한 접근법은 동물 실험보다 더 많은 화학물질을 적용할 수 있으며, 더 광범위한 안전 평가를 할 수 있도록 한다. 그동안은 비용과 윤리적 문제로 소비자 제품에 포함된 약 10만 개의 화학 물질 중 일부만 종합적으로 테스트됐다.

쥐, 토끼, 기니피그, 개와 같은 동물들은 전 세계 실험실에서 수백만 건의 화학 독성 실험에 사용된다. 동물 실험은 소비자를 보호하기 위해 법으로 정해져 있지만, 많은 대중이 도덕적인 이유로 반대하고 있으며, 제조사들 또한 높은 비용과 실험 결과의 불확실성으로 인해 기피하는 실정이다.

4

하위내용영역	배점	예상정답률
일반영어 B형 서술형	4점	45%

모범 답안 In an isolated society like Japan, a powerful technology can be done away with unlike in a connected society. For example, when guns first appeared in Japan they became very popular. However, the threat they posed to the samurai, who controlled the government, and the hatred of foreign things led to increasing restrictions against them. Eventually, Japan was almost without guns.

채점 기준

ⓐ Topic sentence

+ 1.5점: "In an isolated society like Japan, a powerful technology can be done away with unlike in a connected society"를 명확하게 서술하였거나 유사하였다.

ⓑ Summary

+ 2.5점: "when guns first appeared in Japan they became very popular(1점). However, the threat they posed to the samurai, who controlled the government, and the hatred of foreign things led to increasing restrictions against guns. Eventually, Japan was almost without guns(1.5점)."를 서술하였거나 유사하였다.

감점
- 본문에 나오는 연속되는 6단어 이상을 사용하였다. −0.5pt
- 문단을 두 개나 그 이상으로 구성하였다. −0.5pt
- 문법이나 영어 표현을 합쳐 3개 이상 오류가 있다. −0.5pt

한글번역

　오늘날에는 거의 모든 지구상의 사회가 서로 연결돼 있어서 어떤 변덕 때문에 중요한 기술이 버려지는 일을 상상하기 어렵다. 설령 어느 한 사회가 어떤 강력한 기술을 일시적으로 거부하더라도 그 사회는 이웃 사회가 그 기술을 사용하고 있는 것을 계속 보게 될 것이므로 언제든지 재확산을 통해 다시 습득할 수 있다. (만약 그렇게 하지 못한다면 이웃에게 정복당하든지). 그러나 고립된 사회에서는 그러한 변덕이 오랫동안 지속되기도 한다.

　일본이 총을 포기했던 사례는 유명하다. 총기가 일본에 처음 도착한 것은 1543년이었다. 원시적인 화승총으로 무장한 포르투갈 모험가 두 명이 중국 화물선을 타고 상륙했던 것이다. 일본인들은 이 신 무기에 깊은 인상을 받고 토착적으로 생산하기 시작해 총기 제작 기술을 크게 향상시켰으며 1600년 이전에 벌써 세계 어느 나라보다도 우수한 총을 더 많이 갖게 됐다. 하지만 일본에는 총기 도입에 역행하는 요인들도 있었다. 우선 이 나라에는 사무라이라는 전사 계급이 다수 있었다. 그들에게는 칼이 계급의 상징인 동시에 하층 계급들을 복속시키는 수단이었다. 일본에서 전쟁이란 사무라이 사이의 일대일 전투였다. 그들은 탁 트인 곳에서 서서 의례적인 말들을 주고받았으며 우아하게 싸우는 것을 자랑스럽게 여겼다. 우아하지 못하게 마구 총을 쏘아대는 농민 병사들 앞에서 그런 행동을 하는 것은 치명적인 결과를 낳게 됐다. 게다가 총은 외국의 발명품이어서 1600년 이후에 모든 외국 문물이 그랬듯이 차츰 경멸의 대상이 됐다. 사무라이가 지배하던 정부는 우선 총기 생산을 몇몇 도시에 국한시키기 시작했고 정부의 허가를 얻어야 총을 생산할 수 있게 했다. 그다음에는 정부에 납품하는 총에 대해서만 생산을 허락했고 마지막으로 정부의 총기 주문량도 감소시켜 결국 일본은 제대로 작동하는 총이 거의 없는 상태로 돌아가 버렸다.

제36회 모의고사

1

하위내용영역	배점	예상정답률
일반영어 A형 기입형	2점	55%

모범 답안 old knowledge

채점 기준

- 2점: 모범답안과 같다. 이외에는 답이 될 수 없다.
- 0점: 모범답안과 다르다.

한글번역

현대 과학에는 도그마(독단적 신조)가 없다. 하지만 연구 기법에는 공통적인 핵심이 있는데, 늘 경험적 관찰들을 모은 뒤 수학적 도구의 도움을 받아 그것들을 하나로 결합하는 것이다. 여기서 관찰이란 적어도 우리의 감각 기관 중 하나로 관찰할 수 있는 것을 의미한다.

사람들은 역사를 통틀어 경험적 관찰들을 모았지만, 이 관찰의 중요성은 보통 제한적이었다. 우리에게 필요한 모든 답이 수중에 있는데 또다시 새로운 관찰을 얻으려고 귀중한 자원을 낭비할 필요가 어디 있겠는가? 하지만 현대인은 자신들이 매우 중요한 몇몇 질문에 대한 답을 모른다는 사실을 인정하게 됐으므로, 완전히 새로운 지식을 찾아볼 필요가 있다는 사실을 깨달았다. 그 결과, 현대의 지배적인 연구 기법은 오래된 지식이 충분하지 않다는 사실을 당연한 것으로 받아들인다. 오늘날 무게중심은 전통을 연구하기 보다는 새로운 관찰과 실험을 하는 쪽으로 옮겨갔다. 현대의 관찰이 과거의 전통과 배치되는 경우, 우리는 관찰에 우선권을 부여한다. 물론 먼 은하의 스펙트럼을 분석하는 물리학자, 청동기 시대의 도시 유물을 분석하는 고고학자, 자본주의의 출현을 연구하는 정치학자는 옛 지식을 무시하지 않는다. 이들은 과거의 사람들이 말하고 쓴 것을 공부하는 데서 시작한다. 하지만 물리학자, 고고학자, 정치학자가 되려는 사람들은 대학 1학년 때부터 자신의 임무는 아인슈타인, 하인리히 슐리만, 막스 베버가 알았던 것을 뛰어넘는 데 있다고 배운다.

2

하위내용영역	배점	예상정답률
일반영어 A형 서술형	4점	50%

모범 답안 The actions that helped to keep white nationalism in check were the war against Nazism and the civil-rights struggles of the 50s and 60s. Second, the Internet allows white nationalists to use ambiguous irony and humor to spread their message.

채점 기준

+ 2점: 백인민족주의를 제지하는 데 기여한 실천적 행위를 "the war against Nazism(1점) and the civil-rights struggles of the 50s and 60s(1점)"라 서술하였다.
+ 2점: 인터넷과 더불어 백인민족주의가 급속하게 전파되는 이유를 "the Internet allows white nationalists to use ambiguous (obscure) irony and humor to spread their message"라 서술하였거나 유사하였다.

한글번역

전 세계로 확산된 현대의 백인민족주의는 남북전쟁 후 미국에서 처음 탄생했다. 노예제가 끝나면서 (미국의) 각 주들은 서유럽 후손인 백인 프로테스탄트들의 특혜적 지위를 그대로 유지하기 위한 조치를 취했다. 인종 분리 정책을 강요한 짐크로우법 등이 이에 해당한다. 불법무장단체의 폭력이나 린치(사적인 폭력)도 이어졌다. 중국인과 아일랜드 가톨릭 교도, 유대인들의 이민이 증가하면서 백인 정체성에 대한 집착은 더욱 커졌다. 이민을 제한하기 위한 새로운 법이 만들어졌다. 매디슨 그랜트가 1916년에 발간한 "위대한 인종의 소멸"은 이민 배척주의와 우생학을 버무려 백인우월주의와 "인종 자살"이라는 개념을 만들어 냈다. 아돌프 히틀러는 그랜트에게 편지를 써 이 책이 자신에게 성경과도 같다 말했다고 전해진다.

나치즘과의 전쟁, 그리고 1950~60년대의 민권운동을 거치며 불명예를 떠안게 된 백인민족주의는 20세기 말 부흥을 맞이하게 되는데, 이때 유럽과 미국에서 폭력적인 사태가 발생했다.

1988년 데이비드 레인은 "백인 학살 선언"을 써서 그랜트의 "인종 자살론"에 새로운 이름을 붙였다. 이 글로 전 세계에 백인민족주의의 외침이 잘 알려지게 됐다. 백인민족주의자들이 "열네 단어"로 떠받드는 문장("우리 민족의 존속과 백인 아이들의 미래를 지켜야 한다")도 여기에서 나온다. 백인의 우월성에 대한 핵심적인 믿음을 공유하기는 하지만, 백인민족주의도 다양한 갈래로 나뉜다. 연방 정부에 대한 뿌리 깊은 불신을 갖고 있는 이들(주로 민병대들에게서 발견된다)도 있고, 남북 전쟁에 대한 수정주의적 견해를 받아들여 (남북 전쟁 당시) 남부군을 미화하는 이들도 있다. 유대인들이 세계를 지배하려 한다는 반유대주의적 음모론을 떠받드는 이들도 있는데, 이들은 국제주의자 유대인 엘리트가 이민을 장려하는 데 책임이 있다고도 주장한다.

백인민족주의는 인터넷의 탄생과 함께 빠르게 진화하고 있다. 모니터 반대편의 화자가 진지한지, 농담을 하는지를 알 수 없는 인터넷 시대의 아이러니를 흡수한 것이다. 농담 삼아 그런 이야기를 하는 사람들을 통해, 백인민족주의는 더 많은 사람들에게 다가갈 수 있게 됐다.

⊕ 보충설명

"Declined" would be a reasonable alternative, but "refused" is the better choice because it more strongly captures the principled rejection demonstrated throughout the passage. The passage consistently uses forms of "refuse" to describe the actions of these individuals: "he will refuse to write" / "He refused in a letter which breathed hatred and utter contempt" / "He has refused to be photographed and interviewed" / "he has refused to contribute to symposia" / He "refused scornfully the peerage".

While "declined" does appear once in the passage (regarding Bolus declining invitations), "refused" appears more frequently and with stronger emotional context. The passage emphasizes these men's **firm, principled stands against opportunities that would compromise their values**, which aligns more with **the forceful nature of "refused"** rather than **the potentially more polite connotation of "declined."**

3

하위내용영역	배점	예상정답률
일반영어 B형 서술형	4점	45%

모범답안 The word is "refused". Second, the commonality is their avoidance of situations that can benefit them : Henderson refused to work for publications under a boss with a personal scandal, and Bolus declined invitations by houses and press.

채점 기준

+ 2점 : 빈칸에 들어갈 단어를 "refused"라 정확히 기입하였다.
+ 2점 : 핸더슨과 볼러스의 공통점을 "their avoidance of situations that can benefit them" 또는 "both men prioritize their principles and integrity over financial gain or professional advancement."이라 서술하였거나 유사하였다.

한글번역

대부분의 회원들은 실제 돈보다는 직업적 기회를 거절한 남성들이다. 예를 들어 기자나 작가가 여섯 명쯤 된다. 기자의 경우, 회원으로 선출되기 전 반드시 자신이 절대로 글을 쓰지 않겠다고 맹세한 신문사의 목록을 제출해야 한다. 데일리 블랭크지에 실린 조작된 무선 뉴스—이후의 사건으로 보아 몇 푼짜리 신문을 팔기 위해 고의로 만들어낸 것임이 드러난—에 격분한 핸더슨의 사례를 보자. 그는 같은 소유주가 운영하는 어떤 신문에도 다시는 한 줄도 쓰지 않겠다고 서약했다. 흥미롭게도 그로부터 며칠 뒤, 바로 그 출판사가 운영하는 매우 평판 좋은 잡지에서 그에게 연재를 요청했다. 그는 그 제안을 거절하면서, 편지 한 줄 한 줄마다 증오와 철저한 경멸이 배어 있는 답신을 보냈다. 또한 핸더슨은 자신이 근무하던 신문의 사장이 사적인 일로 다소 비도덕적인 행동을 했다는 이유로 연극 평론가직을 사임했다. 그는 이렇게 말했다. "신문 자체가 그 일에 연루된 것은 전혀 아니에요. 하지만 그는 내 고용주이고, 내 급여를 주는 사람이죠. 난 내 고용주에게는 충실하고 싶어요. 그런데 이 사람에게 충실하다면, 세상 사람들에게 그가 비열한 인간이라고 떠들고 다닐 순 없잖아요."

작가 볼러스의 경우도 있다. 그는 사진 촬영과 인터뷰를 거절했으며, 월간지의 좌담 형식 글 요청도 모두 거절했다. 또한 자신을 명성으로만 아는 사교계 여성들이 보낸 초대장 여러 통도 공손히 사양했다. 그의 이런 태도로 인해 경제적으로 손해를 봤을 가능성이 크다. 그러나 설령 그가 직접적으로 돈의 신을 무너뜨리는 데 기여하지는 못하더라도, 독립 정신을 지키기 위한 한 방은 날린 셈이다. 끝으로, 한 국회의원의 경우도 있다. 그는 당 자금으로 만 달러를 기부했으나, 그 대가로 제안된 작위를 경멸스럽게 거절했다.

4

하위내용영역	배점	예상정답률
일반영어 B형 서술형	4점	35%

모범답안 Time blocking, which schedules out a day in advance and dedicates specific hours to achieving specific tasks, can be an effective way to reach all your tasks. In planning, both proactive and reactive time should be allotted, to allow for focusing on important projects and also accommodating requests and interruptions. Time blocking, unlike standard to-do lists which provide only a list of tasks, has the strength of helping you know the exact way and time specific to completing each task as well as listing all.

채점기준

ⓐ Topic sentence

+ 1.5점 : "Time blocking, <u>which schedules out a day in advance and dedicates specific hours to achieving specific works</u>(0.5점), <u>can be an effective way to reach all your tasks</u>(1점)."를 명확하게 서술하였거나 유사하였다.

☞ 정의(schedules out a day in advance and dedicates specific hours to achieve specific works)가 빠져있으면 0.5점 감점한다.

ⓑ Summary

+ 2.5점 : "In planning, <u>both proactive and reactive time should be allotted, to allow for focusing on important projects and also accommodating requests and interruptions</u> (1점). Time blocking method, <u>unlike standard to-do lists which provide only a list of tasks</u>(0.25점), has <u>the strength of helping you know the exact way and time</u>(0.25점) <u>specific to completing each task as well as listing all</u>(1점)."를 서술하였거나 유사하였다.

감점
- 본문에 나오는 연속되는 6단어 이상을 사용하였다. -0.5pt
- 문단을 두 개나 그 이상으로 구성하였다. -0.5pt
- 문법이나 영어 표현을 합쳐 3개 이상 오류가 있다. -0.5pt

한글번역

엄격한 구조 속에서 일하고, 주어진 시간 안에 과제를 완수하도록 자신을 강제함으로써, 모든 활동에 레이저처럼 집중하게 된다. 시간 할당은 특정한 작업을 마치기 위해 미리 특정한 시간을 배정해 놓는 방법이다. 이를 위해서는 해야 할 일에 대해 정확히 알아야 하고 어느 정도의 시간이 걸릴지 예상할 수 있어야 한다. 일단 이 둘을 염두에 뒀다면, 이것들을 달력에 써넣고 하루 중 적절한 시간에 그 일들을 시작하면 된다.

과제 계획을 세울 때는 능동적 시간과 수동적 시간을 구분해 놓는 것이 필요하다. 능동적 시간은 반드시 해야 할 일을 배정하는 시간이다. 중요한 프로젝트를 진행한다든지, 중요한 문서의 초안을 작성한다든지, 또는 다음에 할 중요한 제품의 원형에 대해 기획하는 것과 같은 (집중이 필요한) 일이 여기에 해당한다. 수동적 시간은 이메일이나 즉석 회의처럼 다른 이의 요구에 대응하거나 수시로 발생하는 일을 위한 시간 할당이다. 예를 들어 업무의 첫 두 시간 동안 가장 어려운 일을 마친 다음, 오후에 이메일을 처리하는 방식이 가능하다. 이를 통해 방해받지 않는 시간과 전화나 이메일을 처리할 시간을 모두 얻을 수 있다. 이 (시간 할당) 방법은 당신이 시간을 어떻게 사용하는지, 그리고 언제 그 일을 마칠 수 있는지 분명히 알려주는 장점이 있다. 일반적인 할 일 목록 방식은 끝내야 할 작업 목록(만)을 제시해 주는 반면, 시간 할당법은 (끝내야 할) 작업 목록을 제시하는 것뿐만 아니라 구체적인 시간대까지 제시해 주는 점이 다르다.

제37회 모의고사

1

하위내용영역	배점	예상정답률
일반영어 A형 기입형	2점	50%

모범답안 natural cycle

채점기준

- 2점: 모범답안과 같다. 이외에는 답이 될 수 없다.
- 0점: 모범답안과 다르다.

한글번역

북극에 가까운 고위도 지방이 불타고 있다. 올여름 알래스카에서만 벌써 600건 넘는 들불이 나 1만km²에 가까운 숲을 태웠다. 캐나다 북부도 마찬가지다. 시베리아에서는 계속된 들불로 발생한 연기가 약 5만 2천km² 상공을 뒤덮었다. (역자: 5만 2천km²는 경상도와 전라도를 합친 면적)

이 지역들에서 들불 자체는 원래 흔한 일이다. 알래스카 중부의 가문비나무가 시들거나 불이 나 숲이 뜨거워지면 곧바로 솔방울을 열어 씨를 퍼뜨린다. 숲이 불에 탄 자리에는 먼저 잡목이나 꽃들이 자란다. 이어 야생산딸기나무, 버드나무, 자작나무, 사시나무 등이 아직 죽지 않은 나무 그루터기나 뿌리들 사이에서 자라난다. 그러다 결국에는 이 지역에 불에 잘 타는 침엽수가 다시 숲을 뒤덮는다.

하지만 다양한 연구 결과를 보면 올여름을 비롯한 최근의 추세가 심상치 않다. 최근에 일어난 들불은 기존에 일어나던 양상과 다르다. 너무 자주, 너무 강하게 퍼져 훨씬 심각한 피해를 남긴다. 숲이 불타면서 가뜩이나 이산화탄소가 적정량보다 많아 문제인 지구의 대기에 더 많은 탄소가 쌓인다.

연구자들은 기후 변화와 늘어나는 들불, 그로 인한 초목과 식생의 변화 양상을 연구한다. 알래스카 북극권 기후 변화 시나리오 네트워크가 지역별로 세분화한 기후 데이터와 모델을 활용해 잦아진 들불의 원인을 분석하고 앞으로 일어날 수 있는 상황을 전망해봤다. 그 결과 알래스카 등 고위도 지방에 사는 우리같은 사람들뿐 아니라 지구상의 모든 이들에게 경종을 울릴 만한 결론을 내릴 수밖에 없다.

위에서 설명한 이 과정을 한 번 거치는 데 걸리는 시간은 대략 200년 정도다. 그런데 최근 들어 계속 그 주기가 무려 25%나 빨라졌다. 이는 생태계를 근본적으로 뒤바꿔놓을 수 있는 어마어마한 변화이다.

2

하위내용영역	배점	예상정답률
일반영어 A형 서술형	4점	40%

모범답안 The meaning of "normal" in the context is covering your invited guest's meal as a show of hospitality. Second, the meaning of the underlined words is that the English have become more committed to capitalism than the Dutch were.

채점기준

+ 2점: 글의 주제의 맥락에서 "정상적인"의 의미를 "<u>covering your invited guest's meal as a show of hospitality</u>"라 서술하였거나 유사하였다.

☞ 다음과 같이 서술했어도 2점을 준다.
 – "returning to old habits to show good manners by covering your invited guest's meal"

+ 2점: 밑줄 친 부분의 의미를 "<u>the English have become more committed to capitalism than the Dutch were</u>"이라 서술했거나 유사하였다.

한글번역

일요일 아침 친구들과의 브런치 모임, 즐거운 식사가 끝나고 웨이터가 테이블로 다가와 묻는다. "한꺼번에 계산하시겠어요, 아니면…"

말이 끝나기도 전에 모두가 한목소리로 외친다. "따로따로 계산할게요!" 너무나 당연한 것을 왜 묻지? 각자 자기가 먹은 것을 계산하는 이른바 "더치페이"는 이제 현대인의 관행으로 자리 잡았(기 때문이)다.

하지만 친구들과 식사를 하고 계산서를 나누는 행위가 언제나 규범이었던 것은 아니다. 초기 영국 사회에서는 친구를 외식에 초대하고 음식값을 내지 않는 것이 매우 이기적인 행동으로 여겨졌다.

1651년에 막을 내린 영국의 시민 혁명(내전) 후, 영국인들은 일상을 되찾기 위해 애를 쓰고 있었다. 일상의 회복이란 계급적 위계와 선한 크리스천으로서의 교양을 드러낼 수 있는 일정한 규범들을 따르는 것을 의미했다. 사람들에게 환대를 베풀어 자신의 신사다움을 드러내는 것은 매우 중요한 부분이었다. 후하게 베풀지 않는 것은 왕실과 신에게 누를 끼치는 행위로 여겨졌다.

"더치페이"라는 단어의 기원은 약간 복잡하지만, 몇몇 과거와 현재의 사전편찬 전문가들은 이 단어의 어원을 따져보는 데 도움을 준다.

우선 1600년대로 돌아가 보자. 영국-네덜란드 전쟁 당시 잉글랜드와 네덜란드 사이에는 무역과 해상의 권력을 두고 다양한 갈등이 일어났다. 이런 적대적인 관계는 영어에서 네덜란드를 뜻하는 "더치"를 부정적인 의미로 사용하는 다양한 관용구를 낳았다. "네덜란드인의 용기(Dutch courage)"는 폭음에서 비롯된 헛된 용기를, "더치식 계산(Dutch reckoning)"은 사기를 당해 지불한 터무니없는 가격을 의미하게 됐다. 이는 영국인들이 네덜란드인을 무역상의 적으로 간주했기 때문이고, 나아가 그들의 도덕성을 의심했기 때문이다. 당시 영국인들은 네덜란드인을 자본주의에 대한 신념 때문에 완전히 타락한 사람들로 여겼다. 이런 경향이 바뀐 것을 생각하면 얼마나 웃긴가.

한글번역

존재는 기억을 바탕으로 한다(기억은 우리 인간에게 우리 자신이 누구인지를 알게 해준다). 기억을 통해 우리는 세상을 이해하고 미래를 예측할 수 있다. 과학자들은 기억이 어떻게 형성되며 시간이 흐른 뒤 이를 어떻게 우리가 떠올리는지에 대해 오랫동안 연구해 왔다. 하지만 지금까지의 연구는 실상의 절반만을 바라본 것이었다. 기억에 대해 알기 위해서는 우리가 어떻게, 그리고 왜 기억을 잊는지를 알아야 한다.

10년 전까지만 하더라도 과학자들은 마치 햇볕 아래 사진이 바랜 것처럼, 망각을 기억이 자연스레 사라지는 과정이라 생각했다. 하지만 소수의 연구자들에 의해 그러한 가정이 잘못이라는 사실이 밝혀졌다. 그들은 기억을 제거하는 것이 뇌의 또 다른 기능이라는 혁신적인 아이디어를 내놓았다.

지난 10년 동안 밝혀진 사실들은 망각이 수동적으로 일어나는 현상이 아님을 보여준다. 오히려, 망각은 뇌에서 일상적으로 일어나는 능동적인 활동의 결과이다. 어쩌면 거의 모든 동물은 기본적으로 능동적인 망각 기능을 활성화한 상태일 수 있다. 이러한 망각에 대한 더 깊은 이해는 불안증, 외상후 스트레스 장애(PTSD), 그리고 알츠하이머와 같은 병에 대한 더 나은 치료법으로 이어질 수 있다.

"망각이 없는 기억이 가능할까요?" 기억의 신경 생물학을 연구하는 인지 심리학자인 올리버 하트는 이렇게 말한다. "불가능합니다. 기억이 제대로 작동하기 위해서는 망각 기능 또한 반드시 가져야 합니다."

3

하위내용영역	배점	예상정답률
일반영어 B형 서술형	4점	50%

모범답안) A handful of researchers contradicted the notion that memories are forgotten through a passive process. Second, "forgetting" best fills in the blank.

채점 기준

+ 2점: 소수의 연구자들이 반박한 것을 "the notion (assumption) that memories are forgotten through a passive process"이라 서술하였거나 유사하였다.
+ 2점: 빈칸에 들어갈 단어를 "forgetting"라 정확하게 기입하였다. 이외에는 답이 될 수 없다.

4

하위내용영역	배점	예상정답률
일반영어 B형 서술형	4점	40%

모범답안 Gender-neutral uniform policies should be more thoughtful in their implementation. Schools have been implementing gender-neutral uniforms in order to remove the discomfort and problems skirts can bring about. However, narrowing choice and expression is detrimental and sends a message implying blame on the wearers of skirts. In conclusion, school skirts are allowed when students want to wear them.

채점기준

ⓐ Topic sentence
+ 1점: "Gender-neutral uniform policies should be more wiser, expanding choices rather than limiting them"를 명확하게 서술하였거나 유사하였다.

ⓑ Summary
+ 2점: "Schools have been implementing gender-neutral uniforms in order to remove the discomfort and problems skirts can present(cause)(1점). However, removing(narrowing) choice and expression is detrimental and sends a message implying blame on the wearers of skirts(1점)."를 서술하였거나 유사하였다.

ⓒ Conclusion
+ 1점: "In conclusion, school skirts are allowed when students want to wear them." 또는 "Thus, they should be allowed alongside trousers as options for students."를 서술하였다.

감점
- 본문에 나오는 연속되는 6단어 이상을 사용하였다. −0.5pt
- 문단을 두 개나 그 이상으로 구성하였다. −0.5pt
- 문법이나 영어 표현을 합쳐 3개 이상 오류가 있다. −0.5pt

한글번역

반항의 뜻에서 허리 부분을 접어 올리지 않는다면 언제나 무릎 길이에 머무는 남색이나 검정색의 얌전한 교복치마는 이제 멸종 위기에 처한 것인가? 아마도. 이 문제가 중요한가? 당연히 중요하다. 영국 내 최소 40개 중등학교가 성 중립을 명분으로 교복 치마를 금지한 것이 현실이기 때문이다. 11세에서 16세 사이의 영국 소녀들은 이제 교복으로 바지만을 입을 운명에 처한 듯하다.

어린 학생들의 가치관이 형성되는 장이자, 폭력의 온상이기도 한 학교에서 성 중립적 교복 정책은 큰 의미가 있다. 상식에도 부합할 뿐 아니라, 성 평등, 그리고 트랜스젠더 학생이나 여성도 남성도 아닌 논바이너리 학생까지도 통합할 수 있는 정책이다. (바지 교복은 분명 치마 교복에 비해 모두의 행동반경을 넓힐 수 있는 옵션이다.) 한번 무릎길이의 치마를 입고 정글짐(철골 놀이 기구)을 올라가려 해 봐라. 아니면 다리를 꼰 채 바닥에 앉으려 해 봐라. 또는 평균적인 중·고교생들이 얼마나 쉽게 당혹감을 느끼는지 생각해 봐라. 학생들이 성적 대상화되는 일이 흔하고 다양한 형태의 폭력이 존재하는 환경에서라면 더욱 그렇다. 아마도 월경. 무슨 말인지 알겠지?

하지만 성 중립적 교복 정책이 치마를 금지하는 것을 필수적으로 요구하는 것은 아니다. 더 많은 이를 포괄하기 위한 정책이, 누군가에게 선택지를 줄이는 방향으로 시행되면 안 된다. 교복 정책은 선택의 폭을 넓히는 방향으로 가야지, 여학생들의 옷차림을 단속하는 방향으로 가면 안 된다. 치마를 금지하는 것이 학생들에게 보내는 메시지는 무엇일까? 평등이라는 메시지보다 누군가를 탓한다는 메시지가 더 크게 느껴지지 않을까?

성 중립 교복 정책이 사용하는 언어에서는 빅토리아 시대의 분위기마저 느껴진다. 치마를 "용인할 수 없는 아이템"의 목록에 올린 학교도 있다. 치마를 "부적절하고 당혹스러운 옷차림"이라고 언급한 또 다른 학교도 있다. 이 언어 중 일부는 분명히 빅토리아 시대의 냄새가 난다. 한 학교는 치마를 "용납할 수 없는 물품" 목록에 올려놓았다. 또 다른 학교는 치마를 "품위 없고 창피한 것"이라고 여긴다. 이 복잡한 주제에 뛰어들면 (실용적인 이유로 바지를 입는 것이 좋겠지만), 머지않아 "정숙함"과 "부적절함"과 같은 강렬한 단어들을 마주하게 될 것이다. 하지만 문제는 치마나 치마 교복을 입은 여학생들이 아니다. 여학생의 치마 교복을 문제 삼는 논리는 강간을 당한 여성의 옷차림을 탓하는 정서와 맞닿아 있다. 한마디로, 학생들이 치마를 입기를 원한다면 입을 수 있어야 한다.

제38회 모의고사

1

하위내용영역	배점	예상정답률
일반영어 A형 기입형	2점	50%

모범답안 ambiguous

채점기준
- 2점: 모범답안과 같다.
- 1점: "confusing"이라 답하였다.
- 0점: 모범답안과 다르다.

한글번역

　초기의 문자들은 모호했다. 예를 들면, 가장 오래된 수메르 설형 문자로는 정상적인 산문이 아니라 전보용 약문에 가까운 문장밖에 쓸 수 없었다. 어휘라고는 이름, 숫자, 도량형, 헤아리는 사물을 일컫는 낱말, 몇 개의 형용사 정도가 고작이었기 때문이다. 가령 오늘날 미국의 법원 서기를 예로 들자면 "우리는 존에게 살찐 양 27마리를 정부에 인도할 것을 명령한다"라고 써야 하는데 그 문장에 필요한 낱말이나 문법이 영어에 없어서 그저 "존 27 살찐 양"이라고 쓰는 것과 같은 상황이었다.

　고대 그리스 미케네 문명의 문자였던 선문자 B는 그보다 더 단순한 형태로 90개 가량의 기호로 이뤄진 음절 문자와 표어문자들로 구성돼 있었다. 하지만 선문자 B가 가지고 있던 장점도, 심한 모호함 때문에 상쇄되고 말았다. 이 문자는 낱말 끝에 오는 자음을 모두 생략했고 몇 개의 관련된 자음을 한 개의 기호로 나타냈다 (예를 들면 l과 r, p와 b, ph, g와 k, kh 등을 각각 한 개의 기호로 표시하는 식으로). 일본에서 나고 자란 사람들이 영어를 할 때 l과 r을 제대로 구별하지 않아서 얼마나 헷갈리게 만드는지 잘 알고 있다. 그런데 방금 영어 알파벳에서 언급한 자음들을 구별하지 않고 일본인들처럼 한가지로 쓴다면 그때는 얼마나 더 헷갈리게 될지 상상해 보라. 그렇게 되면 우리는 "rap" "lap" "lab" "laugh"를 모두 똑같은 철자로 써야 할 것이다.

2

하위내용영역	배점	예상정답률
일반영어 A형 서술형	4점	50%

모범답안 Saez and Zucman(They) found the top 0.01 controlled 22% of all wealth in 2012, up from 7% in 1979. Second, the writer mentions the Netherlands because it shows the exceptional wealth inequality of the United States, as the next nearest country has half as much inequality.

채점기준
- +2점: 사에즈와 저크먼이 연구한 것을 "the top 0.01 controlled 22% of all wealth in 2012, up from 7% in 1979"라 서술하였거나 유사하였다.
- +2점: 네덜란드를 언급한 이유를 "because it shows the exceptional wealth inequality of the United States, as the next nearest country has half as much inequality"이라 서술했거나 유사하였다.

한글번역

　부의 불평등에 관한 데이터를 놓고 나라별로 비교해 보면, 미국이 다른 어떤 선진국보다 불평등이 극명하고, 다른 모든 나머지 선진국들의 부의 불평등을 왜소하게 보일 정도로 압도적으로 심하다는 사실이 뚜렷하게 드러난다. 보수 성향 연구 기관인 허드슨 인스티튜트는 2017년 발표한 보고서에서 2013년 재산 기준 미국 상위 5% 가계가 미국 전체 자산의 62.5%를 가지고 있다고 보고했다. 이는 30년 전 54.1%였던 것보다 높아진 수치로, 나머지 95% 가계의 재산이 차지하는 비중도 45.9%였던 것이 37.5%로 줄었다.

　그 결과, 2013년 기준 소득이 높은 가계의 평균 연소득은 639,400달러, 중간에 해당하는 가계의 평균 연소득은 96,500달러였다. 소득 상위 가계 재산의 중간값이 소득 중위 가계 재산의 중간값보다 거의 일곱 배가 많았다. 적어도 지난 30년 사이 해당 격차가 가장 크게 벌어진 것이다.

유희태 | 일반영어 ❹-2

더욱 눈에 띄는 것은, 불평등을 오랫동안 연구해 온 세계적인 학자 에마누엘 사에즈와 가브리엘 저크먼 교수의 연구인데, 그들은 상위 0.01% 부자가 미국 전체 자산의 22%를 소유하고 있다는 점을 밝혀냈다. 2012년을 기준으로 한 데이터를 분석한 결과인데, 1979년과 같은 수치가 7%에 불과했었다. 하지만 소득 불평등에 관한 데이터만 보면 전혀 다른 결론이 나온다. 예를 들어 2013년 상위 5% 가계가 벌어들인 소득은 미국인 전체 소득의 30%에 불과했지만, 재산으로는 이들은 전체의 거의 63%를 소유하고 있었다.

지난 30년 동안 부의 불평등이 심화하고 빈부 격차가 벌어진 나라는 선진국 가운데 미국 말고도 얼마든지 더 있다. 하지만 그 정도에 있어서 미국은 특이하게 심각하다. 재산 상위 5% 가계의 부는 미국 중간 가계의 부보다 91배나 더 많다. 세계에서 가장 잘 사는 나라 18개국 가운데 부의 편중이 단연 가장 심하다. 미국 다음으로 빈부 격차가 큰 나라가 네덜란드였는데, (앞서 계산한 수치를 네덜란드에 적용해 계산하면) 미국의 절반도 되지 않는다.

3

하위내용영역	배점	예상정답률
일반영어 B형 서술형	4점	50%

모범답안 A "major value shift" refers to the decline in Americans prioritization of family, god and nation. Second, the underlined means that the shift in young adults' belief in God is not disturbing if you don't believe that Judeo-Christian values are key to morality.

채점기준

+ 2점: 주요한 가치의 변환이 가리키는 것을 "the decline in Americans prioritization of family, god and nation"이라 서술하였거나 유사하였다.
+ 2점: 밑줄 친 부분의 의미를 "the shift in young adults' belief in God is not disturbing if you don't believe that Judeo-Christian values are key to morality"라 정확하게 서술하였다.

한글번역

지난 1998년 월스트리트저널과 NBC는 18~38세 미국인에게 인생에서 가장 중요한 가치를 꼽으라는 질문을 던졌다. 가장 많은 사람이 "열심히 일하는 것(work ethic)"을 꼽았다. 이어 애국심과 종교, 그리고 아이를 낳아 가정을 꾸리는 것이 중요하다는 답이 나왔다.

21년이 지난 2019년, 같은 연령대 미국인에게 같은 질문을 던졌다. 밀레니얼 세대와 Z세대의 답변은 21년 전과 아주 달랐다. 아이를 낳고 가정을 꾸리는 것이 중요하다고 답한 비율이 10% 낮아졌고, 애국심이나 종교가 중요하다고 답한 사람의 비율은 무려 20%나 낮아졌다.

가족, 신, 국가 이 세 가지는 전통적인 미국인의 가치관을 든든하게 받치던 다리와도 같다. 그런데 (자녀와 부모로 구성된) 핵가족, 신앙, 애국심에 대한 젊은 세대의 충성도가 급전직하하는 것은 미국인의 정체성의 진화에 대한 중요한 어떤 것을 말해 주고 있다.

이번 설문조사 결과는 우선 전통적인 서구적 믿음의 침식으로 해석될 수 있다. 미국의 30세 이하는 전체 종교인의 1/3을 넘는 많은 수치를 차지한다. 그런데 이들은 기독교가 아니라 이슬람교, 불교, 힌두교이다. 이것은 두 가지 측면을 반영하는데, 하나는 1970년대 이후 유럽이 아닌 지역에서의 미국에 이민 온 사람들이 늘어났기 때문이고, 다른 하나는 20세기 하반기에 규모가 큰 기독교 종파의 쇠퇴 때문이다. 이런 상황은 또한 무신론자의 비율이 급격하게 늘어난 것을 반영한다. (Z세대까지 갈 것도 없이) 밀레니얼 세대만 해도 이미 신의 존재를 믿지 않는 사람이 16%로 베이비붐 세대(6%)보다 세 배 가까이 높다. 당신이 유대 기독교로 이어지는 종교적 가치가 서구 사회를 떠받치는 가장 중요한 윤리적 가치라고 당신이 생각한다면, 이런 설문조사에서 나타난 사실들은 당신을 불편하게 할 것이다. 물론 당신이 그렇게 생각하지 않는다면(유대 기독교로 이어지는 종교적 가치가 서구 사회를 떠받치는 가장 중요한 윤리적 가치라고 생각하지 않는다면) 이런 사실들(젊은 세대들 사이에서 기독교가 쇠퇴한다는)은 별문제가 없을 것이다.

두 번째 해석은, 대개 정치와 관련이 있다. 젊은 세대의 애국심, 가족, 종교에 대한 무관심은 전통적 보수주의에 대한 젊은이들의 혐오에 대한 대리물(혐오를 반영하는 것)일 수 있다는 것이다.

4

하위내용영역	배점	예상정답률
일반영어 B형 서술형	4점	30%

모범답안) Placing water bottles in a car during hot weather can be dangerous. Water bottles can focus sunlight as lenses enough to burn things within cars as shown in several cases (such as with Idaho Power and the Holy Water company). Likewise, Madden, who found that adhesive focused lasers in ways that could cause damage, cautioned that even reduced by a car's window glass there could be enough energy remaining to cause burning. In short, we should be careful not to leave a bottle in a car during a summer hot day.

채점 기준

ⓐ Topic sentence
+ 1점 : "Placing water bottles in a car during hot weather can be dangerous"를 명확하게 서술하였거나 유사하였다.

ⓑ Summary
+ 2점 : "Water bottles can focus sunlight as lenses enough to burn things within cars as shown in several cases (such as with Idaho Power and the Holy Water company)(1점). Likewise, Madden, who found that adhesive focused lasers in ways that could cause damage, cautioned that even reduced by a car's window glass there could be enough energy remaining to cause burning(1점)."을 서술하였거나 유사하였다.

ⓒ Conclusion
+ 1점 : "In short, we should be careful not to leave a bottle in a car during a summer hot day"를 서술하였거나 유사하였다.

감점
- 본문에 나오는 연속되는 6단어 이상을 사용하였다. -0.5pt
- 문단을 두 개나 그 이상으로 구성하였다. -0.5pt
- 문법이나 영어 표현을 합쳐 3개 이상 오류가 있다. -0.5pt

한글번역

자동차 안에 생수병을 둔다고 무슨 일이 벌어질까 생각할 수 있지만, 더운 여름날 투명한 플라스틱 물병은 렌즈가 되어 자동차 시트와 같은 내장재에 불을 낼 가능성이 있다. 지난 여름, 아이다호 전력 회사는 생수병이 자동차 시트에 두 개의 구멍을 내는 비디오를 공유했다. 올해 러시아 월드컵에서 러시아의 생수 회사인 홀리워터가 판매한 축구공 모양의 생수병은 완벽한 렌즈 역할을 할 수 있다. (러시아의) 폰탄카 루가 공개한 비디오에서는 이 축구공 모양 생수병이 어떻게 성냥에 불을 붙이고 코팅된 마룻바닥에 구멍을 내는지를 보여줬다. 그 생수병은 차창 밖에서 들어오는 빛을 모으는 렌즈 역할을 하고 있었다.

재료과학자 오딜 매든은 수년 전, 예술 작품에서 투명한 접착제를 레이저를 이용해 떼내면서 이런 빛의 집중이 어떤 힘을 가지는지를 직접 본 적이 있다. 접착제의 주름이 빛을 모으는 렌즈로 작용해 실험을 위해 그녀가 사용하고 있었던 현미경용 유리 슬라이드를 태우거나 그슬리게 하는 것을 봤다. 그녀는 이 결과를 2005년 학술 논문집 "예술 작품 보존을 위한 레이저"에 발표했다.

매든을 놀라게 한 것은 자동차 유리를 통과한 빛에도 여전히 차에 불을 낼 수 있는 충분한 에너지가 남아 있다는 것이었다. "아마도 뜨거운 날씨라든가, 유리 창문이 내려져 있을 때 더욱 안 좋을 수 있는데, 그 이유는 유리는 빛을 차단하기 때문이다. 이는 태양에서 얼마나 많은 에너지가 지구로 쏟아지는지 보여주는 예이다. 이 생수병은 그저 값싼 플라스틱일 뿐이지만 우연히도 거의 완벽한 렌즈 역할을 할 수 있다"고 매든은 덧붙였다. 뜨거운 날 차 안 종이 더미 위에 생수병을 놔두지 않는 것이 좋을 듯하다.

유희태 | 일반영어 ④-2

제39회 모의고사

1

하위내용영역	배점	예상정답률
일반영어 A형 기입형	2점	55%

모범 답안) autonomy

채점 기준

- 2점: 모범답안과 같다. 이외에는 답이 될 수 없다.
- 0점: 모범답안과 다르다.

한글번역

　여성이 머리부터 발끝까지 부르카로 자신을 감싸는 이슬람의 아주 기본적인 전통은, 문화적 관습이 개인의 자율을 증진시키는 정도를 평가하는 데 있어서 봉착하는 본질적 어려움을 보여주는 하나의 사례이다. 부르카와 이에 유사한 복장을 비난하는 사람들, 특히 서구 문화 비평가들은 그 복장들이 육체적으로는 직물의 무게로 인해 신체적 압박을 가하며; 심리적으로는 여성의 개성이 결여돼 보이게 한다는 점에서 억압적이고; 정서적으로는 여성이 종속돼 있는 남성 지배 사회의 또 하나의 표시라는 점에서 억압적이라고 간주한다. 이런 견해에 따르면, 그런 옷을 입는 전통은 여성의 자율을 크게 제한하기 때문에 정당성이 없다.
　그러나 이 관습을 옹호하는 사람들은 반대되는 견해를 주장한다. 그들은 부르카와 같은 피복은 실제로 여러 가지 이유에서 자율을 조장하며 여성들을 자유롭게 해준다고 주장한다. 예를 들어, 부르카는 여성이 성적 대상으로 보이는 것을 막아주고, 여성 이슬람교도들 간의 단결을 장려하며, 성스러운 외모가 되도록 해준다. 부르카 옹호자들은 또 서양 비평가들에게 "왜 두건을 쓰는 것은 억압적인 것이고, 미니스커트를 입는 것은 자유롭게 하는 것으로 여겨지는가?"처럼 그들로 하여금 자신들의 의류 문화를 돌아보게 하는 질문을 한다. 그들은 그 대답이 관련된 여성들과 그들이 선택하는 능력에 대해 각 문화가 만들어 내는 가정에 있다고 주장한다. 그들은 만일 그러한 의복 관습에 관한 그들의 가정이 실제로 잘못됐고, 부르카와 그 변형된 형태의 옷을 입는 것이 실제로 개인의 선호 문제라면, 그것은 완전히 개인의 자율에 대한 적법한 표현으로 정당화된다고 말한다.

2

하위내용영역	배점	예상정답률
일반영어 A형 서술형	4점	45%

모범 답안) The meaning of the underlined "mysterious" is that the exact reasons for the drug's effectiveness is not known. Second, it("intellectual debt") means the practice of using discoveries and innovations—such as medications or treatments—without fully understanding how they work. This debt is incurred when practical applications are implemented based on observed effectiveness, with the expectation that the underlying mechanisms will be researched and understood later.

채점 기준

+ 2점: 밑줄 친 "신비스러운"이 의미하는 것을 "the exact reasons for the drug's effectiveness is not known"이라 서술하였다.
+ 2점: "지적 부채"가 의미하는 바가 "the practice of using discoveries and innovations—such as medications or treatments—without fully understanding how they work. This debt is incurred when practical applications are implemented based on observed effectiveness, with the expectation that the underlying mechanisms will be researched and understood later"라 서술하였다.

☞ 다음과 같이 서술하였어도 맞는 것으로 한다.
- "it("Intellectual debt") is a concept used to describe the situation in which a discovery or innovation is made and put to practical use before the underlying mechanisms or reasons for its effectiveness are fully understood. In the context of the passage, this means that drugs like Provigil are approved and prescribed based on observed benefits, even though the scientific community does not yet have a complete explanation for how they work."

⊕ 보충설명

The "debt" is the accumulated lack of knowledge, which ideally should be "paid off" by subsequent research to fully understand the mechanisms involved. If this intellectual debt is not addressed, it compounds over time, leading to a reliance on knowledge that is not fully comprehended.

In the context, "make for" means to lead to or contribute to something. So, the phrase "make for anodyne reading" means that the contents of the pamphlet (lists of instructions and precautions, a diagram of the drug's molecular structure) result in reading material that is dull or unexciting.

한글번역

다른 많은 의약품처럼 프로비질이라는 이름으로 팔리는 각성제 모다피닐 안에도 작게 접힌 설명서가 들어 있다. 대부분의 내용은 흔한 수면 유도제처럼 사용법과 주의점, 약의 분자 구조에 관한 것이다. 그러나 "작용 기전"이라 불리는 세부 항목에는 잠이 확 달아나게 할 만한 한 문장이 들어 있다. 그것은 바로 "모다피닐이 어떻게 각성 작용을 하는지는 알려져 있지 않다"는 문장이다.

프로비질만 독특하게 신비스러운 것이 아니다. 허가를 받고 널리 사용되는 약들 중에도 그 약이 정확히 우리 몸속에서 어떻게 작용하는지 우리가 알지 못하는 약들이 많이 있다. 이런 신비스러움은 시행착오에 의해 진행되는 약의 발견 과정에 이미 내재돼 있다 (약이 시행착오를 통해 주로 발견되기 때문이라는 의미). 매년 새로운 약물이 배양 세포나 동물들에게 실험이 되고, 그중 가장 효과가 좋고 안전한 약물이 사람에게 시도된다. 때로는 새로 발견된 약이 새로운 연구 분야를 만들어 내고 자신의 작용 기전이 이를 통해 밝혀지는 경우도 있지만, 늘 그런 것은 아니다. 아스피린은 1897년에 발견됐지만, 우리는 1995년이 돼서야 아스피린이 어떻게 우리 몸속에서 작동하는지를 이해하게 됐다. 의학에는 이런 예가 많다. 뇌심부 자극술(DBS)은 전극을 뇌 속에 삽입하는 기술로 파킨슨병처럼 특정한 움직임에 장애가 있는 이들에게 20년 이상 사용돼 왔으며 어떤 이들은 이 시술이 인지 능력 강화에도 유용하리라 생각한다. 하지만 누구도 그 이유(이 약이 어떻게 작용하는지)는 알지 못한다.

발견에 대한 이러한 접근법, 곧 답을 먼저 찾고 설명은 나중에 찾는 방식이 내가 지적 부채라 부르는 것을 축적한다. 어떤 것이 왜 작동하는지 모르는 상태로 언젠가는 그 원리를 알 수 있을 것이라 생각하며 실제로 이를 사용하는 것도 물론 가능하다. 어떤 경우에선 이 지적 부채를 쉽게 갚을 수 있다. 하지만 다른 경우들에서는, 수십 년 동안 이 기술에 의존하고 다른 분야에까지 적용하면서도 그 원리를 충분히 알지 못한 상태로 사용한다.

3

하위내용영역	배점	예상정답률
일반영어 B형 서술형	4점	45%

[모범답안] The meaning of the underlined words is that the formation of data-labor unions, which will protect and monitor their members' data work, sounds futuristic and far-fetched, like science fiction. Next, the inferred reason is that if they have to do it for all people, it will cut into their profits.

채점 기준

+ 2점: 밑줄 친 부분의 의미를 "the formation of data-labor unions, which will protect and monitor their members' data work, sounds futuristic and far-fetched(unlikely), like science fiction"이라 서술하였거나 유사하였다.
+ 2점: 그 둘이 한 것을 "if they have to do it for all people, it will cut into their profits"라 서술하였거나 유사하였다.

한글번역

그런 데이터가 적극적으로든 수동적으로든 어떻게 만들어지는지와 무관하게, 자신이 만들어 낸 데이터가 어떻게 쓰이는지를 추적하거나 그 가치를 매기는 것은 거의 불가능하다. 설사 그것이 가능하다 하더라도, 개인이 인공 지능 기업을 대상으로 이를 거래할 힘을 가지기는 어려울 것이다. 하지만 노동의 역사는 이 문제를 어떻게 해결해야 하는지 알려준다. 역사적으로 노동의 대가가 적절한 수준으로 오를 수 있었던 데에는 노동조합의 역할이 매우 중요했다. 바일은 사람들의 데이터를 관리해 주는 "데이터 노동조합"이 탄생할 것이라 말한다. 바일은 과거 노동조합이 했던 것처럼, 데이터 노동조합 또한 데이터의 가격을 기업과 흥정하며, 회원들의 데이터가 어떻게 쓰이는지를 추적할 뿐 아니라, 명성 점수 등을 이용해 데이터의 품질을 관리하게 될 것이라 말한다. 또한 전문적인 데이터를 조합원에게 이동시키고, 심지어 조합원들의 데이터에 기업의 접속을 막는 식으로 파업을 주동할 수도 있다. 유사한 방식으로, 데이터 노동조합은 조합원들의 데이터를 대신 거래해주는 창구 기능도 할 수 있고, 그 데이터들 추적해서 그 데이터로부터 혜택을 받는 인공 지능 기업에게 비용 청구서를 보낼 수도 있다.

이런 이야기가 그저 공상 과학 소설로 들릴지 모른다. 구글이나 페이스북이 사람들이 공짜로 제공하는 데이터를 바탕으로 광고 수입을 얻는 지금의 모델을 버릴 이유가 있을까? 2017년 이 두 기업은 광고만으로 1,350억 달러를 벌었다. 그들에게 사람들의 데이터에 대해 비용을 내라고 한다면, 그들의 수익은 크게 줄어들 것이다. 또한 시티즌미나 데이타쿠와 같은 초기 형태의 데이터 노동조합은 아직 성공을 거두지 못하고 있다. 한편, 다른 분야에서는 이 거대 인터넷 대기업들이 데이터에 돈을 지불하고 있지만, 이 사실이 공개적으로 알려지지 않도록 조심하고 있다. 이들은 자신들의 알고리즘을 검증하고 불량한 콘텐츠를 제거하는 일을 외주로 맡기고 있다. 사진에 설명을 덧붙이는 일을 아마존의 메커니컬 터크와 같은 집단 고용 플랫폼으로 해결하는 기업도 있다.

4

하위내용영역	배점	예상정답률
일반영어 B형 서술형	4점	45%

모범답안 Polytheism shows much more tolerance than Christianity to other faiths. Polytheistic empires did not try to convert conquered subjects, and often added the other gods to their pantheons. However, since Christians would not respect the gods of Romans, insisting on their own monotheistic view, they was persecuted for political subversion. This was minor, totaling a few thousand deaths over 300 years, in stark compare with the millions slaughtered Christians killed by slightly-different Christian sects since.

채점기준

ⓐ Topic sentence
+ 1.5점 : "Polytheism shows much more tolerance than Christianity to other faiths"를 명확하게 서술하였거나 유사하였다.

ⓑ Summary
+ 2.5점 : "<u>Polytheistic empires did not try to convert conquered subjects, and often added the other gods to their pantheons</u>(1점). However, <u>since Christians would not respect the gods of Romans, insisting on their own monotheistic view, they was persecuted for political subversion</u>(0.75점). This was minor, <u>totaling a few thousand deaths over 300 years, in stark compare with the millions slaughtered Christians killed by slightly-different Christian sects since</u>(0.75점)."를 서술하였거나 유사하였다.

감점
- 본문에 나오는 연속되는 6단어 이상을 사용하였다. −0.5pt
- 문단을 두 개나 그 이상으로 구성하였다. −0.5pt
- 문법이나 영어 표현을 합쳐 3개 이상 오류가 있다. −0.5pt

제40회 모의고사

1

하위내용영역	배점	예상정답률
일반영어 A형 기입형	2점	55%

모범답안 tolerant

채점기준

- 2점: 모범답안과 같다. 이외에는 답이 될 수 없다.
- 0점: 모범답안과 다르다.

한글번역

우리 인간은 (사회적 동물에서 흔히 볼 수 있는 특징 가운데 하나인 집단을 이뤘다가 또 흩어지고 다른 이들과 다른 기준으로 또 뭉치기를 반복하는) 핵분열-융합(fission-fusion)과 같은 사회를 이루는 종들 가운데서도 대단히 관용적인(쉽게 공격하는 대신 참고 견디는) 쪽으로 진화했다. 이렇게 된 이유 중 일부는 다른 영장류보다 훨씬 더 큰 인간의 뇌와 상대적으로 높은 번식력을 들 수 있다. 이 두 가지 특징이 합쳐진 결과 인간은 고품질, 고위험(시공간적으로 어떤 환경에 처할지 예측할 수 없는) 음식과 도구에 절대적으로 의존하게 됐다. 이것은 인간들로 하여금 먹을거리를 찾는 대단히 독특한 전략을 개발하게 했다. 바로 먹을거리를 포함한 자원이 부족해질 때 다른 집단과 무리를 합침으로써 무리를 유지하는 전략이었다. (다른 어떤 영장류나 사회적 동물도 채택하지 않은 이 전략은 특히 어떤 환경에 처할지 예측할 수 없는 상황에서 쓸모 있는 전략이었다.) 그렇다고 인간이 지금은 물론이고 예전에도 항상 평화를 사랑하는 동물이라는 의미는 아니다. (즉, 싸우는 걸 싫어하거나 평화적인 동물이어서 그런 전략을 개발한 것이 아니라, 우리가 가진 자원을 활용해 필요한 식량과 자원을 얻을 수 없을 때 위기를 헤쳐 나가기 위해 다른 무리와 다른 부족의 사람들에게 기대며 이들의 낯선 점을 참아 내고 협력하는 법을 하나의 전략으로 체화한 것이라는 의미) 비지역적 자원에 대한 접근이 중요한 장소와 시기에는, 인간은 종종 적어도 일정 기간 동안에는 다른 공동체 구성원들에게 관용적인 방법을 찾아냈다.

우리 인간의 공격적 경향의 진화론적 기원에 대한 통찰을 얻기 위한 한 방법으로 예전의 연구는 호전적인 침팬지를 주로 연구한 반면, 최근의 연구는 우리 인간의 관용적 본성의 토대를 이해하기 위해선, 더욱 관용적인 영장류들이 타당하다고 생각하고 있다.

한글번역

다신교의 통찰은 폭넓은 종교적 관용을 낳기 쉽다. 다신교도들은 한편으로는 하나의 최고의 권력, 완벽하게 무관심한 권력을 믿고 다른 한편으로는 편견을 지닌 수많은 권력을 믿기 때문에, 하나의 신에 헌신하는 사람이라도 다른 신들의 존재와 효험을 받아들이는 데 어려움이 없다. 다신교는 본질적으로 마음이 열려 있으며 "이단"이나 "이교도"를 처단하는 일이 드물다. 이것은 자신들의 종교 내에서든 밖에서든 자신들의 종교와 다른 종교를 믿는 사람들과 전쟁을 벌여 왔던 기독교와 같은 일신교적 종교와는 대조적이다.

다신교도는 심지어 거대한 제국을 정복했을 때도 피정복민을 개종시키려고 노력하지 않았다. 이집트인, 로마인, 아즈텍인은 오시리스, 유피테르, 우이칠로포치틀리(아즈텍의 최고신)에 대한 신앙을 전파하려 선교사를 외국에 파견하지 않았고, 이를 목적으로 군대를 파견하지도 않았다. 아즈텍 제국에서 피정복민들은 우이칠로포치틀리 신전을 지어야 했지만, 기존의 신전을 대신해서가 아니라 그 옆에 세웠다. 로마인들은 아시아의 키벨레 여신을, 이집트인들은 이시스를 그들의 만신전에 기꺼이 추가했다.

로마인들이 오랫동안 관용을 거부했던 유일한 신은 일신교적이고 개종을 요구하는 기독교의 신이었다. 로마 제국은 기독교인들에게 신앙과 의례를 포기하라고 요구하지 않았다. 하지만 제국의 수호신과 황제의 신성에 경의를 표할 것을 기대했다. 이는 정치적 충성심의 선언이라고 여겨졌다. 기독교인들이 이를 격렬하게 거부하고 화해를 위한 모든 시도를 거절하는 데까지 나가자 로마인들은 박해로 대응했다. 이런 박해조차 주저하는 식이었다. 예수가 십자가에 달린 지 300년 만에 콘스탄티누스 대제가 개종할 때까지 다신교를 믿는 로마 황제가 기독교인을 박해한 사건은 네 차례를 넘지 않았다. 3세기에 걸친 모든 박해의 희생자를 다 합친다 해도 다신교를 믿는 로마인들이 살해한 기독교인들은 몇 천 명을 넘지 않았다. 이와 대조적으로 이후 1500년간 기독교인은 사랑과 관용의 종교에 대한 조금 다른 해석을 지키기 위해 다른 기독교인 수백만 명을 학살했다.

특히, 이러한 영장류 중 (난쟁이 침팬지로도 불리는) 보노보는 서로 다른 무리끼리 합치는 일이 일어났고, 서로 식량을 나누거나 털을 다듬어 주기도 하는 모습이 관찰됐다. 보노보 사회도 다른 무리의 구성원에게 무조건 친절하거나 늘 협력하고 참았던 건 아니다. 서로 다른 무리가 만나게 되면 다른 무리의 구성원과 갈등도 빚어지고 아예 싸움이 격해져 몇몇 무리를 이탈해 버리기도 한다. 그러나 보노보 사회에서도, 인간 사회와 마찬가지로, 서로 다른 무리들 간의 행동에 있어서 유연성—서로 다른 무리를 때로 배척하고 공격하지만, 또 참고 협력하기도 하는 유연성—이 발견됐다.

2

하위내용영역	배점	예상정답률
일반영어 A형 서술형 - 시	4점	60%

모범답안 The cues are a story told in strict chronological order (suggesting rehearsal); excessive linguistic convolution or overcompensation (using too many words); using impersonal phrases or pronouns rather than names; avoiding saying "I"; working hard to appear truthful by smiling at all the right moments and saying all the right. Second, the underlined words mean that a big smile most likely indicates someone who is trying to deceive.

채점기준

+ 2점 : 거짓말인지 구별할 수 있는 모든 신호가 "a story told in strict chronological order; excessive linguistic convolution (or overcompensation); using impersonal phrases or pronouns rather than names; avoiding saying "I"; working hard to appear truthful by smiling at all the right moments and saying all the right"이라 정확하게 서술하였다.

☞ 5개 중 3~4개만 맞은 경우 1점, 0~2개는 0점을 준다.

+ 2점 : 밑줄 친 부분의 의미를 "a big smile most likely indicates someone who is trying to deceive" 또는 "when someone displays an overly perfect smile, it should be seen as dangerous rather than reassuring—similar to how a shark's smile reveals its teeth before an attack"라 서술하였거나 유사하였다.

한글번역

거짓말쟁이라고 의심되는 사람이 보이면, 다음으로는 귀를 기울여보라. 다음은 귀 담아 들어야 할 단서들이다. (첫째) 엄격한 시간 순서대로 이야기하는 것. 복잡한 거짓말을 할 때, 그 대상이 CIA 요원이든, 십대의 부모든, 또는 밥 우드워드와 칼 번스타인이든, 거짓말쟁이들은 종종 이야기를 미리 연습한다. 그 이야기는 일반적으로 논리적으로 처음부터 끝까지 전개된다. 재미있는 골탕 먹이는 방법은 다음과 같다. 허풍떠는 이야기를 듣고 있다고 생각되면, 이야기를 거꾸로 말해달라고 요청하라: "그래서 당신이 도랑에 있는 차를 우연히 봤을 때—그 전에 무슨 일이 있었죠?" 그런 뒤 거짓말쟁이가 당황하는 것을 지켜보라.

(둘째) 언어적으로 너무 복잡해 혼란스러운 것 또는 과잉 보상. 거짓말쟁이로 의심되는 사람이 열 마디면 충분한데도 백 마디를 사용하나? 혹은 여러 절이 있는 공식적인 언어를 사용하나? 예를 들어, 다음 두 문장을 비교해 보자 : "주어진 상황을 고려할 때, 나는 결코, 그리고 절대로 공유 오피스 냉장고에서 당신의 점심을 빼앗지 않았다고 단언할 수 있습니다." 이 문장을 "나는 당신의 점심을 먹지 않았습니다."와 비교해보라.

(셋째) 진실을 말하는 사람은 이름을 언급하지만, 거짓말쟁이는 비인칭 구문이나 대명사를 사용한다; 예를 들어, "미스 르윈스키"란 말 대신에 "그 여자"라고 한다. (넷째) 또한, 거짓말쟁이는 "나"라고 말하는 것을 피한다. 예를 들어, "나는 계산대에서 돈을 빼돌리지 않았어" 대신에 "여기 있는 누구도 계산대에서 돈을 빼돌리지 않았을 거야"라고 말하는 것을 들을 것이다.

거짓말쟁이는 진실하게 보이기 위해 정말 열심히 노력한다. (다섯째) 거짓말쟁이들은 모든 적절한 순간에 미소를 짓고 적절한 것을 말한다. 그러나 그 결과는 종종 인위적이고 가짜처럼 보인다. 실제로 그렇기 때문이다. 만약 당신이 속임수를 당하고 있다고 느낀다면, 아마도 당하고 있을 것이다. 요약하자면, 밝고 치아가 드러나는 미소는 아마도 상어(사기꾼)를 의미할 것이다.

3

하위내용영역	배점	예상정답률
일반영어 B형 서술형	4점	40%

모범답안 Inception's limitation is that it can be tricked by altering the pixels of an image. Despite appearing normal to human eyes, these changes can cause Inception to incorrectly identify the object in the image with high confidence. This highlights a vulnerability where the system can be easily fooled by specially crafted or corrupted data. Second, insurance swindlers could exploit the vulnerabilities in Health-care AI by manipulating images or data to trick the AI into making incorrect classifications, such as misidentifying benign conditions as malignant or vice versa. This could enable them to commit fraud by fabricating or exaggerating medical conditions to claim undue insurance benefits.

채점기준

+ 2점 : Inception의 한계를 "it can be tricked by altering the pixels of an image. Despite appearing normal to human eyes, these changes can cause Inception to incorrectly identify the object in the image with high confidence. This highlights a vulnerability where the system can be easily fooled by specially crafted or corrupted data"라 서술하였거나 유사하였다.

+ 2점 : 보험 사기꾼들이 헬스케어 AI를 어떻게 사용할 것 같은가에 대한 질문에 "insurance swindlers could exploit the vulnerabilities in Health-care AI by manipulating images or data to trick the AI into making incorrect classifications, such as misidentifying benign conditions as malignant or vice versa"라 서술하였거나 유사하였다.

한글번역

이미지 인식의 문제를 생각해 보자. 10년 전, 컴퓨터는 사진 속의 물체를 쉽게 인식하지 못했다. 오늘날, 우리는 일상에서 매우 뛰어난 기계 학습 모델 기반의 이미지 검색 엔진을 사용하고 있다. 구글의 이미지 검색은 인셉션이라 불리는 신경망을 사용한다. 2017년, MIT의 학부생과 대학원생으로 이뤄진 랩식스 팀은 고양이 사진의 픽셀 몇 개를 바꿔 사람 눈에는 여전히 고양이로 보이지만 인셉션은 99.99%의 확률로 과카몰 사진으로 판단하는 사진을 만들었다. 물론 인셉션 신경망은 자신이 어떤 고양이 사진을 왜 고양이 사진으로 판단하는지 말할 수 없기 때문에 특정한 조작이 가해진 이미지에 대해 인셉션이 잘못된 판단을 내릴지를 예측하는 것도 불가능하다. 곧 이런 시스템은 일반적으로 알려진 정확도에 비해 의도적인, 훈련된 공격자에 대해서는 매우 쉽게 뚫리는 단점을 가질 수밖에 없다.

기계 학습 시스템에 의해 만들어진 지식이 널리 사용될수록, 이런 종류의 단점은 필연적으로 발생하게 된다. 의료분야에서 사진 속 피부암이 악성인지 양성인지를 판단하는 인공 지능은 매우 성공적인 기술이다. 하지만 하버드 의대와 MIT의 연구진이 올해 발표한 논문에서 이들은 앞서 고양이를 과카몰로 판단하게 만든 것과 같은 방식으로 이 인공 지능을 속일 수 있음을 보였다. (즉, 보험금을 노리는 이들이 이런 방식의 공격을 할 수 있다.) 기계 학습이 보여주는 놀라운 정확도는 우리로 하여금 인간의 판단보다 이들을 더 믿음직스럽게 여기게 만든다. 하지만 이들은 이런 조작에 취약하며, 우리는 이 시스템의 실수를 확인할 수 있는 다른 쉬운 방법을 가질 수 없다는 문제가 있다.

4

하위내용영역	배점	예상정답률
일반영어 B형 서술형	4점	45%

모범답안 Successful entrepreneurs tend to be middle-aged despite notions that young people dominate the field. Researchers have shown that the mean age of startup founders is 42, and high-growth startups 45, backed by their greater experience in their specific industry. Even considering the high-growth startup states of California, Massachusetts and New York, successful entrepreneurs are middle aged.

채점 기준

ⓐ Topic sentence
+ 1점: "Successful entrepreneurs tend to be middle-aged (despite notions that young people dominate the field)"를 명확하게 서술하였거나 유사하였다.

ⓑ Summary
+ 3점: "Researchers have shown that the mean age of startup founders is 42, and high-growth startups is 45(1점), backed by their greater experience in their specific industry(1점). Even considering the high-growth startup states of California, Massachusetts and New York, successful entrepreneurs are middle aged(1점)."를 서술하였거나 유사하였다.

감점
- 본문에 나오는 연속되는 6단어 이상을 사용하였다. −0.5pt
- 문단을 두 개나 그 이상으로 구성하였다. −0.5pt
- 문법이나 영어 표현을 합쳐 3개 이상 오류가 있다. −0.5pt

한글번역

19세에 마이크로소프트를 창업한 빌 게이츠, 21세에 애플을 창업한 스티브 잡스, 그리고 19세에 페이스북을 창업한 마크 저커버그와 같은 스타 창업자들의 신화와 같은 이야기는 젊음이야 말로 창업에 어울리는 나이라는 오래된 믿음을 강화한다. 하지만 창업가들의 나이를 체계적으로 분석한 데이터가 가리키는 결론은 이런 믿음과 배치된다. 많은 연구자들은 평균적으로 성공한 기업가들이 중년의 사람들이라는 증거를 제공한다.

이들은 미국 통계청 자료를 이용해 적어도 한 명 이상을 고용하고 있는 회사를 창업한 미국의 창업가 270만 명을 분석했다. 창업가들의 평균 나이는 42세였다. 성장 속도에서 상위 1%에 속하는 기업만 놓고 보면 창업가의 평균 나이는 45세로 높아졌다. 게다가, 이 연구는 기업의 성공과 상관관계가 있는 요인들을 분석한다. 스타트업의 특정 산업에 더 가깝고 더 오랜 업무 경험을 가진 이러한 나이 든 설립자들과 그 산업에서 더 오랜 경험을 가진 설립자들은 훨씬 더 높은 성공률을 가지고 있다. 연구진은 "고성장 기업 1,000곳 중 1곳 꼴로 어떤 산업에서 3년 이상의 경험을 한 창업자가 그런 산업에서 경험하지 않은 젊은 창업자보다 2배 높은 성공률을 보인다"고 밝혔다. 이 연구는 또한 지리적 이질성을 고려했으며, 캘리포니아, 매사추세츠, 뉴욕을 별도로 고려했다. 이들 3개 주는 미국 내 고성장 스타트업 활동의 대부분을 차지하고 있으며, 이들 주에서도 성공한 창업자들은 여전히 중장년층이다.

제41회 모의고사

1

하위내용영역	배점	예상정답률
일반영어 A형 서술형	4점	45%

모범답안 The word is "attention". Second, the writer thought he was a complete hypocrite because he had said he didn't use acting for attention earlier, but then he was using it to get attention.

채점 기준

+ 2점: 빈칸에 들어갈 단어를 "attention"이라 정확히 기입하였다. 이외에는 답이 될 수 없다.
+ 2점: 글의 저자가 스스로를 "완전 위선자"라 생각한 이유를 "because he had said he didn't use acting for attention earlier, but then he was using it to get attention"라 서술하였거나 유사하였다.

한글번역

나는 여름 캠프에서 처음으로 관심을 얻기 위해 행동했던 여덟 살 때를 기억한다. 그때 나는 이미 약 1년 동안 오디션을 봤고, TV 쇼와 광고에서 작은 역할을 얻는 행운을 누렸으며, 캠프에서 그 사실을 많이 자랑했다. 처음에는 효과가 있었다. 다른 아이들이 나에게 훨씬 더 많은 관심을 보냈다. 왜냐하면 나는 "패밀리 타이즈"에 출연한 적이 있기 때문이다. 그러나 상황이 변했다—나는 자랑을 너무 과하게 했던 것 같다. 그러자 다른 아이들이 나를 놀리기 시작했다. 기억나는 건 내가 반한 여자아이가 있었다. 이름은 레이첼이었지만, 그녀는 록키라고 불리는 걸 선호했다. 그녀는 아름다웠으며, 가수였고, 나는 그녀에게 푹 빠졌다. 나는 자랑하며 거기 서 있었는데, 그녀가 나를 향해 돌면서 나를 허풍쟁이라고 불렀다. 나는 100% 그렇게 불려도 마땅했다. 하지만 그때 정말 아팠다. 그 이후로 나는 내 연기에 대한 관심을 얻는 것에 대해 약간의 주저함을 느꼈다.

때때로 사람들이 나에게 묻는다, "그런 관심을 싫어한다면서 왜 배우가 된 거야?" 그러면 나는 이렇게 대답한다. "연기는 남에게서 관심을 끄는 것이 아니라, 예술에 관한 것이기 때문이지, 친구." 그러면 그들은 "그래, 그래, 친구."라고 대답한다. 그리고 그때 트위터가 등장했다. 나는 모두가 그렇듯 완전히 중독됐고, 그것은 나를 완전히 위선자로 만들었다. 왜냐하면 그때쯤 나는 내 연기를 통해 관심을 얻고 있었다. 나는 내 팔로워들이 내 통찰력 있는 트윗을 좋아한다고 생각했을까? 실제로 그렇게 생각했다—나는 이렇게 생각했다. "그들은 어떤 영화에서 나를 봤기 때문에 나를 좋아하는 것이 아니라 내가 말하는 것을 좋아하는 거야, 나는 말에 재능이 있어." 그리고 금방 그것은 내가 너무 소중히 생각하는 창의적 과정에 영향을 미치기 시작했다. 지금도 그렇다. 나는 그것이 영향을 미치지 않도록 노력한다.

2

하위내용영역	배점	예상정답률
일반영어 A형 서술형	4점	50%

모범답안) The crucial element is incomplete information. The best tweets and funniest jokes rely on what is left unsaid, requiring the reader to fill in the gaps and understand the context or setup that is not explicitly provided. Second, "Twitter" fills in the blank.

채점 기준

+ 2점: 트위터에서 최고의 트윗과 조크가 되기 위한 필수적인 요소를 "incomplete information"라 서술하였거나 유사하였다.
  ☞ 다음과 같이 서술하였어도 2점을 준다.
  - "<u>understanding the setup, or additional information, such as the genre conventions</u>"
  - "The best tweets are using information that is off-screen."
  - "The best tweets are showing understanding of genre conventions to fill in incomplete information provided."
  - "The best tweets require understanding about Twitter's genre conventions needed to figure out its incomplete information."
+ 2점: 빈칸에 들어갈 단어를 "Twitter"라 정확하게 기입하였다. 이외에는 답이 될 수 없다.

한글번역

다음은 우리가 오늘날 알고 있는 통신 플랫폼을 분해한 것이다: 문자 메시지, 트위터, 인스타그램, 페이스북.

문자 메시지: 아주 차갑다. 특히 젊은이들에게 문자 메시지의 요점은 정보를 거의 드러내지 않는 방식으로 소통하는 것이다. 불확실성과 모호함이 핵심이다. 문자 메시지, 특히 단체 채팅은 자주 "말해진 것 대 말해지지 않은 것" 사이의 게임과 같아서, 빈틈을 채워야 한다. 이는 소통되는 내용을 완성하기 위해 적극적으로 참여해야 한다. (iMessage의 악명 높은 "…"는 아주 적은 정보를 제공하지만 우리를 끌어들이는 차가운 미디어다.)

트위터: 차갑다. 트위터는 사용하는 방식이 다양하기 때문에 까다롭다. 한 예로, 속보 트위터는 매우 뜨겁다. 하지만, 소셜 네트워크로서의 트위터는 매우 차갑다. 낮은 해상도와 문자 제한 형식으로, 소통되는 대부분의 내용이 실제로는 화면 밖, 그림 밖에 있다. 트위터에서 가장 좋은 트윗과 가장 재미있는 농담은 불완전한 정보다. 그것들은 완전히 급소를 찌르는 구절이다. 설정은 말해지지 않고; 우리가 이미 그것을 알고 있어야 하거나, 알아내야 한다. 트위터를 성공적으로 사용하려면 많은 노력이 필요하며, 이해하려면 그 장르의 규칙을 능숙하게 이해해야 한다. 트위터가 완벽하게 사용될 때, 그것은 차가운 미디어다.

인스타그램: 따뜻하다. 교환되는 핵심 콘텐츠는 모두 시각적이어서, 장르의 규칙을 이해할 필요가 적다. 초기 사진 필터 시절의 인스타그램은, 고전적인 사진이 그러하듯, 꽤 뜨거운 미디어였지만, 점점 사실상 사회적 지위 앱으로 진화하면서 식어갔다. 이제 게시물이 무엇인지, 그 게시물이 받는 좋아요 수, 좋아요를 누른 사람, 그리고 다른 사회적 역학관계(예를 들어 비공개 대 공개 게시물) 사이의 상호작용이 있다. 여전히 일부 모호함이 있지만, 매체로서 트위터나 문자 메시지보다 정보가 더 완전하다.

페이스북: 뜨겁다. 속삭이는 듯한 수많은 내부 농담인 트위터나, 여전히 차가운 요소를 가지고 있지만 더 따뜻한 인스타그램과 달리, 페이스북은 신문에 더 가깝다. 그것은 아무것도 숨기지 않는다. 이것을 인정하라! 이것에 화내라! 이것을 축하하라! 라고 외치는 조각 모음이다. 페이스북에는 신비가 많지 않고, 그것을 올바르게 사용하는 데 많은 유창함이 필요하지 않다. 전달되는 정보는 모두 거기에 있다, 당신에게 폭발적으로 쏟아진다. 페이스북은 대학생들이 소셜 지위를 전달하던 그 초창기 시절에는 더 차가웠을지 모른다 (현재 인스타그램이 사용되는 방식처럼). 하지만 그 이후로 꾸준히 뜨거워졌다.

3

하위내용영역	배점	예상정답률
일반영어 A형 서술형	4점	55%

모범답안 It can be inferred that Ms. Porter was nervous because she was afraid to present her ideas to her teacher colleagues who were reluctant to deal with the Thanksgiving. Second, Ms. Tilson refers to Native American students.

채점기준

+ 2점: 포터 선생이 교직원 회의에서 어떤 주제를 논의하기 꺼려하는 이유를 "because she was afraid to present her ideas to her teacher colleagues who were reluctant to deal with the Thanksgiving"라 서술하였거나 유사하였다.
  ☞ 다음과 같이 서술하였어도 2점을 준다.
  - "Because her colleagues were reluctant to deal with the Thanksgiving which is a day of mourning to some Native Americans."
  - "It is because she was concerned about addressing a sensitive and potentially controversial issue. (Her nervousness likely stemmed from her awareness that discussing the myths surrounding Thanksgiving and the perspective of Native Americans could provoke strong reactions from her colleagues, as well as the fear of not receiving support or understanding from them.)"

+ 2점: "those students"이 가리키는 것이 "Native American students"라 정확하게 서술하였다. 이 외에는 답이 될 수 없다.

⊕ 보충설명

The phrase "such as pretending to be Pilgrims and Indians" refers to activities or classroom exercises where students might dress up or act out the roles of Pilgrims and Native Americans. These activities are often part of traditional ways schools teach about Thanksgiving. However, Ms. Porter is concerned that these activities might perpetuate myths and stereotypes about the historical events and cultures involved, and they could alienate or offend some students and families, particularly those who have different perspectives on the Thanksgiving holiday.

한글번역

포터 선생은 긴장된 손을 들어 올렸다. 그녀의 교직원 회의가 시작될 때, 교장인 창 선생님이 누군가 새로운 안건을 추가하고 싶다면 말해보라고 했기 때문이다. "다가오는 추수감사절을 어떻게 가르칠지에 대해 이야기하고 싶습니다." 포터 선생이 말했다.

여러 동료들이 반응했다.

"저는 아예 이야기하지 않을 생각입니다. 추수감사절은 가족과 함께 시간을 보내는 것보다는 소비주의에 더 관련이 있는 것 같아요." 에스피노사 선생이 말했다. 틸슨 선생이 덧붙였다. "저는 음식을 중점적으로 다룹니다. 학생들이 음식에 대해 이야기할 때 정말로 참여도가 높습니다. 우리는 필그림(1620년 메이플라워 호를 타고 영국에서 건너온 초창기 이민자)과 인디언들이 잔치를 나눴다는 이야기를 할 것이고, 우리 학생들 중 일부는 이민자이기 때문에 전통 음식에 대해 배우는 기회로 삼을 수 있습니다."

"저는 추수감사절의 감사에 초점을 맞춥니다," 웹스터 선생이 덧붙였다. "우리는 모두 감사할 일이 많습니다. 저는 긍정적인 면에 집중하는 것을 좋아합니다."

창 선생이 대답했다. "우리가 명절을 기리는 다양한 방법이 있는 것 같군요. 추가적인 논의가 필요하지 않은 것 같아요. 질문이 있으신가요?"

포터 선생의 마음은 동료들이 언급하지 않으려 하는 것들에 가장 관심이 있었다. "저는 첫 번째 추수감사절에 대한 신화를 지속하는 것이 걱정입니다. 저는 일부 미국 원주민들이 이날을 축하가 아닌 애도의 날로 기념한다는 사실을 인정하지 않는 것이 걱정됩니다. 이는 필그림과 인디언을 흉내내는 것과 같은 관습이 일부 학생과 가족들을 소외시킬 수 있다는 점에 대해 학교 커뮤니티 내에서 대화를 촉진할 수 있는 좋은 기회입니다." 그녀가 말했다.

이 말들이 그녀의 입에서 나오는 것을 들으면서, 포터 선생님은 안도감과 후회의 물결을 느꼈다. 그녀는 동료들이 지난 몇 년간 추수감사절을 다루는 방식에 불편함을 느꼈지만, 말할 용기를 내지 못했다.

"우리 학교에는 너무 많은 요구사항들이 있습니다. 추수감사절을 어떻게 가르칠지 세세하게 관리할 필요는 없다고 생각합니다. 우리 학교에는 그런 학생들이 없잖아요." 틸슨 선생이 말했다.

창 선생은 방 안의 긴장을 감지하고 대답했다. "여러분 모두 좋은 점을 지적해 주셨습니다. 의견을 공유해 주셔서 감사합니다. 이 주제는 지금 논의할 시간이 부족한 것 같습니다." 그 말을 끝으로, 그녀는 다음 안건으로 넘어갔다.

포터 선생은 방 안을 둘러보며 동료들의 발언에 좌절감을 느꼈고, 자신이 말한 것에 대해 아무도 지지하거나 말을 보태지 않는 것에 실망했다.

4

하위내용영역	배점	예상정답률
일반영어 A형 서술형	4점	40%

모범 답안) The underlined "a variant" refers to a version of the game in which participants were informed of their assigned co-participant's ethnicity. Second, "don't trust" best completes the blank.

채점 기준

+ 2점: 밑줄 친 부분의 의미를 "a version of the game in which participants were informed of their assigned co-participant's ethnicity"라 서술하였거나 유사하였다.

☞ 다음과 같이 서술하였어도 2점을 준다.
- "an edition of the study in which participants were informed of their assigned co-participant's ethnicity"

+ 2점: 빈칸에 들어갈 단어를 "don't trust"라 정확히 기입하였다. 이외에는 답이 될 수 없다.

◎ 보충설명

In the context of the passage, "tripled" means that the amount of money given by the first participant to the second participant is multiplied by three. For example, if the first participant decides to give $4 to the second participant, the amount the second participant actually receives becomes $12 ($4 × 3). This tripling of the amount is a key part of the trust game, as it creates an incentive for the second participant to potentially share some of the increased money back with the first participant.

유희태 일반영어 ④-2

한글번역

사회 과학자들은 한 사람이 얼마나 신뢰하는지, 얼마나 신뢰할 만한지를 연구할 수 있는 다양한 도구를 가지고 있다. 가장 인기 있는 것은 신뢰 게임인데, 이 게임에서는 두 명의 참가자가 보통 익명으로 플레이한다. 첫 번째 참가자는 예를 들어 10달러와 같은 소액을 받고, 그중 얼마를 다른 참가자에게 줄지 결정한다. 전송된 금액은 세 배로 늘어나고, 두 번째 참가자는 첫 번째 참가자에게 얼마를 돌려줄지 선택한다.

적어도 서구 국가에서는 신뢰가 보상받는다: 첫 번째 참가자가 더 많은 돈을 전송할수록 두 번째 참가자가 더 많은 돈을 돌려주고, 따라서 첫 번째 참가자가 최종적으로 얻게 되는 돈이 많아진다. 그럼에도 불구하고, 첫 번째 참가자들은 평균적으로 받은 돈의 절반만을 전송한다. 일부 연구에서는 참가자들이 서로의 민족을 알고 있는 변형이 도입됐다. 편견으로 인해 참가자들은 특정 그룹—이스라엘의 동양 출신 남성(아시아 및 아프리카 이민자와 그들의 이스라엘 태생 자녀들), 또는 남아프리카의 흑인 학생들—을 신뢰하지 않고, 그들에게 더 적은 돈을 전송했다. 이러한 그룹은 더 잘 평가받는 그룹만큼 신뢰할 수 있음에도 불구하고 말이다.

사람들과 기관들이 우리가 평가하는 것보다 더 신뢰할 수 있다면, 왜 우리는 그것을 올바르게 이해시키지 못할까? 왜 우리는 더 많이 신뢰하지 않을까?

누군가를 신뢰하면, 그들에 대한 신뢰가 정당했는지 아닌지를 알게 된다. 지인이 며칠 동안 자신의 집에서 자도 되냐고 물어본다. 만약 당신이 허락한다면, 그가 좋은 손님인지 아닌지를 알게 될 것이다. 동료가 새로운 소프트웨어 애플리케이션을 추천한다. 만약 당신이 그녀의 조언을 따른다면, 새로운 소프트웨어가 이전에 사용하던 것보다 더 나은지 알게 될 것이다.

대조적으로, 만약 당신이 누군가를 신뢰하지 않는다면, 대부분 당신이 그들을 신뢰했어야 했는지 알지 못하게 된다. 만약 당신이 친구를 초대하지 않는다면, 그가 좋은 손님이었을지 알지 못할 것이다. 만약 당신이 동료의 조언을 따르지 않는다면, 새로운 소프트웨어 애플리케이션이 실제로 더 유용한지, 그리고 따라서 그녀가 이 분야에서 좋은 조언을 해주는지 알지 못할 것이다.

제42회 모의고사

1

하위내용영역	배점	예상정답률
일반영어 A형 서술형	4점	40%

모범답안 The word "intention" best completes the blank. Second, the word "triangle" is used to show that a message doesn't have only two parts with A sending to B, but instead has other influences on it as a third component.

채점기준

+ 2점: 빈칸에 들어갈 단어를 "intention"이라 정확히 기입하였다. 이외에는 답이 될 수 없다.
+ 2점: 저자가 "삼각형"이란 용어를 언급한 이유를 "to show that a message doesn't have only two parts with A sending to B, but instead has other influences on it as a third component"라 서술하였거나 유사하였다.

⊕ 보충설명

In the sentence "The message is a construction of signs which, through interacting with the receivers, creates meanings" means that the message is composed of various signs (such as words, images, symbols, etc.), and these signs interact with the receivers (the audience or readers) to create meanings. The interpretation and understanding of the message are shaped by **how these signs are perceived and understood by the receivers**, considering their cultural backgrounds, experiences, and contexts. Thus, the meaning is not solely embedded by the sender but is co-constructed through the interaction between the signs and the receivers.

The phrase "This negotiation takes place as the reader brings aspects of his or her cultural experience to bear upon the codes and signs which make up the text" means that the process of understanding and interpreting a text involves the reader using their own cultural background and experiences to influence their perception of the text's meaning. The "negotiation" refers to the dynamic interaction between the reader's personal context and the text's symbols and structures. The reader's cultural experiences shape how they decode and understand the signs and codes within the text, leading to unique interpretations and meanings.

The sentence "We have only to see how various newspapers report the same world event differently to perceive how important is this understanding, this view of the world, which each paper shares with its readers" means that by observing how different newspapers cover the same global event in different ways, we can understand **the significance of the perspective and interpretation each newspaper holds and conveys to its readers**. Each newspaper has its own worldview, shaped by its cultural, political, and social context, which influences how it reports news. This shared perspective helps to shape the readers' understanding and interpretation of events. Thus, the way newspapers report events highlights the importance of the underlying views and interpretations they bring to their audience.

The phrase "we might model this structure as a triangle" means that we can use a triangle as a conceptual tool to illustrate the structure of communication.

한글번역

과정 학파는 메시지를 커뮤니케이션 과정에서 전달되는 것으로 본다. 이 학파의 많은 구성원들은 의도가 메시지를 결정하는 주요 요인이라고 믿는다. 따라서 경매인에게 사전에 신호를 보내기 위해 고의로 귀를 잡아당기지 않는다면, 귀를 잡아당기는 것은 메시지가 되지 않는다. 발신자의 의도는 명시되거나 암시될 수 있으며, 의식적일 수도 무의식적일 수도 있지만 분석을 통해 추출할 수 있어야 한다. 메시지는 발신자가 가능한 모든 수단으로 그것(메시지)에 넣은 것이다.

반면에, 기호학에서는 메시지를 기호의 구성으로 보며, 수신자와 상호작용을 통해 의미를 만든다. 메시지의 전달하는 것으로 정의된 발신자의 중요성은 감소하고, 강조점은 텍스트와 그것이 '읽히는' 방식으로 옮겨진다. 읽기는 독자가 텍스트와 상호작용하거나 협상할 때 발생하는 의미를 발견하는 과정이다. 이 협상은 독자가 자신의 문화적 경험을 텍스트를 구성하는 코드와 기호에 영향을 끼치면서 이뤄진다. 또한 텍스트가 무엇을 의미하는지에 대한 공유된 이해를 포함한다. 서로 다른 신문들이 동일한 세계 사건을 다르게 보도하는 것을 보면, 각 신문이 독자들과 공유하는 세계관, 이해가 얼마나 중요한지 알 수 있다. 따라서 서로 다른 사회적 경험을 가진 독자들이나 다른 문화에서 온 독자들은 동일한 텍스트에서 서로 다른 의미를 찾을 가능성이 있다. 이것이 꼭 커뮤니케이션 실패라는 증거는 아니다.

따라서 메시지는 A에서 B로 보내지는 것이 아니라, 외부 현실과 생산자/독자를 포함하는 구조화된 관계의 한 요소이다. 텍스트를 생산하고 읽는 것은, 이 구조화된 관계에서 동일한 위치를 차지한다는 점에서, 병렬적—비록 동일한 것은 아니지만—과정으로 본다. 우리는 이 구조를 상호작용을 나타내는 화살표가 있는 삼각형으로 나타낼 수 있는데, 이 구조는 정적이지 않고 역동적인 실천이다.

2

하위내용영역	배점	예상정답률
일반영어 A형 서술형	4점	40%

모범답안 While the 2004 study (conducted by Glenn Yu) found that children who took music lessons had a significant increase in IQ, (averaging seven points, compared to those in the acting class or control group, who gained an average of 4.3 points), the 2013 study (backed by the Education Endowment Foundation, which involved over 900 students,) failed to find any evidence that music lessons improved math and literacy skills. (This suggests a discrepancy between the results of the two studies, with the latter not corroborating the positive transfer effects of music lessons on general intelligence that the former found.) Second, (It can be inferred that variables such as socioeconomic status should be corrected) because wealthier students often have more support and resources, which can also improve their intelligence, thereby confounding the results if not accounted for. Third, the appropriate word for the blank is "causation".

유희태 | 일반영어 ❹-2

> **채점 기준**

+1점: 2004년과 2013년 연구 결과 사이의 차이를 "<u>While the 2004 study found that children who took music lessons had a significant increase in IQ, the 2013 study failed to find any evidence that music lessons improved math and literacy skills</u>"라 서술하였거나 유사하였다.

+2점: "사회 경제적 지위와 같은 변수"를 보정해야만 하는 이유를 "<u>because wealthier students often have more support and resources, which can also improve their intelligence, thereby confounding the results if not accounted for</u>"라 서술하였거나 유사하였다.

☞ 다음과 같이 서술하였어도 맞는 것으로 한다.

— "Because these variables can influence both access to music education and cognitive development, potentially confounding the results of studies on the impact of music lessons."

— "Because these variables can significantly influence the outcomes of studies on music education and intelligence. Socioeconomic status may affect a child's access to resources, quality of education, parental involvement, and overall learning environment. If these variables are not accounted for, it becomes difficult to isolate the specific impact of music lessons on intelligence, leading to potential biases in the results. (Correcting for these variables helps ensure that any observed differences in intelligence are more likely to be attributed to the music lessons themselves rather than other confounding factors.)"

+1점: 빈칸에 들어갈 단어를 "causation"이라 정확히 기입하였다. 이외에는 답이 될 수 없다.

> **한글번역**

2004년, "음악 레슨이 IQ를 향상시킨다"라는 제목의 에세이가 *심리학* 저널에 실렸다. 저자 글렌 유는 144명의 어린이를 무작위로 네 그룹으로 나눠 실험을 진행했다. 한 그룹은 1년 동안 피아노를 배웠고, 다른 그룹은 노래 레슨을 받았으며, 또 다른 그룹은 연기 수업에 참여했고, 통제 그룹은 별다른 방과 후 활동을 하지 않았다. 음악 그룹에 속한 아이들의 IQ는 1년 동안 평균 7점 상승했지만, 다른 두 그룹은 평균 4.3점 상승에 그쳤다.

유는 오랫동안 음악 교육이 아이들의 추상적 사고, 수학, 또는 언어 능력을 향상시킨다는 주장에 회의적이었다. 피아노를 치는 아이들이 더 똑똑하다면, 그것은 꼭 피아노를 치기 때문이 아닐 수도 있다고 그는 말한다. 피아노를 배우는 학생들이 더 야망이 있거나 집중력이 더 좋은 경우일 수도 있기 때문이다. 상관관계는 인과관계를 증명하지 못한다는 점을 항상 염두에 둬야 한다.

2004년 논문은 이러한 불일치를 해결하기 위해 개발됐다. 그리고 열정적인 음악가였던 유는 음악이 일반 지능에 전이 효과가 있다는 신뢰할 만한 증거를 발견했을 때 기뻤다. 그러나 10년 후인 2013년에 교육 기부 재단은 900명 이상의 학생을 대상으로 한 더 큰 연구를 지원했는데, 그 연구는 유의 발견을 입증하지 못하고 음악 레슨이 수학 및 읽기 능력을 향상시킨다는 증거를 찾지 못했다.

유는 그 소식을 받아들이면서도 자신의 전공 분야에서 진행된 연구들에 계속 회의적인 눈길을 보냈다. 최근 그는 심리학 및 신경과학 연구자들이 음악과 지능 사이의 인과관계를 잘못—혹은 최소한 성급하게—연결하는 경우가 얼마나 자주 있는지 공식적으로 조사하기로 결정했다. 그의 결과는 5월에 발표됐으며, 많은 동료들이 바로 그렇게 하고 있다는 것(인과관계를 잘못—혹은 최소한 성급하게—연결하고 있다)을 보여준다.

시간이 지남에 따라 음악 레슨이 뇌에 어떻게 영향을 미치는지 정확히 파악하기 위해, 이상적으로는 과학자들이 유가 2004년 연구에서 했던 것처럼 학생들을 무작위로 다른 그룹에 배정해야 한다. 한 그룹의 아이들은 몇 년 동안 피아노 레슨을 받도록 하고, 다른 그룹은 전혀 음악 교육을 받지 않도록 하는 것이다. (하지만) 심리학 실험을 위해 이러한 방식으로 진행하는 것은 일반적으로 불가능하기 때문에, 많은 연구자들은 이미 레슨을 받고 있는 아이들과 그렇지 않은 아이들을 비교하는 연구에 의존하며, 사회경제적 지위와 같은 변수를 보정한다. 그러나 이러한 보정을 하더라도, 그러한 연구들은 상관관계만을 발견할 수 있을 뿐, 인과관계를 증명할 수는 없다.

3

하위내용영역	배점	예상정답률
일반영어 B형 서술형	4점	45%

모범 답안) Thin people are have many unpleasant qualities unlike fat people. They are not fun, they do not use their free time enjoyably and always stay busy. Also, they are tiring, always moving and looking for problems to solve, unlike fat people who are so inactive. On the other hand, fat people are nicer than mean thin people and see there is no truth, while thin people are looking for a "key thing" in unsolvable problems. In conclusion, the thin should gain weight to become more likeable.

채점 기준

ⓐ Topic sentence

+ 1점 : "Thin people are have many unpleasant qualities unlike fat people"을 명확하게 서술하였거나 유사하였다.

☞ 다음과 같이 서술하였어도 1점을 준다.
- "Thin people are much more unlikable than fat people."

ⓑ Major supporting details

+ 2점 : "① They aren't fun, they don't use their free time enjoyably and always stay busy. ② They are tiring, always moving and looking for problems to solve, unlike fat people who are so inactive. On the other hand, ③ fat people are nicer than mean thin people and see there is no truth, while thin people are looking for a "key thing" in unsolvable problems"을 명확하게 서술하였다.

☞ 3개 중 3개 모두 정확하게 요약했으면 2점, 2개를 정확하게 요약했으면 1점, 나머지는 0점을 준다.

ⓒ Conclusion

+ 1점 : "In conclusion, the thin should gain weight to become more likeable"을 명확하게 서술하였거나 유사하였다.

감점
- 본문에 나오는 연속되는 5단어 이상을 사용하였다. −0.5pt
- 문단을 두 개나 그 이상으로 구성하였다. −0.5pt
- 문법이나 영어 표현을 합쳐 3개 이상 오류가 있다. −0.5pt

한글번역

카이사르는 옳았다. 마른 사람들은 감시가 필요하다. 나는 성년의 대부분을 그들을 지켜보며 보냈고, 내가 본 것을 좋아하지 않는다. 이 좁아터진 사람들이 나에게 덤벼들 때마다 발끝까지 떨린다. 마른 사람들은 다양한 성격을 가지고 있는데, 대부분이 위협적이다. '정리된' 마른 사람, 기계적인 마른 사람, 거만한 마른 사람, 혀를 차는 마른 사람, 효율성 전문가 마른 사람이 있다.

우선, 마른 사람들은 재미없다. 그들은 제대로 빈둥거리는 방법을 모른다. 항상 무언가를 해야 한다. 커피 브레이크를 주면, 블록을 돌아 뛰어다닌다. 조용한 저녁 시간을 주면, 스크린 도어를 고치고 S&H 그린 스탬프를 핥는다. 그들은 "하루가 충분히 길지 않다" 같은 말을 한다. 뚱뚱한 사람들은 절대 그런 말을 하지 않는다. 뚱뚱한 사람들은 하루가 이미 너무 길다고 생각한다.

마른 사람들은 나를 피곤하게 만든다. 그들은 빠른 신진대사를 가지고 있어서 항상 바쁘게 움직인다. 그들은 항상 뼈만 남은 손을 비비며 새로운 문제를 '해결'하려 한다. 나는 느리고, 비활동적이고, 느긋한 뚱뚱한 사람들, 오늘 청소해도 내일 다시 더러워질 거라고 믿는 사람들로 내 주변을 둘러싸고 싶다.

뚱뚱한 사람들이 하루 종일 크게 웃고 있는 것은 아니지만, 그들은 메마르고 쭈글쭈글한 사람들보다 훨씬 더 친절하다. 마른 사람들은 곧바로 문제의 핵심으로 가며, 뚱뚱한 사람들은 모든 것을 실제로 그렇듯이 흐릿하고 모호하게 둔다. 마른 사람들은 진실을 직시하고 싶어한다. 뚱뚱한 사람들은 진실이 없다는 것을 안다. 마른 사람들은 해결할 수 없는 문제를 직시하며 "중요한 것은…" 같은 말을 한다. 뚱뚱한 사람들은 그런 말을 절대 하지 않는다. 그들은 어떤 것에도 '중요한 것'이라는 것이 없다는 것을 안다. 이러한 차이점을 감안할 때, 만약 당신이 마르다면, 체육관을 건너뛰고, 슈퍼사이즈 점심을 주문하라. 더 커지면, 더 쾌적한 동반자가 될 것이다.

유희태 | 일반영어 ❹-2

제43회 모의고사

감점 본문에 나오는 연속되는 5단어 이상을 사용하였다. -0.5pt

1

하위내용영역	배점	예상정답률
일반영어 A형 서술형	4점	40%

모범 답안 (The writer mentions the words) to illustrate the detrimental effects of sugar, from which they got relief from after quitting sugar. Second, "fructose" best fills in the blank.

채점 기준

+ 2점: 저자가 밑줄 친 부분을 언급한 이유를 글의 핵심 생각과 연관하여 설명하라는 문제에 대해 "to illustrate the detrimental effects of sugar, from which they(젠더가 명확하지 않을 때는 복수 사용) got relief(경감) from after quitting"라 서술하였거나 유사하였다.

☞ 다음과 같이 서술하였어도 맞는 것으로 한다.

- (The writer mentions the words) to highlight the transformative impact of giving up sugar on their life. (By listing the negative symptoms they used to experience—such as feeling "hangry," having mood swings, and experiencing physical slumps etc.—and then stating that these are no longer part of their life, the writer emphasizes the dramatic positive change brought about by eliminating sugar. This underscores the overarching message of the passage : <u>the significant and beneficial effects of removing sugar from one's diet.</u>)
- to highlight the significant positive changes and improvements in their physical and mental well-being after quitting sugar, emphasizing the transformative impact of removing sugar from their diet.

+ 2점: 빈칸에 들어갈 한 단어를 "fructose"라 정확하게 기입하였다. 이외에는 답이 될 수 없다.

한글번역

3년 전, 나는 설탕을 끊었다. 설탕을 끊자 모든 것이 바뀌었다. 실험으로 시작한 일이지만, 곧 새로운 습관이 됐다. 나는 생각지도 못하던 여러 측면에서 변화를 느낄 수 있었다.

나는 조금이라도 허기가 지면 짜증(Hangry)을 내던 사람이었다. 이를 막기 위해 아몬드나 말린 과일을 늘 지니고 다녔다. 설탕을 먹던 시절에는 아침에 달리기를 할 수 없었다. 달리기를 하려고 할 때마다 너무 졸렸고, 다리는 천근만근으로 느껴졌다. 오후에는 머릿속에 안개가 낀 것처럼 피곤했다. 그래서 재택으로 일할 때는 낮잠을 꼭 잤다. 기분이 쉽게 바뀌었고, 즐겁다가도 우울했다. 하지만 나는 이 모든 것을 그저 삶의 일부로 여겼고, 내가 원래 그런 사람이라고, 이것이 내 성격의 단점이라고만 생각했다. 하지만 지금은 이런 모든 것들이 다 사라졌다.

설탕을 끊고 처음 2주 정도는 짜증이 자주 났다. 겨울의 우중충한 날씨 때문인 줄 알았다. 하지만 곧 나는 차분해지고, 행복해지고, 평온해지면서 한 가지 (해로운) 생각이 날 갉아먹기 시작했다. 혹시 그 짜증이 금단 증상은 아니었을까?라는.

화학자에게 설탕은 수소, 탄소, 산소로 이뤄진 몇 종의 분자를 말한다. 이들 중 몇 가지는 생물학적으로 의미가 있다. 예를 들어 젖당(lactose)은 우유에 들어 있다. 설탕의 한 종류인 디옥시리보오스는 DNA의 D에 해당한다. 하지만 일상에서 가장 많이 섭취되는 설탕은 포도당(glucose), 과당(fructose) 그리고 포도당과 과당이 결합한 형태의 자당(sucrose)이다. 이 두 개의 단순 설탕인 포도당과 과당은 6개의 탄소 원자, 12개의 수소 원자, 그리고 6개의 산소 원자라는 같은 원자 구성을 가지고 있지만, 화학적 구조가 다르다. 사람은 혀로 이 둘을 구분할 수 있다. 곧, 과당을 더 달게 느낀다.

포도당은 혈액을 통해 에너지원으로 세포에 전달되며, 혈당(blood sugar)이라고도 불린다. 물론 과일과 야채 속에 과당과 함께 존재하기도 한다. 자당은 사탕수수나 근대(beet)에서 추출되며, 커피에 넣는 하얀 육면체 모양으로 우리에게 익숙하다. 사람들이 흔히 설탕이라고 말하는 것이 바로 이 자당이다. 인간은 역사적으로 우유, 꿀, 과일을 통해 당분을 섭취해 왔다. 사탕수수가 유럽에 등장한 것은 겨우 1천 년 전이며, 그것도 향신료, 의약품, 보존제로 받아들여졌다. 1700년 경, 영국의 평균 설탕 소비량은 연간 1인당 2kg였다. 오늘날 그 양은 10배로 늘었다. 오늘날의 설탕 섭취량은 인간에게 정상이 아니다. 우리는 우리의 입맛에 따라 세상을 바꿨지만, 우리 몸은 그 변화를 따라가지 못하고 있다.

2

하위내용영역	배점	예상정답률
일반영어 A형 서술형	4점	40%

모범답안) It can be inferred that the standard view would see forms of life simpler than mice as not having consciousness. Second, the word is "matter" best fills in the blank.

채점기준

+ 2점: 쥐보다 더 단순한 생명체에 대한 "표준적 시각"은 어떤 것일까에 대해 "the standard view would see forms of life simpler than mice as not having consciousness"라 서술하였거나 유사하였다.

☞ 다음과 같이 서술하였어도 맞는 것으로 한다.

— "(The perspective of the "standard view" toward forms of life simpler than mice can be inferred to be that) these simpler forms of life either lack consciousness entirely or have very rudimentary forms of consciousness, if any at all. This perspective implies that consciousness is a feature that becomes more pronounced and complex in higher organisms and is either minimal or nonexistent in simpler organisms."

+ 2점: 빈칸에 들어갈 한 단어를 "matter"라 정확히 기입하였다. 이외에는 답이 될 수 없다.

감점 본문에 나오는 연속되는 5단어 이상을 사용하였다. −0.5pt

보충설명

The sentence "The basic commitment is that the fundamental constituents of reality—perhaps electrons and quarks—have incredibly simple forms of experience. And the very complex experience of the human or animal brain is somehow derived from the experience of the brain's most basic parts." means that the basic idea (or commitment) of panpsychism is that the smallest parts of reality, such as electrons and quarks, possess very simple forms of experience. This does not imply consciousness as we typically understand it in humans, but rather a basic form of experience or awareness. / The complex experiences that humans and animals have (such as thoughts, feelings, and perceptions) are somehow built upon or emerge from the simple experiences of these fundamental particles. Essentially, the intricate experiences of the brain are thought to be rooted in and arise from the combined experiences of its most basic components.

In summary, the passage explains the idea that all matter, even at its most basic level, has some form of experience, and the complex experiences of more evolved beings are derived from these basic experiences.

한글번역

물질에 대한 우리의 표준적 관점에서, 고도로 진화한 생명체의 뇌만이 의식을 가졌다고 생각하며, 그렇기에 의식은 우주의 극히 일부에만 존재하며 우주의 역사에 있어서도 극히 최근에 등장했다고 생각한다. 하지만 범심론은 그와는 다르게 의식이 우주 전체에 존재하며 우주의 근본적 특성이라고 말한다. 그렇다고 말 그대로 모든 것이 똑같은 의식을 가지고 있다는 뜻은 아니다. 전자나 쿼크와 같은 우주를 구성하는 기본 요소들은 극히 단순한 형태의 경험을 가질 것이고, 반대로 인간이나 동물의 뇌는 매우 복잡한 경험을 가지지만, 그 경험은 뇌의 기본적인 요소들이 겪는 경험으로부터 유도할 수 있다는 뜻이다.

내가 말하는 "의식"이 어떤 뜻인지를 명확히 해야겠다. 사실 이 용어는 매우 모호하다. 어떤 이들은 이 용어가 자각 능력이나 자신의 존재를 반추하는 것과 같은 고도의 정신 상태를 의미한다고 생각한다. 바로 이 점이 우리가 다른 동물이나 물질이 의식을 가지고 있다고 말하기 꺼려하는 이유이다. 하지만 나는 의식이란 그저 즐거움, 고통, 시각·청각적 경험 등에서와 같은 경험을 의미한다고 생각한다.
 인간은 매우 다양하고 복잡한 경험을 한다. 말은 그보다는 덜하고, 쥐는 말보다도 덜할 것이다. 더 단순한 생명체일수록 더 단순한 경험을 가진다. 아마 어떤 수준에 이르면, 그저 불이 꺼지듯 의식은 사라질 것이다. 이런 의식 축소의 연속성이 생명체를 넘어 물질 수준으로 계속 이어질 것이라고, 곧 근본 입자들까지도 자신의 극히 단순한 본질을 반영하는 극도로 단순한 경험을 가질 것이라고 가정한다면, 이는 적어도 어떤 일관성 있는 주장일 것이다. 범심론자들은 바로 이런 생각을 가지고 있다.
 범심론은 물리학이 물질이란 무엇인가에 답하지 못한다는 사실에서 출발한다. 아마 이 말이 이상하게 들릴 것이다. 물리학 교과서에는 공간과 시간, 물질에 대한 놀라운 사실들이 쓰여 있으니까. 하지만 과학 철학자들은 물리학의 그 풍부한 내용에도 불구하고 모든 것이 물질이 어떻게 행동하느냐에 관한 것일 뿐, 물질이란 무엇인가라는 본질에 대한 답은 없다는 것을 깨달았다. 예를 들어 물리학은 물질이 질량과 전하를 가지고 있다고 말한다. 이 두 성질은 인력, 척력, 관성력 등 물질의 행동을 완벽하게 정의한다. 하지만 물리학은 곧 물질이란 무엇인가에 대한 질문에는 전혀 답하지 않는다.

3

하위내용영역	배점	예상정답률
일반영어 A형 서술형	4점	45%

모범답안 The meaning of the underlined selection is that it was an opportunity to instruct Caylee about the complexities of protest. Second, Mr. Harrold is concerned with appearing to endorse the protests, which some view as disrespectful to veterans.

채점 기준

+ 2점: 밑줄 친 부분의 의미를 "it was an opportunity to instruct Caylee about the complexities of protest"라 서술하였거나 유사하였다.
+ 2점: 불공정한 사회에 대한 저항(의 이유나 원인)을 (진지하게) 다룰 때, Mr. Harrold가 걱정하는 반발을 "appearing to endorse the protests, which some view as disrespectful to veterans"라 서술하였거나 유사하였다.

감점 본문에 나오는 연속되는 5단어 이상을 사용하였다. -0.5pt

한글번역

 학생들이 교실로 들어오면서, 해롤드 선생은 전날 저녁의 프로 축구 경기 점수에 대해 학생들이 이야기하는 것을 들었다. 대화가 잠잠해지자, 한 학생인 케일리가 진 팀의 한 선수가 국가 연주 중에 일어서지 않은 것을 언급했다. "국기를 존중하지 않아서 지는 건 업보야."라고 그녀는 선언했다. 몇몇 동급생들은 웃으며 고개를 끄덕였다. 다른 학생은 "그 선수 때문에 팀이 집중을 못 해서 진 거야."라고 덧붙였다.
 "아, 이걸 다뤄야 하나?" 해롤드 선생은 생각했다. 그는 다뤄야 할 모든 내용과 세심하게 계획된 수업을 생각하며, 케일리의 발언에 대해 반응하지 않기로 결정했다.
 그날 저녁 해롤드 선생은 학생들이 이야기한 축구 경기의 하이라이트를 뉴스를 통해 봤다. 기자는 국가 연주 중에 일어서지 않은 선수에 대한 반발을 다뤘다. 그녀는 그 선수의 결정을 지지하는 사람들과 반대하는 사람들 모두를 인터뷰했다. 해롤드 선생은 자신의 결정을 다시 생각하며, 케일리의 발언을 다루지 않은 것이 옳았는지 의문을 가졌다. 그러나 그는 가르칠 수 있는 순간이 지나갔다고 느꼈다.
 몇 주 후 해롤드 선생은 학생들이 그날 아침 국기에 대한 맹세 중에 일어서지 않은 동급생에 대해 이야기하는 것을 엿들었다. 동급생들이 자신의 결정에 대해 물었을 때, 케이트는 "우리나라에 '모두를 위한 자유와 정의'가 존재한다고 믿지 않기 때문"이라고 설명했다.
 몇몇 동급생들은 그녀의 행동에 불쾌감을 표했다. 그들은 케이트가 문화적 또는 정치적 신념 때문이 아니라 단지 주목받고 싶어서 항의한다고 말했다.
 다시 한 번 해롤드 선생은 어떻게 반응해야 할지 확신이 서지 않았다. 그는 이 주제가 어른들 사이에서 열띤 논쟁을 불러일으킨다는 것을 알고 있었고, 조심스럽게 접근해야 한다는 것을 알았다. 그는 또한 자신의 학교가 매년 개최하는 참전용사 기념 프로그램을 자랑스럽게 여기며, 국가나 국기에 대한 맹세 중에 앉아 있는 것에 관련해서 대화를 촉진하는 것이 참전용사를 기리는 학교의 전통과 충돌한다고 보는 사람들이 있을 수 있다는 것을 생각했다.
 그가 이 상황을 다루는 방법에 대해 깊이 고민하고 있을 때, 한 학생이 그의 생각을 끊었다. "해롤드 선생님," 그 학생이 물었다. "국가나 국기 연주 중에 일어서지 않는 것이 불경스럽다고 생각하세요? 우리가 일어서야 한다는 학교 규칙이 있지 않나요?"

4

하위내용영역	배점	예상정답률
일반영어 A형 서술형	4점	40%

모범 답안 The reason for not tricking venture capitalists is when your startup is not a good investment, you are wasting your own time. Second, the implication of the underlined words is that the founders did not truly understand the speaker's point.

채점 기준

+ 2점: 저자가 위험 투자가를 속이지 않아야 하는 주요 이유를 "when your startup is not a good investment, you are wasting your own time"라 서술하였거나 유사하였다.
+ 2점: 창업 기업과 관련하여, 밑줄 친 부분이 말하는 함축 의미를 "the <u>founders did not truly understand (or the founders ignored) the speaker's point</u>"라 서술하였거나 유사하였다.

감점 본문에 나오는 연속되는 5단어 이상을 사용하였다. -0.5pt

한글번역

내가 와이 컴비네이터에서 스타트업 창업자들에게, 주로 젊은 창업자들인데, 조언을 주기 시작한 이후, 이 젊은 창업자들이 문제를 과도하고 복잡하게 생각하는 경향이 있다는 것을 알았다. 그들은 이렇게 묻는다. 어떻게 투자를 받나요? 벤처 투자자들이 투자를 하게 하려면 어떤 요령(trick)을 써야 할까요? 나는 이렇게 설명한다. 벤처 투자자들이 당신에게 투자하게 만드는 가장 좋은 방법은 당신에게 하는 투자가 실제로 좋은 투자가 되게 만드는 것이라고. 당신이 나쁜 스타트업을 가지고 있음에도 어떤 요령을 써서 투자자로 하여금 투자하게 만든다면, 당신은 당신 자신 또한 속이는 것이다. 당신은 투자를 요청한 그 회사(즉, 당신의 회사)에 당신의 시간을 투자하고 있다. 만약 그 투자가 좋은 투자가 아니라면, 당신은 왜 그 회사를 운영하고 있는 것인가?

그들은 아, 하고 내 말을 곱씹은 다음 다시 이렇게 묻는다. 어떻게 해야 좋은 투자가 되게 만들 수 있나요?

나는 투자자의 눈만이 아니라 실제로 스타트업의 장래성을 알 수 있게 하는 것은 바로 성장이라고 말한다. 이상적으로는 매출에서, 그렇지 않으면 사용량에서라도 성장을 해야 한다. 그러니 사용자가 늘어나야 한다.

그럼 어떻게 해야 사용자가 늘 수 있을까? 그들은 이를 위해 여러 가지를 말한다. 많은 이들에게 "노출"될 수 있는 행사를 이야기하고, 영향력 있는 사람들이 자신의 서비스를 언급해야 된다고 말하며, 심지어 서비스를 화요일에 출시해야 사람들의 관심을 가장 많이 받을 수 있다고도 말한다.

그게 아니라고 나는 설명한다. 그건 사용자를 늘리는 방법이 아니다. 사용자를 늘리는 유일한 방법은 정말로 훌륭한 제품을 만드는 것이다. 사람들은 그 제품을 사용할 뿐 아니라 자신의 친구들에게 추천할 것이며, 당신은 기하급수적인 성장을 할 수 있을 것이다.

내가 창업자들에게 한 이야기, 곧 좋은 제품을 만들어서 좋은 회사가 돼야 한다는 것은 너무나 당연한 조언으로 보일 것이다. 그러나 이 말에 대해 그들은 마치 상대성 이론을 처음 들었을 때 많은 물리학자들이 보였을 법한, 그 조언이 가진 명백한 천재성에 대한 놀라움과 그러면서도 그렇게 이상한 말이 답일리 없다는 의심이 섞인 그런 반응을 보인다. 그들은 의무적으로 내게 알았다고 답하면서도, 다시 묻는다. 혹시 이러이러한 유명인을 소개해 줄 수 있나요? 그리고 우리는 화요일에 제품을 출시하고 싶어요.

창업자들이 이 단순한 교훈을 받아들이기까지는 때로 몇 년의 시간이 걸린다. 이는 그들이 게으르거나 어리석기 때문이 아니다. 그저 자신의 바로 눈앞에 있는 것을 보지 못하기 때문이다.

제44회 모의고사

1

하위내용영역	배점	예상정답률
일반영어 A형 서술형	4점	40%

모범 답안) The two words are "drug-resistant bacteria". Second, the way phage therapy works is that specific viruses that eat bacteria are matched to their respective bacteria to help patients fight infections.

채점 기준

+ 2점: 빈칸에 들어갈 두 단어를 "drug-resistant bacteria"라 정확하게 기입하였다. 이외에는 답이 될 수 없다.
+ 2점: "파지 요법"이 기능하는 방식을 "specific viruses that eat bacteria are matched to their respective bacteria to help patients fight infections"라 서술하였거나 유사하였다.

감점 본문에 나오는 연속되는 5단어 이상을 사용하였다. −0.5pt

한글번역

올해 전 세계는 지구상에서 가장 강력하고 정교한 종이 가장 작고 가장 기본적인 생물에게 비극적으로 취약하다는 사실을 깨달았다. 전염병 전문의들은 수십 년 동안 이에 대해 경고해 왔다. 그리고 그 위협은 동물에서 인간으로 넘어오는 COVID-19를 일으키는 바이러스와 같은 새로운 바이러스뿐만 아니라, 항생제를 무분별하게 사용해 우리가 만들어낸 항생제 내성 박테리아인 MRSA(메티실린 내성 황색포도상구균)와 다제내성 아시네토박터 바우마니이와 같은 미생물 괴물에서도 비롯된다. 이 박테리아는 이라크에서 돌아온 많은 군인들이 감염되면서 "이라크박터"라는 별명을 얻었다. 세계보건기구는 내성 슈퍼박테리아로 인한 사망자가 현재 연간 약 70만 명에서 2050년까지 거의 1000만 명에 이를 것으로 예측했다.

하지만 멋진 아이러니로, 종종 우리의 적으로 여겨지는 바이러스가 수많은 치명적인 감염과 싸우는 우리의 구세주가 될 수도 있다. 내성 바이러스의 위협이 커지고 새로운 항생제 개발이 지연되면서, 연구자들은 박테리오파지—말 그대로 박테리아를 먹는 바이러스—에 주목하게 됐다. 이 계열의 바이러스는 지구상에서 가장 오래되고 가장 많은 생물로 여겨진다. 마치 유도 미사일처럼, 각 유형은 특정 박테리아를 찾아 파괴하도록 진화해 왔다. 파지 요법은 동유럽에서 오랫동안 감염 치료에 사용돼 왔지만, 1940년대에 현대 항생제가 등장한 이후로는 거의 무시됐다. "내성 문제가 점점 악화되면서" 이 세기(21세기)에 관심이 다시 높아지기 시작했다고 록펠러 대학의 세균 병원성 및 면역학 실험실을 이끄는 빈센트 피셰티는 말한다. 현대 기술로, 바이러스학자들은 특정 슈퍼박테리아 균주에 정확히 맞는 파지를 정밀하게 매칭할 수 있으며, 때로는 놀라운 결과를 얻을 수 있다.

예를 들어, 톰 패터슨은 그의 아내 스테파니 스트래스디가 그를 구할 파지를 찾아 전 세계를 뒤진 후, 압도적인 이라크박터 감염에서 소생했다. 두 사람 모두 샌디에고 캘리포니아 대학교의 교수로, 이들은 2019년 저서 "완벽한 포식자"에서 그의 이야기를 전한다. 스트래스디는 이후 UCSD의 혁신적인 파지 응용 및 치료 센터를 공동 설립했다.

현재까지는 파지 요법은 실험 단계에 머물러 있다. 대부분, 이는 특정 환자의 박테리아에 대해 시험관 내에서 활성을 보이는 여러 파지를 혼합해 맞춤형 칵테일을 만드는 것을 포함한다. 패터슨의 경우, 9가지 다른 파지를 사용해 18주 동안 하루에 여러 번 그의 혈류에 주사했다. 스트래스디는 이미 정제되고 특성화되었으며 시퀀싱된 수만 개의 파지 도서관을 만들어 의료 믹솔로지스트들이 사용할 수 있도록 하는 것을 상상하고 있다.

2

하위내용영역	배점	예상정답률
일반영어 A형 서술형	4점	30%

모범 답안) The meaning of the underlined is that the speaker will be true to their own nature, even if they are considered "bad" by society. Second, the five words are "integrity of your own mind". Third, "love" best fills the blank.

채점 기준

+ 2점: 밑줄 친 부분의 의미를 "the speaker will be true to their own nature, even if they are considered "bad" by society or law"라 서술하였거나 유사하였다.
+ 1점: "적나라한 진실"에 상응하는 다섯 단어를 "integrity of your own mind"라 정확하게 기입하였다. 이외에는 답이 될 수 없다.
+ 1점: 빈칸에 들어갈 한 단어를 "love"라 정확하게 기입하였다. 이외에는 (philanthropy 등) 답이 될 수 없다.

감점 본문에 나오는 연속되는 5단어 이상을 사용하였다. −0.5pt

한글번역

[A] 누구든지 인간이 되려면 반드시 비영합주의자가 돼야 한다. 불후의 영예를 얻고자 하는 자는 선이라는 이름의 방해를 받아서는 안 되고, 오히려, 그 선이라고 불리는 것이 진정한 선인가를 스스로 검토해 봐야 한다. 궁극에 이르러 세상에는 그대 자신의 마음의 정직 이상으로 신성한 것은 없다. 우선 그대 자신에 대해 자기의 무죄함을 선포하라. 그러면 세계의 승인을 얻을 것이다. 내가 아주 젊었을 때, 존경할 만한 한 조언자에게 불가불하지 않을 수 없었던 한 마디 대답을 아직도 기억하고 있다. 그 사람은 늘 교회의 알뜰히도 낡아 빠진 교리를 가지고 날 귀찮게 구는 것이었다. 내가 "만일 내가 전적으로 내부의 명령에 의해 산다면 전통의 신성과 같은 것이 무슨 소용이 있겠습니까?"하니, 그가 말했다. "그런 충동은 천상의 것이 아니라 지옥의 것인지 모르지"라고. 나는 답했다. "나에겐 그렇게 생각되지 않습니다. 하지만 만일 내가 악마의 아들이라면 나는 그땐 악마에 의해 살겠습니다."라고. 나에겐 내 본성의 법칙 이외엔 그 어떠한 법칙도 신성하지 않다. 선과 악이란 것은 단지 이름뿐일 따름인데, 이것은 매우 용이하게도 이것이었다가 어떤 때는 저것으로 변하는 것이다. 유일한 '옳음'은 나의 체질(본성)에 부합하는 것이고, 유일한 '그름'은 그것에 거스르는 것이다.

[B] 인간은 모든 반대 앞에서, 마치 자기 자신 외의 모든 것이 빈 이름에 지나지 않는 하루살이인 것처럼 행동해야 한다. 우리들이 배지, 이름, 큰 단체, 그리고 죽은 제도 등에 쉽게 굴복하는가를 생각하면 나는 부끄러움을 금할 수 없다. 점잖고 품위 있는 말을 하는 모든 사람들은 필요 이상으로 지나칠 정도로 날 감동시키고 동요시킨다. 나는 곧고 씩씩하게 나아가 모든 면에서 적나라한 진리를 토해내지 않으면 안 된다. 만일 악의와 허영이 박애의 옷을 걸치고 나타난다면 그것이 통하겠는가? 만일, 이제 어떤 비분강개하고 편견이 심한 사람이 노예 폐지라는 자선운동의 임무를 띠고서 바바도스섬으로부터 최근의 소식을 가지고 나에게 온다면 나는 반드시 그에게 이렇게 말하겠다. "가서 너의 자식이나 사랑하고 너의 집 장작 패는 사람이나 사랑하라. 선량하고 겸손하라. 그런 미덕을 가져라. 그리고 천 마일 밖의 먼 곳에 있는 흑인에 대한 이런 믿기 어려운 온정으로써 너의 냉철하고 무자비한 야심을 가장하지 말라. 먼 곳에 대한 너의 사랑은 가까이 있는 것에 대한 증오일 따름이다." 이러한 (나의) 인사는 교양 없고 무례한 것일지도 모르지만, 진리는 사랑의 가식보다 아름답다. 우리들의 선에는 다소의 모난 면이 있어야 한다. 그렇지 않다면 그것은 아무것도 아니다. 사랑의 교훈이 다만 울고불고하는 것을 일삼는다면, 사랑의 교훈의 반대 작용으로서 증오의 교훈을 설교할 필요가 있다.

3

하위내용영역	배점	예상정답률
일반영어 B형 서술형	4점	45%

모범답안 The recent growth of the wellness industry can cause harm if not addressed. Though "The Goop Lab" looks like a promising platform, it prevents proven treatments and puts people in harm's way. Unfortunately, this sort of wellness business has been influenced by the patriarchal nature of medicine, having left out women, who thus become dominant in the wellness industry. In conclusion, to solve this distressing situation, medicine should challenge the wellness claims compassionately and also remove the patriarchal practices helping to grow that market.

채점 기준

ⓐ Topic sentence

+ 1점: "The recent growth of the wellness industry can cause harm if not addressed."를 명확하게 서술하였거나 유사하였다.

ⓑ Major supporting details

+ 2점: ① "Though 'The Goop Lab' looks like a promising platform, it prevents proven treatments and puts people in harm's way. ② Unfortunately, this sort of wellness business has been influenced by the patriarchal nature of medicine, having left out women, who thus become dominant in the wellness industry."을 명확하게 서술하였거나 유사하였다.

☞ 2개 중 2개 모두 정확하게 요약했으면 2점, 1개를 정확하게 요약했으면 1점, 나머지는 0점을 준다.

ⓒ Conclusion

+ 1점: "In conclusion, to solve this, medicine should challenge the wellness claims compassionately and also remove the patriarchal practices helping to grow that market."을 명확하게 서술하였거나 유사하였다.

감점
- 본문에 나오는 연속되는 6단어 이상을 사용하였다. −0.5pt
- 문단을 두 개나 그 이상으로 구성하였다. −0.5pt
- 문법이나 영어 표현을 합쳐 3개 이상 오류가 있다. −0.5pt

한글번역

지난 몇 년간 외과의사로 일하면서, 나는 웰니스 산업이 가져온 재앙을 점점 더 자각하게 됐다. 나는 과학적으로 검증된 치료 대신 덜 매혹적이라는 이유로 식이요법, 보조제, 혹은 기적적인 치료법을 선택하는 환자들을 보게 된다. 다른 사람들과 마찬가지로 나 또한 광고나 선의의 친구들로부터 "이 식단" 혹은 "저 비타민"이 건강, 장수, 아름다움, 사회적 지위의 열쇠라는 메시지를 끊임없이 받아왔다.

'구프 랩'이라는 잘못된 정보와 특권, 반(反)과학적 담론의 플랫폼, 그리고 더 넓게는 수조 달러 규모에 이른 웰니스 산업의 성장은 우려할 만한 일이다. 겉보기에는 그것이 희망과 가능성으로 가득 차 보인다. 그러나 조금만 깊이 파고들면, 천연의 기적이라 주장하는 에너지 치유, 냉치료, 노화 방지 시술 등의 이면에는, 아무리 좋게 봐도 돈 낭비에 불과하며, 나쁘게는 건강을 해칠 수도 있는 위험한 방법들이 숨어 있다. 연구에 따르면 암 환자 중 동종요법이나 특수 식단 같은 대체 요법을 사용하는 사람들은 검증된 치료를 포기할 가능성이 높았고, 그 결과 암으로 사망할 위험이 증가했다.

나 같은 의사들에게 이러한 웰니스의 확산은 불안하고 괴로운 일이다. 그러나 의학이라는 직업과 학문 또한 이 거대 웰니스 산업의 발생과 성장에 일정 부분 책임이 있다. 의학은 그 존재의 거의 전 역사에 걸쳐 여성들을 소외시켜 왔으며, 오늘날에도 정도의 차이는 있지만 그 문제는 여전히 지속되고 있다. 현대 의학이 자율성과 편견 해소를 중시하며 발전해 왔다고는 해도, 여전히 때로는 가부장적이고 온정적인 태도를 보인다. 따라서 여성들이 웰니스 산업에서 소비자이자 공급자로 과도하게 많이 등장하는 것은 전혀 놀라운 일이 아니다.

진정으로 사람들의 안전을 보장하려면, 의학은 위험하고 불필요하며 값비싼 가짜 치료법을 단호히 비판해야 한다. 그러나 동시에 내부를 성찰하고, 사람들이 진정으로 필요로 하고 원하며, 그들의 자율성을 지지하는 방식으로 연민을 담아 소통하는 진료를 제공해야 한다. 의료적 반진실과 해로운 치료로부터 사람들을 보호하기 위해서는, 내 직업은 수많은 사람들을 소외시켜 온 가부장적 관행으로부터 멀리 벗어나야 한다.

제45회 모의고사

1

하위내용영역	배점	예상정답률
일반영어 A형 서술형	4점	40%

모범 답안 The one word is "cancer". Second, it means that the speaker might be able to live longer than predicted by the mean or median.

☞ 출제의도 : 중간 정도 난이도의 글을 읽고, 그 지문을 바탕으로 정확한 추론을 하는지 평가한다.

채점 기준

+ 2점 : 빈칸에 들어갈 한 단어를 "cancer"라 정확하게 기입하였다. 이외에는 답이 될 수 없다.
+ 2점 : "(중간값이나 중위값이 아니라) 변수 그 자체가 현실(실재)"이라는 말이 저자의 상황(암에 걸려 8개월밖에 살지 못하는)에 어떠한 의미를 지니고 있는지 설명하라는 문제에 "the speaker might be able to live longer than predicted by the mean (or median)"라 서술하였거나 유사하였다.

감점 본문에 나오는 연속되는 5단어 이상을 사용하였다. −0.5pt

한글번역

태도는 분명히 암과 싸우는 데 중요한 역할을 한다. 왜 그런지 우리는 잘 모르지만 (내 구식 유물론적 관점에서 보자면, 정신 상태가 면역 체계에 영향을 미친다고 생각한다), 같은 나이, 계층, 건강 상태, 사회경제적 지위를 가진 사람들을 비교해 보면, 일반적으로 긍정적인 태도를 가지고 있고, 강한 의지와 삶의 목적을 가지고 있으며, 투쟁에 헌신하고, 의사들이 말하는 것을 수동적으로 받아들이기보다는 자신의 치료를 돕기 위해 적극적으로 대응하는 사람들이 더 오래 사는 경향이 있다. 몇 달 후 나는 나의 개인 과학 멘토이자 면역학 분야의 노벨상 수상자인 피터 메다워 경에게 암에 대한 성공적인 처방이 무엇일지 물어봤다. 그는 "낙관적 성격"이라고 답했다. 다행히 나는, 굳이 말하자면, 바로 이 문제에선 침착하고 자신감 있는 성격을 가지고 있다.

문제는 간단히 말해질 수 있다 : 우리의 일상 언어에서 "중앙값으로 사망률 8개월"이 무엇을 의미할까? 통계에 대한 교육을 받지 않은 대부분의 사람들은 이 문구를 "나는 아마도 8개월 안에 죽을 것이다"라고 읽을 것 같다. 이는 거짓일 뿐만 아니라 태도가 매우 중요하기 때문에 반드시 피해야 하는 결론이다.

물론 나는 기쁘지 않았지만, 이 문구를 일상 언어로 읽지도 않았다. 내가 가지고 있는 전문적 훈련은 "중앙값으로 8개월 사망률"에 대해 다른 관점을 가지도록 했다. 이 점은 미묘해 보일 수 있지만, 결과는 매우 클 수 있다.

우리는 평균과 중앙값을 냉엄한 "현실"로 보는 경향이 있고, 그 계산을 가능하게 하는 변수(편차)를 일시적이고 불완전한 측정치의 집합으로 본다. 중앙값이 현실이고 중앙값 주위의 변수가 계산을 위한 장치일 뿐이라면, "나는 아마도 8개월 안에 죽을 것이다"라는 해석이 합리적으로 보일 수 있다.

하지만 모든 진화 생물학자들은 변수 자체가 자연의 유일한 본질이라는 것을 알고 있다. 변수는 중심집중경향(변수들의 값이 평균값에 가까워지는 경향)을 위한 불완전한 측정치의 집합이 아니라, (그 자체가) 단단한 현실이다. 평균과 중앙값은 추상적인 개념일 뿐이다. 따라서 나는 그 통계를 다르게 봤다. 낙관주의자로서 구멍을 보지 않고 도넛을 보는 경향이 있기 때문만은 아니다. 오히려 더 근본적으로는 변수 자체가 현실이라는 것을 알기 때문이다. 나는 변수 속에 나 자신을 둬야 했다.

2

하위내용영역	배점	예상정답률
일반영어 A형 서술형	4점	45%

모범답안) It can be inferred that Stephen Jay Gould was very famous and successful in his field. Second, the Civil Rights Movement allows Gould to understand a sudden, surprising evolutionary change.

☞ 출제의도 : 중상 이상 난이도의 글을 읽고, 주어진 정보를 가지고 올바른 추론을 하는지 평가한다.

채점기준)

+ 2점 : 뉴욕 타임스가 스티븐 제이 굴드의 죽음을 1면에 언급한 것이 의미하는 바를 "Stephen Jay Gould was very famous and successful in his field"라 서술하였거나 유사하였다.
+ 2점 : 시민권 투쟁이 굴드의 진화론에 대한 이해에 어떤 면에서 연관이 있느냐는 질문에 "the Civil Rights Movement allows Gould to understand a sudden, surprising evolutionary change"라 서술하였거나 유사하였다.

감점 본문에 나오는 연속되는 4단어 이상을 사용하였다. -0.5pt

한글번역

스티븐 제이 굴드가 사망한 다음 날, 그의 부고 기사가 <뉴욕 타임스> 1면에 실렸다. 이는 그가 미국에서 가장 유명한 과학자였음을 증명하는 것이다. 그의 아이디어와 논쟁을 종합하는 재능, 그의 직업윤리, 그리고—그 자신이 먼저 언급했듯이—운이 그를 유명하게 만들었다.

그는 (원래는) 잡지 <자연사>(미국 자연사박물관에서 발행)의 월간 칼럼 "생명에 대한 관점"을 25년 동안 쓰기로 계획한 것은 아니었다. 하지만, 어린 시절 영웅인 조 디마지오처럼, 굴드는 이 문학적 연재물로 알려지게 됐고, 이는 반쯤 잊혀졌던 대중 과학 에세이란 예술—갈릴레오까지 거슬러 올라가는 (유서 깊은) 전통인—에 새로운 생명을 불어넣었다. 갈릴레오처럼 굴드는 일반 대중을 위해 과학을 해석하는 것 이상을 했다. 그는 또한 획기적인 진화 이론가이자 좌파 운동의 능숙한 정치 조직가였다.

그의 동료 닐스 엘드레드와 함께, 굴드는 생물학자들이 화석 기록을 보는 방식을 변화시켰다. 그의 '단속 평형설' 개념은 새로운 종들이 상대적으로 빠르게 출현한 후 수백만 년 동안 대부분 안정적으로 남아있다고 주장했다. 보다 편협한 동료들의 불만에도 불구하고, 굴드는 부분적으로 이 단속 평형설의 영감을 문자 그대로 "아버지 무릎에서" 마르크스주의를 배웠던 사실에서 찾았다.

이 발언으로 인해 그는 빨갱이로 몰리기도 했지만, 굴드와 엘드레드는 독단주의자가 아닌 다원주의자이자 역사주의자로서 이야기하고 있었다. "우리는 지도적 철학에서 다원주의를 옹호한다. 왜냐하면 그런 지도적 철학들이 (도그마처럼 하나의 생각만 강조한다면) 우리의 모든 사유를 제한한다는 가장 기본적인 원리를 인정하기 때문이다." 역사적 맥락도 새로운 아이디어에 제한을 가한다. 다윈은 자신의 진화론에 스미스와 맬서스의 고전 정치경제학의 영향을 인정했다. 굴드는 자신의 자유주의적 배경과 시민권 운동 혁명에 참여한 경험이 단속 평형설의 갑작스럽고 불연속적인 진화 변화 패턴의 중요성을 인식하게 했다고 언급했다. 굴드는 주체, 개체발생과 개통발생에 대한 영향력 있는 역사적 조사를 통해 진화적 발달에 대한 연구를 재활성화시켰다. 그리고 인간의 진화가 예측 가능한 단계들의 사다리라기보다는 여러 겹치는 계통을 가진 덤불의 가지들에 더 가깝다고 주장함으로써 인류학에도 큰 영향을 끼쳤다.

3

하위내용영역	배점	예상정답률
일반영어 A형 서술형	4점	45%

모범답안) He was reassured because the sleeping dog means that nobody is intruding into his house. Second, the word "fear" best describes the state of the main character.

☞ 출제의도 : narrative 패턴의 글을 읽고, 글쓴이의 주관적 내면의 감정을 정확하게 파악할 수 있는지 평가한다.

채점기준)

+ 2점 : "그"가 개가 잠을 자고 있는 모습에 안심한 이유를 "the sleeping dog means that nobody is intruding into his house"라 서술하였거나 유사하였다.

☞ 다음과 같이 서술하였어도 2점을 준다.

– "The dog was sleeping and not disturbed by an intruder in the house that he imagined was there."

+ **2점**: 빈칸에 들어갈 한 단어를 "fear"라 정확하게 기입하였다. 이외에는 답이 될 수 없다.

감점 본문에 나오는 연속되는 4단어 이상을 사용하였다. −0.5pt

한글번역

한밤중에 그는 이상한 소리—침실 문 바로 밖에서 동물처럼 긁는 소리와 쿵쿵거리는 소리—에 잠에서 깬다. 어떤 야생 동물이 발톱을 갈고 카펫을 찢는 것 같은데, 무거운 숨소리가 동물 같지 않다. 그것은 완전히 그리고 끔찍하게 인간적인 소리이다. 그는 그녀를 향해 팔을 뻗지만, 그의 팔은 어둠 속에서 광활하고 빈 공간을 가로지른다. 그녀는 거기에 없다. 그는 침대에 혼자 있고 집에 이상한 무언가 또는 누군가가 있다. 그는 순간적으로 몸이 굳고 자신의 심장 소리에 귀가 멍멍해진다. 결국 오랜 시간이 지나 집이 다시 조용해지고, 멀리서 냉장고가 덜컹거리는 소리와 개가 잠결에 부드럽게 신음하는 소리만 들린다.

그는 잠든 개에게서 안심을 느끼고, 그 소리가 꿈에서 들렸다는 것을 깨닫는다. 오래된 두려움이 꿈에서 생명력을 얻어 그에게 복수하는 악마처럼 다가온 것이다. 불안하게 하지만, 집에 침입자가 있는 것보다는 낫다. 그런 두려움이 그의 꿈속에서 그를 괴롭히는 것이, 자신의 아이들을 괴롭히는 것보다 낫다. 그는 잠든 아이들을 생각하며 갑작스런 아픔을 느끼고, 그 아픔은 부드러운 감정으로 변해 서서히 사라진다. 그런 다음, 아이들이 더 이상 아이가 아니고, 수년 동안 집에 살지 않았음을 기억하고, 그는 기지개를 켜고 깊이 숨을 쉬고 다시 잠에 든다. 그는 들락날락하며 한동안 졸다가 안도의 감각을 즐긴다. 안도감, 가까스로 피한 듯한 느낌, 비록 잠시일지라도 절벽 가장자리까지 간 듯한 느낌을 즐긴다.

갑자기 날카롭고 추한 감각이 그를 깨어나게 한다. 그는 벌떡 일어나 침대 위에 웅크리고, 공격할 준비를 한다. 문 아래 틈으로 빛이 빠르게 움직인다. 침묵. 부드러운 신음 소리도 잠든 으르렁거림도 없고, 심지어 개도 조용하다. 아니, 침묵당했다. 그는 끔찍하게 거의 인간적인 울음소리를 예상하며, 영화 〈케이프 피어〉의 (사이코패스 살인자) 맥스 캐디가 집안을 배회하며 성령처럼 벽을 통과하는 모습을 상상한다. 그는 침실 문 반대편에 있는 누군가의 존재를 느낄 수 있다. 누군가가 숨을 죽이고 침묵을 듣고 있다. 그의 눈은 어둠에 익숙해졌지만, 그는 지금 어둠 속에서 보고 있는지 느끼고 있는지 알 수 없다.

4

하위내용영역	배점	예상정답률
일반영어 A형 서술형	4점	50%

모범답안 The "hardest workers" were the students that worked very hard no matter what their ability and performed well. Second, the writer thinks "the situation" is ridiculous because David did perfectly on tests and exams but wasn't put on the accelerated track to get into the Advanced Placement Calculus.

☞ **출제의도**: 중급 정도 난이도의 글을 읽고, 글의 내용을 정확하게 이해했는지 평가한다.

채점기준

+ **2점**: "가장 열심히 일하는 일꾼"을 "the students that worked very hard no matter what their ability and performed well"이라 서술하였거나 유사하였다.
+ **2점**: "이 상황이 말도 안 되는 것"이라 생각하는 이유를 "because David did perfectly on tests and exams but wasn't put on the accelerated track (to get into the Advanced Placement Calculus)"라 서술하였거나 유사하였다.

감점 본문에 나오는 연속되는 4단어 이상을 사용하였다. −0.5pt

제46회 모의고사

1

하위내용영역	배점	예상정답률
일반영어 A형 서술형	4점	45%

모범답안 It is odd for them to be successful because they lack genetic diversity. Second, "diversity" best fills the blank. Third, all the elements are as follows: nature, nurture (or environment), and random.

☞ 출제의도 : 중·상급 정도 난이도의 최신 과학적 발견에 대한 글을 읽고, 그 글의 내용을 정확하게 이해했는지, 그리고 그 이해를 바탕으로 논리적 추론력이 충분한지 평가한다.

채점기준

+ 2점: 밑줄 친 "그것들의 성공은 이상한 것"이라는 말이 의미하는 것을 "It is odd for them to be successful because they lack genetic diversity"라 서술하였다.

+ 1점: 빈칸에 들어갈 한 단어를 "diversity"라 정확히 기입하였다. 이외에는 답이 될 수 없다.

+ 1점: 서로 다른 특질을 만들어 내는 데 영향을 미치는 모든 요소를 "① <u>nature</u>, ② <u>nurture (or environment)</u>, and ③ <u>random</u>"이라 정확하게 서술하였다.

☞ 3개 중 2개만 언급했으면 1점, 나머지는 0점을 준다.

감점 본문에 나오는 연속되는 4단어 이상을 사용하였다. −0.5pt

한글번역

태평양 근처의 항상 안개가 끼는 분지에 한적한 곳에 자리 잡은 로웰은 샌프란시스코에서 학업 성적을 기준으로 학생들을 입학시키는 유일한 공립 고등학교이다. 캘리포니아 대학교 시스템에 가장 많은 학생을 보내는 로웰은 많은 졸업생들을 미국에서 가장 뛰어난 대학들로 진학시킨다. 이런 이미지는 최고 수준의 시험 점수와 성적이 없는 아이들보다 훨씬 더 똑똑한 천재들을 떠올리게 할 수 있다. 하지만 내가 발견한 것은 로웰 학생들이 지능보다는 근면함으로 더 두드러진다는 것이었다. 한번은 내가 담임으로 있는 학생들에게 얼마나 공부하는지 물어봤다. 전형적인 대답은? 많은 시간 공부한다고 했다. 일주일이 아니라 하루에. 그럼에도, 다른 학교처럼 학생들이 얼마나 열심히 공부하는지와 얼마나 좋은 결과를 내는지에 대한 엄청난 차이가 있었다. 뉴욕에서 발견한 것처럼, 잘할 거라고 예상했던—그들에겐 수학이 너무 쉽게 느껴졌기에—몇몇 학생들이 반 친구들보다 못했다. 반면에, 몇몇 가장 열심히 공부하는 학생들은 항상 시험과 퀴즈에서 가장 높은 성적을 받았다. 이 매우 열심히 하는 학생들 중 한 명이 데이비드 루옹이었다. 데이비드는 나의 1학년 대수학 수업을 들었다. 로웰에는 두 종류의 대수학 수업이 있었다: 가속 트랙(고급 학습 과정)은 고등학교 졸업 학년 때 AP 미적분으로 이어졌고, 내가 가르치는 일반 트랙은 그렇지 않았다. 내 반 학생들은 로웰의 수학 배치고사에서 가속 트랙에 들어갈 만큼 높은 점수를 받지 못했다. 처음에는 데이비드가 눈에 띄지 않았다. 그는 조용했고 교실 뒤쪽에 앉아 있었다. 그는 손을 자주 들지 않았고 문제를 풀기 위해 칠판으로 나오는 것도 거의 자원하지 않았다. 하지만 내가 과제를 채점할 때마다 데이비드가 완벽한 과제를 제출한 것을 곧 알아차렸다. 그는 내 퀴즈와 시험에서 만점을 받았다. 내가 그의 답 중 하나를 틀렸다고 표시했을 때, 그것은 대부분 나의 실수였다. 그는 배움에 굶주려 있었다.

나는 이 아이가 도대체 왜 내 수업에 있는지 궁금해지기 시작했다. 상황이 얼마나 어이없는지 이해하자마자 나는 데이비드를 교과부장 사무실로 데려갔다. 상황을 설명하는 데 오래 걸리지 않았다. 다행히 그 부장은 관료적인 규칙보다 아이들에게 더 높은 가치를 두는 현명하고 훌륭한 교사였다. 그녀는 즉시 데이비드를 내 수업에서 가속 트랙으로 전환하는 서류 작업을 시작했다.

한글번역

1990년대에 한 떼의 클론이 독일을 침략했다. 10년 안에 그들은 이탈리아, 크로아티아, 슬로바키아, 헝가리, 스웨덴, 프랑스, 일본, 마다가스카르로 퍼져나갔으며, 강과 호수, 논과 늪, 따뜻하고 차가운 물, 산성과 염기성의 물에서 엄청난 피해를 일으켰다. 그 범인은 6인치 길이의 바닷가재처럼 생긴 생물인 대리석무늬 가재였다.

과학자들은 1995년경에 유전적 돌연변이가 애완용 가재가 무성생식을 할 수 있게 만들어 수정되지 않은 알로 자신을 복제할 수 있는 새로운 암컷 종이 생겨났다고 추정한다. 고의적으로 또는 실수로 이 돌연변이들 중 일부가 수족관에서 야생으로 방출됐고, 그곳에서 급격히 수백만 마리로 늘어나 토착 수로 종과 생태계를 위협했다.

그러나 그것들의 성공은 이상하다. 하이델베르크 대학의 생물학자인 귄터 보그트는 "오늘날 존재하는 모든 대리석무늬 가재는 단일 개체에서 파생됐다. 그들은 모두 유전적으로 동일하다."라고 말했다. 일반적으로 유전적 다양성이 없으면 개체군은 예측불가의 환경 변화에 매우 취약해진다. 그럼에도 불구하고 대리석 가재는 전 세계적으로 번성하고 있다.

자세히 살펴보면 가재의 균일성은 유전체 수준에서만 그러할 뿐이다. 2000년대 중반 보그트와 다른 연구자들이 수행한 연구에 따르면 이 수생 클론은 실제로 색상, 크기, 행동 및 수명에 있어 꽤 많은 차이를 보인다. 즉, 유전자 외에 다른 무언가가 그 다양성을 야기하고 있다는 것을 의미한다.

상식적으로 생각해보면 만일 그것이 선천적(자연적)인 것이 아니라면 양육(후천적인 환경) 때문이다. 즉, 다양한 특성의 결과적 차이는 동물의 유전체와 상호작용하는 환경적 영향에서 비롯된다. 하지만 그것이 전부는 아니다. 가재를 비롯한 다른 수많은 생물에 대한 새로운 연구는 변이와 다양성을 일으키지만 흔히 간과돼 온 중요한 역할을 드러내고 있다. 즉, 배아 발달의 첫 번째 날들에 시작되는 우리를 독특하게 만드는 놀라운 기초: 무작위적이고 내재적인 잡음이다.

2

하위내용영역	배점	예상정답률
일반영어 A형 서술형	4점	45%

모범답안 The word "Procrastinate" best fills the blank. Second, work and study is lacking immediate reward.

☞ 출제의도 : 중·상급 정도 난이도의 글을 읽고, 글의 내용을 정확하게 이해했는지 평가한다.

채점기준

+ 2점 : 빈칸에 들어갈 한 단어를 "procrastinate"라 정확하게 기입하였다. 이외에는 답이 될 수 없다.
+ 2점 : 일과 공부가 가지고 있지 못한 것이 "immediate reward"라 서술하였거나 유사하였다.

한글번역

<방해받지 않기-초집중>의 저자 니르 이얄은 산만함은 우리가 계획한 일에서 벗어나게 하는 행동이라고 말한다. 산만함의 반대는 집중이 아니라, 주의를 끄는 것이다. 무엇이든 산만함이 될 수 있는 것처럼, 무엇이든 주의를 끄는 것이 될 수 있다. 큰 프로젝트를 할 계획인데 이메일을 확인하면 산만해진다. 반대로, 비디오 게임을 할 계획이라면, 그 게임은 산만함이 아니다. 그것은 주의를 끄는 것이다. 주의 전환은 주의를 다시 집중시키는 것이다. 주의 전환은 멋질 수 있다. 미루기는 우리가 계획한 일을 하는 대신 산만함에 빠질 때 발생한다.

우리가 왜 미루는지, 그리고 이 원치 않는 습관이 왜 그렇게 깨기 어려운지에 대한 많은 이론이 있다. 1930년대에 심리학자들은 쥐에게 특정 행동, 예를 들어 레버를 누르는 행동을 작은 보상을 주고 훈련시켰다. 훈련이 완료된 후, 과학자들은 쥐에게 보상을 예측할 수 없게 줬을 때, 예를 들어 3~7번마다 보상을 줬을 때, 그들이 훈련된 행동을 더 자주 수행한다는 것을 발견했다. 더 놀라운 것은, 무작위로 보상을 줄 때, 그 행동이 사라지기 어려워졌다는 것이다. 보상을 받는 것은 뇌에서 도파민을 방출하며, 심지어 보상을 기대하는 것만으로도 이 효과가 있다.

유희태 | 일반영어 ❹-2

쥐뿐만 아니라 인간도 무작위성을 원하는 경향이 있다. 우리는 예측 불가능성에 흥분한다. 스포츠를 볼 때—누가 점수를 낼까/이길까? 라디오를 들을 때—다음에 어떤 노래가 나올까? 쇼핑할 때—세일에서 좋은 상품을 찾을 수 있을까? 이 시대에는 클릭 한 번으로 무작위성을 접할 수 있다. 대부분의 사람들은 스마트폰을 항상 가지고 다니며, 그 큰 매력 중 하나는 "새로운 것"을 발견하는 흥분이다. 어떤 사람들에게는 설탕이나 헤로인보다 더 중독성이 있다.

무작위성에 참여하는 것 자체는 나쁜 것이 아니지만, 우리가 그것을 (뭔가를) 미루기 위해 사용할 때는 멈추기 어려울 수 있다. 한 번 더 클릭, 스크롤, 또는 탭. 우리가 계획한 많은 일들, 예를 들어 일, 공부, 집안일 등은 즉각적인 보상이 없다. 일과 공부의 혜택은 미래에 있지만, 인스타그램이나 페이스북을 확인하는 것은 즉각적으로 뇌의 보상 시스템을 자극한다. 내가 올린 게시물에 좋아요가 달렸을까? 종 아이콘 아래에 어떤 이야기가 숨겨져 있을까?

내가 사용하는 인기 있는 미루기 방지 기술 중 하나는 타임박싱, 즉 포모도로 기법이다. 이 기법은 25분 동안 일하고 5분 동안 휴식을 취하는 세션을 규정한다. 엄격한 규칙이 있다. 25분 동안의 작업 세션 동안에는 하나의 작업만 해야 하고, 이메일 확인 등의 방해를 받지 않아야 한다. 산만함 없이 오직 주의를 끄는 일만 해야 한다.

채점 기준

ⓐ Topic sentence
+ 1점 : "Adolescents have brains that are more developed to experience fear and rewards which cause their unique behavior"를 명확하게 서술하였거나 유사하였다.

ⓑ Major supporting details
+ 2점 : ① "These differences mean they experience higher anxiety and also participate in more risky behaviors. ② Likewise, it helps show how therapy is less effective for them and how drugs such as stimulants might disrupt their development into healthy adults"를 명확하게 서술하였거나 유사하였다.
☞ 2개 중 2개 모두 정확하게 요약했으면 2점, 1개만 정확하게 요약했으면 1점, 나머지는 0점을 준다.

ⓒ Conclusion
+ 1점 : "In conclusion, adolescents should be understood as being prone to anxiety and needing proper guidance to grow healthily past this stage"을 명확하게 서술하였거나 유사하였다.

감점
• 본문에 나오는 연속되는 6단어 이상을 사용하였다. −0.5pt
• 문단을 두 개나 그 이상으로 구성하였다. −0.5pt
• 문법이나 영어 표현을 합쳐 3개 이상 오류가 있다. −0.5pt

3

하위내용영역	배점	예상정답률
일반영어 A형 서술형	4점	40%

모범 답안 Adolescents have brains that are more developed to experience fear and rewards, which cause their unique behavior. These differences mean they experience higher anxiety and also participate in more risky behaviors. Likewise, it helps show how therapy is less effective for them and how drugs such as stimulants might disrupt their development into healthy adults. In conclusion, adolescents should be understood as being prone to anxiety and needing proper guidance to grow healthily past this stage.

☞ 출제의도 : 글의 전체적인 내용을 파악한 후, 그 파악에 기초해서 글의 구조를 정확하게 요약하는지 평가한다.

제47회 모의고사

1

하위내용영역	배점	예상정답률
일반영어 A형 서술형	4점	60%

모범답안 The underlined words means the trip was impossible to afford. Second, pursuing high ambitions can lead to satisfying results.

채점 기준

+ 2점: 밑줄 친 부분의 의미를 "the trip was impossible to afford"라 서술하였거나 유사하였다.
  ☞ 다음과 같이 서술하였어도 2점을 준다.
  – "They could not afford to do the trip."
+ 2점: 제니스가 밑줄 친 부분에서 생각한 것을 "pursuing high ambitions (or goals) can lead to satisfying results"라 서술하였거나 유사하였다.

한글번역

뇌 발달의 특이성 때문에, 청소년들은 평균적으로 아이들이나 성인들보다 더 많은 불안과 공포를 경험하며, 두려움을 극복하는 법을 배우는 데 어려움을 겪는다. 뇌의 서로 다른 영역과 회로는 매우 다른 속도로 성숙한다. 공포를 처리하는 뇌 회로인 편도체는 전두엽피질—이성과 실행 제어를 담당하는—보다 훨씬 앞서 발달한다. 이는 청소년들이 불안과 공포에 대한 능력은 높지만, 이성적으로 침착하게 판단하는 능력은 상대적으로 발달이 덜 된 뇌를 가지고 있음을 의미한다.

청소년들이 그러한 높은 불안에 대한 수용력을 가지고 있다면, 왜 그들이 새로운 것을 찾고 위험을 무릅쓰는 경향이 있는지 의문을 가질 수 있다. 두 특성이 서로 모순되는 것처럼 보일 것이다. 그 해답의 일부는 뇌의 보상 센터도 마찬가지로 공포 회로처럼 전두엽피질보다 일찍 성숙한다는 것이다. 그 보상 센터가 많은 청소년들의 위험 행동을 유발한다. 이러한 행동의 역설은 또한 청소년들이 특히 부상과 외상에 취약한 이유를 설명하는 데 도움이 된다. 청소년의 주요 사망 원인 세 가지는 사고, 살인, 자살이다.

뇌 발달의 지연은 불안을 어떻게 생각하고 치료할지에 대한 중요한 시사점을 제공한다. 이는 불안한 청소년들이 인지 행동 치료와 같은 두려움을 극복하는 법을 가르치려는 심리 치료에 잘 반응하지 않을 수 있음을 시사한다. 우리가 배운 것을 통해 청소년들 사이에서 증가하는 자극제 사용에 대해 두 번 생각해 볼 필요가 있다. 이러한 약물은 불안을 악화시키고 청소년들이 발달 과정에서 해야 할 일, 즉 적절한 상황에서 두려움을 극복하는 법을 배우는 데 어려움을 줄 수 있기 때문이다. 자극제의 무분별한 사용은 청소년들이 학습된 공포를 억제하는 능력을 손상시키고, 이들을 더 두려운 성인으로 만들며, 외상을 경험한 청소년들 사이에서 PTSD의 위험을 증가시킬 가능성이 있다.

우리는 청소년들이 단순히 걱정 없는 새로운 것 탐구자와 위험 감수자가 아니라, 고유하게 불안에 취약하며 지나가는 위험에 대한 두려움을 배우기 어렵다는 것을 알고 있다. 부모들은 청소년기의 불안이 예상된다는 것을 깨닫고, 자신과 자녀들을 위로하며, 이들이 곧 성장해서 이 문제들을 극복할 것이라고 상기시켜야 한다. 이러한 점들을 제대로 고려하면, 청소년들이 직면한 위협을 더 잘 이해하고 건강하게 대처할 수 있게 될 것이다.

한글번역

월요일에 갑작스럽게 지역 여행사가 제니스에게 전화해서 그녀가 뉴멕시코에서 열리는 앨버커키 국제 열기구 축제에 갈 수 있는 두 장의 티켓에 당첨됐다고 전했다. 제니스와 그녀의 남편 존은 항상 그 축제에서 열기구를 타고 싶어 했지만, 그런 여행은 그들에게 너무 멀게 느껴졌다. 제니스는 존에게 이 좋은 소식을 전하기 위해 전화를 걸 때 매우 기뻤다. 처음에 존은 제니스가 농담을 하고 있다고 생각하고 믿지 않았다. 그러나 그녀가 꿈을 꾸고 있는 것이 아님을 깨달았을 때, 그의 짜증은 순식간에 사라졌다. 존이 퇴근하자마자, 제니스와 존은 그 여행에 대해 열심히 이야기를 나눴다. 곧 그들의 계획은 급속도로 커졌다. 제니스는 여행과 난생 처음 타는 열기구를 기대하면서 항상 들떠 있었다. 여행 2주 전에, 제니스는 병원으로 급히 이송됐다. 의사가 그녀를 진찰한 후, 수술이 필요하다고 말하면서 그녀의 기대를 꺾었다. 의사의 결정은 매우 실망스러웠다. 제니스는 충격을 받았다. 이제 그들의 열기구 여행 계획은 불확실해졌다. 무료 티켓이 없으면, 여행 비용이 너무 많이 들 것을 알고 있었다. 하지만 제니스는 운이 좋았다. 수술은 심각하지 않았고, 그녀는 의사에게 여행을 허락해달라고 간청했다. 일주일 후, 제니스와 존은 꿈에 그리던 여행을 떠났다. 그들은 열기구가 푸른 하늘로 올라가면서 매우 행복했다. 제니스는 생각했다 : 꿈을 크게 가지는 것이 가치가 있다.

한글번역

매트는 신입 교사로서 빌의 교실에 들어가 그를 관찰할 수 있어 매우 흥분했다. 매트는 빌을 교사로서 매우 존경했고, 효과적인 교실 관리 기법을 실제로 보는 것을 고대하고 있었다. 베테랑 교사인 빌은 학생들과 동료들에게 매우 인기가 있었다. 교장 선생님은 매트에게 학생들을 참여시키는 빌의 방법을 관찰하도록 추천했는데, 이는 규율 방해를 최소화하는 데 중요한 요소였다. 매트는 교실 뒤쪽에 있는 책상에 자리를 잡고 노트를 준비했다.

학생들이 자리에 앉자, 빌은 밝게 인사했다. 그는 다음 날 예정된 기준 시험(학기 중에 주기적으로 실시돼 학생들의 학업 성취도를 평가하고, 특정 기준이나 목표에 도달했는지를 확인하는 시험)에 대해 상기시켰다. 짧게 공부 전략 개요를 설명한 후, 빌은 학생들에게 게임을 하고 싶은지 물었다. "시험 준비가 얼마나 됐는지 보자."

"먼저, 두 팀으로 나눠야 해," 라고 빌은 설명한 후, 학생들에게 어떻게 나눌지 토론해보라고 했다. 학생들이 의견을 나누는 동안, 빌은 교실 뒤쪽으로 가서 매트에게 말했다. "학생들이 결정을 내리도록 하면, 그들은 자신들의 학습에 대한 책임감을 가지게 돼."

한 학생이 성별로 팀을 나누자고 제안했고, "남자 대 여자"라는 의견에 여러 학생들이 열렬히 지지했다. 빌은 남학생들을 교실 한쪽으로, 여학생들을 다른 쪽으로 보내고, 각 팀에게 질문을 하면서 정답 개수를 세기 시작했다.

10분 후, "여자" 팀이 "남자" 팀을 크게 앞서자, 몇몇 남학생들은 "여자들이 이기게 해주고 있다"고 농담을 했다. 몇몇 여학생들은 "여자" 팀이 이전 두 게임에서도 이겼음을 남학생들에게 상기시켰다. 팀들이 몇 분 동안 서로를 조롱한 후, 빌은 "너희들이 진정하지 않으면 게임을 끝낼 거야"라고 공표하며 학생들을 다시 집중시키려고 했다.

수업이 끝난 후, 학생들이 교실을 떠날 때, 매트는 몇몇 학생들이 웃으며 서로에게 경멸적인 말을 하며 어떤 성별이 더 똑똑한지에 대해 논쟁하는 것을 들었다. 빌은 매트에게 다가가 따뜻하게 말했다. "학생들은 경쟁을 좋아하고 그 과정에서 얼마나 많이 배우고 있는지 깨닫지 못하지."

그러고 나서 매트의 노트를 내려다보니, "성별 고정관념"이라고 적고 동그라미 친 것을 발견했다. "와! 그게 자네가 집중하고 있는 거야?" 빌이 물었다. "남자 대 여자 : 그게 학생들이 좋아하는 거잖아요." 그는 매트에게 충고했다. "자넨 아직 이 일이 새롭고, 학생들이 참여하고 배우고 있는 한 다른 것들은 중요하지 않다는 것을 곧 배우게 될 거야."

2

하위내용영역	배점	예상정답률
일반영어 A형 서술형	4점	45%

모범 답안 An example of ownership of learning is that the students formed the two groups on their own. Second, the underlined words refer to the students focusing on gender stereotypes during the class.

채점 기준

+ 2점 : 밑줄 친 부분의 의미를 "the students formed the two groups on their own"이라 서술하였거나 유사하였다.
+ 2점 : 밑줄 친 부분이 가리키는 것을 "(the students focusing on) gender stereotypes (during the class)"라 서술하였거나 유사하였다.

3

하위내용영역	배점	예상정답률
일반영어 A형 서술형	4점	50%

모범답안) It is because it was magma and the water would evaporate into space. Second, the word is "comets".

채점기준

+ 2점: 지구가 물을 지니지 못하고 있었던 이유를 "because it was magma and the water would evaporate into space"라 서술하였거나 유사하였다.
+ 2점: 빈칸에 들어갈 단어를 "comets"라 정확하게 기입하였다. 이외에는 답이 될 수 없다.

한글번역

지구는 어떻게 바다를 가지게 됐을까? 원시 지구는 끓어오르는 마그마 공이었기 때문에, 처음에 있던 물은 증발해 우주로 사라졌을 것이다. 그 결과, 행성 과학자들은 혜성과 소행성 중 어느 쪽이 지구에 물을 전달하는 데 더 큰 역할을 했는지에 대해 오랫동안 논쟁해 왔다.

<사이언스>지에 발표된 새로운 연구에 따르면, 소행성이 그 원천이었다고 한다. 워싱턴 DC의 카네기 연구소의 코넬 알렉산더가 이끈 저자들은 86개의 원시 운석에서 질소와 수소의 동위원소 비율을 분석한 결과, 그것들이 지구의 비율과 일치한다는 것을 발견했다.

소행성은 이미 선호되는 원천이었다. 태양계 역학에 대한 연구는 약 39억 년 전, 후기 대폭격기라고 불리는 기간 동안 지구가 주로 소행성에 의해 폭격을 받았을 것이라고 시사한다.

혜성은 물의 높은 함량과 아미노산이 풍부해 이상적인 원천임에도 불구하고, 몇 가지 단점이 있다. 오르트 구름에서 온 혜성에 대한 여섯 가지 연구는 그것들의 중수소 동위원소 비율이 지구의 비율보다 훨씬 높다는 것을 발견했다. 2011년 <네이처>지에 실린 한 논문이 혜성 *하틀리 2*의 중수소 동위원소 비율이 지구와 유사하다는 것을 발견했을 때, 혜성에서 물이 왔다는 아이디어에 대한 관심이 다시 일어났다. 그러나 알렉산더와 그의 동료들은 하틀리 2 전체에서의 중수소 수준이 (그리고 그 혜성의 얼음에서의 수준뿐만 아니라) 훨씬 더 높을 것이라고 제안한다.

4

하위내용영역	배점	예상정답률
일반영어 A형 서술형	4점	35%

모범답안) The word is "pain". Second, the writer argues that pleasure and pain are independent and not merely relative concepts that exist only in contrast to each other. He believes they can exist on their own without necessarily being defined by the absence or presence of the other.

채점기준

+ 2점: 빈칸에 들어갈 단어를 "pain"라 정확하게 기입하였다. 이외에는 답이 될 수 없다.
+ 2점: 밑줄 친 부분에서 저자가 말하고자 하는 바를 "the writer argues that pleasure and pain are independent and not merely relative concepts that exist only in contrast to each other. He believes they can exist on their own without necessarily being defined by the absence or presence of the other"라 서술하였거나 유사하였다.

보충설명

The sentence "It seems necessary towards moving the passions of people advanced in life to any considerable degree, that the objects designed for that purpose, besides their being in some measure new, should be capable of exciting pain or pleasure from other causes" means that to significantly move the emotions of older people, it is necessary to use objects or experiences that are somewhat new. However, novelty alone isn't enough. These objects or experiences must also have the inherent ability to evoke strong emotions—such as pain or pleasure—due to other reasons or factors. This implies a deeper, more profound connection or impact is required beyond just being new.

The sentences "Pain and pleasure are simple ideas, incapable of definition. People are not liable to be mistaken in their feelings, but they are very frequently wrong in the names they give them, and in their reasonings about them." convey that **pain and pleasure are fundamental, basic experiences that cannot be fully captured or defined by words**. People inherently understand their own sensations of pain and pleasure without error. However, they often make mistakes when **they try to label these sensations with words and when they attempt to reason or theorize about the causes and nature of their feelings**. This highlights the gap between direct emotional experience and the intellectual processes of naming and reasoning about those experiences.

The sentence "pain and pleasure, in their most simple and natural manner of affecting, are each of a positive nature, and by no means necessarily dependent on each other for their existence." conveys that pain and pleasure, **when considered in their most fundamental and straightforward form of impacting (=influencing) individuals**, each have a **definite and distinct** character or importance. Furthermore, the existence of one does not depend on the existence of the other. In other words, pain can exist without pleasure and vice versa; they are not interdependent for their existence. This highlights the idea that **pain and pleasure are separate and distinct experiences, each playing its own role in human life without needing the other to be present**.

한글번역

나이 든 사람들의 감정을 어느 정도로 자극하기 위해서는, 그 목적을 위해 설계된 대상이 어느 정도 새로운 것일 뿐만 아니라, 다른 이유로도 고통이나 즐거움을 불러일으킬 수 있어야 하는 것 같다. 고통과 즐거움은 단순한 개념으로, 정의하기가 불가능하다. 사람들은 자신의 감정에 대해 잘못 판단하지는 않지만, 그 감정에 붙이는 이름과 그것에 대한 추론은 자주 틀린다. 많은 사람들은 고통이 반드시 어떤 즐거움의 제거에서 생긴다고 생각하는 반면, 즐거움은 어떤 고통의 중지나 감소에서 생긴다고 생각한다.

(하지만) 나는 고통과 즐거움이 가장 단순하고 자연스러운 방식으로 영향을 미칠 때, 각각 적극적인 (서로 구별되는) 성질을 가지며, 각자의 존재를 위해 서로에 의존하지 않는다고 생각한다. 인간의 마음은 자주, 그리고 대부분 고통이나 즐거움이 없는 상태에 있다고 생각하며, 나는 이를 무관심 상태라고 부른다. 이 무관심 상태에서 즐거움을 실제로 느끼는 상태로 옮겨질 때, 어떤 종류의 고통을 (매개 즉 중간단계로) 거칠 필요가 있다고는 보지 않는다. 만약 이런 무관심, 평온, 고요함 혹은 다른 어떤 이름으로 부르든지 간에 그런 상태에 있을 때, 갑자기 음악회로 즐거움을 얻거나, 아름다운 모양과 밝고 생기 있는 색깔의 물체가 눈앞에 나타나거나, 장미의 향기로 후각이 만족된다면, 듣기, 후각, 맛보기의 모든 감각에서 분명히 즐거움을 느낄 것이다. 그러나 이러한 만족을 느끼기 전 당신의 마음 상태를 조사해보면, 그러한 만족이 당신을 어떤 고통 속에서 발견했다고 말하기는 어려울 것이다.

반대로, 무관심한 상태에 있는 사람이 갑작스러운 강타를 받거나 쓴 약을 마신다면, 여기에는 어떤 즐거움의 제거가 없다. 그러나 영향을 받은 모든 감각에서 매우 구별되는 고통이 느껴진다. 나는 즐거움과 고통이 단지 대비될 때만 존재할 수 있는 단순한 관계라는 생각을 결코 납득할 수 없다.

제48회 모의고사

1

하위내용영역	배점	예상정답률
일반영어 A형 서술형	4점	45%

모범 답안 The word is "inflammation". Next, (The new findings could lead to new treatments for psoriasis) because certain RNA molecules might replicate(=mimic) the benefits of UV therapy without increasing the risk of skin cancer.

채점 기준

+ 2점: 빈칸에 들어갈 단어를 "inflammation"라 정확히 기입하였다. 이외에는 답이 될 수 없다.
+ 2점: 새로운 발견이 건선 치료에 왜 도움이 될 것인지 묻는 질문에 "because certain RNA molecules might replicate(=mimic) the benefits of UV therapy without increasing the risk of skin cancer"라 서술하였거나 유사하였다.

☞ 다음과 같이 서술하였어도 맞는 것으로 한다.

— "Because certain RNA molecules might be able to provide the same therapeutic benefits as UV therapy, a common treatment for psoriasis, but without the associated increased risk of developing skin cancer."

보충설명

Sun-damaged cells and damaged RNA are not the same things, but they are related in the process of sunburn. Here's the relationship between them:

- Sun-Damaged Cells: When skin cells are exposed to ultraviolet B (UVB) radiation from the sun, some of these cells get damaged.
- Damaged RNA: The UVB radiation specifically damages a type of RNA in these skin cells, called micro-RNA.
- Signal Release: The damaged micro-RNA is then released from the sun-damaged cells as a signal of injury.
- Inflammatory Response: This released, damaged RNA signals to neighboring, healthy cells to produce factors that promote inflammation. This inflammatory response helps to remove the damaged cells, which could become cancerous if not cleared away.
→ So, while sun-damaged cells and damaged RNA are not the same, the damage to the RNA within the sun-damaged cells triggers the body's inflammatory response, leading to the symptoms of sunburn.

The new findings could lead to new treatments for psoriasis and other medical conditions **because they identify the role of damaged RNA molecules in triggering the inflammatory response to UV radiation**. Here's a detailed explanation:

① Identification of a Key Mechanism: The research discovered that damaged micro-RNA, released from UVB-exposed skin cells, acts as a signal for inflammation. This inflammation helps remove sun-damaged cells, preventing potential cancerous changes.

② Alternative to UV Therapy for Psoriasis: Currently, one treatment for psoriasis involves exposure to UV light, which helps relieve symptoms but also increases the risk of skin cancer. **Understanding that damaged RNA can trigger a similar inflammatory response opens the possibility of developing treatments that mimic this process without the harmful effects of UV radiation.** Specifically, treatments could be designed to target and modulate the micro-RNA pathway, providing the benefits of UV therapy without the associated risks.

③ Reducing Inflammation in Autoimmune Conditions: People with certain autoimmune conditions experience a burning sensation with minimal UV exposure, **even before significant cell damage occurs**. By blocking the micro-RNA pathway responsible for this early inflammatory response, it might be possible to reduce or prevent this discomfort.

④ Targeted Treatments : The new insights into **how damaged RNA molecules signal injury** can lead to the development of more targeted therapies that specifically address the inflammation process. This could result in treatments that are more effective and have fewer side effects compared to current options.
→ Overall, these findings suggest that **manipulating the micro-RNA pathway** could provide a novel and safer approach to treating conditions like psoriasis and managing inflammation caused by UV exposure.

염증 반응이 왜 중요한지 과정별 설명

① UVB Exposure : Initial exposure to ultraviolet B radiation from the sun. ② Cell Damage : UVB radiation causes damage to skin cells, leading to the production of damaged micro-RNA. ③ Release of Damaged micro-RNA : The damaged RNA is released from the affected cells, signaling injury. ④ Signal to Neighboring Cells : This signal alerts nearby healthy cells to the damage. ⑤ Inflammatory Response : **Neighboring cells respond by producing inflammatory factors, leading to the redness and pain associated with sunburn.** ⑥ Removal of Damaged Cells : The inflammation helps to remove the damaged cells from the skin, preventing them from accumulating. ⑦ Prevention of Cancer : By removing damaged cells, the body reduces the risk of these cells turning cancerous.

자가면역질환이 있는 사람의 문제

The premature activation of the inflammatory response can lead to unnecessary inflammation. Inflammation is a protective mechanism, but when it occurs without significant cell damage, it can result in tissue damage, increased sensitivity, and other health issues over time.

Misleading Health Signals : If the body initiates an inflammatory response before significant damage occurs, it can mask or complicate the detection and treatment of actual cellular damage or other health conditions. This can lead to confusion in diagnosing and managing the underlying autoimmune condition.
→ Overall, premature inflammation without significant cell damage is problematic because it causes discomfort, unnecessary immune activation, and potential long-term health issues.

한글번역

햇볕에 탄 자국은 우리가 햇빛을 즐겼다는 것과 약간 부주의했다는 것을 잘 보여주지만, 고통스럽고 붉은 염증을 일으키는 세포 내부에서 정확히 무슨 일이 일어나는지는 명확하지 않았다.

이제 연구자들은 햇볕에 탄 자국을 유발하는 분자 신호를 발견했다. 피부 세포가 자외선 B(UVB) 방사선에 노출되면 특정 형태의 RNA인 마이크로 RNA가 손상된다고 연구는 밝혔다. (RNA는 유전자를 구성하는 DNA와 구조가 유사하다.) 이 손상된 RNA는 태양 손상의 신호로 방출돼 인접한 건강한 세포들이 염증을 유발하는 요소들을 생산하도록 자극한다.

전체 과정은 암으로 발전할 수 있는 햇볕에 손상된 세포를 제거하기 위한 것이다. "피부 세포는 죽은 햇볕에 손상된 세포를 감지할 수 있는데, 이는 세포가 손상된 RNA를 방출하기 때문이다,"라고 샌디에이고 캘리포니아 대학교 의과 대학의 교수인 리처드 갈로가 말했다. 다른 요소들도 염증 과정에 역할을 할 가능성이 있지만, 연구 결과에 따르면 손상된 RNA 분자가 방사선에 의한 손상의 표지 역할을 한다고 한다.

연구자들은 이러한 발견이 의학적 상황에 영향을 미칠 수 있다고 말한다. 예를 들어, (현재의 의학적 상황에서) 피부 질환인 건선의 한 가지 치료법은 UV 광선에 노출하는 것이다. 하지만 UV 광선이 증상을 완화할 수는 있지만, 피부암 위험도 증가시킨다. 이 새로운 발견은 특정 RNA 분자(즉, 마이크로 RNA)가 UV 치료 대신 사용될 수 있으며 동일한 혜택을 제공할 수 있음을 시사한다. 또한, 특정 자가면역 질환을 가진 사람들은, 건강하지 않은 세포 손상이 발생하기도 전에, 아주 적은 양의 UV 노출로도 화끈거리는 느낌을 받는다. 마이크로 RNA 경로를 차단하는 것이 이러한 환자들의 염증을 줄이는 방법이 될 수 있다. 그러나 이러한 질환이 없는 건강한 사람들이 단순히 햇볕에 타는 것을 막기 위해 이 경로를 차단하고 싶어 하지는 않을 것이다. 왜냐하면 이것은 신체가 손상된 세포를 치유하고 제거하는 중요한 방법이기 때문이다. "염증 반응은 태양으로부터 우리를 보호하는 정상적인 부분이다,"라고 갈로는 말했다.

2

하위내용영역	배점	예상정답률
일반영어 A형 서술형	4점	40%

모범답안 The word is "ear". Second, it is because the artist used secondhand sources and his own imagination to create the image, not direct observance.

채점기준

+ 2점: 빈칸에 들어갈 단어를 "ear"라 정확하게 기입하였다. 이외에는 답이 될 수 없다.
+ 2점: 저자가 "half-invented"란 표현을 사용한 이유를 "the artist used secondhand sources and his own imagination to create the image, not direct observance"라 서술하였거나 유사하였다.

한글번역

1601년 로마 판화의 자막은 이 판화가 같은 해 안코나 근처에 떠밀려 온 거대한 고래를 묘사한 것이며 "자연 그대로 정확하게 그려졌다"고 주장한다. 그러나 1598년 네덜란드 해안에서 비슷한 '특종'을 기록한 이전 판화가 존재하지 않았다면 이 주장은 더 신뢰할 수 있었을 것이다. 하지만 16세기 후반의 네덜란드 예술가들, 그 사실주의의 대가들이 고래를 제대로 묘사할 수 있었을까? 그렇지 않은 것 같다. 그 생물은 의심스럽게도 마치 귀가 있는 것처럼 보이는데, 내가 (이 분야의) 권위자에 의뢰해서 알아본 결과, 귀가 있는 고래는 존재하지 않는다. 드로잉을 한 사람은 아마도 고래의 지느러미 중 하나를 귀로 착각해 눈에 너무 가깝게 배치했을 것이다. 그 역시 익숙한 도식, 즉 전형적인 머리의 도식에 의해 오도된 것이다. 낯선 장면을 그리는 것은 보통 생각하는 것보다 더 큰 어려움을 초래한다. 그리고 이것이 아마도 이탈리아인이 고래를 다른 판화에서 복사하는 것을 선호한 이유일 것이다. 우리는 안코나에서 온 소식을 전하는 자막의 부분을 의심할 필요는 없지만, 그것을 '실제 삶으로부터 (정확히)' 그리는 것은 (그 화가에겐) 그럴 만한 가치가 없었다.

이 점에서, 사진이 등장하기 전 몇 세기 동안의 삽화책에 등장하는 이국적인 생물들의 운명은 교훈적이기도 하고 재미있기도 하다. 독일 르네상스 시대의 화가인 알브레히트 뒤러가 그의 유명한 코뿔소 목판화를 출판했을 때, 그는 자신의 상상력을 채워 넣어야 했으며, 이는 의심할 여지 없이 가장 유명한 이국적인 짐승인 갑옷을 입은 용에 대해 배운 것에 의해 영향을 받았다. 그러나 이 **반쯤 창조된** 생물이 18세기까지 심지어 자연사 책에서도 코뿔소에 대한 모든 묘사의 모델로 사용됐다는 것이 밝혀졌다. 1790년에 제임스 브루스가 그의 '나일 강의 근원을 발견하기 위한 여행'에서 그 동물의 그림을 출판했을 때, 그는 자신이 그 사실을 알고 있다는 것을 자랑스럽게 보여줬다.

3

하위내용영역	배점	예상정답률
일반영어 B형 서술형	4점	40%

모범답안) Work friendships can lead to a more efficient and happy environment if brought into a company. Americans have less work friendships because long term employment has declined alongside a rise in social media connections with old friends. However, friends working together can make for more happiness and effective output when there is trust and mutual support. In conclusion, these helpful relationships can be established through simple interactions of mutual engagement and trust.

채점 기준

ⓐ Topic sentence

+ 1점: "Work friendships (used to be key and) can lead to a more efficient and happy environment (if brought into a company)"을 명확하게 서술하였거나 유사하였다.

ⓑ Major supporting details

+ 2점: "Americans have less work friendships ① as(because) long term employment has declined alongside ② a rise in social media connections with old friends. However, ③ friends working together can make for more happiness and effective output when there is trust and mutual support"을 명확하게 서술하였거나 유사하였다.
☞ 3개 중 3개 모두 정확하게 요약했으면 2점, 2개만 요약했으면 1점, 나머지는 0점을 준다.

ⓒ Conclusion

+ 1점: "In conclusion, these helpful relationships can be established through simple interactions of mutual engagement and trust"를 명확히 서술하였거나 유사하였다.

감점
- 본문에 나오는 연속되는 6단어 이상을 사용하였다. −0.5pt
- 문단을 두 개나 그 이상으로 구성하였다. −0.5pt
- 문법이나 영어 표현을 합쳐 3개 이상 오류가 있다. −0.5pt

한글번역

한때, 직장(일)은 우정의 주요 원천이었다. 우리는 가족을 회사 소풍에 데려가고 동료들을 저녁 식사에 초대했다. 지금은, 우리는 유대감을 형성하기 위해서가 아니라 효율적으로 일하기 위해 사무실에 간다.

왜 미국인들은 이렇게 열심히 일에만 집중할까? 경제적 설명을 하자면, 장기 고용이 사실상 사라졌기 때문이다. 한 조직에서 경력을 쌓는 대신, 우리는 몇 년마다 직장을 옮길 것을 기대한다. 그래서 오래 머물 계획이 없기 때문에, 동일한 방식으로 투자하지 않는다. 우리는 동료들을 일시적인 인연으로 여기며, 일정한 거리를 두고 예의 있게 행동하고, 진정한 우정은 직장 밖에 예약해 둔다. 항상 소셜 미디어로 옛 친구들과 연결돼 있고 언제든지 그들을 방문할 수 있을 때, 왜 새로운 친구를 사귈 필요가 있을까? 24시간 연결된 상태에서 우리는 점점 더 시간 부족에 시달리며, 일을 처리해야 한다는 압박감이 사회화하려는 욕구를 압도할 수 있다.

우리가 직업을 여가의 수단으로 주로 볼 때, 업무에서 효율성을 최우선으로 여겨 직장 밖의 우정에 시간을 할애하는 것이 쉬워진다. 그러나 우리는 직장 내 우정이 우리의 행복과 효과성에 미치는 영향을 과소평가할 수 있다. 직장에서 우정을 형성할 기회를 제공할 때 직업은 더 만족스럽다. 연구에 따르면, 친구들로 구성된 그룹은 의사 결정과 노력 과제에서 지인들로 구성된 그룹을 능가한다. 친구들이 함께 일할 때, 그들은 서로를 더 신뢰하고 성공을 위해 헌신한다. 이는 더 많은 정보를 공유하고 더 많은 시간을 할애해 도우며, 예의 때문에(즉, 상대방 기분이 상할까봐) 건설적인 비판을 자제하지 않는다면, 더 나은 선택을 하고 더 많은 일을 해낸다는 것을 의미한다.

직장에서 유대감을 형성할지 여부는 개인의 결정이지만, 이는 우리가 생각하는 것보다 더 적은 노력과 더 적은 취약성을 수반할 수 있다. 고품질의 연결은 "깊고 친밀한 관계"를 필요로 하지 않는다. 존중, 신뢰, 상호 참여로 표시된 단일 상호작용만으로도 양측 모두에게 에너지를 생성하기에 충분하다. 아무리 작아 보일지라도, 이러한 연결 순간들은 '거래'를 '관계'로 변모시킬 수 있다.

제49회 모의고사

1

하위내용영역	배점	예상정답률
일반영어 A형 서술형	4점	50%

모범답안 It means that younger people announce their age using fractions to sound older sooner. Second, kids and the very old share the similarity of counting in fractions.

채점기준

+ 2점: 밑줄 친 부분의 의미를 "younger people announce their age using fractions to sound older sooner"라 서술하거나 유사하였다.
+ 2점: 가장 늙은 노인과 아이들 사이의 공통점을 "counting in fractions"라 서술하였거나 유사하였다.

한글번역

우리 삶에서 나이가 드는 것을 좋아하는 유일한 시기가 어린아이일 때라는 것을 알고 있나요? 10살이 채 되지 않은 아이들은 나이가 드는 것에 너무 신나서 나이를 분수로 표현한다. "몇 살이야?" "나는 네 살 반이야!" 서른여섯 살 반이라고 하지는 않는다. 네 살 반에서 다섯 살이 되려고 하는 것이다! 이게 핵심이다. 청소년이 되면, 이제 아무도 너를 막을 수 없지. 다음 숫자로, 아니면 몇 살 더 나아가는 거지. "몇 살이야?" "곧 16살 될 거야!" 13살일 수도 있지만, 곧 16살이 될 거라고 말하는 거야! 그리고 인생에서 가장 위대한 날… 21살이 되는 거야. 이 말 자체가 마치 의식처럼 들리지… 21살이 되는 거야. YESSSS!!!

하지만 그러다가 30살이 돼. 오, 무슨 일이 있었던 거지? 내가 상한 우유가 된 것처럼 들려! "상했다; 버려야 했어." 이제는 재미가 없어, 그냥 시큼한 덤플링일 뿐이야. 뭐가 문제일까? 뭐가 변한 걸까? 21살이 되고, 30살이 되고, 그 다음에는 40살을 향해 가. 와! 브레이크를 밟아, 모든 게 다 사라져가고 있어. 어느새 50살이 되고, 꿈은 사라져. 하지만 잠깐만!!! 60살이 돼. 그럴 줄 몰랐지! 그래서 21살이 되고, 30살이 되고, 40살을 향해 가고, 50살이 되고, 60살이 돼.

그렇게 속도를 내다 보면 70살이 돼! 그 이후로는 하루하루가 중요해져; 수요일이 되는 거야! 80대가 되면 하루하루가 완전한 사이클이 돼; 점심시간이 되고; 4시 반이 되고; 취침 시간이 돼. 그리고 거기서 끝나지 않아. 90대가 되면, 거꾸로 가기 시작해; "막 92살이었어." 그러다가 이상한 일이 일어나. 100살이 넘으면, 다시 어린아이처럼 돼. "나는 100살 반이야!" 모두가 건강하게 100살 반까지 살기를 바란다!

2

하위내용영역	배점	예상정답률
일반영어 A형 서술형	4점	45%

모범답안 It is that the majority of left-handed women also hold their babies on the same side as their right-handed counterparts. Second, "left" fills the blank.

채점 기준

+ 2점: 어떤 연구의 결과가 밑줄 친 부분의 주장을 반박하는가라는 질문에 "the majority of left-handed women also hold their babies on the same side as their right-handed counterparts"라 서술하였거나 유사하였다.
+ 2점: 빈칸에 들어갈 단어를 "left"라 기입하였다. 이외에는 답이 될 수 없다.

한글번역

어머니가 아기에게 행동하는 방식의 한두 가지 측면을 살펴보는 것은 가치가 있다. 일반적인 애무, 포옹 및 씻김은 별다른 언급이 필요 없지만, 어머니가 아기를 안고 있을 때 아기를 몸에 대고 있는 자세는 상당히 의미심장하다. 세심한 미국 연구들에 따르면, 어머니의 80%가 아기를 왼쪽 팔에 안고, 아기를 몸의 왼쪽에 대고 있다는 사실이 밝혀졌다. 이 선호도의 중요성에 대해 설명하라는 질문을 받으면 대부분의 사람들은 오른손잡이가 우세하기 때문이라고 대답한다. 아기를 왼팔에 안으면 어머니들은 지배적인 팔을 자유롭게 사용할 수 있기 때문이다. 그러나 자세한 분석에 따르면 이것이 원인이 아니라는 사실이 드러났다. 물론 오른손잡이 여성과 왼손잡이 여성 간에 약간의 차이는 있지만 충분한 설명을 제공할 만큼은 아니다. 오른손잡이 어머니의 83%가 아기를 왼쪽에 안고 있지만, 왼손잡이 어머니도 78%가 그렇게 한다. 다시 말해, 왼손잡이 어머니의 22%만이 지배적인 손을 자유롭게 사용하고 있다. 분명히 다른, 덜 명백한 설명이 있어야 한다.

유일한 다른 단서는 어머니의 심장이 몸의 왼쪽에 있다는 사실에서 나온다. 어머니의 심장 소리가 중요한 요소일 수 있을까? 어떤 방식으로? 이러한 관점에서 생각해 보면, 아마도 어머니의 몸 안에 있는 동안 자라나는 배아가 심장 소리에 집착하게('각인') 되는 것이 아닐까 추론됐다. 만약 그렇다면 태어난 후에 이 익숙한 소리를 다시 발견하는 것이 아기에게 진정 효과를 줄 수 있을 것이다. 특히 낯설고 무서운 새로운 세상에 갓 내던져진 상태에서는 더욱 그러하다. 만약 그렇다면 어머니는, 본능으로든 혹은 무의식적인 일련의 시행착오를 통해서든, 아기를 왼쪽에 안고 심장에 대면 더 평화로워진다는 사실을 곧 발견하게 될 것이다.

3

하위내용영역	배점	예상정답률
일반영어 A형 서술형	4점	45%

모범답안 The word "history" best fills the blank. Second, it means that history is not unpredictable chaos, but has patterns.

채점 기준

+ 2점: 빈칸에 들어갈 단어를 "history"라 기입하였다. 이외에는 답이 될 수 없다.
+ 2점: 밑줄 친 부분의 의미를 "history is not unpredictable chaos, but has patterns"라 서술하였거나 유사하였다.

한글번역

때때로 역사는 정말로 반복되는 것처럼 보인다. 예를 들어, 미국 남북전쟁 후, 소수민족과 계층의 분노로 인한 도시 폭력이 나라 전체를 휩쓸었고, 이는 1870년경에 절정에 달했다. 내부 갈등은 1920년경에 다시 급증했으며, 인종 폭동, 노동자 파업, 반공 감정의 급증으로 인해 많은 사람들이 혁명이 임박했다고 생각하게 만들었다. 그리고 1970년경에 다시 한번 소요가 절정에 달했는데, 이때는 폭력적인 학생 시위, 정치적 암살, 폭동 및 테러가 발생했다.

코네티컷 대학교 스토스 캠퍼스에서 인구 역학을 연구하는 피터 터친에게, 약 50년 간격으로 세 차례의 정치적 불안정성이 나타나는 것은 우연이 아니다. 지난 15년 동안, 터친은 숲 생태계에서 포식자-피식자 주기를 추적할 수 있게 했던 수학적 기법을 인간 역사에 적용해왔다. 그는 미국의 경제 활동, 인구 동향 및 폭력의 폭발에 대한 역사적 기록을 분석한 결과, 새로운 내부 갈등의 물결이 이미 다가오고 있다고 결론지었다. 그는 그 절정이 약 2020년경에 일어날 것이며, 아마도 1970년경의 것만큼 높을 것이라고 말한다. "1870년만큼 나쁘지 않기를 바란다,"라고 그는 덧붙였다.

터친이 고대 그리스 역사의 뮤즈 클리오(Clio)의 이름을 따서 클리오다이내믹스(cliodynamics)라고 부르는 그의 접근 방식은 터친과 그의 동료들이 모든 인간 사회를 형성한다고 말하는 광범위한 사회적 힘을 식별하고 모델링함으로써 역사에 과학적 방법을 적용하려는 노력의 일환이다. 터친은 이 접근 방식이 "역사는 단순히 일련의 사실들이 하나씩 하나씩 순차적으로 발생하는 그런 것이 아니"라는 것을 보여주려는 시도라고 말하면서 흔히 고(故) 영국 역사가 아널드 토인비가 했다라고 하는 이 말을 인용했다. 클리오다이내믹스는 대부분의 대학에서 역사학을 가르치는 학자들 사이에서 매우 큰 의심을 받고 있는데, 이 학자들은 역사를 우연, 개인의 실수 및 광범위한 '역사의 과학'으로는 결코 포착할 수 없는 독특한 상황들의 복잡한 혼합물로 보는 경향이 있기 때문이다. 하버드 대학교의 문화 역사학자인 로버트 단턴은 "마르크스주의와 사회다윈주의에서 구조주의와 포스트모더니즘에 이르는 한 세기에 걸쳐 있던 거대 이론 이후, 대부분의 역사가들은 일반 법칙에 대한 믿음을 버렸다"고 말했다.

4

하위내용영역	배점	예상정답률
일반영어 A형 서술형	4점	50%

모범답안 It is because the teacher wanted to start with a fun location. Second, the word is "angry".

채점기준

+ 2점: 지리 교사가 자신의 주에서 시작하지 않은 이유를 "because the teacher wanted to start with a fun location"라 서술하였거나 유사하였다.
+ 2점: 빈칸에 들어갈 단어를 "angry"라 기입하였다. 이외에는 답이 될 수 없다.

한글번역

워드 선생님은 지리를 아주 좋아했다. 그녀는 학생들에게 더 나이 많은 학생들을 위해 준비된 자료를 배우고 있다고 말하면서 영감을 주고 동기를 부여했다.

워드 선생님이 새 학년을 위해 계획한 첫 번째 단원은 캘리포니아에 초점을 맞췄다. 워드 선생님이 가르치는 러스틴 학교는 중서부에 위치했지만, 그녀는 캘리포니아가 학년을 시작하기에 재미있는 주라고 생각했다. 러스틴 학교의 학생들은 다양한 사회경제적 및 인종적 배경을 나타냈지만, 그녀는 많은 학생들이 해변에 관심이 있다는 것을 알고 있었다. 그녀 생각에는, 캘리포니아는 이 주제에 잘 들어맞았다.

워드 선생님은 학생들을 카펫 위에 모아놓고 플립 차트에 글을 쓰기 시작했다. 몇몇 학생들은 그녀가 종이 맨 위에 "캘리포니아"라고 쓰자 흥분해서 속삭였다. 워드 선생님은 그들의 흥분을 보고 기뻤지만, 그들에게 조용히 하고 말할 것이 있으면 손을 들라고 상기시켰다. 즉시 몇몇 손이 올라갔다.

"우리가 캘리포니아에 대해 배우는 거예요?" 매디가 물었다.

"맞아," 워드 선생님이 대답했다. "우리는 이번 주 내내 여러 과목에서 캘리포니아에 대해 배울 거야." 학생들은 다시 흥분해서 수다를 떨기 시작했고, 워드 선생님은 그들에게 다시 조용히 하라고 상기시켰다. "너희가 한꺼번에 너무 많이 말하면 내가 이해할 수 없어."

단원을 좀 더 설명한 후, 워드 선생님은 캘리포니아에 가본 적이 있는 사람을 물었다. 드쿼안이 손을 들었다. 워드 선생님이 그를 부르자 그는 말했다, "며칠 전에 나는 할머니 집에서 내 여동생과 함께 TV를 보고 있었는데, 여동생이 울어서 잘 들을 수가 없었어요. 나는 그녀에게 조용히 하라고 하고 장난감을 줬어요, 왜냐하면 TV에 나오는 사람이…"

워드 선생님은 드쿼안을 중단시키고 그녀가 물었던 질문은 캘리포니아에 가본 적이 있는 사람이라고 상기시켰다. 잡담과 드쿼안의 간접적인 대답에 약간 화가 나서, 그녀는 지금은 이야기를 할 때가 아니라고 상기시켰다.

"질문에 답할 수 있는 사람만 손을 들어," 그녀가 말했다. 이 말을 듣고 드쿼안은 화난 목소리로 덧붙였다, "나는 TV에 나오는 사람이 프로그램이 건포도를 만드는 회사에서 후원한다고 말하는 것을 듣고 있었다고 말하려고 했어요, 건포도는 내가 제일 좋아하는 간식이고, 그 건포도는 캘리포니아에서 만들어져요!"

워드 선생님은 드쿼안에게 말할 것이 있으면 손을 들어야 한다고 상기시키고, 그의 말투가 불손함으로 가득 차 있다고 덧붙였다. 그룹을 다시 집중시키려고 노력하며, 그녀는 물었다, "디즈니랜드에 가본 사람 있니?" 매디가 손을 들고 말했다, "저요. 캘리포니아에 있어요, 그리고 거기는 따뜻하고 햇빛이 많아요. 그리고 멀리 있어요, 비행기를 오랫동안 탔거든요."

"맞아," 워드 선생님이 대답하며 "따뜻하다"와 "햇빛이 많다"라는 말과 함께 "러스틴 학교에서 멀다"라는 구절을 플립 차트에 썼다.

"캘리포니아를 묘사할 다른 단어가 있니?" 그녀가 물었다. 몇몇 다른 학생들이 손을 드는 동안, 워드 선생님은 드쿼안이 여전히 화가 난 것을 알아챘다. 또 다른 폭발을 예상하며, 그녀는 기쁜 목소리로 말했다, "드쿼안, 마음을 좀 가라앉히고 그룹과 함께 앉아있을 수 있도록 해줘." 이 말을 듣고 드쿼안은 일어나서 자신의 책상으로 걸어가서 의자에 축 처져 앉았다.

오, 안 돼, 워드 선생님은 생각했다. 그가 내 말을 제대로 듣지 못한 것 같아. 시간이 빨리 지나가고 있었고 수업을 끝내야 한다는 것을 알았기에, 워드 선생님은 계속 수업을 진행했지만, 드쿼안의 부정적인 행동이 계속된다면 어떻게 해야 할지 고민했다.

유희태 | 일반영어 ❹-2

제50회 모의고사

1

하위내용영역	배점	예상정답률
일반영어 A형 서술형	4점	50%

모범 답안 It means that many of the other apple companies have become very angry at the company's attempt to sell a genetically engineered apple. Second, the word is "slices"

채점 기준

+ 2점: 밑줄 친 부분의 의미를 "many other apple (=many of the other apple) companies have become very angry at the company's trying (attempt) to sell a genetically engineered apple"라 서술하거나 유사하였다.
+ 2점: 빈칸에 들어갈 단어를 "slices"라 기입하였다. 이외에는 답이 될 수 없다.

한글번역

한 조그만 회사가 잘라지거나 멍이 들어도 갈변하지 않는 유전자 변형 사과를 시장에 내놓으려고 노력하고 있다. 그러나 이것은 나머지 대부분의 사과 회사들에 많은 반발을 불러일으키고 있다.

오카나간 스페셜티 프루츠란 이름의 이 회사는 갈변하지 않는 사과가 소비자와 식품 서비스 회사들에게 인기를 끌 것이며, 부분적으로는 잘린 사과를 제공하거나 판매하는 것을 더 매력적으로 만들어 사과 판매를 증가시키는 데 도움이 될 것이라고 말한다. 미국인들은 1990년대부터 유전자 변형 식품을 먹어왔지만, 주로 가공식품이었다. 아틱 애플이라고 불리는 이 사과는 사람들이 직접 베어 먹는 최초의 유전자 변형 과일 중 하나가 될 수 있다.

그러나 미국 사과 협회는 미국 사과 산업을 대표하는 일부 다른 산업 단체들과 함께 이 제품의 도입에 반대하고 있다. 그들은 유전자 변형이 위험하다고 믿지 않지만, 유전자 변형이 사과를 건강하고 자연스러운 식품으로서의 이미지를 손상시킬 수 있다고 말한다. 사과는 의사를 멀리하게 하고 미국의 전통 음식인 애플파이만큼이나 미국적이라는 것이다. 회사의 창립자이자 사장인 닐 카터는 갈변하지 않는 사과가 당근 판매에 도움을 준 베이비 캐럿처럼 사과 산업의 판매를 개선할 수 있다고 말했다. 그는 "사과 한 개 전체는 많은 사람들에게 너무 큰 부담이 된다"고 말했다. "만약 회의에서 사과 한 그릇이 있다면, 사람들은 그 그릇에서 사과를 꺼내지 않을 것이다. 하지만 만약 사과 조각이 담긴 접시가 있다면, 모든 사람들이 조각을 하나씩 가져갈 것이다." 미국 농무부에 따르면 미국에서 신선한 사과 소비는 1980년대 후반에 1인당 연간 약 20파운드에서 현재 약 16파운드로 감소했다.

사과 조각은 이미 건강한 간식으로 인기를 끌고 있으며, 슈퍼마켓에서 가방에 담아 판매되거나 맥도날드의 어린이 해피 밀에 포함돼 있다. 사과 조각은 갈변을 방지하고 아삭함을 유지하기 위해 종종 비타민 C와 칼슘으로 코팅돼 있다. 그러나 이는 맛에 영향을 줄 수 있다고 카터 씨는 말했다. 그는 또한 재배자들이 사과를 다루면서 흔히 발생하는 작은 멍 때문에 슈퍼마켓에서 거부당하는 사과가 줄어들 것이라고 말했다. 아틱 애플은 먼저 골든 딜리셔스와 그래니 스미스 품종으로 제공될 예정이며, 갈변의 원인인 폴리페놀 옥시다제 생산을 크게 줄이는 합성 유전자를 포함하고 있다.

2

하위내용영역	배점	예상정답률
일반영어 A형 서술형	4점	45%

모범 답안 The word in ① is "nature" and ② "temperature". Second, it is the scientific challenge of creating a diamond from carbon.

채점 기준

+ 1점: 빈칸 ①에 "nature"라 기입하였다. 이외에는 답이 될 수 없다.
+ 1점: 빈칸 ②에 "temperature"라 기입하였다. 이외에는 답이 될 수 없다.
+ 2점: 밑줄 친 "다이아몬드 수수께끼"를 "the scientific challenge of creating a diamond from carbon"라 서술하거나 유사하였다.

3

하위내용영역	배점	예상정답률
일반영어 B형 서술형	4점	35%

모범답안 The Flexner report was a pivotal reformation to medical education which lead to the deleterious separation of medicine and public health. Commissioned in the early 1900s, it help found the modern medical educational system which focuses on individuals, rather than social and environmental factors. Secondarily, it led to the closing of Black medical schools, so that less doctors looked into the environmental factors of racism and instead noted race itself as a risk factor. In conclusion, the Flexner report needs to be replaced by an approach that unifies public health and medicine to better handle diseases.

채점기준

ⓐ Topic sentence

+1점 : "The Flexner report was a pivotal reformation to medical education which lead to the deleterious separation of medicine and public health"를 명확하게 서술하였다.

ⓑ Major supporting details

+2점 : "Commissioned in the early 1900s, ① it help found the modern medical educational system which focuses on individuals, rather than social and environmental factors. Secondarily, ② it led to the closing of Black medical schools, so that less doctors looked into the environmental factors of racism and instead noted race itself as a risk factor"를 서술하였거나 유사하였다.

☞ 2개 중 2개 모두 정확하게 요약했으면 2점, 1개만 요약했으면 1점, 나머지는 0점을 준다.

한글번역

"진짜처럼 보일 뿐만 아니라 진짜인 보석을 만드는 것이 가능해야 합니다."라고 한 화학자가 여러 해 전 말했다. "유일한 차이점은 하나의 결정은 사람이 만들고, 다른 하나는 자연이 만든다는 것입니다."

처음에는 이것이 그다지 어려운 작업처럼 보이지 않았다. 과학자들은 18세기 말부터 합성 다이아몬드를 만들기 시작했다. 이 시기에 중요한 과학적 사실이 발견됐다 : 다이아몬드는 매우 흔한 원소인 탄소의 한 형태라는 것이다. 여러분의 연필에 사용되는 검은 광물인 흑연도 탄소로 만들어졌다. 오늘날 우리가 아는 유일한 차이점은 탄소 원자가 약간 다른 방식으로 결합돼 있다는 것이다. 화학자들은 열정에 불타올랐다 : 왜 싸고 풍부한 물질인 탄소를 희귀하고 비싼 다이아몬드로 바꾸지 못하겠는가?

여러분은 수 세기 동안 일반 납이나 철을 금으로 바꾸려고 했던 연금술사들에 대해 들어봤을 것이다. 그들은 실패했다. 왜냐하면 금은 납이나 철과 완전히 다르기 때문이다. 그러나 탄소를 다이아몬드로 변형시키는 것은 전혀 비논리적이지 않다. 이 변화는 자연에서 일어나기 때문에 실험실에서도 일어나게 할 수 있을 것이다.

가능할 것이다, 하지만 150년 동안 모든 노력이 실패했다. 이 기간 동안, 몇몇 사람들은 다이아몬드 수수께끼를 풀었다고 믿었다. 그중 한 명은 진짜 같은 결정체를 만든 프랑스 과학자였다. 그러나 그 과학자의 사후에 이상한 소문이 돌기 시작했다. 이야기의 내용은 그 과학자의 조수 중 한 명이 탄소 혼합물에 작은 진짜 다이아몬드 조각을 넣었다는 것이었다. 그는 그 일이 지루했기 때문에 노 화학자를 기쁘게 하고 싶어 했다.

첫 번째 진정한 성공은 60년이 넘은 후, 제너럴 일렉트릭 컴퍼니의 실험실에서 나왔다. 그곳의 과학자들은 자연의 일을 복제하려는 과정에 수년간 매달렸다. 지구 표면 깊은 곳에서 탄소는 엄청난 압력과 극도로 높은 온도에 노출된다. 이러한 조건에서 탄소는 다이아몬드로 변한다. 오랫동안 실험실 시도는 실패했는데, 단순히 적절한 기계가 존재하지 않았기 때문이다. 필요한 것은 탄소를 섭씨 1200도에서 2400도 (화씨 2200도에서 4400도) 사이의 온도에서 평방 인치당 800,000에서 1,800,000 파운드의 압력을 견딜 수 있는 일종의 압력 챔버였다.

ⓒ Conclusion

+ 1점: "In conclusion, the Flexner report needs to be replaced by an approach that unifies public health and medicine to better handle diseases"를 명확하게 서술하였다.

감점
- 본문에 나오는 연속되는 6단어 이상을 사용하였다. −0.5pt
- 문단을 두 개나 그 이상으로 구성하였다. −0.5pt
- 문법이나 영어 표현을 합쳐 3개 이상 오류가 있다. −0.5pt

한글번역

팬데믹, 특히 COVID-19 같은 전염병이 왜 그렇게 큰 영향을 미쳤는지 이해하려면, 질병의 진단과 치료 연구가 질병 예방 연구와 분리된 이유를 살펴봐야 한다. 즉, 의학과 공중 보건이 왜 서로 별개로 여겨지는지 알아봐야 하는데, 이 불행한 분리의 원인은 110년 전인 1910년의 플렉스너 보고서에서 시작된다.

1900년대 초반에 미국 의사 협회는 카네기 재단에 의뢰해 의학교육을 개혁하려고 했다. 함께 아브라함 플렉스너를 고용해서 북미의 모든 의과대학을 평가하도록 했고, 그는 보고서를 작성했다. 이 보고서와 그 구현에 따른 자금은 오늘날 우리가 익숙한 의학교육 시스템을 만들었다 : 경쟁적인 입학 기준, 전통적인 교수법, 그리고 과학적 방법을 중심 원칙으로 삼는 시스템 말이다. 이 보고서는 질병의 생물학적 원인만을 중점으로 하는 개별 생물의학 모델을 표준으로 정립했는데, 사회적 및 환경적 요인은 배제했다.

또한, 이 보고서는 역사적으로 흑인 의과대학의 불균형적인 폐쇄를 초래해서 오늘날까지 존재하는 의사 인력의 불균형을 초래하고, 의학 연구와 공중 보건 연구를 실제적으로 분리시켰다. 그래서 여전히 많은 연구자들은 질병의 위험 요인으로 인종의 개별 속성을 자주 언급하면서도 인종차별이라는 환경적 경험은 조사하지 않는다. 마찬가지로 의학교육에서는 가난은 포함되지만 억압은 포함되지 않고, 인종은 포함되지만 인종차별은 포함되지 않는다.

플렉스너 보고서는 의학과 공중 보건을 다시 결합하는 새로운 문서로 대체돼야 한다. 플렉스너 보고서를 대체할 문서는 구체적인 행동을 촉발하고 보호막을 제공할 수 있다. 그것이 단지 구식 사고 방식을 버린다는 상징적인 제스처일지라도, 미국 의사 협회가 플렉스너의 사고 방식이—비록 그의 시대에는 혁명적이었겠지만—더 이상 적용되지 않는다는 것을 보여주는 또 다른 보고서를 의뢰한다면 현명할 것이다.

제51회 모의고사

1

하위내용영역	배점	예상정답률
일반영어 A형 서술형	4점	50%

모범답안 It can be inferred that Branson had an unconventional character which will either make him successful or get him into trouble. Second, it means that the name of Virgin has held on to this day.

채점기준

+ 2점: 브랜슨의 학창 시절 교장의 말에서 추론할 수 있는 그의 기질을 "Branson had an unconventional character which will either make him successful or get him into trouble"라 서술하였거나 유사하였다.

☞ 다음과 같이 서술하였어도 맞는 것으로 한다.
— "It can be inferred that Branson was seen as a highly unconventional and ambitious individual, someone who would either achieve great success or face significant failure. The headmaster's prediction that Branson would become either a prisoner or a millionaire suggests that Branson had a daring and risk-taking nature."

+ 2점: 밑줄 친 부분의 의미를 "the name of Virgin has held on to this day" 또는 "the name of Virgin has been used since that moment"라 서술하였거나 유사하였다.

☞ 다음과 같이 서술하였어도 맞는 것으로 한다.
— "The underlined phrase "the name stuck" means that the name "Virgin" was accepted and became the permanent name for the business."

한글번역

부자가 되고 싶은가? 페라리를 몰고 다니고, 일등석을 타고, 럭셔리 호텔에 머무는 걸 상상해 본 적이 있는가? 그렇다면 백만장자가 돼야 한다. 하지만 40세까지 백만장자가 되는 가장 좋은 방법은 뭘까? 성공한 사람을 보고 그들이 어떻게 했는지 알아보는 게 좋은 생각이다. 영국에서는 버진 그룹의 수장인 리처드 브랜슨보다 더 좋은 예는 없다.

오늘날 버진은 모두 독립적으로 운영되는 거대한 그룹의 회사들이다. 유일한 통일 요소는 브랜슨의 열정과 버진 브랜드이다. 이 그룹은 200개 이상의 버진 회사를 운영해 왔다. 많은 분석가들은 이것이 브랜드 확장을 너무 멀리 가져가는 것이며, 조만간 고객의 마음에서 버진의 정체성을 잃게 될 것이라고 믿는다. 하지만 브랜슨은 항상 비평가들의 예상을 뒤엎는다.

브랜슨은 17세에 그의 침실에서 제국을 시작했고, 그 이후로 많은 발전을 이뤘다. 모든 것은 브랜슨이 학생 잡지 시장에서 틈새를 발견했을 때 시작됐다. 그때까지 학생 잡지들은 모두 학교에 관한 것이든가 학교나 대학에서 일어나는 일에 관한 것이었다. 브랜슨은 학생들이 학교생활 외에도 다른 것들에 관심이 있다는 것을 깨닫고, 음악과 영화에 관한 기사를 담은 잡지를 발행하기로 결정했다. 그의 어머니는 잡지를 시작할 수 있도록 4파운드를 빌려줬고, 그것이 시작이었다. 나중에 그의 교장 선생님은 이렇게 말했다: "축하해, 브랜슨. 내가 예언하건대, 네가 40세가 되면 감옥에 가거나 백만장자가 될 것이다."

곧 잡지 구독을 판매하는 것보다 음반을 판매하는 것이 더 수익성이 높아졌다. 브랜슨은 가게를 차리기로 결심했지만, 임대료를 낼 돈이 없었다. 그 당시 브랜슨은 아직 십대였고 은행은 그에게 신용을 제공하지 않았다. 대부분의 사람들은 이 시점에서 포기했을 것이다. 하지만 브랜슨은 그렇지 않았다. 그는 신발 가게 위의 빈 사무실을 찾아 그 가게 주인을 설득해 무료로 임대하게 했다. 그는 어떻게 했을까? 그는 그 가게 주인에게 브랜슨의 새 가게를 방문하는 사람들이 많아질 것이며, 그 결과 주인은 더 많은 신발을 팔아 임대료보다 더 많은 이익을 얻을 것이라고 보장했다. 그리고 그것은 성공했다.

이제 그는 경쟁력 있는 가격으로 잘 알려진 제품을 판매하는 성공적인 사업을 갖게 됐지만, 여전히 이름이 없었다. 그를 돕는 사람들로부터 많은 제안이 있었지만, 브랜슨은 그 어떤 것도 마음에 들지 않았다. 그러던 중 그의 동료 중 한 명이 "우리는 사업에 완전한 처녀이다"라고 말하며 "버진"을 제안했다. 그리고 그 이름은 정착됐다.

2

하위내용영역	배점	예상정답률
일반영어 A형 서술형	4점	35%

모범답안 The word is "ideal". Second, the central error is that women were asked the ideal family size rather than about their personal preference.

채점 기준

+ 2점: 빈칸에 들어갈 단어를 "ideal"이라 기입하였다. 이외에는 답이 될 수 없다.
+ 2점: 가족 규모에 대한 정보 수집에서 글쓴이가 언급하는 핵심적 오류를 "<u>women were asked the ideal family size rather than about their personal preference</u>"라 서술하였거나 유사하였다.

✚ 보충설명

The phrase "nudges about when you and your significant other are going to start having children; who doesn't love a serving of guilt about not (yet) having kids to go with the stuffing?" means that during Thanksgiving visits, relatives often bring up or subtly pressure the person and their partner about when they plan to have children. This conversation typically includes making them feel guilty for not having children yet. The phrase humorously compares **this feeling of guilt** to **an extra side dish** served with the Thanksgiving meal, specifically stuffing, highlighting how these conversations are an unwelcome but common part of the holiday gathering.

In this context, "stuffing" refers to a traditional Thanksgiving side dish made of seasoned bread cubes, vegetables, and sometimes meat, which is typically cooked inside a turkey. The phrase humorously suggests that the guilt about not having children is an additional "serving" that accompanies the Thanksgiving meal, much like stuffing is a common accompaniment to the turkey.

유희태 | 일반영어 ❹-2

The phrase "Another dominant assumption in these conversations is the idea of 'competing preferences'—activities, behaviors and statuses that are difficult to combine with having and raising children. For some, this conjures up images of lazy millennials playing video games or spending time shopping and dining out;" means that when discussing declining fertility rates, people often assume that younger generations prefer activities and lifestyles that are incompatible with having and raising children. This stereotype portrays millennials as being more interested in leisure activities like playing video games or social activities like shopping and dining out, rather than starting families. This assumption is criticized as overly simplistic and incorrect.

There are two dominant assumptions discussed in the passage: The first assumption is that the number of children people consider as their "ideal" family size is the same as the number of children they personally want to have. The second assumption is the idea of "competing preferences"—the belief that activities, behaviors, and statuses that people enjoy or pursue are difficult to combine with having and raising children, leading to stereotypes about younger generations prioritizing leisure activities over starting families.

한글번역

추수감사절에 집을 방문하면 정치 싸움에서부터 당신과 당신의 배우자가 언제 아이를 낳을 것인지에 대한 재촉까지 다양한 어색한 대화가 따라온다. 아직 아이가 없다는 죄책감을 곁들인 속을 채운 요리를 누가 좋아하지 않겠는가? 그러나 친척들이 출산율 감소와 아이를 너무 늦게 가지면 어떻게 되는지에 대한 암울한 통계를 들먹이기 시작하더라도 그들을 안심시킬 수 있다 : 사람들이 생각하는 이상적인 자녀 수와 실제로 낳고 있는 자녀 수 사이의 격차는 생각만큼 심각하지 않다. 그리고 낮은 출산율에는 비용뿐만 아니라 이점도 있다.

이상적인 가족 크기의 개념은 직관적이고 간단해 보이기 때문에 매력적이다. 지난 10년 동안 미국에서 보고된 이상적인 가족 크기는 2~3명의 자녀로 안정적으로 유지되고 있다. 그러나 출산율은 계속해서 감소하고 있으며, 평생 출산율 추정치인 총출산율은 현재 1.73으로 낮아졌다. 이는 이상과 현실 사이의 격차가 악화되고 있음을 암시하는 것처럼 보인다.

그러나 이 격차를 어떻게 해석해야 할까? 이러한 논의에서는 종종 개인들이—보통 여성들이—이상적인 가족 크기라고 생각하는 것과 그들이 개인적으로 원하는 자녀 수가 동일하다고 당연하게 여긴다. 그러나 이상적인 가족 크기는 너무 추상적일 수 있다; 예를 들어, 일부 사람들은 자신이 두 명의 자녀를 원해서가 아니라 일반적인 두 자녀 기준에 따라 응답할 수 있다. 대신에, 사람들이 개인적으로 몇 명의 자녀를 갖고 싶어 하는지를 측정하는 것이 더 바람직하다; 특히 많은 사람들이 인생이 전개되면서 장기 계획을 변경하기 때문에 단기적으로 자녀를 갖고자 하는 욕구에 대한 정보가 있다면 더욱 좋다.

이러한 대화에서 또 다른 지배적인 가정은 "경쟁하는 선호"의 개념이다—아이를 갖고 양육하는 것과 결합하기 어려운 활동, 행동 및 지위들. 일부 사람들에게 이는 게으른 밀레니얼 세대가 비디오 게임을 하거나 쇼핑과 외식을 하는 이미지를 떠올리게 한다; 다른 사람들은 이 논리를 개인들—특히 여성들이—가족을 이루는 것보다 다른 목표를 우선시해 이기적이고 자기애적이라는 증거로 해석한다. 이는 잘못된 가정이다.

3

하위내용영역	배점	예상정답률
일반영어 A형 서술형	4점	50%

모범답안 The word is "success". Second, it means that the woman is driven to improve to the highest possible standard by her own opinion without self-gratification.

채점기준

+ 2점 : 빈칸에 들어갈 단어를 "success"라 기입하였다. 이외에는 답이 될 수 없다.
+ 2점 : 밑줄 친 부분의 의미를 "the woman <u>is driven to improve to the highest possible standard by her own opinion without self-gratification (self-satisfaction)</u>"라 서술하였거나 유사하였다.

4

하위내용영역	배점	예상정답률
일반영어 A형 서술형	4점	50%

모범 답안 Ford's motivation for using a higher wage was to stabilize his workforce by reducing chronic absenteeism and worker turnover. Second, the differences in 2014 are that a stabilized workforce is not a priority as it was in 1914, but instead staying competitive and keeping up with technology are priorities.

채점 기준

+ 2점 : 포드가 임금을 올려준 핵심적 동기를 "to stabilize his workforce (by reducing chronic absenteeism and worker turnover)"라 서술하였거나 유사하였다.

+ 2점 : 2014년의 미국 기업들과 노동자들이 1914년과 어떻게 완전히 다른가에 대해 "the differences in 2014 are that a stabilized workforce is not a priority (as it was in 1914), but instead staying competitive and keeping up with technology are priorities"라 서술하였거나 유사하였다.

☞ 다음과 같이 서술하였어도 맞는 것으로 한다.

- "In 2014, the global supply chains and hypercompetitive nature of the auto industry mean that businesses prioritize technology and cost-cutting over stabilizing the workforce. Unlike in 1914, where Ford's strategy of paying higher wages to ensure a reliable workforce led to increased productivity and profits, modern businesses often view the lowest wage as the most competitive, focusing more on staying technologically advanced and competitive globally."

한글번역

대학원생으로서 (성공)의 심리를 탐구하기 시작할 때, 나는 사업, 예술, 운동, 저널리즘, 학계, 의학, 법률 분야의 리더들을 인터뷰하고 있었다. 당신 분야의 최고 사람들은 누구인가요? 그들은 어떤 사람들인가요? 그들을 특별하게 만드는 것은 무엇이라고 생각하나요? 이 인터뷰에서 드러난 몇 가지 특징들은 매우 분야별로 특정돼 있었다. 예를 들어, 여러 비즈니스 인사들은 재정적 위험을 감수하는 욕구를 언급했다. "수백만 달러에 대한 계산된 결정을 내리고도 밤에 잠을 잘 수 있어야 합니다." 하지만 예술가들에게는 이것이 전혀 중요하지 않은 것처럼 보였다. 대신에 창작 욕구를 언급했다. "나는 무언가를 만드는 것을 좋아합니다. 왜 그런지 모르겠지만, 그냥 좋아요." 반면에, 운동선수들은 다른 종류의 동기를 언급했는데, 그것은 승리하는 것에서 느끼는 전율이다. "승자는 다른 사람들과 정면으로 맞붙는 것을 좋아합니다. 승자는 패배를 싫어합니다."

이러한 특수성 외에도, 몇 가지 공통적 성격적 특질이 있었는데, 이것들이 나에게 아주 흥미로웠다. 어떤 분야에서든 가장 성공한 사람들은 운이 좋고 재능이 있었다. 나는 그것을 이전에 들었고, 의심하지 않았다. 하지만 성공 이야기는 거기서 끝나지 않았다. 내가 대화한(인터뷰한) 많은 (성공한) 사람들은 잠재력을 실현하기 전에 탈락하거나 흥미를 잃은 떠오르는 스타들의 이야기를 들려줬는데, 이것은 모든 사람이 놀랄 정도였다. 실패 후에도 계속 앞으로 나아가는 것이 매우 중요하고도 전혀 쉽지 않다는 것은 명확했다. "어떤 사람들은 일이 잘 풀릴 때는 훌륭하지만, 일이 잘 안 풀리면 무너져 버립니다." 이 인터뷰에서 묘사된 높은 성취자들은 정말로 끝까지 버텼다. "이 사람으로 말하자면, 처음에는 사실 최고의 작가가 아니었어요. 제 말은, 우리는 그의 이야기를 읽고 나서는, 글이 너무 서툴고 멜로 드라마 같아서 웃곤 했어요. 하지만 그는 점점 더 나아졌고, 작년에 구겐하임 상을 받았습니다." 그리고 이 성공한 사람들은 끊임없이 향상하려고 노력했다. "그녀는 절대 만족하지 않아요. 지금쯤이면 만족할 것 같지만, 그녀는 자기 자신에게 가장 가혹한 비평가입니다." 이 고도로 성취한 사람들은 끈기의 화신(귀감; 모범)이었다.

한글번역

포드 모델 T의 고향은 미시간주 하이랜드 파크에 있는 우드워드 애비뉴를 따라 있는 현재는 버려진 공장 단지인데, 디트로이트의 다른 산업 폐허지와 별로 다를 게 없는 곳이다. 하지만 이 건물 앞에 가 보면 1925년까지 하루에 9,000대 이상의 포드 모델 T가 이곳에서 생산됐다는 것을 알려주는 역사적 표지판을 볼 수 있다. 그 표지판은 이렇게 끝난다: "대량 생산은 이곳에서 곧 미국의 산업 모든 분야로 퍼져나갔고, 20세기 생활의 풍요로운 패턴을 세웠다." 실제로 그것은 (앞문장) 미국의 20세기 중산층이 급속하게 성장하는 데 큰 도움이 됐다.

1914년 1월은 디트로이트에서 매우 추운 달이었다. 2014년 1월처럼 매우 추웠지만, 수천 명이 쌀쌀한 날씨에도 불구하고 헨리 포드의 특별한 제안에 응하기 위해 밖에서 줄을 섰다: 하루 5달러, 북적거리는 공장에서 8시간 동안 일하는 것에 대해.

당시 평균 공장 임금의 두 배 이상이었고, 미국 노동자들에게는 20세기의 중요한 순간 중 하나였다. 1914년의 5달러는 오늘날의 돈으로 대략 120달러에 해당한다. 많은 경제학자들이 오늘날의 고용주들이 포드에게서 배울 점이 있다고 말하지만, 동시에 그 학자들은 2014년은 미국 기업과 노동자들에게 완전히 다른 세상이라고 말한다. 헨리 포드는 냉혹한 사업가였다. 그는 좋은 사람이어서 5달러 근무제를 도입한 게 아니었다. 그는 그런 사람이 전혀 아니었다.

기업 역사학자인 밥 크레이프키는 포드가 1914년 1월에 이것이 현명한 결정이라고 생각한 이유를 이해하려면 몇 달 전 일어난 또 다른 큰 변화를 돌아봐야 한다고 말한다. 1913년까지 모델 T의 생산량은 200,000대에 달했고, 이는 최초의 이동 조립 라인의 창설로 가능해진 일이었다. 컨베이어 벨트가 작은 부품들을 작업자들에게 운반했고, 각 작업자는 특정 작업을 수행했다. 이는 생산 속도를 엄청나게 가속화했지만, 포드에게는 여전히 문제가 있었다. 생산을 표준화했지만, 노동력을 표준화하지 못한 것이었다. 이제 그는 특별히 숙련된 작업자가 필요하지 않았다; 그저 같은 반복적이고 특화된 작업을 매시간, 매일마다 수행할 작업자가 필요했다. 만성적인 결근과 높은 이직률이 있었다. 그는 노동력을 안정시킬 필요가 있었다. 그래서 포드는 더 높은 임금이 더 나은, 더 신뢰할 수 있는 노동자를 유인할 것이라고 생각했다. 이는 절대적으로 완전히 성공했다. 사실, 그것은 누구도 예상치 못한 일이었다. 이점은 거의 즉각적이었다. 생산성이 급상승했고, 포드 자동차 회사는 2년 이내에 이익을 두 배로 늘렸다. 포드는 결국 이것을 그가 만든 최고의 비용 절감 조치라고 불렀다.

헨리 포드가 임금을 올린 이유가 직원들이 자신이 만든 차를 살 수 있을 만큼 충분한 임금을 지급하려는 것이었다는 것은 널리 알려져 있다. 포드의 주된 동기는 아니었지만, 이는 환영할 만한 부수적인 효과였고, 게임 체인저였다고 버클리 캘리포니아 대학교의 노동 경제학자 할리 셰이켄은 말했다. "그것이 우리에게 준 것은 산업 중산층과 소비자 수요에 의해 구동되는 경제였다"라고 셰이켄은 말했다.

오늘날, 대다수의 고용주들은 최저 임금을 가장 경쟁력 있는 임금으로 간주한다. 요즘에는 글로벌 공급망이 초경쟁적인 자동차 산업을 먹여 살리고, 누구도 조금의 여유도 주고 싶어 하지 않으며, 기술을 따라잡는 것이 노동력 안정보다 우선시된다. 이는 더 이상 헨리 포드의 경제가 아니다.

제52회 모의고사

1

하위내용영역	배점	예상정답률
일반영어 A형 서술형	4점	45%

모범답안 The word is "myth". Second, he argues that the secrets for living a long time are useless because they have no good scientific value and are full of crazy ideas.

채점기준

+ 2점: 빈칸에 들어갈 단어를 "myth"라 기입하였다. 이외에는 답이 될 수 없다.
+ 2점: 슈와츠 박사가 주장하는 바를 "the secrets for living a long time are useless because they have no good scientific value and are full of crazy ideas"라 서술하였거나 유사하였다.

☞ 다음과 같이 서술하였어도 맞는 것으로 한다.

- "He argues that the supposed scientific claims behind treatments to reverse aging and prolong life are unfounded and not credible. He describes these claims as being completely baseless and filled with nonsensical ideas."

한글번역

와인은 시간이 지날수록 좋아지지만, 인간의 몸은 그렇지 않다. 우리는 나이가 들면서 쇠퇴한다. 주름과 백발이 생기고, 피부는 얇아지고 더 쉽게 멍이 들며, 시력과 청력이 감소하고 백내장이 생기며, 혈압이 상승하고, 골밀도가 감소하고, 힘과 민첩성이 감소하며, 허리가 두꺼워지고, 관절염에 걸리며, 기억력이 감퇴하고, 키가 1-2인치 줄어들 수 있다. 우리는 배우고 생각하는 속도가 느려지고, 반응 시간이 줄어들며, 성 기능이 변하고 호르몬 수치가 떨어지며, 암과 당뇨병과 같은 노화와 관련된 질병에 걸릴 가능성이 높아진다.

플로리다주 세인트 오거스틴에서는 $18.00의 입장료를 내고 폰세 데 레온의 젊음의 샘 고고학 공원을 방문할 수 있다. 그곳에서 기적의 물을 한 모금 마실 수 있다. 당신은 조금 젊어진 기분이 들 수 있지만 그것은 당신이 믿고 암시를 받기 쉬운 사람이거나 단지 목이 말랐기 때문일 수 있다. 이 샘은 역사적으로는 흥미로울 수 있지만, 치료적인 가치는 없다.

누구든지 그 물을 마시거나 목욕하면 젊어지는 샘은 선사 시대부터 전해 내려오는 (신화)이다. 헤로도토스는 기원전 5세기에 그것에 대해 썼다. 스페인 정복자 폰세 데 레온은 플로리다에 도착한 최초의 유럽 탐험가였다. 스페인 왕은 그에게 '베니미 섬'을 찾기 위한 원정을 이끌도록 허가했으며, 그는 처음에 플로리다를 그 섬으로 착각했다. 그는 젊음의 샘을 찾고 있지 않았다. 그 신화는 그가 죽은 한참 후에나 그의 이름에 붙게 됐다. 그러나 그가 젊음의 샘을 마셨다고 해도 그는 여전히 죽었을 것이다.

희망은 영원히 솟아나고 역사는 반복된다. 오늘날에는 젊음의 샘의 현대적인 버전이 무수히 많다. 식이 보충제와 기타 치료법은 노화의 영향을 되돌리고 수명을 연장한다고 주장된다. 그들의 홍보자들은 과학이 그 뒤에 있다고 주장한다. 실제로는, 그것들은 단지 더 많은 신화일 뿐이다. 백세 장수자들은 장수의 비결을 공유한다; 그것들은 모두 다르다. 인간을 젊게 유지하거나 더 오래 살게 하는 치료법은 입증된 적이 없다. 맥길 대학의 과학과 사회 사무소의 조 슈와츠 박사는 이렇게 말했다: "그 과학은 모두 허구이며, 터무니없는 생각으로 가득 차 있다."

2

하위내용영역	배점	예상정답률
일반영어 A형 서술형	4점	55%

모범답안 It means that the consecutive records for hottest months are due to an overall changing climate, not mere chance. Second, they increase allergy symptoms, lung inflammation along with worse asthma symptoms. Third, the word is "poor".

채점기준

+ 2점 : 밑줄 친 부분의 의미를 "the consecutive records for hottest months are due to an overall changing climate, not mere chance"라 서술하였거나 유사하였다.

☞ 다음과 같이 서술하였어도 맞는 것으로 한다.
  - "It means that the repeated occurrence of record-high temperatures in July 2019, January 2020, and May 2020 is not happening by chance. Instead, it indicates a consistent and predictable trend, which in this context is the ongoing and systematic increase in global temperatures due to climate change."

+ 1점 : 상승된 이산화탄소 수치가 야기하는 글에 언급되는 모든 공공 건강 결과를 "they ① increase allergy symptoms, ② lung inflammation along ③ with worse asthma symptoms"라 서술하였거나 유사하였다.

☞ 3개 중 2개만 서술했으면 0.5점, 나머지는 0점을 준다.

+ 1점 : 빈칸에 들어갈 단어를 "poor"라 기입하였다. 이것 외에는 답이 될 수 없다.

한글번역

산불 시즌이 맹렬히 시작됐다. 뜨거운 여름이 가뭄을 악화시키고 식물을 말리면서 산불이 번지기에 이상적인 환경을 조성하고 있다. 하지만 이것은 지구 온난화의 한 가지 결과일 뿐이다. 지구 온난화는 홍수, 폭우, 그리고 열사병으로 인한 사망도 초래하고 있다. 사실, 기후 위기는 광범위한 공중 보건 위기를 초래했다.

나는 7월 폭염 동안 예약 시간에 늦게 온 환자를 생생하게 기억한다. 내가 들어갔을 때 그녀는 "정말 죄송해요. 밤새 기차역 주변을 손주와 함께 걸었어요."라고 말했다. 집에 에어컨이 없어서 더위 속에서 아이가 옷이 땀으로 범벅돼 탈수 위험에 처해 있었다.

2019년 7월은 기록상 가장 더운 7월이었고, 2020년 1월은 기록상 가장 더운 1월이었으며, 2020년 5월도 기록상 가장 더운 5월이었다. 이것은 우연이 아니다. 이것은 패턴이다. 지구 온난화에 기여하는 중요한 온실가스인 이산화탄소는 2005년 이후 9% 증가했으며, 1950년 이후로는 31% 증가했다. 유엔 기후변화에 관한 정부간 패널(IPCC) 특별 보고서는 세계가 이미 산업화 이전 수준에서 약 1도 상승했음을 지적하며, 온난화를 1.5도로 제한하기 위해 행동의 긴급성을 강조하고, 2도 상승은 전 세계적으로 전례 없는 극심한 더위, 물 부족, 식량 부족을 초래할 것이라고 경고했다.

내 진료실에서는 환자들에게 기후 위기가 그들의 건강에 미치는 영향을 설명한다. 예를 들어, 이산화탄소 농도가 상승하면 광합성 비율이 높아지면서 식물이 생산하는 꽃가루의 양이 증가한다. 꽃가루 규모의 증가는 알레르기 증상을 악화시킬 수 있다. 또 다른 예는 공기 오염과 관련된 미세 입자(일명 PM2.5)로, 대부분 화석 연료의 연소와 관련이 있으며, 이는 온난화를 촉진시킨다. 우리가 이 입자들을 흡입하면, 그것들은 기도를 통해 내려가 폐의 작은 공기 주머니인 폐포에 쌓여 염증을 일으키고 천식 증상을 악화시킬 수 있다.

더욱 나쁜 것은, 이러한 해악은 가난한 사람들에게 불균형적으로 영향을 미친다. 북미에 사는 부유한 사람들은 저소득층 주민들보다 1인당 탄소 발자국이 25% 더 높으며, 일부 부유한 교외 지역은 인근 지역보다 15배 더 많은 이산화탄소를 배출한다. 이러한 탄소 배출은 지구 온난화에 기여하며, 그로 인한 건강상의 결과는 배기가스를 발생시키는 지역을 훨씬 넘어 영향을 미친다. 유색인종과 가난한 지역 사회는 기후 변화의 건강 영향에 평균적으로 회복력이 덜하다.

3

하위내용영역	배점	예상정답률
일반영어 B형 서술형	4점	35%

모범답안 There are differences between procrastination and pre-crastination in terms of productivity and creativity. Procrastinators are easily distracted, seek instant gratification, and require willpower to overcome these distractions. Pre-crastinators, however, strive to start and complete tasks immediately and struggle with not working. A study found that procrastinators were rated more creative in companies. In conclusion, thus, procrastination can lead to more creative output.

채점 기준

ⓐ Topic sentence
+ 1점: "There are differences between procrastination and pre-crastination in terms of productivity and creativity"를 명확하게 서술하였다.

ⓑ Major supporting details
+ 2점: "① Procrastinators are easily distracted, seek instant gratification, and require willpower to overcome these distractions. ② Pre-crastinators, however, strive to start and complete tasks immediately and struggle with not working. ③ A study found that procrastinators were rated more creative in companies"을 명확하게 서술하였다.
☞ 3개 중 3개 모두 정확하게 요약했으면 2점, 2개만 요약했으면 1점, 나머지는 0점을 준다.

ⓒ Conclusion
+ 1점: "In conclusion, thus, procrastination can lead to more creative output."를 명확하게 서술하였거나 유사하였다.

감점
• 본문에 나오는 연속되는 6단어 이상을 사용하였다. −0.5pt
• 문단을 두 개나 그 이상으로 구성하였다. −0.5pt
• 문법이나 영어 표현을 합쳐 3개 이상 오류가 있다. −0.5pt

✚ 보충설명

The phrase "requiring epic all-nighters to finish papers and prepare for tests" means that because of procrastination, college students often have to stay up all night, putting in an intense and prolonged effort, to complete their assignments and study for their exams at the last minute.

The phrase "We can only guess how much higher the estimate would be if more of them got around to filling out the survey" means that the reported percentage of adults who are chronic procrastinators might actually be higher than the current estimate because many of these individuals may have procrastinated or neglected to complete the survey themselves.

The phrase "procrastinators, on the other hand, are at the mercy of an Instant Gratification Monkey who inhabits their brains, constantly asking questions like 'Why would we ever use a computer for work when the Internet is sitting right there waiting to be played with?'" means that procrastinators are often controlled by a part of their mind that seeks immediate pleasure and satisfaction. This "Instant Gratification Monkey" metaphorically represents the internal voice that distracts them from work by suggesting **more enjoyable activities, like browsing the internet, instead of completing tasks**.

The sentence "while pre-crastinators are steadily productive, using one's whole time for a project might be a boon in a creative undertaking" means that although pre-crastinators consistently make progress and complete tasks early, allowing the entire allotted time for a project, as procrastinators often do, can actually be beneficial for creativity. This suggests that taking more time can lead to more original and innovative ideas.

제53회 모의고사

1

하위내용영역	배점	예상정답률
일반영어 A형 서술형	4점	50%

모범답안 The word is "selfishness". Second, he argues that using non-selfish oriented motives can be effective for a whole group.

채점기준

+ 2점 : 빈칸에 "selfishness"라 정확하게 답하였다. 이외에는 답이 될 수 없다.

+ 2점 : 디에고 리베라의 벽화를 통해 저자가 주장하는 바를 "using non-selfish oriented(other-regarding) motives can be effective for a whole group"라 서술하였거나 유사하였다.

☞ 다음과 같이 서술하였어도 2점을 준다.
  — "(He argues that) organizations can motivate workers more effectively by appealing to their desire to do good work and sense of mutual obligation rather than relying solely on economic incentives."

한글번역

어느 쪽이 창의성에 더 도움이 될까: 미루기(procrastination)와 조기 완수(pre-crastination)? 우리는 미루기를 저주로 생각한다. 80% 이상의 대학생들이 미루는 습관에 시달리는데, 그래서 과제를 끝낸다든가, 시험을 준비하기 위해서는 꼬박 밤샘 작업을 해야 한다. 대략 20%의 성인이 만성적인 미루기 습관을 보고한다. (이 만성적으로 미루기를 하는 사람들이) 설문조사를 작성하기 위해 시간을 낸다면 이 추정치가 얼마나 더 높아질지는 미루어 짐작할 수 있다. 미루기는 생산성에는 악덕이지만, 창의성에는 미덕이다. (하지만) 반대로, 나는 항상 가치 있는 일이라면 빨리 하는 것이 좋다고 믿어왔다. 대학원에서 나는 논문을 2년 앞당겨 제출했다. 대학에서는 논문을 몇 주 일찍 쓰고, 졸업 논문은 기한보다 4개월 일찍 마쳤다. 내 룸메이트들은 내가 생산적인 형태의 강박 장애를 가지고 있다고 농담했다. 심리학자들은 내 상태를 설명하는 용어를 만들어냈다 : 조기 완수.

조기 완수는 작업을 즉시 시작하고 가능한 빨리 끝내려는 충동이다. 진지한 조기 완수자라면 진전이 산소와 같고, 연기는 고통이다. 이메일이 한꺼번에 도착해도 즉시 답하지 않으면 인생이 통제 불능으로 느껴진다. 다음 달에 연설을 해야 하는데 매일 작업하지 않으면 점점 공허한 느낌이 든다. 하지만 미루는 사람들은 뇌에 살고 있는 '즉각적인 만족 원숭이'의 지배를 받으며, "인터넷이 바로 거기서 우리를 기다리고 있는데 왜 컴퓨터로 일을 하겠어?" 같은 질문을 끊임없이 한다. 미루는 사람이라면 그 원숭이를 극복하는 데 엄청난 의지가 필요할 수 있다. 하지만 조기 완수자도 일을 하지 않기 위해 똑같은 의지가 필요할 수 있다.

그런데, 몇 년 전, 나의 가장 창의적인 학생 중 한 명인 써니 박은 내 신속한 습관에 의문을 제기했다. 그녀는 미루기를 한 후에 가장 독창적인 아이디어가 떠오른다고 말했다. 증명해 보라고 도전하자, 그녀는 몇몇 회사에 접근해 사람들에게 얼마나 자주 미루는지 설문조사하고, 상사들에게 그들의 창의성을 평가하게 했다. 미루는 사람들이 조기 완수자보다 훨씬 높은 창의성 점수를 받았다. 요컨대, 조기 완수자는 꾸준히 생산적이지만, 프로젝트에 주어진 시간을 모두 사용하는 것이 창의적 작업에 있어서는 도움이 될 수 있다는 것이다.

한글번역

세계적으로 저명한 미국 경제학자 새뮤얼 보울스는 최근 인간이 이기심과 자기 소득을 극대화하려는 욕구에 의해 동기부여되는 방식과 이타심 및 좋은 일을 하고 타인에게 좋은 평판을 얻으려는 욕구에 의해 동기부여되는 방식을 비교해 연구했다. 실제 세계에서 이뤄진 실험들은 전통적 경제 이론과는 달리, 시장 유인이 협력을 파괴하며 대부분의 경우 이타적 행동보다 비효율적이라는 점을 보여준다. 사람들은 단지 물질적 이익만을 위해 행동하지 않으며, 동시에 스스로를 존엄하고 자율적이며 도덕적인 인간으로 만들기 위해 행동한다.

행동경제학 실험들은 경제적 유인이 오히려 역효과를 낼 수 있다는 점을 시사한다. 특히 이러한 유인이 이기적인 반응이 타당하다는 신호로 작용하고, 사람들이 이타적으로 행동하게 만드는 도덕적 가치를 약화시킬 경우 그렇다. 보울스는 이와 관련된 사례로 이스라엘 하이파의 한 보육시설을 제시한다. 이곳에서는 아이를 늦게 데리러 오는 부모들에게 벌금을 부과했다. 그러나 부모들은 지각을 피하기보다는 지각률을 두 배로 늘려 응답했다. 12주 뒤 벌금이 철회됐지만, 부모들의 지각 빈도는 줄지 않고 그대로 유지됐다. 보울스에 따르면, 이는 경제적 유인과 도덕적 행위 사이에 발생하는 일종의 부정적 상승작용(negative synergy)을 보여준다. 벌금은 부모들이 교사에게 불편을 주지 않기 위해 시간을 지키려 했던 도덕적 책임감을 약화시켰고, 대신 지각을 일종의 '구매 가능한 상품'으로 여기게 만들었다.

보울스는 대부분의 사회 구성원 중 상당수가 도덕적 규범을 자발적으로 따르며, 타인에게 기꺼이 베풀고, 적절한 행동 기준을 위반한 사람들을 물질적 보상 없이, 심지어 자기 희생을 감수하면서도 처벌한다는 사실을 보여준다. 디에고 리베라가 포드사의 리버 루즈(River Rouge) 조립공장에서 일하는 노동자들을 그린 벽화는, 조직이 구성원들에게 일을 잘하려는 욕망이나 구성원 간의 상호 책임 의식과 같은 타인지향적 동기를 통해 어떻게 동기를 부여하는지를 시각적으로 보여준다.

한글번역

훌륭한 일을 해내기 위해서는 타고난 재능과 결단력이 모두 필요하다는 사실을 모두가 알고 있다. 하지만 사람들이 잘 인식하지 못하는 세 번째 요소가 있다. 그것은 바로 어떤 특정한 주제에 대한 집요할 정도의 관심이다.

이 점을 설명하기 위해, 나는 어떤 사람들 집단에 내 평판을 좀 깎아 먹을 필요가 있는데, 그 대상으로 버스 승차권 수집가들을 택하겠다. 오래된 버스표를 모으는 사람들이 있다. 많은 수집가들이 그렇듯, 그들은 자신이 수집하는 대상의 사소한 세부사항에 대해 집착에 가까운 관심을 가진다. 그들은 우리가 기억하기조차 어려운 다양한 종류의 버스표들 사이의 미세한 차이를 구별한다. 왜냐하면 우리는 거기에 별 관심이 없기 때문이다. 대체 옛날 버스표에 대해 그렇게 많은 시간을 들여 생각하는 게 무슨 의미가 있는가?

바로 여기서, 이 집착의 두 번째 특징으로 이어진다. 의미가 없다는 것이다. 버스표 수집가의 애정은 '이해타산적이지 않다'. 그들은 남을 감동시키거나 부자가 되기 위해 그런 일을 하는 것이 아니라, 그 자체를 위해 한다.

위대한 성과를 이룬 사람들의 삶을 들여다보면, 일정한 패턴이 보인다. 그들은 종종 동시대인들이 보기에는 아무런 의미 없어 보이는 것에, 버스표 수집가처럼 집요한 관심을 보이는 것에서 시작했다. 다윈이 비글호 항해에 대해 쓴 책에서 가장 인상적인 점 중 하나는, 자연사에 대한 그의 깊고도 끝없는 관심이다. 그의 호기심은 마치 무한해 보인다. 라마누잔도 마찬가지였다. 그는 몇 시간이고 슬레이트 앞에 앉아 수열을 다루며 계산을 했다.

그들이 나중에 발견하게 될 것들에 대한 '기반을 다지고 있었다'고 생각하는 것은 오해다. 그 은유에는 지나치게 많은 '계획된 의도'가 담겨 있다.

2

하위내용영역	배점	예상정답률
일반영어 A형 서술형	4점	45%

모범답안 The words are "obsessive interest". Second, it means that these two were not intending to reach any success, but were following their own interest in the subject.

채점기준

+ 2점: 빈칸에 들어갈 단어를 "obsessive interest"라 기입하였다. 이외에는 답이 될 수 없다.
+ 2점: 밑줄 친 부분의 의미를 "these two(Darwin and Ramanujan) were not intending to reach any success, but were following their own interest in the subject"라 서술하였거나 유사하였다.

3

하위내용영역	배점	예상정답률
일반영어 A형 서술형	4점	30%

모범답안 The words are "low doses". Second, it can be inferred that currently, doctors have very limited treatment options for radiation sickness and must resort to risky, desperate measures like bone-marrow therapy only when patients face almost certain death.

채점 기준

+ **2점**: 빈칸에 들어갈 단어를 "low doses"라 기입하였다. 이외에는 답이 될 수 없다.
+ **2점**: 추론할 수 있는 내용을 "currently, doctors have very limited treatment options for radiation sickness and must resort to risky, desperate measures like bone-marrow therapy only when patients face almost certain death"라 서술하였거나 유사하였다.

한글번역

히로시마와 나가사키 이후 오랜 세월 동안, 전리 방사선의 영향에 관한 연구는 당연히 갑작스럽게 전신이 노출된 경우의 결과에 집중돼 있었다. 그러나 원자력에 대한 의존이 점점 증가할 것으로 예상되는 세계에서, 낮은 선량이 서서히 흡수되는 경우의 궁극적 영향에 대한 보다 충분한 이해가 분명히 필요하게 됐다. 미국 과학아카데미에서 발표된 세 개의 새로운 보고서는 이러한 만성적인 영향에 대한 연구가 확대되고 있음을 보여준다. 이들 영향은 연구하기 매우 어렵기 때문이다.

방사선과 백혈병 사이의 연관성에 대한 연구는 다른 조사들보다 더 정밀하게 이뤄져 왔다. 그 이유는 백혈병처럼 치명적인 질병은 사망률 비교에 적합하기 때문이다. 반면, 방사선의 또 다른 가능성 있는 영향인 조기 노화의 경우, 그 변화가 미묘하고 불확정적이기 때문에 평가하기가 훨씬 어렵다. 게다가 생리적 노화 자체에 대한 이해도 아직 불완전하다. 역학적 조사—대규모 동물 실험과 저선량 방사선에 노출되는 직업을 가진 사람들을 대상으로 한 전향적 연구—는 평균 기대수명이 감소하는지를 밝혀낼 수 있는 상호 보완적인 방법들이다. 그러나 너무 많은 변수들이 얽혀 있어 그 해답을 얻기까지는 매우 오랜 시간이 걸릴 수 있으며, 동물 실험 데이터를 인간에게 적용하는 데에도 많은 불확실성이 존재한다. 전향적 연구(앞으로 일어날 사건이나 결과를 추적하고 관찰하는 방식의 연구. 즉, 연구 대상 집단을 미래에 걸쳐 관찰하면서 특정 변수(예: 방사선 노출)가 건강이나 행동에 어떤 영향을 미치는지를 살펴보는 것이다.)의 장점 중 하나는 미국과 영국의 대부분의 원자력 기관과 엑스레이 부서들이 직원들의 건강과 방사선 노출 기록을 꼼꼼히 관리하고 있다는 점이다. 표본이 클수록 연구의 유효성은 높아진다. 만약 전 세계적으로 측정 및 기록 방식에 공통된 기준을 적용할 수 있다면, 매우 가치 있는 정보를 얻을 수 있을 것이다. 다양한 기록 방식 때문에 간접적으로밖에 비교할 수 없을 경우에는 감춰져 있을 수 있는 차이점들이, 표준화된 조건 하에서는 드러나고 중요한 새로운 아이디어를 제시할 수도 있다. (전 세계에서 방사선 노출이나 건강 관련 데이터를 서로 다른 방식으로 기록하면, 그 데이터들 간의 비교는 간접적일 수밖에 없고 미묘한 차이들은 감춰질 수 있다. 그러나 기록 방식과 측정 방법을 통일(표준화)하면, 그동안 드러나지 않았던 차이점이 명확하게 드러나고, 이는 새로운 과학적 통찰이나 가설을 제시할 가능성이 있다는 뜻이다.) 이러한 가능성을 탐색하기 위해 방사선 의학 및 역학 전문가들이 국제 회의를 열어야 할 당위성이 존재한다. 급성 방사선 증후군에 대한 최선의 치료법은 대부분의 경우에 대해 일반적으로 합의돼 있다. 논란이 있는 유일한 지점은 골수 치료의 효과에 관한 것이다. 방사선으로 인해 면역 반응이 거의 완전히 억제된 경우, 골수 이식을 통해 조혈계의 일시적인 기능 정지를 극복할 수 있을지도 모른다. 그러나 이식된 조직이 이물 반응을 일으켜, 중증 환자에게 치명적인 결과를 초래할 위험도 있다. 만약 방사선의 선량이 환자의 생존 가능성이 거의 없는 수준으로 높다는 것이 명확하다면, 어떤 수단이라도 시도해 보는 것이 정당화될 수 있다. 일부 전문가들은 이러한 경우에 골수 치료를 적용해야 한다고 권고한다. 현재까지의 지식에 따르면 이는 합리적인 조언이다. 그러나 실험 연구가 진전되어 향후 임상적으로 더 많은 선택지가 가능해지기를 기대할 만하다.

4

하위내용영역	배점	예상정답률
일반영어 A형 서술형	4점	45%

모범답안 The students are told to have a designated place at home to study and are each given a pencil box. Second, it is implied the teacher suspects that the family is not following her idea for at-home learning, and also needs financial support.

채점 기준

+ 2점: 교사에 의해서 모든 학생들에게 주어진 충고와 후원을 "The students are told to have a designated place at home to study and are given a pencil box (or supplies)"라 서술하였거나 유사하였다.
+ 2점: 슈아의 가족에 대한 교사의 의심에 관련하여 추론할 수 있는 것을 "the teacher suspects that the family is not following her idea for at-home learning, and also needs financial support"라 서술하였거나 유사하였다.

한글번역

학교에서 'Back to School Night(학부모 초청의 밤)' 행사가 열리는 날이었다. 그래디 선생님은 여름 방학 동안, 학생들이 집에서 더 좋은 학습 습관을 기를 수 있도록 돕겠다고 결심했다. 그날 많은 학부모들이 그녀의 교실을 찾아왔고, 그녀는 학생들이 집에서 공부할 수 있는 지정된 장소를 마련하고 학습 도구를 정리해 두는 것이 얼마나 중요한지 설명했다.

학생들의 동기를 높이기 위해, 그래디 선생님은 각 학생이 집에 가져갈 수 있도록 필통을 하나씩 준비했다. 그녀는 그 안에 연필과 펜 같은 필기구를 가득 채워 넣었다. 학생 중 한 명인 슈아는 그 필통을 특히 기뻐했다. 슈아의 부모가 학부모 행사 때 그녀의 제안에 긍정적으로 반응했던 것이 떠올라, 그래디 선생님도 기대에 차 있었다.

그러나 새 학년이 시작된 지 한 달쯤 지났을 무렵, 그래디 선생님은 슈아가 제출하는 숙제에 음식 얼룩이 묻어 있는 것을 발견했다. 또 그는 답을 고칠 때 지우개로 지우는 대신 줄을 그어 지우고 있었다. 선생님이 그 이유를 묻자, 슈아는 형제들이 그의 연필과 펜을 함께 쓰고 있다고 설명했다. 그들은 필기구를 제자리에 돌려놓지 않아서, 그는 지우개를 쓸 수 없는 상황이 생겼다고 말했다.

"그럼 음식 얼룩은 왜 있는 거니?" 그래디 선생님이 물었다. 슈아는 형과 함께 부엌 식탁에서 숙제를 하는데, 때로 다른 가족들이 식사를 하고 있는 동안에도 그 자리에서 공부한다고 설명했다.

그래디 선생님은 슈아의 사정을 안타깝게 여겼고, 그의 이름이 적힌 새 필기도구 세트를 다시 마련해 줬다. 그러면서 "식탁 말고 조용하고 따로 있는 공간에서 공부하고, 필통도 식탁에 두지 말고 잘 보관하렴"이라고 당부했다. 슈아는 고개를 끄덕였다.

하지만 몇 주가 지나도 숙제 상태에는 큰 변화가 없었다. 그래디 선생님은 다시 슈아에게 공부하는 장소와 형제들이 아직도 그의 필기구를 쓰는지 물었다. 슈아는 불편한 기색을 보이며 대답했다. "아직도 식탁에서 공부하고 있고, 가끔 형제들이 제 물건을 써요." 그래디 선생님은 그의 솔직함에 고맙다고 말했다.

그날 수업이 끝난 후, 그래디 선생님은 다가오는 학부모 상담 때 슈아의 부모에게 이 문제를 어떻게 이야기해야 할지 고민했다. 그녀는 부모가 처음에는 그녀의 기대에 동의하는 것처럼 보였지만, 실제로는 집에서 이를 실천하지 않았을 수도 있다는 생각에 걱정이 들었다. 만약 부모가 공부 공간과 같은 기본적인 제안조차 지지하지 않는다면, 집에서 학습을 도울 수 있는 그녀의 다른 아이디어들도 받아들이지 않을 가능성이 있다는 생각이 들었다. 또 슈아의 형제들이 그의 학용품을 함께 쓰는 것으로 보아, 혹시 그 가족이 학용품이나 생필품이 부족한 상황일지도 모른다는 판단에, 지역 지원 단체의 도움을 연결해 줄 필요가 있을 수도 있다고 생각했다.

답답한 마음을 안은 채, 그녀는 짐을 챙기고 학교를 나섰다.

제54회 모의고사

1

하위내용영역	배점	예상정답률
일반영어 A형 서술형	4점	45%

모범답안 The word is "soap". Second, the writer mentions the Amish because they show how we can develop more resistance by being raised away from(=being raised removed from) highly sanitized environments.

채점기준

+ 2점 : 빈칸에 들어갈 단어를 "soap"라 기입하였다. 이외에는 답이 될 수 없다.
+ 2점 : 저자가 아미쉬 아이들을 언급한 이유를 "because <u>they show how we can develop more resistance(less vulnerability) by being raised away from highly sanitized environments</u>"라 서술하였거나 유사하였다.
  ☞ 다음과 같이 서술하였어도 맞는 것으로 한다.
  — "The writer mentions Amish children as an example of farm kids who are less prone to allergies compared to children raised in highly sanitized environments, supporting the argument that excessive cleanliness can make immune systems overreact when exposed to microbes."

한글번역

톰 라빈이라는 의사는 수년 전부터 샤워를 끊었다. 그는 가끔 머리에 물을 뿌리긴 하지만, 샴푸나 미국 욕실 선반을 가득 채운 각종 세정 제품들은 전혀 사용하지 않는다.

그의 고백은 점잖은 사람들 앞에서 종종 힌덴버그 참사(1937년 5월 6일, 독일의 대형 비행선 LZ 129 힌덴버그 호가 미국 뉴저지주 레이크허스트(Lakehurst) 해군 항공기지에 착륙하던 중 폭발 및 화재로 추락한 사건이다. 이 사고는 비행선 시대의 종말을 상징하며, 대중교통 수단으로서의 비행선 기술에 대한 신뢰를 결정적으로 무너뜨렸다.)처럼 받아들여진다. 이는 우리가 얼마나 표면적인 청결 개념에 집착하고 있는지, 그리고 그 개념을 부정하는 데 얼마나 주저하는지를 드러낸다. 그러나 라빈은 "정기적으로 몸을 닦아야 한다"는 상식처럼 들리는 생각이 단순하고 근시안적이라고 본다. 우리가 비누를 잔뜩 묻힌 샤워 타월로 기름기 있는 피부(=pelt)를 문지를 때, 실제로는 피부 표면의 상호의존적인 미생물 세계, 즉 마이크로바이옴을 파괴하고 있다는 것이다. 라빈은 이렇게 쓴다. "우리가 몸을 씻을 때, 적어도 일시적으로는 미생물 군집을 변화시킨다. 그것은 곧 미생물을 제거하거나, 그들이 사용할 수 있는 자원을 변화시키는 것이다." 다시 말해, 샤워 직후의 그 상쾌한 느낌을 좇는 행위는, 질병으로부터 우리를 보호하고 외부 침입자를 막기 위해 진화가 마련한 최고의 전략 중 하나를 방해하는 셈이다. 이러한 맥락은 특히 두드러기나 발진 같은 피부 증상이 동반되는 코로나19 시대에 더욱 중요하다.

라빈은 우리가 왜 이처럼 세정제와 피부용 화장품에 집착하게 됐는지 그 기원을 추적하며, 수백 년 전 시작된 "청결은 곧 경건함" 운동을 생생하게 되짚는다. 흑사병이나 다른 전염병이 창궐한 뒤, 개인의 청결 상태는 그 사람이 위험한 존재인지 아닌지를 판단하는 지표로 여겨졌다. 위생 상태는 사회적 지위의 대리 지표가 됐고, '더 청결할수록 더 낫다'는 생각이 지배적이 됐다.

그 후, 전염(오염)물질에 대한 불신과 세정제가 질병 확산을 막는다는 사실의 발견이 결합되면서, 20세기 초에는 비누를 생명을 구하는 도덕적 필수품으로 포장한 마케팅 캠페인이 등장했다.

그러나 이런 비누 홍보자들이 간과한 점은, 우리 몸에 공생하는 미생물들을 제거하면 오히려 예상치 못한 질환에 더 취약해질 수 있다는 사실이다. 예를 들어 아토피 피부염(eczema)의 일차 치료는 항생제 연고, 세정제, 그리고 면역 반응을 억제하는 약물 등인데, 연구자들은 이러한 방식이 장기적으로는 증상을 악화시킬 수 있다고 지적한다. 세정이나 긁기 등으로 피부 장벽이 손상되면, 미생물 군집이 교란되며, 이것이 면역계를 자극해 피부세포가 과도하게 증식하고 염증성 단백질로 가득 차는 현상을 유발할 수 있다.

이러한 관찰은 오래전부터 알려진 사실과도 일치한다. 고도로 살균된 환경에서 자란 아이들이, 아미쉬(Amish) 농장 아이들보다 알레르기에 더 취약하다는 점이다. 몸의 미생물 환경을 너무 지나치게 정리해버리면, 아직 제대로 단련되지 않은 면역 체계가 과잉 반응을 일으킬 수 있다. 이런 면역 반응 과잉은 면역학자들이 말하는 '아토피 행진(Atopic March)'을 유발할 수 있다. 즉, 아토피 피부염, 음식 알레르기, 꽃가루 알레르기 등 한 가지 알레르기 질환이 다른 알레르기 질환으로 이어지는 연쇄 반응이 발생하는 것이다.

2

하위내용영역	배점	예상정답률
일반영어 A형 서술형	4점	45%

모범답안 The underlined "ironically" means that while trusting helps people learn to identify trustworthy individuals, this very benefit makes people hesitant to trust **because they focus on betrayal's visible pain** rather than its learning value. Second, "costs" best fits the blank.

채점기준

+ 2점: 밑줄 친 "ironically"의 의미를 "while trusting helps people learn to identify trustworthy individuals, this very benefit makes people hesitant to trust because they focus on betrayal's visible pain rather than its learning value."라 서술하였거나 유사하였다.

☞ 다음과 같이 서술하였어도 맞는 것으로 한다.

– "Ironically" means that while trusting helps people learn and become better at identifying trustworthy individuals, this very advantage creates a psychological barrier. People become hesitant to trust because they focus on the visible pain of betrayal rather than recognizing the learning value, even though more trusting would benefit them.

+ 2점: 빈칸에 들어갈 단어를 "costs"라 기입하였다. 이외에는 답이 될 수 없다.

한글번역

신뢰와 불신 사이의 정보 비대칭은 우리가 불신할 때보다 신뢰할 때 더 많은 것을 배운다는 것을 보여준다. 더 나아가, 우리가 누군가를 신뢰할 때는 특정한 개인에 대해서만 배우는 것이 아니라, 어떤 종류의 상황에서 신뢰해야 할지 또는 하지 말아야 할지를 더 일반적으로 배우게 된다. 우리는 점점 신뢰하는 데 능숙해진다.

새미 유와 그의 동료들은 신뢰하는 사람일수록 더 많은 학습적 이점을 얻는다는 사실을 실험을 통해 보여줬다. 그들의 실험은 일반적인 신뢰 게임과 유사했지만, 참가자들은 돈을 상대방에게 보낼지 말지를 결정하기 전에 서로 상호작용할 수 있는 기회가 있었다. 이 실험에서 가장 신뢰심이 높은 참가자들이 누구를 신뢰할 수 있을지, 혹은 누구에게 돈을 보내는 것이 좋을지를 더 잘 파악했다.

이와 같은 양상은 다른 영역에서도 나타난다. 언론을 더 신뢰하는 사람들은 정치와 뉴스에 대해 더 많이 알고 있으며, 과학을 더 신뢰하는 사람들은 과학적 소양이 더 높다. 물론 이들 사이의 관계는 인과가 아니라 상관관계 수준의 증거에 불과하지만, 더 많이 신뢰하는 사람이 누구를 신뢰해야 할지를 점점 더 잘 구분하게 된다는 것은 충분히 그럴듯한 주장이다. 신뢰도 다른 모든 것과 마찬가지로, 연습을 통해 숙련된다.

새미 유의 통찰은 우리에게 신뢰해야 할 이유를 제공한다. 그러나 여기서 역설이 발생한다. 신뢰는 학습의 기회를 제공하므로, 우리는 오히려 부족하게 신뢰하기보다는 지나치게 신뢰해야 마땅하다. 그런데도 현실에서는 그렇지 않다. 아이러니하게도, 우리가 신뢰해야 하는 이유—즉, 신뢰를 통해 더 많은 정보를 얻을 수 있다는 사실—때문에 오히려 신뢰를 꺼리게 되기도 한다.

(왜 그럴까?) 우리가 신뢰했다가 배신당할 경우, 그 비용은 매우 분명하고 고통스럽게 느껴진다. 그에 대한 반응은 짜증에서 분노, 절망에 이르기까지 다양하다. 반면, 그로부터 무엇을 배웠는지라는 이점은 쉽게 간과된다. 반대로, 사실은 신뢰할 수 있었던 사람을 신뢰하지 않았을 때의 비용은 대부분 보이지 않는다. 예를 들어, 어떤 지인을 집에 머물게 해줬다면 생겼을지도 모를 우정은 알 길이 없고, 동료가 추천한 소프트웨어를 써봤다면 얼마나 유익했을지를 우리는 결코 알 수 없다.

우리가 충분히 신뢰하지 않는 이유는, 신뢰에 실패했을 때의 대가는 너무 눈에 잘 띄는 반면, 잘못된 신뢰의 (학습적) 이익과 잘못된 불신의 대가는 대부분 드러나지 않기 때문이다. 우리는 이러한 숨겨진 비용과 이점들을 더 고려해야 한다. 신뢰를 통해 무엇을 배우는지, 누구와 우정을 맺을 수 있는지, 어떤 지식을 얻을 수 있는지를 생각해보자. 사람에게 기회를 주는 일은 도덕적으로 옳을 뿐 아니라, 이성적으로도 현명한 선택이다.

3

하위내용영역	배점	예상정답률
일반영어 B형 서술형	4점	50%

모범답안 There are various ways of animal communication, which challenge our conventional assumptions. First, animals use singing for mating calls and territorial warnings, while marine mammals produce sounds traveling hundreds of kilometers. Second, they employ body language through physical gestures, with dominant hyenas raising fur to display power and submissive ones crouching to show surrender. Third, distinctive coloring patterns like zebra stripes serve identification purposes and survival strategies during predator encounters. In conclusion, animals should be considered as more complex beings than previously thought.

채점 기준

ⓐ Topic sentence
+ 1점: "There are various ways of animal communication, (challenging our conventional assumptions about their capabilities)"를 명확하게 서술하였거나 유사하였다.

ⓑ Major supporting details
+ 2점: "① First, animals use singing for mating calls and territorial warnings, while marine mammals produce sounds traveling hundreds of kilometers. ② Second, they employ body language through physical gestures, with dominant hyenas raising fur to display power and submissive ones crouching to show surrender. ③ Third, distinctive coloring patterns like zebra stripes serve identification purposes and survival strategies during predator encounters."을 명확하게 서술하였다.

☞ 3개 중 3개 모두 정확하게 요약했으면 2점, 2개만 요약했으면 1점, 나머지는 0점을 준다.

ⓒ Conclusion
+ 1점: "In conclusion, animals should be considered as more complex beings than previously thought."을 명확하게 서술하였거나 유사하였다.

감점
- 본문에 나오는 연속되는 6단어 이상을 사용하였다. −0.5pt
- 문단을 두 개나 그 이상으로 구성하였다. −0.5pt
- 문법이나 영어 표현을 합쳐 3개 이상 오류가 있다. −0.5pt

제55회 모의고사

1

하위내용영역	배점	예상정답률
일반영어 A형 서술형	4점	45%

모범 답안 It would be attributed to engineers because it has to do with function and concerns the heating and cooling systems. Second, the word is "form".

채점 기준

+ 1점: 밑줄 친 부분에 있는 디자인의 예시가 어느 그룹과 밀접한가에 대해 "engineers"라 서술하였다. 이외에는 답이 될 수 없다.
+ 1점: 위와 같이 선택한 이유에 대해 "because it has to do with function and concerns the heating and cooling systems"라 서술하였거나 유사하였다.
+ 2점: 밑줄 친 부분의 의미에 가장 상응하는 한 단어를 "form"이라 서술하였다. 이외에는 답이 될 수 없다.

한글번역

동물들도 우리가 놀랄 만큼 다양한 방식으로 의사소통을 한다. 우리(인간)처럼, 동물들 간의 상호작용은 언어적일 수도 있고 비언어적일 수도 있다. 그중 노래는 동물들이 서로 소통하는 한 가지 방식이다. 예를 들어, 수컷 검은지빠귀(blackbird)는 멜로디가 풍부한 노래를 불러 암컷의 관심을 끌기도 한다. 이 노래들은 다양한 음정으로 구성돼 있으며, 여러 종류의 메시지를 암호화하고 있다. 또한 노래는 자신의 영역을 경고하고 다른 수컷 검은지빠귀를 쫓아내기 위한 수단으로도 쓰인다. 이 영역은 보통 그들이 거주하고 번식하는 장소이다. 큰 바다 포유류들도 노래를 부른다. 거대한 고래는 신음 소리나 끙끙거리는 소리를 내고, 크기가 작은 돌고래나 쇠돌고래는 핑(ping), 휘파람(whistle), 클릭(click) 소리를 낸다. 놀랍게도, 이러한 소리는 수백 킬로미터 떨어진 동료들에게도 전달될 수 있다.

노래 외에도, 몸짓 언어는 동물들의 중요한 의사소통 방식 중 하나이다. 예를 들어, 지배적인 하이에나는 목과 어깨의 털을 곤두세워 자신의 힘을 과시한다. 반면, 복종적인 하이에나는 고개를 숙이고 입술을 살짝 말아올려 이빨을 보이면서, 일종의 '우호적 미소'를 지으며 복종을 표현한다.

또한, 동물들에게서 가장 눈에 띄는 색상 역시 중요한 상호작용 수단이다. 예를 들어, 얼룩말의 검은색과 흰색이 교차된 줄무늬는 중요한 역할을 한다. 각 얼룩말은 고유한 줄무늬를 갖고 태어나기 때문에, 동료들은 서로를 쉽게 인식할 수 있다. 평온하게 풀을 뜯고 있을 때는 줄무늬가 가지런히 정렬돼, 무리에서 누가 누구인지 잘 구별할 수 있다. 하지만 배고픈 사자 같은 포식자가 접근하면, 얼룩말들은 사방으로 흩어지며 도망치고, 이로 인해 사자는 목표 대상을 정하기 어렵게 된다.

의사소통은 우리의 일상에서 빠질 수 없는 요소다. 우리는 서로 인사를 나누고, 기분에 따라 웃거나 찡그린다. 하지만 우리의 일반적인 생각과 달리, 동물들 또한 소통한다. 이와 같은 특성을 고려할 때, 우리는 동물들을 보다 역동적인 존재로 바라볼 필요가 있다.

한글번역

디자인은 어디에나 있다. 때때로 디자인은 화가가 받아들인 미학 원칙에 따라 풍경을 구성하거나 시인이 엄격한 형식을 따라 소네트를 만들 때처럼 매우 명백하다. 다른 디자인들은 사람이 선호하는 온도를 얻기 위해 수도꼭지의 물 흐름을 조절하거나 목적지에 도달하기 위해 익숙한 거리를 걸을 때처럼 덜 명백하거나 덜 명시적으로 생각된다. 디자인이라는 단어는 수많은 의미와 함축을 가지고 있으며, 이러한 의미의 다양성 때문에 적어도 부분적으로는 이 단어의 사용에 종종 수반되는 혼란과 모호함이 생긴다. 전문 디자이너들의 활동이라는 상대적으로 좁은 범위 내조차도 디자인은 서로 다른 맥락에서 다른 것을 의미한다. 한마디로, 의도적으로 만들어지고 행해지는 모든 것은 필연적으로 디자인된다.

유희태 | 일반영어 ❹-2

[A] 건축가와 엔지니어는 매우 명시적으로 디자인에 참여하며, 일반적으로 서로 다른 목적을 가지고 그렇게 한다. 건축가들은 기능보다 형태에 집중하는 경향이 있는 반면, 엔지니어들은 그 반대를 하는 경향이 있다. 많은 건축가에게 건물의 디자인은 우선적으로 그것이 어떻게 보이는가—내부와 외부 모두—그리고 그것이 근처 건물들과 어떻게 어울리는가와 관련이 있다. 건축가들은 또한 건물이 어떻게 사용될지, 사람들이 그것을 통해 어떻게 이동할지, 그것이 어떻게 느껴질지에 대해 상당한 생각을 하는 것으로 기대되지만, 결과로 판단할 때 그러한 고려사항들이 항상 그들의 마음에 가장 중요한 것처럼 보이지는 않는다. 실제로, 건축 비평을 액면 그대로 받아들인다면, 건축가들은 주로 건물 외관의 질감, 공공 공간의 외양, 그것이 채워지는 가구에 관심을 갖는 것처럼 보인다. 건축가들은 조명 기구의 특성과 문과 창문의 하드웨어에 이르기까지 세부사항에 세심한 주의를 기울이는 것처럼 보이지만, 그것들이 어떻게 작동될지나 어떻게 그들의 목적을 달성할지에 대해서는 항상 그렇지는 않다. 그럼에도 불구하고, 그러한 고려사항들은 집합적으로 건축 및 실내 디자인을 구성한다.

[B] 엔지니어들에게 디자인은 일반적으로 미학과 외양과는 덜 관련이 있고 제작과 성능과 더 관련이 있다. 엔지니어들은 외관 뒤의 구조에 집중하는 경향이 있다. 그들은 건물이 어떻게 지어질 것인지, 어떻게 서 있을 것인지, 바람에 너무 많이 흔들릴 것인지, 지진에서 살아남을 것인지, 갈라지거나 누수가 발생할 것인지에 대해 걱정한다. 호텔 건물의 구조 프레임을 디자인하는 엔지니어들은 많은 군중이 모이고 리듬감 있는 춤이 일어날 볼룸 바닥의 강도와 강성을 고려한다. 엔지니어들은 건물이 어떻게 난방되고 냉방될지, 공기가 공간들 사이에서 어떻게 순환할지, 얼마나 에너지 효율적일지에 대해 생각하는 것으로 기대된다.

2

하위내용영역	배점	예상정답률
일반영어 A형 서술형	4점	55%

모범답안) The word is "ethnic". Second, the specific clothing is a Scottish Kilt.

채점기준

+ 2점 : 빈칸에 들어갈 단어를 "ethnic"이라 정확하게 기입하였다. 이외에는 답이 될 수 없다.
+ 2점 : 지문에 언급된 (민족 문화적) 유산을 보여주는 구체적인 옷을 "(Scottish) Kilt"라 서술하였다.

한글번역

이스턴 학교의 증가하는 인종적, 민족적 다양성을 축하하기 위해 학교의 다양성 위원회는 다문화의 날을 후원하기로 결정했다. 집회와 발표를 위해 수많은 공연자들이 고용됐다. 그날의 주요 행사인 "문화 퍼레이드" 동안 학생들은 복도를 걸으면서 민족 의상을 선보이도록 요청받았다. 교사들은 위원회로부터 미국 밖의 국가들의 의복에 대해 논의하고 그런 옷을 가진 학생들을 초대해 퍼레이드를 위해 학교에 가져오도록 격려받았다.

모리슨 선생은 많은 학생들의 부모가 이민자였기 때문에 다문화의 날에 대해 흥미를 느꼈다. 그녀는 이 날을 그 학생들이 다른 사람들에게 자신의 민족 문화에 대해 가르칠 기회로 상상했다.

행사 일주일 전, 모리슨 선생은 킬트를 교실에 가져와서 학생들에게 그 의미를 설명했다. "이것은 나의 스코틀랜드 혈통을 나타낸다"고 그녀가 말했다. "그리고 오늘 너희들에게 이것을 보여줄 수 있어서 자랑스럽다." 그 후 그녀는 학생들이 집에 자신들의 민족 문화를 나타내는 "특별한 의상"을 가지고 있는지 물었다. 몇몇 학생들이 손을 들었고, 이것이 모리슨 선생으로 하여금 퍼레이드를 포함한 다문화의 날에 계획된 행사들에 대해 논의하게 했다. 퍼레이드 전날 하교 시간에 모리슨 선생은 "내일 너희 의상들을 교실에 가져오는 것을 잊지 마라!"고 공지했다.

다음 날, 모리슨 선생은 몇몇 몽족과 라이베리아 학생들이 민족 의상 가방을 들고 온 것을 보고 기뻤다. 그녀는 다른 두 학생인 에밀리와 키샤도 옷을 가져온 것을 봤기 때문에 그들의 가방에 무엇이 들어있는지 물었다. 백인 학생인 에밀리는 흥미롭게 자신의 축구 유니폼을 꺼냈고, 아프리카계 미국인 학생인 키샤는 청바지와 자신이 가장 좋아하는 스웨트셔츠를 가방에서 꺼냈다. 모리슨 선생은 두 소녀에게 다문화의 날에 대한 그들의 열정을 고맙게 생각하지만 퍼레이드에서 걸을 수는 없을 것이라고 말했다. 그녀는 키샤와 에밀리가 가져온 것은 그들의 (민족적) 혈통을 나타내는 옷이라기보다는 일상복이라고 설명했다.

두 소녀 모두 항의했다. "이 옷은 내 문화를 나타내요"라고 키샤가 주장했다. 모리슨 선생은 소녀들에게 혼란에 대해 몹시 미안하다고 느끼지만 그들의 참여를 허용할 수 없다고 나눴다. "아마 내년에는 퍼레이드를 확장할 것이다"라고 그녀가 말했다.

소녀들이 떠난 후, 모리슨 선생은 마음을 바꿀 것을 고려했다. 하지만 그녀는 다른 학생들이나 교직원들이 그들의 참여에 대해 당황할 것이고 키샤와 에밀리가 지시를 따르지 않았다는 이유로 조롱받을 것을 걱정했다.

remarkably significant to people already fascinated by the number 42."라 서술하였거나 유사하였다.

☞ 다음과 같이 서술하였어도 맞는 것으로 한다.
- "Second, the underlined sentence means that the coincidence becomes more astonishing to geeks obsessed with the number 42 because the ancient Greeks measured the distance in their own units, making it purely accidental that it converts to 42.195 kilometers in our modern system."

⊕ 보충설명

The passage is mainly about **the cultural and symbolic significance of the number 42**, particularly how it originated from Douglas Adams's *The Hitchhiker's Guide to the Galaxy* and became embedded in **popular and geek culture**. It explores how the number has been referenced in various contexts—from literature and film to mythology and education—and how it continues to fascinate people through both intentional references and curious coincidences.

The main point of the passage is that **the number 42** from Douglas Adams's novel *The Hitchhiker's Guide to the Galaxy* has become **a cultural phenomenon** that extends far beyond literature. The author shows how this fictional "answer to everything" has permeated geek culture and technology, appearing in search engines, educational institutions, movies, and various curious coincidences throughout history and culture.

The writer is essentially illustrating how **a single creative choice by an author—picking the number 42 as a humorous "answer to life, the universe, and everything"**—can take on a life of its own and become a widespread cultural reference point that people actively look for and celebrate in unexpected places. The author presents this as **an example of how fictional elements can become deeply embedded in real-world culture**, creating a shared language among "initiates" who understand the reference.

3

하위내용영역	배점	예상정답률
일반영어 A형 서술형	4점	45%

모범답안) The word is "forty-two". Second, the underlined sentence means that the connection between the number 42 and the marathon distance becomes more astonishing to geek culture enthusiasts because the ancient Greeks used their own measurement system, making it purely coincidental that their distance converts to exactly 42.195 kilometers—a coincidence that seems remarkably significant to people already fascinated by the number 42.

채점 기준

+ **2점**: 빈칸에 들어갈 단어를 "forty-two"라 정확하게 기입하였다.
+ **2점**: 밑줄 친 부분의 의미를 "the connection between the number 42 and the marathon distance becomes more astonishing to geek culture enthusiasts because the ancient Greeks used their own measurement system, making it purely coincidental that their distance converts to exactly 42.195 kilometers—a coincidence that seems

The number 42 has been referenced in **various contexts.**

① Literature / Fiction: In Douglas Adams's *The Hitchhiker's Guide to the Galaxy (1979)*, the supercomputer Deep Thought calculates that the answer to the "Great Question of Life, the Universe and Everything" is 42.

② Internet Culture / Technology: Search engines (like Google, Qwant, Wolfram Alpha) and AI chatbots (like Cleverbot) often respond "42" when asked about the meaning of life or similar existential questions—reflecting a running in-joke among users.

③ Education / Programming Schools: The "42 Network," a group of private computer-training institutions (starting in France in 2013), was named in reference to Adams's novel.

④ Film / Pop Culture: The number 42 appears in the animated film *Spider-Man: Into the Spider-Verse* in various visual or narrative elements.

⑤ Ancient Mythology: In ancient Egyptian mythology, during the judgment of souls, the dead had to swear before 42 judges that they had not committed any of 42 sins.

⑥ History / Sports: The marathon distance of 42.195 kilometers is connected (albeit anachronistically) to the legendary run of Pheidippides from Marathon to Athens in 490 B.C. to report a military victory.

한글번역

모든 사람들이 미해결 수수께끼를 좋아한다. 예시로는 1937년 태평양 상공에서의 아멜리아 에어하트의 실종과 1962년 캘리포니아 알카트라즈 섬에서 수감자 프랭크 모리스와 존 그리고 클래런스 앵글린의 대담한 탈옥이 있다. 더욱이 그 수수께끼가 농담에 기반한 것이라 해도 우리의 관심은 지속된다. 작가 더글러스 애덤스의 인기 있는 1979년 공상과학 소설 《은하수를 여행하는 히치하이커를 위한 안내서》를 보자. 책의 끝부분에서 슈퍼컴퓨터 딥 쏘트는 "생명, 우주, 그리고 모든 것"의 "위대한 질문"에 대한 답이 "42"라고 밝힌다.

딥 쏘트는 궁극적인 질문에 대한 답을 계산하는 데 750만 년이 걸린다. 그 답을 얻는 임무를 받은 등장인물들은 그것이 매우 유용하지 않기 때문에 실망한다. 하지만 컴퓨터가 지적하듯이, 질문 자체가 모호하게 공식화됐다. 답이 42인 질문의 올바른 진술을 찾기 위해서는 컴퓨터가 자신의 새로운 버전을 만들어야 할 것이다. 그것 역시 시간이 걸릴 것이다. 그 컴퓨터의 새로운 버전이 바로 지구이다.

작가가 선택한 숫자 42는 괴짜 문화의 고정물이 됐다. 그것은 입문자들 사이에서 교환되는 수많은 농담과 윙크의 기원이다. 예를 들어, 검색 엔진에 "모든 것의 답은 무엇인가?"라는 질문의 변형들을 물어보면 "42"라고 답할 가능성이 높다. 프랑스어나 독일어로 시도해보라. 구글, 콴트, 울프럼 알파, 또는 채팅봇 웹 앱 클레버봇을 사용하든 같은 답을 얻을 경우가 많다. (검색 엔진들이 더글러스 애덤스의 소설 참조를 알고 있어서, "모든 것의 답은 무엇인가?" 같은 질문을 하면 의도적으로 "42"라고 답하도록 프로그래밍됐다는 것이다. 이것은 검색 엔진 개발자들이 이 유명한 문학적 농담을 알고 있어서, 사용자들이 그런 철학적이고 광범위한 질문을 할 때 유머러스한 답변으로 "42"를 제공한다는 뜻이다. 언어를 바꿔서 프랑스어나 독일어로 물어봐도, 그리고 다른 검색 엔진이나 AI 챗봇을 사용해도 같은 답을 얻는다는 것은 이 농담이 기술 업계에서 매우 널리 알려져 있고 받아들여져서, 여러 플랫폼에서 공통적으로 이 참조를 구현했다는 것을 보여준다. 즉, 숫자 42가 대중문화와 기술 분야에서 얼마나 깊이 자리 잡았는지를 보여주는 예시이다.)

2013년 프랑스에서 첫 번째 학교가 창립된 이후로 "42 네트워크"라는 사설 컴퓨터 교육 기관들이 급증했는데, 그 이름은 애덤스의 소설에 대한 명백한 암시이다. 오늘날 이를 창립한 회사(2013년 프랑스에서 첫 번째 "42" 학교를 설립한 그 원래 회사)는 전 세계 네트워크에 15개 이상의 캠퍼스를 보유하고 있다. 숫자 42는 영화 《스파이더맨: 스파이더버스》에서도 다양한 형태로 나타난다. 이 숫자는 또한 그 의미를 파악하려는 노력이 아마도 가치가 없을 일련의 기묘한 우연들에서도 나타난다. 예를 들어: 고대 이집트 신화에서 영혼의 심판 동안 죽은 자들은 42명의 판관 앞에서 42가지 죄 중 어느 것도 저지르지 않았다고 선언해야 했다.

42.195킬로미터의 마라톤 거리는 기원전 490년 페르시아에 대한 승리를 알리기 위해 고대 그리스 전령 페이디피데스가 마라톤과 아테네 사이를 여행한 거리에 대한 전설과 일치한다. 그 당시 킬로미터가 아직 정의되지 않았다는 사실은 그 연결을 더욱 놀랍게 만들 뿐이다.

4

하위내용영역	배점	예상정답률
일반영어 A형 서술형	4점	40%

모범답안 The words for ① are "lithospheric plates" and the words for ② are "plate tectonics". Second, it was formed one hundred eighty million years ago.

채점기준

+ 1점: 빈칸 ①에 들어갈 단어를 "lithospheric plates"라 정확하게 기입하였다. "surface plates"라 했어도 1점을 준다.
+ 1점: 빈칸 ②에 들어갈 단어를 "plate tectonics"라 정확하게 기입하였다. 이외에는 답이 될 수 없다.
+ 2점: 북대서양이 언제 형성되었느냐는 질문에 "one hundred eighty million years ago"라 서술하였다.
  ☞ 다음과 같이 서술하였어도 2점을 준다.
  – "when parts of Laurasia separated from each other"
  – "North America separated from Europe"

한글번역

지구의 가장 바깥 부분을 형성하는 단단하고 딱딱한 판들은 약 100킬로미터 두께이다. 이러한 판들은 지구의 지각과 상부 맨틀을 모두 포함한다. 지각의 암석은 주로 알루미늄과 나트륨 같은 가벼운 원소를 가진 광물들로 구성돼 있는 반면, 맨틀은 철과 마그네슘 같은 더 무거운 원소들을 포함한다. 함께, 표면 판(지표판)을 형성하는 지각과 상부 맨틀은 암석권이라고 불린다. 이 딱딱한 층은 나무 뗏목이 연못에 떠 있는 것처럼 하부 맨틀의 더 밀도가 높은 물질 위에 떠 있다. 이 표면 판들은 연약권이라 불리는 하부 맨틀의 약하고 유연한 층 위에 떠 있다. 또한 연못 위의 뗏목처럼, 암석권 판들은 그들 아래의 이 더 유동적인 층의 느린 해류에 의해 운반된다.

판 구조론에 대한 이해로, 지질학자들은 지구 표면에 대한 새로운 역사를 정리했다. 약 2억 년 전, 지구 표면의 판들은 판게아라고 불리는 "초대륙"을 형성했다. 이 초대륙이 판 이동 때문에 분리되기 시작했을 때, 판게아는 먼저 두 개의 큰 대륙 덩어리로 분리됐고, 함몰이 물로 채워지면서 육지 지역들 사이에서 새로 형성된 바다가 자라났다. 남쪽 것은 남아메리카, 아프리카, 오스트레일리아, 남극 대륙의 현대 대륙들을 포함했으며 곤드와나랜드라고 불린다. 북쪽 것은 북아메리카, 유럽, 아시아를 포함했으며 로라시아라고 불린다. 북아메리카는 약 1억 8천만 년 전에 유럽에서 분리돼 북대서양을 형성했다.

암석권 판들 중 일부는 해저면을 구성하고(여기서 "carry"는 물리적으로 들고 다닌다는 뜻이 아니라, 암석권 판의 표면 부분이 해저면으로 구성됐다는 의미), 다른 암석권 판들은 육지 덩어리를 포함하거나 이 두 종류(해저면과 육지덩어리)의 조합을 포함한다. 암석권 판들의 이동은 지진, 화산 활동, 그리고 지구상의 가장 거대한 산맥들의 형성에 책임이 있다. 서로 다른 판들 간의 상호작용에 대한 현재의 이해는 이러한 현상들이 특정 지역에서 발생하는 이유를 설명한다. 예를 들어, 태평양의 가장자리는 그곳에서 매우 많은 화산 폭발과 지진이 일어나기 때문에 "불의 고리"라고 불려왔다. 1960년대 이전에, 지질학자들은 왜 활성 화산과 강한 지진이 그 지역에 집중돼 있는지 설명할 수 없었다. 판 구조론 이론이 그들에게 답을 줬다.

제56회 모의고사

1

하위내용영역	배점	예상정답률
일반영어 B형 서술형	4점	40%

모범답안 The research is surprising because it contradicts the assumption that life is less valuable than money to poor people when compared to rich people and that poor people gave more weight to an adult provider's life over a child's. Then, it is implied that donation formulas would instead support children more.

채점기준

+ 2점: 연구에서 밝혀진 것이 놀라운 이유를 "because it contradicts the assumption that life is less valuable than money to poor people when compared to rich people and that poor people gave more weight to an adult provider's life over a child's (life)"라 서술하였거나 유사하였다.
+ 2점: 기부 방식의 변화를 "donation formulas would instead support children more"라 서술하였거나 유사하였다.

한글번역

최근 한 단체가 흥미로운 연구 결과를 발표했다. 이 연구는 자선의 수혜자, 즉 그동안 거의 의견을 묻지 않았던 사람들의 관점을 바탕으로, 생명을 구하는 일과 소득을 증대시키는 일을 어떻게 비교하고 우선순위를 정할 수 있을지를 수식으로 나타내려는 시도다. 결과는 다소 뜻밖이었다.

가난한 국가의 사람들도 부유한 국가의 사람들과 마찬가지로, 생명과 소득 사이의 가치를 비슷하게 평가하는 경향을 보였기 때문이다. 지금까지는 신뢰할 만한 데이터가 부족했기 때문에, 경제학자들은 극빈층이 소득 증가를 생명보다 더 중시할 것이라고 추정해왔다. 사실, 사람들은 빈곤 속에서 매우 어려운 문제들에 직면하고 있기 때문에 조금 더 많은 돈이 극빈층 사람들에게 상당히 더 가치가 있을 수 있다.

이 조사를 수행한 비영리 연구 단체 IDinsight는 케냐와 가나의 극빈층 2,000명을 대상으로 설문을 진행했다. 이들은 일종의 기부자 역할을 부여받고, 원조 자금을 어디에 배분하는 것이 가장 타당한지를 묻는 다양한 질문에 답했다. 응답자들은 사망 위험을 약간이라도 줄일 수 있다면 그 대가로 많은 금액을 지불할 의향을 보였으며, 소득을 증대시키는 프로그램보다 생명을 구하는 데 효과적인 프로그램을 더 선호하는 경향이 있었다.

연구자들을 더욱 놀라게 한 것은 아동의 생명을 성인의 생명보다 더 높게 평가한 점이다. 일반적으로 극심한 빈곤 속에서 살아가는 사람들에게는 가족의 생계를 책임지는 성인을 잃는 것이 훨씬 더 타격이 클 것이라 여겨졌기 때문이다. "실제로 일부 연구진은, 공동체가 성인을 가족의 돌봄 제공자이자 경제적 기여자로 인식하고 있기 때문에, 성인의 죽음을 막는 것이 더 중요하다고 판단할 것이라 예측했다."라고 한 연구자가 말한다.

그러나 조사 결과는 달랐다. 응답자들은 5세 미만 아동의 생명을 구하는 일에, 5세 이상 개인의 생명을 구하는 일보다 거의 두 배 가까운 가치를 부여했다. 연구진은 이 결과가 매우 초기적인 단계에 불과하며, 앞으로 더 많은 연구가 필요하다는 점을 강조했다. 그럼에도 불구하고, 이들은 이미 자사의 원조 평가 기준 일부를 수정했다. 예를 들어 이전에는 성인의 생명을 약간 더 우선시했으나, 이제는 아동과 성인의 생명을 동일한 비중으로 평가하기로 했다.

2

하위내용영역	배점	예상정답률
일반영어 B형 서술형	4점	25%

모범답안 The word for ① is "speech" and the word for ② is "eyes". Second, Nixon matched Hot media like radio whereas JFK matched Cool media like TV; so Nixon was better at radio whereas JFK at TV.

채점 기준

+ 1점: 빈칸 ①에 들어갈 단어를 "speech"라 기입하였다. "speaking"이라 했어도 1점을 준다.
+ 1점: 빈칸 ②에 들어갈 단어를 "eyes"라 정확하게 기입하였다. 이외에는 답이 될 수 없다.
+ 2점: 닉슨-케네디 논쟁에 관한 글쓴이의 최근의 생각을 "Nixon matched(=suited; got along with) Hot media like radio whereas JFK matched Cool media like TV; so Nixon was better at radio whereas JFK (was better) at TV"라 서술하였거나 유사하였다.

⊕ 보충설명

- "오디오는 당신이 정말로 의미하는 바를 귀, 헤드폰, 그리고 자동차 라디오로 직접적이고 친밀하게 전달하는 방법이다."
- "음악도 이런 면에서 능숙하지만, 말(speech)은 더욱 뛰어나다."
  → 이 문장은 앞 문맥에서 언급된 "진짜 의미를 친밀하고 직접적으로 전달하는 것"에 대해 음악과 말을 비교하고 있다. 음악도 감정이나 분위기를 잘 전달할 수 있지만, 실제 말(speech)은 억양, 강조, 멈춤, 어조 등을 통해 화자의 진짜 의도와 감정을 더 구체적이고 명확하게 전달할 수 있다는 의미이다. 음악은 추상적인 감정 전달에 뛰어나지만, 말은 구체적인 의미와 함께 미묘한 감정의 차이까지도 전달할 수 있어서 "더욱 뛰어나다"고 표현한 것이다.)

- "문자 메시지나 전화로 다툴 수도 있고(차가운, 말을 주고받는), 이메일이나 보이스 메일(뜨거운, 한 번에 모든 내용을 전달하는)로도 가능하다. 문자 메시지는 문제를 차갑게 식히는 반면, 오디오는 해결을 강요한다."
  → Phone=cooler, back-and-forth dialog(쌍방향 대화) / Voice mail=hot, one-shot blasts (일방향 폭발)
  → Phone이 "cooler"인 이유는 상호작용이 가능하기 때문이다: 전화는 즉시 응답하고 반응할 수 있고, 상대방의 반응을 보고 톤을 조절할 수 있다. 대화가 escalate되면 바로 진정시킬 수 있고, 쌍방향 소통으로 오해를 즉시 해결할 수도 있다. 반면 Voice mail은 "hot"인 이유: 일방적으로 메시지를 남기고 끝낸다. 상대방 반응을 모른 채 감정을 쏟아낸다. 수정이나 보완이 불가능하다. 즉, 같은 audio라도 상호작용 여부에 따라 hot/cool이 달라진다는 것이다. Phone은 audio지만 interactive하기 때문에 상대적으로 "cooler"하다.

본문 핵심요약
오디오는 텍스트나 이미지보다 화자의 **진짜 의미와 감정**을 더 생생하고 직접적으로 전달하는 "뜨거운" 매체이며, 닉슨-케네디 토론 사례는 "뜨거운" 후보(닉슨)는 라디오에서, "차가운" 후보(케네디)는 TV에서 더 효과적이었음을 보여준다.

한글번역

오디오에는 수많은 정보가 들어 있다. 어조, 억양, 암시, 목소리 흉내내기, 강조, 망설임 등 문자에 비해 훨씬 많은 정보가 전달된다. 오디오는 "내가 말하는 방식만 봐도 당신은 내가 무슨 이야기를 하는지 알아야"라는 말이 성립하는 미디어이다. 오디오는 당신이 정말로 의미하는 바를 귀, 헤드폰, 그리고 자동차 라디오로 직접적이고 친밀하게 전달하는 방법이다. 음악도 이런 면에서 능숙하지만, 말(speech)은 더욱 뛰어나다.

"오늘밤"을 스무 가지 다른 방식으로, 각각이 다른 느낌을 가지도록 말해 보자. 흥미롭게, 만족스럽게, 피곤하게, 음란하게, 의기소침하게, 짜증나게, 의문스럽게, 주저하듯, 필사적으로 등 끝없이 다양한 방식으로 말할 수 있다. 게다가 상대방은 이를 다 알아듣는다. 이는 이미지나 글자로는 절대 할 수 없는 일이다. 글자로 쓰여진 오늘밤은 그저 오늘밤일 뿐이다. 단순하면서도 아무런 특별한 의미를 가지지 않는다. 우리 눈은 이를 중립적인 정보로 받아들인다. 하지만 귀는 그렇지 않다. 우리의 귀는 놀라운 구별력을 가지고 있다.

어떤 내용을 이야기하든, 오디오는 이를 뜨겁게 만든다. 집주인과 어떤 문제로 다투는 중이라고 가정해 보자. 문자 메시지나 전화로 다툴 수도 있고 (차가운, 말을 주고받는), 이메일이나 보이스 메일 (뜨거운, 한 번에 모든 내용을 전달하는)로도 가능하다. 문자 메시지는 문제를 차갑게 식히는 반면, 오디오는 해결을 강요한다.

어떤 정보를 오디오 중심의 미디어나 오디오만 존재하는 미디어에 실을 경우, 오디오는 정보를 뜨겁게 데우고 그 내용을 완전하게 전달한다. 문자 메시지나 혼성 미디어를 통해 담담하게, 혹은 모호하게 전달될 수 있는 정보도 오디오를 통할 경우 그 모호함이 사라진다. 우리가 귀를 통해 그 정보를 들을 때, 우리는 그 진짜 의미가 무엇인지 이해하며, 또 그렇기 때문에 오디오는 핫한 콘텐츠를 추구한다.

닉슨과 케네디의 TV 토론은 매우 유명한 예이며, 나는 오랫동안 이 예를 잘못 이해하고 있었다. 리처드 닉슨과 JFK가 대통령 후보 당시 가졌던 TV 토론에서 라디오로 이 토론을 들었던 사람은 닉슨이 토론에서 이겼다고 생각했지만, TV를 본 사람들은 JFK가 이겼다고 생각했다. 나는 처음 이 이야기를 들었을 때, 이 예화의 핵심이 TV는 라디오보다 "외면"을 더 강조하며, JFK의 잘생긴 얼굴과 매력적인 스타일이 토론 자체보다 더 먹혔지만, 라디오에서는 그렇지 않았다는 뜻으로 이해했다.

하지만, 이제 나는 이런 이해가 완전히 잘못됐다는 것을 알고 있다. 저 예에서 두 사람이 어떤 말을 했느냐는 전혀 중요하지 않다. 내용은 중요치 않다. 중요한 것은 닉슨이 핫(Hot)한 후보였다는 것이다 : 날카롭고, 정보로 가득하며, 거칠고, 당신 면전에서 공격적이었다. 반면, 케네디는 쿨(Cool)한 후보였는데, (라디오와 같은 핫 미디어에서는 느리고 말이 없으며 무기력한 사람처럼 보였지만,) TV에서는 오히려 여유롭고, 편안하게 자신의 슬로건을 말하는데, 이렇게 함으로써 수많은 해석을 가능하게 하고, 청중들 스스로가 그 해석의 갭을 채우도록 했다.

3

하위내용영역	배점	예상정답률
일반영어 B형 서술형	4점	40%

모범답안) The form of exchange has evolved over time. Barter trade was the first way of exchange, but had the difficulty of having to find the right partner and dividing goods. This led people to switch over to monetary transactions, using beads, shells and fishing hooks as money at the start, then coins. However, people found carrying coins around troublesome and risky, and thus developed checks with names of the users on them to discourage robbery. In conclusion, along with paper exchange, thanks to technology, there are also credit and cash cards.

채점 기준

ⓐ Topic sentence
+1점 : "The form of exchange has evolved over time"를 명확하게 서술하였다.

ⓑ Major supporting details
+2점 : "①Barter trade was the first way of exchange, but had the difficulty of having to find the right partner and dividing goods. ②This led people to switch over to monetary transactions (using beads, shells and fishing hooks as money at the start, then coins). ③However, people found carrying coins around troublesome and risky, and thus developed checks (with names of the users on them to discourage robbery)"을 명확하게 서술하였다.
☞ 3개 중 3개 모두 정확하게 요약했으면 2점, 2개를 요약했으면 1점, 나머지는 0점을 준다.

ⓒ Conclusion
+1점 : "In conclusion, along with paper exchange, thanks to technology, there are also credit and cash cards"을 명확하게 요약하였다.

감점
- 본문에 나오는 연속되는 6단어 이상을 사용하였다. -0.5pt
- 문단을 두 개나 그 이상으로 구성하였다. -0.5pt
- 문법이나 영어 표현을 합쳐 3개 이상 오류가 있다. -0.5pt

제57회 모의고사

1

하위내용영역	배점	예상정답률
일반영어 A형 서술형	4점	50%

모범답안) First, you should choose logo. Second, the word is "color".

채점기준

+ 2점: 회사의 상품을 더 인식시키기 위해 선택해야 할 것을 "logo"라 답하였다. 이외에는 답이 될 수 없다.
+ 2점: 빈칸에 들어갈 단어를 "color"라 정확하게 기입하였다. 이외에는 답이 될 수 없다.

한글번역

태초의 교환 방식은 물물교환이었다. 이 거래 방식에서는 사람들이 자신이 원하는 물건을 얻기 위해 다른 물건을 사용해 교환했다. 예를 들어, A라는 사람이 펜이 필요하고 여분의 양을 가지고 있다면, 그는 정반대의 상황에 놓인 사람, 즉 여분의 펜을 가지고 있으면서 동시에 양이 필요한 사람을 찾아야 했다. 그 조건에 맞는 사람, 이를테면 B라는 사람을 찾았다고 해서 문제가 끝나는 것은 아니다. 큰 양 한 마리가 펜 한 자루의 가치 이상일 수 있기 때문에, B는 A에게 다른 것을 추가로 제안해야 할지도 모른다. 예컨대 두 마리의 돼지를 제시할 수 있다. 그러나 A가 돼지를 필요로 하지 않는다면 이 제안은 거절될 수 있다.

세월이 흐른 뒤, 이런 번거로운 물물교환은 화폐 개념의 등장과 함께 금전적 교환 방식으로 대체됐다. 초기에는 거의 모든 것이 화폐로서 기능할 수 있었다. 구슬, 조개껍데기, 심지어 낚시 바늘도 사용됐다. 그러다가 터키 근방 지역에서는 금화가 화폐로 사용되기 시작했다. 처음에는 각각의 금화가 서로 다른 가치를 지니고 있었으나, 기원전 약 700년경 리디아의 왕 가이게스(Gyges)가 금화의 가치를 표준화했다.

화폐를 통한 거래는 처음에는 전통적인 물물교환보다 훨씬 효율적이었다. 그러나 시간이 지나면서, 쇼핑을 위해 무거운 동전 주머니를 들고 다니는 일이 귀찮을 뿐 아니라 도둑을 불러들이기까지 한다는 점이 문제로 떠올랐다. 이로 인해 멀리 떨어진 도시들로부터 물품을 사들이던 그리스와 로마의 상인들은 이 문제를 해결하기 위해 '수표'라는 개념을 발명했다. 종이 수표는 가지고 다니기 편리할 뿐만 아니라, 수표에 기재된 사람만이 사용할 수 있기 때문에 도난을 억제하는 효과도 있었다.

오늘날에는 정부가 발행한 지폐를 이용한 교환 방식의 편리함 외에도, 기술 발전으로 인해 신용카드나 직불카드 같은 새로운 거래 수단이 등장하게 됐다.

한글번역

그리스어 로고스(말을 의미)에서 유래한 로고는 이상적으로는 우리가 즉시 인식하고 그것이 대표하는 조직과 연관시키는 상징이다. 하지만 그것은 좀처럼 그렇게 단순하지 않다. 모양과 색깔도 역할을 하며, 글자나 심지어 조직의 전체 이름도 마찬가지다. 어떤 경우든, 로고는 목표 집단이 인식하기 쉬워야 한다. 단지 몇 번만 보고 나서 친숙해져야 한다. 좋은 로고는 단순함과 독특함의 균형을 맞추며 독립적으로 설 수 있다. (독특성(Distinctiveness)은 로고가 다른 로고들과 구별된다는 의미—경쟁사와 차별화되고 독창적이라는 뜻이다. 반면, 독립성(Stand alone)은 로고가 추가적인 텍스트나 맥락 없이도 그 자체로 기능한다는 의미—자립적이라는 뜻이다.) 그것은 기업 본사 앞면부터 홍보 브로셔와 수많은 메모의 편지에 이르기까지 다양한 표면을 장식해야 한다.

로고는 당신이 회사에 부여하는 강점과 가치를 드러낸다. 자신을 진지하게 받아들이는 조직은 분명히 경박한 로고를 선택하지 않을 것이다. 많은 전문가들이 인력파견회사 랜드스타드의 로고의 효과성을 칭찬한다. 그것은 수직과 수평축으로 반사된 양식화된 R이다. 전체적으로 보면, 그것은 새를 닮았고 회사의 활동에 적합한 역동성과 이동성의 느낌을 준다. 인력파견회사는 실제로는 다른 회사들을 위한 근로자들로서 매우 낮은 프로필을 가진다. 그럼에도 불구하고 수년에 걸쳐 랜드스타드는 자신만의 구체적인 이미지를 구축하는 데 성공했다.

유희태 | 일반영어 ❹-2

성공적인 브랜드명처럼, 좋은 로고는 회사의 주요 자산 중 하나이다. 그것은 종종 브랜드명보다 보호하기가 더 쉬우며, 특히 독점적 권리를 주장할 수 없는 개인명보다 그렇다. 게다가 로고는 회사명보다 인식하기가 더 쉬우며, 특히 국제적으로 그렇다. 석유회사 셸의 독특한 조개껍데기 로고는 "셸"이라는 단어의 글자들이 익숙하지 않은 국가들에서조차 어디서나 인식된다. 또한 국제적 차원에서 코카콜라가 떠오르는데, 이 회사는 이름 외에 물결 모양의 선을 사용한다. 이것은 전 세계적으로 인식되는 매우 효과적인 로고를 만든다.

종종 각 회사는 자신의 제품에 대한 색깔에 동의한다. 네덜란드의 유제품 진열대에서는 파란색이 우유를, **빨간색**이 버터밀크를, 초록색이 요구르트를 나타낸다. 그리고 상점의 다른 곳에서는 다크 초콜릿 바들이 빨간 포장지를 자랑하고 밀크 초콜릿은 파란색을 한다. 네덜란드 밖에서는 독일과 오스트리아의 국가 우편 서비스가 노란색 사용으로 잘 알려져 있다.

한글번역

나에게는 성공에 대한 하나의 정의가 있다. 당신은 매일 저녁 거울을 보면서, 인생에 의해 타락하기 시작하는 바로 전인 18세 때의 자신을 실망시키는지 궁금해하는 것이다. 18세 때의 그 자신만을 유일한 심판자로 삼아라. 당신의 평판도, 부도, 지역사회에서의 지위도, 옷깃의 훈장도 아니다. 만약 부끄럽지 않다면, 당신은 성공한 것이다. 다른 모든 성공의 정의들은 현대적 구성물들이며, 취약한 현대적 구성물들이다.

고대 그리스인들의 성공에 대한 주된 정의는 영웅적인 죽음을 맞는 것이었다. 하지만 우리가 덜 호전적인 세상에 살고 있으므로, 우리는 성공의 정의를 집단의 이익을 위해 영웅적인 길을 택한 것으로 조정할 수 있다. 당신이 원하는 대로 좁게든 넓게든 정의된 집단 말이다. 당신이 하는 모든 것이 당신만을 위한 것이 아닌 한 말이다. 비밀 결사들은 '명예로운 사람'에 대한 규칙을 가지고 있었다. 자신을 위해 무언가를 하고 다른 구성원들을 위해 무언가를 하는 것이다. 그리고 미덕은 용기와 분리될 수 없다. 인기 없는 일을 할 용기 같은 것 말이다. 다른 사람들의 이익을 위해 위험을 감수하라. 그것이 인류일 필요는 없으며, 베이루트 마다니타나 지역 시정부를 돕는 것일 수도 있다. 더 미시적일수록, 덜 추상적일수록 더 좋다.

나는 성공에는 취약성의 부재가 필요하다고 믿는다. 나는 언론인들을 두려워하는 억만장자들, 처남이 매우 부유해졌다고 해서 짓눌린 기분을 느끼는 부유한 사람들, 웹상의 댓글을 무서워하는 노벨상 수상 학자들을 봤다. 높이 올라갈수록 추락은 더 심하다. 내가 만난 거의 모든 사람들에게 외적 성공은 증가된 취약성과 함께 왔다. 최악은 4페이지짜리 이력서를 가진 "전직 무엇무엇" 유형들인데, 그들은 퇴임 후 비굴한 관료들의 관심에 중독됐다가 자신들이 버려진 것을 발견한다. 마치 어느 날 저녁 집에 갔더니 누군가가 갑자기 집의 모든 가구를 비워버린 것을 발견하는 것과 같다.

하지만 자존감은 견고하다. 그것이 우연히 페니키아 운동이었던 스토아 학파의 접근법이다. 스토아 철학자들이 누구인지 궁금해하는 사람이 있다면 나는 태도에 문제가 있는 불교도들이라고 말하겠다. 나는 자신들의 부족에 관여하는 지역 시민이라는 것을 자랑스러워했던 내 마을 아미운의 견고한 사람들을 봤다. 그들은 자랑스럽게 잠자리에 들고 행복하게 깨어난다. 또는 어려운 소비에트 붕괴 후 전환기 동안 한 달에 200달러를 벌면서도 20명의 사람들에게 인정받는 일을 하는 것을 자랑스러워했고, 자신의 훈장을 보여주거나 상을 받는 것을 약함과 자신의 기여에 대한 확신 부족의 표시라고 여겼던 러시아 수학자들을 봤다.

2

하위내용영역	배점	예상정답률
일반영어 A형 서술형	4점	45%

모범답안 The word is "fragility". Second, it would be unpopular to make such little money, to be appreciated by only a handful of people and to hide one's decoration or awards.

채점기준

+ 2점: 빈칸에 들어갈 단어를 "fragility"라 정확하게 기입하였다. 이외에는 답이 될 수 없다.
+ 2점: 러시아 수학자들의 삶의 방식이 "인기 없을" 수도 있는 이유를 "it would be unpopular to make such little money, to be appreciated by only a handful of people, and to hide one's decoration (or awards)"이라 서술하였거나 유사하였다.

3

하위내용영역	배점	예상정답률
일반영어 A형 서술형	4점	45%

모범답안) The words are ① "Nunu" ② "Mary". Second, an intuitive reaction might cause a wrong answer because we use a mental shortcut to get an answer instead of rational thinking, such as guessing the wrong number of days to grow lily pads over half the lake by dividing the number to grow over all in half.

채점 기준

+ **2점**: 빈칸에 각각 들어갈 단어를 ① "Nunu" ② "Mary"라 정확하게 기입하였다. 이외에는 답이 될 수 없다.

+ **1점**: 직관적 반응이 오류일 수 있는 이유를 "because we use a mental shortcut to get an answer (instead of rational thinking = without resorting to(depending on) rational thinking)"라 서술하였거나 유사하였다.
  ☞ 다음과 같이 서술하였어도 맞는 것으로 한다.
  - "It is because our brain's fast thinking system tries to force us to accept incorrect responses before we engage in slower, more careful rational thinking that would lead to the correct solutions." "guessing the wrong number of days to grow lily pads over half the lake by dividing the number to grow over all in half" 또는 "giving Nunu as a answer following the vowels sounds" 등

+ **1점**: 오류의 예를 글에 있는 "guessing the wrong number of days to grow lily pads over half the lake by dividing the number to grow over all in half" 또는 "giving Nunu as a answer following the vowels sounds" 4가지 중 하나만 서술하였으면 맞는 것으로 한다.

⊕ 보충설명

컵의 가격 = x
찻주전자의 가격 = x + 100 (컵보다 $100 더 비싸므로)
방정식을 세우면 : 컵 + 찻주전자 = $110
$x + (x + 100) = 110$
$2x + 100 = 110$
$2x = 10$
$x = 5$
따라서 컵의 가격 = $5
찻주전자의 가격 = $5 + $100 = $105
검증 : $5 + $105 = $110
찻주전자($105)가 컵($5)보다 $100 더 비싸다.

핵심 포인트
직관적 답 $10이 틀린 이유는, 만약 컵이 $10이라면 찻주전자는 $110이 되어야 하는데, 그러면 총합이 $120이 되어 조건에 맞지 않는다.

한글번역

우리의 네 가지 질문에 어떻게 답했는가? 아래가 정답들이다.

1. 당신은 경주에 참가하고 있다. 2위를 추월한다. 당신은 몇 위인가? 직관적인 답은 "이제 나는 1위다"이다. 물론 정답은 2위에 있는 사람을 추월하면 그의 자리를 차지하게 돼 이제 2위가 된다는 것이다.
2. 메리의 아버지에게는 다섯 딸이 있다. 그들의 이름은 : 1. 나나, 2. 네네, 3. 니니, 4. 노노 그리고 ?? 다섯 번째 딸의 이름은 무엇인가? 대부분의 사람들이 내는 직관적인 반응은 -a-e-i-o-를 살펴보고 누누(NUNU)로 가는 것이다. 정답은 이미 문제에 주어져 있다 : 메리(MARY).
3. 컵과 찻주전자 세트는 110달러이다. 찻주전자는 컵보다 100달러 더 비싸다. 컵은 얼마인가? 직관인 반응은 110달러 - 100달러 = 10달러이다. 정답은 5달러이다.
4. 호수에 수련잎 한 덩어리가 있다. 매일 그 덩어리는 크기가 두 배가 된다. 그 덩어리가 호수 전체를 덮는 데 48일이 걸린다면, 호수의 절반을 덮는 데는 얼마나 걸릴까? 당신의 첫 번째 반응은 아마도 지름길을 택해서 최종 답을 반으로 나누는 것일 것이다. 그것은 당신을 24일로 이끈다. 하지만 그것은 틀렸다. 정답은 47일이다.

네 문제 모두 맞혔는가? 훌륭하다! 하지만 가능성 상 당신의 뇌는 먼저 틀린 답을 받아들이도록 강요하려 했을 것이다.

유희태 | 일반영어 ❹-2

경제학에서 노벨상을 받은 최초의 심리학자인 다니엘 카네만(2002년)은 직관적 반응이 항상 최선이 아닌 이유를 설명한다. 그의 획기적인 저서 《생각, 빠르고 느리게》에서 그는 직관적(빠른) 사고와 합리적(느린) 사고에 대해 논한다. 그는 직관적 반응이 어떻게 문제로 이어질 수 있는지, 그리고 우리의 상식의 한계가 무엇인지 보여준다.

4

하위내용영역	배점	예상정답률
일반영어 A형 서술형	4점	50%

모범 답안 The word is "preparation". Second, it can be inferred that beginners can expect to get indigestion from the food.

채점 기준

+ 2점: 빈칸에 들어갈 단어를 "preparation"라 정확하게 기입하였다. 이외에는 답이 될 수 없다.
+ 2점: 초심자에게 소화 불량 약을 가져오는 것이 좋을 거라고 말한 이유를 "beginners can expect to get indigestion (or sick) from the food"라 서술하였거나 유사하였다.

한글번역

우리 중 많은 사람들이 불 위에서 고기를 굽는 것을 즐기지만 누구도 불에서 고기를 요리한다는 아이디어를 누가 처음 시작했는지 궁금해하지 않는다. 아마도 우리가 때때로 원시 시대로 돌아갈 필요를 느끼는 것은 인간의 정신에 있는 것으로, 도시화된 삶에서 우리를 해방시키기 위해서일 것이다. 그래서 많은 사람들이 바비큐 모임을 갖는 것을 좋아한다.

바비큐 준비를 위한 첫 번째 단계는 보통 가장 기본적인 필수품들과 함께 제공되는 바비큐 화덕을 빌리는 것이다. 결국 우리는 초기 시대로 돌아가야 하기 때문이다. 물론 학교 방학과 같은 성수기에 화덕이 모두 예약돼 있을 때는 집 뒤뜰에 하나를 파보려고 할 수도 있다. 다음으로 철망을 준비하라. 그렇지 않으면 뜨거운 숯 위에서 고기를 굽고 있는 자신을 발견하게 될 것이다. 고기 조각들을 고정하는 데 중요한 꼬챙이, 포크와 숟가락 같은 음식을 집어 드는 데 필요한 도구들, 종이 접시와 컵들을 빠뜨려서는 안 된다.

다음은 바비큐의 가장 중요한 부분인 음식의 준비가 온다. 사실 어떤 종류의 고기든 적합할 것이다. 닭고기, 쇠고기, 양고기 같은 고기 조각들을 샀다면, 꼬챙이에 꿰기 전에 얇은 조각으로 잘라라. 닭 날개가 최고다. 단순히 날개를 벌려서 꼬챙이를 밀어 넣으면 된다. 그 다음 고기는 양념을 위해 향신료 혼합물에 담가서 맛을 낸다.

모든 것이 준비되면 잔치 시작 한 시간 전에 숯으로 불을 피운다. 불이 피워지면 타오르는 불씨가 남을 때까지 모두 태운다. 그런 다음 철망 위에 고기 꼬챙이를 올려놓으면 바로, 바비큐가 시작된 것이다. 고기를 너무 익히는 것에 대해 걱정하지 마라. 결국 바비큐의 진정한 즐거움은 음식을 먹는 것이 아니라 요리하는 데 있다. 초보자들에게 한 가지 조언을 하자면 : 소화제를 가져가라.

제58회 모의고사

1

하위내용영역	배점	예상정답률
일반영어 A형 서술형	4점	45%

모범답안 The words are ① "collaborators" and ② "flow". Second, the Internet is beautiful because it can aid in facilitating collaboration between people who may have never met.

채점기준

+ 2점: 빈칸에 들어갈 단어를 각각 ① "collaborators" ② "flow"라 정확하게 기입하였다. 이외에는 답이 될 수 없다.
+ 2점: 인터넷의 장점을 "because it can aid in (facilitating) collaboration between people who may have never met"이라 서술하였거나 유사하였다.

한글번역

심리학자들과 신경과학자들은 플로우(몰입)라고 부르는 현상을 연구하는데, 이것은 누군가 창의적인 일을 하는 등 단 하나의 일에 주의를 집중하고 다른 어떤 것에도 방해받지 않게 될 때 인간의 뇌에서 일어나는 일이다. 그리고 일부는 몰입을 더 정기적으로 할수록 더 행복해질 것이라고 말한다.

나는 심리학자도 신경과학자도 아니다. 하지만 나에게는 그것이 매우 사실이라고 말할 수 있다. 항상 쉬운 것은 아니고, 어렵다. 이렇게 정말로 주의를 집중하는 것은 연습이 필요하며, 모든 사람이 자신만의 방식으로 주의를 집중한다. 하지만 내가 집중하고 정말로 주의를 기울이는 데 도움이 된다고 생각하는 것을 하나 공유할 수 있다면, 이것이다 : 나는 다른 창작자들을 내 경쟁자로 보지 않으려고 노력한다. 나는 협력자를 찾으려고 한다. 예를 들어, 장면에서 연기를 하고 있을 때, 다른 배우들을 내 경쟁자로 보기 시작하고 "맙소사, 그들이 나보다 더 많은 관심을 받을 것이고, 사람들이 내 연기보다 그들의 연기에 대해 더 많이 이야기할 것이다"라고 생각한다면, 나는 집중력을 잃은 것이다. 그리고 아마 그 장면에서 형편없을 것이다.

하지만 다른 배우들을 협력자로 볼 때, 집중하는 것이 거의 쉬워진다. 왜냐하면 나는 단지 그들에게 주의를 기울이고 있기 때문이다. 그리고 내가 무엇을 하고 있는지 생각할 필요가 없다. 나는 그들이 하는 것에 반응하고, 그들은 내가 하는 것에 반응하며, 우리는 함께 서로를 그 안에 머물게 할 수 있다. 하지만 이런 식으로 협력할 수 있는 것이 촬영장의 배우들뿐이라고 생각하지 않기를 바란다. 나는 어떤 종류의 창작적 상황에든 있을 수 있다. 그것은 전문적일 수도 있고, 그냥 재미를 위한 것일 수도 있다. 나는 같은 방에 있지도 않은 사람들과 협력할 수도 있다. 사실 내가 만든 것 중에서 가장 좋아하는 것들 중 일부는 물리적으로 만난 적이 없는 사람들과 만든 것이다.

그런데 이것이 나에게는 인터넷의 아름다움이다. 만약 우리가 관심을 끌기 위한 경쟁을 멈출 수 있다면, 인터넷은 협력자를 찾는 훌륭한 장소가 된다. 그리고 일단 내가 다른 사람들과 협력하게 되면, 그들이 촬영장에 있든, 온라인에 있든, 어디에 있든, 그것은 내가 그 플로우를 찾는 것을 훨씬 쉽게 만든다. 왜냐하면 우리 모두가 함께 만들고 있는 그 하나의 일에 주의를 기울이고 있기 때문이다. 그리고 나는 나 자신보다 큰 무언가의 일부라고 느끼며, 우리 모두가 그렇지 않았다면 우리의 주의를 끌 수 있는 다른 어떤 것으로부터 서로를 보호하고, 우리 모두가 그냥 거기에 있을 수 있다.

2

하위내용영역	배점	예상정답률
일반영어 A형 서술형	4점	45%

모범답안 The word is "neocortex". Second, pigeons can differentiate between Picasso and Monet. Third, it can be inferred that this previous understanding of the avian brain structure was incorrect or incomplete, as the new research shows birds actually have brain organization similar to mammals rather than just discrete nuclei.

채점 기준

+ 1점: 빈칸에 들어갈 단어를 "neocortex"라 정확하게 기입하였다. 이외에는 답이 될 수 없다.
+ 1점: 새의 높은 수준의 행위 및 역량의 예를 "pigeons can differentiate between Picasso and Monet"라 서술하였거나 유사하였다.
  ☞ 다음과 같이 서술하였어도 맞는 것으로 한다.
  − "Ravens identify themselves in front of a mirror."
  − "Crows leave walnuts in crosswalks to be opened."
+ 2점: 밑줄 친 부분에 대해서 새로운 연구로부터 추론할 수 있는 것을 "this previous understanding of the avian brain structure was incorrect or incomplete, as the new research shows birds actually have brain organization similar to mammals rather than just discrete nuclei"라 서술하였거나 유사하였다.

한글번역

충분한 훈련을 받으면 비둘기는 피카소와 모네의 작품을 구별할 수 있다. 까마귀는 거울에서 자신을 식별할 수 있다. 그리고 일본의 한 대학 캠퍼스에서 까마귀들은 의도적으로 횡단보도에 호두를 남겨두고 지나가는 차량이 견과를 깨뜨리도록 하는 것으로 알려져 있다. 많은 조류 종들이 믿을 수 없을 정도로 영리하다. 그러나 지능적인 동물들 중에서 "새 대가리"는 종종 별로 존중받지 못한다.

최근 《사이언스》에 발표된 두 편의 논문은 새들이 실제로 이전에 생각했던 것보다 우리의 복잡한 영장류 기관과 훨씬 더 유사한 뇌를 가지고 있다는 것을 발견했다. 수년 동안 조류의 뇌는 신피질이 부족하기 때문에 기능이 제한적이라고 여겨졌다. 포유류에서 신피질은 복잡한 인지와 창의성을 가능하게 하고 척추동물 전체에서 대뇌피질이라고 불리는 것의 대부분을 구성하는 거대하고 진화적으로 현대적인 뇌의 외층이다. 새로운 발견들은 새들이 실제로 다른 모양을 취하고 있음에도 불구하고 신피질과 비교할 만한 뇌 구조를 가지고 있다는 것을 보여준다. 세포 수준에서 그 뇌 영역이 포유류 피질과 매우 유사하게 배열돼 있어서, 많은 새들이 오랫동안 과학자들을 당황시켜온 고차원적 행동과 능력을 보이는 이유를 설명한다는 것이 밝혀졌다. 새로운 연구는 심지어 특정 새들이 어느 정도의 의식을 보인다고 시사한다.

포유류 피질은 수평적으로도 수직적으로도 서로 소통하는 뉴런의 수직 기둥들을 포함하는 6개 층으로 조직돼 있다. 반면에 조류의 뇌는 등쪽 뇌실능선(DVR)이라고 불리는 영역과 불스트라고 명명된 단일 핵을 포함해 핵이라고 불리는 뉴런들의 개별적인 집합체로 배열돼 있다고 생각됐다.

새로운 논문 중 하나에서 수석 저자인 신경과학자 오누르 권튀르쿤과 그의 동료들은 소리와 시각 처리에 관여하는 DVR과 불스트의 영역들을 분석했다. 이를 위해 그들은 3차원 편광 영상(3D-PLI)이라고 불리는 기술을 사용했는데, 이는 뇌 샘플에서 신경 섬유를 시각화하는 데 사용될 수 있는 빛 기반 현미경 기법이다. 연구자들은 비둘기와 올빼미 모두에서 이러한 뇌 영역들이 우리의 신피질과 매우 유사하게 구성돼 있으며, 층 같은 조직과 기둥 같은 조직을 모두 가지고 있고, 수평적 회로와 수직적 회로를 모두 가지고 있다는 것을 발견했다.

3

하위내용영역	배점	예상정답률
일반영어 B형 서술형	4점	45%

모범답안) Transportation modes have changed and improved over time. First, horses and camels were used to move people and goods. Later, railways were developed and allowed for more commerce and commuting to work. Afterward, motor vehicles outshone the railways with their greater flexibility and ability to reach remote areas. In conclusion, human beings will continue to innovate modes of travel.

채점 기준

ⓐ Topic sentence
+ 1점 : "Transportation modes have (changed and) improved over time"를 명확하게 서술하였거나 유사하였다.
  ☞ 다음과 같이 서술하였어도 맞는 것으로 한다.
  - "The means of transportation have changed over many centuries(=over time)."
  - "Transportation methods have evolved significantly throughout human history."

ⓑ Major supporting details
+ 2점 : "①First, horses and camels were used to move people and goods. ②Later, railways were developed and allowed for more commerce and commuting to work. ③Afterward, motor vehicles outshone the railways with their greater flexibility and ability to reach remote areas"을 명확하게 서술하였다.
  ☞ 3개 중 3개 모두 정확하게 요약했으면 2점, 2개를 요약했으면 1점, 나머지는 0점을 준다.

ⓒ Conclusion
+ 1점 : "In conclusion, human beings will continue to innovate modes of travel"을 명확하게 요약하였다.
  ☞ 다음과 같이 서술하였어도 맞는 것으로 한다.
  - "This continuous innovation in transportation will persist as people seek increasingly efficient ways to travel."

감점
- 본문에 나오는 연속되는 6단어 이상을 사용하였다. −0.5pt
- 문단을 두 개나 그 이상으로 구성하였다. −0.5pt
- 문법이나 영어 표현을 합쳐 3개 이상 오류가 있다. −0.5pt

한글번역

오래 전 왕과 기사들의 시대에, 말, 버팔로, 낙타와 같은 동물들이 인간에 의해 운송 목적으로 사용됐다. 이러한 동물들이 의심할 여지 없이 인간이 걸어서 여행하는 수고를 덜어졌지만, 여행을 마치는 데 오랜 시간이 걸렸으며, 특히 화물을 운송할 때는 더욱 그랬다. 운송 수단은 수 세기에 걸쳐 변화하고 개선됐다.

1825년 조지 스티븐슨의 첫 번째 철도 개통은 운송 역사에서 중요한 진전을 의미했다. 철도는 더 많은 사람과 화물을 실을 수 있기 때문에 인기가 높았다. 더 중요하게는, 동물들보다 더 빨리 달렸다. 철도는 통신망을 개선했고, 따라서 상품의 수출입과 일하기 위해 자신의 마을이나 심지어 나라 밖으로 여행하는 사람들이 가능해졌다. 불행히도 자동차의 발명 이후 철도의 인기는 감소했다.

자동차는 18세기에 처음 발명됐다. 이러한 차량들은 선로 위를 달리지 않아서 고정된 경로가 없기 때문에 많은 사람들에게 선호됐다. 따라서 여행자들은 자신의 편의에 맞게 자신만의 경로를 계획할 수 있었다. 이는 특히 목적지가 작은 마을이나 외진 지역과 같은 곳일 때 그렇다. 이런 곳들에는 기차가 거의 또는 전혀 도달하지 않으므로, 자동차로 여행하는 것이 이 문제를 해결할 것이다. 수년간의 개조를 거쳐, 자동차는 이제 가장 일반적으로 사용되는 운송 수단 중 하나이다. 오늘날 우리는 거의 매일 자동차, 택시, 버스, 트럭이나 밴으로 여행한다.

인간은 수 세기에 걸쳐 다양한 운송 수단을 혁신해 왔다. 어딘가에 더 편리하고 안전하게 가는 것은 우리 영혼에 새겨진 기본적인 욕망이다. 따라서 더욱 발전된 형태의 운송 수단의 발명은 인류 역사에서 지속적으로 나타날 것이다.

제59회 모의고사

1

하위내용영역	배점	예상정답률
일반영어 A형 서술형	4점	45%

모범답안 The container model has been applied to more detrimental lengths as it has enabled harmful practices in commercial surrogacy. Specifically, fertility clinics exploited the conceptual separation between gestators and fetuses to create dehumanizing prenatal care that treated surrogate mothers as disposable. Second, the word is "gestator".

채점기준

+ 2점 : 컨테이너 모델이 왜 해로운 방향으로 적용됐는지에 대해 "The container model has been applied to more detrimental lengths as(=because) it has enabled harmful practices in commercial surrogacy. Specifically, fertility clinics exploited the conceptual separation between gestators and fetuses to create dehumanizing prenatal care that treated surrogate mothers as disposable"라 서술하였거나 유사하였다.
+ 2점 : 빈칸에 들어갈 단어를 "gestator"라 정확하게 기입하였다. 이외에는 답이 될 수 없다.

⊕ 보충설명

① "it's through this model that we can speak of a 'bun in the oven' and, to add to her list, depict fetuses as floating astronauts in an empty black space rather than embedded in the uterine wall."
→ "태아 용기 모델(fetal container model)"이 우리의 언어와 시각적 표현에 어떻게 반영되어 있는지를 보여주는 예시들은 다음과 같다.
• "bun in the oven"(오븐 속의 빵): 임신을 표현하는 일상적인 영어 표현이다. 이는 태아를 빵에, 자궁을 오븐에 비유하는 것으로, 태아와 임신한 사람이 분리된 개체라는 용기 모델의 관점을 반영한다.
• "floating astronauts in an empty black space": 태아를 묘사할 때 흔히 사용되는 시각적 표현이다. 태아가 마치 빈 검은 공간에 떠다니는 우주비행사처럼 그려지는 것을 말한다.
• "embedded in the uterine wall": 태아가 자궁벽에 착상되어 밀접하게 연결되어 있다는 생물학적 사실을 말한다.

핵심 메시지
용기 모델은 태아와 임신한 사람을 분리된 존재로 보기 때문에 태아가 마치 독립적으로 존재하는 것처럼 묘사한다. 하지만 **이는 태아와 임신한 사람이 실제로는 생물학적으로 불가분의 관계에 있다는 현실을 왜곡하는 것이다.**

② "Though relatively innocuous in its daily use, the container model has been applied to more detrimental lengths too."
일상적 사용에서는 비교적 무해하지만, 용기 모델이 더욱 해로운 차원으로까지 적용되었다는 뜻이다. 구체적으로, 작가는 용기 모델이 단순히 "오븐 속의 빵"이라는 무해한 표현에서 그치지 않고, 상업적 대리모 산업에서 대리모를 비인간화하고 일회용품처럼 취급하는 훨씬 더 해로운 방식으로 악용되었다고 지적하고 있다.

핵심 메시지
즉, **이론적 모델이 현실에선** 여성을 착취하고 차별하는 등 **더욱 심각하고 해로운 실천으로** 발전했다는 의미이다.

③ "What this shows is that the metaphysical container view might be morally neutral, but its cultural manifestation has developed and is currently utilised in a patriarchal context."
형이상학적 용기 관점 자체는 도덕적으로 중립적일 수 있다. 즉, 태아와 임부를 분리된 개체로 보는 **철학적 관점** 자체는 선악을 판단할 수 없는 중립적 개념일 수 있다. 하지만 이 관점의 문화적 발현은 가부장적 맥락에서 발전하고 현재 활용되고 있다. 즉, 실제 사회에서 이 이론이 적용될 때는 남성 중심적, 여성 억압적 방식으로 사용되고 있음을 뜻한다.

핵심 메시지
추상적 이론은 중립적일 수 있지만, 그것이 현실에서 구현될 때는 기존의 권력 구조(가부장제) 안에서 작동하기 때문에 여성에게 해로운 방식으로 악용되고 있음을 비판한다. 상업적 대리모 산업에서 "용기 모델"이 대리모를 비인간화하고 착취하는 도구로 사용되는 것이 그 예이다.

④ "The plausibility of certain reproductive practices depends upon the kind of conceptual framework we use to understand them."
생식 기술이나 관행에 대한 우리의 판단은 객관적이지 않다. 어떤 생식 기술이 실현 가능하거나 받아들일 만한지는 우리가 임신과 태아를 어떤 관점으로 바라보느냐에 따라 달라진다.
- 용기 모델로 보면 : (태아와 임신한 사람이 분리 가능하므로) 인공 자궁 기술이 타당하고 실현 가능해 보인다.
- 부분 모델로 보면 : (태아와 임신한 사람이 불가분의 관계이므로) 인공자궁 기술이 문제적이거나 불완전해 보인다.

핵심 메시지
기술 자체의 객관적 특성보다는 **우리의 사고 틀**이 그 기술에 대한 평가를 결정한다는 철학적 통찰

⑤ "an alternative view in which the plausibility of artificial-womb technology becomes less of a 'workable concept'—or at least more complicated."
인공 자궁 기술의 타당성이 '실용적인/실행 가능한 개념'이 되지 못하거나, 아니면 적어도 더 복잡해지는 대안적 관점(앞서 언급된 용기 모델에 대한 반대 관점)
→ 이는 Irina Aristarkhova의 부분 모델(parthood model) 관점을 가리킨다.

핵심 메시지
태아를 임신한 사람의 일부로 보는 관점에서는 인공 자궁이 단순한 기술적 해결책이 아니라 매우 복잡하고 문제적인 개념이 된다는 뜻이다.

⑥ "then the extent to which artificial wombs are truly capable of satisfying this role becomes limited."
그렇다면 인공 자궁이 이 역할(임부 gestating person의 역할)을 진정으로 만족시킬 수 있는 정도가 제한적이 된다.

핵심 메시지
태아가 임부의 일부라면, 인공 자궁은 **단순히 물리적 공간만 제공**하는 것으로, 임부와 태아의 생물학적, 감정적 연결은 대체할 수 없다. 따라서 인공 자궁의 역할 대체 능력이 제한적이다.
→ 부분 모델 관점에서는 인공 자궁이 완전한 해결책이 될 수 없다는 의미이다.

⑦ "Of course, one could concede a new fetus-gestator relationship, one that extends into the realms of mechanics and machines."
물론 기계와 기계 장치의 영역으로 확장되는 새로운 태아-임부 관계를 인정할 수도 있다.

핵심 메시지
인공 자궁 기술로 인해 태아와 임부(기계) 사이의 새로운 형태의 관계가 생길 수 있음은 인정한다. 즉, 기계적/기술적 임신 관계의 가능성을 인정하는 것이다.

⑧ "Still, if we're willing to confront the biological realities of pregnancy—that is, the actual inextricability of fetus and gestator—then our future as machines is, in this specific context, one that we'll need to confront eventually."
그러나 임신의 생물학적 현실들—즉, 태아와 임부가 실제로는 분리될 수 없다는 사실—을 정면으로 마주하고자 한다면, 이러한 특정한 상황에서 기계가 된 우리의 미래는 결국 우리가 직면하게 될 미래이다.
→ "our future as machines" 기계로서의 우리의 미래(인공 자궁 기술이 발전하면 임신 과정에서 기계가 인간을 대체하는 미래)
→ "one that we'll need to confront eventually" 결국 우리가 직면해야 할 미래

핵심 메시지
비록 인공 자궁으로 새로운 관계를 만들 수는 있지만, 임신이 본질적으로 분리 불가능한 생물학적 과정이라는 현실을 받아들인다면, 기계가 이 역할을 대체하는 미래는 결국 우리가 직면하게 될 것이라는 뜻이다.

한글번역

사상가 로렌 윤은 현재 서구에서 논의되고 있는 임신에 대한 두 가지 주요 형이상학적 모델에 대해 이야기한다. 첫째 이른바 "부분 모델"이라는 것으로, 태아가 임부의 팔, 다리, 신장과 같은 식으로 임부의 일부라는 시각이다. 둘째 "컨테이너 모델"은 임부와 태아를 각각 독립된 개체로 보며, "태아를 담고 있는 엄마"라는 문화적으로 지배적인 시각으로 이어진다. 이러한 시각을 바탕으로 우리는 "오븐 안에서 구워지고 있는 빵"과 같은 비유에 이르고, 태아를 자궁 내벽에 붙어 있는 존재로 상상하기보다는 어두운 공간에서 떠다니는 우주 비행사와 같은 존재로 그리게 되는 것이다.

"컨테이너 모델"의 일상적인 활용은 해롭지 않지만, 그 모델의 확장은 보다 해로운 방향으로 이뤄지기도 한다. 사회학자 암리타 팬디는 2010년 인도의 (그 이후) 금지된 상업적 대리모 산업에 대한 연구 결과를 발표했는데, 임부와 태아가 별개라는 개념은 대리모 업체들의 비인간적인 산전 케어 관행으로 이어졌다는 것이다. 형이상학적 개념 자체는 도덕적으로 중립일지 몰라도, 그것이 문화적으로 발현되는 모습을 살펴보면 가부장적 맥락에서 활용되고 있는 것이다.

재생산을 둘러싼 특정 관행의 타당성은 우리가 그 과정을 이해하기 위해 어떤 개념적 틀을 사용하는가에 달려있다. 인공 자궁을 활용해 임신의 일부, 또는 전 과정을 대체하겠다는 아이디어는 그 자체로 태아와 임부가 분리가능한 존재라는 것을 전제로 하고 있다. 인공 자궁 기술이 반드시 컨테이너 모델을 수반하는 것은 아니지만, 현재 진행 중인 담론의 수사는 그와 같은 시각을 적극 반영하고 있다. 예를 들어, 자궁을 생식사회학자인 로저 고스던이 명명한 "영리한 인큐베이터"로 비유하는 것 등이 그것이다.

여성학자 이리나 아리스타르코바는 인공 자궁 기술의 타당성에 대한 논의가 "말이 되는 컨셉" 차원이 아닌 조금 더 복잡한 논의가 되도록 하는 대안적 시각을 제안한다. 짐작하건대 태아를 임부의 일부로 이해한다면, 인공 자궁이 그 역할을 진정 만족시킬 가능성은 제한적이다. 물론 역학과 기계의 영역까지 확대된 전혀 새로운 태아-임부 관계를 받아들일 수도 있을 것이다. 하지만 우리가 태아와 임부 간의 실질적인 불가분성이라는 임신의 생물학적 현실을 받아들이고자 한다면 기계로서의 우리 미래는 우리가 언젠가는 반드시 마주하게 될 것이다.

2

하위내용영역	배점	예상정답률
일반영어 A형 서술형	4점	65%

모범답안 Ms. Clark's expectation was subverted when the after school program had active participation and wasn't used to keep students busy. Second, Mr. Stein believes that the Ms. Sutter's students will be unlikely to be able to attend the renowned university.

채점기준

+ 2점: 교사 클락의 기대가 어떤 식으로 전복되었는가에 대해 "the after school program had active participation (and wasn't used to keep students busy)"라 서술하였거나 유사하였다.
+ 2점: 스타인의 밑에 깔려 있는(근본적인) 편견에 찬 전제를 "Ms. Sutter's students will be unlikely to be able to attend the renowned university(=Mr. Stein's school)"라 서술하였거나 유사하였다.

한글번역

서터 선생님은 가족 중 처음으로 대학에 진학할 수 있는 학생들을 위한 방과 후 동아리를 파인우드 학교에 만들게 돼 흥분했다. 그녀는 많은 학생들이 고등교육에 대한 지식이 부족하다는 것을 알게 되면서 그런 동아리의 필요성을 느끼기 시작했다. 많은 부모들이 자녀들에게 대학에 대해 생각해보라고 격려했지만, 그녀의 학생들은 더 부유한 또래들처럼 대학 캠퍼스를 보거나 고등교육 선택지에 대해 배울 기회가 동일하지 않았다.

서터 선생님은 교직원 회의에서 동아리를 제안했다. 일부 교사들은 불필요하다고 생각했지만, 다른 교사들은 흥미를 보이며 지원을 제공했다. 주요 논의 사항은 동아리의 학년 범위였다. 모든 학생들에게 개방해야 할까, 아니면 높은 학년으로 제한해야 할까?

2학년 담임인 베이츠 선생님이 말했다. "경험상 5학년 학생에게 대학에 대해 이야기하기 시작하기에는 너무 이르다. 그들에게는 너무 어려운 일이다."

다른 교사인 클락 선생님이 덧붙였다. "우리 학교의 가정들은 아이들을 바쁘게 하기 위해서만 무료 방과 후 프로그램이라면 무엇이든 등록시킬 것이다. 당신은 넘쳐날 것이고 결국 대학보다는 훈육에 더 많은 시간을 쓰게 될 것이다."

서터 선생님은 동료들의 의견에 동의하지 않았지만, 마지못해 동아리를 5학년 학생들에게만 제공하기로 동의했다.

몇 달 후 서터 선생님은 "대학 동아리" 모임 중에 잠시 멈춰서 일이 얼마나 잘 돼가고 있는지 놀라워했다. 학생들은 정기적으로 참석했고, 부모들은 픽업 시간 전에 도착해 대학 생활에 대한 활발한 토론에 참여했다.

연말 축하 행사로, 서터 선생님은 가이드 투어를 포함한 유명한 지역 대학교로의 현장학습을 계획했다. 캠퍼스에 도착했을 때 그녀는 학생들에게 입학처 사무실 밖에서 기다리라고 하고 자신은 들어가서 접수원에게 일행이 도착했음을 알렸다. 접수원과 이야기한 후, 서터 선생님은 배정된 투어 가이드가 재배정돼 그녀의 일행이 자율 투어를 해야 한다는 사실을 알고 충격을 받았다.

"하지만 저는 이 대학교에 다니지 않았어요! 아이들에게 적절한 투어를 해 줄 수 없어요. 그냥 다른 그룹에 합류하게 해주시면 안 될까요?" 그녀가 애원했다.

"죄송하지만, 가이드는 예비 고등학생들에게 우선순위가 있습니다"라고 접수원이 답했다. 서터 선생님이 계속해서 동아리의 사정을 호소하자, 입학처장인 스타인 씨가 그녀에게 다가왔다.

"도와드릴까요?" 그가 따뜻하게 물었다.

"네"라고 서터 선생님이 답했다. "여기 5학년 학생들 그룹이 있는데, 잠재적인 1세대 대학생들입니다"라고 말하며, 학생들이 투어에 대해 얼마나 흥미를 보이는지 설명했다.

스타인 씨는 서터 선생님에게 자신의 사무실로 들어오라고 했다. 훌륭하다! 서터 선생님이 생각했다. 아마도 그가 우리에게 투어를 해 줄 사람일 것이다. 대신 스타인 씨가 말했다. "투어 가이드가 없어서 죄송합니다. 이런 상황을 피하려고 최선을 다하지만, 여기 진짜 지원 가능한 학생들이 있습니다. 5학년 학생들을 그들보다 우선시해서 그들의 이익을 해칠 수는 없습니다." 그는 잠시 멈춘 후 덧붙였다. "솔직히 말해서, 당신이 학생들을 아마 절대 다니지 않을 곳에 대해 흥미를 갖게 하는 것이 걱정됩니다. 아마도 커뮤니티 칼리지를 투어해야 할 것입니다."

이 말과 함께, 그는 사무실 문을 열어 서터 선생님이 나가도록 했다. 서터 선생님은 창문을 통해 자신의 학생들이 투어를 위해 인내심 있게 기다리고 있는 것을 봤다. 그녀는 그들에게 무엇을 말해야 할지, 그리고 스타인 씨의 발언을 어떻게 다뤄야 할지 생각하며 눈물을 참았다.

3

하위내용영역	배점	예상정답률
일반영어 A형 서술형	4점	50%

모범답안) He didn't believe the invitation to be real at first. Second, it can be inferred they were attracted by to a new type of tough-guy hero and prose, along with unlimited amounts of violence, sexual intrigue, and moral devastation.

채점기준

+ 2점 : 밑줄 친 부분의 의미를 "He didn't believe the invitation to be real at first"라 서술하였거나 유사하였다. 또는 "He first believed the invitation was a prank and unreal"라 서술하였다.
+ 2점 : 해밋의 독자가 (그의 작품에서) 가장 끌린 것을 "<u>a new type of tough-guy hero and prose</u>, along with unlimited amounts of <u>violence, sexual intrigue, and moral devastation</u>"라 서술하였거나 유사하였다.

한글번역

1935년 봄 할리우드의 한 파티에서 대시엘 해밋은 거트루드 스타인으로부터 문학적 미스터리 하나를 해결해달라는 요청을 받았다. 왜, 그녀가 말문을 열었다. 19세기에는 남성(작가)들이 다양한 종류의 남성 캐릭터들을 성공적으로 써냈고 여성(작가)들은 자신들의 단순한 변형에 불과한 여주인공들만 창조할 수 밖에 없었는데—그녀는 샬롯 브론테와 조지 엘리엇을 언급했다—20세기에는 이 상황이 왜 뒤바뀌었느냐는 것이다. (**스타인은 문학사에서 성별에 따른 창작 역할이 시대에 따라 바뀐 현상을 지적하고 있다. 19세기에는 남성 작가들이 다양한 남성 캐릭터를 창조했지만 여성 작가들은 자신의 모습을 투영한 제한적인 여주인공만 만들었는데, 20세기에는 오히려 남성 작가들이 자신만을 반영하는 캐릭터를 쓰게 되었다는 것**) 요즘에는, 남성들이 자기 자신만을 묘사하고 있다고 스타인은 지적하며, 왜 그런지 의문을 제기했다. 스타인은, (해밋 자신이) 술을 많이 마시는 전직 탐정인 데다가 술을 많이 마시는 전직 탐정에 관한 최신 소설 "씬 맨"의 표지에 사진이 실린 해밋이 그 이유를 알 수 있는 입장에 있을 것이라고 합리적으로 생각했다.

그날 저녁 파티는 스타인을 기리기 위해 열렸고, 해밋은 할리우드에서 그녀가 만나달라고 요청한 유일한 사람이었다. 그는 처음에 그 초대를 만우절 농담으로 받아들였지만, 그런 찬사는 더 이상 큰 놀라움이 아니었다. 해밋은 1930년에 출간된 《몰타의 매》가 어울리는 터프가이 문체로 새로운 유형의 터프가이 영웅을 소개한 이래로 "지식인들의 건배 대상(에드먼드 윌슨의 혐오스러운 표현으로는-에드먼드 윌슨이 "duh"라는 비표준 발음을 사용해 지식인들이 해밋을 떠받드는 것을 조롱하며 비하한 표현)"이 돼 있었다. 그는 터프가이 내용에 어울리는 터프가이 문체로 새로운 유형의 터프가이 영웅을 선보였다: 말수가 적고 거리에서 터득한 영리함을 지녔으며, 간혹 재미있는 순간들이 스쳐가도 의도적으로 평면적이고 일반적인 의식의 과정들이 놀랍도록 빠져 있는 스타일이었다. 독자들은 매혹됐고, 비평가들은 미국 언어 창조의 최신 발전을 재빨리 발표했다. (해밋의 독특한 문체가 독자들을 완전히 사로잡았고, 비평가들은 이것이 미국만의 고유한 문학 언어를 만들어가는 과정에서 중요한 새로운 진전이라고 즉시 인정했다는 의미) 이것은 스타인과 다른 문학 급진주의자들이 용감하지만 난해한 작품들과 읽히지 않는 논문들을 통해 애써 이루려 했던 그런 성과였는데, 이 성취가 가장 가능성이 낮은 곳에서 나타났다 : 폭력과 성적 음모, 도덕적 파괴가 무제한으로 수반되는 일을 우연히 하게 된 한 남자의 실제 경험을 바탕으로 한, 많은 사람들이 실제로 읽기를 좋아하는 값싼 탐정소설에서 말이다.

해밋은 활발하게 활동한 12년 동안 약 90편의 단편과 5편의 소설을 썼는데, 그중 많은 작품들이 절실히 필요한 돈을 위해서였다—그는 하루에 5천 단어를 써낼 수 있었다. (매우 빠른 속도로 글을 쓸 수 있는 능력이었다는 의미로, 돈이 필요할 때 신속하게 작품을 대량 생산할 수 있었음을 보여준다. 1930년대 작가들 평균은 하루 500-1000 단어)—그리고 많은 작품들이 명백히 그의 진지한 관심 수준 이하로 집필됐다. 물론 그는 또한 펄프 소설(1890년대부터 1950년대까지 값싼 펄프지에 인쇄돼 대중들에게 저렴하게 판매된 상업적 장르소설로, 탐정, 서부, 공포, 성 등을 주로 다뤘다.)이 제공할 수 있는 최고의 것을 보여주는 기막힌 이야기들과, 해밋 특유의 무표정한 대화의 엄격한 음률 속에서 공식을 초월하는 몇 작품들도 만들어냈다.

4

하위내용영역	배점	예상정답률
일반영어 B형 서술형	4점	40%

모범 답안 It is surprising that neuroscientists are more likely to falsely claim casual relationships without testing than expected, which is usually what psychologists are accused of. Second, the word is "correlation".

채점 기준

+ 2점 : 밑줄 친 "놀람"의 이유를 "neuroscientists are more likely to falsely claim casual relationships without testing than expected, which is usually what psychologists are accused of"라 서술하였거나 유사하였다.
+ 2점 : 음악 연습과 기량 증진 사이의 관계에 대한 루츠 옌케의 의견을 묘사한 한 단어를 "correlation" 또는 "correlational"이라 서술하였다. 이외에는 답이 될 수 없다.

제60회 모의고사

1

하위내용영역	배점	예상정답률
일반영어 B형 서술형	4점	45%

모범답안 The one word is "oligopolies". Second, the misunderstanding of the American Right of European policy is that they believe Europe to be a socialistic nightmare without growth nor innovation. Third, "competition" is the most important characteristic.

채점기준

+ 1점: 빈칸에 들어갈 단어를 "oligopolies"라 정확하게 기입하였다. 이외에는 답이 될 수 없다.
+ 2점: 미국의 우파에 관련해서 "무지"가 의미하는 것을 "they believe Europe to be a socialistic nightmare without growth nor innovation"라 서술하였거나 유사하였다.
+ 1점: 저자가 생각하는 자유 시장에서 가장 중요한 특징이라 추론할 수 있는 것을 "competition"라 서술하였거나 유사하였다.

☞ "no oligopolies"라 했으면 0.5점을 준다.

한글번역

최근 연구를 위해 토마스 라이히는 두 명의 연구 조교에게 음악 교육의 효과에 대한 상관관계 연구를 찾아보라고 요청했다. 그들은 2000년 이후 출판된 총 114편의 논문을 찾았다. 저자들이 어떤 인과관계를 주장했는지 평가하기 위해, 연구자들은 각 논문의 제목과 초록에서 "향상시킨다", "촉진한다", "손쉽게 만든다", "강화한다"와 같은 단서가 되는 동사들을 찾았다. 그 논문들은 연구에서 뇌전도나 자기공명과 같은 뇌 영상 방법을 사용했거나, 제목에 "뇌", "신경과학" 또는 관련 용어가 있는 저널에 게재된 경우 신경과학으로 분류됐다. 그렇지 않으면 논문들은 심리학으로 분류됐다. 라이히는 자신의 조교들에게 정확히 무엇을 증명하려고 하는지 말하지 않았다.

그들의 평가(연구 조교들이 각 논문의 제목과 초록에서 인과관계를 암시하는 동사들을 찾아 분류한 평가 결과들을 의미)를 집계한 후, 라이히는 음악 훈련이 인과적 효과를 가진다는 대다수의 논문이 오류였다고 주장했다. 라이히는 또한 신경과학 연구들 사이에서 과장이 (심리학에서보다) 더 만연했다는 것을 발견했는데, 그중 4분의 3이 음악 훈련과 기술 향상 사이의 단순한 상관관계를 인과관계로 잘못 범주화했다. 이것은 어떤 이들에게는 놀라운 일일 수 있다. 심리학자들은 "진짜" 과학을 하지 않는다는 비난과 한동안 싸워 왔다—주로 고전적 실험들의 많은 발견들이 재현 불가능하다고 판명됐기 때문이다. (심리학이 "진짜" 과학이 아니라는 비판을 받는 주된 이유가 기존의 유명한 심리학 실험 결과들을 다른 연구자들이 같은 실험을 반복했을 때 동일한 결과를 얻을 수 없다는 재현성 문제 때문이라는 것이다.) 반면에 뇌 스캔과 뇌전도로 무장한 신경과학자들은 같은 정도의 비판을 받지 않았다.

라이히의 새로운 연구를 칭찬한 스위스 취리히 대학교의 신경심리학자 루츠 옌케는 "나는 플루트 레슨이 미분방정식을 더 잘 풀게 만든다고 생각한 적이 없다"고 말했다. "그의 비판은 정당하다."

한글번역

1999년 보스턴에 도착했을 때, 미국은 자유 시장의 땅이었다. 많은 재화와 서비스들이 여기 미국에선 유럽보다 더 쌌다. 20년 후, 미국의 자유 시장은 신화가 돼가고 있다. 인터넷 서비스, 휴대폰 요금제, 항공료는 이제 미국보다 유럽과 아시아가 더 싸다. 2018년 광대역 인터넷 연결의 월평균 비용은 프랑스에서 31달러, 영국에서 39달러, 미국에서 68달러였다. 미국 가구는 또한 휴대폰 서비스에 프랑스나 영국 가구의 두 배를 지출한다.

이것은 정책 선택의 결과이다. 1999년 미국은 자유롭고 경쟁적인 시장을 가지고 있었던 반면 유럽 시장들은 독점기업들에 의해 지배되고 있었다. 항공업계가 대표적인 예이다. 지난 20년 동안 일련의 합병이 미국 항공업계를 과점으로 변화시킨 반면, 유럽은 부분적으로 라이언에어와 이지젯 같은 저비용 항공사들 덕분에 경쟁을 위해 하늘을 개방했다.

미국 규제당국은 중요한 이의제기도 없이 이러한 합병들이 일어나도록 허용했다. 반면 EU 규제당국은 저비용 경쟁업체들이 이착륙 슬롯에 접근할 수 있도록 보장함으로써 이들의 진입을 장려했다.

이러한 역사적 역전(미국이 자유 시장의 나라였던 1999년과 달리 현재는 유럽이 더 경쟁적인 시장을 가지게 된 상황의 완전한 뒤바뀜을 의미한다.)에는 여러 층의 아이러니가 있다. 한 가지 아이러니는 오늘날 유럽 소비자들에게 혜택을 주는 자유 시장 아이디어와 비즈니스 모델들이 미국 시장에서 영감을 받았다는 것이다. 또 다른 아이러니는 일부 좌파 미국 정치인들이 이제 대부분의 유럽인들이 극단적이라고 여길 정책들을 고려하고 있다는 것이다. 나는 민간 건강보험 회사들이 폐지돼야 한다고 생각하지 않는다. 나는 부유세를 지지하지만, 그것이 모든 병폐의 치료책이라고 생각하지는 않는다.

정치적 논쟁의 양극화는 부분적으로는 상호 무지의 결과이다. 미국 좌파는 유럽을 무료 의료, 무료 교육, 노동자 권리의 이상향으로 본다. 미국 우파는 유럽을 성장도 혁신도 없는 사회주의적 악몽으로 본다. 둘 다 틀렸으며, 그 결과는 잘못된 정책과 풍차와 싸우는 데 낭비되는 시간이다. (돈키호테에서 나오는 표현으로, 실제로는 존재하지 않는 적이나 잘못된 목표를 상대로 헛된 노력을 기울이는 것을 의미한다.) : 미국 좌파와 우파가 모두 유럽에 대해 잘못 알고 있는 <u>상호 무지</u> → <u>정치적 논쟁의 양극화</u> → 그 결과로 잘못된 정책들과 실제로는 존재하지 않는 문제들을 상대로 헛된 노력을 기울이며 시간을 낭비하게 된다는 논리.

2

하위내용영역	배점	예상정답률
일반영어 B형 서술형	4점	45%

모범답안 The three words are "fish body size" and one word is "ecology". Second, the reasons salmon size may be smaller are climate change, competition with hatchery-raised and wild salmon, and salmon coming from the sea at an earlier age.

채점 기준

+ 2점 : 빈칸에 들어갈 단어를 "fish body size(1점)" and "ecology(1점)"라 정확하게 기입하였다.
+ 2점 : 연어 크기가 작아지는 것 같은 이유를 "<u>climate change</u>, <u>competition with hatchery-raised and wild salmon</u>, and <u>salmon coming from the sea at an earlier age</u>"라 정확하게 서술하였다.

한글번역

매년 연어들은 짝짓기를 하고 알을 낳고 죽기 위해 알래스카의 차가운 강으로 돌아온다. 알래스카의 연어 회유는 세계에서 가장 큰 규모 중 하나다. 하지만 지난 수십 년 동안 그 대규모 연어 회유에는 점점 더 작은 연어들이 특징적으로 나타나고 있다. ("feature"는 "특징으로 하다" 또는 "나타내다"라는 의미)

캘리포니아 대학교 산타크루즈 캠퍼스의 크리스타 오케와 동료들은 1950년대까지 거슬러 올라가는 연어 회유 데이터 기록을 분석했다. 그들은 약 1,250만 마리의 연어에 대한 데이터를 포함시켰다. 그리고 다음에 대해서는 의문의 여지가 없다 : 즉, 연어들의 크기가 줄어들고 있다. 오늘날의 홍연어는 조상들보다 2.1% 더 짧다. 연어는 2.4% 더 짧고 은연어는 3.3% 더 짧다. 킹 연어라고도 불리는 치누크 연어는 8%로 가장 큰 감소를 보였다. 이는 길이에서 평균 2인치 이상의 차이다.

연구자들은 이 경향 뒤에 있는 정확한 이유들을 아직 정확히 밝혀내지 못했다. 하지만 그들의 분석은 기후 변화와 야생 및 부화장에서 기른 연어들과의 경쟁(부화장에서 기른 연어들이 방류되면서 야생 연어들과 함께 제한된 바다 환경에서 먹이와 공간을 두고 경쟁하게 돼, 개체당 이용할 수 있는 자원이 줄어들어 연어 크기가 작아지는 것이다.)이 모두 역할을 한다는 것을 시사한다. 그들은 또한 어류 몸 크기 변화의 대부분이 과거보다 더 어린 나이에 바다에서 돌아오는 물고기들 때문이라는 것을 발견했다. 오케는 물고기들이 어떤 이유로 더 빨리 성숙에 도달하고 있거나 바다가 나이 든 연어들이 생존하기에 더 위험한 곳이 됐기 때문에 더 일찍 돌아올 수 있다고 말한다.

원인이 무엇이든, 이 크기 변화는 사람들과 생태계에 막대한 파급효과를 가져온다. 오케와 그녀의 팀은 더 작은 물고기를 잡는 것이 이미 알래스카 상업적 연어 어업의 가치를 21% 삭감했을 수도 있다고 계산했다. 또한 이는 생계형 어민들—그들 중 많은 이들이 길고 혹독한 겨울을 견디기 위해 연어 저장량에 의존한다—이 이용할 수 있는 식량을 26%만큼 줄였을 가능성이 있다.

생태학 측면에서, 연구자들은 더 작은 물고기들이 16% 적은 알을 낳아 미래에 연어 개체수를 감소시킬 수 있다고 추정했다. 그리고 이 연구에 따르면, 연어들은 그들이 산란하는 유역으로 28% 적은 영양분을 가져온다. "연어들이 번식하고 죽은 후, 연어들의 사체는, 실제로 담수와 육상 생태계를 이 해양 유래 영양분들(연어가 바다에서 먹이를 먹고 성장하면서 체내에 축적한 질소, 인 등의 영양분들이다. 연어가 강으로 돌아와 죽으면 이 바다의 영양분들이 내륙의 담수와 육상 생태계로 전달돼 곰, 새, 나무 등 다양한 생물들의 영양원이 된다.)을 통해서 비옥하게 만드는데, 이는 정말로 중요한 것이며, 곰과 명금류 같은 온갖 종류의 동물들에 의해 사용되기도 하며 심지어 나무들에도 흡수된다."

크기가 작아지는 연어에 대해 비난할 단일 요인이 없기 때문에, 명백한 해결책은 없다고 오케는 말한다.

3

하위내용영역	배점	예상정답률
일반영어 B형 서술형	4점	45%

모범답안 The ubiquity of advertisements presents both advantages and disadvantages for consumers. While ads provide free product information, they can be annoying and misleading. Informative advertisements offer useful details about new products, whereas persuasive ads claim superiority with potentially untrue claims. Excessive advertising from competing brands creates consumer confusion and increases production costs, ultimately leading to higher prices. In conclusion, therefore, while advertisements serve essential functions in providing product awareness, consumers must approach them with critical judgment to navigate their limitations effectively.

채점 기준

ⓐ Topic sentence
+ 1점 : "<u>The ubiquity of advertisements has benefits and concerns</u>" 또는 "<u>Advertisements have benefits and drawbacks</u>"라 서술하였다.

ⓑ Major supporting details
+ 2점 : "<u>Advertisements can be categorized as either informative, offering product details and specifications, or persuasive, encouraging purchases by emphasizing product advantages over competitors. While these provide valuable information for decision-making, especially regarding new products, advertisements often conceal product flaws and present misleading claims. Additionally, excessive advertising from competing brands creates consumer confusion and increases production costs, which are ultimately passed on to buyers through higher prices</u>"을 명확하게 서술하였다.

ⓒ Conclusion
+ 1점 : "<u>In conclusion, due to these circumstances, we can benefit from advertisements but must control how we live with them</u>"을 정확하게 서술하였거나 유사하였다.

감점
- 본문에 나오는 연속되는 6단어 이상을 사용하였다. -0.5pt
- 문단을 두 개나 그 이상으로 구성하였다. -0.5pt
- 문법이나 영어 표현을 합쳐 3개 이상 오류가 있다. -0.5pt

한글번역

사람들은 끊임없이 광고의 폭격을 받고 있다. 판매업체들은 우리의 관심을 끌고 그들의 서비스나 제품을 팔려고 노력한다. 광고는 어디에나 나타난다: 텔레비전, 인터넷, 라디오, 팸플릿 등

광고는 때때로 우리가 좋아하는 텔레비전 프로그램을 방해할 때 짜증을 느끼더라도 매우 유용하다. 광고는 제품과 서비스에 대한 무료 정보를 우리에게 제공한다. 광고에는 두 가지 유형이 있다: 정보 제공형과 설득형. 정보 제공형 광고는 제품이나 서비스의 세부사항을 제공해주는 것들이다. 이러한 정보는 특히 제품이나 서비스가 새로운 것일 때 유용하다. 예를 들어, 컴퓨터를 사야 할 때, 최신 모델들과 그들의 다양한 기능을 설명하는 광고들이 도움이 될 것이다. 하지만 광고의 소수만이 정보 제공형이다. 그들 중 많은 것들은 두 번째 범주인 설득형에 속한다. 이러한 광고들은 제품에 대해 더 많이 말해줄 뿐만 아니라, 동시에 그들의 제품이 경쟁 제품들보다 우수하다고 주장함으로써 고객들이 그것들을 구매하도록 설득한다. 이러한 주장들은 때때로 사실이 아닐 수도 있지만, 진정한 제품 정보를 찾는 소비자들에게는 소수의 진정으로 정보적인 광고들이 여전히 가치가 있다.

광고가 쇼핑에 좋은 도우미가 될 수 있지만, 단점도 있다. 대부분의 광고는 오직 판매만을 목표로 한다. 제품이나 서비스의 결함은 보통 소비자들로부터 숨겨진다. 따라서 때때로, 우리가 구매한 제품이나 서비스가 광고에서 주장하는 것처럼 나오지 않으면 속았다고 느낀다. 때때로, 경쟁업체들의 광고는 매우 치열해질 수 있는데, 특히 유사한 제품을 생산하는 회사들이 많을 때 그렇다. 한 가지 일반적인 예는 세탁 세제이다. 다양한 브랜드에 대한 광고가 너무 많아서 고객들이 때때로 무엇을 사야 할지 혼란스러워한다. 게다가, 더 많은 광고를 하는 것은 회사의 생산 비용이 증가한다는 것을 의미할 것이다. 이러한 비용 증가는 보통 더 높은 가격의 형태로 소비자들에게 전가된다.

광고가 없다면, 우리는 불완전한 정보에 기반해 물건을 사야 하거나 제품이나 서비스를 알기 전에 더 복잡한 방법을 거쳐야 할 수도 있다. 반면에, 너무 많은 광고 또한 우리의 구매 결정을 복잡하게 만든다. 그래서 나는 우리가 광고 없이는 살 수 없지만 그것들과 어떻게 살아야 하는지에 대해서는 조심해야 한다고 말하고 싶다.

제61회 모의고사

1

하위내용영역	배점	예상정답률
일반영어 A형 서술형	4점	50%

모범답안 The First World War marked the transition from Art Nouveau to Functionalism. Second, the word is "glass".

채점기준

+ 2점: 아르누보에서 기능주의로의 이행을 이끈 역사적 사건을 "The First World War"라 서술하였거나 유사하였다.
+ 2점: 빈칸에 들어갈 단어를 "glass"라 서술하였거나 유사하였다.

한글번역

국제적인 아르누보 양식은 구불구불한 선, 꽃과 식물 모티프, 그리고 부드럽고 희미한 색채로 특징지어졌다. 그것은 일본 예술의 요소들, 고대 문화의 모티프들, 그리고 자연 형태들을 함께 가져온 절충주의적인 양식이었다. 이 양식의 유리 제품들은 종종 의도적으로 왜곡됐지만 윤곽이 우아했으며, 창백하거나 무지개빛 표면을 가지고 있었다. 이 양식의 선호되는 기법은 매장됐던 고대 유리에서 보이는 무지개빛 표면을 모방하는 것이었다. 가장 인기가 높았던 시기에 생산된 아르누보 유리의 대부분은 일반적으로 "예술 유리"라고 불렸다. 예술 유리는 장식적 목적을 위한 것이었고 신중하게 선택된 색상 조합과 혁신적인 기법에 그 효과를 의존했다. 미국에서는 루이스 컴포트 티파니가 이 양식의 가장 주목받는 대표자였으며, 당시에 널리 모방됐고 오늘날 매우 귀중하게 여겨지는 다양한 유리 형태와 표면을 생산했다. 티파니는 고대 이집트, 일본, 페르시아 모티프들을 성공적으로 결합한 뛰어난 디자이너였다.

아르누보 양식은 1895년부터 1915년까지 장식 예술에서 주요 세력(주도적 흐름)이었지만, 그 영향은 1920년대 중반까지 계속됐다. 아르누보 양식은 결국 세기 전환기부터 존재해 왔던 기능주의라고 알려진 새로운 사상 학파에 의해 추월당하게 됐다. 처음에는 소수의 전위적인 건축가와 디자이너 그룹에 제한됐던 기능주의는 제1차 세계대전 후 디자이

너들에게 지배적인 영향력으로 등장했다. 이 운동의 기본 신조인 기능이 형태를 결정해야 한다는 것은 새로운 개념이 아니었다. 곧 뚜렷한 미학적 규범이 발전했다 : 형태는 단순해야 하고, 표면은 평범해야 하며, 어떤 장식이든 기하학적 관계에 기반해야 한다. (기능주의 운동의 "기능이 형태를 결정해야 한다"는 기본 원칙 자체는 새로운 개념이 아니었지만, 이 원칙을 바탕으로 곧 구체적이고 독특한 미학적 규범—단순한 형태, 평범한 표면, 기하학적 장식—이 발전했다는 의미이다.) 이 새로운 디자인 개념은 이전 수십 년의 양식과 관습에 대한 날카로운 전후 반발과 결합해 아르누보 유형의 유리를 유행에서 밀려나게 만든 완전히 새로운 대중적 취향을 만들어냈다. 새로운 취향은 대조적이고 뚜렷한 윤곽의 극적인 효과, 그리고 복잡한 질감의 표면을 요구했다. (기능주의 이후 새로운 대중적 취향이 어떤 것을 선호했는지 설명하는 것으로, 아르누보의 부드럽고 곡선적인 특징과 대조되는 강렬하고 명확한 대비, 날카로운 윤곽선, 그리고 복잡한 표면 질감을 원했다는 의미이다.)

- boisterous(=rowdy) campaigns to get a speaking invitation canceled(=rescinded)
- disrupting the speaker by screaming and shouting
- engaging noise makers
- pulling the fire alarm
- keeping(=preventing) the speaker from airing her views
- depriving a person of her tenure or her doctorate

한글번역

60년 이상 동안 미국의 역사는 문화 전쟁에 의해 주도돼 왔다. 이 문화 전쟁은 보통 1960년대의 사회혁명으로 거슬러 올라가지만, 그보다 일찍 시작됐다. 문화 전쟁 1.0은 1950년대에 종교적 열성자들이 급속히 자유주의화되고 세속화되는 사회에서 그리스도를 위해 마음과 정신, 영혼을 얻으려고 노력하면서 시작됐다. 이 전쟁은 최근 2013년 대법원이 동성 결혼을 지지하는 문화적으로 중요한 판결을 내렸을 때 흐지부지한 결말로 흘러간 전쟁이다. 2015년에 대법원은 오버거펠 대 호지스 사건에서 동성 결혼에 제한을 가하는 것이 위헌이라고 판결하며 동성 결혼에 대한 완전한 승인을 했다. 이 시점에서 문화 전쟁 1.0은 끝났다.

이 첫 번째 문화 전쟁은 종교적 신앙과 도덕성에 관한 문제들, 예를 들면, 창조론이 생물학적 진화론에 대한 실행 가능한 대안인지 아닌지 여부와 공적 영역에서 기독교 가치를 제도화하는 것에 대해 제한을 둬야 하는지 여부 등을 놓고 벌어졌다. 문화 전쟁 2.0에서는 초자연적인 것, 형이상학, 심지어 더 광범위한 종교조차 무관해졌다. 기독교 신앙과 도덕의 요구는 계몽주의 원칙에 기반한 사회(계몽주의 원칙은 다음과 같다 : 이성과 합리성-감정이나 전통보다 논리적 사고와 증거에 기반한 판단; 자유로운 토론과 논쟁; 학문의 자유; 관용-서로 다른 견해와 신념을 존중하고 받아들이는 것; 개인의 권리-표현의 자유, 종교의 자유 등 개인의 기본권 보장. 이 문장에서 저자는 Culture War 2.0의 "de-platforming" 전술이 이러한 계몽주의 원칙들을 위협한다고 주장하고 있다. 즉, 상대방과 토론하고 논쟁하는 대신 아예 발언 기회를 차단하려는 행위가 자유로운 토론과 학문의 자유라는 계몽주의의 핵심 가치와 충돌한다는 것으로, 미국 사회는 바로 이러한 계몽주의적 가치들을 바탕으로 건설됐다고 저자는 생각한다.)에 훨씬 더 위협적인 무언가로 대체됐다.

2

하위내용영역	배점	예상정답률
일반영어 A형 서술형	4점	50%

모범답안 The word is "evolutionary biologist". Second, de-platforming is trying to get a speech canceled or to disrupt it aggressively and two examples are boisterous campaigns to get a speaking invitation canceled and disrupting the speaker by screaming and shouting.

채점기준

- 2점 : 빈칸에 들어갈 단어를 "evolutionary biologist"라 서술하였거나 유사하였다. 이외에는 답이 될 수 없다.
- 1점 : "de-platforming"이 "trying to get a speech canceled or to disrupt it(=the speech) aggressively"라 정확하게 서술하였거나 유사하였다.
- 1점 : "de-platforming"의 구체적 예를, 다음의 6가지 가운데 2가지를 선택해 정확하게 서술하였다.

문화 전쟁 2.0은 새로운 교전 규칙을 중심으로 돌아간다. 이 교전 규칙은 의견 불일치를 어떻게 다루는지와 관련이 있다. 문화 전쟁 1.0에서는 진화생물학자가 지질학적 연대 측정 기법에 기반해 지구의 나이에 대한 공개 강연을 한다면, 창조론적 입장을 지닌 반대자들은 반박하고, 그런 연대 측정 기법이 편향됐다고 주장하며, 그 진화생물학자에게 토론을 요구하고, 질의응답 시간에 날카로운—비록 불공정하게 유도된 것이지만—질문을 했을 것이다. (특정한 답변을 유도하거나 상대방을 곤란하게 만들려는 의도가 담긴 편향된 질문이다. 여기서는 창조론자들이 진화생물학자에게 겉보기에는 예리한 질문을 하지만, 실제로는 불공정하게 상대방을 궁지에 몰아넣으려는 의도가 숨어있는 질문들을 한다는 뜻이다.) 문화 전쟁 2.0에서는 연설자와의 의견 불일치가 때때로 플랫폼 박탈 시도로 대응된다. 연설이 전달되기 전에 초청을 철회하도록 하는 소란스러운 캠페인들이 벌어진다. 이 플랫폼 박탈이 성공하지 못하면, 비판자들은 소리를 지르고 외치거나, 소음 발생기를 사용하거나, 화재경보기를 당겨서(실제 화재가 없는데도 화재경보기를 의도적으로 작동시켜서 건물을 대피시키고 강연을 중단시키려는 방해 행위를 의미한다.) 연설자를 방해하는 방법에 호소할 수 있다. 목표는 더 나은 논증으로 연설자에 맞서거나 심지어 대안적 견해를 주장하는 것이 아니라, 연설자가 자신의 견해를 전혀 드러내지 못하도록 방해하는 것이다.

기독교 조직들은 검열의 오랜 역사를 가지고 있으며, 이 검열은 최근 수십 년 동안에도 어느 정도 계속됐다. 그럼에도 불구하고, 학술 논문을 억압하려는 시도는 문화 전쟁 1.0 동안에는 거의 상상할 수 없었을 것이다. 예를 들어 1925년 테네시주의 버틀러 법과 그에 따른 "스콥스 원숭이 재판"을 둘러싼 사건들에서처럼 이 문화 전쟁의 전조 기간 동안 기독교인들 측에서 유사한 시도들이 있었다. (문화 전쟁 1.0 이전에도 기독교도들이 학문적 자유를 억압하려는 비슷한 시도를 했다는 것이다. 버틀러 법은 공립학교에서 진화론 교육을 금지한 법이고, 스콥스 재판은 이 법을 위반한 교사를 기소한 유명한 재판이다. 이는 현재의 "플랫폼 박탈"과 유사한 검열 시도의 역사적 선례라는 뜻이다.) 그리고 문화 전쟁 1.0 동안 종교적 검열 시도자들은 가끔 <그리스도의 마지막 유혹> 같이 신성모독적이거나 외설적으로 해석되는 소설이나 영화에 (검열) 시도를 하기도 했다. 하지만 대부분의 경우, 첫 번째 문화 전쟁의 창조론자들은 진화생물학자가 대학교수 종신 재직권과 박사 학위를 잃기를 원하지 않았다. 그들(창조론자)은 토론하고 그들(진화생물학자들)이 틀렸음을 증명하기를 원했다.

3

하위내용영역	배점	예상정답률
일반영어 A형 서술형	4점	45%

모범답안 Women's aging experience has improved by gaining access to multiple new pathways for earning admiration and recognition, expanding beyond traditional beauty-based validation to include achievements in sports, professional careers, artistic endeavors, and political participation. Second, to fulfill the loyalty, people would need to completely reject and refuse to use modern inventions like motor-cars and wireless technology, actively abstaining from the conveniences of contemporary life to remain truly faithful to the past world they claim to prefer.

채점기준

+ 2점: 여성들에게 나이 들어가는 경험이 어떻게 향상되는지에 대해 "by gaining access to multiple new pathways for earning admiration and recognition, expanding beyond traditional beauty-based validation to include achievements in sports, professional careers, artistic endeavors, and political participation"라 서술하였거나 유사하였다.

+ 2점: 밑줄 친 "충성심"을 충족시키기 위해 취해야 될 것이 무엇이냐는 질문에 "people would need to completely reject and refuse to use modern inventions like motor-cars and wireless technology"라 서술하였거나 유사하였다.

한글번역

우리들 대부분이 햇빛을 필요로 하듯 찬사를 필요로 한다는 것은 부인할 수 없으며, 여성들이 남성들보다 찬사를 얻는 수단으로써 아름다움에 더 크게 의존한다는 것도 사실이다. 하지만 매년 여성들에게는 찬사를 받을 수 있는 길이 점점 더 많이 열리고 있으며, 운동, 전문직, 예술, 공적 생활에서 얻

4

하위내용영역	배점	예상정답률
일반영어 A형 서술형	4점	50%

모범답안 The word is "death". Second, if the premise comes true, wars would become less likely **because people would be more risk-averse with much more at stake**, and it would make little sense to send young soldiers to fight or start wars in the first place. Third, the writer mentions "a fisherman" **to illustrate how passengers on extremely long space journeys might lose sight of their original purpose** (and question whether their goal is still worthwhile,) just as a fisherman might forget that catching fish is the real purpose after **a long period without success**.

채점기준

+ 1점: 빈칸에 들어갈 단어를 "death"라 서술하였다. 이외에는 답이 될 수 없다.
+ 1점: 만일 글의 전제가 실현된다면 전쟁에는 무슨 일이 일어날까라는 질문에 "wars would become less likely because people would be more risk-averse with much more at stake, and it would make little sense to send young soldiers to fight or start wars in the first place"라 서술하였거나 유사하였다.
+ 2점: 저자가 "어부"를 언급한 이유를 "to illustrate how passengers on extremely long space journeys might lose sight of their original purpose (and question whether their goal is still worthwhile,) just as a fisherman might forget that catching fish is the real purpose after a long period without success"라 서술하였거나 유사하였다.

보충설명

어부 비유는 장기간의 여행에서 발생할 수 있는 심리적 문제를 보여준다. 어부가 오랫동안 물고기를 잡지 못하면 "낚시의 진짜 목적이 물고기를 잡는 것인가?"라고 의문을 품게 되듯이, 10만 년간 우주를 여행하는 승객들도 원래 목표를 잃어버리고 "우리가 왜 이 여행을 하고 있는가?"라고 회의할 수 있다는 뜻이다. 즉, 어부는 **목적의식을 잃고 방향감각을 상실한 상태를 나타내는** 예시이다. 작가는 극도로 긴 우주여행에서 승객들이 신념을 잃지 않고 안정된 마음가짐을 유지해야 한다고 강조하면서, 이런 심리적 도전을 어부의 예로 설명한 것이다.

한글번역

최근 과학자들은 1억 년 이상 바다 밑에 묻혀 있었지만 여전히 살아있는 박테리아를 발견했다. 만약 우리가 단지 100만 년만이라도 살 수 있다면 무엇이 바뀔까? 한 가지 생각이 즉시 떠오른다. 학계의 종신재직권은 제한돼야 할 것이다. 대학들은 인재 풀을 새롭게 하고, 낡은 구식 교육 및 연구 독단을 완화하기 위해 교수 임용을 기껏해야 한 세기로 제한해야 할 것이다. (인간이 100만 년을 산다면 한 사람이 수십만 년 동안 같은 자리에 있을 수 있는데, 이는 학문적 발전을 저해하고 새로운 세대의 기회를 막을 것이므로 인위적으로 임용 기간을 100년 이하로 제한해야 한다는 것이다.)

과거 세대들은 자연스러운 죽음을 연기할 수는 없지만 어떻게 살 것인지는 통제할 수 있다고 말하곤 했다. 그들은 또한 "태양 아래 새로운 것은 없다"고 믿었다. 두 진술 모두 현재 우리의 관점에서는 부정확하다. 생명과학과 기술의 발전으로, 대부분의 질병이 치료되고 우리의 수명이 상당히 늘어날 포스트 코로나19 미래를 상상할 수 있다. 그러면 죽음은 더 이상 인간의 적이 될 수 없다.

그런 일이 일어난다면, 우리의 목표는 어떻게 바뀔 것이며, 이것이 우리 삶을 어떻게 형성할 것인가? 장기적인 계획을 추구할 수 있는 여유가 주어진다면, 우리는 더 야심찬 과제들을 성취할 수 있을 것이다. 오염이나 적대감이 장기적인 위험을 수반하므로, 우리는 지구 환경과 인간 서로 간의 협력에 더 많이 신경 쓰기로 결정할 수 있을 것이다. 연장된 인생 경험은 훨씬 더 많은 것이 위험에 처해 있기 때문에 우리를 더 현명하고 위험을 회피하게 만들 수 있을 것이다. ("much more at stake"은 "훨씬 더 많은 것이 위험에 처해 있다, 훨씬 더 많은 것을 잃을 위험이 있다"는 의미로, 100만 년의 긴 수명을 가진 사람들은 잃을 것이 너무 많아서 전쟁 같은 위험한 행동을 피하려 할 것이라는 뜻이다.) 젊은 군인들을 전쟁에 보내거나, 애초에 전쟁을 시작하는 것은 의미가 없을 것이다.

하지만 영리한 전략을 써도 생존이 보장되는 것은 결코 아니다. 예를 들어, 뇌 크기와 체중 사이의 알려진 상관관계가 공룡들을 그들을 죽인 소행성을 막을 만큼 충분히 똑똑하게 만들지는 못했다. (공룡들이 큰 몸집에 비례해서 큰 뇌를 가지고 있었지만, 그것만으로는 소행성 충돌이라는 재앙을 예측하거나 피할 만큼 지능적이지 못했다는 뜻이다. 이는 인간이 아무리 오래 살고 현명해진다고 해도, 예측하지 못한 사고나 재앙은 여전히 생존을 위협할 수 있다는 맥락에서 사용된 예시이다.) 사고는 불가피하며, 치료 센터들은 일상적인 사고로 인한 치명적이지 않은 손상을 수리하느라 계속 바쁠 것이다. (사람들이 100만 년을 산다고 해도 일상생활에서 발생하는 크고 작은 사고들(routine mishaps)은 피할 수 없고, 이런 사고들로 인해 생기는 부상이나 손상들—죽지는 않지만 치료가 필요한—을 고치기 위해 병원이나 치료 시설들이 계속 바쁘게 운영될 것이라는 뜻이다. 긴 수명에도 불구하고 완전히 안전한 삶은 불가능하다는 점을 강조하고 있다.)

좋은 소식은(앞서 언급한 부정적인 측면들—사고의 불가피성, 치료 센터의 바쁜 운영 등—과 대조되는 긍정적인 측면을 도입하는 표현이다. 즉, 100만 년의 수명이 가져올 문제점들을 언급한 후, 이제는 그 긍정적인 측면—우주 여행의 가능성—을 제시하기 위해 사용된 전환 표현이다.) 100만 년만큼 긴 수명에 걸쳐, 우주 여행이 기존의 화학 로켓을 사용해 우리를 가장 가까운 별들까지 데려갈 수 있다는 것이다. NASA의 뉴 호라이즌스 우주선의 속도로 여행하는 우주선으로 프록시마 센타우리 주변의 거주 가능한 행성에 도달하는 데는 단지 10만 년이 걸릴 것이다. 100만 년을 사는 승객들에게 그러한 여행은 현재 우리 수명 내에서 뉴 호라이즌스가 명왕성까지 가는 10년간의 여정과 같이 보일 것이다. (수명이 100만 년으로 늘어나면 시간에 대한 인식이 달라져서, 10만 년이라는 긴 기간도 상대적으로 짧게 느껴질 것이라는 비유다.) 물론 우주선은 이 긴 여행 동안 지속적인 생태계와 편안한 생활 조건을 제공해야 할 것이다. 그리고 승객들은 오랫동안 물고기를 찾지 못한 후 낚시의 진정한 목적이 물고기를 잡는 것인지 묻는 어부처럼, 여행의 목표에 대한 안정된 마음가짐을 유지하고 신념을 잃지 않아야 할 것이다.(이는 목적의식의 상실을 나타내는 비유다. 어부가 너무 오랫동안 물고기를 잡지 못하면 원래 목적(물고기 잡기)을 잊고 낚시 행위 자체에 대해 의문을 갖게 되는 것처럼, 100만 년 동안 우주를 여행하는 승객들도 여행 중에 원래 목적(목적지 도달)을 잊고 "우리가 왜 이 여행을 하고 있는가?"라는 의문을 갖게 될 수 있다는 뜻이다. 즉, 극도로 긴 시간은 사람들로 하여금 원래 목표를 잃게 만들 수 있다는 위험성을 경고하는 것이다. 긴 수명이 가져올 수 있는 심리적 위험을 지적한 것이다.)

제62회 모의고사

1

하위내용영역	배점	예상정답률
일반영어 A형 서술형	4점	40%

모범답안 The word for ① is "mathematics" and ② is "fact". Second, it is because they loved theory.

채점기준

+ 2점: 빈칸에 들어갈 단어를 각각 ① "mathematics(1점)"와 ② "fact(1점)"라 기입하였다. 이외에는 답이 될 수 없다.
+ 2점: 고대 그리스인들이 수학 이론의 발전에 중요한 역할을 할 수 있었던 근본적 이유를 "because they loved theory"라 서술하였거나 유사하였다.

❖ 보충설명

- "allowing for some minor qualifications, nothing had come from it except the intrinsic interest of the study." 몇 가지 사소한 예외를 감안하더라도, 그 연구 자체의 본질적 흥미를 제외하고는 기하학으로부터는 아무것도 나오지 않았다.
  → 기하학이 2천 년 동안 연구되고 정교하게 발전되었지만 실용적인 응용이나 유용한 결과물은 거의 없었다. 오직 학문 자체의 지적 흥미만 있었을 뿐이다. 16세기 이전까지 기하학은 이론적으로는 발달했지만 실제 세계에 응용되지 못했다는 점을 강조하고 있다. 그러다가 케플러, 데카르트, 뉴턴 등이 나타나면서 갑자기 수학이 실용적으로 활용되기 시작했다는 대비를 보여주는 문장이다.

- "Apart from(=without=if it had not been for) the capital of abstract ideas which had accumulated slowly during two thousand years, our modern life would have been impossible." 2천 년 동안 천천히 축적된 추상적 개념들의 자본이 없었다면, 우리의 현대적 삶은 불가능했을 것이다.
  → 앞에서 기하학이 오랫동안 실용성이 없어 보였지만, 결국 16세기에 케플러, 데카르트, 뉴턴 등에 의해 활용되면서 현대 문명의 토대가 되었다는 점을 강조하는 문장이다. 겉보기에 쓸모없어 보이던 추상적 이론들이 결국 현대 문명을 가능하게 만든 필수적 자본이었다는 것이다.

- "There is nothing magical about mathmatices as such. It is simply the greatest example of a science of abstract forms." 수학 그 자체에는 마법적인 것이 전혀 없다. 그것은 단순히 추상적 형태들의 과학 중 가장 위대한 예일 뿐이다.
  → 수학이 특별히 신비롭거나 마법적인 것은 아니다. 수학은 추상적 형태를 다루는 과학들 중 하나의 예시일 뿐, 다만 그중에서 가장 뛰어난(위대한) 사례라는 것이다. 앞서 수학이 현대 문명을 가능하게 했다고 설명한 후, 수학을 신비화하지 말고 객관적으로 바라보자는 취지이다. 수학은 여러 추상적 과학 분야 중 하나이며, 단지 가장 성공적인 사례라는 것이다.

- "The instance of political economy illustrates an important point. Abstract political economy deals with men under an abstraction. It limits its view to the "economic man."" 정치 경제학의 사례가 중요한 점을 보여준다. 추상적 정치 경제학은 추상화된 인간만을 다룬다. 추상적 정치 경제학은 자신의 관점을 '경제적 인간'(경제학에서 사용하는 이상적 모델로, 합리적이고 자기 이익만 추구하는 인간)으로 제한한다.
  → 정치 경제학은 **현실의 복잡한 인간**을 그대로 다루지 않고, "경제적 인간"이라는 단순화된 추상적 모델을 사용한다는 것이다. 즉, 실제 인간의 모든 복잡한 면을 고려하지 않고 경제적 측면만 고려하는 추상화된 접근법을 사용한다는 의미이다.

- 추상화는 **복잡한 현실**에서 특정 측면만을 추출하여 **단순한 모델로 만드는 과정**이다. 정치 경제학에서의 추상화의 의미는 다음과 같다.
  → 현실(실제)의 인간은 감정적, 사회적, 문화적, 도덕적, 심리적 등 복합적 존재로 다양한 동기와 행동 양상을 지니고 있는데, 이런 복잡한 인간에게서 복잡성을 제거하고, **오직 합리적 경제적 계산만 하는 경제적 인간으로 단순화**하는 것이다.
  예시: 현실에서는 사람이 돈보다 가족, 명예, 감정을 우선할 수 있지만, 경제학 모델에서는 **이런 복잡성을 무시하고** 오직 경제적 이익만 고려하는 존재로 추상화한다.

유희태 | 일반영어 ❹-2

- "We have here an example of the necessity of transcending a given morphological scheme. Up to a point the scheme is invaluable. It clarifies thought, it suggests observation, and it explains fact. But there is a strict limit to the utility of any finite scheme. If the scheme be pressed beyond its proper scope, definite error results." 우리는 여기서 주어진 형태학적 체계(여기서는 "경제적 인간" 모델)를 초월할 필요성의 사례를 갖게 된다. 어느 정도까지는 이 체계가 매우 유용하다. 이 체계는 사고를 명확하게 하고, 관찰을 제안하며, 사실을 설명한다. 그러나 어떤 유한한 체계의 유용성에도 엄격한 한계가 있다. 만약 그 체계가 적절한 범위를 넘어서 억지로 적용된다면, 명확한 오류가 발생한다.
    → 정치 경제학의 "경제적 인간" 모델 같은 추상적 체계는 일정 범위 내에서는 매우 유용하지만, 그 한계를 넘어서 무리하게 확장 적용하면 오히려 오류를 낳는다. 따라서 기존 체계의 한계를 인식하고 그것을 초월하는 새로운 접근이 필요하다는 것이다.
        - 형태학적 체계의 장점 : 사고를 정리하고, 관찰 방향을 제시하며, 현상을 설명한다.
        - 형태학적 체계의 한계 : 일정 수준을 넘어서면 한계가 있어서 더 넓은 관점이 필요하다.

왜 "geometry"는 안 되는지:
① 문법적 이유 : "There is nothing magical about _____ as such"에서 빈칸 앞에 관사가 없다. "geometry"라면 "There is nothing magical about the geometry as such"가 되어야 자연스럽다. 하지만 "mathematics"는 불가산 명사로 관사 없이 사용 가능하다.
② 의미적 이유 : 이 문장은 앞 문단의 전체 주제를 요약하는 역할이다. 앞 문단에서 다룬 것은 기하학만이 아니라 수학 전반의 역사와 중요성이고, 케플러, 데카르트, 뉴턴의 예시도 기하학뿐 아니라 수학 전반을 포함하고 있다. "현대 문명을 가능하게 한 것"도 기하학만이 아닌 수학 전체이다.
③ 문맥적 이유 : 다음 문장에서 "추상적 형태들의 과학 중 가장 위대한 예"라고 했는데, 이는 수학 전체를 가리키는 표현이다. 음악, 정치 경제학 등 다른 추상적 과학들과 병렬로 비교하려면 mathematics 전체가 적절하다.

따라서 "mathematics"가 정답이다.

빈칸에 "fact"가 들어가는 논리적 근거:
① 수학 사례에서의 패턴 : 추상적 기하학 이론 발달 (2000년간) → 그 후 케플러, 뉴턴 등이 자연 현상(사실)을 설명
② 정치 경제학 사례에서의 패턴 : "경제적 인간"이라는 추상적 이론 먼저 개발 → 그 이론을 통해 경제 현실(사실)을 이해하려 함
③ 뒷 문단에서의 확인 : "It clarifies thought, it suggests observation, and it explains fact" 추상적 체계의 목적이 결국 사실(fact) 설명임을 명시
④ 논리 구조 : 추상적 이론 개발 → 사실(fact) 이해 / 설명

따라서 "theory precedes the understanding of fact"가 이 글 전체의 핵심 논리이다. 수학과 정치 경제학 모두 이 패턴을 따르므로 "fact"가 정답이다.

한글번역

자, 수학의 초기 단계를 한번 생각해 보자. 기원전 2천년경의 이집트에서 출현했던 몇 개의 기술적으로 (별 것 아닌) 방안이었던 수학! 그 수학은 당대의 이집트라는 위대한 문명의 스케일에 있어서 아주 사소한 요소였다. 그런데 기원전 5백년경 그리스인들은 순수한 이론 그 자체에 대한 사랑 때문에 수학의 이론적 발전을 선취하기 시작했다 (주도적으로 시작했다). 이것은 인간에게 현시된 가장 위대한 예언이었던 솔로몬의 꿈이 나타난 지 4~5백년 후의 사건이었다. 그리스인들의 천재성은 자연의 연구를 위해 수학의 중요성을 명료하게 예측해 낸 선견지명으로 과시되는 것이다. 추상적 형태학의 발전을 촉진시키는 것에 대한 필요성은 16세기가 시작될 즈음 기하학이라는 과학의 상태를 고찰하면 잘 예증된다. 이 기하학은 2천년 동안이나 열심히 연구돼 왔다. 그리고 아주 세부적인 데까지 정교하게 다듬어져 왔다. 하지만 약간의 사소한 예외를 인정한다면, 아무것도 그 학문의 내재적 관심 외의 것은 기하학으로부터 생겨난 것이 없었다. 그러던 것이 갑자기 대문이 활짝 열린 듯이, 케플러가 원추곡선의 수백 가지 이용법 가운데 최초의 중요한 이용법을 제시했고, 데카르트와 데자르그(1591~1661 프랑스의 수학자)는 과학의 방법들을 혁신시켰으며, 뉴턴은 <프린키피아>를 저술했고, 이리하여 봇물 터지듯 문명의 근대기가 발동되기 시작했다. 2천년 동안 서서히 축적돼 온 추상적 관념의 자본 없이는, 우리가 살고 있는 근대적 삶이라고 하는 것이 불가능했을 것이다. 수학이라고 하는 것, 그것 자체로 그 어떤 마술적인 것이라곤 아무것도 없다. 수학은 추상적 형식으로 된 과학의 가장 위대한 표본일 뿐이다.

추상적 음악 이론도 그러한 추상적 과학의 좋은 본보기이다. 정치 경제학의 추상적 이론과 통화의 추상적 이론도 그렇다. 이들에게 공통된 요점은 바로 추상적 이론의 발전이 사실의 이해에 선행한다는 것이다. 정치 경제학의 예는 중요한 점을 보여준다. 정치 경제학은 그 속성상 추상화시킨 인간만을 대상으로 삼는다. 즉 정치 경제학은 그 관점을 "경제적 인간"이라고 하는 전제에 국한시키는 것이다. 그리고 그것은 많은 중요한 인간적 요소를 외면한 채, 시장과 경쟁에 관한 가설을 세우고 있다. 바로 여기에 우리는 주어진 형태론적 도식을 초월해야만 (넘어서야만) 하는 필요성의 한 전형을 발견한다. 어느 정도까지는 이 도식은 매우 소중한 것이다. 그것은 우리의 사유를 명료히 하고, 관찰을 암시하며, 사실을 설명한다. 하지만 그 어떠한 유한한 도식이든지 그 유용성에는 엄격한 한계가 있다. 그 도식이 그것의 적합한 범위를 넘어서서 적용될 때에는 반드시 오류가 필연적으로 발생하게 된다.

한글번역

어떤 남자가 더 정직할 것이라고 예상하는가: 아르마니 정장을 입은 남자인가, 아니면 맨즈 웨어하우스의 스포츠 코트를 입은 남자인가? 옷이 무관해 보일 수도 있지만, 버클리 대학의 사회심리학자 폴 피프의 연구는 사회경제적 지위의 지표들이 신뢰성을 예측할 수 있다고 시사한다. 지위와 권력이 증가하는 것은 정직성과 신뢰성이 감소하는 것과 밀접한 관련이 있다는 것이 밝혀졌다. 예를 들어, 한 실험에서 피프와 동료들은 참가자들에게 채용 담당자 역할을 하도록 요청했다. 참가자들은 최대 6개월까지만 지속될 공개된 임시직과 장기직에만 관심이 있는 자격을 잘 갖춘 지원자에 대해 들었다. 이 지원자를 유혹하기 위한 제안서를 준비하라고 요청받았을 때, 더 높은 지위의 채용 담당자들은 지원자에게 그 일이 임시직이라는 것을 말하지 않았을 뿐만 아니라, 연구 책임자들에게 만약 질문을 받는다면 그 일의 기간에 대해 거짓말을 하겠다고 말했다. (상황 설정: ① 임시직 (6개월 이하) ② 지원자는 장기직만 원함 → 명백한 불일치 상황. 높은 지위 채용담당자들의 행동: ① 은폐: 임시직이라는 중요한 사실을 숨김 ② 의도적 기만: 질문받으면 거짓말하겠다고 공언. 실험의 핵심: 지위가 높을수록 자신의 목적(채용 성공) 달성을 위해 상대방을 속이는 것을 주저하지 않으며, 오히려 그런 행동을 당연하게 여긴다는 것을 증명한 실험이다.)

이것과 다른 연구 결과들로부터 부자들이 단순히 가난한 사람들보다 덜 신뢰할 만하다고 생각할 수도 있지만, 정확히 그런 것은 아니다. 사람의 정직성은 은행에 얼마나 많은 돈을 가지고 있느냐가 아니라 권력이나 취약성에 대한 상대적 감정에 달려 있다. 퀼른 대학교 심리학자 조리스 라머스의 연구가 이 점을 증명한다. 라머스는 사무실 시뮬레이션에서 사람들을 무작위로 "상사"나 "부하"로 배정했고, 일시적으로 더 고위직으로 승진한 대부분의 사람들이 더 높은 정도의 위선적 행동을 보였다는 것을 발견했다. 그들은 비윤리적이고 이기적인 행동에 대해 다른 사람들을 빠르게 비난했지만, 자신의 유사한 행동은 받아들일 만하다고 판단했다.

2

하위내용영역	배점	예상정답률
일반영어 A형 서술형	4점	50%

모범 답안 Joris Lammers proves that untrustworthy and hypocritical behavior comes from having a higher relative feeling of power, not only from wealth. Second, the words are "higher status".

채점 기준

+ 2점: 조리스가 증명한 것을 "untrustworthy and hypocritical behavior comes from having a higher relative feeling of power (or status), not only from wealth"라 서술하였거나 유사하였다.
+ 2점: 빈칸에 들어갈 단어를 "higher status"라 기입하였다. 이외에는 답이 될 수 없다.

> 누군가가 당신보다 더 높은 지위를 가지고 있거나, 심지어 단지 그렇다고 생각하기만 해도, 그의 마음은 당신이 그를 필요로 하는 정도가 그가 당신을 필요로 하는 정도보다 크다고 말한다. 결과적으로 그는 단기적 욕구를 충족시킬 가능성이 더 높고, 신뢰할 수 없는 사람이 되는 것의 장기적 결과에 대해 덜 걱정한다. 따라서 누구를 신뢰할지 결정할 때, 새롭고 일시적인 것들을 포함하여 권력 차이를 고려해야 한다. (권력/지위의 심리적 효과: 높은 지위를 가진 (또는 그렇게 생각하는) 사람은 상대방이 자신에게 더 의존한다고 여긴다. ① 행동 변화: 이런 심리로 인해 단기적 이익을 추구하고 장기적 신뢰 관계를 경시한다. ② 실용적 조언: 신뢰 판단 시 권력 관계의 변화(승진, 성공 등)를 고려해야 한다.) 잠재적 협력자가 방금 승진했거나 큰 거래를 성사시켰다면, 그는 일부 관계들을 덜 중요하다고 여길 수도 있다. 그리고 일류 회사들이 종종 훌륭한 평판을 가지고 있지만, 그것이 그들이 소규모 고객들을 대규모 고객들만큼 잘 대한다는 것을 의미하지는 않는다. (이 문장은 권력/지위 변화가 관계에 미치는 실제적 영향을 보여주는 구체적 사례들이다. ① 첫 번째 예시 (개인 차원): 승진이나 성공 → 기존 관계를 하찮게 여김. 새로운 권력으로 인해 이전 동료나 파트너를 소홀히 함. ② 두 번째 예시 (기업 차원): 큰 회사 → 작은 고객보다 큰 고객을 우대. 평판과 실제 대우는 다를 수 있음 → 권력이나 지위가 높아지면 상대적으로 약한 위치에 있는 사람들을 덜 중요하게 대하게 된다는 앞선 논리의 현실적 적용 사례를 제시한 것이다.)
>
> 요약: 사람의 정직성은 실제 부보다는 상대적 권력 감정에 의해 결정되며, 높은 지위나 권력을 가진 사람일수록 신뢰할 수 없는 행동을 보일 가능성이 크다.

3

하위내용영역	배점	예상정답률
일반영어 B형 서술형	4점	50%

[모범답안] Television has advantages and disadvantages. **First, regarding advantages**, children can learn language faster and develop better pronunciation through watching various programs. In addition, in families where both parents are working, television provides opportunities for family bonding during leisure times. **As regards disadvantages**, the decline in reading habits is detrimental to children's writing abilities, thinking capacities, and analytical skills. In conclusion, selective and controlled television viewing represents the optimal solution.

[채점기준]

ⓐ Topic sentence
+ 1점: "Television has advantages and disadvantages"를 명확하게 서술하였다.

ⓑ Major supporting details
+ 2점: "First, regarding advantages, children can learn language faster and develop better pronunciation through watching various programs. In addition, in families where both parents are working, television provides opportunities for family bonding during leisure times. As regards disadvantages, the decline in reading habits is detrimental to children's writing abilities, thinking capacities, and analytical skills"을 명확하게 서술하였다.

☞ 3개 중 3개 모두 정확하게 요약했으면 2점, 2개만 요약했으면 1점, 나머지는 0점을 준다.

ⓒ Conclusion
+ 1점: "In conclusion, selective and controlled television viewing represents the optimal solution"을 정확하게 요약하였다.

[감점] • 본문에 나오는 연속되는 6단어 이상을 사용하였다. −0.5pt
• 문단을 두 개나 그 이상으로 구성하였다. −0.5pt
• 문법이나 영어 표현을 합쳐 3개 이상 오류가 있다. −0.5pt

한글번역

텔레비전의 출현으로 많은 오락들이 대체됐다. 세계 뉴스와 텔레비전 연속극 같은 생방송 프로그램들이 라디오를 듣거나, 책이나 신문을 읽거나, 심지어 영화를 보러 가고 싶은 우리의 욕구를 제거했다. 실제로 텔레비전은 세상을 우리 집으로 가져다준다. 버튼을 누르면 세계의 사건들이 즉시 우리 앞에 제시된다. 요즘 아이들은 텔레비전 프로그램에 일찍 노출돼 언어 발달이 더 빠르다. 그렇게 어린 나이에는 책이나 신문을 읽기가 어려울 것이다. 따라서 텔레비전 프로그램은 그들에게 좋은 학습원이다. 게다가 뉴스 진행자, 배우나 여배우들의 발음은 보통 표준화돼 있어서, 이러한 프로그램을 보는 어린 아이들도 "올바른" 발음을 배우게 될 것이다. 텔레비전은 또한 보통 너무 바쁘거나 피곤해서 아이들을 데리고 오락을 위해 외출하기 어려운 직장을 다니는 부모들에게 매우 유익하다. 집의 편안함에 둘러싸여 가족이 함께 모여 좋아하는 텔레비전 프로그램을 볼 수 있다.

물론 우리는 텔레비전의 장점에 너무 빠져서는 안 된다. 텔레비전 프로그램을 보는 것은 읽고 싶은 우리의 욕구를 앗아간다. 흥미진진한 영화가 상영되는데 왜 책을 읽는가? 텔레비전 뉴스 보도에서 들을 수 있는데 왜 굳이 신문을 읽는가? 읽기 부족은 특히 어린 아이들에게 건강하지 않는데, 그들이 말하는 능력만 가지고 쓰는 능력은 없이 자라날 것이기 때문이다. 예를 들어, 나는 6세 아이가 "나는 개를 좋아해"와 같은 완전한 문장을 말할 수 있지만 그 문장을 써보라고 하면 그렇게 할 수 없는 이웃이 있다. 아이들의 쓰기 능력이 영향을 받을 뿐만 아니라, 그들의 사고 능력도 손상된다. 텔레비전 프로그램은 생각할 필요를 제거한다. 이야기, 아이디어, 사실들이 텔레비전 기획자들이 원하는 방식으로 짜여진다. 그러한 의견에 노출되고 사고 기회가 부족하면 아이들의 분석 능력이 저해될 것이다.

텔레비전 프로그램 시청의 단점에도 불구하고, 선택적 텔레비전 시청을 하는 "중간 길"을 선택하는 것이 텔레비전의 장점과 단점을 모두 조화시키는 최선의 해결책이어야 한다.

제63회 모의고사

1

하위내용영역	배점	예상정답률
일반영어 A형 서술형	4점	60%

모범 답안 The word is "lack". Second, it is because vitamin A, which human body cannot create, is required from outside sources and crucial for good health and fitness.

채점 기준

+ 2점 : 빈칸에 들어갈 단어를 "lack"이라 정확하게 기입하였다. 이외에는 답이 될 수 없다.
+ 2점 : 균형 잡힌 식습관이 사람에게 중요한 이유를 "(a well-balanced diet is important) because vitamin A, which human body cannot create, is required from outside sources (and crucial for good health and fitness)"라 서술하였거나 유사하였다.

한글번역

달걀 노른자, 유제품, 마가린 등에서 비타민 A를 찾을 수 있다. 그것은 어간유에 풍부하며, 따라서 어간유는 비타민 A 부족으로 인한 질병을 예방하고 치료하는 데 사용된다. 잘 먹고 건강한 인간의 경우, 간은 6개월 동안 신체의 필요를 충족할 충분한 비타민 A를 저장할 수 있다.

비타민 A 자체는 식물에 존재하지 않지만, 많은 식물이 엽록소로부터 형성되는 카로틴이라는 물질을 생산하며, 우리 몸은 이것을 비타민 A로 전환할 수 있다. 카로틴은 당근의 황색색 색소이다. 잎이 더 푸를수록, 보통 더 많은 카로틴을 포함한다. 따라서 카로틴의 공급원으로서 식단에서 푸른 잎채소의 중요성이 있다. 토마토, 파파야, 망고, 바나나는 대부분의 다른 과일들보다 더 많은 카로틴을 포함한다. 붉은 팜유는 너무 많은 카로틴을 포함해 대구 간유 대신 사용된다. 따라서 그것은 식용유와 튀김용 기름으로서 매우 가치가 있다.

비타민 A와 카로틴은 물에 용해되지 않으며 산소가 존재하지 않는 한 열에 의해 파괴되지 않는다. 따라서 물에서 끓이는 것은 비타민 A나 카로틴을 많이 파괴하지 않는다.

비타민 A는 건강한 성장과 체력을 증진시킨다. 어린 동물들은 식단에 그것이 없으면 곧 성장을 멈추고 죽는다. 이 비타민은 소화관, 폐, 기도를 둘러싸는 촉촉한 표면을 건강하게 유지한다. 또한 다양한 선의 관, 눈꺼풀을 덮고 안구 전면을 덮는 조직을 기능적으로 유지하는 데 도움을 준다. 비타민 A가 이러한 조직들이 감염에 대한 저항력을 기르는 데 도움을 주므로, 종종 항감염 비타민이라고 불린다. 사람들의 가장 흔한 질환 중 일부는 촉촉한 조직이 건조하고 거칠어질 때 비타민 A 부족으로 인해 발생한다. 이는 종종 심각한 안질환을 일으키고, 이어서 기도의 감염이 뒤따른다. 피부도 또한 거칠고 각질이 생길 수 있다.

신체가 비타민 A를 생산할 수 없기 때문에, 그것은 외부 공급원에서 와야 한다. 따라서 균형 잡힌 식단이 필요하며 보통 필요한 양을 제공하기에 충분하다. 따라서 알약 형태로 필요량을 보충할 필요가 없다.

한글번역

북태평양 연안의 아메리카 원주민들은 그들의 특수한 환경에 독특한 생산 방식을 발명하면서 매우 복잡한 해양 문화를 창조했다. 그들의 정교한 기술 문화에 더해, 그들은 또한 세계의 어떤 비농업 민족들 중에서도 가장 복잡한 사회 조직 중 하나를 달성했다. 내륙의 수렵민들과 전 세계의 채집민들 사이의 분업과 유사하게, 남성들이 대부분의 어업을 했고, 여성들이 어획물을 가공했다. 여성들은 또한 해안 가까이에 사는 풍부한 생물들을 채집하는 데 특화됐다. 그들은 게, 홍합, 전복, 그리고 조개를 수집했는데, 이것들은 아이들 곁에 머물면서 채집할 수 있었다. 여성들이 수확한 해양 생물은 음식을 제공했을 뿐만 아니라, 남성들이 모은 물고기보다 도구 제작을 위한 원료를 더 많이 공급했다. 금속이 도입되기 전 토착 도구 세트에서 특히 중요했던 것은 큰 홍합 껍질로 만든 넓은 칼과 다른 해양 껍질로 만들 수 있는 다양한 절단날이었다. 여성들은 자신들의 도구를 사용해 남성들이 가져온 모든 물고기와 해양 포유동물을 가공했다. 그들은 물고기를 손질했고, 겨울을 위해 엄청난 양을 말렸다. 실용적일 때는 물고기를 햇볕에 말렸지만, 연안 지역의 비가 많은 기후에서는 연간 수 톤의 물고기와 다른 해산물을 보존하기 위해 훈제실도 사용했다. 각 제품은 고기를 자르거나 말리는 특별한 방법을 요구하는 고유한 특성을 가지고 있었고, 각 작업은 고유한 절단날과 다른 도구들을 필요로 했다. 물고기를 말린 후, 여성들은 그중 일부를 가루로 빻았는데, 이는 신선한 물고기가 없거나 긴 여행 중에 수프, 스튜, 또는 다른 요리에서 단백질과 걸쭉함을 제공하기 위해 사용되는 쉽게 운반할 수 있는 음식이었다. 여성들은 또한 물고기와 어란의 혼합물로 치즈 같은 물질을 만들었는데, 창고에서 숙성시키거나 바위와 나뭇잎으로 안을 댄 나무 상자나 구덩이에 묻어서 만들었다.

2

하위내용영역	배점	예상정답률
일반영어 A형 서술형	4점	55%

모범 답안 The word is "maritime". Second, they used smokehouses to preserve fish in a rainy climate where sun-drying wasn't convenient.

채점 기준

+ 2점: 빈칸에 들어갈 단어를 "maritime"라 정확하게 기입하였다. 이외에는 답이 될 수 없다.
+ 2점: 북미 원주민들이 훈제실을 사용한 이유를 "to preserve fish in a rainy climate where sun-drying wasn't convenient"라 서술하였거나 유사하였다.

3

하위내용영역	배점	예상정답률
일반영어 A형 서술형	4점	40%

모범답안 The writer cites Star Trek to illustrate **how the term "Before Time" has historically been used to describe a pre-plague world**, paralleling how people today refer to the pre-Covid era. Second, it is "superforecasters".

채점기준

+ 2점: 스타트렉을 인용한 이유를 "to illustrate **how the term "Before Time" has historically been used to describe a pre-plague world**, paralleling how people today refer to the pre-Covid era"이라 서술하였거나 유사하였다.
  ☞ The passage's main topic is about how the pandemic has created this sense of temporal disconnection and how we use the term "Before Time" to describe the pre-Covid era.

+ 2점: "견자"의 역할에 대한 가장 최근의 용어를 "superforecasters"라 서술하였다. 이외에는 답이 될 수 없다.

한글번역

글을 쓰고 있는 2020년 여름, 나는 가끔 이 세상이 마치 허먼 멜빌(모비딕의 작가)이 묘사한 소설 속 세상이 아닌가 생각한다.

"미친 에이헙(선장)에게 흰 고래 모비딕은 모든 광기와 고통, 사물의 이면을 자극하는 것, 악의를 품고 있는 진실, 힘줄이 끊어지고 뇌가 구워지는 것, 삶과 생각에 존재하는 모든 미묘한 악, 그리고 순수한 악이 구체화, 의인화된 존재였으며 그럼에도 실제로 공격 가능한 대상이었다. 그는 고래의 등에 인류가 아담 이래 느껴 온 모든 분노와 증오를 쌓았으며, 마치 자신을 폭탄처럼 사용해 그의 뜨거운 심장을 그 위에 터뜨렸다."

중환자실에서 코로나 19로 마지막 숨을 내쉬고 있는 가족에게 마지막 인사조차 할 수 없는 상황에서 누가 광기와 고통을 느끼지 않을까? 몇 달씩이나 고립돼 자신의 생각과 주장이 입막음을 당하고 사회적 활동에 제약을 당하는 상황에서 누가 힘줄이 끊어지고 뇌가 구워지는 경험을 하지 않을까?

우리가 먼 미래를 예상할수록 시야는 점점 더 흐려지고 불활실성의 안개는 짙어진다. 2030년에 2020년은 어떤 의미를 가질까? 30년 뒤인 2050년에는? 백년 뒤인 2120년에는? 베이지안 추론과 빅데이터 분석을 훈련받은 초예측자들이라 하더라도 5년 이상의 미래에 대해서는 그저 동전을 던지는 것 이상을 예측하지 못한다.

1966년 방영된 스타트렉의 "미리" 에피소드에서 아직 어린 소녀인 주인공 미리는 당황한 커크 선장에게 자신의 행성에서 모든 어른들은 죽었으며, 아이들만 남았다고 말한다. "전시대(Before Time)에 어른들은 아프기 시작했어요. 우리는 숨었고, 그들은 모두 죽었어요." 전시대의 어원을 추적한 언어학자 벤 짐머는 이 단어가 종종 전염병이 돌기 전의 세상을 가리키며 킹제임스 버전의 사무엘서에 나올 정도로 오래된 단어라고 말한다. "전시대 이스라엘에서는 어떤 사람이 하나님께 물으러 가려 할 때 이렇게 말했다: '와서 견자에게 가자.' 지금 예언자라고 불리는 자가 옛날에는 견자라고 불렸기 때문이다." 이 어구는 코로나-19 팬데믹에 대한 반응으로 되살아났는데, 애틀랜틱 칼럼니스트 마리나 코렌이 "코로나 바이러스가 전국을 휩쓸기 전 시절들, 즉 많은 사람들이 '이전 시대'라고 부르게 된 그 시절들이 지나간 시대처럼 느껴진다는 감각이 더욱 심해졌다"고 쓴 경우가 그 예다.

4

하위내용영역	배점	예상정답률
일반영어 A형 서술형	4점	40%

모범답안 The words are "quantitative vocabulary". Second, the implication is that physical science's inability to explain consciousness is not **a problem to be solved but an inevitable result** of its deliberate design to exclude qualitative phenomena like consciousness from the beginning.

채점기준

+ 2점: 빈칸에 들어갈 단어를 "quantitative vocabulary"라 정확하게 기입하였다.
+ 2점: 밑줄 친 부분의 함축 의미를 "physical science's inability to explain consciousness is not a problem to be solved but an inevitable result of its deliberate design to exclude qualitative phenomena like consciousness from the beginning"라 서술하였거나 유사하였다.

보충설명

The underlined words imply that the current inability to explain consciousness through physical science is not a failure or limitation that can be overcome by simply improving our methods, but rather an inevitable result of the fundamental design principles of physical science itself. (Galileo deliberately excluded qualitative phenomena (like consciousness) from the domain of science to make it mathematically tractable(다루기 쉬운), so expecting physical science to eventually explain consciousness is fundamentally misguided—it's like expecting a tool to perform a function it was specifically designed to avoid. 갈릴레오는 과학을 수학적으로 다루기 쉽게 만들기 위해 의도적으로 (의식과 같은) 질적 현상들을 과학의 영역에서 배제했다. 따라서 물리 과학이 결국 의식을 설명할 것이라고 기대하는 것은 근본적으로 잘못된 생각이다—이는 어떤 도구가 특별히 피하도록 설계된 기능을 수행하기를 기대하는 것과 같다.

한글번역

뇌에 대한 과학적 이해가 크게 발전했음에도 불구하고, 우리는 여전히 복잡한 전기화학적 신호가 어떻게 해서 각자가 자신의 경우에 알고 있는 색깔, 소리, 냄새, 맛의 내적이고 주관적인 세계를 일으킬 수 있는지에 대해서 전혀 설명하지 못하고 있다. 과학이 말하는 외면의 물질과 내면에서 바라보는 자신을 어떻게 연결시킬 것인가의 문제는 아직도 전적으로 미지의 문제이다.

이 문제에 대해 많은 이들은 우리가 뇌를 연구하던 기존의 방법을 그대로 적용하면 해결될 수 있다고 생각하는 경향이 있다. 하지만 나는 의식의 문제는 우리가 과학 혁명을 시작하던 당시 과학을 설계했던 바로 그 방식 때문에 생긴 문제라고 주장한다.

과학 혁명의 가장 중요한 순간은 갈릴레오가 새로운 과학의 도구로 수학을 택했던 것이다. 곧, 새로운 과학은 순수하게 양(quantity)적인 언어로 기술돼야 했다. 하지만 갈릴레오는 의식을 이런 방식으로는 설명할 수 없다는 것을 잘 알고 있었다. 의식은 전적으로 질(quality)과 관련된 현상이기 때문이다. 붉은색에 대한 경험이나 꽃의 향기, 민트의 맛 등을 생각해 보자. 이런 질적 느낌은 물리학이 사용하는 양적 언어로는 설명할 수 없다. 즉, 갈릴레오는 의식을 과학의 외부에 두기로 결정한 것이다. 그 결정 이후, 의식을 제외한 모든 것은 수학으로 기술될 수 있었다. (의식을 제외시킨 후에야 나머지 모든 현상들을 수학적으로 설명할 수 있게 되었다는 의미이다.)

이 부분은 매우 중요하다. 왜냐하면, 많은 이들이 의식의 문제를 진지하게 생각하면서도, 기존의 과학적 방법으로 이 문제를 풀 수 있다고 생각하기 때문이다. 그 이유는 물론 물리학이 그 방법으로 우리 우주를 설명하는 데 매우 성공적이었기 때문이고, 따라서 언젠가는 이 방법으로 우리의 의식조차도 설명할 수 있을 것이라는 확신을 가지게 됐기 때문이다. 하지만 나는 이러한 생각이 과학의 역사에 대한 잘못된 이해에서 출발했다고 생각한다. 물론 물리학은 믿을 수 없을 만큼 성공적이었다. 하지만 그 성공은 처음부터 의식의 문제를 제외했기 때문이다. 만약 갈릴레오가 타임머신을 타고 이 시대로 와서 물리학을 이용해 의식을 설명하려는 이들을 본다면 이렇게 말할 것이다. "음, 그건 안 될 거예요. 나는 질이 아닌 양을 다루도록 과학을 설계했거든요."

제64회 모의고사

1

하위내용영역	배점	예상정답률
일반영어 A형 서술형	4점	45%

모범답안 The words are "appraisal stage". Second, the strategy is situation modification.

채점기준

+ 2점 : 빈칸에 들어갈 단어를 "appraisal stage"라 정확하게 기입하였다.
+ 2점 : 공부하는 동안 스마트폰을 다른 방에 놓는 것의 가장 적절한 전략을 "situation modification"라 서술하였다.

⊕ 보충설명

"To gorge on delicious cookies at the end of your working week, you first had to go through a situational stage, where you put yourself in a compromising situation with tempting cookies. From there, you transitioned to an attentional stage, where you directed your attention back towards those cookies. After that, you went through an appraisal stage, where you thought about how good those cookies would taste (especially with a glass of milk). All this led to a response stage, where you broke down and eventually ate all the cookies. To put it bluntly, a lot of things had to go wrong for you to end up giving in to temptation."

이 문장은 유혹에 빠지는 과정을 단계별로 설명하고 있다:
① 상황 단계 (situational stage) : 유혹적인 **쿠키가 있는 위험한 상황**에 자신을 노출시키는 단계
② 주의 집중 단계 (attentional stage) : 그 **쿠키들에게 다시 주의**를 돌리는 단계
③ 평가 단계 (appraisal stage) : 쿠키가 얼마나 맛있을지 **상상하고 생각**하는 단계 (특히 우유와 함께 먹으면 얼마나 좋을지)
④ 반응 단계 (response stage) : 결국 참지 못하고 모든 쿠키를 **먹어버리는** 단계

즉, 사람이 유혹에 굴복하는 것이 단순한 의지력 부족이 아니라, **여러 단계를 거치는 복잡한 심리적 과정임**을 보여준다.

"The good news is that this means you could have applied self-control **at several instances** prior to when you tried and failed to exert inhibitory self-control (or 'willpower' in everyday talk)."

유혹에 굴복하는 과정이 여러 단계로 나뉘기 때문에, 마지막 단계에서 억지 자제력(의지력)으로 버티려다 실패하기 전에 이미 **앞선 여러 단계**(순간)들(상황 단계, 주의 집중 단계, 평가 단계)에서 자제력을 발휘할 기회들이 있었다는 뜻이다. 즉, 마지막 순간의 의지력에만 의존하지 말고, 더 이른 단계에서 미리 자제력을 적용하는 것이 더 효과적이라는 것을 시사한다.

"With this in mind, you could have employed 'situational self-control strategies'. For instance, instead of sitting in front of a box of cookies and forcing yourself not to eat them, you could have either not bought them in the first place — known as 'situation selection' or simply removed them from sight by placing them in a cabinet (or thrown them out) — 'situation modification'."

이 문장은 자제력을 발휘하는 두 가지 효과적인 방법을 제시하고 있다.
- 기존 방식 (비효율적) : 유혹 앞에서 **의지력**으로 버티기 (쿠키 앞에 앉아서 참기)
- 새로운 방식 (효율적) :
  ① 상황 선택 (situation selection) : 아예 유혹적인 상황을 만들지 않기 (쿠키를 사지 않기)
  ② 상황 수정 (situation modification) : 유혹을 제거하거나 멀리하기 (쿠키를 숨기거나 버리기)
- 핵심 메시지 : **의지력**에만 의존해서 유혹을 참으려 하지 말고, 애초에 유혹적인 상황 자체를 피하거나 수정하는 것이 훨씬 효과적이라는 것이다. "예방이 치료보다 낫다"는 원리와 같다.
→ "공부하는 동안 스마트폰을 다른 방에 두는 것에 가장 적절하게 들어맞는 전략은 무엇인가?"에 해답이 여기에 있다.

한글번역

힘든 한 주를 보내고 이제 쿠키를 마음껏 먹으려는 순간, 당신은 쿠키의 유혹을 견뎌야 하는 상황 단계에 진입한다. 다음 단계는 쿠키에 관심을 가지게 되는 주의 단계이다. 그리고 쿠키가 우유 한 잔과 함께라면 얼마나 맛있을지를 생각하는 평가 단계를 가지게 되며, 마지막으로 규칙을 깨고 모든 쿠키를 다 먹게 되는 반응 단계에 이르게 된다. 거칠게 말하자면, 쿠키의 유혹에 넘어가기 위해서는 이 모든 단계에서 당신은 잘못된 선택을 해야 한다. 좋은 소식은 당신이 최종 단계에서 억지 자제력(일상에선 '의지력'이란 이름을 지닌)을 사용하지 않을 수 있도록 그 앞의 여러 단계에서 자제력을 발휘할 수 있다.

먼저 상황 단계에서부터 시작해 보자. 상황의 힘을 이해하기 위해 복잡한 사회 심리학을 다 알 필요는 없다. 대부분의 선생님들은 앞자리에 앉은 학생들이 집중을 더 잘한다는 것을 알고 있다. 이를 염두에 두고, 당신은 '상황적 자제력 전략'을 사용할 수 있었을 것이다. 예를 들어, 쿠키 상자 앞에 앉아서 먹지 않으려고 억지로 참는 대신에, 애초에 사지 않았거나—이를 '상황 선택'이라고 한다—아니면 단순히 찬장에 넣어두거나 (또는 버려서) 시야에서 치워버렸을 수도 있었다—이를 '상황 수정'이라고 한다.

이러한 상황 전략이 매우 유용하다는 것을 보이는 연구들이 있다. 예를 들어, 스마트폰을 눈앞에서 치우라는 지시를 받은 고등학생들은 그저 억지 자제력을 발휘해 스마트폰을 사용하지 못하게 된 고등학생들에 비해 더 좋은 점수를 받았다. 다이어트 연구에서도 고칼로리 음식이 보이는 상황을 그저 피하도록 한 방법이 효과가 있었다. 예를 들어 마트에서 음식을 살 때 빵 코너 앞을 지나가지 않는 것이다. 이를 통해 빵의 유혹을 강력하게 만드는 향긋한 냄새와 먹음직한 모양이라는 신호를 피할 수 있었던 것이다. 곧, "눈에서 멀어지면 마음에서도 멀어진다."는 것이다.

상황 전략을 사용하지 못할 때에는 어떻게 해야 할까? 때로는 어쩔 수 없이 빵 코너 앞을 지나가야 하거나, 아니면 쿠키를 버릴 경우 아이가 화를 낼 것 같을 때가 있다. 다행히, 이렇게 상황을 제어할 수 없는 경우라 하더라도 주의 단계와 평가 단계에서 쓸 수 있는 "심리적 전략"이 있다.

2

하위내용영역	배점	예상정답률
일반영어 A형 서술형	4점	50%

모범답안 The word is "performance". Second, the characteristics are the listener's receptiveness, interest or sympathy.

채점기준

+ 2점 : 빈칸에 들어갈 단어를 "performance"라 정확하게 기입하였다.
+ 2점 : 화자가 발표를 할 때 가장 영향을 주는 청자의 특성들을 "the listener's receptiveness, interest or sympathy"라 서술하였거나 유사하였다.

한글번역

소리와 관련된 많은 요인들이 화자의 성격을 드러낸다. 첫째, 목소리는 한 개인의 자아상, 타인에 대한 인식, 그리고 정서적 건강에 대한 심리적 단서를 제공한다. 자아상은 자신감 있는, 가식적인, 수줍은, 공격적인, 외향적인, 또는 활기찬 음조로 나타날 수 있는데, 이는 성격 특성 중 몇 가지만을 말한 것이다. 또한 목소리는 그 사람의 겉모습이나 가면에 대한 단서를 줄 수 있는데, 예를 들어 과도하게 자신감 있는 겉모습 뒤에 숨은 수줍은 사람과 같다. 화자가 어떤 주어진 대화에서 청자의 수용성, 관심, 또는 공감을 어떻게 인식하는지는 화자를 격려하거나 낙담시킴으로써 발표의 음조를 극적으로 바꿀 수 있다. 정서적 건강은 목소리에서 행복한 사람의 자유롭고 선율적인 소리, 화난 사람의 긴장되고 거친 소리, 그리고 우울한 사람의 둔하고 무기력한 특성으로 증명된다. (정서적 건강 상태는 목소리에서 다음과 같이 나타난다 : 행복한 사람은 자유롭고 선율적인 소리; 화난 사람은 조이고 거친 소리; 우울한 사람은 둔하고 무기력한 소리. 즉, 사람의 감정 상태(행복, 분노, 우울)가 목소리의 음색과 특징을 통해 드러난다는 뜻으로, 목소리가 그 사람의 정서적 건강을 보여주는 지표 역할을 한다는 것이다.)

두 번째는 의사소통의 광범위한 영역으로, 언어 사용을 통한 정보 전달과 공연을 통한 전문적 의사소통을 포함한다. 사람은 단어 선택을 통해, 즐겁거나 불쾌하고 부드럽거나 거친 음조를 통해, 언어 자체에 내재된 리듬을 통해, 그리고 흐르듯 규칙적이거나 불규칙하고 주저하는 말의 리듬을 통해, 마지막으로 발화의 높낮이와 억양을 통해 생각과 아이디어를 전달한다. 집단 앞에서 말할 때, 사람의 음조는 불확실함이나 두려움, 자신감이나 침착함을 나타낼 수 있다. 대인 관계 차원에서, 목소리 톤은 선택된 단어들 이상의 생각과 감정들을 반영할 수도 있고, 또는 그것들과 모순될 수도 있다. (말로 표현한 것 이상의, 혹은 말에 담지 못한 추가적인 생각과 감정들을 목소리 톤이 드러낼 수도 있고, 반대로 목소리 톤이 실제 말한 단어들과 다른 의미를 전달하거나 반대되는 느낌을 줄 수 있다는 뜻으로, "belie"는 "거짓으로 보이게 하다, 모순되다"는 의미이다.) 여기서 대화 상대의 음조는 의식적으로 또는 무의식적으로 직관적 공감이나 반감, 관심이나 흥미의 부족, 피로, 불안, 열정이나 흥분을 반영할 수 있으며, 이 모든 것은 보통 예리한 청자에 의해 식별 가능하다.

공연은 목소리나 몸짓으로 효과를 얻기 위한 고유한 기법들을 가진 고도로 전문화된 의사소통 방식이다. 텍스트에서 나오는 동기(그리고 노래의 경우에는 음악)가 공연자의 기술, 성격, 그리고 공감을 창조하는 능력과 결합돼 예술적, 정치적, 또는 교육적 의사소통의 성공을 결정할 것이다.

3

하위내용영역	배점	예상정답률
일반영어 B형 서술형	4점	50%

모범답안 Writing tools have evolved over time. The first writing tools used primitive techniques such as reed pens, clay tablets, animal skins and flattened papaya. Later, in the 1880s, fountain pens were created which held their ink inside, though sometimes the tips broke and ink leaked onto writers' hands. Thus, ball point pens were invented to improve on this problem. In conclusion, at present, writing tools are not likely to develop because the Internet and social media has made them inessential.

채점기준

ⓐ Topic sentence
+ 1점: "Writing tools have evolved(=changed and improved) over time (=over a period of time)"를 명확하게 서술하였다. "The evolution of writing tool has come a long way up to the current era"이라 했어도 1점을 준다.

ⓑ Major supporting details
+ 2점: "① The first writing tools used primitive techniques such as clay tablets, animal skins and flattened papaya. ② Later, in the 1880s, fountain pens were created which held their ink inside, though sometimes the tips broke and ink leaked onto writers' hands. ③ Thus, ball point pens were invented to improve on this problem"을 명확하게 서술하였다.
☞ 3개 중 3개 모두 정확하게 요약했으면 2점, 2개만 요약했으면 1점, 나머지는 0점을 준다.

ⓒ Conclusion
+ 1점: "In conclusion, at present, writing tools are not likely to develop because the Internet and social media has made them inessential(=unnecessary)"을 정확하게 요약하였다.

유희태 | 일반영어 ❹-2

감점
- 본문에 나오는 연속되는 6단어 이상을 사용하였다. −0.5pt
- 문단을 두 개나 그 이상으로 구성하였다. −0.5pt
- 문법이나 영어 표현을 합쳐 3개 이상 오류가 있다. −0.5pt

한글번역

단지 26개의 글자로, 우리는 친구들에게 편지를 쓰거나 시험 문제에 답할 수 있다. 수천 년 전에는 문자 체계와 도구가 전혀 없었다. 필기 도구의 발명은 주요한 전환점이다. 옛날에는 사용된 필기 도구의 종류가 글을 쓰는 재료에 따라 달라졌다. 예를 들어, 점토가 풍부하게 공급되는 중동에서는 초기 사람들이 속이 빈 갈대 '펜'을 사용해 젖은 점토판에 새겼다. 그 후, 이 점토 조각들은 글씨를 영구적으로 만들기 위해 바위처럼 단단해질 때까지 구워졌다. 고대 이집트에서는 이집트인들이 '양피지'라고 불리는 긁어낸 얇은 동물 가죽 조각이나 '파피루스'로 알려진 편평하게 만든 파파야 줄기에 글을 썼다.

만년필이 발명된 것은 1880년대에 이르러서였다. 그전에는 대부분의 사람들이 깃털펜—날카롭게 한 새 깃털이나 펜촉이 있는 펜을 사용했는데, 이것들은 글을 쓰기 전에 잉크에 담갔다. 나중에 발명된 만년필은 장단점이 모두 있다. 작은 잉크 탱크가 들어있는 만년필은 잉크가 그렇게 빨리 떨어지지 않기 때문에 깃털펜이나 펜촉 펜보다 우수하다. 단점은 때때로 만년필의 펜촉이 부러져서 잉크가 새어 작가의 손가락을 더럽힐 수 있다는 것이다.

만년필의 결함은 추가 연구로 이어졌고 1931년 헝가리인 라디슬라오 비로가 최초의 '볼펜'을 성공적으로 발명했다. 그 후 많은 사람들이 그의 볼펜의 외관을 개선하려고 시도했다.

전 세계의 많은 기술자들이 이전 것들을 개선하는 더 나은 필기 도구를 찾으려고 노력해왔다. 하지만 필기 도구의 전망은 낙관적이지 않다. 왜냐하면 인터넷과 소셜미디어의 현재 시대에서 사람들이 더 이상 반드시 그것들에 의존하지 않기 때문이다.

제65회 모의고사

1

하위내용영역	배점	예상정답률
일반영어 A형 서술형	4점	55%

모범답안) The underlined part means that economists haven't usually been the ones to encourage the humanities as fields of study, but are recommending this now. The word is "stories".

채점 기준

+ 2점: 밑줄 친 부분의 의미를 "economists haven't usually been the ones to encourage the humanities as fields of study, but are recommending this now"라 서술하였거나 유사하였다.
  ☞ 인문학의 부활을 요구하는 목소리가 예상치 못한 곳에서 나오고 있다는 뜻이다. 구체적으로, 일반적으로 인문학보다는 실용적이고 기술적인 분야를 중시할 것으로 여겨지는 저명한 경제학자들이 인문학의 중요성을 옹호하고 나서고 있다는 의미이다. 노벨경제학상 수상자인 로버트 실러 같은 경제학자가 인문학 교육의 가치를 강조하는 것이 "놀라운 곳"에서 나오는 요구라고 표현한 것이다.

+ 2점: 빈칸에 들어갈 단어를 "stories"라 정확하게 기입하였다. 이외에는 답이 될 수 없다.

한글번역

미국 대학 캠퍼스에서 거대한 이주가 일어나고 있다. 2008년 가을 이후로, 많은 학생들이 영어와 인문학 강의에서 나와 과학기술공학수학 수업, 특히 컴퓨터 과학과 공학으로 옮겨갔다.

국가 교육 통계 센터가 수집한 자료에 따르면, 대공황 이후 영어 전공자들이 4분의 1 이상(25.5%) 감소했다. 이는 센터가 연간 자료에서 추적하는 모든 전공 중 가장 큰 감소이며, 지난 10년간 대학 등록률이 급증했다는 점을 고려하면 상당히 놀라운 일이다.

초서 공부에서 코딩 공부로의 이런 큰 변화가 왜 일어나고 있는지 어떤 대학생이나 교수에게 물어보면, 그들은 아마도 일자리 때문이라고 말할 것이다. 학생들이 자신들의 취업 전망을 두려워하면서, 그들과 그들의 부모들은 졸업 후 안정적인 급여로 이어질 학위를 원했다. 과학기술공학수학이 취업으로 가는 길이라는 인식이 있다. 컴퓨터 과학과 보건 분야의 전공자들은 2009년부터 2017년까지 거의 두 배가 됐다. 공학과 수학도 큰 증가를 보였다.

인문학 전공자들이 수십 년 만에 최저 수준으로 떨어지면서, 놀라운 곳에서 부활을 위한 요구가 나오고 있다. 일부 저명한 경제학자들은 더 기술적인 분야와 함께 인문학을 전공하거나(적어도 수업을 듣는 것이) 여전히 매우 합리적인 이유를 주장하고 있다.

노벨상 수상자 로버트 실러의 새 책 《서사 경제학》은 그가 미시간 대학교 학부생 시절 들었던 깨달음을 주는 역사 수업을 회상하는 것으로 시작한다. 그는 대공황에 대해 배운 것이 경제학 과정에서 배운 어떤 것보다도 경제적, 재정적 혼란의 시기를 이해하는 데 훨씬 더 유용했다고 썼다.

실러의 책의 전체 전제는 이야기가 중요하다는 것이다. 사람들이 서로에게 하는 말은 시장과 전체 경제에 깊은 영향을 미칠 수 있다. 예시로는 비트코인에 대한 "빨리 부자 되기" 이야기나 주택 거품을 부추기는 데 도움이 된 "누구나 주택 소유자가 될 수 있다"는 이야기들이 있다. "전통적인 경제학적 접근법은 주요 경제 사건에서 대중의 믿음, 즉 서사의 역할을 검토하지 못한다. 경제학자들은 서사 경제학의 기술을 개발하고 그것을 자신들의 학문에 통합함으로써 자신들의 과학(경제학)을 가장 잘 발전시킬 수 있다."

그가 본질적으로 더 많은 영어와 역사 전공자를 주장하는 것인지 질문받았을 때, 실러는 "그렇다고 생각한다"고 말하며 "지적 삶의 구획화는 나쁘다"(학문 분야를 서로 분리해서 생각하는 것은 좋지 않다는 의미)고 덧붙였다. 실러는 주변에 더 많은 이야기꾼들(그리고 이야기 분석가들)이 있기를 바라는 데 있어서 혼자가 아니다.

2

하위내용영역	배점	예상정답률
일반영어 A형 서술형	4점	50%

모범답안 The words are "communication failure". Second, the difference occurs because the writer has a commonality with the culture producing the works as opposed to the Chinese critic, who does not have a commonality.

채점기준

+ 2점: 빈칸에 들어갈 단어를 "communication failure"라 정확하게 기입하였다. 이외에는 답이 될 수 없다.
+ 2점: 중국 비평가와 글쓴이 사이에서 차이가 발생하는 이유를 "because the writer has a commonality with the culture producing the works as opposed to the Chinese critic (, who does not have a commonality with the culture producing the works)"라 서술하였거나 유사하였다.
☞ 둘 사이의 문화의 차이에서 기인한다는 의미가 들어 있으면 2점을 준다.

◆ **보충설명**

문화적 배경이 다른 해석자 – 여기서는 중국인 평론가 – 가 서구 문화의 대표적인 텍스트들(King Lear, Coronation Street)을 비판적으로 해석하는 방식을 보여준다. 이러한 해석은 서구 내부에서는 일반적이지 않은 시각이지만, 타문화적 관점에서 충분히 가능한 읽기 방식이라는 점을 강조하고 있다. 이것은 곧 의미가 텍스트 자체에 고정되어 있는 것이 아니라, 해석자와 문화적 맥락에 따라 달라진다는 '기호학적 커뮤니케이션 관점'을 뒷받침한다.

한글번역

의사소통 연구에는 두 가지 주요 학파가 있다. 첫 번째 학파는 의사소통을 메시지를 전달하는 것으로 본다. 이는 발신자와 수신자가 어떻게 부호화하고 해독하는지, 전송자가 의사소통의 채널과 매체를 어떻게 사용하는지에 관심이 있다. 효율성과 정확성 같은 문제들에 관심이 있다. 의사소통을 한 사람이 다른 사람의 행동이나 마음 상태에 영향을 미치는 과정으로 본다. 효과가 의도했던 것과 다르거나 더 작다면, 이 학파는 의사소통 실패라는 관점에서 말하는 경향이 있고, 실패가 어디서 발생했는지 알아내기 위해 과정의 단계들을 살펴본다. 편의상 나는 이것을 '과정' 학파라고 부르겠다.

두 번째 학파는 의사소통을 **의미의 생산과 교환**으로 본다. (즉, 단순히 정보를 전달하는 것이 아니라, 사람들이 어떻게 의미를 만들어내고 공유하는지를 중심적으로 다룬다.) 이 학파는 메시지나 텍스트가 의미를 생산하기 위해 사람들과 어떻게 상호작용하는지에 관심이 있다("interact with people"은 텍스트가 독자 혹은 수용자에 의해 해석되는 과정을 가리킨다). 즉, 이 학파는 우리 문화 속에서 텍스트가 어떤 역할을 하는지에 주목한다. (텍스트는 고정된 의미를 전달하는 것이 아니라, 문화적 맥락 속에서 의미를 구성하는 주체로 본다.) 이 학파는 의미화 같은 용어를 사용하며,(signification은 "기호가 의미를 생성하고 전달하는 과정"을 의미하며, 기호학에서 **핵심 개념이다**.) 오해를 반드시 의사소통 실패의 증거로 여기지 않는다. 그것들은 발신자와 수신자 간의 **문화적 차이**에서 비롯될 수 있다. 이 학파에게 의사소통 연구는 **텍스트와 문화의 연구**이다. 주요 연구 방법은 기호학(기호와 의미의 과학 : 기호와 의미의 관계를 과학적으로 탐구하는 학문)이며, 나는 이것을 '기호학' 학파라고 부르겠다.

각 학파는 "메시지를 통한 사회적 상호작용"이라는 커뮤니케이션의 정의를 **자기 자신만의 방식으로** 해석한다. 첫 번째 학파(과정 학파)는 사회적 상호작용을 한 사람이 다른 사람과 관계를 맺거나, 그 사람의 행동이나 심리 상태, 감정적 반응에 영향을 미치는 과정으로 본다. 물론 그 반대 방향의 영향도 포함된다. (Process school은 사회적 상호작용을 상호 간의 영향력 행사 과정으로 본다. 여기서 커뮤니케이션은 단지 메시지의 이동이 아니라, 상대방의 생각이나 감정, 행동을 변화시키려는 목적을 가진 작용 과정이다.) 이는 (한 사람이 다른 사람의 행동, 감정, 생각 등에 영향을 미치는 과정) 우리가 일상적인 상식 수준에서 이해하는 "사회적 상호작용"이라는 표현의 의미에 가깝다. ('사회적 상호작용'이라는 표현을 우리가 보통 일상적으로 사용하는 **방식과 거의 유사하다**.) 반면에 기호학은 '사회적 상호작용'을 개인을 특정 문화나 사회의 구성원으로 구성하는 것으로 정의한다. (constitutes는 "형성하다, 정체성을 구성하다"는 의미의 철학·사회학적 용법을 뜻한다.) 나는 내가 서구 산업 사회의 구성원임을 안다. 왜냐하면 많은 동일시의 원천 중 하나를 들자면, 내가 셰익스피어나 코로네이션 스트리트에 내 문화의 동료 구성원들과 대체로 같은 방식으로 반응하기 때문이다. (respond to는 단순한 감상 이상의 의미로, **공유된 의미체계 속에서 특정 텍스트를 해석하고 수용한다는 것**을 의미한다.) 나는 한 중국인 평론가가 『리어왕』을 가족이 사회의 기반이라는 서구적 이상에 대한 신랄하고 파괴적인 공격으로 읽는 것을 들었고(중국 평론가는 『리어왕』이라는 희곡을 단순한 가족 비극이 아니라, 가족이 **개인을 도덕적으로 형성하고, 사회를 안정시키는 가장 중요한 단위라는 서구적 가치관에 대한 강력한 비판**으로 해석하고 있다. 『리어왕』에서는 부성애, 권위, 가족 간의 충성 등 서구적 가족관이 잔혹하게 붕괴된다. 이러한 붕괴를 "서구 가족 이데올로기에 대한 근본적 해체"로 읽는다면, 그것은 곧 그 이상(ideal)에 대한 비판적 해석, 즉 devastating attack으로 볼 수 있는 것이다.) 또 『코로네이션 스트리트』가 서구가 노동자 계급을 자기 자리에 묶어두는 방식이라고 주장하는 것을 들으면 문화적 차이를 인식하게 된다. 이 두 해석 모두 가능하지만, (앞에서 언급된 중국인 평론가의 해석, 즉 『리어왕』을 서구 가족 이데올로기에 대한 공격으로, 『코로네이션 스트리트』를 서구의 계급 유지 장치로 보는 해석) 내가 말하고자 하는 점은, 그것들이 내 문화의 전형적인 구성원으로서의 나의 것이 아니라는 것이다. 코로네이션 스트리트에 더 일반적인 방식으로 반응함으로써, 나는 내 문화의 다른 구성원들과의 공통성을 표현하고 있다. (다른 문화권의 독법은 충분히 가능하지만, 글쓴이는 자신이 속한 문화—즉 서구 문화—의 문해력과 감수성에 따라 텍스트를 해석한다. 예를 들어, 그는 『코로네이션 스트리트』를 서구 문화권 내에서 통용되는 '보통'의 방식으로 수용한다. 다시 말해, 중국인 비평가가 이를 정치적 메시지나 계급 억압의 장치로 읽어내는 반면, 글쓴이는 그것을 일상적인 드라마이자 친숙한 문화 코드로 받아들인다.)

3

하위내용영역	배점	예상정답률
일반영어 A형 서술형	4점	35%

모범답안 The Tuskegee experiment put extra burden on black physicians because of the deceptive nature of that experiment that was conducted on black patients and harmed the trust in the black community toward doctors. Second, the word is "history".

채점기준

+ 1점: 터스키기 실험이 최근에 큰 부담을 드리우는 사람을 "black physicians"라 서술하였다.
+ 1점: 이유를 "because of the deceptive nature of that experiment that was conducted on black patients and harmed the trust in the black community toward doctors"라 서술하였거나 유사하였다.
+ 2점: 빈칸에 들어갈 단어를 "history"라 정확하게 기입하였다. 이외에는 답이 될 수 없다.

한글번역

코로나 바이러스에 맞서 의료진 동료들과 함께 싸우는 과정에서, 흑인 의사들은 많은 흑인 지역사회 내에 존재하는 연방 정부에 대한 광범위한 불신이라는 추가적인 부담에 직면하고 있다.

콜롬비아 특별구(워싱턴 D.C.를 의미. 미국의 수도인 워싱턴이 위치한 연방 직할 특별구를 가리킨다. 어느 주(state)에도 속하지 않는 독립적인 연방 구역이다.)의 전 보건 위원장인 피에르 비질런스 박사는 아프리카계 미국인 불신의 "근원"인 미국 역사상 그 순간—악명 높은 40년간의 터스키기 실험—을 지적할 수 있다고 믿는다.

미국 공중보건청은 1932년 앨라배마주에 있는 전통적인 흑인 대학인 터스키기 대학교(당시 터스키기 연구소)와 협력해 이 연구를 시작했다. ("historically black college/university (HBCU)"는 미국에서 흑인 학생들을 위해 설립된 대학들을 가리키는 용어인데, "역사적"이라고 직역하면 한국어로는 부자연스러워 "전통적인"으로 번역했다.) 연구진은 앨라배마주 메이컨 카운티의 가난한 아프리카계 미국인 소작농 총 600명을 연구 대상자로 등록했다. 이 중 399명은 잠복 매독에 감염됐고, 201명은 감염되지 않은 대조군이었다. 연구는 환자들의 사전 동의라는 보호장치 없이 수행됐다. ("informed consent"는 의학 연구에서 중요한 개념으로, 연구 참여자에게 연구의 목적, 방법, 위험성 등을 충분히 알려준 후 동의를 받는 것을 의미한다.) 연구진은 이들에게 매독, 빈혈, 피로감 등을 가리키는 현지 말인 "나쁜 피" 치료를 받고 있다고 설명했다. (연구진이 의도적으로 정확한 의학 용어 대신 그 지역 사람들에게 친숙한 모호한 표현을 사용해서 참여자들을 속인 것이다. 연구진은 참여자들에게 "매독 연구에 참여하고 있고 치료는 받지 않는다"고 솔직하게 말하지 않고, 대신 "나쁜 피라는 병을 치료받고 있다"고 거짓말을 한 것이다.) 실제로는, 그들은 질병을 치료하는 데 필요한 적절한 치료를 받지 못했다. 연구 참여의 대가로, 남성들은 무료 건강 검진, 무료 식사, 그리고 매장 보험을 받았다. 원래 6개월 동안 지속될 것으로 예상됐지만, 연구는 실제로 40년간 계속돼 1972년까지 이어졌다. 그해 터스키기 연구에 대한 연합통신 기사가 공분을 일으켜 보건과학부 차관보는 연구를 검토할 임시 자문위원회를 임명하게 했고, 남성들이 오도됐으며 연구의 목적이나 목표에 대해 듣지 못했다는 것을 발견했다.

"일부는 잘 알고 있고 그 역사를 안다. 하지만 불신의 많은 촉발 요인들이 '조니 삼촌은 괜찮았는데, 의사에게 갔더니 모든 것이 내리막길을 걸었다'와 같은 가족사로 대체되고 있다. (일부 사람들은 터스키기 매독 실험이라는 역사적 사건을 잘 알고 있지만, 많은 경우 의료진에 대한 불신은 그런 역사적 사건보다는 개인적인 가족 경험담에서 비롯되고 있다는 뜻이다.) 그렇게 보였을 수도 있고, 실제로 그랬을 수도 있지만, 조니 삼촌에게는 그 역사와는 전혀 관계없는 여러 불리한 요소들이 있었다. (가족들은 "조니 삼촌이 병원에 가서 나빠졌다"고 생각하지만, 실제로는 터스키기 실험 같은 역사적 사건과는 무관한 다른 요인들—아마도 건강상 문제, 사회 경제적 요인, 의료 접근성 문제 등—이 조니 삼촌의 상황을 악화시켰다는 뜻이다.) 하지만 그것이 바로 그들의 믿음이다"라고 비질런스 박사는 말했다. "그리고 그것은 의료계와 공중보건계의 악행만큼이나 중요한 부분이다." (사람들이 "조니 삼촌이 병원에 가서 나빠졌다"고 믿는 것 자체가—그것이 사실이든 아니든—터스키기 같은 실제 의료 윤리 위반 사건들만큼이나 의료진 불신에 큰 영향을 미친다는 뜻이다. 즉, 실제 의료계의 잘못된 행위와 사람들의 주관적 믿음·인식 모두가 의료진 불신을 형성하는 데 똑같이 중요한 역할을 한다는 것이다.) 따라서 흑인 의사들이 현재 팬데믹 동안 정부가 추진하는 지침과 서비스를 자신들의 지역 사회가 신뢰하도록 돕는 것은 어려운 일이다.

4

하위내용영역	배점	예상정답률
일반영어 A형 서술형	4점	45%

모범 답안 The two rules are that it should be a long study of several years and it should be conducted closely within the community being studied. Second, the word is "intimacy".

채점 기준

+ 2점: 두 개의 규칙을 "it should be a long study of several years and it should be conducted closely within the community being studied"라 서술하였거나 유사하였다.
  ☞ "unlimited time and ties of intimacy"라고 했어도 2점을 준다.
+ 2점: 상응하는 한 단어를 "intimacy"이라 정확하게 기입하였다. 이외에는 답이 될 수 없다.

한글번역

인류학자의 훈련에 대한 나의 개략적 설명에서, 나는 그가 원시 민족들에 대한 집중적인 연구를 해야 한다고만 말했다. 나는 아직 그가 어떻게 그것들을 수행하는지 말하지 않았다. 원시 민족에 대한 연구는 어떻게 하는가? 나는 이 질문에 매우 간략하고 일반적인 용어로 답하겠으며, 좋은 현장 연구의 필수 규칙으로 우리가 여기는 것만을 서술하겠다.

경험이 증명하기로는 좋은 조사가 수행되려면 특정 조건들이 필수적이다. 초기의 전문 현장 연구자들은 항상 매우 서둘렀다. 토착민들에 대한 그들의 짧은 방문은 때로는 단지 며칠간 지속됐고, 몇 주를 넘는 경우는 거의 없었다. 이런 종류의 조사 연구는 집중적인 연구에 유용한 예비 단계가 될 수 있고 그것으로부터 기초적인 민족학적 분류가 도출될 수 있지만, 사회생활을 이해하는 데는 가치가 거의 없다. 오늘날 상황은 매우 다르다. 단일 민족의 연구에 1년에서 3년이 헌정된다. 이는 일 년의 모든 계절에 관찰이 이루어지고, 사람들의 사회생활이 마지막 세부사항까지 기록되며, 결론들이 체계적으로 검증될 수 있게 한다.

하지만 연구를 위한 무제한의 시간이 주어진다 해도, 인류학자는 그들과 친밀한 유대를 맺을 수 있고, 그들의 공동체 생활의 외부가 아닌 내부에서 그들의 일상 활동을 관찰할 수 있게 해주는 위치에 자신을 둘 수 없다면 연구하고 있는 사람들에 대한 좋은 기록을 만들어내지 못할 것이다.

그는 가능한 한 그들의 마을과 야영지에서 살아야 하며, 그곳에서 다시 가능한 한 물리적으로 그리고 도덕적으로 공동체의 일부가 돼야 한다. 그러면 그는 사람들의 일상적인 생활뿐만 아니라 의례와 법적 사건 같은 덜 일반적인 사건들에서 무슨 일이 일어나는지 보고 들을 수 있다. 그가 적절히 참여할 수 있는 활동들에 참여함으로써 귀와 눈뿐만 아니라 행동을 통해서도 자신의 주변에서 일어나는 일을 배운다. 이는 토착 공동체 밖에서 선교소나 정부 기관에 살면서 주로 몇몇 정보제공자들이 그들에게 말하는 것에 의존해야 했던 초기 인류학적 현장 연구자들이 토착 생활의 기록을 편집했던 상황과는 매우 다르다.

제66회 모의고사

1

하위내용영역	배점	예상정답률
일반영어 B형 서술형	4점	45%

모범 답안 The new discovery suggests there can be life on Venus. Second, "Venus". Third, "phosphine".

채점 기준

+ 2점: 새로운 발견이 시사하는 바를 "there can be life on Venus"라 서술하였거나 유사하였다.
+ 1점: "옆에 있는 자매 행성"을 "Venus"라 서술하였다. 이외에는 답이 될 수 없다.
+ 1점: 빈칸에 들어갈 단어를 "phosphine"이라 정확하게 기입하였다. 이외에는 답이 될 수 없다.

⊕ 보충설명

parts per billion(ppb)는 농도를 나타내는 단위로 "10억분의 몇"을 의미한다.
20ppb = 10억 개 중 20개 = 0.00002%
금성: 20ppb; 지구: 대략 0.02ppb~0.00002ppb
(역산하면) 20 ÷ 1,000 = 0.02ppb (최소값);
20 ÷ 1,000,000 = 0.00002ppb (최대값)

이 엄청난 농도 차이는 왜 과학자들을 놀라게 했는지 보여준다. 지구에서도 포스핀은 극미량으로만 존재하는데, 금성에서는 그보다 훨씬 높은 농도로 발견되었기 때문이다. 이는 금성에 **포스핀을 대량으로 생성하는 무언가(생명체일 가능성)**가 있는 것을 시사한다.

한글번역

금성의 구름에서 뭔가 이상한 일이 벌어지고 있다. 망원경들이 포스핀 분자의 비정상적으로 높은 농도를 탐지했다. 포스핀은 악취가 나고 가연성인 화학물질로, 일반적으로 대변, 방귀, 그리고 썩어가는 미생물 활동과 관련 있다. 이 물질이 금성 표면의 작열하는 온도보다 훨씬 높은 대기층에서 발견된 것이다.

이 발견이 흥미로운 이유는 지구에서 포스핀이 본질적으로 항상 생명체와 연관이 있기 때문이다. 포스핀은 신진대사 과정의 부산물이거나 산업용 훈증제나 메스암페타민 제조소 같은 인간 기술의 산물로 나타난다. 많은 유기체에게 독성이 있음에도 불구하고, 포스핀 분자는 일반적인 지질학적 또는 대기적 작용으로는 만들어내기가 매우 어렵기 때문에 생명의 명확한 신호로 여겨져 왔다.

황산 구름에 싸여 있고 압도적인 표면 압력과 납을 녹일 정도로 뜨거운 온도를 가진 금성은 지옥 같은 세계다. 하지만 포스핀이 존재하는 특정 구름층은 상당히 온화한 편으로, 충분한 햇빛과 지구와 비슷한 대기압 및 온도를 가지고 있다. 이러한 결과들은 과학계의 신중한 검증을 거쳐야 할 것이다. 그럼에도 불구하고 이 발견은 우리의 이웃 행성인 금성을 탐사하는 데 대한 새로운 관심을 불러일으킬 것으로 보인다.

워싱턴 대학교의 우주생물학자 마이클 웡은 "포스핀이 금성 대기에 존재해야 할 화학물질 종류에 대한 우리의 개념에 맞지 않기 때문에 정말 당황스러운 발견"이라고 말한다. (과학자들이 예상하는 금성 대기 구성 성분들 중에 포스핀은 포함되지 않았는데, 실제로는 발견됐기 때문에 당황스럽다는 뜻이다.) 위스콘신 대학교 매디슨 캠퍼스의 행성과학자 산제이 리마예도 동의한다. 리마예는 "결론적으로 우리는 무슨 일이 일어나고 있는지 모른다"고 말한다. (웡과 산제이 모두 이 연구에는 참여하지 않았다.)

태양과 달 다음으로, 금성은 지구 하늘에서 육안으로 볼 수 있는 가장 밝은 천체다. 수천 년 동안 사람들은 일출과 일몰 무렵에 나타나는 반짝이는 보석에 대한 이야기를 전해왔다. 금성의 밝기는 웨일스 카디프 대학교의 전파천문학자 제인 그리브스의 관심을 끈 것이었다. 그리브스는 보통 멀리 떨어진 신생 행성계에 주의를 집중하지만, 우리 우주의 뒷마당에 있는 세계들(태양계: 금성 등이 포함돼 있는)에서 분자 식별 능력을 테스트하고 싶어 했다.

2017년 그리브스는 하와이 마우나케아에 있는 제임스 클러크 맥스웰 망원경(JCMT)으로 금성을 관측했다. 그리브스는 금성의 스펙트럼에서 바코드 같은 선 패턴을 찾아 서로 다른 화학물질의 존재를 나타내는 신호를 찾고 있었다. (천체에서 오는 빛을 분광기로 분석하면, 그 천체에 포함된 각각의 화학 원소나 분자들이 특정 파장의 빛을 흡수하거나 방출한다. 이때 스펙트럼에 나타나는 흡수선이나 방출선들이 마치 바코드의 검은 선들처럼 보인다.) 관측 중에 그리브스는 포스핀과 관련된 선을 발견했다. 데이터에 따르면 그 분자(포스핀)가 금성 대기에서 약 10억분의 20 농도로 존재했는데, 이는 지구 대기의 농도보다 1,000배에서 100만 배 높은 수치였다. 그리브스는 "깜짝 놀랐다"고 말한다.

포스핀은 인 원자 하나와 수소 원자 세 개로 구성된 비교적 단순한 분자다. 포스핀은 마늘이나 썩은 생선 냄새가 나는 것으로 알려져 있지만, 인간이 냄새를 맡을 수 있는 농도에 도달하면 폐 손상을 일으킬 가능성이 높다.

2

하위내용영역	배점	예상정답률
일반영어 B형 서술형	4점	50%

모범답안 The word is "cheat". Second, the writer would propose managers and negotiators to trust their intuitions.

채점기준

+ 2점: 빈칸에 들어갈 단어를 "cheat"이라 정확하게 기입하였다. 이외에는 답이 될 수 없다.
+ 2점: 관리자들과 협상가들에게 제안하는 변화를 "managers and negotiators to trust their intuitions (or their gut feelings)"라 서술하였거나 유사하였다.

한글번역

최근에 코넬 대학교와 MIT의 동료들과 함께 진행한 한 실험에서, 연구진은 참가자들이 경제 게임을 시작하기 직전에 짧은 '서로 알아가는' 대화를 나누는 장면을 촬영했다. 참가자들은 두 가지 방식으로 대화를 나눴는데, 하나는 직접 얼굴을 맞대고, 다른 하나는 온라인 채팅을 통해서였다. 이 경제 게임은 개인의 이익 추구와 협력 사이에서 선택을 요구하는 구조였다. 전체적으로 봤을 때, 두 그룹 모두 협력의 평균 수준은 비슷했지만, 사람들이 상대방과 금전적 교환을 할 때, 상대가 얼마나 공정하게 행동할지를 예측한 것은, (온라인 채팅을 통해 대화한 경우보다) 사전에 직접 얼굴을 마주하고 대화한 경우 훨씬 더 정확했다. (이는 직접 대면한 상호작용이 신뢰 판단에 중요한 비언어적 단서를 제공했다는 실험의 핵심 결과 중 하나이다.) 이것은 (앞 문장의 전체 내용을 가리킴) '신뢰와 관련된 (신뢰 판단에 영향을 미치는) 어떤 신호'가 반드시 존재해야 한다는 점을 의미했다. ("얼굴을 맞댄 상호작용이 예측의 정확성을 높였다"는 실험 결과로부터 비언어적이거나 직관적인 신뢰 관련 신호가 실제로 작동하고 있다는 논리적 귀결을 이끌어내는 연결 문장이다.)
(*참고: 구체적으로 이 글에서 말하는 "신뢰와 관련된 신호"는 다음과 같다. 비언어적 행동(예 몸을 뒤로 젖히기, 팔짱 끼기, 손/얼굴 만지기 등)이 반복적으로 나타날 경우, 사람들은 그 상대를 덜 신뢰하게 되었고 실제로도 그 상대는 이익을 공유하지 않는 이기적인 행동을 보였다. 즉, 여기서 말하는 "신뢰와 관련된 신호"란 바로 이러한 일련의 비언어적 행동 패턴을 의미한다.)

이 신호가 무엇인지 알아내기 위해, 연구진은 사전에 수집해 둔 비언어적 단서(nonverbal cues)들을 비교 분석했다. 그 결과, 다음의 네 가지 행동—① 상대방에게서 몸을 멀리 기울이는 행동 ② 팔짱을 끼는 행동 ③ 자신의 손을 만지는 행동 ④ 자신의 얼굴을 만지는 행동—이 신뢰할 수 없는 행동을 예측하는 데 있어 신뢰도 높은 지표로 작용한다는 사실을 발견했다. 어떤 사람이 이 네 가지 비언어적 단서들(몸을 뒤로 젖히기, 팔짱 끼기, 손 만지기, 얼굴 만지기)을 더 자주 나타낼수록, 파트너와 이익을 나누기를 거부함으로써 더 큰 자기중심적 행동을 보였다. 또한, 파트너가 그 네 가지 단서들을 상대방에게서 더 자주 목격할수록, 그 사람(상대방)이 자신을 속일 것이라고 더 강하게 예상했다. (비언어적 신호를 본 횟수가 많을수록 불신이 더 커졌다는 뜻이다.) 가장 흥미로운 점은, 얼굴을 맞대고 대화한 참가자들이 자신이 이러한 단서를 활용해 상대방의 신뢰 가능성을 추론하고 있다는 사실을 전혀 인식하지 못했다는 것이다. 다시 말해, 이들은 자신도 모르게 보다 정확한 '직관'을 발전시키고 있었던 셈이며, 왜 그런 판단을 하게 됐는지 설명할 수는 없었다.

연구진은 이후 동일한 실험을 다시 수행하되, 한 가지 중요한 변화를 줬다. 이번에는 참가자들이 사람과 대화하는 것이 아니라, 사람처럼 생긴 '휴머노이드 로봇'과 대화하게 했다. 이 로봇은 두 가지 중 하나로 사전에 프로그래밍됐다. 하나는 앞서 언급한 네 가지 단서를 표현하는 방식, 다른 하나는 감정이 담기지 않은 중립적인 몸짓을 표현하는 방식이었다. 로봇을 사용한 이유는 통제의 정밀성 때문이다. 로봇은 사람 배우(human actor)보다 훨씬 더 정확하고 일관되게 특정 제스처를 반복할 수 있기 때문에, 네 가지 단서가 실제로 신뢰 판단에 어떤 영향을 주는지 정밀하게 분석할 수 있었다. 그리고 그 결과는 연구진의 예측과 같았다. 참가자들이 로봇이 그 네 가지 단서를 표현하는 것을 봤을 때, 그 로봇을 덜 신뢰한다고 보고했고, 또한 그 로봇이 자신을 속일 것이라고 더 많이 예상했다.

이러한 일련의 발견들은 인간의 마음이 타인의 신뢰성을 감지하는 기능을 본능적으로 갖추고 있다는 점을 보여준다. 동시에, 이러한 직관, 즉 '직감(gut feelings)'이 얼마나 소중한지를 뒷받침하는 증거이기도 하다. 하지만 문제는 다음과 같다. 관리자나 협상가들은 종종 자신의 직관적인 판단 체계를 억누르는 경향이 있다는 것이다. 그들은 신뢰성을 예측할 때, 직관보다 평판이나 지위 같은 보다 이성적이라고 여겨지는 지표에 의존하려 하거나, 혹은 잘못된 비언어적 신호(어떤 사람의 신뢰성을 판단하려 할 때, 실제로 유의미한 신호(예 팔짱, 몸 기울임 등) 대신, 표현 방식이 다를 뿐 전혀 상관없는 신호를 믿고 해석하려는 잘못된 시도를 지칭하는 말)를 신뢰하는 실수를 저지르기도 한다.

3

하위내용영역	배점	예상정답률
일반영어 B형 서술형	4점	50%

감점
- 본문에 나오는 연속되는 6단어 이상을 사용하였다. −0.5pt
- 문단을 두 개나 그 이상으로 구성하였다. −0.5pt
- 문법이나 영어 표현을 합쳐 3개 이상 오류가 있다. −0.5pt

모범답안 Child abuse stems from multiple causes both inside and outside the home. Within families, it often arises from emotional stress, financial pressure, or a lack of support, which prevents parents from managing their anger. Abuse can also occur in childcare settings, especially when babysitters or nursery staff are overwhelmed. Substance abuse further increases the risk by impairing judgment or triggering violent behavior. In conclusion, early detection and intervention are crucial, as they offer the best chance to protect the child and help the abuser.

채점기준

ⓐ Topic sentence
+ 1점: "Child abuse stems from multiple causes both inside and outside the home"를 명확하게 서술하였다. 또는 "There are several reason for child abuse"라 했어도 1점을 준다.

ⓑ Major supporting details
+ 2점: "Within families, it often arises from emotional stress, financial pressure, or a lack of support, which prevents parents from managing their anger. Abuse can also occur in childcare settings, especially when babysitters or nursery staff are overwhelmed. Substance abuse further increases the risk by impairing judgment or triggering violent behavior"을 명확하게 서술하였다.
☞ 3개 중 3개 모두 정확하게 요약했으면 2점, 2개만 요약했으면 1점, 나머지는 0점을 준다.

ⓒ Conclusion
+ 1점: "In conclusion, early detection and intervention are crucial, as they offer the best chance to protect the child and help the abuser"을 정확하게 요약하였다.

한글번역

가정은 아이가 안전하고 보호받는다고 느껴야 할 피난처가 돼야 한다. 불행히도, 가정은 대부분의 경우 아이가 학대받는 곳이기도 하다.

가해자들은 자신들의 스트레스와 좌절감 때문에 그런 일을 한다고 주장한다. 아동 학대를 하는 부모들은 우는 아이에게 괴롭힘을 당한다고 느끼며 자신들의 분노를 억제할 수 없다. 특히 누구로부터도 지원을 받지 못한다면 더욱 그렇다. 아동 학대 피해자에게는 가해자보다 더 쉽게 지원이 제공되므로 이는 놀라운 일이 아니다. 때때로, 부모들이 서로 싸우고 다툴 때 자녀에게 좌절감을 발산할 수 있다. 구체적으로, 재정적 문제가 아동 학대로 이어질 수 있다. 먹여야 할 입이 너무 많을 때, 부모들은 압박감을 느끼고 아이에게 분노를 발산한다.

부모 모두가 보통 직업을 가지고 있는 이 현대 시대에서, 아이들은 보육사와 어린이집에 맡겨진다. 이러한 돌봄 제공자들에 의한 학대는 돌봐야 할 아이들이 너무 많을 때 발생한다. 약물 남용은 아동 학대 사건을 증가시키는 또 다른 요인이다. 알코올이나 마약의 영향 하에서, 부모는 자신이 무엇을 하고 있는지 모를 수 있다. 또는 오히려, 자신이 무엇을 하고 있는지 알지만 전혀 신경 쓰지 않는다. 마약 중독자는 기분 변화를 겪을 수 있고 자녀들의 사소한 실수에 쉽게 자극받는다. 우리는 아이가 잔혹하게 고문당하고 쓰레기처럼 다른 곳에 버려지는 끔찍한 보고서들을 보고 읽는다.

학대의 이유가 무엇이든, 잔혹함을 멈추기 위해 무언가가 이뤄져야 한다. 아이가 학대로 고통받고 있다고 의심된다면, 목소리를 내는 것이 중요하다. 가능한 한 빨리 문제를 발견함으로써, 아이와 가해자 모두 도움받을 더 나은 상태에 있게 된다.

제67회 모의고사

1

하위내용영역	배점	예상정답률
일반영어 A형 서술형	4점	45%

모범답안 The word is "starvation". It means that she wants to get revenge on nature by abandoning life and the illness it gave her.

채점기준

+ 2점: 빈칸에 들어갈 단어를 "starvation"라 정확하게 기입하였다. 이외에는 답이 될 수 없다.
+ 2점: 밑줄 친 부분의 의미를 "she wants to get revenge on nature by abandoning life and the illness it gave her"라 서술하였거나 유사하였다.

한글번역

안락사 합법화를 위해 캠페인을 벌여온 한 여성이 더 이상 자신의 쇠약한 심폐 질환을 견딜 수 없다며 스스로 굶어 죽기로 결정했다. 2주 전부터 식사를 중단한 28세의 켈리 테일러는 자신의 삶이 너무 제한적이라 "사회에 어떤 기여도 할 수 없다"고 말했다. 그녀의 질환인 아이젠멩거 증후군은 그녀가 산소에 의존해야 하고 쓰러지지 않고는 몇 걸음 이상 걸을 수 없음을 의미한다. 그녀는 굶주림이 남편 리처드를 자살 방조 혐의로 기소당하게 하지 않을 죽음의 방법이라고 믿었기 때문에 굶주림을 선택했다고 말했다. 그녀는 안락사가 합법인 나라로 여행하는 것을 고려했지만, 남편이 영국으로 돌아왔을 때 기소될 것을 우려한다고 말했다. 그녀는 "제 마음은 오랫동안 준비돼 있었습니다. 저는 제가 가진 삶을 계속하고 싶지 않습니다. 너무 제한적입니다. 저는 사회에 전혀 기여하지 못합니다. 그것이 제게 가장 큰 부담이었습니다. 저는 일을 할 수 없었습니다. 저는 결코 회복되지 않을 것임을 압니다. 제 상태는 서서히 악화되고 있습니다. 안락사가 합법인 곳에 가서 죽을 수 있는 약을 받는 것을 고려했지만 제 남편에게 법적 영향이 있을 것임을 압니다. 그런 일이 일어나게 할 수는 없었습니다."라고 말했다.

테일러 부인이 목숨을 끊겠다는 결심은 마요르카에서 휴가를 보내던 중 남편과 부모님과 함께 바다에 들어갈 수 없었을 때 더욱 굳어졌다. "그들을 지켜보는 것을 견딜 수 없었습니다"라고 그녀는 말했다. "저는 물에 들어가고 싶었지만 할 수 없다는 것을 알았습니다. 제 삶의 질이 얼마나 악화됐는지 깨달았고 계속할 수 없었습니다." 단식 시위를 시작한 후 며칠 동안, 테일러 부인은 체중이 1스톤(약 6.4kg) 줄었다고 말했다. "제가 스스로 굶기 시작했을 때는 다르게 느끼지 않았습니다. 3일째 되는 날 제 배가 꾸르륵거렸습니다. 이제 저는 더 약해졌고 더 많이 잠을 자야 합니다. 물론 죽음에 대한 두려움은 있지만 장기간의 고통스러운 삶을 사는 것에 대한 두려움이 훨씬 더 무섭습니다. 저는 이것을 단식 시위나 자살로 생각하지 않고 자연에게 한 방 먹이는 것으로 생각합니다." 테일러 부인은 이 희귀한 퇴행성 질환을 가지고 태어났고 어릴 때부터 휠체어가 필요했다. 아이젠멩거 증후군을 가진 사람들은 심장에 구멍이 있어 폐의 동맥에 압력을 가한다. 그녀는 9년간 심폐 이식 대기자 명단에 있었다. 하지만 이제 위험이 너무 높다는 말을 들었다.

2

하위내용영역	배점	예상정답률
일반영어 A형 서술형	4점	50%

모범답안 The words are "first exposure". The understanding has evolved in that it was believed that pets were good for mental health but new studies have created doubt about this.

채점기준

+ 2점: 빈칸에 들어갈 단어를 "first exposure"라 정확하게 기입하였다. 이외에는 답이 될 수 없다.
+ 2점: 애완동물을 소유함으로 인해 발생하는 정신 건강상의 혜택이 어떻게 진전(변화)되어 왔는지에 대해 "it was believed that pets were good for mental health but new studies have created doubt about this"라 서술하였거나 유사하였다.

한글번역

고고학적 기록들은 우리가 애완동물과 오랫동안 가까운 관계를 유지해왔음을 시사한다. 약 1만 년 전 우리는 농장 주변을 뛰어다니는 잘 먹은 설치류들에게 끌린 고양이들과 함께 살기 시작했다. 고대 이집트에서는 수백만 마리의 애완견들이 비싼 선물과 비문으로 장식된 정교한 무덤에 묻혔다. 그 결과, 우리는 아마도 여러 세대에 걸쳐 길들여진 동물들과 포옹을 나누는 동시에 미생물 생물체들을 교환해왔을 것이다.

오늘날 그러한 애완동물들은 여전히 명백히 우리 집에서 편안하게 지내고 있다. 그리고 많은 기사들은 애완동물이 포옹과 동반자 관계를 넘어서 정신적, 신체적 건강 개선과 같은 다른 이익들을 제공한다고 선전한다.

하지만 성급하게 결론내리지 말자. 최근 연구들의 급증은 애완동물이 우리 삶에 가져다주는 것—우리의 장내 환경을 바꿀 수 있는 미생물 교환부터 정서적 안녕까지—에 대한 더 혼란스러운 그림을 제시한다.

먼저, 알레르기에 대해 이야기해보자. 수많은 연구들이 개를 기르는 것이 생애 매우 이른 시기에 첫 노출이 일어나면 애완동물 알레르기 발생률을 줄이는 것으로 보인다고 말한다. 많은 미생물체 연구자들은 유아기 동안 애완동물 비듬 형태로 애완동물의 미생물 환경에 노출되는 것이 구체적으로 면역 체계가 애완동물과 다른 알레르기 유발 물질들을 다루도록 훈련시킬 수 있다고 믿는다. (이론은 다음과 같다: 특정 세균과 감염 병원체에 대한 조기 노출 없이는 면역 체계의 자연스러운 발달이 본질적으로 저해된다.) 하지만 수천 명의 아이들과 성인들을 대상으로 한 2017년 5월 연구가 결론짓듯이, 그러한 노출의 시기가 핵심인 것으로 보인다. 십대나 젊은 성인으로서 첫 노출이 일어날 때, 애완동물 알레르기의 위험이 실제로 증가하는 것으로 보인다.

더 나쁜 소식이 있다. 애완동물들은 또한 다른 문제들을 일으킬 수 있다. 도마뱀과 거북이는 살모넬라균을 옮길 수 있다. 앵무새는 인간에게 심각한 폐렴을 일으키는 앵무병의 병원체를 옮길 수 있다. 그리고 우리의 털 달린 친구들 중 많은 수가 "슈퍼박테리아" 메티실린 내성 황색포도상구균, 지아르디아, 그리고 다른 병원체와 기생충들을 포함한 심각한 감염 병원체들을 옮길 수 있다는 증거가 축적됐다.

애완동물 소유로부터 오는 정신 건강상의 이익에 대한 우리의 현대적 이해조차 계속 발전하고 있다. 수십 년 동안 애완동물과 함께 긴장을 푸는 것의 정신 건강상 이익에 대한 광범위한 수용이 있었다. 하지만 그 그림은 스웨덴의 거의 4만 명을 대상으로 한 2010년 연구에 의해 복잡해졌는데, 이 연구는 애완동물 소유자들이 애완동물이 없는 사람들보다 신체적으로 더 건강했지만 애완동물이 없는 동료들보다 더 많은 정신 건강 문제를 겪었다는 것을 발견했다. 이제 과학은 누가 애완동물 소유로부터 이익을 얻을 수 있는지 또는 심지어 그러한 관계가 왜 도움이 될 수 있는지에 대해 여전히 불확실하다.

3

하위내용영역	배점	예상정답률
일반영어 A형 서술형	4점	45%

모범 답안 The word is "novelty". Curiosity appears as giddiness, restlessness, as well as anxiety.

채점 기준

+ 2점: 빈칸에 들어갈 단어를 "novelty"라 정확하게 기입하였다. 이외에는 답이 될 수 없다.
+ 2점: 의미를 "giddiness, restlessness, as well as anxiety"라 서술하였거나 유사하였다.

한글번역

인간의 마음속에서 제일 먼저 발견되는 가장 단순한 감정은 호기심이다. 여기서 호기심은 새로운 것에 대한 욕구나 거기서 얻게 되는 즐거움을 통틀어 이르는 말이다. 어린아이들은 끊임없이 무언가 새로운 것을 찾아다닌다. 자신 앞에 나타나는 것은 대상을 가리지 않고 아주 열심히 살핀다. 이렇듯 어린아이들은 모든 새로운 사물에 관심을 보이는데, 그 시기에는 새로운 것이면 무엇이든 나름의 매력을 지니기 때문이다.

하지만 우리는 단지 새롭다는 이유만으로 관심의 대상이 되는 사물에는 그다지 오래 애착을 느끼지 않는다. 따라서 호기심은 인간의 감정들 가운데서 가장 피상적이다. 호기심의 대상은 끊임없이 바뀐다. 호기심은 아주 강한 욕구지만 다른 한편 매우 쉽게 충족되기 때문이다. 그래서 호기심은 언제나 경박하며 침착하지 못하고 불안한 감정이라는 인상을 준다.

호기심은 본질적으로 매우 활동적이다. 호기심은 대부분의 대상들을 빠르게 스쳐 지나간다. 따라서 아무리 다양한 대상들이 있더라도—다양성과 호기심은 본질적으로 서로 잘 어울리는 개념이다—순식간에 전부 살펴보고 나서는 곧 싫증을 느낀다. 동일한 사물이 자주 반복해서 나타나면 우리가 거기서 느끼는 즐거움은 점점 줄어든다. 인생에서 벌어지는 어떤 일에 대해 점점 더 알아갈수록 우리에게는 혐오나 권태의 감정밖에 남지 않는다. 이와 다른 감정을 느끼려면 새로움과는 다른 성질이나 호기심 외의 다른 감정을 통해서 우리의 마음이 움직여야 한다.

하지만 이런 성질이 무엇이든 또는 어떤 원리에 따라 이 성질이 우리의 마음을 움직이든, 이것이 우리의 마음을 움직이기 위해서 반드시 필요한 조건이 있다. 이런 성질이 진부한 대상에서 나타나서는 안 된다는 것이다. 진부한 대상은 일상적으로 사용하는 것이라서 친숙하기는 하지만 별 감동은 주지 못하기 때문이다. 따라서 어떤 대상이 인간의 마음을 움직이려면 어느 정도 새로운 것이어야 한다. 호기심은 많든 적든 우리의 마음을 움직이는 모든 감정에 수반되는 감정인 것이다.

4

하위내용영역	배점	예상정답률
일반영어 A형 서술형	4점	45%

[모범답안] It means that most younger British people would be surprised when a person talks to them about forgetting to use polite phrases such as "thank you" or "please". Second, the word is "Britain".

[채점기준]

+ 2점: 밑줄 친 부분의 의미를 "<u>most younger British people would be surprised when a person talks to them forgetting to use polite phrases such as 'thank you' or 'please'</u>"라 서술하였거나 유사하였다.
+ 2점: 빈칸에 들어갈 단어를 "Britain"라 정확하게 기입하였다. 이외에는 답이 될 수 없다.

한글번역

냉전이 절정에 달했을 때, 데일리 미러는 전면에 걸쳐 소비에트 연방의 화를 잘 내고 떼를 쓰는 지도자인 니키타 흐루시초프에게 직접 전하는 질책을 다뤘다. 신문은 찾을 수 있는 가장 큰 활자로 이렇게 외쳤다: "오래된 영국 표현을 용서해 주시길 바라며, 흐루시초프 씨, 그렇게 지독하게 무례하게 굴지 마십시오." 같은 말이 이제 영국 전체 인구에게 전해져야 한다. 운전자들이 실제로 차에서 내려 서로를 죽이고 있는 번잡한 도로의 광고판에서 우리에게 외쳐야 한다. 그들이 자신들의 야만적이고 광적인 분노, 빨간 신호등을 먼저 통과하겠다는 결심을 통제할 수 없을 정도로 말이다. 그것들은 모든 공공건물의 밖과 안, 상점 계산대, 학교 운동장 문, 버스와 기차역, 호텔과 지역 술집의 바 위에 표시돼야 한다. 텔레비전 방송국들은 모든 프로그램을 "그렇게 지독하게 무례하게 굴지 마라"는 슬로건으로 시작해야 한다. 여기에 아마도 "무례함은 삶을 지옥으로 만든다"는 부가 설명을 덧붙일 수 있을 것이다.

영국의 모든 계층의 대부분 사람들이 서로에게 부탁합니다와 감사합니다를 말하는 것을 중단했다. 당신이 그 누락을 언급하면 아이들과 청소년들은 놀라서 당신을 바라본다. 그들은 이러한 간단하지만 매우 필수적인 말들을 구식이고 아첨하는 것으로 여긴다. 하지만 제공된 서비스나 베풀어진 호의에 대해 다른 사람들에게 감사하기를 거부하는 것은 거칠고 고집스럽게 무례한 행동의 가장 덜 해로운 표출이다. 사람들이 공공장소에서 행동하는 방식이 훨씬 더 위협적이고, 국가 문화에 더 해롭다. 쇼핑객들이 냄새나는 조깅복을 입고 슈퍼마켓 식품 계산대에서 줄을 선다. 티셔츠를 입은 배가 나온 바보들이 유행하는 바에서 병맥주를 벌컥벌컥 마신다. 기차에서 승객들의 행동은 혐오스럽다. 한때는 진흙투성이 부츠나 신발을 좌석에 올려놓는 것은 오직 하층민과 부랑자들과 보수당 지지자들뿐이었다. 오늘날 줄무늬 양복을 입은 경영진들이 일등석을 타고 가면서 그렇게 한다. 그리고 팝 음악 팬들이 있다. 그들은 헤드셋을 착용하고 있는데, 이론적으로는 소음을 자신들의 바보 같은 귀에만 가두도록 설계된 것이다. 하지만 착용자들은 항상 볼륨을 최대로 올려서 20야드 내의 누구든지 드럼 섹션의 무의미하고 미치게 하는 쿵쿵거림과 충돌음을 공유할 수 있도록 한다.

요즘 영국은 이기심, 공격성, 그리고 영구적인 불안의 사회적 분위기에서 서로 팔꿈치로 밀치는 찌푸린 얼굴의 무례한 야만인들의 땅이 됐다.

제68회 모의고사

1

하위내용영역	배점	예상정답률
일반영어 A형 서술형	4점	50%

모범답안 Creativity is being focused and having nothing take away one's attention. Second, the words are "getting attention".

채점기준
+ 2점: 창의력을 "being focused and having nothing take away one's attention"라 서술하였거나 유사하였다.
+ 2점: 빈칸에 들어갈 단어를 "getting attention"라 정확하게 기입하였다. 이외에는 답이 될 수 없다.

한글번역

나는 연기할 때 단 한 가지에만 관심을 쏟을 수 있도록 집중한다. 내가 촬영장에서 준비가 끝나면 조감독은 "롤링"을 외치고, 뒤이어 "스피드", "마커", "셋" 소리가 들린 뒤 감독의 "액션!" 지시를 듣는다. 이 순서가 너무 익숙해서 이제 나는 파블로프의 개처럼 여기에 반응한다. 나에게도 어쩔 수 없는 내면의 무언가가 시작되고 오직 한 가지에만 관심을 쏟게 되는 것이다. 나머지 모든 것, 나를 신경 쓰게 하고 내 주의를 앗아가던 모든 것들이 그 순간 사라진다. 그 순간 나는 그저 그 장소에 존재하는 사람이 된다. 바로 이 감정이 내가 너무 사랑하는 감정이며, 나는 이 감정을 창의력이라 느낀다. 내가 연기자가 된 것이 감사한 가장 큰 이유다.

그러니까 관심을 끄는 것과 관심을 쏟는 것의 두 가지 아주 강력한 감정이 있는 것이다. 사실 지난 10년 동안 등장한 새로운 기술은 점점 더 많은 이들이 사람들의 관심을 끌 때 느끼는 강력한 감정을 느낄 수 있게 만들었다. 연기만이 아니라 글쓰기, 사진, 그림, 음악 등 모든 분야의 창조적인 이들은 사람들의 관심을 끌 수 있게 됐다. 문화가 전달되는 채널이 다양해졌고 이는 좋은 일이다.

하지만 이런 현상은 의도치 않은 결과를 만들었다. 곧, 많은 이들에게 창조적으로 보여야 한다는 압력으로 작용하게 된 것이다. 여기에는 나도 포함된다. 나는 지금 이 세상의 창조적인 작업이 점점 더 한 가지 목적을 위한 어떤 수단으로 바뀌고 있다고 느낀다. 그 목적은 바로 사람들의 관심을 끄는 것이다. 그래서 나는 사람들에게 내 경험을 통해 이런 이야기를 하려 한다. 바로, 내가 관심을 쏟을 때의 강력한 감정을 쫓을 때 나는 더 행복해졌지만, 남들의 관심을 받을 때의 강력한 감정을 쫓을 때 내가 더 불행해졌다는 것이다.

2

하위내용영역	배점	예상정답률
일반영어 A형 서술형	4점	35%

모범답안 Making quick predictions about a possible "snake" is required for being able to react fast and survive better. Second, the words are "makes predictions".

채점기준
+ 2점: 밑줄 친 부분의 의미를 "Making quick predictions (about a possible "snake") is required for being able to react fast and survive better"라 서술하였거나 유사하였다.
+ 2점: 빈칸에 들어갈 단어를 "makes predictions"라 정확하게 기입하였다. 이외에는 답이 될 수 없다.

한글번역

　심리학 교수인 바렛은 우리의 뇌를 어둡고 조용한 상자, 그러니까 두개골 속에 갇힌 죄수라고 이야기한다. 이 죄수가 바깥세상에 대해 얻을 수 있는 정보는 빛(시각), 기압(청각), 화학 물질(미각과 후각)밖에 없다. 무엇이 이 감각의 변화를 일으키는지도 알지 못하며, 따라서 지금 가진 정보만으로 무엇을 할지 결정해야 한다.

　어떻게 해야 할까? 뇌는 과거의 비슷한 감각과 이를 비교해, 앞으로 어떤 일이 벌어질지 예측한다. 당신이 숲속을 걷고 있다고 상상해 보자. 나뭇가지 사이로 비치는 얼룩덜룩한 햇볕은 당신 앞에 줄무늬의 그림자를 만든다. 당신은 과거에 수많은 뱀을 봤고, 또 숲속에는 뱀이 살고 있다는 사실을 알고 있다. 당신의 뇌는 이런 일련의 예측을 계속하도록 만들어져 있다.

　이 이야기의 핵심은, 이러한 예측 활동이 바로 의식이며, 곧 세상에 대한 끊임없는 예측, 그리고 새로운 감각 정보에 의해 그 예측이 확인되거나 혹은 오류로 판명되는 과정을 계속 반복하는 것이다. 얼룩덜룩한 햇볕은 (숲속의 검은 줄무늬는) 당신이 한 발을 내딛음으로써 그저 바닥에 떨어진 나뭇가지였음을 알게 되며, 이로써 그 줄무늬가 뱀이라는 예측은 그 신호가 너무 강해 당신의 시각 신호가 뱀이 그곳에 있다는 사실을 당신에게 말하기 전에 오류로 판명된다. 즉, 우리는 자신을 둘러싼 세상을 매 순간 만들어 간다. 이런 활동이 없다면, 우리는 이 세상에서 살아남지 못했을 것이다. 만약 "뱀"에 대한 예측이 뇌에 새겨져 있지 않았다면, 실제로 뱀을 보고 나서 당신을 도망가게 만들 아드레날린 호르몬은 이미 늦었을 것이다.

　뇌는 우리의 심장 박동, 폐의 활동과 면역계, 호르몬 수치 등을 또한 정보로 받아들인다. 인체의 상태에 대한 상시적인 관찰 정보를 말하는 "내부감각 수용기"는 일반적으로 의식보다 낮은 수준의 상태에서 처리된다. 하지만 이 정보는 앞서 이야기한 우리의 감정을 결정하는 정서(affect), 곧 쾌감과 불쾌감, 흥분의 정도를 결정하기 때문에 매우 중요한 정보이다.

　뇌는 신체 내부로부터 오는 정보 또한 외부로부터 오는 정보를 처리할 때와 같은 방법으로 처리한다. 곧, 무엇이 이런 변화를 일으켰는지를 과거의 경험으로부터 예측한다는 것이다.

3

하위내용영역	배점	예상정답률
일반영어 B형 서술형	4점	50%

모범답안) There are two major types of leaders with their own strengths and roles within a group. First, instrumental leaders are fixed on completing tasks and achieving overall goals, while expressive leaders focus on collective well-being. The former holds a distant relationship to members. On the other hand, expressive leaders are closer and interact with sympathy and humor more than orders. In conclusion, neither type is better suited to all groups and situations, but understanding the difference can help.

채점기준

ⓐ Topic sentence
+1점: "There are two major types of leaders with their own strengths and roles within a group"를 명확하게 서술하였다.

ⓑ Major supporting details
+2점: "① First, instrumental leaders are fixed on completing tasks and achieving overall goals, while expressive leaders focus on collective well-being. ② The former holds a distant relationship to members. On the other hand, expressive leaders are closer and interact with sympathy and humor more than orders."을 명확하게 서술하였다.
☞ 2개 중 2개 모두 요약했으면 2점, 1개만 요약했으면 1점, 나머지는 0점을 준다.

ⓒ Conclusion
+1점: 글의 conclusion "In conclusion, neither type is better suited to all groups and situations, but understanding the difference can help"을 요약하였거나 유사하였다.

감점
• 본문에 나오는 연속되는 6단어 이상을 사용하였다. −0.5pt
• 문단을 두 개나 그 이상으로 구성하였다. −0.5pt
• 문법이나 영어 표현을 합쳐 3개 이상 오류가 있다. −0.5pt

한글번역

지도자들이 종종 특별한 개인적 능력을 가진 사람들로 생각되지만, 수십 년간의 연구는 "타고난 지도자"라는 범주가 있다는 일관된 증거를 만들어내지 못했다. 모든 지도자들이 공통으로 가지고 있는 개인적 자질의 집합은 없는 것 같다; 오히려, 사실상 누구든지 그 특정 집단의 필요를 충족하는 자질을 가지고 있다면 지도자로 인정받을 수 있다.

더 나아가, 사회 집단이 단일한 지도자를 가지고 있다고 일반적으로 여겨지지만, 일반적으로 서로 다른 개인들이 맡는 두 가지 다른 지도력 역할이 있다. 도구적 지도력은 사회 집단에 의한 과업 완수를 강조하는 지도력이다. 집단 구성원들은 도구적 지도자들이 "일을 해내기"를 기대한다. 반면에 표현적 지도력은 사회 집단 구성원들의 집단적 복지를 강조하는 지도력이다. 표현적 지도자들은 집단의 전반적인 목표보다는 집단 구성원들에게 정서적 지원을 제공하고 그들 사이의 긴장과 갈등을 최소화하려고 시도하는 것에 덜 관심이 있다. 집단 구성원들은 표현적 지도자들이 집단 내에서 안정적인 관계를 유지하고 개별 구성원들에게 지원을 제공하기를 기대한다.

도구적 지도자들은 다른 집단 구성원들과 다소 이차적인 관계를 가질 가능성이 높다. 그들은 명령을 내리고 집단의 목표 달성을 방해하는 집단 구성원들을 훈계할 수 있다. 표현적 지도자들은 집단의 다른 사람들과 더 개인적이거나 일차적인 관계를 기른다. 그들은 누군가가 어려움을 겪거나 훈계를 받을 때 동정을 제공하고, 유머로 진지한 순간을 빠르게 밝게 만들며, 집단을 분열시킬 위험이 있는 문제들을 해결하려고 노력한다.

이 두 역할의 차이가 시사하듯이, 표현적 지도자들은 일반적으로 집단 구성원들로부터 더 많은 개인적 애정을 받는다; 도구적 지도자들은, 집단 목표를 촉진하는 데 성공한다면, 더 거리를 둔 존경을 누릴 수 있다. 말하자면, 이러한 차이들을 이해하는 것은 팀 관계를 형성할 때 도움이 된다.

제69회 모의고사

1

하위내용영역	배점	예상정답률
일반영어 A형 서술형	4점	45%

모범 답안 The words are "low credit scores". Second, it is a history of paying on schedule.

채점 기준

+ 2점: 빈칸에 들어갈 단어를 "low credit scores"라 정확하게 기입하였다. 이외에는 답이 될 수 없다.
+ 2점: 의미를 "a history of paying on schedule"라 서술하였거나 유사하였다.

한글번역

신용점수는 대출 기관이 차용자가 대출을 제때 상환할 가능성을 평가하기 위해 사용하는 숫자이다. 대출 기관들은 신용점수를 사용해, 첫째로는 개인에게 돈을 빌려줄지 여부를, 둘째로는 어떤 이자율로 빌려줄지를 결정한다. 신용점수가 낮은 사람들은 대출을 거부당하거나 더 높은 이자율을 지불해야 한다. 신용점수의 사용은 광범위하며, 사람들이 자동차 대출, 자동차 보험, 신용카드, 또는 주택 구매 대출을 신청하면, 대출 기관은 신용 연장에 동의하기 전에 그들의 신용점수를 살펴볼 것이다.

신용점수에는 두 가지 유형이 있다: 일반 점수와 맞춤 점수. 맞춤 점수는 일부 개별 대출 기관들이 자신들의 회사에서 사용하기 위해 개발한다. 예를 들어, 백화점은 어떤 고객들이 매장 신용카드 승인을 받을지 결정하기 위해 자체 맞춤 신용점수 시스템을 개발할 수 있다. 반면에, 일반 점수는 하나 이상의 회사에서 사용되며 특정 개인이 대출을 제때 상환하지 않을 위험에 대한 통계적 모델에 기반한다. 많은 상점들과 다른 사업체들은 누구에게 신용을 제공할지 결정할 때 일반 신용점수에 의존한다. 중간값 일반 신용점수 이상을 가진 개인은 일반적으로 대출에서 가장 유리한 금리를 받을 것이다. 예를 들어, 어떤 사람이 250,000달러짜리 주택을 사기 위해 주택담보대출을 받고 싶다고 가정해보자. 개인의 신용점수에 따라, 대출 기관이 부과하는 이자율과 30년 주택담보대출의 월 상환금이 달라질 것이다. 자동차 대출과 신용카드 같은 다른 유형의 신용에서도 유사한 상황이 적용된다. 추가적으로, 보험회사와 공공요금 회사들은 고객들을 위한 요금을 설정하기 위해 신용점수를 사용한다. 신용점수가 낮은 사람들은 더 많은 요금을 부과받는다.

2

하위내용영역	배점	예상정답률
일반영어 A형 서술형	4점	50%

모범답안 The words are "political resistance". Second, it is used as an instrument of social control by regulating the sale prices, location, times and people allowed in order to divide races and classes and to control women's actions.

채점기준

+ 2점: 빈칸에 들어갈 단어를 "political resistance"라 정확하게 기입하였다. 이외에는 답이 될 수 없다.
+ 2점: 술이 어떻게 사회적 통제를 부과하는 도구로 사용됐는가에 대해 "by regulating the sale prices, location, times and people allowed in order to divide races and classes and to control women's actions"라 서술하였거나 유사하였다.

한글번역

맥주는 종종 정치로부터 휴식처럼 선전되지만 실제로는 그렇지 않다. 사실, 양조장들은 대학 캠퍼스를 분열시킨 논란이 되는 문제들에 대해 입장을 취해왔다. 최근에, 플로리다주 게인즈빌의 앨리게이터 양조장은 플로리다 대학교에서 열린 리처드 스펜서의 논란이 된 행사에 대한 사용하지 않은 티켓 한 쌍을 가져오는 고객에게 무료 맥주를 제공함으로써 그의 강연을 비우려고 시도했다. 앨리게이터는 맥주를 사용해 현대의 백인 우월주의에 반대 목소리를 냈고, 그렇게 함으로써 주변 집단이든 정부 자체든 인지된 억압에 맞서는 무기로 맥주를 사용해온 오랜 역사를 이어나갔다. 맥주는 음식처럼 민주적 참여를 촉진한다. 맥주를 만들고 소비하는 것은 미국에서 도덕성, 법률, 다양성, 그리고 자본주의에 대한 논쟁으로 이어졌다. 그리고 정치적 저항의 도구로서, 맥주는 개인들이 자신들의 권리를 표현하고 보호하는 데 도움을 줬다.

수 세기 동안, 맥주는 사회적 윤활유 이상의 것이었다. 그것은 정치적 저항의 도구였다. 맥주는 사실상 우리나라 건국의 중심이었다. 주점들은 식민지 사회에서 교회보다 더 흔했다. 그들은 사람들이 먹고, 마시고, 지역 소식을 듣고, 그것에 대해 논쟁하고, 공개 모임을 열고, 사업 거래를 하는 정치적, 사회적 삶의 중심지였다. 예를 들어, 맥아 제조업자였던 새뮤얼 애덤스를 생각해보자. 그는 독립에 대한 지지를 얻기 위해 식민지 음주 문화를 이용했다. 그는 보스턴 주변의 주점들을 이용해 자유의 아들들을 조직하고 영국 왕실에 대한 정치적 저항 행위를 계획했다. 술집과 정치가 너무 얽혀 있어서 1785년부터 1790년까지, 뉴욕시가 신생 미국의 수도였을 때, 맨해튼의 한 주점이 국무부, 재무부, 그리고 전쟁부를 수용했다.

그러나 이 시기에 건강한 영양분으로 여겨졌던 물질인 알코올을 통제하는 것은 1700년대 후반에 사회적 통제를 가하는 메커니즘이 됐다. 법률들은 맥주와 다른 알코올이 언제, 어디서, 어떤 가격에 판매될 수 있는지, 그리고 주점이 누구를 접대할 수 있는지를 규제했다. 이들은 지배층이 인종과 계층 간의 혼합을 방지하고, 여성의 행동을 통제하기 위한 의도적인 노력이었다.

맥주는 1800년대 내내 사회적 통제를 가하는 도구이자 정치적 저항의 도구로 계속 사용됐다. 금주 개혁가들은 알코올을 사회의 범죄, 빈곤, 그리고 광기의 주요 원인으로 봤고, 오늘날 미국인들이 소비하는 것의 두 배 이상을 평균적으로 섭취했던 국가의 엄청난 알코올 섭취량을 줄이기 위해 열성적으로 캠페인을 벌였다.

3

하위내용영역	배점	예상정답률
일반영어 A형 서술형	4점	45%

모범답안 It doesn't accurately capture the true lower levels of childlessness such as when people have children later in life. Second, the word is "delaying". Third, the meaning is that the economy is not accommodating to raising children.

채점 기준

+ **1점**: 총출산율 방식이 한계가 있는 이유를 "It doesn't accurately capture the true lower levels of childlessness such as when people have children later in life"라 서술하였거나 유사하였다.
+ **1점**: 빈칸에 들어갈 단어를 "delaying"이라 정확하게 기입하였다. 이외에는 답이 될 수 없다.
+ **2점**: 밑줄 친 부분의 의미를 "(this means that) the economy is not accommodating (or hospitable or friendly) to raising (or having) children (or families)"라 서술하였거나 유사하였다.
  ☞ 다음과 같이 서술하였어도 맞는 것으로 한다.
  – "Having children is related to economic circumstances rather than personal preferences"라 서술하였다.

한글번역

미국은 역사적으로 의도치 않은 높은 출생률의 나라였다. 사람들은 원하는 것보다 일찍, 또는 전혀 원하지 않는 상황에서도 아이를 낳았다. 최근 들어서야 그처럼 원치 않거나, 계획에 없던 출산이 줄어드는 현상이 나타나기 시작했다. 사람들은 아이를 원하지만, 상황이 됐을 때 낳기를 원한다. 즉, 교육을 마치고, 경제적인 안정과 안정적인 파트너십을 이뤘을 때 아이를 낳기를 원한다. 개인적으로 중요시하는 조건을 충족시키기 어렵다는 것은 아이를 낳지 않을 수도 있다는 의미이기도 하지만, 동시에 사람들이 자신의 재생산 행위를 보다 더 주도적으로 관리해 준비가 됐을 때 아이를 낳게 된 것이 엄청난 성취라는 뜻이기도 하다. 이는 개인에게만 좋은 것이 아니라, 미래 세대나 사회 전체에도 도움이 되는 현상이다.

미국과 전 세계에서 일어나고 있는 저출생 현상은 "아기의 종말"이 아니다. 보다 많은 사람들이 준비가 될 때까지 아이 갖기를 미루고 있다는 의미다. 합계 출산율과 같은 흔히 쓰이는 지표로는 이 같은 현상을 잘 잡아낼 수 없다. 하지만 아이 없이 평생을 지내는 사람이 오히려 줄어들고 있고, 대부분의 사람들이 가임기 중에 약 2명의 아이를 갖는다는 것을 보여주는 지표들도 찾아볼 수 있다. 기술의 발전으로 인한 다른 목표들 때문에 출산을 미루는 사람들이 늦게 아이를 갖는 것이 앞으로 더 쉬워질 수도 있다.

사람들이 원하는 가정을 이룰 수 있도록 돕는 것이 목표라면 인구 감소에 대한 패닉을 자극해 출생률을 끌어올리려는 시도보다는 출산과 양육을 교육 및 노동과 양립할 수 있도록 하는 정책을 도입해야 한다. 현재 아이를 낳아 기르는 데 걸림돌이 되는 문제들, 즉 학자금, 높은 부동산 가격, 비싼 의료 보험 제도, 만연한 소득 불평등 등을 바로잡아야 한다. 그러니 명절 식사 자리에서 친척이 아이는 언제 낳을건지, 둘째는 언제 가질 계획인지 물으면 화살을 돌려라. 미국 경제의 구조 조정을 위해 무슨 일을 할 계획인지를 물어보라.

4

하위내용영역	배점	예상정답률
일반영어 A형 서술형	4점	35%

모범답안 The word for ① is "opinions" and ② is "others". Second, diversity is no longer acceptable when one's actions cause harm to others.

채점 기준

+ **1점**: 빈칸 ①에 들어갈 단어를 "opinions"라 정확하게 기입하였다. 이외에는 답이 될 수 없다.
+ **1점**: 빈칸 ②에 들어갈 단어를 "others"라 정확하게 기입하였다. 이외에는 답이 될 수 없다.
+ **2점**: 의미를 "(diversity is no longer acceptable) when one's actions cause harm to others"라 서술하였거나 유사하였다. 또는 "it is when human beings can recognize the total truth"라 서술하였다.

한글번역

사람들은 자유롭게 자기 의견을 가져야 하며, 또 그 의견을 아무런 제약 없이 표현할 수 있어야 한다. 인간은 자신의 의견에 따라 행동하는 데 있어서 자유로워야 한다. 그에 따르는 모든 위험과 불확실성을 스스로 책임지는 한, 다른 사람에게 일체의 물리적, 도적적 방해를 받지 않고 각자 자신의 생각대로 행동하는 자유가 필요하다.

(자신의 행동에 대해 책임진다는) 이 단서는 두말할 것 없이 매우 중요하다. 행동하는 것이 의견을 가지는 것처럼 자유로워야 한다고 주장하는 사람은 아마 없을 것이다. 반대로, 다른 사람들이 해로운 행동을 하도록 적극적으로 부추기는 상황이라면, 의견의 자유라 해도 무제한적으로 허용될 수는 없다. 어떤 사람이 곡물 중개상들이 가난한 사람들의 배를 곯린다거나 또는 사유 재산은 강도짓이나 다름없다는 의견을 신문 지상에 발표한다면, 이런 행동을 방해해서는 안 된다. 그러나 곡물 중개상의 집 앞에 모여든 흥분 상태의 폭도들을 상대로 그런 의견을 개진하거나 그들이 보는 데서 그 같은 내용의 벽보를 붙인다면, 그런 행동을 처벌하는 것은 불가피하다.

어떤 종류의 행동이든 정당한 이유 없이 다른 사람에게 해를 끼치는 것은 강압적인 통제를 받을 수 있으며, 사안이 심각하다면 반드시 통제를 받아야 한다. 나아가 필요하다면 사회 전체가 적극적으로 간섭해야 한다. 이렇게 되면 개인의 자유가 심각하게 제한받게 된다. 그렇지만 사람을 성가시게 해서는 안 되기 때문에 이는 불가피하다. 하지만 다른 사람들이 관심을 가지는 문제에 대해 그들을 괴롭히지 않는 한편, 그저 자신에게만 관계되는 일에 대해 자기 스스로의 기분과 판단에 따라 행동한다면, 각자가 자유롭게 자기 의견을 가질 수 있어야 하는 것과 마찬가지로, 자신의 책임 아래 남의 방해를 받지 않고 자기 생각에 따라 행동하는 자유가 허용돼야 한다. 인간은 오류를 범하지 않는 절대적인 존재가 아니다. 인간이 아는 진리란 대부분 반쪽짜리 진리일 뿐이다. 인간이 진리의 모든 측면에 대해 지금보다 훨씬 더 잘 알 수 있을 때까지는, 의견 일치도 반대쪽 의견이 최대한 자유롭게 피력된 끝에 이루어진 것이 아니라면 바람직하다고 할 수 없다. 다양함은 나쁜 것이 아니라 오히려 좋은 것이라는 사실은 개인의 의견 못지않게 행동 양식에도 적용될 수 있다.

인간이 불완전한 상태에서는 서로 다른 의견이 존재하는 것이 유익하듯이, 삶의 실험도 다양하게 이뤄지는 것이 필요하다. 다른 사람에게 피해를 주지 않는 한, 각자의 개성을 다양하게 꽃피울 수 있어야 한다. 누구든지 시도해보고 싶다면 자기가 원하는 삶의 양식이 얼마나 가치 있는 것인지 실천적으로 증명해볼 수 있어야 한다. 예컨대, 다른 사람들에게 기본적으로 우려(걱정)거리가 되지 않는 한에서는, 각자의 개별성은 자기주장을 하는 것이 바람직하다.

제70회 모의고사

1

하위내용영역	배점	예상정답률
일반영어 A형 서술형	4점	50%

모범답안 Burning is mentioned to show the relative financial success of Parasite. Second, the OK Boomer generation would like the class outrage the movie demonstrates.

채점기준

+ 2점 : 영화 <버닝>을 언급한 이유를 "to show the relative financial success of Parasite"라 서술하였거나 유사하였다.
+ 2점 : 오케이 부머 세대에 호소력이 있는 부분을 "the OK Boomer generation would like the class outrage (or haves-versus-have-nots discourse) the movie demonstrates"라 서술하였거나 유사하였다.

한글번역

봉준호 감독의 <기생충>이 개봉 다섯 번째 주말에 전국적으로 상영관 수가 확대되면서 천만 달러 임계점을 꾸준히 상승하며 돌파했다는 소식을 할리우드 업계지 헤드라인들이 일제히 보도했다. 보통은 그것이 할리우드에서 샴페인 코르크를 터뜨릴 만한 수치는 아니지만, 현재 시장의 자막 영화에게는 힘든 상황이다 : 기생충의 현재 수익은 올해 미국에서 비영어권 영화 중 최고치이다. (작년에 비평적으로 사랑받고 칸에서 인정받은 한국 스릴러인 이창동의 <버닝>은 미국에서 초라하게 719,000달러를 벌었다.)

작년, 알폰소 쿠아론의 넷플릭스 지원 멕시코 회상작 <로마>는 91년간의 오스카 역사에서 어떤 비영어권 영화도 해내지 못한 일, 즉 작품상 수상에 근접했다. 시상식에 유력한 우승 후보로 진입해, 영원히 영미권 중심적인 기관에서 또 다른 최초인 감독상을 수상하며 역사를 만들었지만, 마지막 고비에서 <그린 북>의 안전하고 퇴행적이며 강조적으로 순미국적인 위안에 의해 넘겨졌다. 이후 이어진 업계의 대체로 불만스러운 사후 분석에서, 전문가들은 쿠아론의 더 호평받은 영화가 왜 졌는지에 대한 다양한 이론들을 주고받았다.

<기생충>은 애정 어린 리뷰들에도 불구하고 <로마>가 결코 완전히 달성하지 못한 무언가를 점진적으로 획득하고 있다: 진정한 대중적 명성으로, 이는 돈으로 사거나 조작할 수 없지만, 영화의 문화적 발자취를 박스오피스보다 더 크게 보이게 만들 수 있는 종류의 것이다. 그것은 칸에서부터 시작됐는데, 그곳에서 영화에 대한 과대광고는 비평계의 아첨하는 리뷰들에 의해서만이 아니라, 더 젊고, 매우 온라인에 능숙하며 매우 목소리가 큰 Z세대 영화광 집단에 의해 만들어졌고, 이들은 신속히 스스로를 #봉하이브라고 명명하고 영화가 황금종려상을 수상하거나 국제적으로 개봉하기 전에도 즉각적인 소셜 미디어 존재감을 부여했다.

그 이후로, <기생충>은 긍정적인 밈 생산 기계가 됐다: 아직 영화를 보지 않았지만 트위터를 정기적으로 이용한다면, 깨닫지도 못한 채 영화의 이미지와 움짤들을 정기적으로 마주쳤을지도 모른다. "제시카 징글"—영화의 젊은 등장인물 중 한 명이 자신의 거짓 정체성을 기억하는 데 도움이 되도록 전달하는 짧은 주문으로, 그 자체가 한국 학생들을 위한 표준 기억 보조 도구에 기반한 것—이 팬들에게 너무 널리 차용돼 지금은 휴대폰 벨소리로도 이용 가능하며, 이는 천만 달러보다 훨씬 더 가치 있는 현상적 지위로의 영화 승격을 신호하는 맥락에서 벗어나면 설명할 수 없는 내부 농담의 종류이다.

어떤 비미국 영화든 이런 종류의 보편적 통용성을 달성하는 것은 드물다. 봉준호 감독의 영화가 계층 분노의 전 세계적 우물을 깔끔하게 활용했다는 것이 사회의식이 있는 젊은 관객들에게 보편적 공명을 줬고, 이들은 전 세계적 정치적 혼란 속에서 가진 자 대 못 가진 자 담론을 먹여 살릴 텍스트에 굶주려 있었다: <기생충>의 계층 기반 공감은 다세대적일 수 있지만, 여전히 "오케이 부머" 세대에게는 뼈에 가깝게 파고든다.

2

하위내용영역	배점	예상정답률
일반영어 A형 서술형	4점	40%

모범답안 The word is "discount". Second, the major drawbacks of verification are that it is slow and costly and personal ability has been shown to be only somewhat better than chance.

채점 기준

+ 2점: 빈칸에 들어갈 단어를 "<u>discount</u>"라 정확하게 기입하였다. 이외에는 답이 될 수 없다.
+ 2점: 의미를 "<u>the major drawbacks of verification are that it is slow and costly and personal ability has been shown to be only somewhat better than chance</u>"라 서술하였거나 유사하였다.

한글번역

대형 회사에 아웃소싱 서비스를 제공하는 다년 계약을 협상하고 있다고 상상해보라. 고객이 그녀의 회사가 특정 수준의 서비스에 계약하기를 원하지만, 필요에 따라 추가 자원에 대한 조건을 해결할 수 있을 것이라고 믿으면서 즉석에서 더 많은 것을 기꺼이 제공해 주기를 바란다고 말한다. 당신은 동의해야 할까?

또는 잠재적 사업 파트너가 당신으로부터 1,200만 달러 상당의 서비스를 구매하고 싶어하지만 일시적인 예산 제약 때문에 1,000만 달러만 쓸 수 있다고 상상해보라. 그는 할인에 대한 대가로 장기적인 수익 기회의 전망을 내밀지만 아직 아무것도 약속할 수 없다고 말한다. 당신은 그에게 그 거래를 해줘야 할까?

이런 상황들은 어떤 관리자에게든 딜레마를 제시한다. 답은 명확하지 않다. 새로운 고객, 계약자, 또는 협력자를 신뢰하기로 선택한다면, 당신은 스스로를 취약하게 만든다: 당신의 결과는, 재정적으로든 다른 면에서든, 이제 그들의 신의에 달려 있다. 하지만 계약이 체결되기 전에 각각의 주장을 검증하고 모든 세부사항을 확인하기를 고집한다면, 과정을 늦추고 비용을 증가시켜 잠재적으로 스스로를 불리한 위치에 놓게 될 것이다.

위의 두 시나리오는 세계 최대 컨설팅 회사 중 한 곳의 파트너인 내 친구—토니라고 부르자—로부터 나온 것이다. 그가 두 고객의 제안 모두에 동의했지만, 신뢰하기로 한 결정들은 매우 다른 결과를 가져왔다. 첫 번째 고객은 토니의 동의를 그녀와 그녀의 매우 큰 회사가 관계에서 권력을 쥐고 있으므로 향후 작업에 대한 조건을 지시할 수 있다는 확인으로 받아들였다. 시간이 지나면서, 그녀는 회사의 점점 더 비합리적인 요구가 충족되지 않으면 단순히 더 기꺼이 응하는 다른 제공업체로 옮겨갈 것이라고 분명히 했다. 반면에 두 번째 고객은 신뢰할 만함을 증명했고, 그것이 토니의 회사에 창출한 장기적인 수익은 초기 합의에서 부여한 할인을 충분히 보상하고도 남았다.

사업에서의 성공은 의심할 여지없이 다른 사람들과 협력하고 그들을 믿으려는 어느 정도의 의지를 필요로 한다. 문제는, 얼마나 많은 믿음을 누구에게 가져야 하는가이다. 수십 년간의 과학적 연구는 다른 사람이 신뢰할 수 있는지 결정하는 데 있어서 사람들의 정확도가 우연보다 겨우 조금 나은 정도에 그치는 경향이 있음을 보여준다.

감점
- 본문에 나오는 연속되는 6단어 이상을 사용하였다. -0.5pt
- 문단을 두 개나 그 이상으로 구성하였다. -0.5pt
- 문법이나 영어 표현을 합쳐 3개 이상 오류가 있다. -0.5pt

한글번역

동굴 탐험은 종종 동굴학 또는 동굴 탐사라고 불리며, 재미있고 모험적이며 보람 있는 활동이 될 수 있다. 하지만 동굴 탐험을 시작하는 것은 도전이 될 수 있다. 동굴 탐험을 위한 준비를 해야 한다. 그렇지 않으면 매우 끔찍한 경험이 될 수 있다.

들어가고 나오는 정확한 길을 알지 못한 채로 동굴을 탐험하러 가지 마라. 동굴에서 길을 잃는 것은 당신의 최악의 악몽과 비슷할 수 있는 매우 위험한 상황이다. 동굴에 들어갈 계획이라면, 경로를 알고 있는지 확인하라. 또한, 동굴에서의 시간을 최대 8시간으로 제한하라. 그보다 더 오래 있으면 매우 피곤해지고 경계심이 떨어질 것이다. 카바이드 1킬로그램은 대략 6시간에서 8시간 동안 충분한 조명을 제공할 것이다. 심장이 약하거나 밀실 공포증을 앓고 있는 사람이라면, 관광용 동굴로만 제한해야 한다.

동굴 다이빙이나 차가운 물에서 만들어진 드라이 수트를 가져오는 것이 좋은 생각일 수 있다. 수트 자체는 목과 손목에 방수 라텍스 밀봉이 있는 적층된 방수 소재로 만들어진다. 양쪽에 있는 주머니는 안전 장비를 넣을 수 있다. 또한, 손잡이 줄과 수직 하강을 위해 밧줄이 필요하다. 이를 위해 안전장치로 사용하기 전에 모든 밧줄의 상태와 보관 방법을 항상 고려하라. 밧줄 보호대는 밧줄과 그것을 마모시킬 수 있는 모든 표면 사이의 완충재로 사용돼야 한다.

동굴 탐험은 일생에 한 번의 스릴일 수 있다. 하지만 동굴은 적절한 준비 없이는 영구적으로 영향을 받거나 부상을 야기할 수 있는 섬세하고 잠재적으로 위험한 환경이다. 동굴 탐험을 시작하는 가장 일반적이고 일반적으로 받아들여지는 표준 과정은 당신이 사는 곳 근처의 동굴 탐험 클럽을 찾아 모임에 참석하고 "초보자" 동굴 탐험 여행에 가고 싶다는 관심을 표현하는 것부터 시작하는 것이다.

3

하위내용영역	배점	예상정답률
일반영어 B형 서술형	4점	50%

모범 답안 To ensure safe and pleasant caving, you have to make preparations. First, plan a cave trip by knowing the exact route and limiting your time inside the cave to safe areas. In addition, a well-maintained dry suit, rope and rope protectors are also essential gear for staying safe inside caves. In conclusion, a common way to begin caving is to find a local caving club and join a meeting.

채점 기준

ⓐ Topic sentence

+ 1점 : "To ensure safe and pleasant caving, you have to make preparations"를 명확하게 서술하였다.

ⓑ Major supporting details

+ 2점 : "First, plan a cave trip by ① knowing the exact route and ② limiting your time inside the cave to safe areas. In addition, ③ a well-maintained dry suit, ④ rope and rope protectors are also essential gear for staying safe inside caves"을 명확하게 서술하였다.
☞ 4개 중 4개 모두 정확하게 요약했으면 2점, 2~3개를 요약했으면 1점, 나머지는 0점을 준다.

ⓒ Conclusion

+ 1점 : "In conclusion, a common way to begin caving is to find a local caving club and join a meeting"을 정확하게 요약하였다.

MEMO

2S2R

유희태 일반영어 ④-2 문제은행
● 모범답안 및 번역

초판 1쇄	2014년 4월 14일	
2판 1쇄	2016년 6월 15일	
3판 1쇄	2019년 2월 20일	
2쇄	2019년 5월 10일	
3쇄	2019년 7월 10일	
4판 1쇄	2020년 10월 23일	
2쇄	2021년 7월 30일	
3쇄	2022년 4월 15일	
5판 1쇄	2023년 1월 10일	
6판 1쇄	2026년 1월 15일	

저자와의
협의하에
인지생략

저자 유희태　**발행인** 박 용　**발행처** (주)박문각출판
표지디자인 박문각 디자인팀
등록 2015. 4. 29. 제2019-000137호
주소 06654 서울시 서초구 효령로 283 서경 B/D
팩스 (02) 584-2927
전화 교재 문의 (02) 6466-7202　동영상 문의 (02) 6466-7201

이 책의 무단 전재 또는 복제 행위는 저작권법 제136조에 의거, 5년 이하의 징역 또는 5,000만원 이하의 벌금에 처하거나 이를 병과할 수 있습니다.

정 가 42,000원(분권 포함)
ISBN 979-11-7519-529-5
ISBN 979-11-7519-527-1(세트)